CASEBOOK

Company Law

CONSULTANT EDITOR: LORD TEMPLEMAN
EDITOR: CHRIS SHEPHERD
LLB, MA, CertEd, Barrister
Senior Lecturer in Law at South Bank University

OLD BAILEY PRESS

OLD BAILEY PRESS
200 Greyhound Road, London W14 9RY

1st edition 1997

© Old Bailey Press Ltd 1997

Previous editions published under The HLT Group Ltd.

ISBN 1 85836 260 1

British Library Cataloguing-in-Publication.
A CIP Catalogue record for this book is available from the British Library.

Acknowledgement
The publishers and author would like to thank the Incorporated Council of Law Reporting for England and Wales for kind permission to reproduce extracts from the Weekly Law Reports, and Butterworths for their kind permission to reproduce extracts from the All England Law Reports.

Extracts from British Company Cases (BCC) are reproduced with kind permission of CCH Editions Limited.

Extracts from Butterworth's Company Law Cases (BCLC) are reproduced with kind permission of Butterworths.

Printed and bound in Great Britain

Contents

Preface

Old Bailey Press casebooks are intended as companion volumes to the textbooks but they also comprise invaluable reference tools in themselves. Their aim is to supplement and enhance a student's understanding and interpretation of a particular area of law and provide essential background reading. Companion Revision WorkBooks and Statutes are also published.

Important recent decisions covered in the *Company Law* casebook include the Court of Appeal decisions in *George Fischer (Great Britain) Ltd* v *Multi-Construction Ltd* (on whether a shareholder can claim damages for the losses of a subsidiary) and in *Barrett* v *Duckett and Others* (where a derivative action was struck out as there was a more appropriate remedy available to the shareholder). The Privy Council has formulated a number of rules to determine which acts are attributed to a company in *Meridan Global Funds Management Asia Ltd* v *Securities Commission*, and there have also been potentially far reaching first instance decisions, such as that in *Re Farmizer (Products) Ltd*, dealing with the limitation period for wrongful trading.

Cases reported on or before 1 January 1996 have been taken into account.

Table of Cases

1 Introduction and Corporate Personality

Corporate personality

Attorney-General's Reference (No 2 of 1982) [1984] 2 All ER 216 Court of Appeal (Watkins and Kerr LJJ)

Theft of company property by sole shareholder/directors

Facts

The defendants (X and Y) were the sole shareholders and directors of various companies involved in property speculation in the early 1970's. With the collapse of the property market in 1974 the companies went bankrupt owing £2.5m and X and Y also went bankrupt owing millions. However, while the companies had been functioning X and Y lived extravagantly and much of the money to finance this lifestyle was drawn by X and Y from the accounts of the companies despite warnings from accountants that it was illegal to do so. As a result charges were brought against X and Y alleging theft by them of the companies' property. The trial judge directed the jury to acquit both defendants on the basis of *Tesco Supermarkets* v *Nattrass* [1972] AC 153 on the ground that X and Y were the company, and therefore could not steal from it. The Attorney General referred the point to the Court of Appeal as to whether a person, or persons acting in concert, who had total control of a company were capable of stealing therefrom. At the trial the defendants conceded that, with the exception of 'dishonestly', all the ingredients of the definition of theft had been prima facie satisfied. In defence X and Y claimed that as they were the sole owners of the company and, through their shareholdings, the sole owners of all its property they could not be charged with stealing from themselves so that there was no issue to go to the jury on the element of 'dishonestly'.

Held

Persons in total control of a company who act illegally or dishonestly in the management of the company's affairs were not to have their knowledge of, or consent to, the illegal or dishonest acts imputed to the company. They could, therefore, be guilty of stealing from the company.

Kerr LJ:

'... The basic fallacy in the submission on behalf of the defendants is the contention that, in effect, in a situation such as the present a jury is bound to be directed that, when all the members and directors of a company act in concert in appropriating the property of their company, they cannot, as a matter of law, be held to have acted dishonestly, or that, on such facts, any reasonable jury is bound to reach this conclusion. We entirely disagree with both these propositions ...

... The speeches in the House of Lords in *Tesco Supermarkets* v *Nattrass* [1972] AC 153 merely illustrate that in situations like the present the defendants "are" the company in the sense that any offences committed by them in relation to the affairs of the company would be capable of being treated as offences committed by the company itself. The decision has no bearing on offences committed against the company ...'

Lee v Lee's Air Farming Ltd [1961] AC 12 Privy Council (Viscount Simonds, Lords Reid, Tucker, Denning and Morris)

A principal shareholder and sole governing director can contract with his company

Facts

Mrs Lee's husband formed Lee's Air Farming Ltd in 1954 one of whose objects was to carry on the business of aerial top-dressing. Of the £3,000 £1 shares in the company all but one share were held by Mr Lee and he was the sole governing director of the company. In accordance with powers granted in the articles Mr Lee as director of the company employed himself to be the chief pilot of the company and the articles stated that the rules of master and servant were to apply to any contract of employment entered into by the company. Mr Lee, as governing director, arranged insurance policies for the benefit of the company and its employees and these included personal accident cover. The premiums were paid by the company and debited to the company's accounts. In March 1956 while Mr Lee was flying the company aircraft used for top-dressing, it stalled and crashed to the ground killing him. Mrs Lee claimed compensation for her husband's death under New Zealand's Workers' Compensation Act 1922 s3(1) which made an employer liable to pay compensation if personal injury was caused to a 'worker' by reason of an accident in the court of employment. The insurers, who were liable to indemnify the company under this Act if the claim succeeded, disputed that Mr Lee was an 'employee' of the company.

Held

Mr Lee was a 'worker' within the meaning of the Workers' Compensation Act. His position as principal shareholder and governing director did not stop him from making a contract of employment on behalf of the company between himself and the company.

Lord Morris:

'… Their Lordships conclude, therefore, that the real issue in the case is whether the position of the deceased as sole governing director made it impossible for him to be the servant of the respondent company in the capacity of chief pilot of that company. In their Lordships' view, for the reasons which have been indicated, there was no such impossibility. There appears to be no greater difficulty in holding that a man acting in one capacity can give orders to himself in another capacity than there is in holding that a man acting in one capacity can make a contract with himself in another capacity. The respondent company and the deceased were separate legal entities. The respondent company had the right to decide what contracts for aerial top-dressing it would enter into. The deceased was the agent of the respondent company in making the necessary decisions. Any profits earned would belong to the respondent company and not to the deceased. If the respondent company entered into a contract with a farmer then it lay within its right and power to direct its chief pilot to perform certain operations. The right to control existed even though it would be for the deceased, in his capacity as agent for the respondent company, to decide what orders to give. The right to control existed in the respondent company and an application of the principles of *Salomon* v *Salomon & Co* demonstrates that the respondent company was distinct from the deceased. As pointed out above, there might have come a time when the deceased would remain bound contractually to serve the respondent company as chief pilot though he had retired from the office of sole governing director. Their Lordships consider, therefore, that the deceased was a worker and that the question posed in the Case Stated should be answered in the affirmative …'

Macaura v *Northern Assurance Co* [1925] AC 619 House of Lords (Lords Buckmaster, Sumner, Wrenbury, Atkinson and Phillimore)

An unsecured creditor who is also a principal shareholder has no insurable interest in the company's property

Facts

Macaura owned a large estate in Co Tyrone with the timber thereon. In December 1919 he assigned the whole of the timber on the estate to a company known as Irish Canadian Saw Mills Ltd for a total price of £42,000 this being satisfied by the issue of 42,000 £1 shares to Macaura in the company.' At various dates in January and February 1922 he insured the timber against fire with five insurance companies in his own name since most of it had been felled. On 22 February 1922 the timber was destroyed by fire and Macaura claimed on the policies. The questions arose as to whether he had an insurable interest in the timber by reason of (a) owning almost all the shares in the company or (b) by reason of being a creditor of the company.

Held

He had no insurable interest.

Lord Buckmaster:

'... It must, in my opinion, be admitted that at first sight the facts suggest that there really was no person other than the plaintiff who was interested in the preservation of the timber. It is true that the timber was owned by the company, but practically the whole interest in the company was owned by the appellant. He would receive the benefit of any profit and on him would fall the burden of any loss. But the principles on which the decision of this case rests must be independent of the extent of the interest he held. The appellant could only insure either as a creditor or as a shareholder in the company, and if he was not entitled in virtue of either of these rights he can acquire no better position by reason of the fact that he held both characters. As a creditor his position appears to me quite incapable of supporting the claim. If his contention were right it would follow that any person would be at liberty to insure the furniture of his debtor, and no such claim has ever been recognised by the courts ...

... Turning now to his position as shareholder, this must be independent of the extent of his share interest. If he were entitled to insure because he held all the shares in the company, each shareholder would be equally entitled, if the shares were all in separate hands. Now, no shareholder has any right to any item of property owned by the company, for he has no legal or equitable interest therein. He is entitled to a share in the profits while the company continues to carry on business and a share in the distribution of the surplus assets when the company is wound-up. If he were at liberty to effect an insurance against loss by fire of any item of the company's property, the extent of his insurable interest could only be measured by determining the extent to which his share in the ultimate distribution would be diminished by the loss of the assets – a calculation almost impossible to make. There is no means by which such an interest can be definitely measured and no standard which can be fixed of the loss against which the contract of insurance could be regarded as an indemnity ...'

Lord Sumner:

'... He owned almost all the shares in the company, and the company owed him a good deal of money, but, neither as creditor, nor as shareholder, could he insure the company's assets. The debt was not exposed to fire nor were the shares, and the fact that he was virtually the company's only creditor, while the timber was its only asset, seems to me to make no difference. He stood in no "legal or equitable relation to" the timber at all. He had no "concern in" the subject insured. His relation was to the company, not to its goods, and after the fire he was directly prejudiced by the paucity of the company's assets, not by the fire. No authority has been produced for the proposition that the appellant had any insurable interest in the timber in any capacity, and the books are full of decisions and dicta that he had none ...'

Salomon v Salomon & Co [1897] AC 22 House of Lords (Lord Halsbury LC, Lords Watson, Herschell, Macnaghten, Morris and Davey)

A company has a separate legal personality from that of its members

Facts

For about 30 years Aron Salomon carried on business as a leather merchant and wholesale boot manufacturer under the style A Salomon & Co. He had a wife and daughter, and five sons. Four of the sons worked with Mr Salomon in the business and in 1892 in order to satisfy their requests for a share in the business he turned his business into a limited company. The company had a share capital of £39,000 'a sum which represented the sanguine expectations of a fond owner rather than anything that can be called a businesslike or reasonable estimate of value'. The subscribers to the memorandum were Mr Salomon, his wife and daughter and four of his sons and 20,007 shares were issued, of which Mr Salomon received 20,001 and the other subscribers one each. The company paid the purchase price of the business by, inter alia, issuing debentures of £10,000 to Mr Salomon. The business was solvent at the date it was transferred to the company but shortly afterwards there was a great depression in the boot and shoe trade and strikes too. As a result the business suffered heavy losses and despite injections of cash by Mr Salomon and his mortgaging his debenture for a £5,000 loan for the business it eventually collapsed. The company was ordered to be wound up in October 1893 and after payment of the mortgage debt and interest thereon there was only £1,055 to satisfy unsecured debts of £7,773 plus the amounts owed to Mr Salomon on his debentures. Mr Salomon claimed the £1,055 and the liquidator counterclaimed alleging that Mr Salomon was liable to indemnify the company against the whole of the unsecured debts. At first instance Vaughan Williams J took the view that the company was Mr Salomon's agent and held him liable to indemnify the company. The Court of Appeal upheld this decision but on different grounds, namely, that the relationship of the company to Mr Salomon was that of trustee to cestui que trust. On appeal to the House of Lords:

Held

The company had been validly formed under the Companies Act 1862 and on the terms of that Act the company was a different person from the subscribers to the memorandum. The company's property was its property and its debts were its alone and in its activities it was not the agent of Mr Salomon but instead he was the agent of the company.

Lord Halsbury LC:

'... I will, for the sake of argument, assume the proposition that the Court of Appeal lays down, that the formation of the company was a mere scheme to enable Aron Salomon to carry on business in the name of the company. I am wholly unable to follow the proposition that this was contrary to the true intent and meaning of the Companies Act. I can only find the true intent and meaning of the Act from the Act itself, and the Act appears to me to give a company a legal existence with, as I have said, rights and liabilities of its own, whatever may have been the ideas or schemes of those who brought it into existence. I observe that Vaughan Williams J held that the business was Mr Salomon's business and no one else's, and that he chose to employ as agent a limited company, and he proceeded to argue that he was employing that limited company as agent, and that he was bound to indemnify that agent – the company. I confess it seems to me that that very learned judge becomes involved by this argument in a very singular contradiction. Either the limited company was a legal entity or it was not. If it was, the business belonged to it and not to Mr Salomon; if it was not, there was no person and no thing to be an agent at all; and it is impossible to say at the same time that there is a company and there is not. Lindley LJ, on the other hand, affirms that there were seven members of the company, but, he says, it is manifest that six of them were members simply in order to enable the seventh himself to carry on business with limited liability, so that the object of the whole arrangement was to do the very thing which the legislature intended not to be done ...'

Lord Macnaghten:

'... When the trial came on before Vaughan Williams J, the validity of Mr Broderip's claim was admitted, and it was not disputed that the 20,000 shares were fully paid up. The case presented by the liquidator broke down completely. But the learned judge suggested that the company had a right of indemnity against

Mr Salomon. The signatories of the memorandum of association were, he said, mere nominees of Mr Salomon, mere dummies. The company was Mr Salomon in another form. He used the name of the company as an alias. He employed the company as his agent; so the company, he thought, was entitled to indemnity against its principal. The counterclaim was, accordingly, amended to raise this point, and on the amendment being made the learned judge pronouned an order in accordance with the view he had expressed.

The order of the learned judge appears to me to be founded on a misconception of the scope and effect of the Companies Act, 1862. In order to form a company limited by shares, the Act requires that a memorandum of association should be signed by seven persons, who are each to take one share at least. If those conditions are complied with, what can it matter whether the signatories are relations or strangers? There is nothing in the Act requiring that the subscribers to the memorandum should be independent or unconnected, or that they or any one of them should take a substantial interest in the undertaking, or that they should have a mind and will of their own, as one of the learned lords justices seems to think, or that there should be anything like a balance of power in the constitution of the company. In almost every company that is formed, the statutory number is eked out by clerks or friends, who sign their names at the request of the promoter or promoters without intending to take any further part or interest in the matter.

When the memorandum is duly signed and registered, though there be only seven shares taken, the subscribers are a body corporate "capable forthwith", to use the words of the enactments, "of exercising all the functions of an incorporated company". Those are strong words. The company attains maturity on its birth. There is no period of minority; no interval of incapacity. I cannot understand how a body corporate thus made "capable" by statute can lose its individuality by issuing the bulk of its capital to one person, whether he be a subscriber to the memorandum or not. The company is at law a different person altogether from the subscribers to the memorandum, and, though it may be that after incorporation the business is precisely the same as it was before, the same persons are managers, and the same hands receive the profits, the company is not in law the agent of the subscribers or trustees for them. Nor are the subscribers as members liable, in any shape or form, except to the extent and in the manner provided by the Act. That is, I think, the declared intention of the enactment. If the view of the learned judge were sound, it would follow that no common law partnership could register as a company limited by shares without remaining subject to unlimited liability.

Mr Salomon appealed, but his appeal was dismissed with costs, though the appellate court did not entirely accept the view of the court below. The decision of the Court of Appeal proceeds on a declaration of opinion embodied in the order which has been already read. I must say that I, too, have great difficulty in understanding this declaration. If it only means that Mr Salomon availed himself to the full of the advantages offered by the Companies Act, 1862, what is there wrong in that? Leave out the words "contrary to the true intent and meaning of the Companies Act, 1862," and bear in mind that "the creditors of the company" are not the creditors of Mr Salomon, and the declaration is perfectly innocent. It has no sting in it. In an early case (*Re Baglan Hall Colliery Co* (1870) 5 Ch App 346 which in some of its aspects is not unlike the present, the owners of a colliery (to quote the language of Giffard LJ in the Court of Appeal) "went on working the colliery not very successfully, and then determined to form a limited company, in order to avoid incurring further personal liability". The lord justice adds: "It was the policy of the Companies Act to enable this to be done." And so he reversed the decision of Malins VC, who had expressed an opinion that if the laws of the country sanctioned such a proceeding they were "in a most lamentable state," and had fixed the former owners with liability for the amount of the shares they took in exchange for their property.

Among the principal reasons which induce persons to form private companies as is stated very clearly by Mr Palmer in his treatise on the subject, are the desire to avoid the risk of bankruptcy, and the increased facility afforded for borrowing money. By means of a private company, as Mr Palmer observes, a trade can be carried on with limited liability and without exposing the persons interested in it in the event of failure to the harsh provisions of the bankruptcy law. A company too can raise money on debentures which an ordinary trader cannot do; any member of a company acting in good faith is as much entitled to take and hold the company's debentures as any outside creditor. Every creditor is entitled to get and to hold the best security the law allows him to take. If, however, the declaration of the Court of Appeal means that Mr Salomon acted fraudulently or dishonestly, I must say that I can find nothing in the evidence to support such an imputation. The purpose for which Mr Salomon and the other subscribers to the memorandum were associated was "lawful". The fact that Mr Salomon raised £5,000 for the company on debentures that belonged to him seems to me strong evidence of his good faith and of his confidence in the company.

The unsecured creditors of A Salomon & Co Ltd may be entitled to sympathy, but they have only themselves to blame for their misfortunes. They trusted the company, I suppose, because they had long dealt with Mr Salomon and he had always paid his way; but they had full notice that they were no longer dealing with an individual, and they must be taken to have been cognisant of the memorandum and of the articles of association. For such a catastrophe as has occurred in this case some would blame the law that allows such a thing as a floating charge. But a floating charge is too convenient a form of security to be lightly abolished. I have long thought and I believe some of your Lordships also think, that the ordinary trade creditors of a trading company ought to have a preferential claim on the assets in liquidation in respect of debts incurred within a certain limited time before the winding-up. But that is not the law at present. Everybody knows that when there is a winding-up, debenture holders generally step in and sweep off everything. And a great scandal it is.

It has become the fashion to call companies of this class "one-man companies". That is a taking nickname, but it does not help one much in the way of argument. If it is intended to convey the meaning that a company which is under the absolute control of one person is not a company legally incorporated, although the requirements of the Act of 1862 may have been complied with, it is inaccurate and misleading; if it merely means that there is a predominant partner possessing an overwhelming influence and entitled practically to the whole of the profits, there is nothing in that that I can see contrary to the true intention of the Act of 1862, or against public policy, or detrimental to the interests of creditors. If the shares are fully paid up it cannot matter whether they are in the hands of one or many. If the shares are not fully paid it is as easy to gauge the solvency of an individual as to estimate the financial ability of a crowd ...'

Commentary
See also *Adams* v *Cape Industries plc* [1991] 1 All ER 929, below.

Seaboard Offshore Ltd v *Secretary of State for Transport* [1994] 1 WLR 541 House of Lords (Lords Keith, Bridge, Jauncey, Browne-Wilkinson and Nolan)

A company was not vicariously liable for the acts of all its employees

Facts
Seaboard Offshore Ltd were the charterers and managers of the mv *Safe Carrier,* which set sail from the River Tyne bound for Aberdeen. The vessel broke down three times within a period of 24 hours, leaving her drifting at sea. The chief engineer, who was responsible for the mechanical running of the ship, boarded the vessel only 2 hours and 50 minutes before she put to sea. The minimum time needed to familiarise himself with the vessel was in fact three days. The company was charged with failing 'to take all reasonable steps to secure that the ship was operated in a safe manner', pursuant to s31 of the Marine Shipping Act 1988.

The issue that the House of Lords had to decide was whether s31 imposed vicarious liability on the company for the acts of all its employees.

Held
The appeal was dismissed.

Section 31 imposed a personal duty on the owner, charterer or manager of a ship to take all reasonable steps to secure that the ship was operated in a safe manner. Construed properly, Parliament could not have intended that s31 made the owner of a ship always liable for any act or omission by any officer of the company or member of the crew, which led to the unsafe operation of the ship.

Lord Keith of Kinkel:

'... As Staughton LJ observed in the course of his judgment in the Divisional Court, it would be surprising if by the language used in s31 Parliament intended that the owner of a ship should be criminally liable for any act or omission by any officer of the company or member of the crew which resulted in unsafe operation of the ship, ranging from a failure by the managing director to arrange repairs to a failure by the bosun or cabin steward to close portholes (see [1993] 3 All ER 25 at 33, [1993] 1 WLR 1025 at 1033). Of particular relevance in this context are the concluding words of s31(4), referring to the taking of all such steps as are reasonable for *him* (my emphasis) to take, ie the owner, charterer or manager. The steps to be taken are to be such as will secure that the ship is operated in a safe manner. That conveys to me the idea of laying down a safe manner of operating the ship by those involved in the actual operation of it and taking appropriate measures to bring it about that such safe manner of operation is adhered to. Where the owner, charterer or manager is a corporation which can act only through natural persons, the natural persons who are to be treated in law as being the corporation for the purpose of acts done in the course of its business are those who by virtue of its constitution or otherwise are entrusted with the exercise of the powers of the corporation: see per Lord Diplock in *Tesco Supermarkets Ltd* v *Nattrass* [1971] 2 All ER 127 at 155, [1972] AC 153 at 199–200.

In the judgment of the Divisional Court there is some discussion as to whether or not the offence provided for by s31 is one of strict liability, involving no necessary element of mens rea. It is not, however, helpful to seek to categorise the offence as either being or not being one of strict liability. It consists simply in failure to take steps which by an objective standard are held to be reasonable steps to take in the interests of the safe operation of a ship, and the duty which it places on the owner, charterer or manager is a personal one. The owner, charterer or manager is criminally liable if he fails personally in the duty, but is not criminally liable for the acts or omissions of his subordinate employees if he has himself taken all such reasonable steps.

My Lords, for these reasons I would dismiss the appeal.'

Commentary

The Secretary of State also argued that there had been a breach of s31 of the Marine Shipping Act 1988 in that there was no established system to ensure that the chief engineer had had sufficient opportunity to familiarise himself with the ship's equipment and machinery. It was argued that this was the responsibility of those whom the company had entrusted with the exercise of its powers. This was rejected by their Lordships because the case was not originally argued on this basis before the justices. Therefore, they did not consider it and it could not now be the basis for an appeal. This case illustrates that where criminal responsibility of a company is based on vicarious liability, the company may not be liable for all of the acts of all of its employees.

Taylor v *Pace Developments Ltd* (1991) The Times 7 May Court of Appeal (Lloyd, Nourse and Ralph Gibson LJJ)

Director's liability for costs

Facts

The plaintiffs had been successful in proceedings against the defendant company, which was insolvent, but their application for an order for costs against, inter alia, the managing director and sole beneficial shareholder of the company had been dismissed. The plaintiffs appealed against this decision.

Held

The court would not disturb the judge's exercise of his discretion as to costs under s51(1) of the Supreme Court Act 1981. Although Lloyd LJ accepted that the controlling director of a one-man company was inevitably the person who caused the costs to be incurred, by causing the company to defend the proceedings, it could not be right that in every such case he should be made personally liable for costs, even if he knew that the company would not be able to meet the plaintiff's costs should the company lose its case. That would be far too great an inroad on the principle of limited liability. In the great majority of cases the directors of an insolvent company, which defended proceedings brought against it, should not be at personal risk for costs.

Lifting the veil of incorporation by the courts

Adams v *Cape Industries plc* [1991] 1 All ER 929 Court of Appeal (Slade, Mustill and Ralph Gibson LJJ)

Refusal to lift the corporate veil between a group of companies

Facts

Mr Adams and 204 other plaintiffs sought to enforce in England a United States judgment against the defendants, Cape Industries plc and its wholly owned subsidiary Capasco Ltd, both of which were incorporated in the United Kingdom. The plaintiffs' injuries had been caused by exposure to asbestos dust in a factory to which the defendants had supplied asbestos. The defendants had taken no part in the United States proceedings because they had no assets in that country, but they marketed asbestos there through a United States subsidiary and an independent Illinois corporation (CPC) which acted as a marketing agent. In order to succeed in England, the plaintiffs had to show, inter alia, that the defendants had been present in the United States when proceedings were there commenced. The judge dismissed the plaintiffs' claim and they appealed.

Held

The appeal would be dismissed because, inter alia, the corporate veil would not be lifted so that the presence of the subsidiary and independent corporation could be treated as the presence of the defendants.

Slade LJ:

'The relationship between Cape/Capasco and CPC is the crucial factor, since CPC was undoubtedly carrying on business in the United States. We have already indicated our acceptance of the judge's findings that CPC was a company independently owned ... These findings by themselves make it very difficult to contend that the operation of CPC involved a facade which entitles the court to pierce the corporate veil between CPC and Cape/Capasco and treat them all as one. Is the legal position altered by the facts that Cape's intention, in making the relevant arrangements (as we infer), was to enable sales of asbestos from the South African subsidiaries to be made while (a) reducing if not eliminating the appearance of any involvement therein of Cape or its subsidiaries, and (b) reducing by any lawful means available to it the risk of any subsidiary or of Cape as a parent company being held liable for United States taxation or subject to the jurisdiction of the United States courts and the risk of any default judgment by such a court being held to be enforceable in this country?

We think not. [Counsel for the plaintiffs] submitted that the court will lift the corporate veil where a defendant by the device of a corporate structure attempts to evade (i) limitations imposed on his conduct by law, (ii) such rights of relief against him as third parties already possess and (iii) such rights of relief as third parties may in the future acquire. Assuming that the first and second of these three conditions will suffice in law to justify such a course, neither of them apply in the present case. It is not suggested that the arrangements involved any actual or potential illegality or were intended to deprive anyone of their existing rights. Whether or not such a course deserves moral approval, there was nothing illegal as such in Cape arranging its affairs (whether by the use of subsidiaries or otherwise) so as to attract the minimum publicity to its involvement in the sale of Cape asbestos in the United States. As to condition (iii), we do not accept as a matter of law that the court is entitled to lift the corporate veil as against a defendant company which is the member of a corporate group merely because the corporate structure has been used so as to ensure that the legal liability (if any) in respect of particular future activities of the group (and correspondingly the risk of enforcement of that liability) will fall on another member of the group rather than the defendant company. Whether or not this is desirable, the right to use a corporate structure in this manner in inherent in our corporate law. [Counsel] urged on us that the purpose of the operation was in substance that Cape would have the practical benefit of the group's asbestos trade in the United States without the risks of tortious liability. This may be so. However, in our judgment, Cape was in law entitled to organise the group's affairs in that manner and ... to expect that the court would apply the principle of *Salomon* v *A Salomon & Co Ltd* [1897] AC 22 in the ordinary way.'

Atlas Maritime Co SA v *Avalon Maritime Ltd, The Coral Rose (No 1)* [1991] 4 All ER 769 Court of Appeal (Neill, Stocker and Staughton LJJ)

Refusal to lift the corporate veil between a group of companies

Facts
Marc Rich, of Switzerland, was offered the ship Coral Rose. It declined to buy the vessel in its own name, but advanced the necessary funds to Avalon, a Gibraltar company purchased for that purpose by a Marc Rich Liberian subsidiary. Avalon duly bought the Coral Rose for $7.92m. Atlas claimed that Avalon had agreed to sell it the Coral Rose for $15.5m and had wrongfully repudiated the contract. Steyn J granted a Mareva injunction which allowed Avalon to sell the Coral Rose provided $3m was paid into a bank account in London. Avalon sold the ship to a third party for about $10.7m and, apart from the $3m, paid over the proceeds to Marc Rich. The $3m was the amount of damages for which it was considered Atlas had a good arguable case. Avalon sought to have the injunction discharged or varied.

Held
The application had properly been refused. Staughton LJ said that there was no justification for piercing the corporate veil so as to treat Avalon's liabilities as liabilities of Marc Rich. It was enough to lift or look behind it to ascertain that Marc Rich was as to 100 per cent the ultimate parent of Avalon. It was wholly proper, in deciding whether to permit payment by Avalon of the moneys claimed by Marc Rich, to have regard to the fact that Marc Rich was the ultimate parent as to 100 per cent. It was just and convenient to continue the injunction, and not to permit the variation sought. The nature of the debt was repayment of loan capital.

Neill LJ said that there were cases where, notwithstanding the principle of *Salomon* v *Salomon & Co Ltd* [1897] AC 22, the 'corporate veil' between two companies could be pierced so that one company was to be regarded as the alter ego of the other. But this was not such a case. Nevertheless, in the exercise of a discretion in relation to injunctive relief 'the eye of equity' (see *Jones* v *Lipman* [1962] 1 All ER 442 at 445 per Russell J) could look behind the corporate veil in order to do justice. This approach was recognised by Danckwerts LJ in *Merchandise Transport Ltd* v *British Transport Commission* [1961] 3 All ER 495 at 518 where he said: '... where the character of a company, or the nature of the persons who control it, is a relevant feature the court will go behind the mere status of the company as a legal entity, and will consider who are the persons as shareholders or even as agents who direct and control the activities of a company which is incapable of doing anything without human assistance.'

Neill LJ noted that in *Adams* v *Cape Industries plc* [1991] 1 All ER 929 at 1024, Slade LJ accepted this approach as being correct in an appropriate case. In his Lordship's (Neill LJ's) view, the court had to look at all the circumstances of the case. As Slade LJ explained in *Adams* v *Cape Industries plc* [1991] 1 All ER 929 at 1020 a holding company is free to choose to arrange the affairs of its group in such a way that the business of the group in a particular country or for a particular project is carried on by a subsidiary. In such an event there was no presumption of agency and the company and the subsidiary could be regarded as two separate entities. But when it came to considering the exercise of a discretion and the scope of injunctive relief it was then legitimate to look at all the circumstances and to examine the nature of the debt and the identity of the creditor. In the present case he had no doubt that justice required that the Mareva injunction should be maintained in respect of the sum of $3m.

Bugle Press Ltd, Re [1961] Ch 270 Court of Appeal (Harman and Donovan LJJ)

Lifting the veil – the company formed was a 'sham'

Facts
Two of the three shareholders held 9,000 out of the 10,000 issued shares in Bugle Press. The third shareholder, one Treby, held the other 1,000 shares and the other two shareholders wished to get rid of him. There was no way in which they could lawfully dispossess him of his shares since he did not wish to part with them. A scheme was devised by which the two shareholders formed another company in which they had all the shares and they made a takeover bid for Bugle Press using this company. Under s209 of the Companies Act 1948 if a takeover bid is made and accepted by 90 per cent of the shareholders within four months the dissenting 10 per cent can be bought out against their will by acquiring the company. The two shareholders accepted the offer from their company and demanded the right to buy the other 10 per cent of the shares through their company. At first instance Buckley J refused to approve the scheme. The two shareholders appealed.

Held
The appeal was dismissed on the ground that it was an attempt to use the newly formed company to perpetrate a fraud on the minority.

Harman LJ:

'… In my judgment this is a barefaced attempt to evade that fundamental rule of company law which forbids the majority of shareholders, unless the articles so provide, to expropriate a minority. It would be all too simple if all one had to do was to form a £2 company and sell to it one's shares, and then force the outsider to comply. … The transferee company is nothing but a little hut built round his two co-shareholders, and that the so-called scheme was made by themselves as directors of that company with themselves as shareholders and the whole thing, therefore, is seen to be a hollow sham …'

DHN Food Distributors v *London Borough of Tower Hamlets* [1976] 1 WLR 852 Court of Appeal (Lord Denning MR, Goff and Shaw LJJ)

Lifting the veil between a group of companies

Facts
Tower Hamlets Borough served a compulsory purchase order on a warehouse which they wished to demolish so that the site could be used to build houses on it. The warehouse was used as a 'cash and carry' carried on by three companies of which DHN was the parent company and owned all the shares in the other two companies, Bronze Investments Ltd, which owned the warehouse, and DHN Food

Transport Ltd, which collected and delivered goods for the business. Under the provisions of the Land Compensation Act 1961 a firm whose business is affected by a compulsory purchase order is entitled to compensation for the value of the land and also compensation for disturbance of the business. In this case if all of the business had been owned by one company it could have claimed under both of these heads. The local authority was prepared to pay Bronze Investments £360,000 for the land but refused to pay anything for disturbance of business as Bronze Investments merely owned the land and the business in the warehouse was carried on by DHN itself. Therefore, it was claimed, Bronze Investments had no business which had been disturbed and DHN, being a separate entity, could not recover for disturbance of business, as this was only recoverable if it had an interest in the land. DHN argued that the corporate veil should be lifted and the three companies treated as one.

Held

The veil should be lifted on the three companies; the realities of the situation had to be looked at and the group of companies was, in essence, a partnership.

Lord Denning MR:

'... We all know that in many respects a group of companies are treated together for the purpose of general accounts, balance sheet and profit and loss account. They are treated as one concern ... This is especially the case when a parent company owns all the shares of the subsidiaries, so much so that it can control every movement of the subsidiaries. These subsidiaries are bound hand and foot to the parent company and must do just what the parent company says. A striking instance is the decision of the House of Lords in *Harold Houldsworth & Co (Wakefields) Ltd* v *Caddies* [1955] 1 WLR 352; so here. This group is virtually the same as a partnership in which all three companies are partners. They should not be treated separately so as to be defeated on a technical point. They should not be deprived of the compensation which should justly be payable for disturbance. The three companies should, for present purposes, be treated as one, and the parent company, DHN, should be treated as that one ...'

Gilford Motor Co v *Horne* [1933] Ch 935 Court of Appeal (Lord Hanworth MR, Lawrence and Romer LJJ)

Lifting the veil – company formed was a 'sham'

Facts

Horne was employed as the managing director of the Gilford Motor Co under an agreement for a period of six years from 1 September, 1928. The business of the Gilford Motor Co was assembling motor cars and selling the same together with any spare parts needed for them. Clause 9 of Horne's contract of employment provided that he was not after leaving the company to, inter alia, 'solicit, interfere with, or endeavour or entice away from the company any person, firm or company ... in the habit of dealing with the company'. Horne resigned as managing director in November 1931 and immediately afterwards set up in the same line of business at his home in Highgate. However, he was worried as to whether he was in breach of cl 9 and before he received legal advice on this he formed a company under the name of his wife which solicited business from customers of the Gilford Motor Co and enticed some of their employees away. The Gilford Motor Co sought an injunction against Horne and the company he formed for breach of the covenant. At first instance Farwell J accepted the claim that the company was a 'sham' but concluded that the covenant in cl 9 was invalid. On appeal

Held

The covenant was enforceable and as the company was a sham the injunction would be issued against both it and Horne.

Lord Hanworth MR:

'... I am quite satisfied that this company was formed as a device, a stratagem, in order to mask the effective carrying on of a business of Mr E B Horne. The purpose of it was to try to enable him, under what is a cloak or sham, to engage in business which, on contemplation of the agreement which had been sent to him just about seven days before the company was incorporated, was a business in respect of which he had a fear that the plaintiffs might intervene or object ...'

Jones v *Lipman* [1962] 1 WLR 832 High Court (Russell J)

Lifting the veil – company a 'sham'

Facts
The defendant had contracted to sell his house to the plaintiff and, having changed his mind, he tried to avoid completion by conveying the house to a company which had always been under his complete control. The plaintiff sought specific performance against either the defendant or the company.

Held
Specific performance would be decreed against both of them.

Russell J:

'The ... company is the creature of the ... defendant, a device and a sham, a mask which he holds before his face in an attempt to avoid recognition by the eye of equity. The case cited (*Gilford Motor Co Ltd* v *Horne* [1933] Ch 935) illustrates that an equitable remedy is rightly to be granted directly against the creature in such circumstances.'

Multinational Gas and Petrochemical Co v *Multinational Gas and Petrochemical Services* [1983] Ch 258 Court of Appeal (Lawton, May and Dillon LJJ)

Lifting the veil – multinational companies

Facts
Three multinational oil companies formed the plaintiff company in Liberia for a joint commercial enterprise involving the purchase, transportation, storage and sale of liquefied petroleum gas and liquefied natural gas and similar products. It was originally intended that the plaintiff should carry on business in and from London. However, tax counsel advised that this would make the plaintiff's profits, wherever earned, liable to British taxation and, accordingly, the defendant company was incorporated in England to act as the plaintiff's agent and in doing so to give the plaintiff financial information and provide managerial and executive services to the plaintiff. The three oil companies were at all times the sole shareholders in both the plaintiff and defendant companies and the directors of each were employees and nominees of the three oil companies. The plaintiff began trading in 1971 but it ran into financial difficulties and in 1978 it was ordered to be wound up with debts of over £114m. As a result of the plaintiff's financial difficulties the defendant also ran into difficulties and was ordered to be wound up with assets of only £34,000. It was alleged by the liquidator of the plaintiff that the plaintiff's financial problems were caused by a highly speculative decision to build or acquire six oil tankers for trade in the oil spot market. Accordingly, the plaintiff brought an action in negligence against the defendant and its directors, the plaintiff's directors and the three oil companies. Since the only parties able to satisfy a monetary judgment were outside the jurisdiction (ie the directors and the three oil companies) the plaintiff applied for leave to serve writs on those defendants outside the jurisdiction under RSC Ord 11

r 1 (j) on the ground that the action was based on a tort committed within the jurisdiction. The master granted leave but Peter Gibson J set aside his order. The plaintiff appealed.

Held

(May LJ dissenting) No tort was committed inside the jurisdiction and leave to serve outside the jurisdiction was refused. Although the three oil companies were the sole shareholders of the plaintiff and directed it accordingly, they were not liable for the losses it sustained.

Lawton LJ:

... 'The submission in relation to the defendants was as follows. No allegation had been made that the plaintiff's directors had acted ultra vires or in bad faith. What was alleged was that when making the decisions which were alleged to have caused the plaintiff loss and giving instructions to (Multinational Gas) Services to put them into effect they had acted in accordance with the directions and behest of the three oil companies. These oil companies were the only shareholders. All the acts complained of became the plaintiff's acts. The plaintiff, although it had a separate existence from its oil company shareholders, existed for the benefit of those shareholders who, provided they acted intra vires and in good faith, could manage the plaintiff's affairs as they wished. If they wanted to take business risks through the plaintiff which no prudent businessman would take they could lawfully do so. Just as an individual can act like a fool provided he keeps within the law so could the plaintiff, but in its case it was for the shareholders to decide whether the plaintiff should act foolishly. As shareholders they owed no duty to those with whom the plaintiff did business. It was for such persons to assess the hazards of doing business with them. It follows, so it was submitted, that the plaintiff, as a matter of law, cannot now complain about what they did at their shareholders' behest.

This submission is based on the assumption, for which there was evidence, that Liberian company law was the same as English company law and on a long line of cases starting with *Salomon v Salomon & Co Ltd* [1897] AC 22 and ending with the decision of this court in *Re Horsley & Weight* [1982] 3 Ch 442. In my judgment these cases establish the following relevant principles of law. First, that the plaintiff was at law a different person from the subscribing oil company shareholders and was not their agent (see *Salomon v A Salomon & Co Ltd*). Second, that the oil companies as shareholders were not liable to anyone except to the extent and manner provided by the Companies Act 1948. (See *Salomon v A Salomon & Co Ltd*. Third, that when the oil companies acting together required the plaintiff's directors to make decisions or approve what had already been done, what they did or approved became the plaintiff's acts and were binding on it (see by way of examples *A-G for Canada & Standard Trust Co of New York* [1911] AC 498; *Re Express Engineering Works Ltd* [1920] 1 Ch 466; and *Re Horsley & Weight Ltd* . When approving whatever their nominee directors had done, the oil companies were not, as the plaintiff submitted, relinquishing any causes of action which the plaintiff may have had against its directors. When the oil companies, as shareholders, approved what the plaintiff's directors had done there was no cause of action because at that time there was no damage. What the oil companies were doing was adopting the directors and acts and as shareholders, in agreement with each other, making those acts the plaintiff's acts.'

National Dock Labour Board v Pinn & Wheeler Ltd and Others [1989] BCLC 647
Queen's Bench Division (MacPherson J)

Refusal to lift corporate veil between three related companies

Facts

P Ltd operated a wharf at which cargoes of timber belonging to S Ltd were unloaded and taken to the mill of K & B Ltd for processing. The National Dock Labour Board (NDLB) claimed that the work carried out by P Ltd was dock work subject to the national dock labour scheme. The scheme exempted waterside manufacturers from its application. An industrial tribunal held that P Ltd, S Ltd and K & B Ltd should be treated as a single entity and as a consequence qualified as waterside manufacturers and therefore were outside the operation of the national dock labour scheme.

The NDLB appealed.

Held

As a matter of principle there were no grounds for piercing the corporate veil of P Ltd, K & B Ltd and S Ltd and treating the three companies as a single entity. In addition even if the work of the three companies could be aggregated, because of the geographical location of K & B Ltd's factory some distance from the wharf there was no basis for finding that it constituted the business of a waterside manufacturer. Accordingly, the activities of the companies were not exempt from the national dock labour scheme.

MacPherson J:

'... It is only in special circumstances which indicate that there "is a mere facade concealing the true facts" that it is appropriate to pierce the corporate veil. See per Lord Keith in *Woolfson* v *Strathcylde Regional Council* (1978) 38 P & CR 521. In *Alex Lobb (Garages) Ltd* v *Total Oil GB* [1985] 1 All ER 303 at 309, Dillon J did refer to the proposition that: "The court has ample power to pierce the corporate veil." That is true, and in the context of that case he was referring to the unveiling of "a palpable device in an endeavour to evade the doctrine of restraint of trade" so that there was a facade concealing the true facts.

In my judgment, there was (to quote Lord Keith's word's) "no basis consonant with principle"on which on the facts of this case "the corporate veil can be pierced ..." It does indeed seem to me perhaps to be unseemly that the three companies should be allowed to unveil themselves in order to try and avoid the effect of the Dock Labour Scheme.

Where the companies are kept alive as separate legal entities for good commercial or historical reasons in order to keep the company's name fully alive and in order to maintain the loyalty of employees for example, and also probably to avoid redundancy and other problems, I see no reason why the veil should be pierced.'

Smith, Stone & Knight Ltd v *Birmingham Corporation* [1939] 4 All ER 116 King's Bench Division (Atkinson J)

Lifting the corporate veil between a group of companies

Facts

The plaintiff company purchased a partnership involved in the manufacture of paper and incorporated it running it as a wholly owned subsidiary in which it held all the shares but five, these five being held by nominees. All the profits of this company were treated as the profits of the parent company and it was under the control of the parent company. In 1935 Birmingham Corporation wished to compulsorily acquire the buildings belonging to the subsidiary to use the land on which they stood to build a technical college. The parent company claimed compensation pursuant to statute for disturbance but the corporation claimed that the subsidiary was the proper claimant.

Held

Where, in the circumstances, the subsidiary company was operating on behalf of the parent company the parent company could claim the compensation.

Atkinson J:

'... It seems therefore to be a question of fact in each case, and those cases indicate that the question is whether the subsidiary was carrying on the business as the company's business or as its own. I have looked at a number of cases – they are all revenue cases – to see what the courts regarded as of importance for determining that question ... and I find six points which were deemed relevant for the determination of the question: Who was really carrying on the business? In all the cases, the question was whether the company, an English company here, could be taxed in respect of all the profits made by some other company, a subsidiary company, being carried on elsewhere. The first point was: Were the profits treated as the profits of the company? – when I say "the company" I mean the parent company – secondly, were the persons conducting the business appointed by the parent company? Thirdly was the company the head and the brain of the trading venture? Fourthly, did the company govern the adventure, decide what should be done and what capital should be embarked on the venture? Fifthly, did the company make the profits by its skill and direction? Sixthly, was the company in effectual and constant control? Now, if the judgments in those cases are analysed, it will be found that all those matters were deemed relevant for consideration in determining the main question, and it seems to me that every one of those questions must be answered in favour of the claimants. Indeed, if ever one company can be said to be the agent or employee, or tool or simulacrum of another, I think the Waste company was in this case a legal entity, because that is all it was. There was nothing to prevent the claimants at any moment saying: "We will carry on this business in our own name". They had but to paint out the Waste company's name on the premises, change their business paper and form, and the thing would have been done. I am satisfied that the busines belonged to the claimants; they were, in my view, the real occupiers of the premises ...'

Lifting the veil of incorporation by statute

Blum v OCP Repartition SA [1988] BCLC 170 Court of Appeal (May and Balcombe LJJ)

Section 345 of the Companies Act 1985 – incorrect company name – personal liability on a company cheque

Facts

Bomore Medical Supplies Ltd, an English limited company of which Blum was a director, ordered and received from a French company a substantial quantity of pharmaceutical products. By way of par payment, cheques were drawn on an English bank, personalised in the name 'Bomore Medical Supplies' (ie, the word 'Limited' was omitted) and signed by Blum. Bomore encountered financial difficulties and was wound up before the cheques were paid.

Held

By virtue of s108 of the Companies Act 1948 (see now s349 of the Companies Act 1985), Blum was liable personally on the cheques.

May LJ:

'The defence which Blum sought to raise below ... has been one wholly of law ... This is based on what is said to have been a mutual mistake between all concerned. That is to say they ... were all aware that the cheques sued on in these proceedings were the cheques of the limited company; consequently when they were drawn without the inclusion of the word "Limited" on them they did not give effect to the clear, common intention of all concerned because of that mistake; consequently, it is contended, the cheques can and should be rectified to insert the word "Limited" on them. Thereafter as the rectification would have retroactive effect, Blum's liability by virtue of s108 of the 1948 Act would determine ...

As to the question of rectification, I quote the basic principle from *Snell's Principles of Equity* (28th edn, 1982) p610:

"If by mistake a written instrument does not accord with the true agreement between the parties, equity has the power to reform or rectify that instrument so as to make it accord with the true agreement."

It is on that basic principle that Blum relies ...

One may have sympathy for Blum in the predicament in which he finds himself, but the statutory provision is clear. The facts of this case are not in dispute and as a matter of law ... I do not think that the claim to rectification can afford him any defence. I respectfully agree with the submission which was made on behalf of the respondent that the true fallacy which lies behind Blum's contentions based upon rectification is that they are based on the premise that the respondent's rights arise from the cheques themselves. They do not. They arise from the application of the statutory provision to the signature of Blum in person.'

Commentary
See also *Lindholst & Co A/S* v *Fowler* [1988] BCLC 166.

Lindholst & Co A/S v *Fowler* [1988] BCLC 166 Court of Appeal (Sir John Donaldson MR, Neill and Ralph Gibson LJJ)

Section 349 of the Companies Act 1985 – incorrect company name – personal liability on bills of exchange

Facts
Four bills of exchange were drawn to cover instalments of the price of equipment supplied by the plaintiffs for a poultry processing plant under a written contract. The parties to the contract were expressed to be on the one hand the plaintiffs and on the other 'Corby Chicken Co' – the word 'Limited' was omitted. The contract was signed by the defendant as 'Managing Director' and the bills of exchange bore his signature by way of acceptance. The plaintiffs had prepared the contract and they had put forward the bills of exchange addressed to 'Corby Chicken Co': they alleged that the bills of exchange were intended to be and were accepted on behalf of Corby Chicken Co Ltd and with this the defendant agreed, saying also that the entire contract was with Corby Chicken Co Ltd.

Held
By virtue of s349 (4) of the Companies Act 1985 the defendant was personally liable to the plaintiffs.

Sir John Donaldson MR:

'Mr Fowler accepts that, as a consequence of that section, he is prima facie personally liable to the plaintiffs. But, he says, this is an exceptional case in which he should not be held liable because of the principles of estoppel, which I applied as a trial judge in *Durham Fancy Goods Ltd* v *Michael Jackson (Fancy Goods) Ltd* [1968] 2 QB 839 ...

For my part I am quite unable to accept that. Once it is admitted that the contract was with Corby Chicken Co Ltd, the obligation under the contract was to accept in a proper form for Corby Chicken Co Ltd as prescribed by the statute. What occurred was not a compliance ...

Furthermore, I am quite unable to apply the doctrine of estoppel which I applied in Durham Fancy Goods to this case because, whereas in Durham Fancy Goods the form of words for acceptance was prescribed by the plaintiffs and they were estopped by what they had prescribed, in this case the form of words for acceptance was not prescribed by the plaintiffs or by the contract. The plaintiffs simply put forward bills of exchange addressed by the Corby Chicken Co, which both they and the defendant knew meant Corby Chicken Co Ltd, and it was for the defendant to accept that bill in the proper form as required by the statute.'

Commentary

See also *Blum* v *OCP Repartition SA* [1988] BCLC 170.

Nisbet v *Shepherd* [1994] BCC 91 Court of Appeal (Balcombe, Leggatt and Hoffmann LJJ)

Liability under s24 CA 1985 – membership fell below two

Facts

Until 22 April 1983 KM & Co Ltd had two members with equal shareholdings. On that date the other member sold his shares to S and purported to execute a stock transfer. The instrument, however, was defective in that it was undated, the consideration was not mentioned and the address of the transferor and transferee were omitted. N, the liquidator of the company, sought an order that from 22 October 1983 S was personally liable jointly and severally with the company for the payment of all its unsatisfied debts, pursuant to s24 CA 1985. S contended that due to the defects the stock transfer was not effective to transfer the shares so that he was not therefore a sole member to which s24 could apply.

Held

The defects in the stock transfer amounted to a mere irregularity and did not affect the transfer of legal title to the shares. S was therefore the sole member of the company and s24 applied to him. Leggatt LJ said the case served as a useful reminder to small traders that, because of s24, they would not succeed in limiting their liability by setting up a company if they failed to ensure that no more than six months went by without the company having at least one member. Hoffmann LJ said he had considerable sympathy with S, who had fallen foul of an ancient and obsolete rule of company law. He could have avoided its effect by transferring a single share to his wife to hold on trust for him but he had not done so.

Commentary

Section 24 was amended from 15 July 1992 by the Companies (Single Member Private Limited Companies) Regulations 1992 (SI 1992/1699), and now only applies to public limited companies.

Rafsanjan Pistachio Products Co-operative v *S Reiss* (1989) The Times 4 December; [1990] BCLC 352 Queen's Bench Division (Potter J)

Section 349 of the Companies Act 1985 – absence of company name – personal liability on company cheques

Facts

The defendant had signed three separate cheques on behalf of Firegreen Ltd, now in receivership. The cheques were delivered to the plaintiff under an agreement it had with Firegreen but they did not bear Firegreen's name. Three of the cheques had not been honoured. The defendant was not a party to the agreement. She signed the cheques for the company and not in her own personal capacity. Her liability under s349 arose only as a result of the receivership.

Held

The liability of a director under s349 on a cheque which misnames or omits the company arises from the statutory rule as to the signing of the cheque rather than the cheque itself, and so rectification of the cheque is not permitted. To permit rectification would negate the plain intention of the Act by depriving the recipient of the cheque of the statutory liability imposed on the signatory. The Act could impose hardship on a director innocent of moral blame.

Thorne v *Silverleaf* [1994] BCC 109 Court of Appeal (Ralph Gibson and Peter Gibson LJJ)

Restrictions on re-using the name of an insolvent company: ss216 and 217 IA 1986

Facts
T had been a director of three companies which had all gone into insolvent liquidation. All of the companies had the name 'Mike Spence' as part of their name. S was a creditor of the company to the sum of £133,338 and claimed that T was jointly and severally liable with the company for this debt under ss216 and 217 of the Insolvency Act 1986. S obtained summary judgment and T appealed.

Held
The appeal was dismissed. Peter Gibson LJ said that S was not prevented from relying on ss216 and 217 on the basis that he had aided and abetted T to commit the crime in s216 (acting as a director of a company using a prohibited name). 'The monies claimed by Mr Silverleaf are not something to which but for the crime of aiding and abetting he would have no right or title.'

Criminal and civil liability of companies

Criminal liability

Deutsche Genossenschaftsbank v *Burnhope & Others* [1995] 1 WLR 1580 House of Lords (Lords Keith, Lloyd, Nicholls, Steyn and Hoffmann)

Theft by a company – whether an insurance policy covered theft by a company not on the premises

Facts
The Wallace Smith Company ('WSM') had a credit facility with the appellant bank for £9 million. This was secured, with the bank holding physical possession of £9 million worth of paper securities. WSM wanted to give the bank alternative securities, and to this end gave a letter of undertaking to the bank, which guaranteed delivery of the new securities by the close of business on that particular day. This was arranged by WSM's chairman but the letter was delivered by Towers, an innocent, temporary and junior employee of WSM. In return, the bank gave back the existing securities and allowed WSM to draw on the credit. The alternative securities were never delivered and a winding up petition was presented against WSM. In addition, Smith, WSM's chairman and directing mind and will, was arrested and charged with fraudulent trading. The bank was insured with the defendants and clause 2 of the policy gave protection against 'A (a) burglary, robbery or hold-up, or (b) theft ... committed by persons present on the premises of the assured ...'. When the bank made a claim under the policy, the defendants refused to pay.

    The majority of the Court of Appeal, with Staughton LJ dissenting, felt that the company committed the theft and that it was present on the bank's premises through Towers, even though he was not the directing mind and will of the company. Staughton LJ dissented on the basis that the policy only covered theft by natural persons on the premises. However, the only natural person on the premises was Towers and since he was innocent and not a thief, his Lordship found for the insurance company. The insurers appealed.

Held

The appeal was allowed, with Lord Steyn dissenting. The insurance policy only covered theft by a natural person who was physically present on the bank's premises. Here the company had committed the theft through its chairman, who did not enter the bank. The only natural person on the premises was Towers, but he was an innocent employee who was not a thief. The definition of 'person' contained in s61 Law of Property Act 1925 includes a corporation, but this was not adopted.

Lord Keith:

'The reason why the company was guilty of theft in the circumstances of this case was that its directing mind and will, Mr Smith, was himself guilty of theft. It was he who formed the dishonest intention of permanently depriving the bank of the securities, and who arranged for the innocent Mr Towers to deliver to the bank his letter containing false representations and to uplift the securities against it. If there had been no company involved and if it had been Mr Smith as an individual to whom the bank had granted the loan and who had deposited his own securities with the bank, so that the theft was committed by Mr Smith alone, then it could not be said, consistently with the ordinary use of language, that Mr Smith was present in the bank when the securities were uplifted by Mr Towers. Section 61 of the Law of Property Act 1925 provides that in all contracts and other instruments "person" included a corporation unless the context otherwise requires. No doubt if Mr Smith himself had, in this case, taken delivery of the securities in the premises of the bank, the company, as well as Mr Smith himself, would have been criminally liable for the theft, and it could be said that the company had been present in the premises of the bank within the meaning of clause 2. That is because Mr Smith was the directing mind and will of the company. But the company's liability would be irrelevant, since theft would in any event have been committed by a real live person on those premises, in the shape of Mr Smith. In the situation where Mr Smith could not be said to be present on the bank's premises then neither could that be said of the company.

It is apparent that the purpose of clause 2A(a) was to limit in some way the liability of the insurers for theft from the bank. What precisely was in contemplation is a matter of conjecture. It may have been some form of abstraction by electronic means, carried out by persons operating away from the bank's premises. Clause 2A(a), referring to burglary, robbery or hold-up, can only relate to crimes committed by natural persons on the bank's premises. Clause 2A(b), on a natural reading, has the same concept in view. It is not reasonable to suppose that the parties had in view section 61 of the Act of 1925, so as to have in contemplation that a company might be present on the premises of the bank and commit theft there. As Staughton LJ said, what was in contemplation was theft by a real live person in the bank.

My Lords, for these reasons I would allow the appeal and restore the order of Hobhouse J.'

Lord Steyn (dissenting):

'In my view as a matter of business common sense the theft took place at the bank's premises where the company through its agent appropriated the securities. The insurers' contrary argument is a literalist argument devoid of any redeeming commercial sense.'

R v Philippou [1989] Crim LR 585 Court of Appeal (O'Connor LJ, Caulfield and Eastham JJ)

Directors and shareholders – the 'mind and will' of a company

Facts

The two directors were the sole directors and shareholders of Budget Holiday Group in London. The three principal companies went into liquidation in October 1984 with deficiencies; one was Sunny Tours.

In 1983/4 the two directors bought a block of flats in Spain which had been used by Sunny Tours. The flats were put into a Spanish company's name, with the two directors as sole shareholders. The purchase price was paid with money drawn from Sunny Tours in London.

The defence argued that the two directors as sole shareholders and directors were the 'mind and will' of Sunny Tours. When they gave instructions to the bank to transfer the money, the instructions were those of the company. So that the company had consented to the transfer in the sense that the transfer could not be said to be adverse to any right of the company.

Held

That where a defendant and his co-accused were the sole directors and shareholders of a company it was possible in law for them to steal from their own company.

Lord Justice O'Connor giving the reasons of the court said:

'... the order to the bank was only one part of a composite transaction. The other component was the fact that the money was being used to put the block of flats into the pockets of the appellant and his co-accused through the Spanish company.

That component was the fact from which the jury could infer not only the transaction was dishonest but was intended to deprive Sunny Tours permanently of its money.

... Once the two components were put together the drawing of the money from the bank was shown to be adverse to the rights of the company and there was an appropriation.'

P & O European Ferries (Dover) Ltd, Re (1991) 93 Cr App R 72 Central Criminal Court (Turner J)

Criminal liability of a company – corporate manslaughter

Facts

On March 6 1987 a ferry, the Herald of Free Enterprise, sank, resulting in loss of life. Seven defendants together wth the owners of the vessel, P & O European Ferries (Dover) Ltd, were charged with manslaughter. One of the issues at the trial was whether or not English law recognised the offence of corporate manslaughter.

Held

It is possible to include in an indictmet a charge of corporate manslaughter. Manslaughter is not restricted to when one natural person kills another natural person. After reviewing the authorities, Mr Justice Turner felt that his decision did not increase the scope of the criminal law, but merely reflected the developments in the existing law. In reaching his decision, Turner J referred to *Her Majesty's Coroner for East Kent, ex parte Spooner* [1989] 88 Cr App R 10, and the words of Bingham LJ who said:

'I am, however, tentatively of the opinion that on appropriate facts the mens rea required for manslaughter can be established against a corporation. I see no reason in principle why such a charge may not be established.'

Tesco Supermarkets Ltd v *Nattrass* [1972] AC 153 House of Lords (Lords Reid, Morris, Viscount Dilhorne, Lords Pearson and Diplock)

A branch manager is not the 'directing mind and will' of a company

Facts

Tesco displayed an advertisement in one of their supermarkets offering 'Radiant' washing powder at a special offer price of 2s 11d instead of the normal price of 3s 11d. An old age pensioner saw the advertisement and went to buy a pack but he could only find packs marked 3s 11d: when he took one to the cashier he was told there were none in stock for sale at 2s 11d so he paid 3s 11d and complained to the inspector of weights and measures who brought a prosecution against Tesco under s11(2) of the Trade Descriptions Act 1968 for offering goods for sale at a price indicated to be less than that at which they were in fact offered. The mistake as to pricing the washing powder arose because the 2s 11d packs were out of stock and a shop assistant had put the 3s 11d packs on display without informing the shop manager. The justices fined Tesco for the offence and the Divisional Court dismissed an appeal by Tesco who then appealed to the House of Lords arguing, inter alia, that the failure of their shop manager to exercise his supervisory function to see prices were correct could not be regarded as a failure by the company as he was not the 'directing mind and will' of the company.

Held

The appeal would be allowed.

Lord Reid:

'... Where a limited company is the employer difficult questions do arise in a wide variety of circumstances in deciding which of its officers or servants is to be identified with the company so that his guilt is the guilt of the company.

I must start by considering the nature of the personality which by a fiction the law attributes to a corporation. A living person has a mind which can have knowledge or intention or be negligent and he has hands to carry out his intentions. A corporation has none of these; it must act through living persons, though not always one or the same person. Then the person who acts is not speaking or acting for the company. He is acting as the company and his mind which directs his acts is the mind of the company. There is no question of the company being vicariously liable. He is not acting as a servant, representative, agent or delegate. He is an embodiment of the company, or, one could say, he hears and speaks through the persona of the company, within his appropriate sphere, and his mind is the mind of the company. If it is a guilty mind then that guilt is the guilt of the company. It must be a question of law whether, once the facts have been ascertained, a person in doing particular things is to be regarded as the company or merely as the company's servant or agent. In that case any liability of the company can only be a statutory or vicarious liability.

In *Lennard's Carrying Co Ltd* v *Asiatic Petroleum Co Ltd* [1915] AC 705 the question was whether damage had occurred without the "actual fault or privity" of the owner of a ship. The owners were a company. The fault was that of the registered managing owner who managed the ship on behalf of the owners and it was held that the company could not dissociate itself from him so as to say that there was no actual fault or privity on the part of the company. Viscount Haldane LC said:

"For if Mr Lennard was the directing mind of the company, then his action must, unless a corporation is not to be liable at all, have been an action which was the action of the company iself within the meaning of s502 ... It must be upon the true construction of that section in such a case as the present one that the fault or privity of somebody who is not merely a servant or agent for whom the company is liable upon the footing respondeat superior, but somebody for whom the company is liable because his action is the very action of the company itself."

Reference is frequently made to the judgment of Denning LJ in *HL Bolton (Engineering) Co Ltd* v *TJ Graham & Sons Ltd* [1957] 1 QB 159. He said:

"A company may in many ways be likened to a human body. It has a brain and nerve centre which controls what it does. It also has hands which hold the tools and act in accordance with directions from the centre. Some of the people in the company are mere servants and agents who are nothing more than hands to do the work and cannot be said to represent the mind or will. Others are directors and managers who represent the directing mind and will of the company, and control what it does. The state of mind of these managers is the state of mind of the company and is treated by the law as such."

In that case the directors of the company only met once a year; they left the management of the business to others, and it was the intention of those managers which was imputed to the company. I think that was right. There have been attempts to apply Denning LJ's words to all servants of a company whose work is brain work, or who exercise some managerial discretion under the direction of superior officers of the company. I do not think that Denning LJ intended to refer to them. He only referred to those who "represent the directing mind and will of the company, and control what it does". I think that is right for this reason. Normally the board of directors, the managing director and perhaps other superior officers of a company carry out the functions of management and speak and act as the company. Their subordinates do not. They carry out orders from above and it can make no difference that they are given some measure of discretion. But the board of directors may delegate some part of their functions of management giving to their delegate full discretion to act independently of instructions from them. I see no difficulty in holding that they have thereby put such a delegate in their place so that within the scope of the delegation he can act as the company. It may not always be easy to draw the line but there are cases in which the line must be drawn. *Lennard's* case was one of them.

In some cases the phrase alter ego has been used. I think it is misleading. When dealing with a company the word alter is I think misleading. The person who speaks and acts as the company is not alter. He is identified with the company. And when dealing with an individual no other individual can be his alter ego. The other individual can be a servant, agent, delegate or representative but I know of neither principle nor authority which warrants the confusion (in the literal or original sense) of two separate individuals ...'

Civil liability

C Evans & Sons Ltd v Spritebrand Ltd [1985] 1 WLR 317; Court of Appeal (Cumming-Bruce, O'Connor and Slade LJJ)

Tort committed by company – directors procured infringement of copyright – whether director personally liable

Facts
The defendant company Spritebrand and one of its directors called Sullivan were sued for infringement of copyright by the plaintiff company. Sullivan applied to have the action against him struck out on the ground that it disclosed no reasonable cause of action against him. The application was refused by the Master and, on appeal, by a Chancery udge. The matter was appealed to the Court of Appeal. Because of the manner in which the plaintiff company pleaded its case the issue upon which the Court of Appeal was asked to decide the case was based on the proposition 'that a director of a company who personally directs and procures the company to commit a tort is himself liable to the victim in tort no less than the company.'

Held
The application to have the action struck out was refused.

Slade LJ:
The mere fact that a person is a director of a limited liability company does not by itself render him liable for torts committed by the company during the period of his directorship; see, for example, *Rainham Chemical Works Ltd v Belvedere Fish Guano Co Ltd* [1921] AC 465 at 488 per Lord Parmoor and *Pritchard & Constance (Wholesale) Ltd v Amata Ltd* (1924) 42 RPC 63. Nevertheless, judicial

dicta of high authority are to be found in the English decisions which suggest that a director is liable for those tortious acts of a company which he has ordered or procured to be done.

'In *Performing Rights Society Ltd* v *Ciryl Theatrical Syndicate Ltd* [1924] 1 KB 1 Atkin LJ referred to a statement of principle by Lord Buckmaster in the *Rainham Chemical Works* case and said at p14:

"Prima facie a managing director is not liable for tortious acts done by servants of the company unless he himself is privy to the acts, that is to say unless he ordered or procured the acts to be done. That is authoritatively stated in *Rainham Chemical Works Ltd* v *Belvedere Fish Guano Co Ltd* where it was sought to make a company liable for an explosion upon their works in the course of manufacturing high explosives. The company were held liable on the principle of *Rylands* v *Fletcher* (1868) LR 3 HL 330. It was also sought to charge two directors with liability. They were eventually held responsible because they were in fact occupiers of the works. It was contended that they were liable on the ground that they were managing directors of the company, that the company was under their sole control as governing directors, and that they were responsible for the work done by their servants. Lord Buckmaster said 'I cannot accept either of these views. If the company was really trading independently on its own account, the fact that it was directed by Messrs Feldman and Partridge would not render them responsible for its tortious acts unless, indeed, they were acts expressly directed by them. If a company is formed for the express purpose of doing a wrongful act or if, when formed, those in control expressly direct that a wrongful thing be done, the individuals as well as the company are responsible for the consequences, but there is no evidence in the present case to establish liability under either of these heads.' Perhaps that is put a little more narrowly than it would have been if it had been intended as a general pronouncement without reference to the particular case; because I conceive that express direction is not necessary. If the directors themselves directed or procured the commission of the act they would be liable in whatever sense that did so, whether expressly or impliedly ..."

... The authorities, as I have already indicated, clearly show that a director of a company is not automatically to be identified with his company for the purpose of the law of tort, however small the company may be and however powerful his control over its affairs. Commercial enterprise and adventure is not to be discouraged by subjecting a director to such onerous potential liabilities. In every case where it is sought to make him liable for his company's torts, it is necessary to examine with care what part he played personally in regard to the act or acts complained of. Furthermore, I have considerable sympathy with judges, particularly when dealing with commercial matters, who may be anxious to avoid or discourage unnecessary multiplicity of parties by the joinder of directors of limited companies as additional defendants in inappropriate cases. As Mr Watson emphasised, the very fact of such joinder could in some cases operate to put unfair pressure on the defendants to settle. In some instances, where the joinder is demonstrably a mere tactical move, a striking out application may well be justified ...'

Lennard's Carrying Co Ltd v *Asiatic Petroleum Co Ltd* [1915] AC 705 House of Lords (Viscount Haldane, Lords Dunedin, Atkinson, Parker and Parmoor)

Directing mind and will of a company – managing director

Facts

The appellants owned a bulk oil carrier, the Edward Dawson, which went aground in heavy seas and eventually burst into flames whilst transporting benzine from Novorossisk in the Black Sea to Rotterdam. The cause of the fire was due to the ship's boilers being in poor condition and unable to generate sufficient energy to avoid the ship going aground and the consequent bumping caused the tanks to crack resulting in benzine leaking into the ship's furnace. The judge at first instance found the ship to be unseaworthy and the question arose whether the ship owners could invoke the protection of s502 of the Merchant Shipping Act that they be not 'liable to make good to any extent whatever any loss or damage happening without his actual fault or privity' when they were sued by the cargo owners for its loss. The management of the ship was entrusted to a Mr Lennard, who was the company's managing director, and his name appeared as such in the ship's register. He knew or ought to have known of the condition of the ship's boilers, but had given no instructions regarding their supervision to the ship's captain or chief engineer. He also took no steps to avoid the ship commencing its voyage in an unseaworthy condition. The issue was whether what happened was without the fault or privity of the appellants so that they could rely on the defence in s502.

Held

The House of Lords held that Mr Lennard was the directing mind and will of the company and that his actions were those of the company. The ship owners could not, therefore, rely on the defence.

Viscount Haldane LC:

'... A corporation is an abstraction. It has no mind of its own any more than it has a body of its own; its active and directing will must consequently be sought in the person of somebody who for some purposes may be called an agent, but who is really the directing mind and will of the corporation, the very ego and centre of the personality of the corporation. That person may be under the direction of the shareholders in general meeting; that person may be the board of directors itself, or it may be, and in some companies it is so, that that person has an authority co-ordinate with the board of directors given to him under the articles of association, and is appointed by the general meeting of the company, and can only be removed by the general meeting of the company. Whatever is not known about Mr Lennards's position, this is known for certain, Mr Lennard took the active part in the management of this ship on behalf of the owners, and Mr Lennard, as I have said, was registered as the person designated for this purpose in the ship's register. Mr Lennard, therefore, was the natural person to come on behalf of the owners and give full evidence not only about the events of which I have spoken, and which related to the seaworthiness of the ship, but about his own position and as to whether or not he was the life and soul of the company. For if Mr Lennard was the directing mind of the company, then his action must, unless a corporation is not to be liable at all, have been an action which was the action of the company itself within the meaning of s502. It has not been contended at the Bar, and it could not have been successfully contended, that s502 is so worded as to exempt a corporation altogether which happened to be the owner of a ship, merely because it happened to be a corporation. It must be upon the true construction of that section in such a case as the present one that the fault or privity is the fault of somebody who is not merely a servant or agent for whom the company is liable upon the footing respondeat superior, but somebody for whom the company is liable because his action is the very action of the company itself.'

Meridian Global Funds Management Asia Ltd v *Securities Commission* [1995] BCC 942 Privy Council (Lords Keith, Jauncey, Mustill, Lloyd and Hoffmann)

Company's state of mind – whether the knowledge of employees can be attributed to the company

Facts

Meridian Global National Corporation Ltd ('Meridian') acquired 49 per cent of the shares in Euro-National Corporation Ltd ('ENC'), a company listed on the New Zealand Stock Exchange. This was implemented by two Meridian employees; Koo, the chief investment officer, and Ng, a senior portfolio manager. As a result Meridian became a 'substantial security holder' in ENC. As such, Meridian was required to notify ENC and the New Zealand Stock Exchange of its holding under s20 (New Zealand) Securities Amendment Act 1988. This it failed to do and it raised the question whether Meridian knew it had become a substantial security holder.

The Court of Appeal of New Zealand held that Koo was the directing mind and will of Meridian and so his knowledge ought to be attributed to Meridian, who was thus in breach of s20. Meridian appealed to the Privy Council on the grounds that only its board of directors or its managing director could be considered as its directing mind and will.

Held

The appeal was dismissed. The knowledge of Koo and Ng was to be attributed to Meridian for the purposes of s20 of the 1988 Act. Meridian knew it had become a substantial security holder when that was known to the person who had authority to buy the shares. It made no difference that Koo did the deal for a corrupt purpose and did not give the relevant notice because he did not want his employers to find out about the shares. This did not affect the attribution of knowledge. To hold otherwise would be to defeat the policy of the Act.

Lord Hoffmann:

'Once it is appreciated that the question is one of construction rather than metaphysics, the answer in this case seems to their Lordships to be as straightforward as it did to Heron J. The policy of s20 of the Securities Amendment Act 1988 is to compel, in fast moving markets, the immediate disclosure of the identity of persons who become substantial security holders in public issuers. Notice must be given as soon as that person knows that he has become a substantial security holder. In the case of a corporate security holder, what rule should be implied as to the person whose knowledge for this purpose is to count as the knowledge of the company? Surely the person who, with the authority of the company, acquired the relevant interest. Otherwise the policy of the Act would be defeated. Companies would be able to allow employees to acquire interests on their behalf which made them substantial security holders but would not have to report them until the board or someone else in senior management got to know about it. This would put a premium on the board paying as little attention as possible to what its investment managers were doing. Their Lordships would therefore hold that upon the true construction of s20(4)(e), the company knows that it has become a substantial security holder when that is known to the person who had authority to do the deal. It is then obliged to give notice under s20(3). The fact that Koo did the deal for a corrupt purpose and did not give such notice because he did not want his employers to find out cannot in their Lordships' view affect the attribution of knowledge and the consequent duty to notify.

It was therefore not necessary in this case to inquire into whether Koo could have been described in some more general sense as the "directing mind and will" of the company.

But their Lordships would wish to guard themselves against being understood to mean that whenever a servant of a company has authority to do an act on its behalf, knowledge of that act will for all purposes be attributed to the company. It is a question of construction in each case as to whether the particular rule requires that the knowledge that an act has been done, or the state of the mind with which it was done, should be attributed to the company. Sometimes, as in *Ready Mixed Concrete* [1995] 1 AC 456 and this case, it will be appropriate. Likewise in a case in which a company was required to make a return for revenue purposes and the statute made it an offence to make a false return with intent to deceive, the divisional court held that the mens rea of the servant authorised to discharge the duty to make the return should be attributed to the company: see *Moore* v *I Bresler Ltd* [1944] 2 All ER 515. On the other hand, the fact that a company's employee is authorised to drive a lorry does not in itself lead to the conclusion that if he kills someone by reckless driving, the company will be guilty of manslaughter. There is no inconsistency. Each is an example of an attribution rule for a particular purpose, tailored as it always must be to the terms and policies of the substantive rule.'

2 Memorandum of Association

The memorandum

Guinness v Land Corporation of Ireland (1882) 22 Ch D 349 Court of Appeal (Cotton and Bowen LJJ)

Relationship between a memorandum and the articles

Facts

The company was formed with the general object, appearing from the memorandum, of cultivating land in Ireland. It had a share capital of £1,050,000 divided into 140,000 A shares of £5 each and 3,500 B shares of £100 each. Clause 8 of the articles provided that the interest produced by the B shares was, so far as necessary, to be applied in giving the holders of the A shares a 5 per cent preferential dividend on the amounts paid up on their shares. The holder of some B shares objected to this on the ground that an application of the income from the capital of the B shares would be ultra vires as an application of capital inconsistent with the memorandum of association.

Held

Clause 8 of the articles was invalid as it purported to apply capital of the B shares for purposes which were not within the objects of the company as set out in the memorandum. Further, the articles could not modify the memorandum in respect of any matters required to be stated in the memorandum by the Companies Acts.

Bowen LJ:

' ... There is an essential difference between the memorandum and articles. The memorandum contains the fundamental conditions upon which alone the company is allowed to be incorporated. They are conditions introduced for the benefit of the creditors, and the outside public, as well as of the shareholders. The articles of association are the internal regulations of the company. How can it be said that in all cases the fundamental conditions of the charter of incorporation, and the internal rgulations of the company are to be construed together? *Harrison* v *Mexican Railway Company* (1875) LR 19 Eq 358 was cited as showing that the Master of the Rolls was willing to read the two together, but the distinction is obvious that in that case the matter was one with which the creditors had no concern whatsoever. In any case, it is, as it seems to me, certain that for anything which the Act of Parliament says shall be in the memorandum you must look to the memorandum alone. If the Legislature has said that one instrument is to be dominant, you cannot turn to another instrument and read it in order to modify the provisions of the dominant instrument.'

New Zealand Guardian Trust Co Ltd v Keneth Stewart Brooks and Others [1995] 1 WLR 96 Privy Council (Lords Keith of Kinkel, Oliver of Aylmerton, Mustill, Lloyd of Berwick and Nicholls of Birkenhead)

Whether company vicariously liable for directors' negligence

Facts

A company (Budget) borrowed money from a consortium of financiers which was secured by a debenture trust deed. The deed required the company to provide the trustee with quarterly reporting certificates which required, among other things, the directors to state whether any matters had arisen which would adversely affect the lender's position. The certificates were prepared and signed by the company's directors. When the company was unable to pay back the monies advanced, two of the debenture holders accepted a sum less than the amount owed in full and final settlement of the loan. The two debenture holders then sued the trustee for the shortfall, amounting to £2,712,000. They alleged breaches of duties owed to them by the trustee under the trust deed. The trustee, NZGT Ltd, joined Budget's directors as third parties, alleging that the quarterly reporting certificates were prepared negligently. NZGT Ltd had previously released Budget from all liabilities towards it, but the release did not cover the directors of Budget.

Held

The directors of Budget were joint tortfeasors with Budget in negligently preparing the certificates. The release of Budget's liability also released the directors from further liability. The directors were properly struck out as third parties to the proceedings.

Lord Keith of Kinkel:

'The directors of Budget were its agents, and the question is whether or not they were acting in the course of their agency when they prepared the certificates. There can be no doubt that they were acting in their capacity as directors when they did so, and indeed this was conceded by counsel for the NZGT. Further, they were acting within the scope of their agency. They could not have prepared the certificates if they had not been authorised by Budget to do so, and their doing so was for the benefit of Budget because the rendering of the certificates was necessary to the maintenance of the loans to it. It is to be accepted that the directors assumed a personal responsibility towards NZGT to see that the certificates complied with the requirements of the trust deed and to exercise reasonable care in their preparation, but in most if not all cases where the acts of an employee or agent render the employer or principal vicariously liable it is because the employee or agent was in breach of a duty which he personally owed to the injured party.'

After referring to *Cassidy* v *Ministry of Health* [1951] 2 KB 343 and *Kuwait Asia Bank EC* v *National Mutual Life Nominees Ltd* [1991] 1 AC 187, his Lordship concluded:

'In their Lordships' opinion Budget was vicariously liable for the negligence of its directors in the preparation of the certificates and was accordingly a joint tortfeasor with them. The release of Budget therefore had the effect of releasing also the directors.'

Ultra vires

Ashbury Railway Carriage and Iron Co v *Riche* (1875) LR 7 HL 653 House of Lords (Lord Cairns LC, Lords Chelmsford, Hatherley, O'Hagan and Selbourne)

Effect of a company acting outside its objects clause

Facts

The company was registered under the Joint Stock Companies Act 1862 for the following objects – 'to make and sell, or lend on hire, railway carriages and waggons, and all kinds of railway plant, fittings, machinery, and rolling stock, to carry on the business of mechanical engineers and general contractors; to purchase, lease, work and sell mines, minerals, land and buildings; to purchase and sell, as merchants, timber, coal, metals, or other materials, and to buy and sell any such materials on commission or as agents.' The directors of the company agreed to purchase a concession for the making of a railway line in Belgium. As the work progressed on the line difficulties arose about payment and the shareholders differed from the directors as to the profitability of the venture. To settle these differences it was agreed that the directors would purchase from the company all its interest in the railway line. Later, however, the company repudiated the contract for constructing the line on the ground that it was ultra vires.

Held

The contract was one which by its nature was not included in the memorandum. It was ultra vires not only of the directors but the company.

Lord Cairns LC:

'... I will ask your Lordships to observe ... the marked and entire difference there is between the two documents which form the title deeds of companies of this description – I mean the memorandum of association on the one hand, and the articles of association on the other hand. With regard to the memorandum of association, your Lordships will find, as has often already been pointed out, although it appears somewhat to have been overlooked in the present case, that that is, as it were, the charter and defines the limitation of the powers of a company to be established under the Act. With regard to the articles of association, those articles play a part subsidiary to the memorandum of association. They accept the memorandum of association as the charter of incorporation of the company, and so accepting it, the articles proceed to define the duties, the rights and the powers of the governing body as between themselves and the company at large, and the mode and form in which the business of the company is to be carried on, and the mode and form in which changes in the internal regulations of the company may from time to time be made. With regard, therefore, to the memorandum of association, if you find anything which goes beyond that memorandum or is not warranted by it, the question will arise whether that which is so done is ultra vires, not only of the directors of the company, but of the company itself. With regard to the articles of association, if you find anything which, still keeping within the memorandum of association, is a violation of the articles of association, or in excess of them, the question will arise whether that is anything more than an act extra vires the directors, but intra vires the company ...'

His Lordship then referred to the various provisions in the Joint Stock Companies Act 1862 concerning the memorandum and continued:

'... Now, my Lords, if that is so – if that is the condition upon which the corporation is established – if that is the purpose for which the corporation is established – it is a mode of incorporation which contains in it both that which is affirmative and that which is negative. It states affirmatively the ambit and the extent of vitality and power which by law are given to the corporation, and it states, if it is necessary so to state, negatively, that nothing shall be done beyond that ambit, and that no attempt shall be made to use the corporate life for any other purpose than that which is so specified ...

... Now, my Lords, bearing in mind the difference which I have just taken the liberty of pointing out to your Lordships between the memorandum and the articles, we arrive at once at all which appears to me to be necessary for the purpose of deciding this case. I have used the expressions extra vires and intra vires. I prefer either expression very much to one which occasionally has been used in the judgments in the present case, and has also been used in other cases, the expression "illegality".

In a case such as that which your Lordships have now to deal with, it is not a question whether the contract sued upon involves that which is malum prohibitum or malum in se, or is a contract contrary to public policy, and illegal in itself. I assume the contract in itself to be perfectly legal, to have nothing in it obnoxious to the doctrine involved in the expressions which I have used. The question is not as to the legality of the conract; the question is as to the competency and power of the company to make the contract. Now, I am clearly of opinion that this contract was entirely, as I have said, beyond the objects in the memorandum of association. If so, it was thereby placed beyond the powers of the company to make the contract. If so, my Lords, it is not a question whether the contract ever was ratified or was not ratified. If it was a contract void as its beginning, it was void because the company could not make the contract. If every shareholder of the company had been in the room, and every shareholder of the company had said, "That is a contract which we desire to make which we authorise the directors to make, to which we sanction the placing the seal of the company", the case would not have stood in any different position from that in which it stands now. The shareholders would thereby, by unanimous consent, have been attempting to do the very thing which, by the Act of Parliament, they were prohibited from doing.

But, my Lords, if the shareholders of this company could not ab ante have authorised a contract of this kind to be made, how could they subsequently sanction the contract after it had, in point of fact, been made? I endeavoured to follow as accurately as I could the very able argument of Mr Benjamin at your Lordships' Bar on this point; but it appeared to me that this was a difficulty with which he was entirely unable to grapple. He endeavoured to contend that when the shareholders had found that something had been done which ought not to have been done, they might be authorised to make the best they could of a difficulty into which they had thus been thrown, and therefrom might be deemed to possess power to sanction the contract being proceeded with. My Lords, I am unable to adopt that suggestion. It appears to me that it would be perfectly fatal to the whole scheme of legislation to which I have referred, if you were to hold that, in the first place, directors might do that which even the whole company could not do, and that then, the shareholders finding out what had been done, could sanction, subsequently, what they could not antecedently have authorised.

My Lords, if this be the proper view of the Act of Parliament, it reconciles, as it appears to me, the opinion of all the judges of the Court of Exchequer Chamber; because I find Mr Justice Blackburn, whose judgment was concurred in by two other judges who took the same view, expressing himself thus (1874) LR 9 Ex 262: "I do not entertain any doubt that if, on the true construction of a statute creating a corporation it appears to be the intention of the Legislature, expressed or implied, that the corporation shall not enter into a particular contract, every court, whether of law or equity, is bound to treat a contract entered into contrary to the enactment as illegal, and therefore wholly void, and to hold that a contract wholly void cannot be ratified." My Lords, that sums up and exhausts the whole case.'

Commentary
See now ss108–112 of the Companies Act 1989.

Aveling Barford Ltd v *Perion Ltd and Others* [1989] BCLC 626 Chancery Division (Hoffmann J)

Sale of company property – unauthorised return of capital which was ultra vires

Facts
In March 1987 the balance sheet of Aveling Barford Ltd (now in liquidation) showed that on a going concern basis its assets exceeded its liabilities but it had an accumulated deficit on its profit and loss account and therefore could not make any distribution to its shareholders. The company owned a site known as 'Arnoldfield' comprising around 18 acres and valued independently in October 1986 at £650,000. The property was sold to the first defendant company in February 1987 for £350,000. The first defendant company Perion Ltd was controlled by L who also controlled Aveling Barford Ltd. The purchase was financed in part by a mortgage and the mortgage company valued the property at £1,150,000. There also appeared to be an agreement that if Perion Ltd sold the property within a year of the transaction, then they would pay Aveling Barford Ltd £400,000 if the sale price exceeded £800,000. It was sold within the year at a sale price of £1,526,000. Aveling Barford Ltd obtained judgment in default on the ground that the first defendant was a constructive trustee of the proceeds of sale. The first defendant sought to have the judgment set aside.

Held

As L knew that the property was worth £650,000, it was a breach of L's fiduciary duty to arrange to sell the property for £350,000 and, since the first defendant was aware of the facts constituting the breach, it was accountable as a constructive trustee. The sale to the defendant was not a genuine exercise of the power of the plaintiff to sell its property. It was a sale at undervalue for the purpose of enabling L, the sole beneficial owner of the plaintiff, to obtain an unauthorised return of capital and hence was ultra vires and unratifiable. As there was no arguable defence to the plaintiff's claim, the motion to set aside the judgment was dismissed.

Hoffmann J:

'... The general rule is that any act which falls within the express or implied powers of a company conferred by its memorandum of association, whether or not a breach of duty on the part of the directors, will be binding on the company if it is approved or subsequently ratified by the shareholders: see *Rolled Steel Products (Holdings) Ltd* v *British Steel Corporation* [1984] BCLC 466 at 507. But this rule is subject to exceptions created by the general law and one such exception is that a company cannot without leave of the court or the adoption of a special procedure return its capital to its shareholders. It follows that a transaction which amounts to an unauthorised return of capital is ultra vives and cannot be validated by shareholder ratification or approval. Whether or not the transaction is a distribution to shareholders does not depend exclusively on what the parties choose to call it. The court looks at the substance rather than the outward appearance.

... So it seems to me in this case that looking at the matter objectively, the sale to Perion was not a genuine exercise of the company's power under its memorandum to sell its assets. It was a sale at a gross undervalue for the purpose of enabling a profit to be realised by an entity controlled and put forward by its sole beneficial shareholder. This was as much a dressed-up distribution as the payment of excessive interest on *Ridge Securities Ltd* v *IRC* [1964] 1 All ER 275 or excessive remuneration in *Re Halt Garage (1964) Ltd* [1982] 3 All ER 1016.'

Construction of the objects clause

Bell Houses v *City Wall Properties* [1966] 2 QB 656 Court of Appeal (Sellers, Danckwerts and Salmon LJJ)

Subjectively worded object clauses

Facts

The plaintiff company had, inter alia, the objects of carrying on business as general, civil and engineering contractors and, in particular building houses and by clause 3 (c) 'to carry on any other trade or business whatever, which can, in the opinion of the board of directors be advantageously carried on by the company in connection with or as ancillary to any of the above business or the general business of the company...' The defendants were also property developers whom the plaintiffs had agreed to introduce to a financier prepared to lend the defendants £1m of short-term credit for property development. The agreed fee for the plaintiffs was £20,000. The introduction was effected and the defendants received the desired credit but they then refused to pay the £20,000 fee to the plaintiffs, alleging that the whole contract was ultra vires the plaintiffs and void. At first instance Mocatta J upheld the defendants' contention on the construction of the objects clause. The plaintiffs appealed.

Held

The appeal would be allowed as clause 3(c) allowed the company to carry on any trade or business which the directors bona fide believed could be advantageously carried on by it in connection with or ancillary to its main business. The contract was within the ambit of clause 3(c) and, accordingly, intra vires.

Salmon LJ (after reading clause 3(c)):

'As a matter of pure construction, the meaning of these words seems to me to be obvious. An object of the plaintiff company is to carry on any business which the directors genuinely believe can be carried on advantageously in connection with or as ancillary to the general business of the company. It may be that the directors take the wrong view and in fact the business in question cannot be carried on as the directors believe. But it matters not how mistaken the directors may be. Providing they form their view honestly, the business is within the plaintiff company's objects and powers. This is so plainly the natural and ordinary meaning of the language of sub-clause (c) that I would refuse to construe it differently unless compelled to do so by the clearest authority. And there is no such authority.'

Cotman v *Brougham* [1918] AC 514 House of Lords (Lord Finlay LC, Lords Atkinson, Parker and Wrenbury)

The use of lengthy objects clauses – independently worded objects clauses

Facts
The Essequibo Rubber and Tobacco Estates Company was registered in 1910 with a memorandum of association which 'set out a vast variety of objects'. The company's actual business was rubber and tobacco plantations. Shortly after it was registered the Essequibo company underwrote shares in the Anglo-Cuban Oil Company. In 1912 an order was made to wind up the Anglo-Cuban Oil Company and it was ordered in this liquidation that the Essequibo company should be placed on the list of contributories in respect of £14,046 due on these shares. The Essequibo company also went into liquidation and its liquidator applied for its name to be removed from the list of contributories on the ground that the underwriting transaction was ultra vires.

Held
The transaction was not ultra vires as the objects clause was wide enough to permit the company to enter into underwriting transactions.

Lord Parker:

'... It may well be that the memorandum of association in the present case is not framed on the lines contemplated by the Companies (Consolidation) Act 1908. This point would no doubt have been open to argument on proceedings for a mandamus had the registrar refused to accept it ...

... The truth is that the statement of a company's objects in its memorandum is intended to serve a double purpose. In the first place, it gives protection to subscribers, who learn from it the purposes to which their money can be applied. In the second place, it gives protection to persons who deal with the company and who can infer from it the extent of the company's powers. The narrower the objects expressed in the memorandum the less is the subscribers' risk, but the wider such objects the greater is the security of those who transact business with the company. Moreover, experience soon showed that persons who transact business with companies do not like having to depend on inference when the validity of a proposed transaction is in question. Even a power to borrow money could not always be safely inferred, much less such a power as that of underwriting shares in another company. Thus arose the practice of specifying powers as objects, a practice rendered possible by the fact that there is no statutory limit on the number of objects which may be specified. But even thus, a person proposing to deal with a company could not be absolutely safe, for powers specified as objects might be read as ancillary to and exercisable only for the purpose of attaining what might he held to be the company's main or paramount object and on this construction no one could be quite certain whether the court would not hold any proposed transaction to be ultra vires. At any rate, all the surrounding circumstances would require investigation. Fresh clauses were framed to meet this difficulty, and the result is the modern memorandum of association with the multifarious list of objects and powers specified as objects, and its clauses designed to prevent any specified object being read as ancillary to some other object ...'

Lord Wrenbury:

'... There has grown up a pernicious practice of registering memoranda of association which under the clause relating to objects contain paragraph after paragraph not specifying or delimiting the proposed trade or purpose, but confusing power with purpose and indicating every class of act which the corporation is to have power to do. The practice is not one of recent growth. It was in active operation when I was a junior at the Bar. After a vain struggle I had to yield to it, contrary to my own convictions. It has arrived now at a point at which the fact is that the function of the memorandum is taken to be, not to specify, not to disclose, but to bury beneath a mass of words the real object or objects of the company, with the intent that every conceivable form of activity shall be found included somewhere within its terms. The present is the very worst case of the kind that I have seen. Such a memorandum is not, I think, a compliance with the Act ...'

German Date Coffee Co Ltd, Re (1882) 20 Ch D 169 Court of Appeal (Sir George Jessel MR, Baggallay and Lindley LJJ)

Objects clause – impossibility of carrying on the business of the company

Facts
The company was formed having, according to the first object in the objects clause, the purpose of acquiring 'a German patent granted to one Henley for manufacturing from dates a substitute for coffee'. The objects contained several sub-clauses which were effectively ancillary to this object and on reading could be regarded as related to it. The patent proved to be unobtainable, and a subscriber for shares in the company petitioned for its winding-up. At first instance Kay J ordered that the company be wound up. On appeal:

Held
The whole substratum of the company had gone; it should, therefore, be wound up.

Baggallay LJ:

'... It appears to me that the principle involved in the decision in *Re Suburban Hotel Co* (1867) 2 Ch App 737 by Lord Cairns amounts to this, that if you have proof of the impossibility of carrying on the business contemplated by the company at the time of its formation, that is a sufficient ground for winding-up the company. That gives rise in the present case to the question whether there was an impossibility in carrying out the objects of the company at the time the company was formed. I cannot entertain any doubt, having regard to the memorandum of association – and the view I take from a consideration of the memorandum is verified by the surrounding circumstances – that the real contemplated object was to carry out the manufacture of German date coffee to be manufactured from dates in Germany under a patent that was actually granted or was about to be granted. The contemplation of all the parties was that the granting of the letters patent in Germany for the working of this invention was the contemplated object of the company.

No doubt in this case, and in many other cases, you have a variety of general words added which, if they were to be construed by themselves, would give rise to giving power to carry on almost any business which might possibly be suggested. That has been guarded within certain limits, and those limits are that the other objects must be regarded as ancillary to the purpose of the scheme for which the company was formed. It appears to me, from the memorandum of association, that the purpose of the company was the manufacturing of this coffee by virtue of a patent already obtained or to be obtained, and also any improvement that might be made by the patentee, or the company themselves, in connection with that particular patent. Is there an utter impossibility in carrying on the business of the company? It appears from the evidence that there is. There is this very strong evidence that the actual obtaining of these letters patent was contemplated by all the parties who took shares – that the holders of more than one quarter of the shares of the company, of 27,000 shares, directly they found it was not true that the patent had been already obtained (although possibly at that period it was not clear it might not be obtained) retired from the company. It appears to me, beyond all question, that there is an impossibility in carrying on the business of the company, and I think that the order appealed from is quite correct. I feel bound to add that I entirely agree with the learned judge in his enunciation of the law applicable to the case, and his criticisms ...'

Introductions Ltd, Re [1970] Ch 199 Court of Appeal (Harman, Russell and Karminski LJJ)

Objects and powers

Facts
The company was formed in 1951 to provide facilities for visitors to the Festival of Britain. In 1953, after the Festival was over, it was in the business of providing deck chairs at seaside resorts and in 1960, following the election of a new board, it went into the business of pig-breeding. The company became heavily indebted to its bankers who demanded and obtained a debenture over all the company's assets. The bank had a copy of both the memorandum and articles of the company and was expressly aware of the pig-breeding business. The company eventually went into liquidation and the question arose whether the borrowing from the bank was intra vires the company. The bank admitted that pig-breeding was ultra vires the memorandum but argued that as the objects clause contained an express power to borrow money and that this was an object by virtue of a clause which declared that each clause in the objects was to be construed independently of others and regarded as an independent object of the company.

Held
Borrowing money was a power and not an object regardless of what the objects clause stated; it could only be used for purposes intra vires the company. Thus, money could not be borrowed by the company for an ultra vires purpose such as pig-breeding, and, as the bank was aware of this ultra vires purpose, the debentures were void.

Harman LJ:

'... It was argued that the only obligation of the defendant bank was to satisfy itself that there was an express power to borrow money and that this power was converted into an object by the concluding words which I have read. It was said that if this was so not only need the defendant bank enquire no further but they were unaffected by knowledge that they had that activity on which the money was to be spent was one beyond the company's powers.

The judge rejected this view, and I agree with him. He based his judgment, I think, on the view that a power or an object conferred on a company to borrow cannot mean something in the air: borrowing is not an end in itself and must be for some purpose of the company; and as this borrowing was for an ultra vires purpose that is an end of the matter ...'

Kitson & Co Ltd, Re [1946] 1 All ER 435 Court of Appeal (Lord Greene MR, Morton and Tucker LJJ)

Objects clause – loss of substratum

Facts

The company was incorporated in 1899 and its objects provided that it was (i) to acquire and take over as a going concern the business carried on at the Airedale Foundry, Leeds under the style of 'Kitson & Co', to carry on the business of general engineers. In 1945 the company sold the business of Kitson & Co to a purchaser. Some shareholders presented a petition for the winding-up of the company on the ground that the substratum of the company had failed as the main object was to acquire, take over and carry on the business of Kitson & Co and everything else in the objects clause was ancillary to this. At the date of the petition it was the declared purpose of the company to carry on the business of engineers by acquiring another company.

Held

The main object of the company was to carry on the business of general engineers, not Kitson & Co, and therefore the disposal of Kitson & Co did not destroy the substratum of the company.

Lord Greene MR:

'... I cannot bring myself to construe this memorandum as limiting the paramount object and restricting the contemplated adventure of the shareholders to the carrying on of what could be called the business of Kitson & Co. The impossibility of applying such a construction seems to me to be manifest when one remembers that a business is a thing which changes. It grows or it contracts. It changes; it disposes of the whole of its plant; it moves its factory; it entirely changes its range of products and so forth. It is more like an organic thing. Counsel for the respondents quoted to us a number of very well known authorities on which it has been held that on particular facts the substratum of particular companies had gone. I do not propose to examine those authorities, because they do not assist me in construing this particular memorandum. It must be remembered in these substratum cases that there is every difference between a company which on the true construction of its memorandum is formed for the paramount purposes of dealing with some specific subject-matter and a company which is formed with wider and more comprehensive objects. I will explain what I mean. With regard to a company which is formed to acquire and exploit a mine, when you come to construe its memorandum of association you must construe the language used in reference to the subject-matter, namely, a mine, and, accordingly, if the mine cannot be acquired or if the mine turns out to be no mine at all, the object of the company is frustrated, because the subject-matter which the company was formed to exploit has ceased to exist. It is exactly the same way with a patent, as, in the well known *German Date Coffee* case (1882) 20 Ch D 169. A patent is a defined subject-matter, and, if the main object of a company is to acquire and work a patent and it fails to acquire that patent, to compel the shareholders to remain bound together in order to work some other patent or make some unpatented article is to force them into a different adventure to that which they contracted to engage in together; but, when you come to subject-matter of a totally different kind like the carrying on of a type of business, then, so long as the company can carry on that type of business, it seems to me that prima facie at any rate it is impossible to say that its substratum has gone. So far as this stage of the argument is concerned, it is to my mind quite impossible upon the true construction of this memorandum of association to limit the paramount object of this company to the specific business of Kitson & Co, so as to lead to the result that as soon as Kitson & Co's business was sold the substratum of the company had gone. ...'

Commentary

See now s3A CA 1985.

R v Registrar of Companies, ex parte Attorney-General [1991] BCLC 475 High Court (Ackner LJ and Skinner J) (judgment delivered 17 December 1980)

Company formed for immoral purpose – striking off register

Facts

Knowing that the main object of a company would be that of organising the services of a prostitute – its first stated object was 'To carry on the business of prostitution' – the registrar accepted registration in the name 'Linda St Claire (Personal Services) Ltd'. The Attorney General applied for judicial review of the decision to incorporate and register the company and for the incorporation and registration to be quashed.

Held

The application would be allowed.

Ackner LJ:

'This application has many of the indicia that one might expect to find in a student's end of term moot ... Section 15 of the Companies Act 1948 [see now s13(7)(a) of the Companies Act 1985] ... would appear to be a difficulty in the way of this application, but the matter was dealt with in the case of *Bowman* v *Secular Society Ltd* [1917] AC 406 ... so clearly the Attorney General is entitled to bring these proceedings ...

Mr Simon Brown on behalf of the Attorney General concedes that, if the company should not be deemed valid, then it should not have been registered in the first place ... and therefore the issue with which we are concerned is the validity of the registration.

That takes us to s1(1) of the Companies Act 1948 [see now s1(1) of the 1985 Act] ...

It is well settled that a contract which is made upon a sexually immoral consideration or for a sexually immoral purpose is against public policy and is illegal and unenforceable. The fact that it does not involve or may not involve the commission of a criminal offence in no way prevents the contract being illegal, being against public policy and therefore being unenforceable. Here, as the documents clearly indicate, the association is for the purpose of carrying on a trade which involves illegal contracts because the purpose is a sexually immoral purpose and as such against public policy.

Mr Simon Brown submits that if that is the position, as indeed it clearly is on the authorities, then the association of the two or more persons cannot be for "any lawful purpose".

To my mind this must follow. It is implicit in the speeches in the *Bowman* case to which I have just made reference. In my judgment, the contention of the Attorney General is a valid one and I would order that the registration be therefore quashed.'

Ultra vires and constructive notice

David Payne & Co Ltd, Re [1904] 2 Ch 608 Chancery Division (Buckley J) Court of Appeal (Vaughan Williams, Romer and Cozens Hardy LJJ)

Ultra vires and the doctrine of constructive notice

Facts

The company was formed in 1894 to acquire the business of a printers' and stationers' engineer and machinist. The memorandum permitted the company, inter alia, to borrow and raise money for the purpose of the company's business and to povide security on the company's property, if necessary. In 1900 the company got into financial difficulties and from then until its winding-up it was in the control of one Johnston, who also owned three other companies in the same business. Johnston needed £6,000 to push through an amalgamation scheme for these companies and to pay £2,000 due to an American company in respect of patents he had purchased. It was arranged by a friend of Johnston's that the Exploring Land and Minerals Company would lend the £6,000 to the company on a debenture which could then be applied for the desired purposes. Exploring Land and Minerals was not told of the purpose although the friend was a director of this company. The liquidator sought a declaration that the debenture was void as it was for a purpose ultra vires the company.

Held
The debenture was a valid security.

Romer LJ:

'... where you have a limited company with a memorandum of association authorising the company to embark on a series of transactions, if among those purposes you find a power to borrow generally for the purposes of the company, I take it to be clear beyond controversy at the present day that, when money is being borrowed within the limits of the power of borrowing as to amount, the person who lends the money is not bound to inquire to what purpose the borrowing company is to apply the money so borrowed ...'

Buckley J:

'... A corporation cannot do anything except for the purposes of its business, borrowing or anything else; everything else is beyond its power and is ultra vires. So that the words "for the purposes of the company's business" are a mere expression of that which would be involved if there were no such words. If you found a power to borrow which would arise only on the happening of a particular event, then I think it would lie upon the lender to say, "I cannot lend you until you can satisfy me that the condition has been complied with"; but where the power is merely a general power to borrow, limited only as it must be, for the purposes of the company's business, I think the matter is to be treated in this way – that the lender cannot investigate what the borrower is going to do with the money; he cannot look into the affairs of the company and say, "Your purposes do not require it now; this borrowing is unnecessary; you must show me exactly why you want it", and so on. That is all matter lying between the shareholders and the directors ...'

Commentary
See now s142 CA 1989.

Ultra vires and abuse of directors' powers

Rolled Steel Products Ltd v *British Steel Corporation* [1985] 2 WLR 908 Court of Appeal (Lawton, Slade and Browne-Wilkinson LJJ)

Objects and powers – ultra vires and abuse of directors' powers

Facts
Rolled Steel Products (RSP) had capacity under its objects clause (cl 3k) inter alia: 'To lend and advance money ... and to give guarantees and become security' to those dealing with the company. RSP borrowed money from a company (SSS Ltd) to build a steel plant. SSS Ltd in turn borrowed money from another company (C Ltd) from whom SSS Ltd purchased steel. A Mr Shenkman was a director of RSP and SSS Ltd and the owner of the majority of shares in RSP and all the shares in SSS Ltd. C Ltd was taken over by British Steel Corporation (BSC) who insisted that Shenkman had sufficient assets to cover the debt. RSP was therefore used to give a further guarantee as it had sufficient assets. Shenkman saw to it that the guarantee was given by RSP and also procured the execution of a debenture by RSP in favour of C Ltd. SSS Ltd defaulted on repayment of the debt and C Ltd appointed a receiver under the debenture given to it by RSP. When C Ltd's debenture was realised there were insufficient assets left for the unsecured creditors of RSP. RSP brought this action claiming (1) that the giving of the guarantee and

the debenture to C Ltd was ultra vires RSC and, therefore void, not being for the purposes or benefit of RSP (2) that the execution of the guarantee was an improper exercise of RSP powers and in breach of the directors' duties. At first instance Vinelott J held that cl 3k was not an object but an ancillary power to be exercised in the furtherance of the main objects of the company. He went on to distinguish between ultra vires in the narrow sense and ultra vires in the wider sense. 'It is used in a narrow sense to describe a transaction which is outside the scope of the powers expressed in the memorandum ... or which can be implied as reasonably incidental to the furtherance of the objects thereby authorised'. It is used in a wider sense 'to describe a transaction which, although it falls within the scope of the powers of a company, express or implied, is entered into in furtherance of some purpose which is not an authorised purpose'. Vinelott J held that the giving of the guarantee and debenture did not fall within cl 3k because they were ultra vires in the wider sense, not being given in furtherance of a purpose or object authorised by the memorandum. BSC appealed and RSP cross-appealed.

Held

1. Whether a particular transaction is ultra vires is a matter of construction of a company's memorandum. If it falls within the objects of the company or is capable of being treated as reasonably incidental to the objects it is not ultra vires.
2. A transaction which falls within the objects of a company or which is reasonably incidental to them is not ultra vires merely because the directors enter into that transaction in excess or abuse of the powers of the company.
3. Clause 3k of RSP's memorandum was, on its true construction, a power not an object which had not been used in furtherance of RSP's purposes in this case. This was an abuse of the directors' powers and not ultra vires. But, as C Ltd knew that the guarantee and debenture were an abuse of power by RSP's directors, RSP was entitled to disclaim the transaction.

Slade LJ:

'... The statutory requirement that the objects of a company shall be specified in the memorandum marks one important difference between objects and powers. In my judgment, however, whether a particular transaction, carried out in purported exercise of an express or implied power contained in a company's memorandum of association, is within the capacity of the company must still depend on the true construction of that memorandum ... The question whether cl 3k of the plaintiff's memorandum contains a separate independent object of the company is purely one of construction of that memorandum ... Attention, however, has been directed to the particular wording of cl 3k.

... which authorise the company to – "lend and advance money or give credit to such persons, firms or companies and on such terms as may seem expedient, and in particular to customers of and others having dealings with the company ..."

The phrase "as may seem expedient" necessarily implies that there is some criterion by which expediency is to be tested. The only possible criterion, in my opinion, can only mean "as may seem expedient" for the furtherance of the objects of the company. The references in cl 3k to the giving of credit and to customers of and persons having dealing with the company, make it additionally clear that the sub-clause in its context was intended to comprise merely a series of ancillary powers. It follows that, in my opinion, the power to give guarantees and become security, which are the relevant powers in the present case, are not to be construed as independent objects of the plaintiff and the judge was right in so holding ...

... What, then, is the position if, as I have concluded, the power to give guarantees and to become security are to be regarded as mere powers ancillary to the objects of the plaintiff? Even on this footing, the plaintiff in executing the guarantee and the debenture was performing acts of a nature which, at least seemingly, it was expressly authorised by cl 3k and 1 of its memorandum to perform. The particular exercises of these powers were, on the face of them, well capable of falling within the objects of the plaintiff.

The judge, as I have read his judgment, accepted that these transactions were capable of falling within the scope of the wording of the powers conferred on the plaintiff by its memorandum. Nevertheless, he considered that there is a general principle of company law that a transaction, which ostensibly falls within the scope of the wording of a company's memorandum but is in fact entered into for some purpose not authorised by that memorandum, will be ultra vires the company in what he called the "wider sense" and will confer rights on another party only if he can show that he dealt with the company in good faith and did not have notice that the transaction was entered into for an unauthorised purpose. It was primarily on the basis of this principle that the judge ultimately held the defendants in the present case liable to restore the moneys which they had received.

As Lord Selbourne said in *Ashbury Railway Carriage and Iron Co Ltd v Riche* (1875) LR 7 AL 653 at 693:

> "a statutory corporation, created by Act of Parliament for a particular purpose, is limited, as to all its powers, by the purposes of its incorporation as defined in that Act."

Strict logic might therefore appear to require that any act purported to be done by a company in purported exercise of powers ancillary to its objects conferred on it by its memorandum of association, whether express or implied, (eg a power to borrow) would necessarily and in every case be beyond its capacity and therefore wholly void if such act was in fact performed for purposes other than those of its incorporation. However, the practical difficulties resulting from such a conclusion for persons dealing with a company carrying on a business authorised by its memorandum would be intolerable. As Buckley J put it, in regard to a power to borrow, in *In Re David Payne & Co Ltd* [1904] 2 Ch 608 at 61:

> "A corporation, every time it wants to borrow, cannot be called upon by the lender to expose all its affairs, so that the lender can say, 'Before I lend you anything, I must investigate how you carry on your business, and I must know why you want the money, and how you apply it, and when you do have it I must see you apply it in the right way'. It is perfectly impossible to work out such a principle."

The *David Payne* decision, in my opinion, indicates the proper alternative approach. In that case, the company concerned had express power under its memorandum of association "to borrow and raise money for the purpose of the company's business". It borrowed money and issued a debenture to secure the loan. Its liquidator claimed that the debenture was ultra vires and void because there was evidence that the borrowing had not in fact been made for the purposes of the company's business. Buckley J in his judgment considered the force of the phrase "for the purposes of the company's business". He asked the question, at p612:

> "is it a condition attached to the exercise of the power that the money should be borrowed for the purposes of the business, or is that a matter to be determined as between the shareholders and the directors?"

In the course of answering this question he said, at p612:

> "A corporation cannot do anything except for the purposes of its business, borrowing or anyting else; everything else is beyond its power, and is ultra vires. So that the words 'for the purposes of the company's business' are a mere expression of that which would be involved if there were no such words."

This passage has been frequently echoed in later cases and, perhaps not surprisingly, has on occasion been read as referring to the capacity of the company. However, I think that in using the phrase "ultra vires" in this particular context Buckley J can only have meant "ultra vires the directors". This, in my opinion, is made clear by what followed. He accepted that if the phrase, "for the purpose of the company's business" was a condition attached to the exercise of the power, a loan would be ultra vires and void if the condition had not been complied with. He did not, however, regard it as such a condition; in his view it did no more than state the obvious. In these circumstances, his conclusion was, at p613:

> "If this borrowing was made, as it appears to me at present it was made, for a purpose illegitimate so far as the borrowing company was concerned, that may very well be a matter on which rights may arise as between the shareholders and directors of that company. It may have been a wrongful act on the part of the directors. But I do not think that a person who lends to the company is by any words such as these

required to investigate whether the money borrowed is borrowed for a proper purpose or an improper purpose. The borrowing being effected, and the money passing to the company, the subsequent application of the money is a matter in which the directors may have acted wrongly; but that does not affectthe principal act, which is the borrowing of the money."

In these circumstances he held, at p 614, that the defendants:

"who have paid this money and taken this debenture without notice that the money was going to be applied as it was, are not affected by anything arising in regard to that."

The most relevant passages in the judgment of the Court of Appeal in the *David Payne* case [1904] 2 Ch 608 are cited in Vinelott J's judgment and I will not repeat them. Vaughan Williams and Cozens-Hardy L JJ expressly approved the manner in which Buckley J had approached the problem. Vaughan Williams LJ expressly, at p615, and the other members of the court implicitly rejected the borrowers' first argument that, since the debenture was not issued to raise money for the purposes of the company, it was ultra vires altogether "in such a sense that nothing could make it right." All three members of the court considered that the plaintiff company could succeed if, but only if, it showed that, at the time of the loan, the lending company knew that the money was going to be applied by the borrowers for an improper purpose and that this had not been proved.

The one crucially important point to which Buckley J and the Court of Appeal in *David Payne* did not expressly advert is the basis upon which the lenders would have lost their security if they had known of the improper purpose for which the money lent were going to be applied. The basis is, in my opinion, this. The directors of the borrowing company in fact had no authority from the company to take the loan and grant the debenture because these transactions were not effected for the purposes of the company. Nevertheless, as a general rule, a company incorporated under the Companies Acts holds out its directors as having ostensible authority to do on its behalf anything which its memorandum of association expressly or by implication gives the company the capacity to do. In *David Payne* the company's memorandum gave it the capacity to borrow. As a matter of construction of the company's memorandum, the court was not prepared to construe the words "for the purposes of the company's business" as limiting its corporate capacity but construed them simply as limiting the authority of the directors.

In the absence of notice to the contrary, the lenders would thus have been entitled to assume, on the authority of the principle in *Turquand's* case 6 E & B 327 and on more general principles of the law of agency, that the directors of the borrowing company were acting properly and regularly in the internal management of its affairs and were borrowing for the purposes of the company's business: see, for example, In *Re Hampshire Land Co* [1896] 2 Ch 743, a decision of Vaughan Williams J which was cited in the *David Payne* case and *Bowstead on Agency*, 14th ed (1976) pp 241-242 and the cases there cited. However, a party dealing with a company cannot rely on the ostensible authority of its directors to enter into a particular transaction if it knows they in fact have no such authority because it is being entered into for improper purposes. Neither the rule in *Turquand's* case nor more general principles of the law of agency will avail him in such circumstances: see *Bowstead on Agency* 14th ed p243. The various passages in the judgments in both courts in the *David Payne* case which refer to the extent of the lender's obligations, if any, to inquire as to the purposes for which the loan is to be used, in my opinion are not directed at all to the corporate capacity of the borrowing company; they are directed to the right of the lender to rely on the ostensible authority of the borrower's directors.

In *Introductions Ltd* v *National Provincial Bank Ltd* [1970] Ch 199 the Court of Appeal again had to consider the validity of debentures granted by a company as security for a loan. The company under its memorandum of association had a general ancillary power to borrow money and to issue debentures to secure its repayment. But this power was not an independent object of the company. As Harman LJ put it, at p210, "borrowing is not an end in itself and must be for some purpose of the company." The power was not expressed in terms to be exerciseable only "for the purposes of the company" but, following the reasoning of Buckley J in *In Re David Payne & Co Ltd* the court held that the words necessarily had to be implied. The company had borrowed money from a bank and granted debentures to secure the loan. But the only business carried on by it was that of pig-breeding which was a purpose not authorised by its memorandum of association. On the liquidation of the company a question arose as to the validity of the debentures. Harman LJ who gave the leading judgment, after deciding that the power to borrow conferred by the memorandum was a mere ancillary power not an independent object, proceeded to cite at p210, the following passage from the speech of Lord Parker of Waddington in *Cotman* v *Brougham* [1918] AC 514 at 521..

"A person who deals with a company is entitled to assume that a company can do everything which it is expressly authorised to do by its memorandum of association, and need not investigate the equities between the company and its shareholders."

This passage, it will be seen, closely echoes some of the language used by Buckley J in his judgment in the *David Payne* case and is, I think, an expression of the rule in *Turquand's* case, and the more general principles of agency to which I have already referred. Harman LJ went on to say:

"I would agree that, if the bank did not know what the purpose of the borrowing was, *it need not inquire*" – the emphasis is mine – "but it did know, and I can find nothing in *Cotman* v *Brougham* to protect it notwithstanding that knowledge."

The words "it need not inquire", in my opinion, make it clear that Harman LJ did not regard the borrowing as having been beyond the *capacity* of the company. However, he then went on to point out that the *David Payne* decision shows that the protection afforded by the principle stated by Lord Parker affords no protection to a lender who knows that the money is intended to be misapplied. The absence of any express provision in the company's memorandum of association requiring the loan to be applied for the purposes of the company, in his judgment, did not improve the bank's position, since such a provision would fall to be implied anyway. He concluded, at p211:

"This borrowing was not for a legitimate purpose of the company: the bank knew it and *therefore*" – the emphasis is mine – "cannot rely on its debentures."

As I read his judgment, therefore, Harman LJ reached his decision that the bank could not rely on the debentures following the ratio of the *David Payne* decision, that is to say, not because they had been granted by the company in excess of its corporate capacity, but because the bank knew that the directors of the company, in purporting to grant them, had exceeded the authority conferred on them by the company by entering into the transaction for purposes other than the cmpany's corporate purpose ...

... it follows that, in my opinion, the decisions of this court, in *David Payne* and *Introductions Ltd* on their true analysis, lend no support to the plaintiff's submission that the relevant transactions in the present case were beyond the corporate capacity of the plaintiff simply because they were effected for improper purposes not authorised by its memorandum of association. Nor does this argument derive any support from the powerful judgment of Pennycuick J in *Charterbridge Corporation Ltd* v *Lloyds Bank Ltd* [1970] Ch 62 ...

... My conclusions from these authorities on these questions of principle may be summarised as follows:

(1) The basic rule is that a company incorporated under the Companies Acts only has the capacity to do those acts which fall within its objects as set out in its memorandum of association or are reasonably incidental to the attainment or pursuit of those objects. Ultimately, therefore, the question whether a particular transaction is within or outside its capacity must depend on the true construction of the memorandum.

(2) Nevertheless, if a particular act (such as each of the transactions of 22 January 1969 in the present case) is of a category which, on the true construction of the company's memorandum, is *capable* of being performed as reasonably incidental to the attainment or pursuit of its objects, it will not be rendered ultra vires the company merely because in a particular instance its directors, in performing the act in its name, are in truth doing so for purposes other than those set out in the memorandum. Subject to any express restrictions on the relevant power which may be contained in the memorandum, the state of mind or knowledge of the persons managing the company's affairs or of the persons dealing with it is irrelevant in considering questions of corporate capacity.

(3) While due regard must be paid to any express conditions attached to or limitations on powers

contained in a company's memorandum (eg a power to borrow only up to a specified amount), the court will not ordinarily construe a statement in a memorandum that a particular power is exercisable "for the purposes of the company" as a condition limiting the company's corporate capacity to exercise the power; it will regard it as simply imposing a limit on the authority of the directors; see *David Payne* case [1904] 2 Ch 608.

(4) At least in default of the unanimous consent of all the shareholders (as to which see below), the directors of a company will not have actual authority from the company to exercise an express or implied power other than for the purposes of the company as set out in its memorandum of association.

(5) A company holds out its directors as having ostensible authority to bind the company to any transaction which falls within the powers expressly or impliedly conferred on it by its memorandum of association. Unless he is put on notice to the contrary, a person dealing in good faith with a company which is carrying on an intra vires business is entitled to assume that its directors are properly exercising such powers for the purposes of the company as set out in its memorandum. Correspondingly, such a person in such circumstances can hold the company to any transaction of this nature.

(6) If, however, a person dealing with a company is on notice that the directors are exercising the relevant power for purposes other than the purposes of the company, he cannot rely on the ostensible authority of the directors and, on ordinary principles of agency, cannot hold the company to the transaction ...'

Browne-Wilkinson LJ:

'... I summarise my conclusions as follows. To be ultra vires a transaction has to be outside the capacity of the company, not merely in excess or abuse of the powers of the company. (2) The question whether a transaction is outside the capacity of the company depends solely upon whether, on the true construction of its memorandum of association, the transaction is capable of falling within the objects of the company as opposed to being a proper exercise of the powers of the company. (3) Notwithstanding the fact that the provision authorising the company to enter into the particular transaction is found in the objects clause and there is a provision requiring each paragraph to be construed as a separate object, such provision may be merely a power, and not an object, if either it is incapable of existing as a separate object or it can only be construed as a power ancillary to the other objects in the strict sense. (4) If a transaction falls within the objects, and therefore the capacity, of the company, it is not ultra vires the company and accordingly it is not absolutely void. (5) If a company enters into a transaction which is ultra vires (as being within its capacity) but in excess or abuse of its powers, such transaction will be set aside at the instance of the shareholders. (6) A third party who has notice – actual or constructive – that a transaction, although intra vires the company, was entered into in excess or abuse of the powers of the company, cannot enforce such transaction against the company and will be accountable as constructive trustee for any money or property of the company received by the third party. (7) The fact that a power is expressly or impliedly limited so as to be exercisable only "for the purposes of the company's business" (or other words to that effect) does not put a third party on inquiry as to whether the power is being so exercised, ie such provision does not give him constructive notice of excess or abuse of such power ...'

Corporate gifts

Charterbridge Corporation Ltd v *Lloyd's Bank Ltd* [1970] Ch 62 Chancery Division (Pennycuick J)

Granting of a legal charge as security for giving a guarantee

Facts
A company referred to as Castleford created a legal charge on land it owned in Yorkshire to secure a

guarantee of the liability of another company, referred to as Pomeroy, to Lloyd's Bank. Pomeroy and Castleford were property development companies comprised in a group of which Pomeroy was the principal company; the other companies in the group, including Castleford, were not subsidiaries of Pomeroy but had a common shareholding, directorate and offices. Castleford's objects expressly included:

> 'To secure or guarantee by mortgages, charges or otherwise the performance and discharge of any contract, obligation or liability of (Castleford) or of any other person or corporation with whom or which (Castleford) is concerned or interested whether directly or indirectly.'

The memorandum of association also included a separate objects clause. About a month after Castleford granted the legal charge to Lloyd's Bank it entered into a contract for the sale of the land subject to the charge to the plaintiff company, Charterbridge, for £30,000. Charterbridge paid £20,000 of the price on account which was applied by Castleford in discharging a legal charge on the property ranking in priority to the charge granted to Lloyd's Bank. Subsequently, Charterbridge learned of the bank's legal charge and that Castleford could not give them a good title free from encumbrances. In addition, the bank was demanding payment from Castleford under the guarantee and threatening to realise the security. Charterbridge claimed a declaration that the legal charge created by Castleford was ultra vires and void since it was created for purposes outside the scope of its business and not for its benefit and an injunction to prevent the bank realising the alleged security.

Held

The legal charge granted by Castleford to the bank was not ultra vires; it was within the scope of the objects of Castleford and as Castleford had an express power to grant it in the circumstances it was irrelevant that it was not for the benefit and to promote the prosperity of Castleford.

Pennycuick J:

> '... The plaintiff company's contention is formulated under two heads, namely: (i) that the guarantee and legal charge were created for purposes outside the scope of Castleford's business; and (ii) that the guarantee and legal charge were created for purposes which were not for the benefit of Castleford. This second contention is intended to mean, and is accepted as being intended to mean, that the directors of Castleford in creating those obligations were not acting with a view to the benefit of the company. Counsel for the plaintiff company based his contention under both heads primarily on *Re Lee, Behrens & Co Ltd* [1932] 2 Ch 46, to which I shall refer in a minute. But where as here a company is carrying on the purposes authorised by its memorandum and a transaction is effected pursuant to an express power conferred by the memorandum, counsel for the plaintiff company found difficulty in attaching any significant meaning to the expression "purposes outside the scope of Castleford's business" in the first head. He suggested as alternatives: (i) not for the purpose of carrying on Castleford's business; (ii) not reasonably connected with Castleford's business; and (iii) not done for the benefit of and to promote the business; and (iii) not done for the benefit of and to promote the prosperity of Castleford. But (i) is tautology; (ii) could not be asserted on the facts of the present case; and (iii) is a paraphrase of the second head. I think I need say no more about the first head.
>
> The second head, namely that the guarantee and legal charge were not created for the benefit of Castleford in the sense which I have indicated, formed the real basis of the argument of counsel for the plaintiff company. As I have said, he founded that argument primarily on the decision in *Re Lee, Behrens & Co Ltd* and I will now turn to the case: The headnote is as follows: (His Lordship read the headnote). I think it is really clear that the last sentence (viz That the grant of the pension in that case "was therefore void and ultra vires the company") does not fully reflect the content of the judgment. The liquidator rejected the proof so far as now material on two distinct grounds: (i) that it was ultra vires the company and void: (ii) alternatively, that it could only be authorised by the company in general meeting and that no such meeting was summoned or held. Neither in the arguments as reported nor in the judgment are

these two grounds kept clearly distinct. The passage principally relied on by counsel for the plaintiff company runs as follows:

"It is not contended, nor in the face of a number of authorities to the contrary effect could it be, that an arrangement of this nature for rewarding long and faithful service on the part of the persons employed by the company is not within the power of an ordinary trading company such as this company was, and indeed in the company's memorandum of association is contained (clause 3) an express power to provide for the welfare of persons in the employment of the company or formerly in its employment, and the widows and children of such persons and others dependent upon them by granting money or pensions, providing schools, reading rooms or places of recreation, subscribing to sick or benefit clubs or societies or otherwise as the company may think fit. But whether they be made under an express or implied power, all such grants involve an expenditure of the company's money, and that money can only be spent for purposes reasonably incidental to the carrying on of the company's business, and the validity of such grants is to be tested, as is shown in all the authorities, by the answers to three pertinent questions: (i) Is the transaction reasonably incidental to the carrying on of the company's business? (ii) Is it a bona fide transaction? and (iii) Is it done for the benefit and to promote the prosperity of the company? Authority for each of the foregoing propositions is to be found in the following cases: *Hampson* v *Price's Patent Candle Co* (1876) 45 LJ Ch 437; *Hutton* v *West Cork Railway Co* (1883) 23 Ch D 654; and *Henderson* v *Bank of Australasia* (1888) 40 Ch D 170."

It seems to me, on the best consideration I can give to this passage, that the learned judge must have been directing his mind to both the issues raised by the liquidator, without differentiating them. In truth (i), the first of the three pertinent questions which he raises, is probably appropriate to the scope of the implied powers of a company where there is no express power. Question (ii) is appropriate in part again to the scope of implied powers, and in part, and perhaps principally, to the duty of directors. Question (iii) is, I think, quite inappropriate to the scope of express powers and notwithstanding the words "whether they be made under an express or implied power" at the beginning of the paragraph, I doubt very much whether the learned judge really intended to apply this last question to express powers. None of the cases cited by him would support such an application. If he did so intend, his statement is obiter, and with greater diffidence I do not feel bound to follow it. Finally, I would observe that the whole passage proceeds on the footing that the transaction might have been ratified, which would not be possible if it had been ultra vires the company ...'

Halt Garage, Re (1964) Ltd [1982] 3 All ER 1016 Chancery Division (Oliver J)

Ultra vires – payment of a director's remuneration was a disguised gift of capital

Facts

The company was formed in 1964 to carry on a garage business near the M1 motorway. It had £2 issued share capital of which Mr and Mrs Charlesworth held one each. They were the only directors and worked in the business. The company had an express power to grant remuneration to the directors as was from time to time determined by the company in general meeting. Mr and Mrs Charlesworth determined the sums to be paid. In 1967 Mrs Charlesworth became seriously ill and because of continuing illness she took no further part in the running of the business as she was unable to. However, she continued to be a director and received her director's fees. The company went into voluntary liquidation in 1971 and was subsequently compulsorily wound-up. The liquidator in the winding-up brought proceedings under s333 of the Companies Act 1948 on the ground that certain payments Mr and Mrs Charlesworth authorised for themselves as remuneration in the accounting years 1967/68, 1968/69, 1969/70 and 1970/71 were gratuitous payments out of capital and ultra vires. In these periods the company had traded at a loss and the liquidator claimed the whole of the remuneration received by Mrs Charlesworth in this period and such amounts as Mr Charlesworth received were in excess of reasonable remuneration.

Held

1. The liquidator's claim against Mr Charlesworth failed because where remuneration was awarded to a director pursuant to an express power without fraud and was in all the circumstances genuine director's remuneration then it was not for the court to determine the reasonableness of such remuneration. Further, such payments were not to be tested by reference to any benefit to the company.
2. Because Mrs Charlesworth was so inactive during the period a part of the amounts she received could not be regarded as genuine remuneration for her office as director. This part was a disguised gift of capital or payment of dividends to her and was ultra vires the company.

Oliver J (after referring to *Hutton* v *West Cork Railway Co* (1883) 23 Ch D 654 and *Re Lee, Behrens & Co* [1932] 2 Ch 62 in some detail):

'... It is interesting to see that Eve J in fact carries the matter one stage further than *Hutton's* case, where Bowen LJ has postulated (at 671) the test as "what is reasonably incidental to, and within the reasonable scope of carrying on, the business of the company", or (at 672) "reasonably incidental to the carrying on of the company's business for the company's benefit". The test of whether the power is exercised "for the benefit and to promote the prosperity of the company" is added by Eve J as a separate and distinct matter and must, I think, be derived from the judgment of North J in *Henderson* v *Bank of Australasia* (1888) 40 Ch D 170 and from the line of cases relating to the power of a company in general meeting to alter its articles. It is, of course, wholly appropriate to a consideration of the propriety of the exercise of a fiduciary power and, indeed, it appears from the report that it is in relation to an exercise of the power by directors that Eve J is considering the question. He said (at 891):

"The conclusion to which in my opinion such evidence as is available irresistibly points is that the predominant, if not the only, consideration operating in the minds of the directors, was a desire to provide for the applicant, and that the question what, if any, benefit would accrue to the company never presented itself to their minds."

He then went on to the alternative ground of decision, namely that this being, as he put it (at 891) "a gift or reward given out of the company's assets by the directors to one of their own body", it could be done only under an express power (of which there was none) or with the sanction of a general meeting (which had not been obtained). The applicant was not in fact "one of their own body" but the widow of a former director, but that does not affect the principle ...

... I confess that I have not found it easy to understand the logical basis for the doctrine which emerges from *Re Lee, Behrens & Co Ltd* as it was applied in that case and has been applied in subsequent cases.

It is frequently spoken of as a facet of the ultra vires doctrine, but I doubt whether that is strictly correct. If it were, it would involve this, that every power, express or implied, would have to be read and qualified by some such words as "if (but only if) it is for the benefit of the company's business and to promote its interests"; and if that has to be read into every power, it is difficult to see how the company (at least in the case of a company whose affairs are not public knowledge and whose status or credit could not be affected by its dividend record) could ever declare a dividend, which must necessarily reduce the assets available for the promotion of the company's business.

I cannot help thinking, if I may respectfully say so, that there has been a certain confusion between the requirements for a valid exercise of the fiduciary powers of directors (which have nothing to do with the capacity of the company but everything to do with the propriety of acts done within that capacity), the extent to which powers can be implied or limits be placed, as a matter of construction, on express powers, and the matters which the court will take into consideration at the suit of a minority shareholder in determining the extent to which his interests can be overridden by a majority vote. These three matters, as it seems to me, raise questions which are logically quite distinct but which have sometimes been treated as if they demanded a single, universal answer leading to the conclusion that, because a power must not be abused, therefore, beyond the limit of propriety it does not exist ...

... Counsel for the liquidator submits, however, that, even given a bona fide unanimous resolution in general meeting, it still must be a resolution to do something which the company can lawfully do. It cannot, for instance, lawfully return money to its shareholders out of capital. That is plainly right, and *Ridge Securities Ltd* v *IRC* [1964] 1 WLR 479 illustrates the proposition. That was a case of what Pennycuick J in the *Charterbridge* case ([1970] Ch 62) described as a "dressed-up gift" of a company's funds to its parent company ... Counsel for the liquidator submits that since (at any rate during most of the material time) there were no profits available in the company for distribution and since directors' emoluments are always gratuities, except where possible under contract, and since the directors were shareholders as well, every payment to them constituted an illegal reduction of capital except to the extent to which it can be justified by the test of benefit to the company. One difficulty about that, even accepting the submission for the moment, is that if "the benefit of the company" means, as Plowman J suggested in *Parke* v *Daily News* [1962] Ch 927, "the benefit of the shareholders as a whole", it leads him nowhere.

I accept entirely the submission of counsel for the liquidator that a gratuitous payment out of the company's capital to a member, qua member, is unlawful and cannot stand, even if authorised by all the shareholders. What I find difficulty in accepting is that, assuming a sum to be genuinely paid to a director-shareholder as remuneration under an express power, it becomes an illegal return of capital to him, qua member, if it does not satisfy some further test of being paid for the benefit of the company as a corporate entity. If he genuinely receives the money as a reward for his directorship, the question whether the payment is beneficial to the company or not cannot, as I see it, alter the capacity in which he receives it; see, for instance, *Cyclists' Touring Club* v *Hopkinson* [1910] 1 Ch 179 (at 188).

Now, there is no presumption that directors' remuneration is payable only out of divisible profits. That appears clearly from *Re Lundy Granite Co Ltd*, *Lewis's* case (1872) LT 673 where an alternative ground for the decision was that the company in general meeting had indeed sanctioned the payment of directors' remuneration out of capital, the company never having made any profits.

... I do not think that in circumstances such as those in the instant case the authorities compel the application to the express power of a test of benefit to the company which, certainly construed as Plowman J held that it should be construed, would be largely meaningless. The real test must, I think, be whether the transaction in question was a genuine exercise of the power. The motive is more important than the label. Those who deal with a limited company do so on the basis that its affairs will be conducted in accordance with its constitution, one of the express incidents of which is that the directors may be paid remuneration. Subject to that, they are entitled to have the capital kept intact. They have to accept the shareholders' assessment of the scale of that remuneration, but they are entitled to assume that, whether liberal or illiberal, what is paid is genuinely remuneration and that the power is not used as a cloak for making payments out of capital to the shareholders as such ...'

Horsley & Weight Ltd, Re [1982] Ch 442 Court of Appeal (Buckley, Cumming-Bruce and Templeman LJJ)

Ultra vires and the provision for pensions

Facts

The company was formed in 1950 to take over a business of shopfitters which until then was carried on by Mr Stephen Horsley and Mr Weight in partnership. Mr Horsley was in name one of the directors of the company, although he was really an employee of the company. About 1973 Mr Horsley made it plain to the then directors of the company that he intended to retire on his 65th birthday on 2 May 1976.

About September 1975 two of the directors, who owned all the shares in the company between them, arranged with an insurance company for a pension policy for the benefit of Mr Horsley in recognition of his service to the company. The cost of the pension policy to the company was £9,000 plus annual premiums of £1,000. The two directors arranged the pension without the authority of the board or general meeting, but acted in good faith in regard to the company's affairs. In 1977 the company was compulsorily wound up owing substantial sums to creditors. The liquidator claimed against Mr Horsley a declaration that he was guilty of misfeasance and breach of trust in respect of the acquisition by the company of the pension policy for his benefit and that it was a disposition of the company's property ultra vires the company. However, cl 3(o) of the company's objects clause stated that it was established:

'(o) To grant pensions to employees and ex-employees and directors and ex-directors or other officers or ex-officers of the company, their widows, children and dependants, and to subscribe to benevolent and other funds for the benefit of any such persons and to subscribe to or assist in the promotion of any charitable benevolent or public purpose or object.'

At first instance Oliver J dismissed the summons, which then only referred to misfeasance and breach of trust. The liquidator appealed having amended his claim to include the ultra vires point. On appeal:

Held

The appeal would be dismissed because (i) the company had as an express object the making of pensions; this was on its construction a substantive object and not an incidental power and in such circumstances it was irrelevant whether or not it was of any benefit to the company. (ii) On the evidence the directors were not guilty of misfeasance but in the circumstances the provision of the pension was an unauthorised act done without the consent of the board of directors or general meeting. But as the two directors who arranged it held all the shares it had, accordingly, the unanimous consent of all the corporators and was binding on the company. See *Parker & Cooper Ltd* v *Reading* [1926] Ch 975.

Buckley LJ:

'... Ex hypothesi an implied power can only legitimately be used in a way which is ancillary or incidental to the pursuit of an authorised object of the company, for it is the practical need to imply the power in order to enable the company effectively to pursue its authorised objects which justifies the implication of the power. So an exercise of an implied power can only be intra vires the company if it is ancillary or incidental to the pursuit of an authorised object. So also, in the case of express "objects" which, on construction of the memorandum or by their very nature, are ancillary to the dominant or main objects of the company, an exercise of any such power can only be intra vires if it is in fact ancillary or incidental to the pursuit of some such dominant or main object.

On the other hand, the doing of an act which is expressed to be, and is capable of being, an independent object of the company, cannot be ultra vires, for it is by definition something which the company is formed to do and so must be intra vires. I shall use the term "substantive object" to describe such an object of a company.

The question, therefore, is whether cl 3(o) of the company's memorandum of association in the present case contains a substantive object or merely an ancillary power. Having regard to the presence of the separate objects clause, the former of these alternatives must be the case unless the subject matter of cl 3(o) is of its nature incapable of constituting a substantive object ...

Counsel for the liquidator relying principally on the judgment of Eve J in *Re Lee, Behrens & Co Ltd* (1) submits that, properly construed, para (o) should be read as conferring a mere ancillary power.' (His Lordship then referred to the test set out in Eve J's judgment in *Re Lee, Behrens & Co Ltd*).

Counsel for the liquidator submits that that passage from the judgment of Eve J is applicable to the present case and provides, as he submits, an aid to construction of any memorandum of association which contains a paragraph such as we have in cl 3(o) of the company's memorandum. It is true that Eve J's observation expressly refers to both express and implied powers, but in relation to the former it was no more than an obiter dictum. It is worthy of note that the judge used the word "power", not the word "object". Counsel for the liquidator, however, submits that the decision indicates that a capacity to grant pensions to employees or ex-employees or to directors or ex-directors, is of its nature a power enabling the company to act as a good employer in the course of carrying on its business, and as such is an incidental power which must be treated as though it were expressly subject to a limitation that it can only be exercised in circumstances in which a grant of pension will benefit the company's business. I do not feel able to accept that contention. Clause 3(o) must be read as a whole. It includes not only pensions and other disbursements which will benefit directors, employees and their dependants but also making grants for charitable, benevolent or public purposes or objects. The objects of a company do not need to be commercial: they can be charitable or philanthropic; indeed, they can be whatever the original incorporators wish, provided they are legal. Nor is there any reason why a company should not part with its funds gratuitously or for non-commercial reasons if to do so is within its declared objects.

Counsel for the liquidator relies on the finding of Oliver J that there is no evidence that the company did or could derive any benefit or that the question was considered by anyone connected with the transaction. He says that the provision of the pension must accordingly be accepted as having been purely gratuitous, that is to say, a gift which could and did confer no consequent benefit on the company. Accepting this to have been the case, the transaction none the less falls, in my view, precisely within the scope of cl 3(o) and, in my judgment, the purposes referred to in that clause are such as to be capable of subsisting as substantive objects of the company and having regard to the separate objects clause, must be so construed. For these reasons the liquidator fails on the ultra vires point.'

Lee, Behrens & Co Ltd, Re [1932] 2 Ch 46 Chancery Division (Eve J)

Ultra vires and the provision of pensions

Facts

The company was formed in 1909 and in 1931 a resolution was passed for voluntary liquidation. A Mr Southerden had been the managing director of the company for some years. He died in 1923. At his death Mr Southerden owed the company money; it was resolved to release his debts in 1928. In addition the company agreed to pay his widow an annuity of £500 for life from November 1927. The widow lodged a proof in the winding-up for £8,000 being the capitalised value of her annuity. The liquidator rejected it on the grounds that (1) it was ultra vires the company and void; (2) alternatively, it could only be authorised by a general meeting and no such meeting had been held; (3) it was a mere gratuity which could only be paid out of profits and there were no profits to pay it. The widow sought to have the liquidator's decision reviewed. Under art 3 of the company's articles the company had express power to provide for the welfare of persons in the employment of the company or formerly in its employment and the widows and children of such persons by granting, inter alia, money or pensions, etc.

Held

The grant of the pension to the widow was ultra vires and void because it was not given for the benefit of the company nor was it reasonably incidental to the company's business. It did not come within art 3 either because that did not include a managing director or other director; they were not in the employment of the company.

Eve J:

'... But whether they (the payments) be made under an express or implied power, all such grants involve an expenditure of the company's money, and that money can only be spent for purposes reasonably incidental to the carrying on of the company's business, and the validity of such grants is to be tested as is shown in all the authorities by the answers to three pertinent questions: Is the transaction reasonably incidental to the carrying on of the company's business? (ii) Is it a bona fide transaction? and (iii) Is it done for the benefit and to promote the prosperity of the company? Authority for each of the foregoing propositions is to be found in the following cases: *Hampson* v *Price's Patent Candle Co* (1876) 45 LJ Ch 437; *Hutton* v *West Cork Railway Co* (1883) 23 Ch D 654; *Henderson* v *Bank of Australasia* (1888) 40 Ch D 170.

In the present case the court is left entirely without any material for determining whether the transaction was characterised by any of these several attributes. Assuming, as I am prepared to do, that there are no grounds for impugning the bona fides of the board or the applicant, not one of them has given evidence to suggest that the course adopted was taken for the benefit or to promote the prosperity of the company or that the execution of the deed of covenant and the assumption of so burdensome a liability was reasonably incidental to the carrying on of the company's business. ... Neither of the two directors who authorised the sealing of the deeds has made any affidavit. The only material paragraphs in the applicant's affidavit are paragraphs 2 and 3, where she says: "(2) My late husband was for many years prior to his death managing director of the company. (3) After the decease of my said husband considerable negotiations took place between me and the directors of the company and S L Behrens Ltd, with a view to providing me with a pension and eventually it was agreed that the company and S L Behrens Ltd and myself should enter into a deed of covenant under which the company and S L Behrens Ltd were to jointly and severally pay me an annuity of £500."

The conclusion to which in my opinion such evidence as is available irresistibly points is that the predominant, if not the only, considerations operating on the minds of the directors, was a desire to provide for the applicant, and that the question what, if any, benefit would accrue to the company never presented itself to their minds ...'

Effect of ultra vires

Bell Houses v *City Wall Properties* [1966] 1 QB 207 Queen's Bench Division (Mocatta J)

Reliance on ultra vires by a defendant

Facts
The facts of this case and the decision of the Court of Appeal are set out above in 2.3. The Court of Appeal reversed Mocatta J on the ultra vires point and, consequently, found it unnecessary to discuss the issue whether a defendant could plead ultra vires in his defence.

Mocatta J:

'... In my judgment, a defendant, when sued on a contract by a company, is entitled to take the point by way of defence that the contract was ultra vires the company. In short my reasons are that any other conclusion would be inconsistent with the reasoning in the *Ashbury Railway* case (1875) LR 7 HL 653 that the contract is void and in the eyes of the law non-existent; that to hold a defendant liable under a non-existent contract would be to act contrary to all principle; that there are no authorities which, properly understood, support the argument of counsel for the plaintiffs; and that the authorities relied on by counsel for the defendants, though perhaps not conclusive, point strongly the other way.

As to the second point, counsel for the plaintiffs argued that the ultra vires doctrine could not be invoked or successfully relied on by way of defence by a defendant when the plaintiff company, under the contract made by it ultra vires, had performed its part of the contract. The doctrine only had application to the plaintiffs' alternative claim in this action for damages. It would, however, apply to the first way in which their claim is pleaded – namely, that the fee of £20,000 is due to them, they having completely performed their part of the contract. In support of this argument, counsel for the plaintiffs relied on the statement in Mr Furmston's article already cited (1961) 24 MLR 715 that in America

"once the contract has been completely performed, the law lets it alone and any property rights acquired by either party thereunder will be protected, and most jurisdictions will give some relief either in contract or in quasi-contract where the contract has been partly performed".

He also relied on *Copper Miners of England* v *Fox* (1851) 16 QB 229) where there was certainly some argument about the difference between executory and executed contracts and Lord Campbell CJ said: "the cases respecting executed contracts are here wholly inapplicable".

The argument of counsel for the plaintiffs can be summarised as the submission that if the defendant has had the benefit of money, goods or services under a contract made by a company ultra vires, the company can notwithstanding sue in respect thereof and the fact that the contract was made ultra vires is irrelevant. I can say at once that in my view *Copper Miners of England* v *Fox* is irrelevant on this matter. There was no decision there about the law relevant to executed contracts and no expression of judicial opinion on it. If the point had arisen, it would have been in relation to the exception from the rule that corporations could not sue on contracts not under seal established eventually in the case of non-trading corporations (see *Cheshire and Fifoot on Contracts* (5th Edn), pp352 and 353). In my judgment, there is no ground in principle for distinguishing between executory and executed contracts in the manner contended for by counsel for the plaintiffs. If the plaintiff company that has made an ultra vires contract has to rely on the terms of that contract in order to succeed in its action, it must in my judgment fail, since the contract was void ab initio and the defendant is entitled to raise the point. I need not repeat my reasoning on the first point, which is equally applicable here.

That, however, does not necessarily in every case exhaust such a company's remedies. In an appropriate case that company may be able to obtain relief quasi ex contractu in an action for money had and received: see, for example, *Re Coltman* (1881) 19 Ch D 64; *Brougham* v *Dwyer* (1913) 108 LT 504 and the remarks of Myers CJ in the New Zealand case mentioned earlier. In other cases relief may be obtained on a quantum meruit basis; see the decision of the Court of Appeal in *Craven-Ellis* v *Canons Ltd* [1936] 2 KB 403. In that case it was held that a plaintiff, who had done work for the defendants under a void agreement, was entitled to recover something on a quantum meruit. As was said by Greer LJ at p412:

> "... the obligation to pay reasonable remuneration for the work done when there is no binding contract between the parties is imposed by a rule of law, and not by an inference of fact arising from the acceptance of services or goods."

There is, however, no claim put forward on a quasi-contractual basis in the present action, nor must anything I say in this judgment be taken as indicating any view on the question whether any such claim could in the circumstances of this case succeed. On this preliminary issue I can deal only with the claims raised on the pleadings before me. On those pleadings, which are based exclusively on the alleged contract between the parties, the defendants are in my judgment entitled to take the point that the contract sued on, whether executory or executed, was ultra vires the plaintiffs, and, if that be right, the claims must fail ...'

International Sales and Agencies Ltd v *Marcus* [1982] 3 All ER 551 Queen's Bench Division (Lawson J)

Ultra vires – statutory protection

Facts

In April 1973, Marcus loaned £30,000 through one of his moneylending companies to a Mr Fancy who was then in financial difficulties. The loan was arranged by one Munsey, a friend of Marcus' and a director of International Sales, one of several companies owned by Mr Fancy. Mr Fancy became ill in July 1973 and Marcus was told by him, in the presence of Munsey, that Munsey would see he was repaid if anything happened. Mr Fancy died in October 1973 and his estate was insolvent to the extent of £200,000. Munsey was in effective control of International Sales after Mr Fancy's death and he arranged for cheques to be drawn on the company in favour of Marcus. These were stated to be 'loans' but were really to pay off the £30,000 debt and Marcus knew the payments were a breach of Munsey's duties as a director, as International Sales was not liable for Mr Fancy's debts in any way. After Munsey died in 1978 the beneficiaries of Mr Fancy's estate brought these proceedings to recover the £30,000 on the ground, inter alia, that it was money had and received. Marcus pleaded s9(1) ECA 1972 (now s35 CA 1985) in defence.

Held

The £30,000 must be repaid because (i) Munsey had breached his duty as a director to the knowledge of Marcus who was therefore accountable as a constructive trustee of corporate assets. (ii) The payments were ultra vires in any event as such handouts could not fall under the stated objects of the company. (iii) Marcus could not rely on s9(1) ECA 1972 since it only protected innocent parties 'dealing with the company in good faith' not those who knowingly received company property in breach of trust.

Lawson J:

'... I now turn to the question raised by the amended defence, which is whether the defendant's liability to the plaintiffs to account for the moneys they knowingly received in breach of trust is affected by the provisions of s9(1) of the European Communities Act 1972. This Act was passed to give effect in England to EEC Council Directive 68/151 of 9 March 1968. Section 9(1) of the 1972 Act reads as follows:

His Lordship read s9(1) and continued:

It is to be observed that the section (indeed the Act in which it is set) does not in fact reproduce, first, the statement of purposes which precedes the text of the actual articles in the directive; second, the heading of Section II of the directive (this is the section of the directive which contains art 9 which is the ancestor of s9(1) of the 1972 Act) is: "Validity of obligations entered into by a company"; third, there is an important qualification in the first paragraph of art 9 of the directive (which broadly corresponds with s9(1) of the 1972 Act) which appears in the second paragraph of art 9. The introductory words of Directive 68/151 make it clear that what the directive is concerned with is the obligations of companies. For example, one of the recitals provides:

"Whereas the co-ordination of national provisions concerning disclosure, the validity of obligations entered into by, and the nullity of, such companies is of special importance ... (and further on): whereas the protection of third parties must be ensured by provisions which restrict to the greatest possible extent the grounds on which obligations entered into in the name of the company are not valid ..."

In my judgment, those passages and the heading of Section II of the directive are reflected effectively in the words: "In favour of a person dealing with a company in good faith, any transaction decided on ..." This is directed at transactions with companies which obviously will result in the companies being under obligations which before the enactment of the 1972 Act they might have been able to avoid by the application of the old ultra vires doctrine. The other passage in the directive which is not reflected in s9(1) relates to the state of mind of the person dealing with the company. The second paragraph of art 9(1) reads:

"However, Member States may provide that the company shall not be bound where such acts are outside the objects of the company, if it proves that the third party knew that the act was outside those objects ... (and it goes on): or could not in view of the circumstances have been unaware of it ..."

Whilst art 9(1) reflects, if it proves that the third party knew the act was outside those objects, it does not directly reflect or reflect in so many words, the alternative, "or could not in view of the circumstances have been unaware of it". Which seems to me very close to turning a blind eye. In my judgment I am entitled to look at the Council's directive as an aid to the interpretation of s9(1) of the 1972 Act. I conclude, first that s9(1) relates only to legal obligations of the company under transactions with third parties, whether or not they be within or without its powers; second, that s9(1) is designed to give relief to innocent third paties entering into transactions with companies against the operation in England of the old ultra vires doctrine; third, that the test of lack of good faith in somebody entering into obligations with a company will be found either in proof of his actual knowledge that the transaction was ultra vires the company or where it can be shown that such a person could not in view of all the circumstances, have been unaware that he was party to a transaction ultra vires.

It seems to me, so far as the amended defence is concerned, I have to ask a number of questions. First, does s9(1) of the 1972 Act at all affect the principles of constructive trust in relation to the recipients of companies' moneys knowingly paid in breach of trust, as happened, I find, in this case? Second, if the answer to the first question be No, then there is no need to go any further; but, if the answer to the first question were Yes, one must then answer a number of further questions and these, in my judgment, are: were the defendants in this case "dealing" with the plaintiff companies (I emphasise the word "dealing"); if so were the "handouts", the result of these dealings, decided on by the directors of the plaintiff companies, to use the terms of s9(1)? Third, if so, has it been proved by the plaintiffs in this action that the defendants were not acting in good faith in relation to the "handouts" which they received?

The onus of proof is on the defendants in relation to dealing with the companies in relation to the decision of the directors, but it is on the plaintiffs in relation to the absence of good faith. The first question: does s9(1) of the 1972 Act affect the application of the principles of constructive trust in cases like the present? In my judgment, the answer to this question is No. Constructive trust situations may or may not arise in an ultra vires context. The basic principles governing the two doctrines are, I find, quite different. I am satisfied that s9(1) of the 1972 Act was designed to deal not with the operation of the doctrine of constructive trust, but only with the effect of the doctrines of ultra vires. In my judgment in the light of the EEC Council's directive, this conclusion is a plain one.

In the absence of any decided cases on the point (although I have referred to the text books, particularly Goff and Jones *The Law of Restitution* (2nd ed 1978) and *Gower's Principles of Modern Company Law* (4th ed 1979), which discuss this section) it is necessary for me to consider the further questions which would arise if my judgment that s9(1) of the 1972 Act has no effect on the application of the doctrines and principles of constructive trusts. I may be wrong. So I ask whether the defendants in this case were dealing with the plaintiff companies. In my judgment, the answer to this is No. The payments here did not arise from dealings with the plaintiff companies; they arose clearly from dealings with Mr Munsey. Although the companies' cheques and moneys were used by Mr Munsey, they were used by him as a vehicle for his generosity to the defendants. Mr Marcus conceded that the plaintiff companies had no obligations to him in relation to the debt of Aziz Fancy's estate to the second defendants for £30,000 arising out of the April 1973 transaction.

Should I be wrong in my last conclusion, I have to answer the question whether these dealings were decided on by the plaintiffs' directors. In my judgment, although at the material times there were two other directors of the first plaintiffs (Mrs Fancy and Ismat Fancy) and three other directors of the second plaintiffs (the two Fancys and Mr Day), it is clear on the evidence that Mr Munsey was the sole effective director to whom all actual authority to act for the companies was effectively delegated. I conclude therefore that these dealings, if they were in fact dealings with the companies, were in fact decided on by the directors within the terms of s9(1) of the 1972 Act.

The last question relating to the application of s9(1) is whether the plaintiffs have proved that the defendants did not act in good faith as that expression in the 1972 Act is to be construed. My earlier findings are that the defendants had actual knowledge that the payments to them were in breach of duty and trust and were ultra vires the companies (and according to Mr Marcus's evidence, for example, he said specifically that he knew that company directors must not give away a company's money); alternatively, at the lowest, that the defendants could not in all the circumstances have been unaware of the unlawful nature of the payments that they received.'

Commentary
See now s35A(2)(a) of the Companies Act 1985 as inserted by s108(1) of the Companies Act 1989.

TCB Ltd v *Gray* [1986] 1 All ER 587 Chancery Division (Browne-Wilkinson V-C)

Ultra vires – statutory protection

Facts
In January 1982 TCB, a secondary bank, lent £5 million to two companies. Gray was the principal shareholder in both. One of the companies granted TCB a debenture as security but TCB insisted that Gray should give an unlimited personal guarantee in respect of the loan and he gave this guarantee which was supported by a charge over his personal share portfolio which was valued at over £4m. Gray's solicitor executed all the documentation for the loan, including the debenture by the company and the personal guarantee, under a power of attorney. The two companies to whom the loan was made collapsed in February 1983 and the debenture granted by one of them was insufficient to cover the TCB's loan in full. Consequently, TCB demanded that Gray pay the deficency, amounting to £1.8m under his personal guarantee. In defence Gray claimed that as the power of attorney had not been properly sealed he was not bound by it. He also claimed that the articles of association of the company which granted the debenture required the company's seal to be signed by a director and said nothing about a director delegating his duties. On these points he claimed the guarantee and debenture were invalid. On the facts it was found that Gray was estopped from denying that the power of attorney was properly sealed. On the argument that the debenture was invalid TCB pleaded s9(1) European Communities Act (which became s35(1) Companies Act 1985: see now ss35, 35A and 35B, as substituted by s108(1) of the Companies Act 1989).

Held
The validity of the debenture could not be challenged. TCB were entitled to rely on s9(1). In particular it could not be argued that they lacked 'good faith' under s9(1) by showing that they ought to have inquired into the capacity of the company or its articles to see if it was entitled to enter into the transaction.

Browne-Wilkinson V-C:

'... Apart from s9(1) of the European Communities Act 1972, there would have been much force in these submissions. But in my judgment that section provides a complete answer. Under the old law, a person dealing with a corporation was required to look at the company's memorandum and articles to satisfy himself that the transaction was within the corporate capacity of the company and was to be carried through in accordance with the requirements of its articles. The vigour of those requirements was only tempered to the extent that the rule in *Royal British Bank* v *Turquand* (1855) 5E & B 248 allowed third parties to assume that acts of internal management had been properly carried out.

It has been generally assumed that the old law has to a large extent been swept away by s9(1) of the 1972 Act ... In approaching the construction of the section, it is in my judgment relevant to note that the manifest purpose of ... the section is to enable people to deal with a company in good faith without being adversely affected by any limits on the company's capacity or its rules for internal management. Given good faith, a third party is able to deal with a company through its "organs" ... or directors. Section 9(1) achieves this in two ways. First, it "deems" all transactions to be authorised. Second, it "deems" that the directors can bind the company without limitations. The second part of the section reinforces this by expressly abolishing the old doctrine of constructive notice of the contents of a company's memorandum and articles. It being the obvious purpose of the section to obviate the commercial inconvenience and frequent injustice caused by the old law, I approach the construction of the section with a great reluctance to construe it in such a way as to reintroduce, through the back door, any requirement that a third party acting in good faith must still investigate the documents of a company.

Mr Brodie ... submitted that TCB did not act in "good faith" within the meaning of the section since TCB was put on inquiry by the unusual manner in which the debenture had been executed. He said that TCB should have looked at the articles and would then have discovered the irregularity. On further consideration Mr Brodie abandoned this argument, to my mind rightly. The last words of the second part of the subsection expressly provide that good faith is to be presumed; the second part further provides that the person dealing with the company is *not* bound to inquire as to the limitations on the powers of the directors. In my judgment it is impossible to establish lack of "good faith" within the meaning of the section solely by alleging that inquiries ought to have been made which the second part of the subsection says need not be made.

The next submission of Mr Brodie was that, in order for the section to apply at all, the first requirement is that there must be a transaction by the company. Since Link (the company which granted the debenture) never sealed the debenture in the only way authorised by the articles, there was here no transaction by Link at all: the debenture was not the act of Link. If this argument is right, it drives a coach and horses through the section: in every dealing with the company the third party would have to look at its articles to ensure that the company was binding itself in an authorised manner. In my judgment the section does not have that effect. The section is dealing with purported actions by a company which, having regard to its internal documents, may be a nullity eg acts outside its corporate capacity. In such a case under the old law the purported act of the company would not be the act of the company at all. Yet the first part of s9(1) of the 1972 Act "deems" it to be. Similarly a document under seal by the company executed otherwise than in accordance with its articles was not, under the old law, the act of the company; but s9(1) deems it so to be since the powers of the directors are deemed to be free from limitations, ie as to the manner of affixing the company's seal. In my judgment, s9(1) applies to transactions which a company purports to enter into and deems them to be validly entered into. Mr Brodie also submitted that art 113 (regulating the way in which Link can seal documents) is not a "limitation" on the powers of the directors to bind the company but a mandatory direction as the only way in which the company can bind itself. I reject this submission also. Link has either actual or, under s9(1), deemed capacity to enter into the debenture. Being an artificial person, Link can only enter into the debenture by its agents, the directors. Any provision in the articles as to the manner in which the directors can act as agents for the company is a limitation on their power to bind the company and as such falls within the first part of s9(1).

Finally, Mr Brodie submitted that in order to rely on the section it has to be shown that the debenture was a transaction "decided on by the directors". I agree ... The evidence clearly established that no ... meeting of the directors of Link ever took place. But in fact all the directors of Link individually had decided to grant the debenture, although not at a meeting at which they were all present ... In my judgment ... the grant of the debenture was a "transaction decided on by the directors ...".'

Liability for acts of officers and agents

The rule in Turquand's case

B Liggett (Liverpool) Ltd v Barclays Bank Ltd [1928] 1 KB 48 King's Bench Division (Wright J)

Non-application of the rule where the person claiming the benefit of it is put on enquiry

Facts

The company was incorporated in 1923 and the first directors were Mr Liggett and Mr Melia. The defendant bank were the company's bankers and when the company was formed the branch of the defendant bank at which the company's account was opened received instructions to honour cheques if they were signed by any two directors for the time being and specimen signatures of Mr Liggett and Mr Melia were appended. In 1925 Mr Melia had reason to believe that demands were being made by Mr Liggett to the bank to honour cheques with his signature only. Mr Melia saw the bank manager and told him not to honour any cheques unless they were signed by him. A few months later Mr Liggett sent a note to the bank that his wife had also been appointed a director of the company, appended her specimen signature and confirmed that cheques should only be honoured if signed by two directors for the time being. As all these matters appeared to be in order in accordance with the articles the bank honoured cheques bearing the signature of Mr and Mrs Liggett. No inquiry was made of Mr Melia despite his instruction that no cheques were to be paid if they did not bear his signature. No thought was given either to the point that a quorum might not have been present at the meeting at which Mrs Liggett was appointed a director. The company sued the bank for over £500 paid on cheques signed by Mr and Mrs Liggett.

Held

(Inter alia) the bank was liable as it should have been put on inquiry in the circumstances.

Wright J:

'... The rule as relied on by the defendant bank is that, the defendant bank having had the articles of association, were entitled to assume that the notice of September 1, 1925, regarding the appointment of Mrs Liggett as a director, sent to them by the chairman was a valid and proper notice because, according to the articles of association, it was possible, if the proper steps in the matter of internal management had been taken by the directors of the company, that Mrs Liggett had been duly appointed an additional director as the notice stated. I am relieved from any examination of the exact definition of this very respectable, but perhaps somewhat ambiguous, rule of law, because the plaintiff company in answer to that contention have alleged that the defendant bank in any case is not entitled to the benefit of that rule by reason of the fact that the defendant bank were put on inquiry by the circumstances of the case and were negligent in not investigating the position before they accepted and acted upon the notice of the appointment of a new director. On that issue I put two questions to the jury, and the questions were these: "Was the bank put on inquiry whether the appointment of Mrs Liggett was in order?" The jury answered: "Yes". Secondly, "Was the bank guilty of negligence in paying the bills and cheques complained of?" and again the jury answered "Yes". Whatever may be the exact scope of the rule in *Turquand*'s case (1856) 6 E & B 327, I think it is quite clear on the authorities I have already referred to that it can never be relied upon by a person who is put on inquiry. The rule proceeds on a presumption that certain acts have been regularly done, and if the circumstances are such that the person claiming the benefit of the rule is put on inquiry, if the circumstances debar that person from relying on the prima facie presumption, it is clear that he cannot claim the benefit of the rule. If, therefore, the answers of the jury to the questions which I put to them stand, it is clear, I think, that this defence will not avail the defendants here ...'

Mahony v *East Holyford Mining Co Ltd* (1875) LR 7 HL 869 House of Lords (Lord Cairns, LC, Lords Chelmsford, Hatherley and Penzance)

Turquand's case and the non-appointment of directors

Facts

The East Holyford Mining Co was formed by one Wadge, to purchase a mine from him above its true value. A prospectus was issued naming the directors and secretary of the proposed company, its bank as the National Bank, Dublin and stating the address of the registered office in Grafton Street, Dublin. Almost £4,000 was raised on the prospectus and paid into the National Bank to the credit of the company. The memorandum and articles were then registered; these were subscribed by seven persons, namely, Hoare, Wall, Tully, McKenna, Murphy, Hughes and McNally. Of these Tully, McKenna, Murphy and Hughes were clerks in constant attendance at the company's office and Hoare, Wadge and Wall also attended there regularly. Under Article 53 the first seven persons who signed the articles were to be the first directors. No directors were ever appointed and no regular meetings of members or directors were ever held but Wadge, Hoare and Wall acted as if they were directors. In order that the money could be drawn out of the company's account Wall wrote a letter to the bank, signed by him as company secretary and directing the bank to pay all cheques drawn on the company's account signed by two of three directors, namely, McNally, Wadge and Hoare and countersigned by the company secretary. The bank acted on the faith of this letter and paid out on cheques signed in accordance with the letter. The company went into liquidation and the liquidator sought to recover from the bank the moneys it had paid out of the company's account.

Held

The bank was not liable to replace the money drawn from the company's account. It was entitled to assume that the persons who had acted as directors of the company had been properly appointed in all the circumstances. Further, it had no right to insist on inquiries to show that these conclusions were true.

Lord Hatherley:

'... It is settled by a series of decisions of which *Ernest* v *Nicholls* (1857) 6 HL Cas 401 is one, and the *Royal British Bank* v *Turquand* (1856) 6 E & B 327, a later one, that those who deal with joint stock companies are bound to take notice of that which I may call the external position of the company. Every joint stock company has its articles of association, and nearly every one has its partnership deed under which it acts. Those articles of association and that partnership deed are open to all who are minded to have any dealings with the company, and those who so deal with them must be affected with notice of all that is contained in those two documents; after that the company, entering upon its business and dealing with persons external to it, is supposed on its part to have all those powers and authorities which by its articles and deed it appears to possess. All that they do with reference to what I may call the indoor management of their own concern is a thing known to them only, subject to this observation, that no person dealing with them has a right to suppose that anything has been done, or can be done, which is not permitted by the articles or by the deed.

This being the case, a banker dealing with a company must be taken to be acquainted with the manner in which, under the articles, the moneys of the company may be drawn out of his bank for the purposes of the company. My noble and learned friend on the woolsack has read those articles by which in this case the bank were informed that cheques might be drawn by three directors of the company. The bank must also be taken to have had knowledge from the articles of the duties of the directors, and the mode in which they were to be appointed. But after that, when there are persons conducting the affairs of the company in a manner which is perfectly consonant with the articles of association, supposing all to have been rightly done by those who had the management of the company internally, then those dealing with them externally are not to be affected by any irregularities which may take place in the internal management of the company. They are entitled to presume that that of which only they can have knowledge, namely, the external acts, are rightly done when those acts purport to be performed in the mode in which they ought to be performed. For instance, when a cheque is signed by three directors, they are entitled to assume that those directors are persons properly appointed for the purpose of performing that function. Of course the case is open to any observation arising from gross negligence or fraud. I pass that by as not entering into the consideration of the question at the present time.

Outside persons when they find that there is an act done by a company will, of course, be bound in the exercise of ordinary care and precaution to know whether or not that company is actually carrying on business, or whether it is a company which has been stopped and wound-up, and which has parted with its assets, and the like. All those ordinary inquiries which mercantile men would, in the course of their business, make, I apprehend would have to be made on the part of persons dealing with the company. But what do the bank find in the case now before us? They find how the directors are to be appointed. They find both by the articles of association and by the prospectus which was issued that the place of business was 12, Grafton Street. That was an external fact upon which they might well acquaint themselves. They go to 12, Grafton Street, and they find there an office, and they find there a person acting as secretary, who is the same person as the person described as secretary in the prospectus. They find there certain persons in constant attendance, namely, six out of the seven persons who signed the articles of association. Finding them a certain number of persons acting as directors who had been represented to them to be directors, and finding four other persons who might well have elected them to be directors, having the authority and the power to do so, on the spot daily, sitting by and seeing them performing those functions, what conclusion could they come to but that those directors had been duly appointed? And I apprehend that cl 85 of the articles of association covers any defect there might have been in that appointment.

Then the bank gets a notice from a gentleman who calls himself the secretary and says he gives them a resolution under which the cheques are to be drawn. The mode of providing for the drawing of cheques is treated of in the articles, and it is there laid down that the duty is to be performed by directors. The bank was furnished with the names of three so-called "directors", who sent their signatures in order that the bank might have an opportunity of verifying the signatures upon any cheques that might be drawn. If the bankers went there and found the secretary sitting there as the evidence tells us he did all day long, performing the duties of a secretary, and if they found some of these other gentlemen sitting there performing the duties of directors, and if they saw those four other gentlemen who might have appointed them as directors sitting there also, witnessing them performing the duties of directors, I must ask what more could be required on the part of those dealing with the company, who had obtained all the external information they could upon the subject? If we are not now to hold that the bank is to be protected in honouring the drafts of these three persons who, they were informed, were authorised to draw cheques, I do not know how any person dealing with a company can be safe against being bound to inquire into all the minute transactions which may have taken place indoors, and any defect in which it appears to me cl 85 of the articles in this case, independently of any general law upon the subject, was intended to cover.'

Morris v *Kanssen* [1946] AC 459 House of Lords (Viscount Simon, Lords Thankerton, Simonds and Uthwatt)

Reliance on *Turquand*'s case by directors

Facts

Rialto (West End) Ltd was incorporated in 1939 to run a cinema. It had a share capital of 100 £1 shares and the directors were Kanssen and one Cromie, each of whom held one share. Kanssen and Cromie fell out and Cromie purported to appoint one of his friends called Strelitz to the board in 1940. This appointment was ineffective because it was only carried against Kanssen's objections by Strelitz voting in favour of his own appointment. The purpose of the appointment was to put Cromie in a position to call on Kanssen to resign. In 1942 the company needed finance and Morris was prepared to help. He was appointed a director by Cromie and Strelitz at a directors' meeting and at the same meeting Morris voted with Cromie and Strelitz to issue a further 90 shares in the company. Of these 34 were allotted to Morris, 32 to Strelitz and 24 to Cromie. Later Strelitz transferred 17 of his shares to Morris. Kanssen issued writs claiming that only two shares were validly allotted in the company, viz the one each originally allotted to himself and Cromie, and that he and Cromie were the only directors. Cohen J held that in addition to the two shares initially allotted the 51 shares held by Morris were validly allotted as he could rely on s143 CA 1929 and table A art 88. He also held that the company had no directors since 1941 because all were due to go out of office then and no annual general meeting had been held to replace them. Kanssen appealed to the Court of Appeal claiming that the allotment to Morris was ineffective. His appeal was allowed. Morris appealed to the House of Lords relying on s143 CA 1929 and table A art 88 as well as on *Turquand*'s rule.

Held

Morris could not rely on s143 CA 1929 or table A art 88 as these were concerned with the validity of actions of directors where there was a defect in their appointment and not cases such as the present where the directors who made the allotment to him were not appointed at all. In Cromie's case his office had expired and in Strelitz's case he never had been a director. Therefore the allotment by them was ineffective.

Morris could not rely on the rule in *Turquand*'s case (1) either because this was in relation to an allotment to himself in which he purported to act as a director.

Lord Simonds:

'... The question is whether he can nevertheless, under the rule in *Turquand*'s case (1856) 6 E & B 248, claim that he is entitled, as between himself and the company to treat that act as done with the authority of the company, which was in fact and in law done without its authority ...

... One of the fundamental maxims of the law is the maxim omnia praesumuntur rite esse acta. It has many applications. In the law of agency it is illustrated by the doctrine of ostensible authority. In the law relating to corporations its application is very similar. The wheels of business will not go smoothly round unless it may be assumed that that is in order which appears to be in order. But the maxim has its proper limits. As ostensible agent cannot bind his principal to that which the principal cannot lawfully do. The directors or acting directors or other officers of a company cannot bind it to a transaction which is ultra vires. Nor is this the only limit to its application. It is a rule designed for the protection of those who are entitled to assume, just because they cannot know, that the person with whom they deal has the authority which he claims. This is clearly shown by the fact that the rule cannot be invoked if the condition is no longer satisfied ie if he who would invoke it is put upon his inquiry. He cannot presume in his own favour that things are rightly done if inquiry that he ought to make might tell him that they were wrongly done.

What then is the position of the director or acting director who claims to hold the company to a transaction which the company had not, though it might have, authorised? Your Lordships have not in this case to consider what the result might be if such a director had not himself purported to act on behalf of the company in the unauthorised transaction. For here Morris was himself purporting to act on behalf of the company in a transaction in which he had no authority. Can he then say that he was entitled to assume that all was in order? My Lords, the old question comes into my mind: Quis custodiet ipsos custodes? It is the duty of directors and equally of those who purport to act as directors, to look after the affairs of the company, to see that it acts within its powers and that its transactions are regular and orderly. To admit in their favour a presumption that that is rightly done which they have themselves wrongly done is to encourage ignorance and condone dereliction from duty. It may be that in some cases, it may be that in this very case, a director is not blameworthy in his unauthorised act. It may be that in such a case some other remedy is open to him, either against the company or against those by whose fraud he was led into this situation, but I cannot admit that there is open to him the remedy of invoking this rule and giving validity to an otherwise invalid transaction. His duty as a director is to know; his interest, when he invokes the rule, is to disclaim knowledge. Such a conflict can be resolved in only one way.'

Commentary

1. Distinguished in *Hely-Hutchinson* v *Brayhead Ltd* [1968] 1 QB 549.
2. See now s285 Companies Act 1985 and table A, art 2.

Royal British Bank v *Turquand* (1856) 6 E & B 327; Court of Exchequer Chamber (Jervis CJ, Pollock CB, Alderson B, Cresswell and Crowder JJ and Bramwell B)

Those dealing with a company are entitled to assume that matters of 'indoor management' have been complied with

Facts

A company formed to operate a mine and railway and created by deed of settlement and registered under the Joint Stock Companies Act 1844 empowered its directors to borrow on mortgage, bond or otherwise such sums for such periods and at such rates of interest they deemed expedient, provided they were authorised to do so by a resolution passed at a general meeting. A bond under seal signed by two directors acknowledged the company's indebtedness to the plaintiff bank in the sum of £2,000. The plaintiff sought to recover this but the company alleged in defence that a resolution had not been passed authorising the making of the bond.

Held

The company was liable on the bond whether or not the resolution had been passed.

Jervis CJ:

'... We may now take for granted that the dealings with these companies are not like dealings with other partnerships, and that the parties dealing with them are bound to read the statute and the deed of settlement. But they are not bound to do more. The party here, on reading the deed of settlement, would find, not a prohibition from borrowing, but a permission to do so on certain conditions. Finding that the authority might be made complete by a resolution, he would have the right to infer the fact of a resolution authorising that which on the face of the document appeared to be legitimately done.'

Ruben v *Great Fingall Consolidated* [1906] AC 439 House of Lords (Lord Loreburn LC, Lords Macnaghten, Davey, James, Robertson and Atkinson)

The rule in *Turquand*'s case does not apply in the case of forgery

Facts

Rowe, the company secretary of Great Fingall, applied to Ruben, a firm of stockbrokers, for a loan of £20,000 to enable him to buy 5,000 shares in Great Fingall. The loan was arranged with a bank who agreed to advance the money upon the shares being transferred into their name. Rowe forged a transfer in the name of one Storey as transferor and the bank duly executed this as transferees. Ruben then delivered the transfer to Rowe on behalf of the bank in exchange for a share certificate. The share certificate was also forged; it purported to be signed by two directors, their signatures were forged by Rowe, and he fraudulently affixed the company's seal to it and signed it as company secretary. The bank advanced the £20,000. When the fraud was discovered Ruben were obliged to repay the £20,000 to the bank and they brought this action to recover the money from the company on the ground that they were liable for the fraud of Rowe who was the proper person to deliver certificates on behalf of the company.

Held

The company could not be estopped from denying that the certificate was genuine. Rowe was not held out as having authority to make any such representation or to give any such warranty and no such authority could be derived from his holding the office of company secretary.

Lord Loreburn LC:

'... I cannot see upon what principle your Lordships can hold that the respondent company is liable in this action. The forged certificate is a pure nullity. It is quite true that persons dealing with limited liability companies are not bound to inquire into their indoor management, and will not be affected by irregularities of which they had no notice. But this doctrine, which is well established, applies only to irregularities that otherwise might affect a genuine transaction. It cannot apply to a forgery.

Another ground was pressed upon us – namely, that this certificate was delivered by Rowe in the course of his employment, and that delivery imported a representation or warranty that the certificate was genuine. He had not nor was held out as having authority to make any such representation or give any such warranty. And certainly no such authority is given by the simple fact that he held the office of secretary and was a proper person to deliver certificates. Nor am I able to see how the respondent company is estopped from disputing the genuineness of this certificate. That, indeed, is only another way of stating the same contention. From beginning to end the company itself and its officers with the exception of the secretary had nothing to do either with the preparation or issue of the document. No precedent has been quoted in support of the appellants' contention except *Shaw v Port Philip Gold Mining Co* (1884) 13 QBD 103. I agree with Stirling LJ in regarding that decision as one that may possibly be upheld upon the supposition that the secretary there was in fact held out as having authority to warrant the genuineness of a certificate. If that be not so, then, in my opinion, the decision cannot be sustained. For these reasons the judgment of the Court of Appeal ought to be affirmed.'

Lord Macnaghten:

'This case was argued at some length and with much ingenuity of the learned counsel for the appellants. In my opinion there is nothing in it. Ruben and Ladenburg are the victims of a wicked fraud. No fault has been found with their conduct. But their claim against the respondent company is, I think, simply absurd. The thing put forward as the foundation of their claim is a piece of paper which purports to be a certificate of shares in the company. This paper is false and fraudulent from beginning to end. The representation of the company's seal which appears upon it, though made by the impression of the real seal of the company, is counterfeit and no better than a forgery. The signatures of the two directors which purport to authenticate the sealing are forgeries pure and simple, and every statement in the document is a lie. The only thing real about it is the signature of the secretary of the company, who was the sole author and perpetrator of the fraud. No one would suggest that this fraudulent certificate could of itself give rise to any right or bind or affect the company in any way. It is not the company's deed, and there is nothing to prevent the company from saying so. Then, how can the company be bound or affected by it? The directors have never said or done anything to represent or lead to the belief that this thing was the company's deed. Without such a representation there can be no estoppel. The fact that this fraudulent certificate was concocted in the company's office, and was uttered and sent forth by its author from the place of its origin cannot give it an efficacy which it does not intrinsically possess. The secretary of the company, who is a mere servant, may be the proper hand to deliver out certificates which the company issues in due course, but he can have no authority to guarantee the genuineness or validity of a document which is not the deed of the company.

I could have understood a claim on the part of the appellants if it were incumbent on the company to lock up their seal and guard it as if it were a dangerous beast, and as if it were culpable carelessness on the part of the directors to commit the care of the seal to their secretary or any other official. That is a view which once commended itself to a jury, but it has been disposed of for good and all by *Bank of Ireland v Evans' Charities Trustees* (1855) 5 HLC 389 in this House. Of all the numerous cases that were cited in the opening, none, I think, is to the point but *Shaw v Port Philip Gold Mining Co*, and that, as it seems to me, cannot be supported unless a forced and unreasonable construction is to be placed on the admissions which were made by the parties in that action. I think that the appeal must be dismissed with costs.'

The doctrine of 'holding out'

Freeman & Lockyer v Buckhurst Park Properties (Mangal) Ltd [1964] 2 QB 480
Court of Appeal (Willmer, Pearson and Diplock LJJ)

Agency – company holding out a person as a managing director

Facts

Buckhurst Park Properties was formed for the purpose of purchasing Buckhurst Park Estate and making a quick and profitable resale. The proposed resale was not achieved and afterwards the aim of the company was to dispose of the property as advantageously as possible. There was power in the articles to appoint a managing director but none was in fact appointed. However, one of the directors, a Mr Kapoor, to the knowledge of the board of directors acted as if he were the managing director, both in trying to resell the property quickly and, after this failed, in trying to dispose of the property as advantageously as possible. In the course of carrying out the company's business, Kapoor instructed the plaintiffs, a firm of architects and surveyors, to obtain planning permission for the property and to survey and prepare plans of the property. The plaintiffs claimed the fees earned by them. The question was whether the company was liable for these fees or Kapoor. Proceedings were brought against the company alone as Kapoor disappeared without trace.

Held

The company was liable for the fees because it had held out Kapoor as being managing director. There was authority in the articles to appoint a managing director and Kapoor had acted within the scope of authority normally conferred on a managing director in engaging the services of the plaintiffs. The fact that the plaintiffs had not read the articles or made any enquiries as to whether Kapoor was properly appointed was irrelevant.

Diplock LJ:

'This makes it necessary to enquire into the state of the law as to the ostensible authority of officers and servants to enter into contracts on behalf of corporations. It is a topic on which there are confusing and, it may be, conflicting judgments of the Court of Appeal, which are elaborately analysed and discussed by Slade J in *Rama Corporation Ltd* v *Proved Tin and General Investments Ltd* [1952] 2 QB 147. If, when properly understood, the judgments of the Court of Appeal in the previous cases do conflict, this court is entitled to decide which of them it should follow; see *Young* v *Bristol Aeroplane Co Ltd* [1944] KB 718. We are concerned in the present case with the authority of an agent to create contractual rights and liabilities between his principal and a third party whom I will call "the contractor". This branch of the law has developed pragmatically rather than logically, owing to the early history of the action of assumpsit and the consequent absence of a general jus quaesitum tertii in English law. But it is possble (and for the determination of this appeal I think it is desirable) to restate it on a rational basis. It is necessary at the outset to distinguish between an "actual" authority of an agent on the one hand and an "apparent" or "ostensible" authority on the other. Actual authority and apparent authority are quite independent of one another. Generally they co-exist and coincide, but either may exist without the other and their respective scopes may be different. As I shall endeavour to show, it is on the apparent authority of the agent that the contractor normally relies in the ordinary course of business when entering into contracts.

An "actual" authority is a legal relationship between principal and agent created by a consensual agreement to which they alone are parties. Its scope is to be ascertained by applying ordinary principles of construction of contracts, including any proper implications from the express words used, the usages of the trade, or the course of business between the parties. To this agreement the contractor is a stranger; he may be totally ignorant of the existence of any authority on the part of the agent. Nevertheless, if the agent does enter into a contract pursuant to the "actual" authority, it does create contractual rights and liabilities between the principal and the contractor. It may be that this rule relating to "undisclosed principals", which is peculiar to English law, can be rationalised as avoiding circuity of action, for the principal could in equity compel the agent to lend his name in an action to enforce the contract against the contractor, and would at common law be liable to indemnify the agent in respect of the performance of the obligations assumed by the agent under the contract.

An "apparent" or "ostensible" authority, on the other hand, is a legal relationship between the principal and the contractor created by a representation, made by the principal to the contractor, intended to be and in fact acted on by the contractor, that the agent has authority to enter on behalf of the principal into a contract of a kind within the scope of the "apparent" authority, so as to render the principal liable to perform any obligations imposed on him by such contract. To the relationship so created the agent is a stranger. He need not be (although he generally is) aware of the existence of the representation. The representaton, when acted on by the contractor by entering into a contract with the agent, operates as an estoppel, preventing the principal from asserting that he is not bound by the contract. It is irrelevant whether the agent had actual authority to enter into the contract.

In ordinary business dealings the contractor at the time of entering into the contract can in the nature of things hardly ever rely on the "actual" authority of the agent. His information as to the authority must be derived either from the principal or from the agent or from both, for they alone know what the agent's actual authority is. All that the contractor can know is what they tell him, which may or may not be true. In the ultimate analysis he relies either on the representation of the principal, ie apparent authority, or on the representation of the agent, ie warranty of authority. The representation which creates "apparent" authority may take a variety of forms of which the commonest is representation by conduct, ie by permitting the agent to act in some way in the conduct of the principal's business with other persons. By so doing the principal represents to anyone who becomes aware that the agent is so acting that the agent has authority to enter on behalf of the principal into contracts with other persons of the kind which an agent so acting in the conduct of his principal's business has normally "actual" authority to enter into.

In applying the law, as I have endeavoured to summarise it, to the case where the principal is not a natural person, but a fictitious person, viz, a corporation, two further factors arising from the legal characteristics of a corporation have to be borne in mind. The first is that the capacity of a corporation is limited by its constitution, ie in the case of a company incorporated under the Companies Act, by its memorandum and articles of association; the second is that a corporation cannot do any act, and that includes making a representation, except through its agents. Under the doctrine of ultra vires the limitation of the capacity of a corporation by its constitution to do any acts is absolute. This affects the rules as to the "apparent" authority of an agent of a corporation in two ways. First, no representation can operate to estop the corporation from denying the authority of the agent to do on behalf of the corporation an act which the corporation is not permitted by its constitution to do itself. Secondly, since the conferring of actual authority on an agent is itself an act of the corporation the capacity to do which is regulated by its constitution, the corporation cannot be estopped from denying that it has conferred on a particular agent authority to do acts which, by its constitution, it is incapable of delegating to that particular agent. To recognise that these are direct consequences of the doctrine of ultra vires is, I think, preferable to saying that a contractor who enters into a contract with a corporation has constructive notice of its constitution, for the expression "constructive notice" tends to disguise that constructive notice is not a positive, but a negative doctrine, like that of estoppel of which it forms a part. It operates to prevent the contractor from saying that he did not know that the constitution of the corporation rendered a particular act or a particular delegation of authority ultra vires the corporation. It does not entitle him to say that he relied on some unusual provision in the constitution of the corporation, if he did not in fact so rely.

The second characteristic of a corporation, viz that unlike a natural person it can only make a representation through an agent, has the consequence that, in order to create an estoppel between the corporation and the contractor, the representation as to the authority of the agent which creates his "apparent" authority must be made by some person or persons who have "actual" authority from the corporation to make the representation. Such "actual" authority may be conferred by the constitution of the corporation itself, as for example, in the case of a company, on the board of directors, or it may be conferred by those who under its constitution have the powers of management on some other person to whom the constitution permits them to delegate authority to make representations of this kind. it follows that, where the agent on whose "apparent" authority the conractor relies has no "actual" authority from the corporation to enter into a particular kind of contract with the contractor on behalf of the corporation, the contractor cannot rely on the agent's own representation as to his actual authority. He can rely only on a representation by a person or persons who have actual authority to manage or conduct that part of the business of the corporation to which the contract relates. The commonest form of representation by a principal creating an "apparent" authority of an agent is by conduct, viz, by permitting the agent to act in the management or conduct of the principal's business. Thus, if in the case of a company the board of directors who have "actual" authority under the memorandum and articles of association to manage the company's business permit the agent to act in the management or conduct of the company's businss, they thereby represent to all persons dealing with such agent that he has authority to enter on behalf of the corporation into contracts of a kind which an agent authorised to do acts of the kind which he is in fact permitted to do normally enters into in the ordinary course of such business. The making of such a representation is itself an act of management of the company's business. Prima facie it falls within the "actual" authority of the board of directors, and unless the memorandum or articles of the company either make such a contract ultra vires the company or prohibit the delegation of such authority to the agent, the company is estopped from denying to anyone who has entered into a contract with the agent in reliance on such "apparent" authority that the agent had authority to contract on behalf of the company.

If the foregoing analysis of the relevant law is correct, it can be summarised by stating four conditions which must be fulfilled to entitle a contractor to enforce against a company a contract entered into on behalf of the company by an agent who had no actual authority to do so. It must be shown: (a) that a representation that an agent had authority to enter on behalf of the company into a contract of the kind sought to be enforced was made to the contractor; (b) that such representation was made by a person or persons who had "actual" authority to manage the business of the company either generally or in respect of those matters to which the contract relates; (c) that he (the contractor) was induced by such representation to enter into the contract, ie that he in fact relied on it; and (d) that under its memorandum or articles of association the company was not deprived of the capacity either to enter into a contract of the kind sought to be enforced or to delegate authority to enter into a contract of that kind to the agent.

The confusion which, I venture to think, has sometimes crept into the cases is, in my view, due to a failure to distinguish between these four separate conditions, and in particular to keep steadfastly in mind (first) that the only "actual" authority which is relevant is that of the persons making the representation relied on, and (second) that the memorandum and articles of association of the company are always relevant (whether they are in fact known to the contractor or not) to the questions (i) whether condition (b) is fulfilled, and (ii) whether condition (d) is fulfilled, and (but only if they are in fact known to the contractor) may be relevant (c) as part of the representation on which the contractor relied.

In each of the relevant cases the representation relied on as creating the "apparent" authority of the agent was by conduct in permitting the agent to act in the management and conduct of part of the business of the company. Except in *Mahony v East Holyford Mining Co Ltd* (1875) LR 7 HL 869, the conduct relied on was that of the board of directors in so permitting the agent to act. As they had, in each case, by the articles of association of the company full "actual" authority to manage its business, they had "actual" authority to make representations in connexion with the management of its businesss including representations as to who were agents authorised to enter into contracts on the company's behalf. The agent himself had no "actual" authority to enter into the contract, because there had not been compliance with the formalities prescribed by the articles for conferring it on him. In *British Thomson-Houston Co Ltd v Federated European Bank Ltd* [1932] 2 KB 176, where a guarantee was executed by a single director, it was contended that a provision in the articles, requiring a guarantee to be executed by two directors, deprived the company of capacity to delegate to a single director authority to execute a guarantee on behalf of the company, ie that condition (d) ante was not fulfilled; but it was held that other provisions in the articles empowered the board to delegate the power of executing guarantees to one of their number, and this defence accordingly failed.

In *Mahony's* case no board of directors or secretary had in fact been appointed, and it was the conduct of those who, under the constitution of the company, were entitled to appoint them which was relied on as a representation that certain persons were directors and secretary. Since they had "actual" authority to appoint these officers, they had "actual" authority to make representations who the officers were. In both these cases the constitution of the company, whether it had been seen by the contractor or not, was relevant in order to determine whether the persons whose representations by conduct was relied on as creating the "apparent" authority of the agent had "actual" authority to make the representations on behalf of the company. In *Mahony's* case if the persons in question had not been persons who would normally be supposed to have such authority by someone who did not in fact know the constitution of the company, it may well be that the contractor would not have succeeded in proving condition (c), viz, that he relied on the representations made by those persons unless he proved that he did not know the constitution of the company. This, I think, accounts for the passages in the speeches of Lord Chelmsford and Lord Hatherley which are cited by Slade J in *Rama Corpn v Proved Tin and General Investments Ltd*.

The cases where the contractor's claim failed, viz, *JC Houghton & Co v Nothard, Lowe and Wills Ltd* [1927] 1 KB 247, *Kreditbank Cassel GmbH v Schenkers Ltd* [1927] 1 KB 826 and the *Rama Corpn* case; were all cases where the contract sought to be enforced was not one which a person occupying the position in relation to the company's business, which the contractor knew that the agent occupied, would normally be authorised to enter into on behalf of the company. The conduct of the board of directors in permitting the agent to occupy that position on which the contractor relied, thus did not of itself amount to a representation that the agent had authority to enter into the contract sought to be enforced, ie condition (a) was not fulfilled. The contractor, however, in each of these three cases sought to rely on a provision of the articles, giving to the board power to delegate wide authority to the agent, as entitling the contractor to treat the conduct of the board as a representation that the agent had had delegated to him wider powers than those normally exercised by persons occupying the position in relation to the company's business which the agent was in fact permitted by the board to occupy. Since this would involve proving that the representation on which he in fact relied as inducing him to enter into the contract comprised the articles of association of the company as well as the conduct of the board, it would be necessary for him to establish, first, that he knew the contents of the articles (ie that condition (c) was fulfilled in respect of any representation contained in the articles) and, secondly, that the conduct of the board in the light of that knowledge would be understood by a reasonable man as a representation that the agent had authority to enter into the contract sought to be enforced, ie that condition (a) was fulfilled. The need to establish both these things was pointed out by Sargant LJ in Houghton's case, in a judgment which was concurred in by Atkin LJ; but his observations, as I read them, are directed only to a case where the contract sought to be enforced is not a contract of a kind which a person occupying the position which the agent was permitted by the board to occupy would normally be authorised to enter into on behalf of the company.

I find some confirmation for this view of Sargant LJ's judgment in the dictum of Atkin LJ in the *Kreditbank Cassel* case, another case of an "abnormal" contract. He says:

"If you are dealing with a director in a matter in which a director normally would have power to act for the company you are not obliged to enquire whether or not the formalities required by the articles before he exercises that power have in fact been complied with."

I therefore disagree with the conclusion that Slade J draws in the *Rama Corpn* case as to the law laid down in *Houghton's* case and the *Kreditbank Cassel* case; but, if I am wrong as to this, I think that *Houghton's case* as construed by Slade J, is contrary to the decisions of the Court of Appeal in *Biggerstaff v Rowatt's Wharf Ltd, Howard v Howatt's Wharf Ltd* [1896] 2 Ch 93 and the *British Thomson-Houston* case, and I prefer, and would follow, the latter.

In the *Biggerstaff* case the agent (who had never been appointed managing director) had been permitted by the board to manage the affairs of the company, ie to perform the functions of a managing director, although it does not appear whether the board knew that he described himself to the contractor as such. In the *British Thomson-Houston* case the agent was the chairman of the board, who was permitted by them to manage the affairs of the company. In each case the contract was a normal contract, ie of a kind which a director managing the affairs of the company (whether described as a "managing director" or not) would be authorised to enter into on behalf of the company. In each case it was held that, by permitting a person holding the office of director to manage the affairs of the company, the board had represented that he had authority to enter into the "normal" contract sought to be enforced. The only relevance of the articles, in my view, was to show that the delegation of powers of management to the agent which the board had by their conduct represented that they had made was not one which was prohibited by the articles, ie that condition (d) was fulfilled.

In the present case the findings of fact by the county court judge are sufficient to satisfy the four conditions, and thus to establish that the second defendant had "apparent" authority to enter into contracts on behalf of the defendant company for their services in connexion with the sale of the company's property, including the obtaining of development permission with respect to its use. The judge found that the board knew that the second defendant had throughout been acting as managing director in employing agents and taking other steps to find a purchaser. They permitted him to do so and by such conduct represented that he had authority to enter into contracts of a kind which a managing director or an executive director responsible for finding a purchaser would in the normal course be authorised to enter into on behalf of the defendant company. Condition (a) was thus fulfilled. The articles of association conferred full powers of management on the board. Condition (b) was thus fulfilled. The plaintiffs, finding the second defendant acting in relation to the defendant company's property as he was authorised by the board to act, were induced to believe that he was authorised by the defendant company to enter into contracts on behalf of the company for their services in connexion with the sale of the company's property, including the obtaining of development permission with respect to its use. Condition (c) was thus fulfilled. The articles of association, which contained powers for the board to delegate any of the functions of management to a managing director or to a single director, did not deprive the company of capacity to delegate authority to the second defendant, a director, to enter into contracts of that kind on behalf of the company. Condition (d) was thus fulfilled. I think that the judgment was right, and would dismiss the appeal.'

Hely-Hutchinson v *Brayhead Ltd* [1968] 1 QB 549 Queen's Bench Division (Roskill J) Court of Appeal (Lord Denning MR, Lords Wilberforce and Pearson)

Agency – authority of a managing director

Facts
The plaintiff (Viscount Suirdale) was for many years the chairman and managing director of an electronics company called Perdio and had guaranteed a loan of £50,000 to Perdio by a merchant bank. Brayhead was also involved in electronics. In 1964 Perdio was in financial difficulty and Brayhead was willing to help as it wished to gain control of Perdio. As a result the plaintiff sold 750,000 of his shares in Perdio to Brayhead at 3s 3d per share, thus giving Brayhead a 60% holding in Perdio. Brayhead proposed to lend Perdio £150,000 and the plaintiff was appointed a director of Brayhead on 25 January 1965 as part of the agreement, but did not attend any board meetings until 19 May 1965. Perdio's financial position deteriorated and at the beginning of May 1965 it was clear that it needed more money if it was to survive. The chairman of Brayhead, a Mr Richards, discussed with the plaintiff the possibility of the plaintiff advancing money to Perdio. This matter was not mentioned at the board meeting on 19 May but immediately after that meeting it was agreed that the plaintiff would advance money to Perdio. As part of this agreement Mr Richards wrote two letters to the plaintiff: (i) in the event of him having to fulfil his guarantee in relation to the loan of £50,000 in consideration of a loan of up to £10,000 by the plaintiff to Perdio and (ii) Brayhead would guarantee repayment of any personal loans by the plaintiff to Perdio. The plaintiffs advanced some £45,000 in reliance on the letters. Perdio continued to suffer losses and was wound up in September 1965. The plaintiff was called upon to honour his £50,000 guarantee and he sought to recover this and the £45,000 he had advanced to Perdio from Brayhead under the letters. In defence Brayhead claimed (i) that the letters were not binding on it as Mr Richards had no authority, actual or ostensible, to write those letters and that the plaintiff as a director of Brayhead had notice of his want of authority and (ii) if there was a contract by the company the plaintiff could not enforce it as he was a director and had failed to disclose his interest in a contract with the company to the board as required by the articles.

Held
1. The agreements of indemnity and guarantee between the plaintiff and Brayhead were enforceable as Mr Richards had actual authority to enter into these agreements.
2. (Per Roskill J) the plaintiff was an 'outsider' in the circumstances of the case since he was acting otherwise than in his capacity as a director of Brayhead in making the agreements. He was not, therefore, presumed to know that Richards did not have authority. The Court of Appeal in (1) above found that Richards did have authority so this question was not considered on appeal.

Roskill J:

'Lord Suirdale did not act on behalf of Brayhead in relation to the allegedly unauthorised transaction. But both Mr Finer and, in his admirable argument following his leader, Mr Instone said it was enough to exclude the operation of the rule in *Turquand*'s case ((1856) 6 E &B 327) that Lord Suirdale was a party to the transaction and was a director of Brayhead, even though he did not act for Brayhead. With the utmost respect to that argument and the skill with which it was advanced both by Mr Finer and Mr Instone, I find nothing in these cases which compels me to go so far as they have invited me to go. In some cases – and of course *Morris*'s case ([1946] AC 459) is one and *Howard*'s case (*Howard* v *Patent Ivory Manufacturing Co* (1888) 38 Ch D 156) is another – a director is quite plainly anything but a "stranger," or an "outsider," or a "third party," but I do not think the mere fact that a man who is a director of a company makes a contract with that company in a capacity other than that of a director automatically affects him in the capacity in which he is contracting, with constructive knowledge of such disabilities and limitations as he might be deemed to know were he also acting for the company in the transaction in question. As Mr MacCrindle said in the course of his reply, to extend this doctrine in the way suggested would have very far-reaching ramifications on ordinary day-to-day business transactions and would or might involve very often considerable inquiry before a contract could be signed as to what the respective position and authority was of a particular individual by whom it was proposed that a contract should be signed. I regard the decisions in *Morris* v *Kanssen* [1946] AC 459 and in *Howard*'s case as decisions where, on the facts of those particular cases, the rights sought to be enforced by the plaintiffs concerned arose from acts done by them as directors which were so closely interwoven with their duties and acts as directors as to make it impossible for the directors involved to say that they were not for all purposes to be treated as possessed of knowledge of the limitations upon their powers as directors. In the present case Brayhead's agreement with Lord Suirdale had nothing to do with his duties and obligations as a director of Brayhead. What he was doing was to agree to advance money to an associated company of Brayhead of which he was chairman and managing director against a guarantee and indemnity from Brayhead, who were expected to become the parent company of that associated company. He was acting, as I think, otherwise than in his capacity as a director of Brayhead in making that agreement. He was acting as an individual, for it was he who was going to advance the money in consideration of the agreement into which Mr Richards was purporting to enter on behalf of Brayhead. He was going to be the other contracting party. I think, therefore, that this argument fails.'

Lord Denning:

'I need not consider at length the law on the authority of an agent, actual, apparent, or ostensible. That has been done in the judgments of this court in *Freeman & Lockyer* v *Buckhurst Park Properties (Mangal) Ltd* [1964] 2 QB 480; [1964] 2 WLR 618; [1964] 1 All ER 630 CA. It is there shown that actual authority may be express or implied. It is *express* when it is given by express words, such as when a board of directors pass a resolution which authorises two of their number to sign cheques. It is *implied* when it is inferred from the conduct of the parties and the circumstances of the case, such as when the board of directors appoint one of their number to be managing director. They thereby impliedly authorise him to do all such things as fall within the usual scope of that office. Actual authority, express or implied, is binding as between the company and the agent, and also as between the company and others, whether they are within the company or outside it.

Ostensible or apparent authority is the authority of an agent as it *appears* to others. It often coincides with actual authority. Thus, when the board appoint one of their number to be managing director, they invest him not only with implied authority, but also with ostensible authority to do all such things as fall within the usual scope of that office. Other people who see him acting as managing director are entitled to assume that he has the usual authority of a managing director. But sometimes ostensible authority exceeds actual authority. For instance, when the board appoint the managing director, they may expressly limit his authority by saying he is not to order goods worth more than £500 without the sanction of the board. In that case his actual authority is subject to the £500 limitation, but his *ostensible* authority includes all the usual authority of a managing director. The company is bound by his ostensible authority in his dealings with those who do not know of the limitation. He may himself do the "holding-out". Thus, if he orders goods worth £1,000 and signs himself "Managing Director for and on behalf of the company", the company is bound to the other party who does not know of the £500 limitation, see *British Thomson-Houston Co Ltd* v *Federated European Bank Ltd* [1932] 2 KB 176 CA, which was quoted for this purpose by Pearson LJ in *Freeman & Lockyer* [1964] 2 QB 480, 499. Even if the other party happens to be a director of the company, nevertheless the company may be bound by the ostensible authority. Suppose the managing director orders £1,000 worth of goods from a new director who has just joined the company and does not know of the £500 limitation, not having studied the minute book, the company may yet be bound. Lord Simonds in *Morris* v *Kanssen* [1946] AC 459; 62 TLR 306; [1946] 1 All ER 586 HL(E), envisaged ([1946] AC 459, 475, 476) that sort of case, which was considered by Roskill J (above) in the present case.

Apply these principles here. It is plain that Mr Richards had no express authority to enter into these two contracts on behalf of the company: nor had he any such authority implied from the nature of his office. He had been duly appointed chairman of the company but that office in itself did not carry with it authority to enter into these contracts without the sanction of the board. But I think he had authority implied from the conduct of the parties and the circumstances of the case. The judge did not rest his decision on implied authority, but I think his findings necessarily carry that consequence. The judge finds that Mr Richards acted as de facto managing director of Brayhead. He was the chief executive who made the final decision on any matter concerning finance. He often committed Brayhead to contracts without the knowledge of the board and reported the matter afterwards. The judge said:

"I have no doubt that Mr Richards was, by virtue of his position as de facto managing director of Brayhead or, as perhaps one might more compendiously put it, as Brayhead's chief executive, the man who had, in Diplock LJ's words [1964] 2 QB 480, 506, 'actual authority to manage', and he was acting as such when he signed those two documents".

And later he said

"the board of Brayhead knew of and acquiesced in Mr Richards acting as de facto managing director of Brayhead."

The judge held that Mr Richards had ostensible or apparent authority to make the contract, but I think his findings carry with it the necessary inference that he had also actual authority, such authority being implied from the circumstance that the board by their conduct over many months had acquiesced in his acting as their chief executive and committing Brayhead Ltd to contracts without the necessity of sanction from the board.

This finding makes it unnecessary for me to go into the question of ostensible authority; or into the rule in *Royal British Bank* v *Turquand* (1856) 6 E & B 327; or into the question whether a director has constructive notice. I do not say that the judge was in error in what he said on these subjects. All I say is that I do not find it necessary to express any opinion on it.

Panorama Developments (Guildford) Ltd v *Fidelis Furnishing Fabrics Ltd* [1971] 2 QB 711 Court of Appeal (Lord Denning MR and Salmon, LJ)

Agency – authority of a company secretary

Facts

The plaintiffs ran a car-hire business, hiring large cars such as Rolls-Royces and Jaguars. The company secretary of the defendant company hired cars from the plaintiffs on the pretext that they were needed for meeting important customers, etc at airports and so on. Each time the secretary signed all the necessary forms as 'company secretary' and told the plaintiffs that they should send in an account to the company. The cars were in fact used by the company secretary for his own purposes; he told the plaintiffs a pack of lies. When the fraud was eventually discovered the plaintiffs sued for the amount of hire; the defendants argued that the secretary had no authority to hire cars. Judgment was given for the plaintiffs at first instance. The defendants appealed.

Held

The appeal would be dismissed. It was within the scope of the usual authority of a company secretary to hire cars.

Lord Denning MR:

'... Mr Hames' second point is this: he says that the company is not bound by the letters which were signed by Mr Bayne as "company secretary". He says that, on the authorities, a company secretary fulfils a very humble role: and that he has no authority to make any contracts or representations on behalf of the company. He refers to *Barnett, Hoares & Co* v *South London Tramways Co* (1887) 18 QBD 815 at 817 where Lord Esher MR said:

"A secretary is a mere servant; his position is that he is to do what he is told, and no person can assume that he has any authority to represent anything at all ..."

Those words were approved by Lord Macnaghten in *George Whitechurch Ltd* v *Cavanagh* [1902] AC 117 at 124. They are supported by the decision in *Ruben* v *Great Fingall Consolidated* [1906] AC 439. They are referred to in some of the textbooks as authoritative.

But times have changed. A company secretary is a much more important person nowadays than he was in 1887. He is an officer of the company with extensive duties and responsibilities. This appears not only in the modern Companies Acts, but also by the role which he plays in the day-to-day business of companies. He is no longer a mere clerk. He regularly makes representations on behalf of the company and enters into contracts on its behalf which come within the day-to-day running of the company's business. So much so that he may be regarded as held out as having authority to do such things on behalf of the company. He is certainly entitled to sign contracts connected with the administrative side of a company's affairs, such as employing staff, and ordering cars, and so forth. All such matters now come within the ostensible authority of a company's secretary.

Accordingly I agree with the judge that Mr R L Bayne, as a company secretary, had ostensible authority to enter into contracts for the hire of these cars and, therefore, the company must pay for them. Mr Bayne was a fraud. But it was the company which put him in the position in which he, as company secretary, was able to commit the frauds. So the defendants are liable. I would dismiss the appeal, accordingly.'

3   Articles of Association

The distinctive features of the s14 contract

Bratton Seymour Service Co Ltd v *Oxenborough* [1992] BCC 471 Court of Appeal (Dillon and Steyn LJJ and Sir Christopher Slade)

Articles – statutory contract – can a term be implied into the articles?

Facts

Mr Oxenborough was appealing against a county court order that he had to make a contribution towards expenses incurred by the company. A management company was formed to manage the common parts of a small housing development known as Bratton House estate. Each owner of the flats became a shareholder in the company. Liability on each resident to contribute towards the upkeep of the common parts, such as the driveway into the development, was imposed in the conveyances of the property to them. The conveyance did not however impose liability to contribute towards the upkeep of the amenity areas such as the swimming pool, tennis courts and garden area. When Mr Oxenborough refused to pay his part of these expenses, the company brought an action against him and argued that he ought to be liable on the basis of an implied term which should be incorporated into the articles of association of the company.

Held

The articles of association are different from a normal contract and a term cannot be implied in order to give it business efficacy. The Court of Appeal allowed Mr Oxenborough's appeal from the county court.

Steyn LJ:

> 'The question is whether it is ever permissible to imply into articles of association a term not on the basis of a construction or implication derivable purely from the consideration of the language of an instrument, but on the basis of extrinsic evidence of surrounding circumstances.
>
> Section 14(1) of the Companies Act 1985 provides that:
>
> > "… the memorandum and articles, when registered, bind the company and its members to the same extent as if they respectively had been signed and sealed by each member …"

By virtue of s14 the articles of association become, upon registration, a contract between a company and its members. It is, however, a statutory contract of a special nature with its own distinctive features. It derives its binding force not from a bargain struck between parties but from the terms of the statute. It is binding only in so far as it affects the rights and obligations between the company and the members acting in their capacity as members. If it contains provisions conferring rights and obligations on outsiders, then those provisions do not bite as part of the contract between the company and the members, even if the outsider is coincidentally a member. Similarly, if the provisions are not truly referable to the rights and obligations of members as such it does not operate as a contract. Moreover, the contract can be altered by a special resolution without the consent of all the contracting parties. It is also, unlike an ordinary

68

contract, not defeasible on the grounds of misrepresentation, common law mistake in equity, undue influence or duress. Moreover, as Dillon LJ has pointed out, it cannot be rectified on the grounds of mistake.

Turning now to the present case, the question is whether the implied term of requiring members to contribute to maintenance of the amenities can be implied not on the basis of any language to be found in the articles, but on the basis of extrinsic circumstances. The question is, is it notionally ever possible to imply a term in such circumstances? I will readily accept that the law should not adopt a black-letter approach. It is possible to imply a term purely from the language of the document itself: a purely constructional implication is not precluded. But it is quite another matter to seek to imply a term into articles of association from extrinsic circumstances.

Here, the company puts forward an implication to be derived not from the language of the articles of association but purely from extrinsic circumstances. That, in my judgment, is a type of implication which, as a matter of law, can never succeed in the case of articles of association. After all, if it were permitted, it would involve the position that the different implications would notionally be possible between the company and different subscribers. Just as the company or an individual member cannot seek to defeat the statutory contract by reason of special circumstances such as misrepresentation, mistake, undue influence and duress and is furthermore not permitted to seek a rectification, neither the company nor any member can seek to add to or to subtract from the terms of the articles by way of implying a term derived from extrinsic surrounding circumstances. If it were permitted in this case, it would be equally permissible over the spectrum of company law cases. The consequence would be prejudicial to third parties, namely, potential shareholders who are entitled to look to and rely on the articles of association as registered. Despite Mr Asprey's lucid and incisive argument, I take the view that on this ground alone the implication cannot succeed.

For this reason, and also for the reasons given by *Dillon* LJ, I agree that the appeal ought to be allowed.'

Scott v *Frank F Scott (London) Limited and Others* [1940] Ch 794 Court of Appeal (Scott, Clauson and Luxmoore LJJ)

Articles – the statutory contract – rectification

Facts
The company's business was that of shipping butchers and the whole of the share capital was owned by three brothers, Stuart, Reginald and Frank Scott. Frank Scott died and under the terms of his will his widow became entitled to all of his shares. The surviving two brothers, however, refused to enter her name in the register of members, and sought rectification of the articles on the basis that they did not accord with the intention of the three brothers, that ordinary shares held by a deceased member should be offered at par to the principal shareholders.

Held
The court has no jurisdiction to rectify the articles. The articles can only be altered according to the statute which creates the contract in s14, that is, by special resolution under s9 of the Companies Act 1985. The widow was entitled to have her name entered in the register of members.

Luxmoore LJ:

'The next question which falls to be considered is whether the defendants are entitled to have the articles of association rectified in the manner claimed by them. Bennett J said he was prepared to hold that the articles of association as registered were not in accordance with the intention of the three brothers who were the only signatories of the memorandum and articles of association, and down to the date of Frank Stanley Scott's death the only shareholders therein. Bennett J, however, held that the court has no jurisdiction to rectify articles of association of a company, although they do not accord with what is proved to have been the concurrent intention of all the signatories therein at the moment of signature. We are in complete agreement with this decision. It seems to us that there is no room in the case of a company incorporated under the appropriate statute or statutes for the application to either the memorandum or articles of association of the principles upon which a Court of Equity permits rectification of documents whether inter partes or not.'

Parties to the s14 contract

Hickman v Kent or Romney Marsh Sheep-Breeders' Association [1915] 1 Ch 881
Chancery Division (Astbury J)

The articles bind the company as well as the members

Facts
The association was non profit making and was incorporated in 1895 to encourage the breeding of Kent or Romney Marsh sheep and maintain the purity of the breed. The plaintiff became a member of the association in 1905 and in doing so signed a form by which he, inter alia, agreed to conform with the rules and regulations of the association. Under art 49 of the articles of association it was provided that all differences between the association and any of the members were to be referred to an arbitrator or two arbitrators appointed by the parties. A dispute arose between the plaintiff and the association which refused to register his sheep in their pedigree flock books and proposed to expel him. The plaintiff issued a writ in 1914 claiming an injunction to restrain the association from expelling him, damages for refusing to register his sheep and a declaration that he was entitled to have his sheep registered. The association issued a summons to stay proceedings on the ground that the matters should be referred to arbitration under art 49. The question arose as to the effect of the articles generally and whether, in particular, art 49 was binding on the plaintiff.

Held
1. The plaintiff's application for membership of the association and its subsequent acceptance was a contract between the plaintiff and the association and by it he had agreed in writing to conform with its rules and regulations and was bound thereby.
2. General articles dealing with the rights of members 'as such' amounted to a statutory agreement between them and the company as well as between themselves inter se and as art 49 was such a general article it bound the plaintiff to submit his case to arbitration in the circumstances.

Astbury J:

'In the present case the defendants contend, first, that art 49, dealing as it does with the members of the company in their capacity of members only, constitutes a submission within the meaning of the Arbitration Act, or, alternatively, that the contract contained in the plaintiff's application for membership and the company's acceptance of it amounts to such a submission. The plaintiff contests both these propositions. Independently of the particular dispute in this case, the arguments, especially upon the first of these contentions, have raised questions of far-reaching importance and of great difficulty.

I will deal with the question as to the effect of art 49 first. Section 14(1) of the Companies (Consolidation) Act 1908 (now s14 of Companies Act 1985) says:

"The memorandum and articles shall, when registered, bind the company and members thereof to the same extent as if they respectively had been signed and sealed by each member, and contained covenants on the part of each member, his heirs, executors, and administrators, to observe all the provisions of the memorandum and of the articles, subject to the provisions of this Act."

It is laid down in text-books of the highest authority that the articles are not a contract between the members and the company, but a contract with the other members. The articles are a contract only as between the members inter se in respect of their rights as shareholders. The exact nature of this covenant – that is, the covenant referred to in s14 – has given rise to considerable discussion and is even now very difficult to define; but it is now settled that it is not equivalent to a contract between the company, on the one part, and the members, on the other, on which either a member can sue the company or the company can sue a member.

The principal authorities in support of these propositions are *Re Tavarone Mining Co, Prichard's Case* (1873) 8 Ch App 956; *Melhado v Porto Alegre Railway Co* (1874) LR 9 CP 503; *Eley v Positive Government Security Life Assurance Co* (1875) 1 Ex D 20; and *Browne v La Trinidad* (1888) 37 Ch D 1. In *Prichard's Case* by the articles of association of a mining company it was provided that the company should immediately after incorporation enter into an agreement with the vendor of the mine for the purchase of the mine, and the price was fixed. The articles were signed by the vendor and six other persons, and the directors allotted shares to the vendor, but no further agreement was made with him. It was held, affirming the decision of Wickens VHC, that the articles of association did not constitute a contract in writing between the vendor and the company within s25 of the Companies Act 1867, and that certain shares should not, therefore, be considered as fully paid up. Mellish LJ in giving judgment said (1873) 8 Ch App at p960:

> "But I am of opinion that the articles of association cannot be considered as a contract in writing between De Thierry and the company for the sale of the mine to them. It may no doubt be the case if no other contract was entered into, and if De Thierry signed these articles and they were acted upon, that a court of equity would hold that as between him and the company – from their acting upon it – there was a binding contract; but in themselves the articles of association are simply a contract as between the shareholders inter se in respect of their rights as shareholders. They are the deed of partnership by which the shareholders agree inter se."

In *Melhado v Porto Alegre Railway Co* the articles of association of a joint stock company provided that the company should defray such expenses incurred in its establishment as the directors should consider might be deemed and treated as preliminary expenses to an amount not exceeding a sum named. The plaintiffs, who were promoters of the company, had incurred preliminary expenses in its establishment, and it was held that no action would lie at the suit of the plaintiffs against the company under the articles. Lord Coleridge CJ said (1874) LR 9 CP 503 at 505:

> "The action is brought on a clause in the articles of association, by which the directors are authorised to pay certain expenses if they should consider them to be properly deemed preliminary expenses. The declaration avers that all conditions were performed necessary to entitle the plaintiffs to be paid their expenses; and therefore I think we must take it that they were expenses which, if the directors had thought proper to pay them, the articles would have justified them in paying. The question therefore is whether an action will lie for the payment of these expenses, in pursuance of the articles of association, to which the plaintiffs were not parties. I have come to the conclusion that no such action will lie – I must say somewhat reluctantly, because though I wish to express no opinion on the merits of this particular case, having no materials for forming such an opinion, it does seem just, in general, if a company taking the benefit of the work and expenditure by which its existence has been rendered possible, and voluntarily comes into existence on the terms that it shall be liable to pay for such work and expenditure, that a cause of action should be given. I can find however, no legal principle upon which such an action can be maintained. It appears to me that there is no contract between the plaintiffs and the defendants. The doctrine of ratification is inapplicable, for the reasons given in the judgments in *Kelner v Baxter* (1866) LR 2 CP 174."

Mellor J, said ((1874) LR 9 CP 503 at 506):

> "The plaintiffs were not in any way parties to the articles of association, and there was not, therefore, any express contract to pay them."

Brett J, said (1874) LR 9 CP 503 at 507:

> "There is no contract, in my judgment, of any sort upon which they can sue, and unless there be a contract of some sort between them and the company I do not see that they can have any cause of action. No contract made with them before the existence of the company can be ratified by the company for the reasons pointed out in the case of *Kelner* v *Baxter*, with which I fully agree."

In *Eley* v *Positive Government Security Life Assurance Co* the articles of association contained a clause in which it was stated that the plaintiff, a solicitor, should be the solicitor to the company and transact its legal business. The articles were registered and the company incorporated. The plaintiff was not appointed solicitor by any resolution of the directors, nor by any instrument bearing the seal of the company, but he acted as such for a time. Subsequently the company ceased to employ him, and he brought an action for breach of contract against the company for not employing him as its solicitor. The first count of the declaration stated that it was agreed by and between the plaintiff and the defendants that the plaintiff should be employed by the defendants as, and appointed by them to the office of, solicitor of the company. During the argument it was contended that the contract declared for was not the contract purported to be contained in the articles. Amphlett B, in his judgment, said ((1874) 1 Ex D 20 at 26, 28):

> "The articles, taken by themselves, are simply a contract between the shareholders inter se, and cannot, in my opinion, give a right of action to a person like the plaintiff, not a party to the articles, although named therein. If authority were wanted for this proposition, the cases cited in the argument, *Prichard's Case* and *Melhado* v *Porto Alegre Railway Co* are, in my opinion, quite conclusive on the subject ... For these reasons, I think that there was no contract at all between the plaintiff and the company to the effect stated in the declaration."

Cleasby B confined his judgment to the last points raised in the case and said ((1874) 1 Ex D 20 at 30):

> "I am of opinion that cl 118 of the articles cannot by itself be taken to operate as a contract between the solicitor and the company."

Kelly, CJ said ((1874) 1 Ex D 20 at 31, 32):

> "I forbear to pronounce any opinion as to whether these articles, with the fact of the subsequent employment, constitute a contract on the terms contained in them, because, were I to so hold, there would be a difficult question behind, whether it was not ultra vires for the directors to attempt to bind the company to employ a solicitor to transact, for all his life, all the legal business of the company. Passing by this, I come to consider the objection raised under s4 of the Statute of Frauds. I do not see how anyone can doubt that this agreement was not to be performed within a year. It was for the life of the plaintiff, subject to a defeasance on the possibility of his being guilty of some misconduct. But, assuming, as I think we must, that this was not to be performed in a year, the question arises whether there is any memorandum or note in writing of it signed by the defendants. The signatures affixed to the articles were alio intuitu and it can hardly be suggested that the directors had any idea that in signing the articles they were signing a note of this contract."

This case went to the Court of Appeal, and Lord Cairns LC said ((1874) 1 Ex D at 89, 90):

> "I wish to say, in the first place, that in my opinion a contract of the kind suggested to exist in this case ought not to receive any particular favour from the court. The statement is that Baylis was endeavouring to form a joint stock insurance company upon a new principle, and applied to the plaintiff to make advances to meet the expenses of getting up the company, and it was arranged between them that in the event of the company being formed the plaintiff should be appointed permanent solicitor to the company. That is to say, a bargain is made between a professional man and Baylis, which, so far as the case is concerned does not appear to have been communicated to those who were invited to join the company, that if the former will advance money for the formation of the company he shall be appointed permanent solicitor, and the company shall be obliged to employ him as their professional adviser. When the articles are prepared, they are so by the plaintiff, and in them he inserts a clause which no doubt informs those who signed the articles of the arrangement, but does not appear to have been brought to the notice of those who joined from receiving circulars. This, I repeat, is not a proceeding which the court would encourage in any way. I also

wish to reserve my judgment as to whether a clause of this kind is obnoxious to the principles by which the courts are governed in deciding on questions of public policy ... This case was first rested on the 118th article. Articles of association, as is well known, follow the memorandum, which states the object of the company, while the articles state the arrangement between the members. They are an agreement inter socios, and that view, if the introductory words are applied to at 118, it becomes a covenant between the parties to it that they will employ the plaintiff. Now, so far as that is concerned, it is re inter alios acta, the plaintiff is no party to it. No doubt he thought that by inserting it he was making his employment safe as against the company, but his relying on that view of the law does not alter the legal effect of the articles. This article is either a stipulation which would bind the members or else a mandate to the directors. In either case, it is a matter between the directors and shareholders, and not between them and the plaintiff."

In *Browne* v *La Trinidad* before the formation of the company an agreement was entered into between B and a person as trustee for the intended company by which it was stipulated (inter alia) that B should be a director and should not be removable till after 1888. The sixth clause of the articles provided that the directors should adopt and carry into effect the agreement with or without modification, and that subject to such modification (if any) the provisions of the agreement should be construed as part of the articles. The agreement was acted upon, but no contract adopting it was entered into between the plaintiff and the company. Held, that treating the agreement as embodied in the articles, still there was no contract between B and the company that he should not be removed from being a director, the articles being only a contract between the members inter se and not between the company and B. Cotton LJ towards the end of his judgment said ((1888) 37 Ch D 1 at 13, 14):

"Assuming that an unlimited power is given to the meeting by art 91, ought we, having regard to the contract entered into by the memorandum of 24 November, 1884, and art 6, to interfere by injunction to restrain the company in general meeting from acting under that power? I do not give any opinion upon the question how far the court would have interfered by injunction in order specifically to enforce an agreement between the company and the plaintiff that he should be an irremovable director. That point raises questions upon which I should not like to give any opinion without having them fully discussed. In my opinion we ought not to interfere in the present case, because there is no such contract between the plaintiff and the company. The memorandum of agreement of 24 November, 1884, is in no way a contract between the plaintiff and the company. It is said that it was adopted and incorporated into the articles, but I cannot accede to that. The company by its directors acted upon the agreement, but that does not make it binding on the company. Then is it incorporated into the articles in such a way as to entitle the plaintiff to say, 'I have such a contract between me and the company as can be enforced by a court of law, and as I might enforce in equity by way of specific performance'? That point is clearly settled, I think, by *Eley* v *Positive Government Security Life Assurance Co* . There two of the members of the court of first instance held, and the other member did not express dissent, that the articles are merely a contract between the shareholders inter se, and that though a person in whose favour a stipulation is made in the articles may afterwards have shares allotted to him, he does not by that means become in the same position as if he had entered into a contract with the company."

Lindley LJ said:

"Having regard to the construction put upon s16 of the Companies Act of 1862 in the case of *Eley* v *Positive Government Security Life Assurance Co* (and subsequent cases, it must be taken as settled that the contract upon which he relies is not a contract upon which he can maintain any action, either on the common law side or the equity side. There might have been some difficulty in arriving at that conclusion if it had not been for the authorities, because it happens that this gentleman has had shares allotted to him, and is therefore a member of the company. Having regard to the terms of s16, there would be some force, or, at all events, some plausibility, in the argument that, being a member, the contract which is referred to in the articles has become binding between the company and him. Of course, that argument is open to this difficulty, that there could be no contract between him and the company until the shares were allotted to him, and it would be remarkable that upon the shares being allotted to him a contract between him and the company, as to a matter not connected with the holding of shares, should arise."

In these four cases the article relied upon purported to give specific contractual rights to persons in some capacity other than that of shareholder, and in none of them were members seeking to enforce or protect rights given to them as members in common with the other corporators. The actual decisions amount to this, that an outsider to whom rights purport to be given by the articles in his capacity as such outsider, whether he subsequently becomes a member or not, cannot sue on such articles treating them as contracts between himself and the company to enforce such rights. Such rights are not part of the general regulations of the company applicable alike to all shareholders and can only exist by virtue of some contract between such non-member and the company, and the subsequent allotment of shares to an outsider in whose favour such an article is inserted does not enable him to sue the company on such an article to enforce rights which are res inter alios acta and not part of the general rights of the corporators as such. The language of some of the judgments appears, however, to go further, as recognised, for instance, by Sargant J, in *Re Famatina Development Corporation* [1914] 2 Ch 271 at 279.

The wording of s14(1) of the Companies (Consolidation) Act 1908, which is in the same terms as s16 of the Act of 1862 (now s20(1) of Companies Act 1948) is difficult to construe or understand. The company cannot in the ordinary course be bound otherwise than by statute or contract, and it is in this section that its obligations must be found, so far as the members are concerned. The section does not say with whom they are to be deemed to have covenanted, but the section cannot mean that the company is not to be bound when it says it is to be bound, as if, etc, nor can the section mean that the members are to be under no obligation to the company under the articles in which their rights and duties as corporators are to be found. Much of the difficulty is removed if the company be regarded, as the framers of the section may very well have so regarded it, as being treated in law as a party to its own articles. It seems clear from other authorities that a company is entitled as against its members to enforce and restrain breaches of its regulations: see, for example, *MacDougall v Gardiner* (1875) 1 Ch D 13, *Pender v Lushington* (1877) 6 Ch D 70 and *Imperial Hydropathic Hotel Co, Blackpool v Hampson* (1882) 23 Ch D 1 at 13. In the last case Bowen LJ said:

> "The articles by s16 are to bind the company and all the shareholders as much as if they had all put their seals to them."

It is also clear from many authorities that shareholders as against their company can enforce and restrain breaches of its regulations, and in many of these cases judicial expressions of opinion appear which, in my judgment, it is impossible to disregard.

In *Johnson v Lyttle's Iron Agency* (1877) 5 Ch D 687 at 693, in an action by a shareholder against the company, James LJ said:

> "The notice did not comply strictly with the provisions of the contract between the company and the shareholders which is contained in the regulation of table A."

In *Bradford Banking Co Ltd v Briggs & Co Ltd* (1886) 12 App Cas 29 at 318 the articles gave the company a lien on its members' shares, and, in an action by the company to enforce such lien, Lord Blackburn said:

> "The only one of the articles of association which I think it material to notice is the 103rd article, which is as follows:

The company shall have a first and permanent lien and charge, available at law and in equity, upon every share of every person who is the holder or one of several joint owners thereof of all debts due from him, either alone or jointly with any person, whether a shareholder or not in the company.'

> "John Faint Easby, a coal merchant, became a proprietor of a number of shares in the respondent company, and obtained certificates for them. This property in the shares was, by virtue of s16 of the Companies Act 1862, already quoted, I think, bound to the company as much as if he had (at the time he became holder of these shares) executed a covenant to the company in the same terms as art 103, but I do not think it was bound any further."

In *Wood v Odessa Waterworks Co* (1889) 42 Ch D 636 at 642, which was an action by the plaintiff on behalf of himself and all other shareholders against the company, Stirling J said :

"The articles of association constitute a contract not merely between the shareholders and the company, but between each individual shareholder and every other."

In *Salmon* v *Quin and Axtens Ltd* [1909] 1 Ch 311 at 318, Farwell LJ, referring to this last statement, said:

"I think that that is accurate subject to this observation, that it may well be that the court would not enforce the covenant as between individual shareholders in most cases."

In *Welton* v *Saffery* [1897] AC 299 at 315 Lord Herschell, who dissented on the main question from the rest of the House, made the following general observation:

"Section 16 of the Act of 1862 provides that the articles of association, when registered, shall bind the comany and the members thereof to the same extent as if each member had signed his name and affixed his seal thereto, and there were in such articles contained a covenant on the part of himself, his heirs, executors, and administrators, to conform to all the regulations contained in such articles, subject to the provisions of this Act. The articles thus become in effect a contract under seal by each member of the company, and regulate his rights. They cannot, of course, diminish or affect any liability created by the express terms of the statute; but, as I have said, the statute does not purport to settle the rights of the members inter se; it leaves these to be determined by the articles (or the articles and memorandum together), which are the social contract regulating those rights. I think it was intended to permit perfect freedom in this respect. It is quite true that the articles constitute a contract between each member and the company, and that there is no contract in terms between the individual members of the company; but the articles do not any the less, in my opinion, regulate their rights inter se. Such rights can only be enforced by or against a member through the company, or through the liquidator representing the company; but I think that no member has, as between himself and another member, any right beyond that which the contract with the company gives."

'In all these last-mentioned cases the respective articles sought to be enforced related to the rights and obligations of the members generally as such, and not to rights of the character dealt with in the four authorities first above referred to. It is difficult to reconcile these two classes of decisions and the judicial opinions therein expressed, but I think this much is clear – first, that no article can constitute a contract between the company and a third person; secondly, that no right merely purported to be given by an article to a person, whether a member or not, in a capacity other than that of a member, as, for instance, a solicitor, promoter, or director, can be enforced against the company; and, thirdly, articles regulating the rights and obligations of the members generally as such do create rights and obligations between them and the company respectively ...

... In the present case the plaintiff's action is, in substance, to enforce rights as a member under the articles against the company. The 49th article is a general article applying to all the members as such, and, apart from technicalities, it would seem reasonable that the plaintiff ought not to be allowed, in the absence of any evidence filed by him, to proceed with an action to enforce his rights under the articles which in itself is a breach of his obligation contained therein to submit his disputes with the company to arbitration ... In my judgment, art 49, for the reasons above referred to, creates rights and obligations enforceable as between the plaintiff and the company respectively, and such rights and obligations are contained in a written document, but whether such document is a contract or agreement between the plaintiff and the defendants within s27 of the Arbitration Act, 1889, depends upon whether the decision in *Eley* v *Positive Government Security Life Assurance Co* and the other cases of a similar character above referred to ought to be regarded as only dealing with and applying to articles purporting, first, to contain an agreement with the company and a third person, or, secondly, to define the rights of a shareholder in some capacity other than that of a member of the company. To reconcile the decisions and expressions of judicial opinion above mentioned, some such view should, I think, be adopted and general articles dealing with the rights of members "as such" treated as a statutory agreement between them and the company as well as between themselves inter se, and in my judgment art 49 in the present case does constitute a submission to arbitration within the true meaning and intent of the Arbitration Act ...'

New British Iron Company, Re, ex parte Beckwith [1898] 1 Ch 324 Chancery Division (Wright J)

Articles – supplying terms into an extrinsic contract with outsiders

Facts
Article 62 of the company provided that the remuneration of the board of directors was to be £1,000 per year to be divided in such manner as the board of directors determined from time to time. The company went into liquidation with Beckwith and other directors being owed directors' fees under art 62. In the winding-up they claimed to rank as ordinary creditors in respect of this sum.

Held
The directors' claim succeeded.

Wright J:

'Article 62 fixes the remuneration of the directors at the annual sum of £1,000. That article is not in itself a contract between the company and the directors; it is only part of the contract constituted by the articles of association between the members of the company inter se. But where on the footing of that article the directors are employed by the company and accept office the terms of art 62 are embodied in and form part of the contract between the company and the directors. Under the article as thus embodied the directors obtain a contractual right to an annual sum of £1,000 as remuneration ... It is not due to them by their being members of the company, but under a distinct contract with the company. The claim must therefore be allowed.'

Quin & Axtens Limited v *Salmon* [1909] AC 442 House of Lords (Lord Loreburn LC, Lords Macnaghten, James and Shaw); [1909] 1 Ch 311 Court of Appeal (Cozens-Hardy MR and Farwell LJ)

Reliance on s14 by a director

Facts
The company was incorporated in 1905 to acquire and take over a business of drapers, furnishing and general warehousemen in Brixton. Of 50,007 ordinary shares which had been issued Axtens held 27,240 and Salmon 22,085, 250 by another director, 250 by Salmon's brother and the remainder by various small holders. Article 75 of the articles entrusted the management of the company to the board while art 80 provided, inter alia, that no resolution of a meeting of the directors to purchase or lease property was valid or binding unless 24 hours' notice had been given to each of Axtens and Salmon of such resolution and neither of them had dissented therefrom in writing before or at the meeting at which the resolution was to be put to the vote. The board proposed a resolution under which the company would purchase certain premises for over £2,000. Salmon dissented from this resolution in writing in accordance with art 80. A board meeting was held and the resolutions passed even though Salmon also dissented from these in writing. Subsequently, an extraordinary general meeting was called and the resolutions submitted to it. They were lost on a show of hands but a poll was eventually demanded and taken and the resolutions passed by the weight of Axten's votes. Salmon sought an injunction to stop the company acting on the resolutions.

Held
The resolutions were inconsistent with the provisions of the articles and an injunction would be issued to stop the company acting on it.

Farwell LJ:

'... It appears to me to be plain that this is a contract by which the business of the company shall be managed by the board. The articles, by s16 of the Act of 1862, are made equivalent to a deed of covenant signed by all the shareholders. The Act does not say with whom that covenant is entered into, and there have no doubt been varying statements by learned judges, some of them saying it is with the company, some of them saying it is both with the company and with the shareholders. Stirling J in *Wood* v *Odessa Waterworks Co* (1889) 42 Ch D 636 at 642 says: "The articles of association constitute a contract not merely between the shareholders and the company, but between each individual shareholder and every other." I think that that is accurate subject to this observation, that it may well be that the Court would not enforce the covenant as between individual shareholders in most cases. Now the general power of the board to manage here is qualified by the stipulation which follows, that it is to be subject to the provisions of these articles. I therefore turn to art 80, and I find this provision to which these general powers of management are made subject: (His Lordship read the article.) In the present case Mr Salmon did so dissent according to the terms of that article, and therefore the veto therein provided came into operation. That was met by the company being called together by a requisition of seven shareholders and by passing general resolutions for the acquisition of this property and the letting of the vacant premises. It is said that those resolutions are of no effect, and I am of opinion that that contention is right. I base my opinion on the words of art 75, "subject, nevertheless, to the provisions of any Acts of Parliament or of these articles", which I read to be "subject, nevertheless, to art 80", "and to such regulations (being not inconsistent with any such provisions of these articles) as may be prescribed by the company in general meeting". That is to say, "subject also to such regulations not inconsistent with art 80 as may be prescribed by the company in general meeting". But these resolutions are absolutely inconsistent with art 80; in truth this is an attempt to alter the terms of the contract between the parties by a simple resolution instead of by a special resolution ...'

Rayfield v *Hands* [1960] 1 Ch 1 Chancery Division (Vaisey J)

The articles constitute a contract between the members inter se

Facts

The company, Field-Davis Ltd, whose business was builders and contractors, had 4,000 issued £1 shares of which the plaintiff held 725. Under art 11 of the company's articles it was provided: 'Every member who intends to transfer shares shall inform the directors who will take the said shares equally between them at a fair value ...' The articles also contained restrictions on transfer of shares to a non-member. In April 1955 the plaintiff notified the defendants in writing that as directors of the company he intended to transfer his 725 shares to them. The defendants refused to take up and pay for the shares and the plaintiff claimed an order that they should take them.

Held

Article 11 affected the plaintiff and the directors both in their capacity qua members and the articles required the directors to purchase the shares.

Vaisey J:

'The next and most difficult point taken by the defendants, as to which it would appear that there is no very clear judicial authority, is that art 11, as part of the company's articles of association, does not do what it looks like doing, that is, to create a contractual relationship between the plaintiff as shareholder and vendor and the defendants as directors and purchasers. This depends on s20(1) of the Companies Act, 1948 (now s14 CA 1985) ...

... In *Re Leicester Club and County Racecourse Co* (1885) 30 Ch D 629 Pearson J, referring to the directors of a company, said that they "continue members of the company, and I prefer to call them working members of the company ..." and on the same page he also said: "directors cannot divest themselves of their character of members of the company. From first to last ... they are doing their work in the capacity of members, and working members of the company ..." I am of opinion, therefore, that this is in words a contract or quasi-contract between members, and not between members and directors.'

Commentary

Considered by Scott J in *Cumbrian Newspapers* v *Cumberland Herald* [1986] 2 All ER 816.

Wood v *Odessa Waterworks Company* (1889) 42 Ch D 636 Chancery Division (Stirling J)

Company and members are bound by the terms of the articles

Facts

The defendant company for many years had not paid any dividends but instead applied its profits in extending its mains water system and constructing waterworks. In 1889 the accounts showed an excess of receipts over expenditure of £45,959 but all of this money had been used in extending the mains and construction work. Instead of paying a dividend the directors recommended giving the shareholders debenture bonds bearing interest repayable at par, by annual drawings, extending over 30 years. A resolution of an ordinary meeting was passed adopting this recommendation. The plaintiff who was not present at the meeting, objected to what had been done on the ground that it breached the articles which referred to 'a dividend to be paid to the members'.

Held

The resolution was not in accordance with the articles and an injunction would be granted to stop the directors issuing the debenture bonds.

Stirling J:

'The question, simply, is whether it is within the power of a majority of shareholders to insist against the will of a minority that the profits which have actually been earned shall be divided, not by the payment of cash but by the issue of debenture bonds of the company bearing interest at £5 per cent and repayable at par by an annual drawing extending over 30 years ... Now the rights of the shareholders in respect of a division of the profits of the company are governed by the provisions in the articles of association ... Section 50 of the Act (Companies Act 1862 – now s9 CA 1985) provides the means for altering the regulations of the company contained in the articles of association by passing a special resolution, but no such resolution has in this case been passed or attempted to be passed; and the question is, whether this is a matter as to which the majority of the shareholders can bind those shareholders who dissent. The articles of association constitute a contract not merely between the shareholders and the company, but between each individual shareholder and every other; and the question which I have just stated must, in my opinion, be answered in the negative if there be in the articles a contract between the shareholders as to a division of the profits, and the provisions of that contract have not been followed ... That brings me to consider whether that which is proposed to be done in the present case is in accordance with the articles of association of the company. Those articles provide (101) that the directors may, with the sanction of a general meeting, declare a dividend to be paid to the shareholders. Prima facie that means to be paid in cash. The debenture bonds proposed to be issued are not payments in cash; they are merely agreements or promises to pay; and if the contention of the company prevails a shareholder will be compelled to accept in lieu of cash a debt of the company payable at some uncertain future period ...'

4 Alteration of Memorandum of Association and Articles

Alteration of the memorandum

Hampstead Garden Suburb Trust Ltd, Re [1962] Ch 806 Chancery Division (Pennycuick J)

Alteration of the memorandum under old s4(e) of the Companies Act 1985

Facts

The company was formed in 1906 to purchase, develop and lay out as a garden suburb an estate at Hendon, Middlesex. Under cl 3 sub-cl T of the memorandum directions were given as to the application of the balance of the company's funds on winding-up. It read: 'Upon any winding-up or dissolution of the company, if there remains any balance ... to give or transfer the said balance to some institution or institutions to be determined by the members at or before the time of dissolution, and if and so far as effect cannot be given to the aforesaid provision, then to some charitable object.' It was proposed to alter this sub-clause so that on a winding-up the balance of the company's assets should go to the Hampstead Garden Suburb Community Trust Ltd. The National Trust which held 25 per cent of the company's shares and the various holders of another 1,135 ordinary shares in the company petitioned the court that the resolution effecting this alteration should be cancelled on the grounds that (i) the alteration was not one authorised by the section, and (ii) it should not be confirmed by the court.

Held

The National Trust which held more than 15 per cent of the shares was entitled to bring a petition under s5(2) CA 1948 (now s5(2) CA 1985) but the various holders of 1,135 shares, which together amounted to less than 15 per cent in total had no locus standi to do so. The alteration would be cancelled as it was not within the ambit of s5(1) (e) (now s4(e) as it was alleged to be but was merely a variation of the sub-clause.

Pennycuick J:

'... Counsel, at the opening of his contentions for the company, not by way of a preliminary point at the opening of the hearing, took a point of importance. The National Trust clearly have a right to present a petition, being the holder of 25 per cent of the deferred shares in the company, that is to say, not less than 15 per cent, in nominal value of one class of the company's issued share capital. On the other hand the individual petitioners who hold ordinary shares in the company have no locus standi to present a petition. They hold in all 1,135 ordinary shares, which is much less than 15 per cent of the nominal value of the issued ordinary shares of the company. Again, the National Trust, together with the petitioning ordinary shareholders, hold much less than 15 per cent of the total issued share capital of the company. On those facts counsel for the company submitted, first, that the petition was wholly ill-founded and secondly, that the court should only have regard to the complaints of the National Trust. I do not accept the first of these contentions, but I do accept the second of them. It seems to me that if the petitioners who are holders of ordinary shares have no locus standi in their own right to present this petition, they can only be heard in support of the National Trust's contentions, and cannot put forward grounds of complaint which are not made by the National Trust ...'

... The first issue then, is whether the resolution altering cl 3 (T) of the memorandum comes within s5 (now s4 CA 1985 as substituted by s110(2) of the Companies Act 1989) of the Act. The only sub-para in s5(1) (now s4) which, it is suggested by counsel for the company, is applicable, is sub-para (e), namely, to restrict or abandon any of the objects specified in the memorandum. No suggestion is made on either side that sub-cl (T) is for any reason ineffectual. There is no evidence as to the existence or otherwise of institutions having objects similar to the objects of the company. What is sought to be done by the alteration in sub-cl (T) is, first, to exclude altogether any institution or institutions there may be having objects similar to the objects of this company, ie the primary beneficiary under sub-cl (T), and secondly, to make the balance go to a specified charity, ie one of the class of default beneficiaries.

It seems to me impossible to regard the promotion in this way of a default beneficiary to the status of the primary beneficiary as being within the ambit of the words, "to raise or abandon any of the objects specified in the memorandum". Counsel for the company contended that the resolution first abandons one object, namely, the institution or institutions having objects similar to the objects of the company, and then restricts the remaining objects, namely, the charitable objects, by confining them to a certain named charity. It seems to me that this ingenious way of putting it disregards one essential element in the alterations, namely, the promotion of the default beneficiary to be a primary beneficiary, irrespective of whether or not there exists an institution or institutions having objects similar to the objects of the company. The point may be illustrated by supposing a rather simpler provision, comparable to that in sub-cl (T). Suppose that the provision is to transfer the balance to hospital X if then existing, that is, existing at the date of the winding-up; but if hospital X is not then existing, to hospital Y. It seems to me that a resolution that the balance shall go to hospital Y whether or not hospital X then exists, would clearly not be a provision restricting or abandoning any of the objects specified in the memorandum within the meaning of those words in s5(1)(e) of the Act.'

Commentary
New s4 of the Companies Act 1985 no longer requires the alteration to fall within one or more of seven grounds.

Alteration of the articles

Allen v *Gold Reefs of West Africa Ltd* [1900] 1 Ch 656 Court of Appeal (Sir Nathaniel Lindley MR, Vaughan Williams and Romer LJJ)

Alteration of articles – test of bona fide of the company as a whole

Facts
The company had an issued share capital of 360,000 shares of 5s or 25p each and some were issued as fully paid up, but many were issued unpaid-up under a power in the memorandum. A deceased shareholder named Zuccani held 27,885 fully paid-up and 36,435 unpaid up shares at his death. At one time he had 60,000 unpaid-up shares but he had from time to time paid up the sums due on some of these and sold them at a profit. Zuccani, despite his profits, was regularly in arrears in payment of calls made by the company from time to time on the shares and at his death over £6,000 was owing in respect of calls. The articles of the company gave it a power to forfeit shares in respect of money due to the company. An attempt was made to forfeit some of Zuccani's shares on this ground but because of

mistakes the court held that the forfeiting only extended to unpaid-up shares. Article 29 provided that the company had 'no lien whatever on fully paid-up shares' while art 30 gave an lien on unpaid-up shares for money due on these. The directors of the company wished to extend the lien to Zuccani's fully paid-up shares in order to recover the full £6,000 due to them. Accordingly, a meeting was convened and a special resolution was passed altering art 29 so as to give a lien on fully paid up shares. Zuccani's executors challenged this alteration on the ground, inter alia, that it was oppressive to them as Zuccani's shares were the only shares affected by it.

Held

The alteration was valid as it was carried out bona fide for the benefit of the company as a whole in that it was intended to recover the large debt due to the company from Zuccani.

Sir Nathaniel Lindley MR:

'The articles of a company prescribe the regulations binding on its members. They have the effect of a contract; but the exact nature of this contract is even now very difficult to define. Be its nature what it may the company is empowered by the statute to alter the regulations contained in its articles from time to time by special resolutions (ss50 and 51); and any regulation or article purporting to deprive the company of this power is invalid on the ground that it is contrary to the statute: (*Walker* v *London Tramways Co* (1879) 12 Ch D 705). The power thus conferred on companies to alter the regulations contained in their articles is limited only by the provisions contained in the statute and the conditions contained in the company's memorandum of association. Wide, however, as the language of s50 is, the power conferred by it must, like all other powers, be exercised subject to those general principles of law and equity which are applicable to all powers conferred on majorities and enabling them to bind minorities. It must be exercised, not only in the manner required by law, but also bona fide for the benefit of the company as a whole, and it must not be exceeded. These conditions are always implied, and are seldom, if ever, expressed. But if they are complied with, I can discover no ground for judicially putting any other restrictions on the power conferred by the section than those contained in it. How shares shall be transferred, and whether the company shall have any lien on them, are clearly matters of regulation properly prescribed by a company's articles of association. This is shown by table A in the schedule to the Companies Act, 1862 (c11. 8, 9, 10).

Speaking, therefore, generally, and without reference to any particular case, the section clearly authorises a limited company, formed with articles which confer no lien on fully paid-up shares and which allow them to be transferred without any fetter, to alter those articles by special resolution, and to impose a lien and restrictions on the registry of transfers of those shares by members indebted to the company. But then comes the question whether this can be done so as to impose a lien or restriction in respect of a debt contracted before and existing at the time when the articles are altered. Again, speaking generally, I am of opinion that the articles can be so altered, and that, if they are bona fide for the benefit of the company, they will be valid and binding as altered on the existing holders of paid-up shares, whether those holders are indebted or not indebted to the company when the alteration is made. But, as will be seen presently, it does not by any means follow that the altered article may not be inapplicable to some particular fully paid-up shareholder. He may have special rights against the company which do not invalidate the resolution to alter the articles, but which may exempt him from the operation of the articles as altered.

The conclusion thus arrived at is based on the language of s50, which, as I have said already, the court, in my opinion, is not at liberty to restrict. This conclusion, moreover, is in conformity with such authorities as there are on the subject. *Andrews* v *Gas Meter Co* [1897] 1 Ch 361 is an authority that, under s50 of the Companies Act, 1862, a company's articles can be altered so as to authorise the issue of preference shares taking priority over existing shares, although no power to issue preference shares was conferred by the memorandum of association or by the original articles. The answer to the argument that the company could not alter existing rights is that, within the limits set by the statute and the memorandum of association, the rights of shareholders in limited companies, so far as they depend only on the regulations of the company, are subject to alteration by s50 of the Act.

The decision of Chitty LJ in *Pepe* v *City and Suburban Permanent Building Society* [1893] 2 Ch 311 is in principle also clearly in point. A member of a building society who had given notice of withdrawal, and who by the rules, as they then stood, became entitled to a certain sum of money, was held to be deprived of his right to that sum by an alteration made in the rules before he had ceased to be a member. This case went very far, but it has been treated as correct in *Botten* v *City and Suburban Permanent Building Society* [1895] 2 Ch 441 It was urged that a company's articles could not be altered retrospectively, and reliance was placed on the observations of Rigby LJ in *James* v *Buena Ventura Nitrate Grounds Syndicate* [1896] 1 Ch 456. The word "retrospective" is, however, somewhat ambiguous, and the concurrence of Rigby LJ in *Andrews* v *Gas Meter Co* shows that his observations in *James* v *Buena Ventura Nitrate Grounds Syndicate* are no authority for saying that existing rights, founded and dependent on alterable articles, cannot be affected by their alteration. Such rights are in truth limited as to their duration by the duration of the articles which confer them. But, although the regulations contained in a company's articles of association are revocable by special resolution, a special contract may be made with the company in the terms of or embodying one or more of the articles, and the question will then arise whether an alteration of the articles so embodied is consistent or inconsistent with the real bargain between the parties. A company cannot break its contracts by altering its articles, but when dealing with contracts referring to revocable articles, and especially with contracts between a member of the company and the company respecting his shares, care must be taken not to assume that the contract involves as one of its terms an article which is not to be altered.

It is easy to imagine cases in which even a member of a company may acquire by contract or otherwise special rights against the company which exclude him from the operation of a subsequently altered article. Such a case arose in *Swabey* v *Port Darwin Gold Mining Co* (1889) 1 Meg 385 where it was held that directors, who had earned fees payable under a company's articles, could not be deprived of them by a subsequent alteration of the articles, which reduced the fees payable to directors. I take it to be clear that an application for an allotment of shares on the terms of the company's articles does not exclude the power to alter them, nor the application of them when altered to the shares so applied for and allotted. To exclude that power or the application of an altered article to particular shares, some clear and distinct agreement for that exclusion must be shown, or some circumstances must be proved conferring a legal or equitable right on the shareholder to be treated by the company differently from the other shareholders.

This brings me to the last question which has to be considered – viz, whether there is in this case any contract or other circumstance which excludes the application of the altered article to Zuccani's fully paid-up share and another. Whether a share is paid for in cash or is given in payment for property acquired by the company appears to me quite immaterial for the present purpose. In either case the shareholder pays for his share, and in either case he takes it subject to the articles of association and power of altering them, unless this inference is excluded by special circumstances.

Next let us consider whether a vendor, who makes no special bargain except that he is to be paid in fully paid-up shares, is in any different position from other allottees of fully paid-up shares. I fail to see that he is, unless he stipulates that his shares shall be specially favoured. Zuccani bargained for fully paid-up shares, and he got them. The imposition of a lien on them did not render them less fully paid-up than they were before. They remained what they were. Zucanni did not bargain that the regulations relating to paid-up shares should never be altered, or that if altered his shares should be treated differently from other full paid-up shares. I cannot see that the company broke its bargain with him in any way by altering its regulations or by enforcing the altered regulations as it did. I have already drawn attention to cl 5 of the memorandum of association. Having regard to its plain language, no allottee of shares, whether a vendor or an ordinary applicant, can justly complain of injustice or even hardship if his rights under the original articles are modified to his disadvantage. Every allottee was told by the memorandum that his rights as a shareholder were subject to alteration, and no allottee acquired any rights except on these terms, unless, of course, some special bargain was made with him. If Zuccani had not been indebted to the company, could he have successfully maintained that the company had no power to alter the articles and so make his shares liable to a lien, and, consequently less marketable than before? I take it that it is clear that he could not. But I arrive at this conclusion only because the bargain with him has not been broken.

Zuccani's indebtedness to the company confers on him or his executors no rights against it. But it is his indebtedness which creates the embarrassment from which they seek to escape. The fact that Zuccani's executors were the only persons practically affected at the time by the alterations made in the articles excites suspicion as to the bona fides of the company. But, although the executors were the only persons who were actually affected at the time, that was because Zuccani was the only holder of paid-up shares who at the time was in arrear of calls. The altered articles applied to all holders of fully-paid shares, and made no distinction between them. The directors cannot be charged with bad faith.

After carefully considering the whole case, and endeavouring in vain to discover grounds for holding that there was some special bargain differentiating Zuccani's shares from others, I have come to the conclusion that the appeal from the decision of the learned judge, so far as it relates to the lien created by the articles, must be allowed. His decision as to the forfeiture having, however, been affirmed, each party should be left to pay his own costs.'

Commentary
The references to s50 are to that section in the Companies Act 1862 which is a predecessor of the present s9 in the 1985 Act.

Cane v *Jones* [1980] 1 WLR 1451 Chancery Division (Michael Wheeler QC sitting as a deputy judge of the High Court)
Alteration of articles without holding a meeting or passing a resolution

Facts
The company, Kingsway Petrol Station Ltd, was a family company incorporated in 1946 by two brothers, Percy and Harold Jones, who were appointed directors for life by the articles. Of the 30,000 £1 shares issued by the company 15,000 were held by Percy's children at the date of the action and 15,000 were held by Harold's daughter, Mrs Cane. The articles provided, inter alia, that the chairman was to be elected by the directors and that he was to have a casting vote at board meetings and, where he presided at general meetings, he was to have a casting vote there also. Provisions as to the appointment and retirement of directors and the chairman were not observed because of failure to hold annual general meetings for several years. There was a dispute between Percy's side of the family and Harold's side of the family as to whether Percy was the chairman. This dispute was magnified because the two sides of the family had fallen out and as the shares were held fifty-fifty, the chairman's casting vote could be crucial. In 1967 the then shareholders in the company had agreed that the chairman of the company should not exercise the casting vote in the event of an equality of votes occurring, that an independent chairman should be appointed instead. Harold's daughter, Mrs Cane, sought, inter alia, a declaration that the 1967 agreement had altered the articles of association and that an attempt by Percy's side of the family to put Percy's son, Ronald, on the board using the casting vote was void being in breach of the alteration effected by the 1967 agreement.

Held
The alteration of the articles by the 1967 agreement was effective because all the corporators of a company could, acting together, do anything which was intra vires the company. Section 10(1) of the 1948 Act (now s9(1) CA 1985) did not undermine this principle, it merely laid down a procedure under which some only of the shareholders can validly alter the articles.

Michael Wheeler QC:

'... Now as to the arguments about the effect of the 1967 agreement. Counsel for the plaintiff contends that it operated as an alteration of the articles on what was conveniently called in argument "the *Duomatic* principle" based on *Re Duomatic Ltd* [1969] 2 Ch 365 and the principle is, I think, conveniently summarised in a short passage in the judgment of Buckley J in that case, where he says:

> "... I proceed on the basis that where it can be shown that all shareholders who have a right to attend and vote at a general meeting of the company assent to some matter which a general meeting of the company could carry into effect, that assent is as binding as a resolution in general meeting would be."

Applying that principle to the present case, counsel for the plaintiff says that the agreement of all the shareholders embodied in the 1967 agreement had the effect, so far as requisite, of overriding the articles. In other words, it operated to deprive the chairman for the time being of the right to use his casting vote except, perhaps, in so far as an independent chairman contemplated by cl 1 might need to do. I should add here that it is quite clear that Percy, who was actually chairman of the company at the time, was well aware of the terms of the 1967 agreement.

For the first and third defendants, counsel has two answers to counsel's argument for the plaintiff: first, that on its true interpretation in relation to a special or extraordinary resolution the *Duomatic* principle only applies if there has been (i) a resolution and (ii) a meeting; and that here he says, with some truth, there was neither a resolution nor a meeting of the four shareholders; second, he stresses that the agreement does not in terms purport to alter the articles at all; it rests, he says, solely in contract and Gillian, not being a party, cannot take either the benefit or the burden of the agreement.

On the first of these two arguments, counsel for the first and third defendants helpfully reminded me of the line of cases in which the effect of the unanimous consent of the corporators has been considered, starting with *Baroness Wenlock v River Dee Co* (1883) 36 Ch D 675n. I do not propose to refer to all these cases in detail but, for the record, I will list them.

The other cases are *Re George Newman & Co* [1895] 1 Ch 674. Then there is *Re Express Engineering Works Ltd* [1920] 1 Ch 466, *Re Oxted Motor Co Ltd* [1921] 3 KB 32, *Parker and Cooper Ltd v Reading* [1926] Ch 975, *Re Pearce Duff & Co Ltd* [1960] 1 WLR 1014, *Re Duomatic*, to which I have already referred, and finally a decision of Slade J in *Re Moorgate Mercantile Holdings Ltd* [1980] 1 WLR 227.

Counsel for the first and third defendants pointed out, correctly, that of these cases only three were concerned with special or extraordinary resolutions, namely *Re Pearce Duff & Co Ltd* and *Re Moorgate Mercantile Holdings Ltd* (both of which were concerned with special resolutions) and *Re Oxted Motor Co Ltd* (which was concerned with an extraordinary resolution). All the rest were concerned with matters which, if capable of ratification at all, could have been validated by ordinary resolutions.

The starting point of counsel for the first and third defendants is s10 of the Companies Act 1948 which provides for the alteration of articles by special resolution; and from that he goes on to s141, mentioning sub-ss (1) and (2) and including the particular proviso, laying down how special and extraordinary resolutions are to be passed.

(His Lordship then read ss10 and 141 and continued):

'Thus, says counsel for the first and third defendants, you can only alter the articles by special resolution. That is his first argument. Secondly, a special resolution must be passed at a meeting; thirdly, here there was neither a resolution nor a meeting.

Re Pearce Duff & Co Ltd, he says, does not help counsel for the plaintiff because in that case there had been a resolution and a meeting: and all that was later cured by the unanimous (but separate) consents of the shareholders was a defect in the consent to short notice under the proviso of s141(2).

Re Moorgate Mercantile Holdings Ltd was concerned with the extent to which, if at all, a resolution which is to be proposed as a special resolution could be amended at the meeting, and its relevance for present purposes lies solely in the fact that Slade J referred to *Re Pearce Duff & Co Ltd* and *Re Duomatic Ltd* (and also to s143(4) of the Act to which I too shall refer in a moment) and stated that the proposition which he had laid down earlier in his judgment for the amendment of special resolutions might be subject to modification where the members unanimously agreed to waive the requirements of notice.

Re Oxted Motor Co Ltd was a case of an extraordinary resolution for voluntary winding-up. There were only two shareholders, who were also the two directors. They met and passed a resolution that the company be wound up and they signed a minute to that effect; but no notice to propose the resolution as an extraordinary resolution had ever been given. The Court of Appeal upheld the resolution on the ground that it was competent for the shareholders of the company acting together to waive the formalities required by what is now s141(1) of the 1948 Act ...

The first of counsel's two arguments for the first and third defendants (namely that there must be a "resolution" and a "meeting") does not appear to have been raised in any of the three reported cases which were concerned with special or extraordinary resolutions. But it is not an argument to which I would readily accede because in my judgment it would create a wholly artificial and unnecessary distinction between those powers which can, and those which cannot, be validly exercised by all the corporators acting together.

For my part I venture to differ from counsel for the first and third defendants on the first limb of his argument, namely that articles can *only* be altered by special resolution. In my judgment, s10 of the Act is merely laying down a procedure whereby *some only* of the shareholders can validly alter the articles; and, if, as I believe to be the case, it is a basic principle of company law that all the corporators, acting together, can do anything which is intra vires the company, then I see nothing in s10 to undermine this principle. I accept that the principle requires all the corporators to "act together", but with regard to this I respectfully adopt what Astbury J said in *Parker and Cooper Ltd* v *Reading*:

"Now the view I take of both these decisions (those were in *Re Express Engineering Works Ltd* and *Re George Newman & Co*) is that where the transaction is intra vires and honest, and especially if it is for the benefit of the company, it cannot be upset if the assent of all the corporators is given to it. I do not think it matters in the least whether that assent is given at different times or simultaneously ...'

Commentary
In relation to private companies see now s381A of the Companies Act 1985.

Greenhalgh v *Arderne Cinemas Ltd* [1951] Ch 286 Court of Appeal (Sir Raymond Evershed MR, Asquith and Jenkins LJJ)

Alteration of articles – meaning of bona fide in the interest of the company test

Facts
In 1941 the plaintiff provided substantial financial assistance to the defendant company, which was then in financial difficulties, after being approached by the controllers of the company, the Mallard family. The plaintiff advanced money which was secured by a debenture and unissued shares in the company were allotted to him. Disputes arose between the plaintiff and the Mallard family as to the running of the company which led to a series of actions over various issues; some of these are reported (see [1943] 2 All ER 234; [1946] 1 All ER 512; [1947] 2 All ER 255), others are unreported. The present action was concerned with an alteration to the articles. The Mallard family entered an agreement in June 1948 to sell all their shares which represented the controlling interest in the company to one, Sheckman. But under art 10 it was provided that a member who wished to sell his shares must give notice to the company and the shares would be offered to other members pro rata, at a price fixed by the auditors. This article was an obstacle to the sale to Sheckman who was a non-member. The Mallard family arranged an extraordinary general meeting of the company to pass a special resolution altering the articles by adding to art 10 the following:

'Notwithstanding the foregoing provisions of this article any member may with the sanction of an ordinary resolution passed at any general meeting of the company transfer his shares or any of them to any person named in such resolution as the proposed transferee, and the directors shall be bound to register any transfer so sanctioned.'

This special resolution was passed and afterwards an ordinary resolution was passed authorising the sale to Sheckman. The plaintiff attended this meeting where 'a certain amount of commotion occurred' and he asked questions which the head of the Mallards, Mr Mallard 'so far as he could, avoided answering them'. The plaintiff sought a declaration inter alia, that the resolutions passed were void because they sacrificed the interests of the minority to the interests of the majority without any benefit to the company and were accordingly, a fraud on the minority. At first instance Roxburgh J dismissed the action. On appeal:

Held

The resolution was valid because although it deprived the minority of their rights of pre-emption under the articles, it was not shown by the plaintiff that it was not bona fide for the benefit of the company and it did not unfairly discriminate between the majority and the minority. The minority were in no worse position than under the old articles if they wished to obtain leave to sell their shares to a non-member because under these the directors had a discretion to refuse registration.

Sir Raymond Evershed, MR:

'... I now come to the case as it has been presented in this court. I have stated that the burden of the case is that the resolution was not passed bona fide and in the interests of the company as a whole, and there are, as counsel for the plaintiff has urged, two rather distinct approaches. The first line of attack is one to which, counsel complains, Roxburgh J paid no regard. This is a special resolution, and on authority, counsel says, the validity of a special resolution depends on the fact that those who passed it did so in good faith and for the benefit of the company as a whole. The cases to which counsel referred are *Sidebottom v Kershaw, Leese & Co* [1929] 1 Ch 154; the decision of Peterson J in *Dafen Tinplate Co v Llanelly Steel Co* [1920] 2 Ch 124; and, finally, *Shuttleworth v Cox Bros & Co (Maidenhead) Ltd* [1927] 2 KB 9. Certain things, I think, can be safely stated as emerging from those authorities. In the first place, it is now plain that "bona fide for the benefit of the company as a whole" means not two things but one. It means that the shareholder must proceed on what, in his honest opinion, is for the benefit of the company as a whole. Secondly, the phrase, "the company as a whole" does not (at any rate in such a case as the present) mean the company as a commercial entity as distinct from the corporators. It means the corporators as a general body. That is to say, you may take the case of an individual hypothetical member and ask whether what is proposed is, in the honest opinion of those who voted in its favour, for that person's benefit. I think the thing can, in practice, be more accurately and precisely stated by looking at the converse and by saying that a special resolution of this kind would be liable to be impeached if the effect of it were to discriminate between the majority shareholders and the minority shareholders so as to give to the former an advantage of which the latter were deprived. When the cases are examined where the resolution has been successfully attacked, it is on that ground that it has fallen down. It is, therefore, not necessary to require that persons voting for a special resolution should, so to speak, dissociate themselves altogether from the prospect of personal benefit and consider whether the proposal is for the benefit of the company as a going concern. If, as commonly happens, an outside person makes an offer to buy all the shares, prima facie, if the corporators think it is a fair offer and vote in favour of the resolution, it is no ground for impeaching the resolution because they are considering the position of themselves as individual persons.

But, accepting all that, as I think counsel for the plaintiff did, he said that there are still grounds for impeaching this resolution – first, because when you look at it the resolution goes further than was necessary to give effect to the sale of the shares, and, secondly, because it prejudiced the plaintiff and minority shareholders in that it deprived them of the right which, under the subsisting articles, they would have of buying the shares of the majority if the latter desired to dipose of them. Counsel says that if you pass a resolution altering the articles merely to give effect to a particular transaction, it is quite sufficient (and generally is the case) to limit it to that transaction, but this resolution provides that anybody who wants at any time to sell his shares can go direct to an outsider, provided that there is an ordinary resolution of the company approving the proposed transferee. He says that if it is one of the majority who is selling, of course he will get the resolution. It, so to speak, franks the shares for holders of majority interests, but makes it more difficult for a minority shareholder, because the majority will probably look with disfavour on his choice. But, after all, this is merely a relaxation of the very stringent restrictions on transfer in the existing article, and it is to be borne in mind that the directors, as the articles stood, could always refuse to register a transfer. A minority shareholder, therefore, who produced an outsider was always liable to be met by the directors (who presumably act according to the majority view), saying: "We are sorry, but we will not have this man in". Although I follow the point, and it might, perhaps, have been possible to do it the other way, I think this is very far removed from the type of case in which what is proposed, as in the *Dafen* case (2), is to give a majority the right to expropriate a minority shareholder, whether he wanted to sell or not, merely on the ground that the majority shareholders wanted the minority man's shares.

As to the second point, I felt at one time sympathy for the plaintiff's argument, because, after all, as the articles stood Mr Greenhalgh could have said: "Before you go selling to Mr Sheckman you have to offer your shares to the existing shareholders, and that will enable me, if I feel so disposed, to buy in, in effect, the whole of the shareholding of the Arderne company." I think the answer to that is that, when a man comes into a company, he is not entitled to assume that the articles will always remain in a particular form, and, so long as the proposed alteration does not unfairly discriminate in the way I have already indicated, I do not think it is an objection, provided the resolution is bona fide passed, that the right to tender for the majority holding of shares would be lost by the lifting of the restriction. I do not think it can be said that that is such a discrimination as falls within the scope of the principle I have tried to state ...'

Russell v *Northern Bank Development Corporation Ltd* [1992] 1 WLR 588 House of Lords (Lord Griffiths, Lord Jauncey of Tullichettle, Lord Lowry, Lord Mustill and Lord Slynn of Hadley)

Agreement not to increase share capital – validity

Facts

Tyrone Brick Ltd (TBL) and its four shareholders had entered into an agreement, inter alia, that 'No further share capital shall be created or issued in the company or the rights attaching to the shares already in issue in any way altered ... without the written consent of each of the parties hereto.'

Held

While accepting the principle that 'a company cannot forgo its right to alter its articles' (see *Southern Foundries (1926) Ltd* v *Shirlaw* [1940] AC 701), an agreement outside the articles between shareholders as to how they will exercise their voting rights on a resolution to alter the articles is not necessarily invalid. Here, the company's undertaking was unenforceable, but not that of the shareholders.

Lord Jauncey of Tullichettle:

'Turning back to [the relevant clause] of the agreement it appears to me that its purpose was twofold. The shareholders agreed only to exercise their voting powers in relation to the creation or issue of shares in TBL if they and TBL agreed in writing. This agreement is purely personal to the shareholders who executed it and ... does not purport to bind future shareholders. It is, in my view, just such a private agreement as was envisaged by Lord Davey in *Welton* v *Saffery* [1897] AC 299. TBL on the other hand agreed that its capital would not be increased without the consent of each of the shareholders. This was a clear undertaking by TBL in a formal agreement not to exercise its statutory powers for a period which could, certainly on one view of construction, last for as long as any one of the parties to the agreement remained a shareholder and long after the control of TBL had passed to shareholders who were not party to the agreement. As such an undertaking it is, in my view, as obnoxious as if it had been contained in the articles of association and therefore is unenforceable as being contrary to the provisions of [the Northern Ireland statute]. TBL's undertaking is, however, independent of and severable from that of the shareholders and there is no reason why the latter should not be enforceable by the shareholders inter se as a personal agreement which in no way fetters TBL in the exercise of its statutory powers.'

Shuttleworth v *Cox Bros & Co (Maidenhead) Ltd* [1927] 2 KB 9 Court of Appeal (Bankes, Scrutton and Atkin LJJ)

Alteration of articles in order to remove a director upheld

Facts
The company was formed in 1921 to take over a partnership business of timber and builders' merchants which had been carried on by the plaintiff and two named Beare and Norris. Article 22 of the articles of the company provided that the company was to have five directors, including all three of the former partners and added:

'each of them shall be entitled to hold such office so long as he shall live unless he become disqualified from any of the causes specified in art 22.'

The plaintiff, as well as being a director was appointed as the works manager of the company at a salary. In 1924 and 1925 he failed to account for moneys he had received on 22 occasions and after an inquiry into the matter he was dismissed as works manager. In the circumstances the other directors wished to get rid of the plaintiff as a permanent director and held an extraordinary general meeting to alter the articles to include in art 22 the words: 'if he shall be requested in writing by all the other directors to resign his office.' About ten months after the alteration all the other directors duly requested the plaintiff to resign. The plaintiff issued a writ claiming wrongful dismissal and that the alteration of the articles was invalid. At first instance a jury found that he had been wrongfully dismissed (a matter with which Avory J, the trial judge, disagreed) and when Avory J left them the question as to whether the alteration was made bona fide in the interests of the company they answered: (i) it was not bona fide; (ii) incidentally it was in the interests of the company. Avory J, holding that there was no evidence of lack of good faith, entered judgment for the company. The plaintiff appealed.

Held
The appeal would be dismissed. It was for the majority of shareholders voting to decide whether the alteration was what they considered to be bona fide for the benefit of the company as a whole.

Scrutton LJ:

'... First of all was Avory J right in holding that there was no evidence of lack of good faith in the directors who proposed this resolution? I have come to the conclusion that he was and that there was no evidence on which a reasonable jury could find that the directors acted otherwise than in good faith. I am quite unable to take the view that this failure to account for these 22 items continuing up to date of writ, and for some very considerable time after writ, the items being ultimately all admitted, was other than a very serious matter in the management of the company. It appears to me that the action of the directors in considering this alteration was taken under careful advice, with no precipitation, and with a genuine desire to provide a remedy for an evil which was forced upon them namely, that the man whom they admittedly could have dismissed by notice from the position of manager was still sitting with them as a director in spite of his serious laxity in the management of the business entrusted to him. I can see no evidence whatever on which the jury were justified in finding that the determination was taken maliciously or with a desire to spite the plaintiff, or from any other motive than that of doing what the directors thought best in the interests of the company. If there was no evidence of lack of good faith, the other finding of the jury appears to me to defeat the appeal. They find that the alteration was for the benefit of the company. It is true they say it was "incidentally" for the benefit of the company, but I suppose that must mean that the primary motive was lack of good faith or malice, but that maliciously they were doing a thing which was for the benefit of the company. Once one has got that there is no evidence of malice it remains that they were doing the thing for the benefit of the company.

But for the argument which counsel for the plaintiff then suggests – which is the only reason why I am giving a separate judgment – there would apparently be an end of the case. The third point taken was, as I understand, that these articles of association amount to a contract with the plaintiff that he shall be a permanent director for life except in the conditions named in art 22; being a contract, it could not be varied without the consent of both parties, and the plaintiff never consented to the variation which was made in art 22. That position is quite sound if you can show a contract outside the articles. If you can show a contract ouside the articles, it is no good altering the articles because you cannot alter the contract outside the articles. The best instance of that is *Nelson* v *James Nelson & Sons Ltd* [1914] 2 KB 770 where there was an article that the directors might appoint a managing director with power to revoke his appointment, and they did appoint, by a separate document in writing, a managing director for a named term. Then during the named term they tried to use the article to revoke his appointment, although the term named in the agreement was still continuing. There the court held, the judge of first instance, that there was an outside contract and the company could not alter that without the consent of both parties; it was no good the company saying that it had in the articles a power to revoke it when it had made an independent contract appointing the manager for a named term.

But in the absence of an outside contract, an appointment under an article is subject to the power of varying the articles given by s18 of the Act of 1908, and, consequently, the contract is not a contract to be a permanent director, but a contract to be a permanent director subject to the power of terminating the appointment given in the articles, or any modification of the articles, which may thereafter be made, under the powers of the Companies (Consolidation) Act, 1908. Therefore, so far, on those three points, it appears to me that the appeal fails.

But if I understand the argument which was put forward by counsel for the plaintiff, based upon an expression of Peterson J's, in *Dafen Tinplate Co Ltd* v *Llanelly Steel Co* [1907] Ltd [1920] 2 Ch 214, it was this. It does not matter whether the directors thought that this alteration was for the benefit of the company; the question is whether the court thinks it was for the benefit of the company. I suppose he must further say that it does not matter that the jury say it was for the benefit of the company; the question is whether the court thinks it was genuinely for the benefit of the company, and the court, on the materials before it, ought to think that it was not genuinely for the benefit of the company, and, therefore, reject both the honest opinion of the directors and the equally honest opinion of the jury, and say that the alteration was invalid. To adopt any view of that sort would be to make the court manager of the affairs of innumerable companies instead of the directors to whom the shareholders have entrusted that right of management. I think, with respect to Peterson J, and counsel for the plaintiff, that that view is based on a misunderstanding of the expression used by Lindley MR in *Allen* v *Gold Reefs of West Africa Ltd* [1900] 1 Ch 656, and by Lord Sterndale MR in *Sidebottom* v *Kershaw, Leese & Co Ltd* [1920] 1 Ch 154. Lindley MR in *Allen's* case says (at p671) that the power of alteration

"must be exercised, not only in the manner required by law, but also bona fide for the benefit of the company as a whole."

The material language there is "exercised ... bona fide for the benefit of the company". I do not read that as two separate ingredients: (i) You must find it to be bona fide, and (ii) whether bona fide or not, you must find that it is in fact in your, the court's, opinion, for the benefit of the company. I read it as being that the directors must act honestly having regard to, and endeavouring to effect, the benefit of the company as a whole. I think some light is thrown upon that by the way in which Lord Sterndale MR treats it in *Sidebottom's* case. He repeats the language, in effect, of Lindley MR (1920) 1 Ch at p165): "Did they do it bona fide for the benefit of the company?"; and then he goes on to say ((1920) 1 Ch at p167), commenting on the decision of Astbury J in *Brown* v *British Abrasive Wheel Co Ltd* [1919] 1 Ch 290:

> "He (the learned judge) found as a fact that the majority shareholders ... were not doing this for the benefit of the company or in the interests of the company at large, but entirely for their own benefit, and in their own interests. If that finding be right, and as to that I say nothing, it was not bona fide; it was not done for the benefit of the company, but for the benefit of themselves."

As I understand, the learned judge there is contrasting the acts of people who, acting honestly, consider the thing that they ought to consider, namely, the benefit of the company as a whole, and endeavour to decide what will be for the benefit of the company as a whole, with the acts of those who approach the matter, not from that point of view, but from the point of view of considering what will be for the benefit of the majority of the company or themselves as distinguished from the people against whom they are legislating. From that point of view, provided there are grounds on which reasonable people could come to a decision, considering the matters I have indicated only, it does not seem to me to matter at all whether the court would not have come to the same conclusion. It is not the court which manages the affairs of the company; it is the shareholders through the directors whom they appoint; and so long as the shareholders act honestly and endeavour to consider only the matters they should legitimately consider, namely, the interests of the company as a whole and such action as will promote those interests, it seems to me quite immaterial that the court would come to a different conclusion. The absence of any reasonable ground for a decision that a certain action is conducive to the benefit of the company may be, first of all, a ground for finding lack of good faith, because it may be said that there were no grounds on which honest people could have come to this decision and you may infer bad faith; but, secondly, given honesty, the fact that the company has come to a decision for which there are no reasonable grounds may show that they have not considered the matters that they ought to have considered. On both those grounds you may set a decision aside, but, in my view, if they act honestly, and if the decision is such that honest and reasonable people might come to, the fact that the court would have come to a different decision is no ground whatever for the court interfering. I should be very sorry if the court took upon itself to manage matters which the directors usually understand far better than the court does. So when I find, in the case to which counsel for the plaintiff referred – *Dafen Tinplate Co Ltd* v *Llanelly Steel Co (1907) Ltd* – Peterson J saying (at p140):

> "It has been suggested that the only question in such a case as this is whether the shareholders bona fide or honestly believed that the alteration was for the benefit of the company. But this is not in my view, the true meaning of the words of Lindley MR in *Allen* v *Gold Reefs of West Africa Ltd* , or of the judgment in *Sidebottom's* case . The question is whether in fact the alteration is genuinely for the benefit of the company."

If he means that, whatever the honest decision of the directors is, it is what the court thinks, and not what the directors think, which is to be the governing matter, I respectfully disagree with the interpretation put upon Lord Lindley's words. If he merely means that the court will interfere if the decision of the directors, though honest, is such that no reasonable people could have come to it upon proper materials, then I do not object to the explanation, and I should be prepared to act in a case like that; but in the way in which the judgment is reported, I think that the test is erroneous, for the reasons I have given.

As I say, I have only added a separate judgment of my own because I think the point I have last dealt with is of considerable importance in the management of companies by the court. For these reasons, I think, the appeal fails and must be dismissed, with the usual consequences.'

Sidebottom v *Kershaw, Leese & Co Ltd* [1920] 1 Ch 154 Court of Appeal (Lord Sterndale MR, Warrington LJ and Eve J)

Alteration of articles to allow a competing shareholder to be bought out upheld

Facts

Kershaw was a private company involved in cotton spinning and manufacturing with 7,620 issued shares of which the directors held 4,396 and the plaintiffs 711. In June 1919 a special resolution was passed at an extraordinary meeting adopting a new set of articles to replace the existing articles. The resolution was duly carried with the plaintiffs voting against it. The new articles contained, inter alia, art 40, giving the directors power to require any shareholder who carried on any business in direct competition with the company to transfer his shares, at their full value, to nominees of the directors. The plaintiffs carried on a business in competiton with Kershaws but Kershaws did not realise this at the date the new articles were adopted. The aim of this art 40 was to get rid of a certain Mr Bodden who held 70 shares in the company and who had two businesses in keen competition with Kershaws. The plaintiffs sought a declaration that art 40 was invalid.

Held

Article 40 was valid as it was bona fide for the benefit of the company as a whole on the available evidence before the court.

Lord Sterndale, MR:

'... In my opinion the whole case comes down to a rather narrow question of fact, which is this: When the directors of this company introduced the alteration giving power to buy up the shares of members who were in competing business did they do it bona fide for the benefit of the company or not? It seems to me quite clear that it may be very much to the benefit of the company to get rid of members who are in competing businesses ... I cannot have any doubt that in a small private company like this the exclusion of members who are carrying on competing businesses may well be of great benefit to the company. That seems to me to be precisely a point which ought to be decided by the voices of the business men who understand the business and understand the nature of the competiton, and whether such a position is or is not for the benefit of the company. I think, looking at the alteration broadly, that it is for the benefit of the company that they should not be obliged to have amongst them as members persons who are competing with them in business, and who may get knowledge from their membership which would enable them to compete better ...'

Effect of alteration to the articles

Baily v *British Equitable Assurance Company* [1904] 1 Ch 384 Court of Appeal (Vaughan Williams, Stirling and Cozens-Hardy LJJ)

Alteration of the articles may amount to a breach of an extrinsic contract

Facts

The plaintiff took out an insurance policy on his own life with the defendant company in reliance on a prospectus which stated that the whole of the profits made in the department of the company's business to which the policy was attached would be divided among the policy-holders in that department. The proposal form which the plaintif signed before he took out the policy contained an undertaking by him to 'conform to and abide by' the rules and regulations of the company. The company had distributed the profits for many years as bonuses to the policies until 1903 when it was decided to change it from a company with unlimited liability to one with limited liability. As part of this scheme a reserve fund of £37,500 was to be created by altering the by-laws so that some of the profits could be transferred to this with the balance only being distributed to the policy-holders. The plaintiff and other policy-holders objected and sought a declaration that it was a breach of the contract made with policy-holders to distribute all the profits. At first instance Kekewich J granted a declaration that the company ought to distribute the entire profits. The company appealed.

Held

The appeal was dismissed. Although a company is free to change its articles it may lead to a breach of an extrinsic contract, as the promise made in the prospectus was to issue the whole of the profits to the policy-holders. The declaration that the company ought to distribute the entire profits was upheld.

Cozens-Hardy LJ:

'... It is, however, contended that, as the company was registered under s209 of the Companies Act, 1862, it thereby acquired power by special resolution to alter all or any of the provisions of the deed of settlement, not being in the nature of a memorandum of association, and all or any of the by-laws, and that the plaintiff is seeking to restrain the company from altering by-law No 4 in exercise of this statutory power. And is it is said that, apart from the statute, the deed of settlement itself contained a power to alter the by-law, of which power the plaintiff had notice. We cannot assent to this argument. As between the members of a company and the company, no doubt this proposition is to some extent true. The rights of a shareholder in respect of his shares, except so far as they may be protected by the memorandum of association, are by statute made liable to be altered by special resolution: see *Allen* v *Gold Reefs of West Africa* [1900] 1 Ch 656.

But the case of a contract between an outsider and the company is entirely different, and even a shareholder must be regarded as an outsider in so far as he contracts with the company otherwise than in respect of his shares. It would be dangerous to hold that in a contract of loan or a contract of service or a contract of insurance validly entered into by a company there is any greater power of variation of the rights and liabilities of the parties than would exist if, instead of the company, the contracting party had been an individual. A company cannot, by altering its articles, justify a breach of contract ...

... In the present case there was a contract for value between the plaintiff and the company, relating to the future profits of a particular branch of the company's business, and the company ought not to be allowed, by special resolution or otherwise, to break that contract. The appeal must be dismissed ...'

Commentary

Followed in *British Murac Syndicate Ltd* v *Alperton Rubber Co Ltd* [1915] 2 Ch 186.

British Equitable Assurance Company Ltd v *Baily* [1906] AC 35 House of Lords (Lords Macnaghten, Robertson and Lindley)

Whether alteration of the articles amounts to a breach of an extrinsic contract

Facts

The facts were the same as in the Court of Appeal above.

Held

The House of Lords reversed the Court of Appeal's decision on the ground that there was no contract between the company and the policy-holders not to alter the practice of distributing the entire profits made on life policies to them. The contract between the company and the policy-holders was not contained in the prospectus but in the policies themselves. The policies incorporated the terms of the articles from time to time and as such were alterable without causing a breach of contract.

Lord Macnaghten:

'... The judgment of the Court was delivered by Cozens-Hardy LJ. The ground of the decision is to be found expressed in a single sentence: "A company cannot by altering its articles justify a breach of contract." No one, I should think, would be inclined to dispute the proposition thus asserted; but with all deference that is not the question. The simple question is what was the contract between the parties. ...

I am at a loss to understand how the Court of Appeal came to the conclusion that the statements in this prospectus consituted a collateral contract, or are to be treated as incorporated in the contract of insurance, limiting the powers of the company in the full and free exercise of which the plaintiff bound himself to acquiesce.'

Lord Lindley:

'... These contracts are to be found in the policies themselves. By each policy the company agree to pay to the executors of the assured a fixed sum out of the funds of the company, "and all such other sums, if any, as the said company by their directors may have ordered to be added to such amount by way of bonus or otherwise, according to their practice for the time being. Provided always, that this policy is made subject to the conditions and regulations hereon indorsed". That is the contract between the parties; but the indorsed conditions and regulations are part of it, and the fifth is important. The company was formed as long ago as 1854, and the object of the fifth regulation is to limit the liability of the members of the company. But the regulation throws light on the position of the policy-holders and on what they can claim under their policies. The fifth indorsed condition or regulation in effect provides that the funds of the company, "after satisfying prior claims and charges according to the provisions of the deed of settlement and by-laws of the company for the time being, shall alone be liable for the payment of the moneys payable under the policy, and that no shareholder, member, director, or other officer of the company shall be liable to any demand in respect of the policy beyond or otherwise than out of the payment in the manner and at the times provided for by the deed of settlement and the then by-laws of the company of the amount then remaining unpaid of the shares held by him". The reference to the deed of settlement and by-laws for the time being is all-important; for the by-laws determine how the profits of the company are to be disposed of, and those by-laws are subject to alteration from time to time by an extraordinary meeting of the shareholders of the company (see clauses 9, 24, 56 of the deed of settlement). The policy-holders are not shareholders, and have no voice in making or altering by-laws; but the sum payable under any policy, in addition to the fixed sum mentioned in it, is made by the policy itself to depend upon what the directors may have ordered to be added to such sum, and that depends upon their practice for the time being. The practice of the directors in its turn depends on how the profits are to be ascertained and divided in accordance with the by-laws, which may be altered from time to time, as above pointed out.'

British Murac Syndicate Ltd v *Alperton Rubber Co Ltd* [1915] 2 Ch 186 Chancery Division (Sargant J)

Injunction granted to prevent alteration of articles

Facts
In a sale agreement made in 1910 between British Murac as vendors and Alperton Rubber as purchasers a clause provided that so long as British Murac held at least 5,000 shares in Alperton Rubber it should have the right to nominate two directors to the board of Alperton Rubber. This term of the agreement was also included in new articles of Alperton Rubber which were adopted at the same time. Differences arose between various members of Alperton Rubber as to whether it should continue its existing manufacturing policy or take up an invention and exploit it. In 1915 British Murac wished to nominate the inventor of the invention to the board and abandoned this idea in the interests of the company and nominated two persons unconnected with the invention. However, the company refused to accept the nomination of these persons and shortly afterwards a meeting was called at which a special resolution was passed cancelling the article recognising British Murac's right to nominate two directors. The reason given for the alteration was that British Murac wished to change the policy of the company in a manner detrimental to it. British Murac sought a declaration that its nominees had become directors, an injunction to stop them being excluded from the board, specific performance of the agreement and an injunction to prevent the alteration of art 88.

Held

An injunction should be granted to restrain the alteration of art 88 because this would lead to a breach of contract.

Sargant J:

'... As I understood counsel for the Alperton company, he did not contend that the alteration of the articles of association by the striking out of this art 88 would, in fact, get rid of the right of the syndicate to nominate the directors and the obligation of the Alperton company to accept the directors. He took the view as I understand it that that right and obligation would subsist, and that, although the article might have gone, the syndicate would still be at liberty, by virtue of their contractual rights, to nominate the two directors and the Alperton company would still be bound to accept them; I mean, of course, apart from the second objection. Therefore there really does not seem to me to be very much in this objection. But it is said: "Well, at any rate, it does get rid of one fetter on the company" – namely, the fetter of complying with their obligations. The principal case on the subject is *Allen* v *Gold Reefs of West Africa Ltd* [1900] 1 Ch 656; but in that case the court seems to me to have quite clearly recognised that a company cannot alter its articles so as to commit a breach of contract, and that it might be that it would be unfair for the company to alter. Here I have not to consider the question, because there is here both the provision in the articles and the express obligation in the contract under which the syndicate are to have this express right. It seems to me that the real gist of the decision in *Allen* v *Gold Reefs of West Africa Ltd* is to be found in the judgment of Lord Lindley MR. He says:

> "But, although the regulations contained in a company's articles of association are revocable by special resolution, a special contract may be made with the company in the terms of or embodying one or more of the articles, and the question will then arise whether an alteration of the articles so embodied is consistent or inconsistent with the real bargain between the parties. A company cannot break its contracts by altering its articles, but, when dealing with contracts referring to revocable articles, and especially with contracts between a member of the company and the company respecting his shares, care must be taken not to assume that the contract involves as one of its terms an article which is not to be altered."

I think that clearly recognises that if the court sees that a contract involves as one of its terms that an article is not to be altered, then the company is not at liberty to alter its articles so as to break that contract. In my judgment, on the facts of the case the contract between the syndicate and the Alperton company clearly involved as one of its terms that art 88 was not to be altered – that is, that the syndicate were to have a perpetual right of nominating two directors of the company.

It has been said that *Punt* v *Symons* [1903] 2 Ch 506 is an express authority in favour of the defendants' contention. I think, looking at the case, that it is an express authority in favour of that contention; but so far as this part of *Punt* v *Symons* is concerned, it seems to me that it has been overruled by the decision of *Baily* v *British Equitable Assurance Co* [1904] 1 Ch 374 where the Court of Appeal considered, on the view which they took that there was a contract with the policy-holders of the company, that the full profits should be applied in declaring bonuses on the policies of the various holders, that on that view of the existence of the contract the company was disqualified from altering its articles as to provide that a certain portion of the profits should be carried to a reserve fund. Although that decision was reversed by the House of Lords, it is clear to me that it was not reversed through any quarrel by the House of Lords with that principle. Indeed, they seem to me in their judgment to have recognised that principle. All that the House of Lords held was that, on the true interpretation of the bargain between the policy-holder and the company, there was, in fact, no contract between them that the allocation of the whole of the profits to the policies by way of bonus should be a perpetual arrangement. This is an authority clearly in favour of this, that a company may be restrained from altering articles for the purpose of committing a breach of a definite contract, one of the terms of which is that the articles shall not be altered ...

... What the company are doing is trying to get rid altogether of a general right of nomination, not merely objecting to receiving in the capacity of director any particular individual. Everybody who has had anything to do with companies must know that arrangements of this kind, under which either preference shareholders or holders of debentures or other persons who have a permanent stake in a company, have a right to appoint one or more directors of the company for the purpose no doubt of protecting their interests, are extremely common. This also is quite obvious, that to enforce an agreement of that kind merely by giving damages for the breach of it would be a wholly inadequate and illusory remedy. I am not going to be the first to hold here that an agreement for good consideration under which a shareholder in a company, whilst he holds his shares or a certain number of them, shall in virtue of that holding have the right of appointing or nominating a director of the company, is one that cannot be enforced by an injunction of this court. In my opinion the right is one which ought to be so enforced, and the enforcement of which by way of declaration or injunction is not in conflict with the ordinary rules against the specific performance of contracts of service.

It is not here as if the syndicate had had the power of nominating an absolute majority of the board of the company. To that there might possibly be objections, though I have not to deal with the matter now, inasmuch as it would be putting the control of the company in the power of an outsider. Here, all that is secured by the nomination of a director by the syndicate is that there shall be some person or persons on the board, not a majority of the board, and that accordingly the views advocated by the syndicate shall have expression on the board of the company. That being so, I think that I ought to accede to the claim of the plaintiffs by declaring that by virtue of the nomination made by them Dr George Thomson and Mr Thomas Warwick have become directors of the defendant company, and I think that I ought also to grant an injunction as I do to restrain the holding of the confirmatory meeting for the purpose of getting rid of Art 88 of the articles of association of the company ...'

Cumbrian Newspapers Group Ltd v *Cumberland and Westmorland Herald Newspaper and Printing Co Ltd* [1986] 2 All ER 816 High Court (Scott J)

Alteration of articles – granting of injunctions

Facts
The plaintiff had been given special pre-emption rights in the defendant's articles. The defendant proposed to call an extraordinary general meeting to cancel these rights. The plaintiff sought, inter alia, an injunction to restrain the defendant from convening the meeting or acting on any special resolution which affected the plaintiff's rights. The plaintiff's contention was based on alleged agreement by the defendant not to alter the plaintiff's special rights.

Held
There was no such agreement between the parties so the claim for the injunctions would fail. However, Scott J observed, in summarising the law:

'Where a company has contracted that its articles will not be altered, I can see no reason why it should not, in a suitable case, be enjoined from initiating the calling of a general meeting with a view to the alteration of the articles. But an injunction could not, in my view, be properly granted so as to prevent the company from discharging its statutory duties in respect of convening meetings.'

Punt v *Symons & Co* [1903] 2 Ch 506 Chancery Division (Byrne J)

A company cannot contract out of its statutory right to alter its articles

Facts
The company was formed in 1898 to acquire and carry on a furniture business then carried on by Mr G G Symons. The company had a share capital of 11,000 £1 shares of which 9,377 were issued, of which

Mr G G Symons held 8,300, a Mr Jay 537 and a Mr G R Symons 536. All three were directors. The agreement between Mr G G Symons and the company for the sale of the business provided, in cl 6:

'The company shall not at any time alter or attempt to alter the clauses of the articles of association relating to the appointment of the vendor as governing director as originally framed or suffer anything to be done in contravention of the provisions of these clauses respectively.'

The articles conferred various powers and privileges on Mr G G Symons and also stated that if he died whilst holding the office of governing director the trustees of his will should have the same powers so long as they held at least 2,000 shares. After his death disputes arose between Mr G G Symons' trustees and the other two directors who, inter alia, passed a special resolution at an extraordinary general meeting depriving the trustees of these powers. Further issues of shares by the directors enabled them to do this. The trustees sought an injunction.

Held

The company could not contract itself out of its statutory right to alter its articles by an agreement which was independent of the articles; the injunction would not be granted.

Byrne J:

'The first point taken is that passing the resolution would be a breach of contract which was entered into with the testator; and the plaintiffs as executors are entitled to enforce the terms of the agreement by restraining any alteration of the articles. I think the answer to this argument is that the company cannot contract itself out of the right to alter its articles though it cannot, by altering its articles, commit a breach of contract. It is well established as between a company and a shareholder, the right not depending upon a special contract outside the articles, that this is the case. It has not been, so far as I know, the precise subject of reported decision, as between a contractor and a company, where the contract is independent of and outside the articles ...'

His Lordship then referred to the judgment of Lindley MR in *Allen* v *Gold Reefs of West Africa* (1) and to a note of an unreported decision *Re Ladies' Dress Association Ltd* where the company issued ten founder's certificates which stated that the company would not alter or vary the articles without the written consent of the holder. The Court of Appeal dismissed the case on the ground that such a covenant could not be sued upon. He then continued:

'... That appears, so far as I can judge, to be a decision on the point now before me. Whether that be so or not, I am prepared to hold that in the circumstances of the present case the contract could not operate to prevent the article being altered under s50 of the Companies Act, 1862, whatever the result of the alteration may be. It may be that the effect of an alteration after a contract is retrospective. It may be that the remedy is in damages only, or it may be that the stipulation of the contract can be enforced notwithstanding the alteration of the articles. I think that the result of the alteration depends upon the special circumstances in each case, but, speaking generally, and without saying that there may not be some exceptions, any illustration of which does not at present occur to me, I consider that the principle of the decision in *Allen* v *Gold Reefs of West Africa* [1900] 1 Ch 656 applies to a case between the company and an outside party on a separate contract, as well as to a case between a company and a shareholder on the contract contained in the articles, and that it applies in the present case.'

Southern Foundries (1926) Ltd v *Shirlaw* [1940] AC 701 House of Lords (Viscount Maugham, Lords Atkin, Wright, Romer and Porter)

Alteration of the articles may amount to a breach of an extrinsic contract

Facts

Shirlaw was appointed managing director of Southern Foundries for a period of 10 years from 1 December, 1933 under a written agreement. The agreement was not expressed to be subject to the articles. The articles of Southern Foundries provided that the managing director should be subject to the same powers of removal as other directors, eg bankruptcy, lunacy, etc, but 'subject to the provision of any contract between him and the company'. In 1936 several companies, including Southern Foundries, in the iron foundries trade were reorganised and their share capital acquired by Federated Foundries Ltd. Federated Foundries adopted new articles for Southern Foundries which included a power to remove any director on notice. In April 1937 Southern Foundries purported to remove Shirlaw from his office as director which under other articles meant that his office as managing director terminated automatically. Shirlaw sued for damages for breach of contract. At first instance Humphreys J decided in favour of Shirlaw; the Court of Appeal affirmed this decision. On appeal by Southern Foundries to the House of Lords:

Held

(By a majority of three to two) the plaintiff was entitled to damages for wrongful dismissal since the removal of Shirlaw under the altered articles amounted to a breach of contract. This contract was not stated to be subject to the articles and even if it had been there was nothing in the original articles which would have given the company the right to dismiss Shirlaw in the circumstances.

Lord Porter:

'... The general principle, therefore, may, I think, be stated thus. (i) A company cannot be precluded from altering its articles thereby giving itself power to act upon the provisions of the altered articles, but so to act may nevertheless be a breach of contract if it is contrary to a stipulation in a contract validly made before the alteration. (ii) Nor can an injunction be granted to prevent the adoption of the new articles. In that sense, they are binding on all and sundry, but for the company to act upon them will none the less render it liable in damages if such action is contrary to the previous engagements of the company. If, therefore, the altered articles had provided for the dismissal without notice of a managing director previously appointed, the dismissal would be intra vires the company, but would nevertheless expose the company to an action for damages if the appointment had been for a term of (say) 10 years and he were dismissed in less. Once it is established that the appointment is for a time certain and the dismissal before its termination, the result follows, and I do not understand the appellants to contend to the contrary. The complication lies in the facts (i) that the respondent has been dismissed, not from his office of managing director, but has been removed from his position of director, and (ii) that the removal has been effected, not by the Southern Company, but by the Federated Company. So far as the first matter is concerned, the decision must, I think, be reached by applying the well-kown principle laid down by Cockburn CJ in *Stirling v Maitland* (1864) 5 B & S 841:

> "I look on the law to be that, if a party enters into an arrangement which can only take effect by the continuance of a certain existing state of circumstances, there is an implied engagement on his part that he shall do nothing of his own motion to put an end to that state of circumstances, under which alone the arrangement can be operative. I agree that if the company had come to an end by some independent circumstance, not created by the defendants themselves, it might very well be that the covenant would not have the effect contended for; but if it is put an end to by their own voluntary act, that is a breach of covenant for which the plaintiff may sue. The transfer of business and the dissolution of the company was certainly the act of the company itself, so that they have by their act put an end to the state of things under which alone this covenant would operate."

If, therefore, the Southern Company had altered their articles in such a way as to enable them to remove the respondent from his directorship at will, and had so removed him, I, in common, I believe, with all your Lordships, would regard their action as coming under the dictum of Cockburn CJ, as an actionable breach of contract.

In reaching this conclusion I find myself unable to accept the dissenting judgment of Sir Wilfred Greene MR who took the view that under the contract the plaintiff was expressly appointed managing director, not for 10 years, but only for such a period not exceeding 10 years as he remained a director, and that no term could be implied which would prevent the company from terminating the respondent's directorship, with the result that he ceased to be capable of retaining his position as managing director.

However, no such alteration was made. The new articles did away with all former grounds of removal and termination of the director's office, and left it to the Federated Company at their absolute discretion to keep or remove a director of the Southern Company. That change, it is said, is no breach, or, at any rate, is not contended to be a breach, of the respondent's contract, and his later removal is the act of Federated, and not of the Southern Company, and one, therefore, for which the latter company is not responsible. This contention was negatived by Sir Wilfred Greene MR as well as the other two members of the Court of Appeal. As, however, the main argument appears to have been grounded upon the question of the true construction of the contract, the matter now under consideration was treated as subsidiary, with the consequence that it was dealt with very shortly in the Court of Appeal ...'

5   Company Formation

Who is a promoter?

Emma Silver Mining Co v *Lewis & Son* (1879) 4 CPD 396 Court of Appeal (Lord Coleridge CJ, Denman and Lindley JJ)

Definition of promoter

Facts
The defendants, a firm of metal brokers, who had previously sold silver ore from an American mine on a commission of 2 1/2 per cent, arranged with the owner to assist him in selling the mine to a company to be promoted in England. The proprietor was to procure the appointment of the defendants as metal brokers of the company and promised them at least £5,000 remuneration because they knew the mine was of doubtful character. This payment was, in effect, to buy the defendants' silence on the doubts surrounding the mine. The mine was sold to the company for £100,000 and the defendants were named in the prospectus as willing to answer all enquiries relating to the mine. They did so but kept silent on the doubts surrounding it. When payment was made to the proprietor of the mine he transferred 250 fully paid shares of £20 each to the defendants who sold these and kept the proceeds. This transaction was not disclosed to the company. The company sought to recover this secret profit from the defendants on the ground that they were promoters. At the trial the judge left the question of promotership, without any definition, to the jury who found that the defendants were promoters and gave a verdict for the plaintiff.
On appeal:

Held
The judge was not bound to give the jury a definition of the term 'promoter' since it had no very definite meaning and there was ample evidence on which the jury could conclude that the position held by the defendants involved the duties of a so-called promoter. The defendants were therefore in a fiduciary position to the company and liable to refund the secret profit.

Lindley J:

'With respect to the word "promoter" we are of opinion that it has no very definite meaning: see *Twycross* v *Grant* (1877) 2 CPD 469. As used in connection with companies the term "promoter" involves the idea of exertion for the purposes of getting up and starting a company (of what is called "floating" it) and also the idea of some duty towards the company imposed by or arising from the position which the so-called promoter assumes towards it. It is now clearly settled that persons who get up and form a company have duties towards it before it comes into existence ...'

Twycross v *Grant* (1877) 2 CPD 469 Court of Appeal (Cockburn CJ, Kelly CB, Bramwell and Brett LJJ)

Who is a promoter?

Facts

The Duke de Saldantha held certain concessions from the King of Portugal to build railways from Lisbon to various Portuguese towns and cities. An English company, Clark, Punchard & Co, involved in the manufacture of railway and tramway equipment, were given the contract to build the railways and a company was formed by Grant called the Lisbon Steam Tramways Company Ltd for the purpose of purchasing the concession from the Duke. The company proved to be unsuccessful and the plaintiff, who had purchased shares in it on the faith of a prospectus, brought this action to recover the amount paid by him on his shares on the ground of the fraud of the promoters of the company, in omitting from the prospectus two contracts entered into by them and promoters. One was a contract between Clark, Punchard & Co and the Duke for the sale of the concessions to Clark, Punchard & Co and the other a contract between Clark, Punchard & Co and Grant under which Clark, Punchard & Co paid Grant £30,000 and, in return, received the contract to build the railways and provide the rolling stock from the newly promoted company. The jury found that both contracts were material to be made known to intending shareholders of the company.

Held

The contracts ought to have been mentioned in the prospectus and the defendants were liable.

Cockburn CJ:

'... But were the defendants promoters at the time of issuing? It is contended that even if promoters in the outset, they ceased to be so the moment the company was constituted and the governing body, the directors, were appointed. This contention was mainly founded on a provision of the 7 & 8 Vict c 110, s3, which says that promoters shall continue to be such till the complete registration of the company at which time directors would be appointed. But that Act, which had reference to a system of registration widely differing from the present, has been repealed, and there is now no statutory limitation to the functions of a promoter. The question as to when one who in the outset was a promoter of a company continues or ceases to be so, becomes, therefore, as it seems to me, one of fact. A promoter, I apprehend, is one who undertakes to form a company with reference to a given project and to set it going and who takes the necessary steps to accomplish that purpose. That the defendants were the promoters of the company from the beginning can admit of no doubt. They framed the scheme; they not only provisionally formed the company, but were, in fact, to the end its creators; they found the directors, and qualified them; they prepared the prospectus; they paid for printing and advertising, and the expenses incidental to bringing the undertaking before the world. In all these respects the directors were passive; without saying that they were in a legal sense the agents of the defendants, they were certainly their instruments. All the things I have just referred to were done with a view to the formation of the company, and so long as the work of formation continues, those who carry on that work must, I think, retain the character of promoters ...'

Whaley Bridge Calico Printing Co v *Green* (1879) 5 QBD 109 Queen's Bench Division (Bowen J)

Who is a promoter?

Facts

Green purchased a calico printing works for £15,000. Green then joined forces with one Smith, to form a company which would purchase the calico printing works from Green. This scheme was carried out and the calico printing works sold to the company for £20,000 but this was done by Green selling the works to Smith under a sham contract, who then sold them to the company. It was agreed between Green and Smith that Smith would receive £3,000 for his trouble out of the purchase money. However, the latter agreement was not communicated to the company when the sale to the company was effected. The company sought, inter alia, to recover the payment of £3,000 to Smith on the ground it was a secret payment.

Held

Smith was a promoter of the company and was therefore not entitled to secure any profit to himself out of the formation of the company without the knowledge of the directors, and that such being the case the company were entitled to treat the agreement made between Green and Smith as made by Smith on their behalf and recover the £3,000.

Bowen J:

'The term promoter is a term not of law, but of business, usefully summing up in a single word a number of business operations familiar to the commercial world by which a company is generally brought into existence. In every case the relief granted must depend on the establishment of such relations between the promoter and the birth, formation and floating of the company, as to render it contrary to good faith that the promoter should derive a secret profit from the promotion. A man who carries about an advertising board in one sense promotes a company, but in order to see whether relief is obtainable by the company what is to be looked to is not a word or name, but the acts and the relations of the parties. In the present instance, Green and Smith agreed to, and did, bring out the present company for the purpose of purchasing the chemical works and premises on their own terms. The board of directors consisted of their nominees, and in order to make the purchase run more smoothly a sham contract of purchase was on 19 September flashed before the eyes of the directors as if it were a real contract by both Smith and Green. The relation in which Smith by these acts placed himself towards the company is one in which equity will not allow him to retain any secret advantage for himself. He had a perfect right to agree with Green that he should be remunerated to the extent of £3,000 provided the agreement was made with the knowledge and assent of the company ...'

Duties of a promoter

Erlanger* v *New Sombrero Phosphate Co (1878) 3 App Cas 1218 House of Lords (Lord Penzance, Lord Cairns LC, Lords Hatherley, O'Hagan, Selborne, Blackburn and Gordon).

Breach of duty

Facts

A syndicate headed by Erlanger purchased from the official liquidator of an insolvent company an island for £55,000, said to obtain valuable reserves of phosphate. Erlanger then formed a company to which he proposed to sell the island for £110,000. Five persons were named as directors of the company; two of these were abroad and the other three were entirely under the control of Erlanger and he gave them the shares to qualify as directors. The sale of the island to the company was made by a nominee who had no interest in the matter either as a member of the syndicate or as a member of the company. A prospectus was issued by the company which gave a very favourable picture of the likely profits of the concern and there were many subscribers for shares. At the first shareholders' meeting no mention was made of the circumstances of the purchase of the island by the company but the purchase was adopted by the shareholders then present. The company was not successful and within six months the original directors were removed and a committee of investigation appointed. The new directors sought the recission of the contract of sale of the island to the company and repayment of the £110,000 plus interest.

Held

The contract would be rescinded.

Lord Cairns LC:

'... In the whole of this proceeding up to this time the syndicate, or the house of Erlanger, as representing the syndicate, were the promoters of the company, and it is now necessary that I should state to your Lordships in what position I understand the promoters to be placed with reference to the company which they proposed to form. They stand, in my opinion, undoubtedly in a fiduciary position. They have in their hands the creation and moulding of the company; they have the power of defining how, and when, and in what shape, and under what supervision, it shall start into existence and begin to act as a trading corporation. If they are doing all this in order that the company may, as soon as it starts into life, become, through its managing directors, the purchaser of the property of themselves, the promoters, it is, in my opinion, incumbent upon the promoters to take care that in forming the company they provide it with an executive, that is to say, with a board of directors, who shall both be aware that the property which they are asked to buy is the property of the promoters, and who shall be competent and impartial judges as to whether the purchase ought or ought not to be made. (I do not say that the owner of property may not promote and form a joint stock company, and then sell his property to it, but I do say that if he does he is bound to take care that he sells it to the company through the medium of a board of directors who can and do exercise an independent and intelligent judgment on the transaction, and who are not left under the belief that the property belongs, not to the promoter, but to some other person) ...'

Lord O'Hagan:

'... The original purchase of the island of Sombrero was perfectly legitimate – and it was not less so because the object of the purchasers was to sell it again, and to sell it by forming a company which might afford them a profit on the transaction. The law permitted them to take that course, and provided the machinery by which the transfer of their interest might be equitably and beneficially effected for themselves and those with whom they meant to deal. But the privilege given them for promoting such a company for such an object, involved obligations of a very serious kind. It required, in its exercise, the utmost good faith, the completest truthfulness, and a careful regard to the protection of the future shareholders. The power to nominate a directorate is manifestly capable of great abuse, and may involve, in the misuse of it, very evil consequences to multitudes of people who have little capacity to guard themselves. Such a power may or may not have been wisely permitted to exist. I venture to have doubts upon the point. It tempts too much to fraudulent contrivance and mischievous deception; and, at least, it should be watched with jealousy and restrained from employment in such a way as to mislead the ignorant and the unwary. In all such cases the directorate nominated by the promoters should stand between them and the public, with such independence and intelligence, that they may be expected to deal fairly, impartially, and with adequate knowledge in the affairs submitted to their control. If they have not those qualities, they are unworthy of trust. They are betrayers and not the guardians of the company they govern, and their acts should not receive the sanction of a Court of Justice.

Now, my Lords, for reasons repeatedly given by my noble and learned friends, which I shall not detail again, I think that the promoters in this case failed to remember the exigencies of their fiduciary position when they appointed directors who were in no way independent of themselves, and who did not sustain the interests of the company with ordinary care and intelligence ...'

Gluckstein v *Barnes* [1900] AC 240 House of Lords (Earl of Halsbury LC, Lords Macnaghten and Robertson)

Breach of duty

Facts

In 1893 a company owning Olympia was wound up. A syndicate was formed to buy and resell Olympia to a company or some other purchaser. The syndicate proposed to raise a fund for this purpose and this fund was to be in the name of two trustees for the syndicate. Money was raised from many persons for the fund and in February 1893 the trustees bought Olympia for £140,000 by auction. A company was duly registered and Olympia was sold to it for £180,000. A prospectus was then issued inviting applications for debentures and shares and this stated that the promoters constituted the entire board of the company and had bought Olympia for £140,000 and would be selling as vendors to the company for £180,000. However, before the syndicate purchased Olympia four of its members had bought up debenture bonds and a mortgage on the property at a discount. These charged the property with a debt of over £20,000 but the trustees paid only £500 for them. That some profit had been made in buying up the charges might have been discovered by a close examination of a contract which was referred to in the company's articles and memorandum and in the prospectus. Shares were issued and in 1897 the company went into liquidation. The liquidator claimed to recover the share of the secret profit that Gluckstein, a member of the syndicate and a director, had received from the charges when they realised them.

Held

The profit of £20,000 made on realising the charges ought to have been disclosed to the company. The fact that the company could not now rescind this contract was no bar to relief and Gluckstein was bound to replace that share of the £20,000 he had received.

Earl of Halsbury LC:

'... My Lords, I am wholly unable to understand any claim that these directors, vendors, syndicate, associates, have to retain this money. I entirely agree with the Master of the Rolls that the essence of this scheme was to form a company. It was essential that this should be done, and that they should be directors of it, who would purchase. The company should have been informed of what was being done and consulted whether they would have allowed this profit. I think the Master of the Rolls is absolutely right in saying that the duty to disclose is imposed by the plainest dictates of common honesty as well as by well-settled principles of common law.

Of the facts there cannot be the least doubt; they are proved by the agreement, now that we know the subject-matter with which that agreement is intended to deal, although the agreement would not disclose what the nature of the transaction was to those who were not acquainted with the ingenious arrangements which were prepared for entrapping the intended victim of these arrangements.

In order to protect themselves, as they supposed, they inserted in the prospectus, qualifying the statement that they had bought the property for £140,000, payable in cash, that that did not sell to the company, and did not intend to sell, any other profits made by the syndicate from interim investments.

Then it is said there is the alternative suggested upon the agreement that the syndicate might sell to a company or to some other purchaser. In the first place, I do not believe they ever intended to sell to anybody else than a company. An individual purchaser might ask inconvenient questions, and if they or any one of them had stated as an inducement to an individual purchaser that £140,000 was given for the property, when in fact £20,000 less had been given, it is a great error to suppose that the law is not strong enough to reach such a statement; but as I say, I do not believe it was ever intended to get an individual purchaser, even if such an intention would have had any operation. When they did afterwards sell to a company, they took very good care there should be no one who could ask questions. They were to be sellers to themselves as buyers, and it was a necessary provision to the plan that they were to be both sellers and buyers, and as buyers to get the money to pay for the purchase from the pockets of deluded shareholders.

My Lords, I decline to discuss the question of disclosure to the company. It is too absurd to suggest that a disclosure to the parties to this transaction is a disclosure to the company of which these directors were the proper guardians and trustees. They were there by the terms of the agreement to do the work of the syndicate, that is to say, to cheat the shareholders; and this, forsooth, is to be treated as a disclosure to the company, when they were really there to hoodwink the shareholders, and so far from protecting them, were to obtain from them the money, the produce of their nefarious plans.

I do not discuss either the sum sued for, or why Gluckstein alone is sued. The whole sum has been obtained by a very gross fraud, and all who were parties to it are responsible to make good what they have obtained and withheld from the shareholders ...'

Lord Macnaghten:

'... For my part, I cannot see any ingenuity or any novelty in the trick which Mr Gluckstein and his associates practised on the persons whom they invited to take shares in Olympia Limited. It is the old story. It has been done over and over again.

These gentlemen set about forming a company to pay them a handsome sum for taking off their hands a property which they had contracted to buy with that end in view. They bring the company into existence by means of the usual machinery. They appoint themselves sole guardians and protectors of this creature of theirs, half-fledged and just struggling into life, bound hand and foot while yet unborn, by contracts tending to their private advantage, and so fashioned by its makers that it could only act by their hands and only see through their eyes. They issue a prospectus representing that they had agreed to purchase the property for a sum largely in excess of the amount which they had, in fact, to pay. On the faith of this prospectus they collect subscriptions from a confiding and credulous public. And then comes the last act. Secretly, and therefore dishonestly, they put into their own pockets the difference between the real and the pretended price. After a brief career the company is ordered to be wound up. In the course of the liquidation the trick is discovered. Mr Gluckstein is called upon to make good a portion of the sum which he and his associates had misappropriated. Why Mr Gluckstein alone was selected for attack I do not know any more than I know why he was only asked to pay back a fraction of the money improperly withdrawn from the coffers of the company.

However that may be, Mr Gluckstein defends his conduct, or, rather I should say, resists the demand, on four grounds, which have been gravely argued at the bar. In the first place, he says that he was not in a fiduciary position towards Olympia Limited before the company was formed. Well, for some purposes he was not. For others he was. A good deal might be said on the point. But to my mind the point is immaterial, for it is not necessary to go back beyond the formation of the company.

In the second place, he says, that if he was in a fiduciary position he did in fact make a proper disclosure. With all deference to the learned counsel for the appellant that seems to me to be absurd. "Disclosure" is not the most appropriate word to use when a person who plays many parts announces to himself in one character what he has done and is doing in another. To talk of disclosure to the thing called the company, when as yet there were no shareholders, is a mere farce. To the intended shareholders there was no disclosure at all. On them was practised an elaborate system of deception.

The third ground of defence was that the only remedy was rescission. That defence, in the circumstances of the present case, seems to me to be as contrary to common sense as it is to authority. The point was settled more than 60 years ago by the decision in *Hichens v Congreve* (1831) 4 Sim 420, and, so far as I know, that case has never been questioned.

The last defence of all was that however much the shareholders may have been wronged, they have bound themselves by a special bargain, sacred under the provisions of the Companies Act 1862, to bear their wrongs in silence. In other words, Mr Gluckstein boldly asserts that he is entitled to use the provisions of an Act of Parliament, which are directed to a very different purpose, as a shield and shelter against the just consequences of his fraud ...'

Lagunas Nitrate Co v *Lagunas Syndicate* [1899] 2 Ch 392 Court of Appeal (Lindley MR, Rigby and Collins LJJ)

Promoter – breach of duty

Facts
The syndicate promoted and formed the company in 1889 in order that it could purchase land containing nitrate deposits in Chile which the syndicate purchased from a Colonel North for £110,000, together with a factory for manufacturing nitrate of soda. The purchase price to the company was to be £850,000. The directors of the syndicate prepared and signed the memorandum and articles of association of the company and the articles nominated them as the directors and specifically stated that they were also directors of the syndicate. The directors prepared both the prospectus and the purchase contract. Two years after the sale of the land and factory to the company, some shareholders believing the purchase to have been at an overvalue and that there had been misrepresentations in the prospectus and contract, appointed an independent board of directors who investigated the facts and with the sanction of a general meeting decided to bring an action against the syndicate and the directors for recission of the contracts and damages for misrepresentation, misfeasance, breach of trust and concealment of facts. At first instance Romer J dismissed the action. On appeal:

Held
(Rigby LJ dissenting) the company was not entitled to recission or damages for (i) it had at the date of the contract notice that the directors were also vendors and the mere fact that they did not constitute an independent board was not a sufficient ground for setting aside the contract; (ii) there was no misrepresentation to or concealment of facts from any person who was a member of the company at the date of the contract since the only persons who were members then were the directors themselves; (iii) although the contract and prospectus were misleading the company was not in a position to repudiate here because restitution by it was not possible; (iv) the directors had not been guilty of negligence or breach of trust such as to render them liable for any loss.

Lindley MR:

'This appeal involves the proper application to a company peculiarly formed, and to a large number of disputed facts, of a few well-settled principles of law, which, in their application to this case, appear to me to conflict with each other.

The first principle is that in equity the promoters of a company stand in a fiduciary relation to it, and to those persons whom they induce to become shareholders in it, and cannot in equity bind the company by any contract with themselves without fully and fairly disclosing to the company all material facts which the company ought to know. *Erlanger* v *New Sombrero Phosphate Co* (1878) 3 App Cas 1218 is the leading authority in support of this general proposition.

The second principle is that a company when registered is a corporation capable by its directors of binding itself by a contract with themselves as promoters if all material facts are disclosed. *Salomon* v *Salomon & Co* [1897] AC 22 is the leading authority for this principle.

The third principle is that the directors of a company acting with their powers, and with reasonable care, and honestly in the interest of the company, are not personally liable for losses which the company may suffer by reason of their mistakes or errors in judgment. *Overend, Gurney & Co* v *Gibb* (1872) 5 HL 480 is the leading authority on this head.

A fourth principle, not confined to companies, but extending to them, is that a contract can be set aside in equity on proof that one party induced the other to enter into it by misrepresentations of material facts, although such misrepresentations may not have been fraudulent.

A fifth principle is that a voidable contract cannot be rescinded or set aside after the position of the parties has been changed, so that they cannot be restored to their former position. Fraud may exclude the application of this principle, but I know of no other exception. With these preliminary observations I proceed to examine the facts of this case.

His Lordship then examined the facts and continued:

'The first ground relied upon is the formation of the nitrate company itself without an independent body of directors. Notwithstanding all that has been said in *Erlanger* v *New Sombrero Phosphate Co* (1) about the duties of the promoters of a company to furnish it with an independent board of directors, that decision does not require or indeed justify the conclusion that if a company is avowedly formed with a board of directors who are not independent, but who are stated to be the intended vendors, or the agents of the intended vendors, of property to the company, the company can set aside an agreement entered into by them for the purchase of such property simply because they are not an independent board. What vitiated the agreement in *Erlanger's* case were the concealment of the fact that two out of the three managing directors were agents of the vendors and promoters, and the untrue statement that a provisional contract had been entered into by the directors, whilst, in fact, it had only been framed by the promotors and adopted by three directors, two of whom were not known to be their agents, and the third of whom knew nothing about the matter. In the present case there is no secrecy or concealment of the true position of the first directors, and no untrue statement as to what they did for the company. In the face of the memorandum and articles of association it is impossible to treat the nitrate company or the members thereof as ignorant of the real truth as to the position of its directors.

After *Salomon's* case I think it impossible to hold that it is the duty of the promoters of a company to provide it with an independent board of directors, if the real truth is disclosed to those who are induced by the promoters to join the company. Treating promoters of companies as in a fiduciary relation to them, and as having a power of appointing trustees (namely, directors), I cannot treat companies or their shareholders as so many cestuis que trusts under disability, nor even as cestuis que trusts for whom trustees are appointed without their consent. No one need join a company unless he likes, and if a person knows that if he becomes a member he will find as directors who, in his opinion, ought not to be directors, he should not join the company. If he does, he has no right to redress on the ground that improper persons were appointed trustees. "Volenti non fit injuria" applies in such a case to the members of the company, and *Salomon's case* shows that the company in its corporate capacity is in this respect in no better position. On these grounds the nitrate company is not, in my opinion, entitled to relief against the syndicate or its directors on the ground that they did wrong in creating the nitrate company with such provisions as are contained in the instruments by which it was created, and which govern its existence. The principles on which *Salomon's case* was decided by the House of Lords are quite consistent with those on which *Erlanger* v *New Sombrero Phosphate Co* was decided, but are quite inconsistent with such an extension of those principles as would be necessary to give the nitrate company relief against those who formed it, on the ground that they formed it with an objectionable constitution. But it by no means follows that the nitrate company has no rights against the syndicate or its directors for misrepresentation or breach of duty as promoters. Notwithstanding the memorandum and articles of association of the nitrate company, that company may have a right to repudiate the contract into which it entered with the syndicate. It is necessary, therefore, to consider the principles on which such right must be rested ...'

Pre-incorporation contracts

Contronic (UK) Ltd v *Dezonie* [1991] BCC 200 Court of Appeal (Dillon, Balcombe and Ralph Gibson LJJ)

Contract with non-existent company

Facts

Wendaland Builders Ltd, a company controlled by Mr Dezonie, was incorporated in 1973 but struck off and dissolved in 1981, a fact of which Mr Dezonie was unaware until 1987. Mrs Osborne entered into a contract with Wendaland Builders Ltd in March 1986 and a new company bearing the same name was incorporated in 1988.

Held

The contract was invalid and a nullity and it could not be saved by s36(4) of the Companies Act 1985 as there had been no intention of forming the new company when the contract was made. Dillon LJ said that where there was a contract at a pre-incorporation date of a company, a contract to which that company was ostensibly a party was void unless a fresh contract was made by the company after its incorporation to adopt it as a new contract. The contract in question was plainly intended to be a contract of a company, not a personal contract by Mr Dezonie. At the time the contract was signed no one had thought about forming a new company and it was not possible to say that the contract was purported to have been made by the new company.

Commentary

Section 36 of the 1985 Act was substituted by s130(4) of the Companies Act 1989.

Kelner v *Baxter* (1866) LR 2 CP 174 Common Pleas Division (Erle CJ Willes, Byles and Keating JJ)

Liability on a pre-incorporation contract

Facts

The Gravesend Royal Alexandra Hotel Co was proposed to be formed by the defendants to carry on the business of an hotel. The plaintiff entered into a contract to sell wine to the company when it was formed and the wine was sold to and received by the defendants on terms that the contract would be adopted by the company when formed. The terms of the contract were – 'January 27 1866. To A, B and C on behalf of the proposed Gravesend Royal Alexandra Hotel Company, I hereby propose to sell the extra stock as per schedule hereto for the sum of £900, payable on 28 February, 1866' (signed by the plaintiff). The defendants replied – 'We have received your offer to sell the extra stock, as above, and we hereby agree to accept the terms proposed' (signed) 'A, B and C on behalf of the Gravesend Royal Alexandra Hotel Company.' The wine was handed over to the representatives of the company and was consumed in the business. The company obtained a certificate of incorporation on 20 February, 1866 but collapsed before the money was paid. The plaintiff sued the defendants for the money who claimed that they were not liable since the debt was not their debt but the company's debt.

Held

The defendants were personally liable on their agreement, for the price of the wine sold and delivered.

Erle CJ:

'... I agree that if the Gravesend Royal Alexandra Hotel Company had been an existing company at this time, the persons who signed the agreement would have signed as agents of the company. But, as there was no company in existence at the time, the agreement would be wholly inoperative unless it were held to be binding on the defendants personally. The cases referred to in the course of the argument fully bear out the proposition that, where a contract is signed by one who professes to be signing "as agent", but who has no principal existing at the time, and the contract would be altogether inoperative unless binding upon the person who signed it, he is bound thereby; and a stranger cannot by a subsequent ratification relieve him from that responsibility. When the company came afterwards into existence it was a totally new creature, having rights and obligations from that time, but no rights or obligations by reason of anything which might have been done before. It was once, indeed, thought that an inchoate liability might be incurred on behalf of a proposed company, which would become binding on it when subsequently formed; but that notion was manifestly contrary to the principles upon which the law of contract is founded. There must be two parties to a contract; and the rights and obligations which it creates cannot be transferred by one of them to a third person who was not in a condition to be bound by it at the time it was made. The history of this company makes this construction to my mind perfectly clear. It was no doubt the notion of all the parties that success was certain: but the plaintiff parted with his stock upon the faith of the defendants' engagement that the price agreed on should be paid on the day named. It cannot be supposed that he for a moment contemplated that the payment was to be contingent on the formation of the company by 28 February. The paper expresses in terms a contract to buy. And it is a cardinal rule that no oral evidence shall be admitted to show an intention different from that which appears on the fact of the writing. I come, therefore, to the conclusion that the defendants, having no principal who was bound originally, or who could become so by a subsequent ratification, were themselves bound, and that the oral evidence offered is not admissible to contradict the written contract.'

Newborne v *Sensolid (Great Britain) Ltd* [1954] 1 QB 45 Court of Appeal (Lord Goddard CJ, Morris and Romer LJJ)

Liability on a pre-incorporation contract – style of signature

Facts
Leopold Newborne Ltd entered into a contract to sell a quantity of tinned ham to Sensolid. The contract was signed 'Leopold Newborne (London) Ltd' and on the back of it were set out the names of Leopold Newborne and M Newborne as directors of the company. The market fell and Sensolid refused to take delivery of the goods and, consequently, Leopold Newborne Ltd issued a writ against Sensolid claiming damages for breach of contract. While the case was in progress it was discovered that Leopold Newborne Ltd had not been registered as a company at the time the contract was made and steps were taken to substitute Leopold Newborne for his company. Sensolid then contended that Leopold Newborne was attempting to sue on a contract which he had not made but which purported to be made by a company which had not been registered.

Held
Leopold Newborne did not enter the contract to sell the ham either as principal or agent. Instead the contract purported to be made by a company which was not yet in existence by one of its future directors; the contract was therefore a nullity.

Lord Goddard CJ (his Lordship referred to *Kelner* v *Baxter* and continued):

> '...They took delivery of the goods and, therefore, it was held that as they had contracted on behalf of a principal who did not exist they must, having received the wine, pay for it. That decision seems to me to stop far short of holding that every time an alleged company purports to contract – when there is no company in existence – everybody who is signing for the company is making himself personally liable.
>
> Mr Diplock has also relied strongly on *Schmaltz* v *Avery* (1851) 6 QB 655 which lays down a principle, which has been acted on in other cases, notably in *Harper & Co* v *Vigers Brothers* [1909] 2 KB 549 that where a person purports to contract as agent he may nevertheless disclose himself as being in truth a principal. If he entered into a contract as agent he can bring an action in his own name and show that he was in fact the principal. All those cases are well established and we are not departing in any way from those decisions any more than did Parker J.

What we cannot find in this case is that Mr Newborne ever purported to contract to sell as agent or as principal. The contract was one which he was making for the company, and although Mr Diplock has argued that in signing as he did Mr Newborne must have signed as agent, since the company could only contract through agents, that was not really the true position.

The company makes the contract. No doubt the company must do its physical acts, and so forth, through the directors, but it is not the ordinary case of principal and agent. It is a case in which the company is contracting and the company's contract is authenticated by the signature of one of the directors. This contract purports to be a contract by the company; it does not purport to be a contract by Mr Newborne. He does not purport to be selling his goods but to be selling the company's goods. The only person who had any contract here was the company, and Mr Newborne's signature merely confirmed the company's signature. The document is signed "Yours faithfully, Leopold Newborne (London) Ltd" and then the signature underneath is the signature of the person authorised to sign on behalf of the company.

In my opinion, unfortunate though it may be, as the company was not in existence when the contract was signed there never was a contract, and Mr Newborne cannot come forward and say: "Well, it was my contract." The fact is, he made a contract for the company which did not exist. It seems to me, therefore, that the defendants can avail themselves of the defence which they pleaded and the appeal must be dismissed.'

Oshkosh B'Gosh Inc v Dan Marbel Inc Ltd [1988] 4 BCC 442 Court of Appeal (Parker, Nourse and Balcombe LJJ)

Pre-incorporation contract with a wrongly named company

Facts
The plaintiff had claimed against both defendants for goods supplied to the first defendant in 1984 and 1985. The second defendant was a director of the first defendant and controlled its activities. Default judgment was given against both defendants. An appeal by the first defendant had been allowed and the second defendant now appealed further. The first defendant had been incorporated in England in 1979 under the name 'Egormite Ltd'. By a special resolution in 1980 it had resolved to change its name to 'Dan Marbel Inc Ltd'. It was not until June 1985 that the certificate of incorporation with the company's new name was duly issued and that was after the goods in respect of which the plaintiff's claim related were supplied. However, at all material times the first defendant had traded and acted under its new name. A company's change of name took effect only on the issue of the altered certificate (see now s28(6) of the Companies Act 1985) so at all material times the first defendant's name was Egormite Ltd. If the first defendant had 'not been formed', at the material times, within s9(2) of the European Committees Act 1972 (see s36(4) of the 1985 Act, now substituted by s130(4) of the Companies Act 1989), the second defendant was liable and his further appeal would be dismissed.

Held
His appeal would be allowed as the issue of an altered certificate did not effect a reformation or re-incorporation of the company and it followed that it could not be said that the first defendant had 'not been formed' when the contracts were made.

Phonogram Ltd v Lane [1982] QB 938 Court of Appeal (Lord Denning MR, Shaw and Oliver LJJ)

Pre-incorporation contracts – style of signature – s36c(1) of the Companies Act 1985

Facts

In 1973 some 'pop' artists decided to form a pop group under the name of 'Cheap Mean and Nasty' and also to form a company to run the group to be called 'Fragile Management Ltd.' Before the company was formed Lane, who acted on behalf of the proposed company, entered into negotiations to obtain finance for the venture. Phonogram Ltd advanced £6,000 and the contract was signed by Lane 'for and on behalf of Fragile Management Ltd'. The cheque was made payable to 'Jelly Music Ltd' at Lane's request; Lane was a director of this company. Fragile was never formed and when the £6,000 was not repaid on the due date Phonogram Ltd tried to discover who was liable to repay it. They sued Lane and at first instance Phillips J held that Lane had contracted personally. On appeal by Lane:

Held

Lane was personally liable to repay the money.

Lord Denning MR (his Lordship referred to s9(2) of the European Communities Act 1972 which became s36(4) Companies Act 1985 which was itself substituted by s130(1) of the Companies Act 1989 and continued):

'That seems to me to cover this very case. The contract purports to be made on behalf of Fragile Management Ltd, at a time when the company had not been formed. It purports to be made by Mr Lane on behalf of the company. So he is to be personally liable for it.

Counsel for Mr Lane argued very skilfully that s9(2) did not apply. First, he said: "Look at the directive under the European Community law which led to this section being introduced." It is the directive of 9 March 1968 (EEC Council Directive 68/151). It was written in French. (In 1968 English was not one of the official languages of the European Community). So counsel for Mr Lane referred us to the French text of art 7 of the directive:

His Lordship read the French text and continued:

'Mr Lane's counsel says that, according to the French text, that directive is limited to companies which are "en formation", that is companies which have already started to be formed. His submission is reinforced by a passage from a French textbook, Ripert et Roblot, *Traite Elementaire de Droit Commercial* (1970). As I read the passages at pp601 and 604 of that treatise, interpreting the French as best I can, in the case of a French company or societe there may be, recognised by law, a period of time while a company is in the course of formation when people have put their signatures to what I may call "the articles of association". That period is called the period when the societe is "en formation". A parallel is drawn (at p604) with a baby at the time of gestation, ie between the time of conception and at the time of birth and a company when it is "en formation".

I reject the submission of counsel for Mr Lane. I do not think we should go by the French text of the directive. It was drafted with regard to a different system of company law from that in this country. We should go by s9(2) of our own statute, the European Communities Act 1972. Under art 189 of the EEC Treaty, those directives are to be binding only in so far as the spirit and intent are concerned. Article 189 says:

"A directive shall be binding, as to the result to be achieved, upon each Member State to which it is addressed, but shall leave to the national authorities the choice of form and methods."

Section 9(2) is in accordance with the spirit and intent of the directive. We should go by our own statute, and not by the directive.

That brings me to the second point. What does "purports" mean in this context? Counsel for Mr Lane suggests that there must be a representation that the company is already in existence. I do not agree. A contract can purport to be made on behalf of a company, or by a company, even though that company is known by both parties not to be formed and that it is only about to be formed.

The third point made by counsel for Mr Lane was that a company can be "a person" within the meaning of that expression where it first occurs in s9(2). He says that Jelly Music Ltd was "a person" which was purporting to contract on behalf of Fragile Management Ltd. I do not agree. Jelly Music Ltd were not entering into a contract. Mr Lane was purporting to do so.

So all three points made by Mr Lane's counsel fail.

But I would not leave the matter there. This is the first time the section has come before us. It will have much impact on the common law. I am afraid that before 1972 the common law had adopted some fine distinctions. As I understand *Kelner v Baxter* (1866) LR 2 CP 174 it decided that, if a person contracted on behalf of a company which was non-existent, he himself would be liable on the contract. Just as, if a man signs a contract for and on behalf "of his horses", he is personally liable. But, since that case was decided, a number of distinctions have been introduced by *Hollman v Pullin* (1884) Cab & E11 254; *Newborne v Sensolid (Great Britain) Ltd* [1954] 1 QB 45 and *Black v Smallwood* (1965) 117 CLR 51 in the High Court of Australia. Those three cases seem to suggest that there is a distinction to be drawn according to the way in which an agent signs a contract. If he signs it as "agent for X company", or "for and on behalf of X company", and there is no such body as X company, then he himself can be sued on it. On the other hand, if he signs it as X company per pro himself the managing director, then the position may be different; because he is not contracting personally as an agent, it is the company which is contracting.

That distinction was disliked by Windeyer J in *Black v Smallwood* . It has been criticised in *Treitel on the Law of Contract* (5th ed, 1979, p559). In my opinion the distinction has been obliterated by s9(2) of the European Communities Act 1972. We now have the clear words, "Where a contract purports to be made by a company, or by a person as agent for a company, at a time when the company has not been formed." That applies whatever formula is adopted. The person who purports to contract for the company is personally liable.

There is one further point on s9(2) which I must mention. In *Cheshire and Fifoot's Law of Contract* (9th ed, 1976, p462), after reciting s9(2), it says:

"How far (s9(2)) in fact (increases the number of cases where the agent is personally liable) will depend on the meaning given to the words 'subject to any agreement to the contrary' since it could be argued that words showing that A signs as agent express an agreement that he is not to be personally liable. If this were correct *Newborne v Sensolid (Great Britain) Ltd* would still be decided the same way. But it may be suspected that the courts will try to give more content to the subsection."

We certainly will. The words "subject to any agreement to the contrary" mean, as Shaw LJ suggested in the course of the argument, "unless otherwise agreed". If there was an express agreement that the man who was signing was not to be liable, the section would not apply. But, unless there is a clear exclusion of personal liability, s9(2) should be given its full effect. It means that in all cases such as the present, where a person purports to contract on behalf of a company not yet formed, then however he expresses his signature he himself is personally liable on the contract ...'

Commentary

See now new s36c(1) of the Companies Act 1985.

Rover International Ltd and Others v *Cannon Film Sales* [1987] BCLC 540
Chancery Division (Harman J)

Section 36c(1) of the Companies Act 1985 has no application to companies incorporated outside the UK

Facts

Rover International Ltd (Rover), the first plaintiff, purported to enter into a contract with Cannon Film Sales Ltd, the defendant. It was later discovered by Cannon, when Rover sought relief for alleged breaches of the contract, that Rover had only been incorporated after the contract had been entered into.

Cannon argued that it was therefore not bound by the contract on the grounds that either the contract had been accepted by Cannon after Rover had been incorporated or, alternatively, as the parties had conducted themselves on the basis that the contract was valid and enforceable, Cannon was estopped from denying that it was bound by the contract. Rover claimed in the alternative, that by virtue of s36(4) of the Companies Act 1985 their agent, the fourth plaintiff, who purported to act on Rover's behalf, was entitled to enforce the contract against Cannon.

Held

The defendant was not bound by the contract. The contract had been signed before Rover had been incorporated and there was no basis for finding that the contract had been accepted by Cannon after Rover had been incorporated. The principle of estoppel by convention was not appropriate here as that principle required both parties to act on the basis of assumed facts. That condition was not satisfied as Rover was not in existence at the time the estoppel was alleged to have arisen. In addition, as Rover was a foreign company, s36(4) of the 1985 Act did not apply.

Commentary

For s36(4) of the 1985 Act, see now s36C of that Act as substituted by s130(4) of the Companies Act 1989.

Flotation

Criminal sanctions

R v *Kylsant* [1932] 1 KB 442 Court of Criminal Appeal (Avory, Branson and Humphreys JJ)

Prospectus – criminal liability

Facts

Lord Kylsant, a director of the Royal Mail Steam Packet Co, was charged under s84 of the Larceny Act 1861 (now s19 of the Theft Act 1968) with issuing a prospectus which he knew to be false in a material particular the purpose of which was to invite subscriptions to a debenture issue. The prospectus stated the history of the company and the purpose of the issue and proceeded:

> 'The interest on the present issue of debenture stock will amount to £100,000 per annum. Although this company, in common with other shipping companies, has suffered from the depression in the shipping industry, the audited accounts of the company show that during the past ten years the average annual balance available (including profits of the insurance fund), after providing for depreciation and interest on existing debenture stocks, has been sufficient to pay the interest on the present issue more than five times over. After providing for all taxation, depreciation of the fleet, etc, adding to the reserves and payment of dividends on the preference stocks, the dividends on the ordinary stock during the last 17 years have been as follows:'

The prospectus then set out a table of dividends paid from 1911 to 1927 inclusive, those dividends varying from 5 up to 8 per cent and down to 4 per cent in 1926 but up to 5 per cent in 1927. But, the prospectus did not state that for several years the company had made losses on both its trading and investment income or that the dividends on debentures for those years had been paid out of abnormal income received in the war years (1914 – 18 war) which was of a non-recurring nature. A jury convicted him on this evidence.

Held

An appeal against conviction was unsuccessful. The offence could be committed where a written statement omitted or concealed information and was not restricted to what was actually written.

Avory J:

'... In the opinion of this court there was ample evidence upon which the jury could come to the conclusion that this document, the prospectus, was false in a material particular, in that it conveyed a false impression, the falsity in this case consisting in putting before intending investors as material upon which they could exercise a judgment as to the existing position of the company, figures which apparently disclose the existing position but in fact conceal it. In other words, the document implied that the company was in a sound financial position, and that a prudent investor could safely invest in its debentures. This implication arises particularly from the statement that the dividends have been regularly paid over a term of years, although times have been bad, a statement which is entirely misleading when the fact that they were paid not out of current earnings but out of earnings in the abnormal war period is omitted.

The further question is whether there was evidence upon which the jury could properly find that the appellant knew that this document was false. If there was evidence that the document was false in the particulars already indicated, there was ample evidence upon which the jury could find that the appellant knew of its falsity, knowing as he did of the means by which the dividends had been paid; and it is not, and cannot be, disputed that the prospectus was published with intent to induce persons to entrust or advance money to the company, which was sufficient to satisfy the section. But the learned judge told the jury, in the passage that I have already read, that upon this third count also they must find the intention to defraud, and he repeated this, after the jury had retired, and sent their written question to him. In these circumstances the jury must be taken to have found that what was done in this case was done with an intent to defraud ...'

Commentary

See now s19 of the Theft Act 1968.

R v *Markus* [1976] AC 35 House of Lords (Lord Wilberforce, Viscount Dilhorne, Lords Diplock, Kilbrandon and Salmon)

Misleading statements – invitations to invest in shares

Facts

The Agri-Fund, a trust, was supposedly established in Panama for the purpose of encouraging investment in food producing industries. The public were to be invited to invest in the fund by purchasing share units. The fund was managed by a Panamanian company of which Markus was a director and a company was established with offices in London with the purpose of obtaining investments. Markus was also a director of the London based company. Salesmen were sent out to canvas investors in West Germany and investors were shown brochures which gave a glowing account of the fund's prospectus. The fund was in fact entirely bogus and the brochure was false and fraudulent in respect of its statements. Markus was charged under s13 of the Prevention of Fraud (Investments) Act 1958 with 'conniving at a corporation fraudulently inducing the investment of money'. He was convicted and appealed.

Held

The House of Lords was satisfied that Markus had induced the investment of money by false representations that the Panamanian company was carrying on an honest business and that monies invested could be redeemed immediately.

Lord Diplock:

'... the Court of Appeal ... certified that the following point of law of general importance was involved in their decision:

"Whether upon the true construction of s13(1)(b) of the Prevention of Fraud (Investments) Act 1958 (as amended by the Protection of Depositors Act 1963, ss1 and 21) the offence of fraudulently inducing a person to offer to take part in an arrangement with respect to property other than securities is an offence separate and distinct from the offence under the same paragraph of fraudulently inducing a person to take part in an arrangement with respect to such property so that if the facts disclose the former offence it is not open to the prosecution to charge the latter offence by reason of the subsequent acceptance of the victim's offer."

This is a short point of construction. The offence of inducing another person to take part in any arrangements of the kind described in s13(1)(b) is clearly a separate and distinct offence from that of inducing another person to offer to take part in any such arrangements. The use of the conjunction "or" shows that they are alternative offences; but not that to have committed one precludes the possibility of subsequently committing the other. In many cases the actual taking part in the arrangements by the victim of the fraudulent inducement will have been preceded by an offer by him to take part and will have resulted from an acceptance of that offer. The question posed by the Court of Appeal is whether, in such a case, where the person charged is the person who fraudulently induced the victim to take part in the arrangements despite the fact that this was both the actual and the intended consequence of the inducement. When stated in this form the question itself invites the answer, No. No plausible reason has been suggested for ascribing to the words of the statute a meaning which would have so absurd a result. In statutes which make acts done with the intention of achieving a particular result punishable as crimes it is a common practice to provide that there shall be alternative offences depending on the stage to which the offender has managed to get towards achieving that result.

I do not find it credible that Parliament, by doing this, should have intended that an offender who has actually succeeded in achieving the prescribed result should not be charged with that offence because at some intermediate stage he had done something which, if he had been stopped then, would have constituted one of the alternative offences.

So I would answer the question that was certified, No ...'

Commentary

Section 13 of the Prevention of Fraud (Investments) Act 1958: see now ss47 and 47A of the Financial Services Act 1986.

Civil remedies

Addlestone Linoleum Company, Re (1888) 37 Ch D 191 Court of Appeal (Cotton, Lindley and Lopes LJJ)

Issue of shares at a discount – claim for damages refused

Facts

The company issued preference shares in 1881, after only about one-third of its ordinary shares had been taken up in a public issue, in order to raise sufficient capital to start business. The existing shareholders were offered £10 preference shares at 25 per cent discount and some of them took up this offer paying £7 10s per preference share. In 1885 the company was ordered to be wound up and the preference shareholders who had taken their shares at a discount were placed on the list of contributories and calls made on them for the unpaid £2 10s per share; this they paid. However, a number of these preference shareholders applied for leave to prove in the winding-up 'in damages for breach of contract or otherwise, in respect of the issue of the preference shares'.

Held

If the contract for the issue of the preference shares was one under which they were to be treated as fully paid up then the shareholders could have rescinded on discovering that in point of law they were not fully paid up. But since the company had been ordered to be wound up it was too late to rescind and, therefore, they had no remedy because they could not sue in damages.

Lopes LJ:

'Then *Houldsworth* v *City of Glasgow Bank* (1880) 5 App Cas 317 decides that a shareholder cannot claim damages against the company of which he is a member for misrepresentations by which he was induced to take his shares, his proper remedy is rescission of the contract. Here rescission has become impossible, so the shareholder has no remedy at all against the company. It is urged that this may be distinguished from *Houldsworth's* case, because there damages were claimed for misrepresentation, here for breach of contract, but that does not appear to me to be a substantial distinction ...'

Commentary
See now s100 of the Companies Act 1985.

Al-Nakib Investments (Jersey) Ltd v *Longcroft* [1990] 1 WLR 1390 High Court (Mervyn Davies J)

Prospectus – duty of care

Facts
The plaintiff was a shareholder in Combined Technologies Corp plc (CT) which developed an electronic information storage and retrieval system. Mnemos Ltd (M), a subsidiary of CT, was incorporated to exploit this system. CT decided to float M on the unlisted securities market and it issued a prospectus inviting CT shareholders to subscribe for shares in CT and M by way of rights. The plaintiff subscribed for 400,000 shares in M – the first transaction. After the issue of interim reports, the plaintiff purchased through the stock market further shares in both CT and M – transactions 2 to 6. In an action against CT and its directors, the plaintiff alleged the prospectus and the interim reports contains misrepresentations. The defendants applied to strike out the statement of claim in respect of transactions 2 to 6, but not the claim to compensation in respect of the first transaction.

Held
The claims arising from transactions 2 to 6 would be struck out as the defendants had not owed a duty of care to persons, shareholders or otherwise, who purchased shares through the stock market.

Mervyn Davies J:

'... it was said that the document in the Caparo case, an auditor's report, was to be contrasted with the documents now under consideration, ie the prospectus and the interim reports. The documents, of course, do differ but the question whether statements in a document give rise to liability is the same whatever may be the nature of the document; that is, was the document written for a particular purpose and to be communicated to a particular person or class of persons? ...

I am confirmed in my view that the defendants did not owe to the plaintiffs a duty of care in respect of transactions 2 to 6; in that the prospectus (and the interim reports) having been addressed to the first plaintiff for a particular purpose (ie considering the rights issue) it was used by the plaintiffs for another purpose (ie buying shares in the market): see Lord Jauncey in the *Caparo* case [1990] 2 WLR 358 at 404 where he refers to "the fundamental question of the purpose".'

Commentary
Applied: *Caparo Industries plc* v *Dickman* [1990] 2 WLR 358 and *Smith* v *Eric S Bush* [1989] 2 WLR 790.

Andrews v *Mockford* [1896] 1 QB 372 Court of Appeal (Lord Esher MR, A L Smith and Rigby LJJ)

Prospectus liability – claim for damages

Facts
The defendants published a prospectus inviting subscriptions in a gold mining company in the Transvaal and sent one to the plaintiff. The plaintiff kept the prospectus and did not apply for or have any shares allotted to him. Instead he observed carefully the movements in price of the shares on the market over a period of seven months. An article appeared in the Financial Times which stated that there had been a big jump in the value of the shares as the company's engineer had sent a telegram that a shaft had been sunk 50 feet and a large body of pay ore assayed by Government assay 24 ounces to the ton had been discovered. The plaintiff then purchased 50 shares in the company. Thereafter the shares declined in value and the company was wound up within a year of the plaintiff's purchase without ever having paid a dividend. The prospectus was full of fraudulent statements and the statements in the telegram which had been published were untrue having been concocted by the defendants. One of the purposes of the telegram was that it might be sent to the Financial Times so that it might be published and induce those to whom the prospectus had already been sent to purchase shares by strengthening the statements in the prospectus. The plaintiff claimed damages and these were awarded by a jury at the trial. One of the issues on appeal was whether the plaintiff was entitled to rely on the prospectus.

Held
He could since the defendants had intended to induce him to purchase shares on the strength of it.

Rigby LJ:

'... I do not wish to avoid the question arising on the issue of the prospectus as it has been argued before us. In my judgment, there is nothing in Peek v Gurney (1873) LR 6 HL 377, or in any other case, which precisely meets the present one. Undoubtedly, if there be a prospectus issued for the sole purpose of obtaining subscriptions for the original capital of the company, or subscriptions for any issue of shares about to take place, and if that can be treated as a separate transaction, people who did not respond to that invitation, and did not act upon it in the way which it was intended to be acted upon, but who afterwards bought shares in the open market, cannot rely on statements in the prospectus, which they may be able to establish as being fraudulent misrepresentations. It is, however, a totally different matter when the conclusion is arrived at that the prospectus was not intended solely, or even primarily, for the purpose of getting the public to subscribe to the shares. If the object was, in pursuance of a deliberate scheme of fraud, to impress the minds of all persons who read the prospectus with the idea that the sham company which was created was a real and most prosperous company – if that was a part of the scheme, and if, after the issue of the prospectus, that scheme was continued by other devices intended to produce the same results, it is idle to say there is any rule of law or any principle which should lead us to shut our eyes to that portion of the fraud which was contained in the prospectus ...'

Houldsworth v *City of Glasgow Bank* (1880) 5 App Cas 317 House of Lords (Earl Cairns LC, Lords Selbourne, Hatherley and Blackburn)

Prospectus liability – claim for damages

Facts

In February 1877 Houldsworth purchased £4,000 of stock in the bank, an unlimited company. In October 1878 the bank went into liquidation with immense liabilities and Houldsworth was entered on the list of contributories and paid very large calls. In December 1878 Houldsworth commenced this action claiming damages against the company (through the liquidator) on the ground that he had been induced to purchase the stock by reason of fraudulent mis-representations made to him by the directors and others connected with the bank. He did not claim rescission since it was too late to do so. The total claim was for (i) £9,046 being the price of the stock and stamp duty, (ii) £20,000 paid by him on the first call and (iii) £200,000 being the amount of estimated future calls.

Held

Even if Houldsworth proved that he had been induced by fraud to purchase the shares he could not obtain damages for fraudulent misrepresentation from the company whilst he remained a member of it.

Earl Cairns LC:

'The question, therefore, mainly argued at your Lordships' Bar, upon which the decision of the case must depend, was this: Can a man induced by the fraudulent misrepresentations of agents of a company to take shares in the company, after he has discovered the fraud elect to retain the shares and to sue the company for damages? There is no doubt that, according to the law of England, a person purchasing a chattel or goods concerning which the vendor made a fraudulent misrepresentation may, on finding out the fraud, retain the chattel or the goods and have his action to recover any damages he has sustained by reason of the fraud. I will assume that the law of the two countries is the same in the case of a chattel. But does that same rule apply to the case of shares or stock in a company? We are accustomed to use language as to such a sale and purchase as if the thing bought or sold were goods or chattels, but it certainly is not. The contract which is made is a contract by which the person called the buyer agrees to enter into a partnership already formed and going, taking his chance of past liabilities and his chance of future profits or losses. He has not bought any chattel or piece of property for himself; he has merged himself in a society to the property of which he has agreed to contribute, and the property of which, including his own contributions, he has agreed should be used and applied in a particular way, and no other. Does, then, the principle which in the case of a chattel admits of an action for damages, apply to the case of a partnership contract such as I have described? It may go some way to answer this question to observe that, although during the last quarter of a century actions in every shape and form have been brought, or have been attempted to be brought, arising out of dealings in shares alleged to be fraudulent, no case could be mentioned at the Bar in which an action for damages has been sustained, the plaintiff retaining his position in the company.

I will, however, ask your Lordships to look at the case on principle. A man buys from a banking company shares or stock of such an amount as to become, say, the proprietor of one-hundredth part of the capital of the company. A representation is made to him on behalf of the company that the liabilities of the company are £100,000, and no more. His contract as between himself and those with whom he becomes a partner is that he will be entitled to one-hundredth part of all the property of the company, and that the assets of the company shall be applied in meeting the liabilities of the company contracted up to the time of his joining them, whatever their amounts may be, and those to be contracted afterwards, and that, if those assets are deficient, the deficiency shall be made good by the shareholders rateably in proportion to their shares in the capital of the company. That is the contract, and the only contract, made between him and his partners and it is only through this contract and through the correlative contract of his partners with him that any liability of him or them can be enforced.

It is clear that among the debts and liabilities of the company to which the assets of the company and the contributions of the shareholders are thus dedicated by the contract of the partners, a demand that the company – that is to say, these same assets and contributions – should pay the new partner damages for a fraud committed on him by the company in inducing him to enter into the contract, which alone could make them liable for that fraud, cannot be intended to be included. Any such application of the assets and contributions would be, not in accordance, but at variance, with the contract into which the new partner had entered. He finds out, however, after he joins the company that the liabilities are not £100,000 but £500,000. He is entitled thereupon, I will assume, to rescind his contract and to leave the company, and to recover any money he has paid or any damage he has sustained; but he prefers to remain in the company and to affirm his contract – that is to say, the contract by which he agreed that the assets of the company should be applied in paying its antecedent debts and liabilities. He then brings an action against the company to recover out of its assets the sum, say £4,000, which it would fall to his share to provide for the liabilities over and above what his share would have had to provide had the liabilities been as they were represented to him. If he succeeded in that action this £4,000 would be paid out of the assets and contributions of the company. But he has contracted, and his contract remains, that those assets and contributions should be applied in payment of the debts and liabilities of the company, against which this £4,000 cannot be reckoned. The result is he is making a claim which is inconsistent with the contract into which he has entered, and by which he wishes to abide. In other words, he is in substance, if not in form, taking the course which is described as "approbating and reprobating" – a course which is not allowed either in English or Scottish law.'

Commentary
See now s111A (s131 CA 1989).

Nash v *Lynde* [1929] AC 158; House of Lords (Lord Hailsham LC, Viscount Sumner, Lords Buckmaster, Carson and Warrington)

What is a prospectus?

Facts
The company (British and Foreign Industrials Ltd) needed further capital and Nash, the managing director, prepared a document, which was signed by the other directors, which stated the position of the company, that it was proposed to issue 20,000 preference shares and gave an estimate of the profits after new capital was available. There was attached an application for preference shares. Nash also prepared a second document on the company's notepaper which was addressed to a fellow director and marked 'Strictly private and confidential'. This document set out the nominal and issued capital of the company, the reasons why the additional capital was needed, had an application form for ordinary shares attached and concluded: 'I shall be very happy to discuss this proposition in all its details with anyone who is really interested.' Nash gave several copies of this document to a fellow director who sent one of them to a solicitor, together with a request that he find a client prepared to invest in the company. The solicitor sent the document to Lynde's brother-in-law who sent them to Lynde, knowing he was looking for a business investment. Lynde, in reliance on the documents, purchased 3,000 ordinary shares in the company. However, it subsequently transpired that many of the shares in the company had been issued for a non-cash consideration and this was not revealed in the documents. Lynde sued for damages and loss under s81(1)(e) of the Companies (Consolidation) Act 1908, (ie failure to state the number and amount of shares issued within the previous two years as fully or partly paid up otherwise than in cash). (See now s56 and Parts I and II of Schedule 3 of the Companies Act 1985. The provisions

of s81(1)(e) referred to a 'prospectus' and the question arose whether the documents in question were a prospectus.

Held
The documents were not a 'prospectus'.

Lord Buckmaster:

'... The sole point upon which I desire to express my view is the true construction of ss81 and 285 of the Companies Act of 1908. The first of these sections states what it is necessary that a prospectus issued by, or on behalf of a company or by any person who is or has been engaged or interested in the formation of the company, must contain, and the second defines what a prospectus means. The first thing necessary to notice is that s81 contains no reference of any issue to the public. It is sufficient that the prospectus should be issued. The question of what does or does not amount to an issue is a question of fact in each case and is not capable of a rigid and exact definition, but in my opinion it certainly does not necessarily involve a general application impartially made to all members of the public. A distribution of a prospectus among a well defined class of the public would be an issue within the meaning of s81. Many illustrations might be given of such a use of a prospectus, for example: A company like the Army and Navy Stores Ltd originally confined its membership to members of His Majesty's forces; the Civil Service Stores in a similar way was I believe originally limited to members of the Civil Service. There may be, there probably are, assurance companies whose membership is similarly limited to members of the legal or clerical profession; in each of these instances the only source from which membership could originally be obtained would be from a class of people selected out of the general body of the public and having marked and definite characteristics. A prospectus, the distribution of which was so limited would none the less be issued, and that this is the meaning of the statute is I think made plain by considering that subs7 of s81 excludes from the application of the section a circular inviting existing members of a company to subscribe for shares. This would be unnecessary if an issue to such a limited class were not prima facie included. The definition gives rise to greater difficulty. A document is not a prospectus unless it is an invitation to the public, but if it satisfied this condition it is not the less a prospectus because it is issued to a defined class of the public. Whether a prospectus so limited in its invitation that only a special set of people were invited could be properly defined as a prospectus, it is not necessary for the present case to decide, for the documents A and B were in terms quite general.

They did, in fact, satisfy all the necessary requisites of a prospectus for the purposes of s285. The remaining point is, was it issued within the meaning of ss81? Now it is, I think, clear that the issue there mentioned involves issues as a prospectus; a document answering in all respects to the definition of s285 may be used by placing it before people to inform them of some of the facts it contains without its issue as a prospectus. If following on such use application is made for shares in response to the invitation contained, and such application were accepted, the company and the person named in s81 might then be prevented from saying that the original use was not an issue, but that does not arise here.

The letter accompanying the documents A and B shows that the original communication to Mr Alcock was not intended as the issue of a prospectus at all, but merely as a convenient means of enabling him to place facts before people who either on the basis of the document itself or on some modification of its terms might be prepared to come to the assistance of the company.

It was in this sense that it was actually used, and the ultimate arrangement by which the appellant took shares was not a response to the definite invitation in the documents. In these circumstances there was never an issue of a prospectus ...'

Commentary
The definition of prospectus in s285 of the Companies Act 1908 referred to by Lord Buckmaster is the same as that now to be found in s744(1) of the 1985 Act.

Peek v *Gurney* (1873) LR 6 HL 377 House of Lords (Lords Chelmsford, Colonsay and Cairns)

Prospectus liability – subsequent dealings in shares do not give the tranferees the right to maintain an action on the prospectus

Facts

The company was formed in July 1865 and a prospectus issued inviting subscription for its shares. Peek was not an original allottee but purchased his shares (2,000 in all) in the market between October and December 1865. The company was in the business of bill brokers and money dealers and was wound up in June 1866 with Peek declared liable as a contributory; he paid over £100,000 on this basis. In March 1868 Peek brought these proceedings against the directors of the company claiming from them an indemnity for the losses he had suffered by reason of his having become a purchaser of the 2,000 shares in the company. He alleged that he had been deceived and misled by the prospectus which had been put forth by the directors since it contained several misrepresentations and suppressed important facts and materials. One of the questions which arose on the appeal before the House of Lords was whether Peek, as a purchaser of the shares rather than an original allottee, could in the circumstances recover his losses on the basis of the misrepresentations in the prospectus.

Held

The proper purpose of a prospectus of a company is to invite persons to become allottees of the shares, or original shareholders in the company. When it has served this function it is exhausted. In order for a third party who is neither an allottee nor original shareholder to maintain an action on the prospectus it is necessary that he show some direct connection between those responsible for it and himself in the communication of the prospectus.

Lord Cairns:

'... The object of the prospectus on the face of it is clearly to invite the public to take shares in the new company. The prospectus is, as is usual in such cases, an invitation, and there is appended to it a form of application for shares which was to be filled up, and upon which form the invitation was to be answered. It is a prospectus in this shape, addressed to the whole of the public, no doubt, and any one of the public might take up the prospectus and appropriate it in that way to himself by answering it upon the form upon which it is intended by the prospectus that it should be answered. The appellant, however, did not take up and did not appropriate the prospectus in this way. For reasons which it is unnecessary to inquire into he declined to take, or at all events he did not originally take any shares in the company ...'

... The allotment having been completed, the prospectus, as it seems to me, had done its work; it was exhausted. The share list was full; the directors had obtained from the company the money which they desired to obtain. The appellant subsequently, upon 17 October, several months afterwards, bought 1,000 shares at a premium of something over £7, and again, on 6 December, he bought 1,000 other shares at a premium of something over £6. He bought them on the Stock Exchange, and he, of course, did not know in the first instance from whom he bought them. In point of fact, it appears that as to the greater part of them they were shares which had originally been allotted to one of the old partners, Samuel Gurney, by whom they were transferred to a nominee for himself, in whose name they were registered; they were then sold upon the market, and re-sold apparently several times, because the premium seems to have risen from a much smaller to much larger sum, and ultimately they were sold, at the premium which I have stated, to the appellant, and were registered in his name.

Now, my Lords, I ask the question, how can the directors of a company be liable, after the full original allotment of shares, for all the subsequent dealings which may take place with regard to those shares upon the Stock Exchange? If the argument of the appellant is right, they must be liable ad infinitum, for I know no means of pointing out any time at which the liability would, in point of fact, cease. Not only so, but if the argument be right, they must be liable, no matter what the premium may be at which the shares may be sold. That premium may rise from time to time from circumstances altogether unconnected with the prospectus, and yet, if the argument be right, the appellant would be entitled to call upon the directors to indemnify him up to the highest point at which the shares may be sold, for all that he may expend in buying the shares. My Lords, I ask, is there any authority for this proposition? I am aware of none ...'

R v International Stock Exchange of the United Kingdom and the Republic of Ireland Ltd, ex parte Else (1982) Ltd [1993] 2 WLR 70 Court of Appeal (Sir Thomas Bingham MR, Cowan and Leggatt LJJ)

Delisting of shares – rights of shareholder to be notified and heard in advance of delisting

Facts

The shares of Titaghur plc had been listed on the Stock Exchange since 1912. In May 1988 the Stock Exchange suspended the shares because annual listing charges had not been paid. After this was rectified listing recommenced one month later. In June 1989 the company's shares were again suspended due to the arrest of the chairman on suspicion of insider dealing offences. He was later charged and acquitted. Suspension of the company's shares continued as the Stock Exchange was concerned, inter alia, with the adequacy of the company's accounts and the financial information provided by it. In November the matter was referred to the Panel of the Quotations Committee of the Stock Exchange and it was decided to cancel the listing permanently. An appeal was made to the Quotations Committee. The company was represented by a director and two representatives of its brokers. The Committee upheld the Panel's decision in December 1990. Three shareholders of the company sought judicial review, having bought shares off-market during the period when the listing was suspended and before it was cancelled. The judge held that it was necessary to refer the matter to the Court of Justice of the European Communities under art 177 of the EEC Treaty. On appeal the main issue was whether the shareholders were entitled to be notified of and given an opportunity to make representations about the committee's impending decision whether the company's shares should be cancelled.

Held

The applicants had no right to be notified of an impending decision on discontinuation of listing or to be heard before such a decision was made. The EEC Directive governing such matters did not require an opinion from the Court of Justice of the European Communities.

Leggatt LJ:

'It is the policy of the EEC Treaty to abolish restrictions on freedom of establishment. One way of furthering this policy is to co-ordinate safeguards for the protection of individuals by rendering the safeguards "equivalent" throughout the Community. A series of Directives has applied this principle to companies. But that does not detract from the distinction which English law recognises between a company and its members. The court cannot interfere with the internal management of a company acting within its powers. Although the court will interfere to prevent fraud on a minority of shareholders, it will not ordinarily recognise any independent right of action by an individual shareholder based on an allegation of damage to the value of his shareholding, whether caused by the directors or by third parties. Nothing in Community law departs from that principle unless the applicants' submission in the present case is correct that Council Directive (79/279/EEC) accords to individual shareholders the right to apply to the court for the purpose of objecting to the discontinuance of the listing of the company of which they are members.

Community legislation about stock exchanges is mainly concerned with the listing of securities. Directive (79/279/EEC) has been followed by Directives dealing with requirements for furnishing particulars of securities for which listing has been applied, and with information which must be published regularly by companies with listed shares. These Directives are intended to protect investors as well as to facilitate access to the markets of the member states. By force of the Stock Exchange (Listing) Regulations 1984 (SI 1984 No 716) these Directives apply to the United Kingdom.

The scheme of the relevant Community legislation, and Directive (79/279/EEC) in particular, is to provide for the co-ordination of conditions for admission to listing by designating a competent authority in each member state to police the process. Ancillary provision is made for the suspension of listing and for discontinuance of listing. But although one of the main aims of controlling admission to listing is the protection of investors, the Directive is concerned with the means of control by the competent authority rather than with conferring rights on investors so that they may look out for themselves.

The function of Directive (79/279/EEC), known as "the Admission Directive" is "co-ordinating the conditions for the admission of securities to official stock exchange listing." The recitals show that this process is likely to provide protection for investors by rendering more uniform the practices in the member states. The general approach is prescribed by art 3 which says:

"Member states shall ensure that: – securities may not be admitted to official listing on any stock exchange situated or operating within their territory unless the conditions laid down by this Directive are satisfied, and that – issuers of securities admitted to such official listing, whether admission takes place before or after the date on which this Directive is implemented, are subject to the obligations provided for by this Directive."

Article 4 provides that the admission of securities to official listing is subject to the conditions set out in Schedules A and B relating to shares and debt securities, and that the issuers of listed securities must fulfil the obligations in the corresponding Schedules C and D. Schedule A therefore contains conditions for the admission of shares, and Schedule C deals with the obligations of companies whose shares are admitted. Paragraph 2 of Schedule C is concerned with treatment of shareholders. By sub-para (4) –

"The company must ensure, at least in each member state in which its shares are listed, that all the necessary facilities and information are available to enable shareholders to exercise their rights."

This includes information about shareholders' meetings and notices about dividends and new shares.

Section II of the Directive is headed "Authorities Competent to Admit Securities to Official Listing." In that section art 9 by para 1 requires member states to designate the competent authority "to decide on the admission of securities to official listing." Paragraph 3 provides:

"Without prejudice to the other powers conferred upon them, the competent authorities may reject an application for the admission of a security to official listing if, in their opinion, the issuer's situation is such that admission would be detrimental to investors' interests."

Article 10 applies to any special condition to which the competent authority may make the admission of a security subject, and of which they have informed the applicant, that is, the person applying for the admission. Article 11 refers to a refusal to admit. Articles 12 and 13 apply to failure by the issuer to comply with obligations and to publish information. Article 14 is concerned with suspension and discontinuance of the listing. Finally, para 2 of art 15 relates to notification to an applicant of a decision regarding his application for admission, and para 3 provides that a deemed rejection of the application "shall give rise to the right to apply to the courts provided for in para 1." The would-be issuer is both the applicant for admission and the person with the right to apply to the courts. Paragraph 1 itself says that:

"Member states shall ensure decisions of the competent authorities refusing the admission of a security to official listing or discontinuing such a listing shall be subject to the right to apply to the courts."

"Decisions" are made under art 9.1; "decisions refusing" may be made under art 9.3 or under art 11; and "decisions discontinuing" may be made under art 14.2.

In my judgment as a matter of construction the fact that the decisions have to be "subject to the right to apply to the courts" means that as with a deemed rejection under art 15.3, it is the giving to the applicant of an adverse decision by the competent authority that also gives to the applicant a right to apply to the courts. There is no other person to whom that right is given: it is given solely to the applicant. Miss Allan argues that because the Directive is for the protection of investors it is they who must have a right to apply to the court. That is a non sequitur. Nothing in the language of the Directive accords such a right to investors, actual or potential. I am fortified in this conclusion by the fact that, if the law were otherwise, the consequences of extending to persons other than the company the right to apply to the court would be commercially intolerable. If the number of shareholders were large, the process of identifying and communicating with them might be onerous, protracted and expensive. As Mr Henderson has pointed out, it might jeopardise confidentiality. It might even allow the will of a majority to be thwarted, if not overborne, by the protestation of an individual shareholder. I therefore conclude that the correct application of Community law in this case is so obvious as to leave no scope for any reasonable doubt; that recourse to the Court of Justice is unnecessary; and that the appeal should be allowed and the cross-appeal dismissed.'

Tennent v City of Glasgow Bank (1879) 4 App Cas 615 House of Lords (Earl Cairns LC, Lords Hatherley, Selbourne and Gordon)

Loss of the right to rescind – allotment of shares

Facts
On 5 October the company directors sent out notices of an extraordinary general meeting. A fortnight later, this action was started by the plaintiff to rescind an allotment on the basis of fraudulent misrepresentation by the directors to induce him to take the shares. The day after his action was filed a resolution to wind up the company was passed.

Held
It was too late for the plaintiff to rescind.

Earl Cairns LC:

'... The case of *Oakes* v *Turquand* (1867) LR 2 HL 235 however, while it decided negatively that a contract could not be rescinded on the ground of fraud after a winding up had commenced, did not decide affirmatively the converse proposition, that up to the time of the commencement of a winding up a contract to take shares could be rescinded upon the ground of fraud. Whether it can or not be so rescinded up to that time must, I think, depend upon the particular circumstances of the case.

In an ordinary partnership, not formed on the joint stock principle, it is impossible, as a general rule, for a partner at any time to retire from or repudiate the partnership without satisfying, or remaining bound to satisfy, the liabilities of the partnership. He may have been induced by his co-partners by fraud to enter into the partnership, and that may be a ground for relief against them, but it is no ground for getting rid of a liability to creditors. This is the case whether the partnership is a going concern, or whether it has stopped payment or become insolvent. In the case of a joint stock company, however, the shares are in their nature and creation transferable, and transferable without the consent of creditors, and a shareholder, so long as the company is a going concern, can, by transferring his shares, get rid of his liability to creditors, either immediately or after a certain interval. The assumption is that, while the company is a going concern, no creditor has any specific right to retain the individual liability of any particular shareholder.

It is on the same or on a similar principle that, so long as the company is a going concern, a shareholder who has been induced to take up shares by the fraud of the company has a right to throw back his shares upon the company without reference to any claims of creditors. He would have a right to transfer his shares without reference to creditors. The company, as a going concern, is assumed to be solvent, and able to meet its engagements, and to have a surplus, and the company being solvent, its duty to pay the repudiating shareholder what is due to him, and to take the shares off his hands, is an affair of the company and not of its creditors.

But if the company has become insolvent, and has stopped payment, then, even irrespective of winding up, a wholly different state of things appears to me to arise. The assumption of new liabilities under such circumstances is an affair not of the company but of its creditors. The repudiation of shares which, while the company was solvent, would not or need not have inflicted any injury upon creditors must now of necessity inflict a serious injury on creditors. I should, therefore, be disposed in any case to hesitate before admitting that, after a company has become insolvent and stopped payment, whether a winding up has commenced or not, a rescission of a contract to take shares could be permitted as against creditors …'

6 Capital

What is a share?

Borland's Trustee v *Steel Brothers & Co Ltd* [1901] 1 Ch 279 Chancery Division (Farwell J)

Restriction on transfer of shares in articles – definition of a share

Facts
The articles of the defendant company provided that the shares of a member who became bankrupt should be compulsorily transferable upon the giving of notice by the company, at a fair price not exceeding the par value. The plaintiff was the trustee in bankruptcy of Borland, and he was seeking a declaration that the transfer article was void on the grounds that it was repugnant to absolute ownership, or as tending to perpetuity.

Held
The provision in the articles was valid. It was not repugnant because to treat it as such was to misconceive what a share in a company really is. It was not tending to perpetuity because the rule against perpetuities had no application to person al contracts such as this.

Farewell J:
(after stating the facts and referring to the articles of association:)

'It is said that the provisions of these articles compel a man at any time during the continuance of this company to sell his shares to particular persons at a particular price to be ascertained in the manner prescribed in the articles. Two arguments have been founded on that. It is said, first of all, that such provisions are regugnant to absolute ownership. They are likened to the case of a settlor or testator who settles or gives a sum of money subject to executory limitations which are to arise in the future, interpreting the articles as if they provided that if at any time hereafter, during centuries to come, the company should desire the shares of a particular person, not being a manager or assistant, he must sell them. To my mind that is applying to company law a principle which is wholly inapplicable thereto. It is the first time that any such suggestion has been made, and it rests, I think, on a misconception of what a share in a company really is. A share, according to the plaintiff's argument, is a sum of money which is dealt with in a particular manner by what are called for the purpose of argument executory limitations. To my mind it is nothing of the sort. A share is the interest of a shareholder in the company measured by a sum of money, for the purpose of liability in the first place, and of interest in the second, but also consisting of a series of mutual covenants entered into by all the shareholders inter se in accordance with s16 of the Companies Act 1862 [now s14 of the Companies Act 1985].

The contract contained in the articles of association is one of the original incidents of the share. A share is not a sum of money settled in the way suggested, but is an interest measured by a sum of money and made up of various rights contained in the contract, including the right to a sum of money of a more or less amount. ...

125

Then it is said that this is contrary to the rule against perpetuity. Now, in my opinion the rule against perpetuity has no application whatever to personal contracts.'

Classes of shares

Andrews v *Gas Meter Company* [1897] 1 Ch 361 Court of Appeal (Lindley, A L Smith and Rigby LJJ)

Creation of different classes of shares by an alteration of the articles

Facts

The company was incorporated with a nominal capital of £60,000 divided into 600 shares of £100 each and it had power under its articles to increase its capital. In 1865 the company wished to purchase a business of manufacturing meters from the estate of one John West. The articles were amended to permit the company to issue preference shares carrying a 5 per cent preferential non-cumulative dividend but no further shares rights of participation in profits. The company then issued 100 such shares of £100 each to the estate of John West. The company prospered and from the issue of the preference shares in 1865 it paid the 5 per cent dividend regularly but was able to pay dividends on the ordinary shares of between 6 and 17 1/2 per cent. In addition, over £35,000 profits had been applied to capital purposes which the company now intended to re-transfer to the revenue account and distribute among the members. The question arose whether the preference shareholders had any rights in this £35,000. On behalf of the preference shareholders it was argued, inter alia, that the company had no power to create a preference between different classes of share and that the preference shareholders were entitled to rank as ordinary shareholders. Kekewich J held that he was bound by *Hutton* v *Scarborough Cliff Hotel Co* where it was held that a company had no power to alter its articles to create new preferential shares as this was an alteration of the constitution of the company. However, he concluded that the holders of the so-called preferential shares were not members of the company and that they were only entitled to restitution of the money they had contributed to the company. The preference shareholders appealed claiming only that they were entitled to a preferential dividend of 5 per cent.

Held

A company which did not have power in its memorandum or articles to issue preference shares could alter its articles by special resolution to permit the issue of such shares by way of increase of capital. *Hutton* v *Scarborough Cliff Hotel Co* (1865) 2 Dr & Sm 521 overruled.

Lindley LJ:

'... By s8 of the Act the memorandum is to state the amount of the original capital and the number of shares into which it is divided, yet in other respects the rights of the shareholders in respect of their shares and the terms on which additional capital may be raised are matters to be regulated by the articles of association rather than by the memorandum, and are, therefore, matters which (unless provided for in the memorandum, as in *Ashbury* v *Watson* (1885) 30 Ch D 376) may be determined by the company from time to time by special resolution pursuant to s50 of the Act. This view, however, clearly negatives the doctrine that there is a condition in the memorandum of association that all shareholders are to be on an equality unless the memorandum itself shows the contrary. That proposition is, in our opinion, unsound. Its unsoundness was distinctly pointed out by Lord Macnaghten in *British and American Trustee and Finance Corporation* v *Couper* [1894] AC 416 ...'

Birch v *Cropper* (1889) 14 App Cas 525 House of Lords (Lords Herschell, Fitzgerald and Macnaghten)

Distribution of surplus assets on a winding up

Facts

The Bridgewater Navigation Co was formed in 1872 and at first its capital was to be £1,300,000 being 130,000 shares of £10 each. In April 1880 100,000 shares had been issued as ordinary shares and it was determined that the remaining 30,000 shares should be issued as preference shares with a 5 per cent preferential dividend. These shares were issued on terms that they were paid up in full while the ordinary shares were only paid up as to £3 10s per share. In 1887 the Manchester Ship Canal Co purchased the company's undertaking for £1,710,000 and a resolution was passed for the voluntary winding-up of the Bridgewater Co. The liquidator repaid the amount of capital due to the preference and ordinary shareholders as paid up on their shares and afterwards had a surplus of about £550,000. The question arose as to how this surplus should be distributed between the preference and ordinary shareholders. The Court of Appeal held that distribution should be in proportion to the amounts paid up on the shares.

On appeal:

Held

Reversing the Court of Appeal, that the surplus should be divided among all the shareholders in proportion to the shares held by them respectively.

Lord Macnaghten:

'... The question before your Lordships is this. In the liquidation of a company limited by shares, what is the proper mode of distributing assets not required for payment of debts and liabilities, or for the costs of the winding-up, or for the adjustment of the rights of the contributories among themselves, so far, at any rate, as such rights have hitherto been understood and recognised? As incidental to that question, your Lordships have to consider whether the mode of distribution can be in any way affected by one or more of the following circumstances: (i) That the shares of the company were paid up unequally, some being fully-paid up, others being paid up only in part. (ii) That the fully-paid up shares were issued separately as preference shares, carrying a preferential dividend of 5 per cent, without any further right to participate in the profits of the business. (iii) That by the regulations of the company dividends on the company's shares were payable in proportion to the amounts paid up thereon.

The answer, as it seems to me, must depend on the principle applicable to companies limited by shares, and on the provisions contained in the Companies Act 1862. It is perhaps rather beside the mark to discuss the general doctrines of partnership, and to examine particular cases of partnership contracts. The scheme of the Act and the directions to be found there are, I think, a safer guide than any analogies can be. Every person who becomes a member of a company limited by shares of equal amount becomes entitled to a proportionate part in the capital of the company, and, unless it be otherwise provided by the regulations of the company, entitled, as a necessary consequence, to the same proportionate part in all the property of the company, including its uncalled capital. He is liable in respect of all moneys unpaid on his shares to pay up every call that is duly made upon him. But he does not by such payment acquire any further or other interest in the capital of the company. His share in the capital is just what it was before. His liability to the company is diminished by the amount paid. His contribution is merged in the common fund; and that is all.

When the company is wound up new rights and liabilities arise. The power of the directors to make calls is at an end; but every present member, so far as his shares are unpaid, is liable to contribute to the assets of the company to an amount sufficient for the payment of its debts and liabilities, the costs of winding-up, and such sums as may be required for the adjustment of the rights of the contributories among themselves ...

... In the case of winding up everything is changed. The assets have to be distributed. The rights arising from unequal contributions on shares of equal amounts must be adjusted, and the property of the company, including its uncalled capital not required to satisfy prior claims, must be applied for that purpose. But when those rights are adjusted, when the capital is equalised, what equity founded on inequality of contributions can possibly remain? The rights and interests of the contributories in the company must then be simply in proportion to their shares. This was the view of Stirling J, in the case I have referred to. Your Lordships, however, were reminded more than once that "the Act does not say so". You were told that, if that had been the meaning of the legislature, nothing would have been more easy than to have said so in so many words. It is easy, no doubt, to make a slip; but I should have been rather surprised if the framers of this Act, which is a model of careful and accurate drafting, had forgotten that the provisions for voluntary liquidation apply to some companies which have not a capital divided into shares.

The ordinary shareholders say that the preference shareholders are entitled to a return of their capital, with 5 per cent interest up to the day of payment, and to nothing more. That is treating them as if they were debenture-holders liable to be pad off at a moment's notice. Then they say that at the utmost the preference shareholders are only entitled to the capital value of a perpetual annuity of 5 per cent upon the amounts paid up by them. That is treating them as if they were holders of irredeemable debentures; but they are not debenture-holders at all. For some reason or other, the company invited them to come in as shareholders, and they must be treated as having all the rights of shareholders, except so far as they renounced those rights on their admission to the company. There was an express bargain made as to their rights in respect of profits arising from the business of the company. But there was no bargain – no provision of any sort – affecting their rights as shareholders in the capital of the company.

Then the preference shareholders say to the ordinary shareholders: "We have paid up the whole of the amount due on our shares; you have paid but a fraction on yours. The prosperity of a company results from its paid-up capital; distribution must be in proportion to contribution. The surplus assets must be divided in proportion to the amounts paid up on the shares." That seems to me to be ignoring altogether the elementary principles applicable to joint-stock companies of this description. I think it rather leads to confusion to speak of the assets which are the subject of this application as "surplus assets", as if they were an accretion or addition to the capital of the company capable of being distinguished from it, and open to different considerations. They are part and parcel of the property of the company – part and parcel of the joint-stock or common fund – which at the date of the winding-up represented the capital of the company. It is through their shares in the capital, and through their shares of the property of the company, that members of a company limited by shares became entitled to participate in the property of the company. The shares in this company were all of the same amount. Every contributory who held a preference share at the date of the winding up must have taken that share, and must have held it on the terms of paying up all calls duly made upon his respect thereof. In paying up his shares in full he has done no more than he contracted to do. Why should he have more than he bargained for? Every contributory who was the holder of an ordinary share at the date of the winding up took his share and held it, on similar terms. He has done all he contracted to do; why should he have less than his bargain? When the preference shareholders and the ordinary shareholders are once placed on exactly the same footing in regard to the amounts paid up upon their shares, what is there to alter rights which were the subject of express contract?

Observe how unreasonable this contention on the part of the preference shareholders is. They do not propose to unravel the accounts of the company or to inquire how long the company had the benefit of the contributions from each of the two classes of shareholders, or what was the position of the company when those contributions were made. It may be that the founders of the company made a lucky hit at the outset. Good management may have had something to do with the success of the company. And after all, something may perhaps be put down to the fact that the Ship Canal company was forced to buy a property which lay directly in the track of its undertaking. The preference shareholders discard all these considerations. They take the date of the winding up as the date which governs the rights of the shareholders in the distribution of what they call surplus assets. They say: "Our payments then were in excess of the payments of the ordinary shareholders". But that is a mere accident. There was a time not very long ago when the contributions of the ordinary shareholders were in advance of those of the preference shareholders. If the company had gone on they might soon have been on a level again. The prosperity of the company was not due to the contributions of the preference shareholders. They did not come on the scene till just before the last act. It so happens that the very same directors' report which records their final payment calls attention to the ship canal as a practical project. When the preference shareholders were invited to come in the prosperity of the company was assured. The business was flourishing; The shareholders were receiving dividends of 8 per cent, with occasional bonuses, and the directors were in a position to borrow at 4 per cent. Instead of borrowing, the company resolved to issue these preference shares, on the condition that they should be fully paid up within a limited time. As the company chose to admit the preference shareholders as shareholders, they must have the rights of shareholders; but I cannot see why they should claim more.

Then it was said on behalf of the preference shareholders that the provision for payment of dividends in proportion to the amount paid up on the shares leads to an inference that the distribution of surplus assets was to be made in the same proportion. I do not think that it leads to any inference of the kind. It is a very common provision nowadays, though it is not what you find in table A; and it is a very reasonable provision, because during the continuance of the company, and while it is a going concern, it prevents any sense of dissatisfaction on the part of those who have paid more on their shares than their fellow shareholders of a different issue. But when it has come to an end I cannot see how it can be used to regulate or disturb rights with which it had nothing to do even while it was in force ...'

F De Jong & Co Ltd, Re [1946] Ch 211 Court of Appeal (Lord Greene MR, Morton and Somervell LJJ)

Payment of cumulative preference dividend on a winding up

Facts
The company was incorporated in 1905 with a capital of £25,000 divided into 10,000 preference shares of £1 each and 15,000 ordinary shares of £1 each. Of these shares 5,006 of the preference shares and all of the ordinary shares had been issued. A special resolution was passed in March 1944 for the voluntary winding up of the company. All the creditors were paid in full and after the capital on the preference shares was repaid there was a balance of £3,370. The liquidator took out a summons that it might be determined whether on the true construction of the articles the preference shareholders were entitled to receive out of this balance the arrears of the cumulative preference dividend.

Held
On the true construction of the memorandum and articles the preference shareholders had priority over the ordinary shareholders in respect of arrears of the preference dividends.

Morton LJ:

'The question which we have to determine is stated in the summons accurately as follows: "Whether upon the true construction of the articles of association of the company the holders of the preference shares are entitled to receive out of the net surplus assets of the company a sum equivalent to the amount of the arrears of the cumulative preferential dividend thereon accrued since June 30, 1940." Prima facie, and in the absence of words making provision for it in the memorandum and articles of association, cumulative preference dividends are not payable out of the assets in a winding up. It is a question of construction in each case whether the memorandum or articles provide that such arrears of dividend shall be payable in a winding up.

I turn to art 15. The vital sentence in it falls into three parts and I shall consider each part separately, and then their combined effect. The first part is this: "The said preference shares shall carry a right to a fixed cumulative preferential dividend at the rate of 6 per cent per annum on the capital for the time being paid up thereon respectively." That part of the sentence is clear. It is dealing with dividends payable out of the profits of the company, that is, dividends in the true and ordinary sense while the company is a going concern. It is to be noted that the word "preferential" clearly shows that the dividend on those preference shares is to have priority over the dividend on the ordinary shares. The next part of the sentence is: "and shall have priority as to dividend and capital over the other shares in the capital for the time being." To what does that portion of the sentence refer? To my mind it refers to the rights in a winding up. I say that for three reasons. First, the provision giving priority as to dividend must, I think, refer to a winding-up because the word "preferential" has already established the priority of the preference shareholders as to dividend, while the company is a going concern. Secondly, the words "priority as to ... capital" refer naturally to a distribution of the assets in the winding up. It was suggested by Mr Berkeley, in his excellent argument for the appellant, that those words might refer to a return of capital, or a reduction of capital, while the company was a going concern. But I cannot think it is a natural construction to refer those words to that event. I think the natural construction is that they refer to the time when it is contemplated that the assets will be distributed, that is to say, the winding up. The third reason is that one would expect to find somewhere in the articles provisions dealing, not only with the rights of the preference shareholders as to dividends while the company is a going concern, but also with the rights of the preference shareholders in a winding up. Unless the passage which I have just read deals with those rights in a winding up there is no provision at all informing the preference shareholders what their rights in a winding up are to be. Mr Berkeley placed some reliance on the words "for the time being", but I do not think they really assist his argument. The words "in the capital for the time being" refer merely, I think, to the capital at the time when it becomes relevant to consider what are the respective rights of the shareholders inter se.

Further, if that passage refers to a winding up, I think the word "dividend" must mean "arrears of dividend". The prima facie meaning of dividend was thus stated by Stirling LJ in *In re Crichton's Oil Co* [1902] 2 Ch 86: "A dividend means prima facie a payment made to the shareholders while the company is a going concern." But, in the present case, finding, as I do, this word in a passage which refers to a winding up, it seems to me that one must give the meaning of "arrears of dividend" to it; the priority as to dividend in the true sense has been already provided for by the first of the three passages.

I now come to the third passage, "but shall not carry any further right to participate in the profits or assets". That passage to my mind rounds off the description of the rights of the preference shareholders, and prevents them from having, firstly, any more than their fixed cumulative preferential dividend out of the profits of the company, and secondly, any more than the arrears of dividend and return of capital in a winding up. In other words, it provides that the preference shareholders are to have no further right to share in the surplus profits while the company is a going concern, or in the surplus assets in a winding-up. So read, I think that the whole sentence is given a coherent and sensible meaning, and the whole of its provisions are well balanced and result in a comprehensive definition of the rights of the preference shareholders. That was the conclusion at which Cohen J, as he then was, arrived, and I entirely agree with his decision.

We were referred to two recent cases where the wording of the relevant clause in the memorandum bore some resemblance to the article in the present case. I shall refer to them briefly because, as a rule, little assistance is gained from considering provisions in different language when the court is dealing with a question of construction. In *In re Walter Symons Ltd* [1934] Ch 308, which came before Maugham J, as he then was, the relevant clause of the memorandum of association provided: the preference shares "shall confer the right to a fixed cumulative preferential dividend at the rate of 12 per cent per annum on the capital for the time being paid up thereon, and to half the distributable surplus profits which in respect of each year shall remain after paying or providing for the payment of a dividend for such year at the rate of 10 per cent per annum on the capital for the time being paid up on the ordinary shares, and shall rank both as regards dividends and capital in priority to the ordinary shares, but shall not confer the right to any further participation in profits or assets". Maugham J came to the conclusion that the word "dividend" in the phrase "shall rank both as regards dividend and capital in priority to the ordinary shares" was intended to refer to the arrears of dividend in a winding up. It is true that he placed some reliance on the word "rank" in that clause, but his reasoning is, I think, of assistance in the present case. It is to be noted that he found no difficulty in deciding that the word "dividend" in that case meant arrears of dividend. The other case is *In re Wood Skinner & Co* [1944] Ch 323. In that case Cohen J on the wording of the article before him, came to the conclusion that the preference shareholders were not entitled to have priority as to arrears of their dividends in a winding-up. For my part, I see no reason to differ from either of these decisions. In the latter case the clause in the memorandum of association was as follows: "Such preference shares shall confer the right to a fixed cumulative dividend" – not, it is to be noted, preferential dividend or preference dividend – "of £6 per cent per annum on the capital paid up thereon and shall rank both as regards dividends and capital in priority to the ordinary shares with power to increase the capital." In that case it was not necessary for Cohen J to treat the words "shall rank both as regards dividends and capital" as conferring priority in respect of the arrears of the cumulative preferential dividend in a winding up, because up to that point there had been no statement that the preference shareholders were to have a preference dividend. I think that is a point which distinguishes *In re Wood Skinner & Co* from the present case, in which the court is almost driven to the conclusion that the words "shall have priority as to dividend" must refer to a winding up, since priority as to dividend while the company is a going concern has already been provided for.

In my view, this appeal should be dismissed.'

Isle of Thanet Electricity Supply Co Ltd, Re [1950] Ch 161 Court of Appeal (Sir Raymond Evershed MR, Asquith LJ and Wynn-Parry J)

Right to participate in surplus assets on a winding up

Facts
The company was incorporated in 1896 but adopted new articles in 1929 and under these art 3 defined the rights of the shareholders which provided: 'The issued preference shares shall confer on the holders the right to a fixed cumulative preferential dividend at the rate of £6 per cent per annum ... in priority to the ordinary shares and the profits ... after paying or providing for the said preferential dividend ... and the preference shares shall confer a right in a winding up of the company to repayment of capital, together with arrears (if any) and whether earned or not of the preferential dividend to the date of the commencement of the winding up in priority to the ordinary shares.' The company's undertaking was nationalised in 1946 and it went into voluntary liquidation. At that date the company's capital consisted of £282,000 preference stock and £150,000 ordinary stock. The arrears of dividend on preference stock was paid as was the capital on both the preference and the ordinary stock. There was a surplus of assets. The question arose as to how this surplus should be distributed between the preference and ordinary stockholders. Roxburgh J held that both preference and ordinary stockholders were entitled to participate in it. On appeal

Held
The onus of proof was on the preference stockholders to show that they were entitled to participate in the surplus assets since they had failed to show that there was anything in the articles which entitled them to do so.

Wynn-Parry J:

'Having regard to the view which I take of the opinions of the majority of the House of Lords in the *Scottish Insurance Corporation Case*, it appears to me to be unnecessary to embark on any review of the earlier authorities, all of which were considered in that case, and, in my judgment, the effect of the authorities as now in force is to establish the two principles for which counsel for the ordinary stockholder contended: first, that, in construing an article which deals with rights to share in profits, ie dividend rights and rights to share in the company's property in a liquidation, the same principle is applicable; and, secondly, that that principle is that, where the articles set out the rights attached to a class of sharess to participate in profits while the company is a going concern, or to shares in the property of the company in liquidation, prima facie, the rights so set out are in each case exhaustive.'

Scottish Insurance Corporation Ltd v *Wilsons & Clyde Coal Company Ltd* [1949] AC 462 House of Lords (Viscount Maugham, Lords Simonds, Normand and Morton)

Return of capital – right to surplus assets on winding up

Facts

Wilson's & Clyde was incorporated in 1876 to operate certain collieries in Lanarkshire. In 1947 the assets of the company were nationalised under the Coal Industry Nationalisation Act 1946 and vested in the National Coal Board. Since the company's business was at an end it was its intention to go into voluntary liquidation. In 1947 the company's share capital stood at £850,000 and the issued capital at £725,000 being £1 shares of which 40,000 were first preference 7 per cent cumulative stock, 10,000 second preference cumulative stock and 675,000 ordinary stock. The shares had been converted into stock in 1937. Since compensation was payable to the company under the Coal Industry Nationalisation Act 1946 the liquidation of the company was to be postponed until this was paid. In September 1947, before the compensation was paid, an extraordinary general meeting was held at which a resolution was passed by which the share capital of the company was to be reduced from £850,000 to £462,500 being £337,500 of ordinary stock and 125,000 £1 ordinary shares. All the preference shareholders were to be repaid in full and the ordinary stockholders repaid 10s in respect of each £1 share they held. Some preference shareholders voted for and some against this resolution. The company lodged a petition with the court to have the reduction confirmed. Scottish Insurance, who held about 45 per cent of the preference stock, opposed the reduction on the following grounds; (i) they were deprived of the advantages of their investment which had a value well above par for many years; (ii) it deprived them of the right to participate in the liquidation and in the division of the company's surplus assets; (iii) it deprived them of the opportunity of their right to adjustments to compensate them for the loss of expected income yield under the Coal Industry Nationalisation Act 1946. Under the company's articles art 17 gave it the right to reduce its capital by special resolution. Article 128 provided that profits could be set aside in a reserve fund or written off and any surplus thereafter was to be applied in paying the cumulative dividend to the preference shareholders and the residue of profits were to be divisible among ordinary shareholders. Article 139 enabled the directors to set aside out of profits such sum as they thought proper as a reserve fund and which might be used in paying off the preference capital. Article 141(a) enabled the company to convert any individual profits into capital and to distribute it among ordinary stockholders. Articles 159 and 160 provided that in the event of winding up the preference stock ranked before the ordinary stock to the extent of repayment of the amounts called up and paid thereon.

Held

The reduction would be confirmed as it was neither unfair nor inequitable because in any event the preference stockholders would not be entitled to participate in the surplus assets in a winding up; they would only receive a return of their paid up capital in such circumstances. Thus, they could not object to a return of their capital if this was done via a reduction instead of a liquidation.

Lord Simonds:

'… It is clear from the authorities, and would be clear without them, that, subject to any relevant provision of the general law, the rights inter se of preference and ordinary shareholders must depend on the terms of the instrument which contains the bargain that they have made with the company and each other. This means that there is a question to be determined and, undesirable though it may be that fine distinctions should be drawn in commercial documents such as articles of association of a company, your Lordships cannot decide that the articles here under review have a particular meaning, because to somewhat similar articles in such cases as Re William Metcalfe & Sons Ltd [1933] Ch 142 that meaning has been judicially attributed. I have earlier in this opinion stated the relevant articles, and, reading them as a whole, I come to the conclusion that arts 159 and 160 are exhaustive of the rights of the preference shareholders in a winding up. The whole tenor of the articles, as I have already pointed out, is to leave the ordinary stockholders masters of the situation. If there are "surplus assets", it is because the ordinary stockholders have contrived that it should be so, and, though this is not decisive in determining what the parties meant by their bargain it is of some weight that it should be in the power of one class so to act that there will or will not be surplus assets. There is aother somewhat general consideration which also, I think, deserves attention. If the contrary view of arts 159 and 160 is the right one and the preference stockholders are entitled to a share in surplus assets, the question will still arise what those surplus assets are. For the profits, though undrawn, belong, subject to the payment of the preference dividend, to the ordinary stockholders, and, in so far as surplus assets are attributable to undrawn profit, the preference stockholders have no right to them. This appears to follow from the decision of the Court of Appeal in Re Bridgewater Navigation Co [1891] 2 Ch 317 in which the judgment of the House of Lords in Birch v Cropper (1889) 14 App Cas 525 is worked out. This again is not decisive, but I am unwilling to suppose that the parties intended a bargain which would involve an investigation of an artificial and elaborate character into the nature and origin of surplus assets.

Apart, however, from those more general considerations the words of the specifically relevant articles, "rank before the other shares on the property of the company to the extent of repayment of the amounts called up and paid thereon" appear to me apt to define exhaustively the rights of the preference stockholders in a winding up. Similar words, in *Will v United Lankat Plantations Co Ltd* [1914] AC 11 "rank, both as regards capital and dividend, in priority to the other shares", were held to define exhaustively the rights of preference shareholders to dividend, and I do not find in the speeches of Viscount Haldane LC or Lord Loreburn in that case any suggestions that a different result would have followed if the dispute had been in regard to capital. I do not ignore that in the same case in the Court of Appeal the distinction between dividend and capital was expressly made by both Cozens-Hardy MR and Farwell LJ, and that in *Will's* case and *Re William Metcalfe & Sons Ltd* respectively. In *Collaroy Co Ltd v Giffard* [1928] Ch 144 Astbury J, after reviewing the authorities, including his own earlier decision in *Re Fraser and Chalmers Ltd* [1919] 2 Ch 114 said, in regard to capital and dividend preference respectively:

"But whether the considerations affecting them are 'entirely different' is a question of some difficulty."

He approved the proposition there urged by the ordinary shareholders that a fixed return of capital to shareholders in a winding up is just as artificial as a provision for a fixed dividend, and that, if the latter is regarded as exhaustive, there is no prima facie reason why the former should not be similarly regarded. So, also, that learned judge was influenced by the consideration which appears to me to have much weight, that, if such an article as our art 159 is regarded as a complete definition of the rights of the preference stockholders in a winding up, then there is a logical consistency between their rights before and after the company is put into liquidation. In effect, I prefer the reasoning of Astbury J in *Collaroy Co Ltd v Giffard* to that of Eve J and the Court of Appeal in *Re William Metcalfe & Sons Ltd.* Counsel for the appellants in the present case sought to draw a distinction between the right to repayment of capital and the right to some further share in surplus assets and pointed to the fact that arts 159 and 160 said nothing about surplus assets. But this distinction is not, in my opinion, in the present context a valid one. Articles 159 and 160 are the first two in a number of articles headed "Distribution of assets on winding up", and there is nothing in them to suggest a distinction between "property of the company", the expression in fact used in arts 159 and 160, required for repayment of capital or distributable as surplus assets. Nor, I think, is the latter expression used throughout the articles: it is perhaps an expression which is better avoided.

Finally, on this part of the case I ought to deal with an observation made by Lord Macnaghten in *Birch v Cropper* on which counsel for the appellants relied. Lord Macnaghten said:

"... they (the preference shareholders) must be treated as having all the rights of shareholders, except so far as they renounced those rights on their admission to the company."

But, in my opinion, Lord Macnaghten can have meant nothing more than that the rights of the parties depended on the bargain that they had made and that the terms of the bargain must be ascertained by a consideration of the articles of association and any other relevant document, a task which I have endeavoured in this case to discharge. I cannot think that Lord Macnaghten intended to introduce some new principle of construction and to lay down that preference shareholders are entitled to share in surplus assets unless they expressly and specifically renounce that right. For these reasons I reject the assumption on which the appellants' first plea is founded.

I can deal shortly with the other element of unfairness on which the appellants rely, viz. that they have been prematurely deprived of a favourable investment. Much that I have already said is equally applicable here. Funds being available for payment off of capital, the natural order is to pay off that capital which has priority and I see no glimmer of unfairness in the company doing so at the earliest possible moment, particularly if, their undertaking having been wrested from them, they can no longer earn 7 per cent or anything like it on their money ...'

Staples v *Eastman Photographic Materials Co* [1896] 2 Ch 303 Court of Appeal (Lindley, Lopes and Kay LJJ)

Preference shares – whether dividends were cumulative

Facts
The memorandum of the company provided by cl 5: 'The capital of the company is £150,000 divided into 10,000 ordinary shares of £10 each and 5,000 preference shares of £10 each. The holders of preference shares shall be entitled out of the net profits of each year to a preference dividend at the rate of £10 per cent per annum on the amount for the time being paid or deemed to be paid thereon. After payment of such preferential dividend the holders of ordinary shares shall be entitled to a like dividend at the rate of £10 per cent per annum on the amount paid on such ordinary shares. Subject as aforesaid, the preference and ordinary shares shall rank equally for dividend.' In 1892, 1893 and 1894 the company either did not pay dividends or was only able to pay part of the dividend on the preference shares due to low profits. In 1895 there were substantial profits and some of the preference shareholders sought a declaration that they were entitled to arrears of dividend.

Held
On the construction of cl 5 the dividends were not cumulative.

Lindley LJ:

'... The ordinary meaning of the language in this clause appears to me to be this: that the profits of each year are to be divided as follows – give 10 per cent first to the preference shareholders, and then, if the profits are sufficient for the purpose, 10 per cent to the ordinary shareholders, and then, if there is a surplus, that it is to be divided equally amongst the shareholders. That is the view which I take, and I do not think any of the cases warrant a decision to the contrary. The language in *Henry* v *Great Northern Railway Co* (1857) 1 De G & J 606 was such as to make it tolerably plain that what was there promised to the preference shareholders was 10 per cent, and it was called interest or dividend. In the case of *Webb* v *Earle* (1875) LR 20 Eq 556 the words were "a dividend of 10 per cent per annum payable half-yearly" without any context as we have here – without anything to show out of what it was to be paid ...'

Webb v *Earle* (1875) LR 20 Eq 556 Court of Chancery (Sir George Jessel MR)

Preference shares – the payment of dividends

Facts

The West India and Panama Telegraph Co Ltd was registered in 1870 with 65,000 shares of £10 each. In 1873 the directors under the authority of the articles and with the sanction of a general meeting issued 25,000 preference shares of £10 each which were to carry a dividend of £10 per cent per annum. All the preference shares were allotted. A further issue of preference shares was made in 1874. The plaintiff, who held 50 ordinary shares in the company, claimed that where there were insufficient profits to pay the preference shareholders in one year that they had no right to have their back dividends made good out of subsequent profits to the detriment of ordinary shareholders.

Held

If the profits of any year were insufficient to pay the dividend on the preference shares in full, the deficiency might be made good out of subsequent profits.

Sir G Jessel MR

'... Now it has been said in *Henry* v *Great Northern Railway Company* , that there is no magic in the word "dividend"; it may be interest, or it may be an aliquot proportion of dividend, or it may be the dividend itself, that is, the fund to be divided; what it means can only be decided by looking at the words used in the case in question. Here the shareholders are told that the new capital carries dividend at the rate of £10 per cent per annum, payable half-yearly. What, then, does "dividend" here mean?

When you look at the resolution, articles, and letter together, it clearly means this, that the dividend on the preference shares is to be paid out of the dividend declared, if there is one, in other words, that the right is restricted to this, that it is to be paid out of what is declared so far as it will go, and that the preference shareholders cannot get any more, and that they cannot get it when there is no dividend declared. They are to have it if there is anything to pay; if there is nothing to pay they are to go without until there is something to pay; but it does not mean that if there is not enough to pay one half year they are not to have it the next half year, or the third or fourth or fifth half year.

The case is exactly the same as that put by Lord Justice Knight Bruce in *Henry* v *Great Northern Railway Company* (1857) 1 De G & J 606, from which this case, in my opinion, is not fairly distinguishable. He says this: "A, B and C, are partners in a trade, each having contributed an equal share of capital, but they agree that out of the profits £5 per cent per annum shall preferably, and in the first instance, be paid to A on his portion of the capital. The division of the profits among them is agreed to be and is periodically made. At one of the periodical divisions the profits fall short of a sufficiency to pay this amount to A, from the time to which out of the profits his interest had previously been paid. Is the deficiency not afterwards to be made good to him from profits more than adequate to answer it? I have heard no reason why not."

It really comes to nothing more than that. The preference shareholders are to have a dividend of £10 per cent per annum, but it is to be paid as on preference capital, that is, so far as the profits shall extend; there is nothing to prevent them going to the profits of a subsequent period when they are sufficient to make it up. I therefore allow the demurrer.'

Wharfedale Brewery Co Ltd, Re [1952] Ch 913 Chancery Division (Wynn-Parry J)

Preference shares – arrears of dividends paid out of surplus assets on winding up

Facts

The company was incorporated in 1906 with a capital of £30,000 divided into 3,000 £10 shares.

Subsequently the capital was increased to £80,000 by the creation of 4,000 preference shares of £10 each and 1,000 ordinary shares of £10 each. The preference shares were created with the right to a fixed cumulative dividend and were to rank 'both as regards dividend and capital in priority to the other shares but shall not confer any further right to participate in profits or surplus assets'. The company went into voluntary liquidation in January 1952 and, at that date, the arrears of dividend on the preference shares amounted to over £112,000 but the profits available for distribution amounted to only £1,700. But, there was a surplus of £62,887 in the hands of the liquidator after meeting the claims of creditors. The liquidator took out a summons to determine whether the preference shareholders were entitled to arrears of dividend out of the surplus.

Held

The surplus assets were distributable to the preference shareholders as arrears of dividend.

Wynn-Parry J:

'There is a conflict of authority on the point which I am called on to decide, namely, whether, under a provision in these terms, the preference shares are entitled to arrears of dividend, irrespective of whether or not profits were available to pay that dividend at the commencement of the liquidation.

The first case to which I have to refer is *In re WJ Hall & Co Ltd* [1909] 1 Ch 521. In that case the articles of association provided that, in the event of the company being wound up, the surplus divisible assets for the time being remaining "after paying the liabilities of the company shall be applied first, in repaying the capital paid up on the said 500 preference shares or so many thereof as may be issued for the time being, and secondly, in paying the arrears (if any) of the 5 per cent preferential dividends thereon to the commencement of the winding up" and that the balance should belong to the ordinary shareholders. The accumulated profits at the commencement of the liquidation were less than the arrears of the preference dividend, at the date. Two points were decided by Swinfen Eady J. First, he held that the preference shareholders were not entitled to claim arrears of dividend beyond the amount of the accumulated profits. Secondly, he held that arrears of dividend were payable whether declared or not. At the end of his judgment his Lordship says this: "Reading the memorandum and articles together, I hold that the preference shareholders are entitled to the arrears on their 5 per cent dividends, whether declared or not, but so far only as profits are now available."

It is difficult, with all respect to the learned judge, to see by what process of reasoning he arrived at that decision, because he was dealing with an article which provided that, in the event of the company being wound up, the surplus divisible assets should be applied inter alia in paying the arrears of the 5 per cent preferential dividend thereon. The surplus divisible assets represent no doubt a mixed fund, but a fund which for all purposes in a winding up must be treated as assets and not as partly assets and partly profits.

That decision was unfavourably commented on first by Neville J, in *In re New Chinese Antimony Co Ltd* [1916] 2 Ch 115. In that case the articles of association were substantially in a form similar to that in the earlier case. Neville J in the course of his judgment said that the rights of the preference shares were determined by the special resolution under which they were issued. He read the relevant clause, and said: "The meaning of those words is to my mind perfectly clear. We have to deal with a fund which is not capital or income or profits, but surplus assets. That is what we have to distribute. There is nothing to make any distinction between capital and income. The only point is what is meant by "arrears of the preferential dividend aforesaid".

Having discussed further the meaning of the clauses in question and having referred for support to one of the points made by Swinfen Eady J in his judgment in *In re WJ Hall & Co Ltd* so far as concerned the suggested limitation of the dividends to declared dividends, Neville J went on and said: "In that case Swinfen Eady J went on to decide that there could be no arrears of dividends payable except so far as there had been profits. With all deference, I fail to follow that part of the decision, but it does not apply to this case. I am dealing with the decision of surplus assets, not with the declaration of a dividend. I cannot see that it makes any difference whether there are profits or not." That observation, it is true, was obiter, but it is as clear an indication as a judge could give that he disagreed with the reasoning of Swinfen Eady J in the earlier case.

The case of *In re WJ Hall & Co* was further criticised in the later case of *In re Springbok Agricultural Assets Ltd* [1920] 1 Ch 563 (PO Lawrence J) ...

There is the conflict. In my judgment, I am in the same position as regards the case of *In re WJ Hall & Co Ltd* as that in which both Neville J and P O Lawrence J, respectively found themselves. That is, I am not bound by it. Indeed, it appears to me that I am in a position to say that the weight of authority, notwithstanding that the observations of both these learned judges were, in each case, obiter, is against the view of Swinfen Eady J.

Speaking with all respect to his judgment, I for myself cannot agree with his conclusion, and I find myself unable to follow the reasoning by which he arrived at that conclusion on the second point, and I therefore prefer to follow the two later decisions.

Turning back to the relevant resolution in this case, I am unable to discover any ground of distinction between the language used in this resolution which I have to consider and the material provisions in each of the three cases to which I have referred. As I have said, the effect of the modern authorities is that I must read this resolution as if after the words "and such preference shares shall rank" there were inserted "in a winding up", the resolution continuing "both as regards dividend and capital in priority to the other shares but shall not confer any further right to participate in profits or surplus assets".

In my view, the word "profits" there refers back to the phrase "to confer on the holders thereof the right to a fixed cumulative preferential dividend at the rate of 6 per cent per annum on the capital paid up thereon, respectively" – that is, it refers back to the right of the preference shareholders while the company is a going concern. Similarly, the phrase "surplus assets" refers to the provision which follows, which I have already read, beginning "and such preference shares shall rank."

Thus in my judgment it is clear that on the true construction of these resolutions, when one comes to consider the position in a winding up, the fund, and the only fund, which is to be considered is the fund which constitutes the surplus assets, and it is that fund only the distribution of which falls to be considered.'

Variation of class rights

Cumbrian Newspapers Group Ltd v Cumberland and Westmorland Herald Newspaper and Printing Co Ltd [1986] 2 All ER 816 Chancery Division (Scott J)

What is a class right? – procedure to vary a class right

Facts
Cumbrian Newspapers (CN) owned 10.67 per cent of the shares in Cumbrian Herald (CH). When CN acquired these shares in 1968 CH adopted new articles of association which gave CN (i) rights of pre-emption over other ordinary shares in CH, (ii) rights in respect of unissued shares and (iii) so long as CN held not less than 10 per cent of the shares in CH, the right to appoint a director to the board of CH. The object of these provisions was to ensure that CH would not be taken over without CN's consent. The directors of CH proposed to convene an extraordinary general meeting for the purpose of cancelling the special rights given to CN in the articles. CN claimed, inter alia, that as the rights conferred on it by the articles were class rights they could not be varied or abrogated without its consent under s125 CA 1985.

Held
The rights conferred on CN were 'rights attached to a class of shares and, therefore could not be altered except under s125 which required the consent of CN under s125(2).

Scott J:

'... Rights or benefits which may be contained in the articles can be divided into three different categories. First, there are rights or benefits which are annexed to particular shares. Classic examples of rights of this character are dividend rights and rights to participate in surplus assets on a winding up. If articles provide that particular shares carry particular rights not enjoyed by the holders of other shares, it is easy to conclude that the rights are "attached to a class of shares", for the purpose of s125 and of art 4 of table A ... Mr Howarth submitted at first that this category should be restricted to rights that were capable of being enjoyed by the holders for the time being of the shares in question. Such a restriction would exclude rights expressly attached to particular shares issued to some named individual, but expressed to determine on transfer of the shares by the named individual. Palmer's Company Precedents (17th ed 1956) Pt I, p818 contains a form for the creation of a life governor's share in a company. Mr Howarth accepted that the rights attached to a share in accordance with this precedent would be "rights attached to a class of shares". He accepted, rightly in my judgment, that a provision for the defeasance of rights on alienation of the share to which the rights were attached would not of itself prevent the rights, pre-alienation, from being properly described as "rights attached to a class of shares". The plaintiff's rights ... cannot, however, be brought within this first category. The rights were not attached to any particular shares ... The rights conferred on the plaintiff under art 12 are dependent on the plaintiff holding at least 10 per cent of the issued ordinary shares in the defendant ... Any ordinary shares in the defendant, if sufficient in number and held by the plaintiff, would entitle the plaintiff to exercise the rights.

A second category of rights or benefits which may be contained in the articles (although it may be that neither "rights" nor "benefits" is an apt description) would cover rights or benefits conferred on individuals not in the capacity of members or shareholders of the company but for ulterior reasons, connected with the administration of the company's affairs or the conduct of its business. *Eley v Positive Government Security Life Assurance Co Ltd* (1875) 1 Ex D 20 was a case where the articles of the defendant company had included (such) a provision ... They cannot be described as "rights attached to a class of shares"... it is pleaded that the plaintiff's rights ... "are privileges personal to the plaintiffs, whether or not they hold any shares in the defendant company. If this plea were well founded, the rights would fall into this second category and would not be class rights ... The purpose of the rights and privileges conferred on the plaintiff by those articles was to enable the plaintiff in its capacity as shareholder in the defendant, to obstruct an attempted take-over of the defendant. In my judgment the plaintiff's rights under those articles do not fall within this second category.

This leaves the third category. This category would cover rights or benefits that, although not attached to any particular shares, were none the less conferred on the beneficiary in the capacity of member or shareholder of the company ... In the present case the rights conferred on the plaintiff ... were ... conferred on the plaintiff as a member or shareholder of the defendant. The rights would not be enforceable by the plaintiff otherwise than as the owner of ordinary shares in the defendant. If the plaintiff were to divest itself of all its ordinary shares in the defendant, it would not then in my view, be in a position to enforce the rights in the articles. But, the rights were not attached to any particular share or shares. Enforcement by the plaintiff of the rights granted ... would require no more than ownership by the plaintiff of at least some shares in the defendant. Enforcement by the plaintiff of the rights granted under art 12 require the plaintiff to hold at least 100 per cent of the issued shares in the defendants. But any shares would do. It follows in my judgment, that the plaintiff's rights under the articles in question fall squarely within this third category. The question for decision is whether rights in this third category are within the meaning of the phrase in s125 of the 1985 Act and in art 4 of table A, "rights attached to a class of shares" ...

... A number of considerations lead me to the conclusion that the purpose of s125 ... was to deal comprehensively with the manner in which class rights in companies having a share capital could be varied or abrogated. They are these.

First, Chapter II of Part V of the 1985 Act (which includes ss125-129) is headed "Class rights". The sidenote to s125 reads "Variation of class rights". The language seems to treat "class rights" as synonymous with rights attached to any class of shares ...

Second, the use in s17(2)(b) of the 1985 Act of the expression "rights of any class of members" in connection both with companies having a share capital and with companies having no share capital, underlines the point that the expression "rights attached to any class of shares" in s125, must have been regarded by the legislature as synonymous with the former phrase, so far as companies with a share capital were concerned.

Third, the evident intention of the legislature to protect "rights attached to any class of shares" against variation or abrogation by the mere alteration of articles, would, if coupled with an intention to provide no such protection against variation or abrogation of class rights of the third category, be anomalous and arbitrary.

Fourth, if the variation of abrogation of third category rights are not dealt with by s125, then the conclusion would seem to follow that, if the rights were contained in the memorandum, the rights could not be varied or abrogated at all. The enabling provisions of s125 would obviously not apply, nor would the enabling provisios of s17. The terms of s17, to my mind, strongly suggest a legislative belief that s125 would deal with the variation or abrogation of any "special rights of any classs of member" contained in the memorandum.

Fifth, the combination of the considerations thirdly and fourthly above mentioned, leads to a further point. What sense could there be in a result under which the third category rights contained in articles were more freely alterable than "rights attached to any class of shares" contained therein, but under which third category rights contained in the memorandum were less freely alterable than "rights attached to any class of shares" contained in the memorandum? The distinction would not be merely anomalous: it would, to my mind, be perverse. For these reasons I conclude that s125 was intended by the legislature to cater for the variation or abrogation of any special rights given by the memorandum or articles of a company to any class of members, this is to say not only rights falling into the first category I have described, but also rights falling into the third category.'

Greenhalgh v *Arderne Cinemas* [1946] 1 All ER 512 Court of Appeal (Lord Greene MR, Morton and Somervell LJJ)

Variation of class rights – subdivision of shares

Facts
The plaintiff as part of a transaction for advancing money to the defendants, was allotted a number of unissued shares which were subdivided from 10s shares to 2s shares and given one vote each. Thus, the plaintiff obtained increased voting power in this way and his shares were, as regards voting, to rank pari passu with the other ordinary shares in the company. He had five times as many votes as any other shareholder for the amount of capital he contributed. Differences arose between the plaintiff and the other major shareholders, who proposed to subdivide all the other shares from 10s to 2s and thereby to make their voting power five times as great. The plaintiff objected and claimed this could only be done if a separate class meeting was first called in accordance with the articles which provided: 'If at any time the share capital is divided into different classes of share, the rights may be varied with the consent in writing of the holders of three fourths of the issued shares of that class, or with the sanction of an extraordinary resolution passed at a separate meeting of the holders of the shares of the class. The question was whether the plaintiff's rights were being 'varied'.

Held
There was no variation of class rights.

Lord Greene MR:

'Looking at the position of the original 2s ordinary shares, one asks oneself: What are the rights in respect of voting attached to that class within the meaning of art 3 of table A which are to be unalterable save with the necessary consents of the holders? The only right of voting which is attached in terms to the shares of that class is the right to have one vote per share pari passu with the other ordinary shares of the company for the time being issued. That right has not been taken away. Of course, if it had been attempted to reduce that voting right, eg by providing or attempting to provide that there should be one vote for every five of such shares, that would have been an interference with the voting rights attached to that class of shares. But nothing of the kind has been done; the right to have one vote per share is left undisturbed. In order, therefore, to make good the argument that what was done was an interference with the voting rights of that class of shares, it had to be argued, in effect, that those shares had attached to them a right within the meaning of art 3 to object to the other ordinary shares being split so as to increase their voting power: in other words, that it was a right attached to these 2s shares that they could object to any increase in the voting power attached to the 10s shares resulting from a sub-division of those shares. If an attempt had been make, without subdividing the 10s shares, to give them five votes per share, it may very well be that the rights attached to the original 2s shares would have been varied, because one of the rights attached to that class of shares was that they should have voting powers pari passu with the other ordinary shares of the company and that right might well have been affected if in the result you had two kinds of ordinary shares, one a 10s share carrying five votes and the other a 2s share carrying one vote. But that is not what was done. The present position under the resolution which is attacked is that the ordinary shares are now all 2s ordinary shares and each of them has one vote per share, and accordingly the voting power of the original 2s shares in in fact entirely pari passu with the other ordinary shares. It only shows that these things are of a technical nature; but I cannot myself see how it can be said that there is attached to the original 2s shares a right to object to the other ordinary shares having more than one vote, provided that is done, as I say, by the method of subdivision, which was the method employed here.

I now come to a point which to my mind, throws a good deal of light on the validity of the argument. It was conceded by counsel for the appellant that if the company had created a number of new ordinary shares of 2s each and had issued them, each share carrying one vote, that would not have been an interference with the rights of the original 2s shares. Had that been done, of course, it would have been just as possible to swamp the appellant's voting rights as it has turned out to be by the passing of these resolutions. I do not find anything in the answers of counsel which satisfactorily explains why it would be an interference with the 2s shares in the one case and not in the other case, because, if the 2s shares had the right to prevent the voting equilibrium being upset in the way in which it has been upset, I cannot see why they could not object to the creation of new shares which would have the same result ...'

House of Fraser v *ACGE Investments Ltd and Others* [1987] BCLC 478 House of Lords (Lord Keith of Kinkel, Lord Fraser of Tulleybelton, Lord Brandon of Oakbrook, Lord Griffiths and Lord Ackner)

Variation of class rights – return of capital preference shareholders

Facts
By special resolution the company decided to reduce its preference share capital but no class meeting of the preference shareholders was held despite art 12 of the company's articles of association. This provided that special rights attached to any class of shares could only be 'modified, commuted, affected or dealt with' with the consent of the holders of the class of shares which could be given in a number of ways. The appellants who were preference shareholders appealed against the court's decision that the preference shareholders' approval did not have to be obtained because the proposed reduction was not a variation of the class rights of the appellants under either the articles of association or under s125 of the Companies Act 1985.

Held

The appellants' appeal was dismissed. The preference shareholders were to be repaid the capital on their shares according to the article of association and consequently their rights were being fulfilled. Article 12 did not cover the situation where there was a complete cancellation of the company's shares.

Northern Engineering Industries plc, Re [1994] BCC 618 Court of Appeal (Neill, Leggatt and Millett LJJ)

Whether a reduction of capital amounted to a variation of class rights – variation and relationship with the articles

Facts

The company was seeking the court's approval of a reduction of capital, which involved paying off all of the preference shares and cancelling them. The reduction was opposed by a preference shareholder.

The company's articles provided in article 7(B) that 'rights attached to any shares shall be deemed to be varied by a reduction of capital paid up on such shares'. Article 6 required such variation to be consented to by the preference shareholders or by an extraordinary resolution passed at a separate meeting of the preference shareholders.

The preference shareholders argued that in the absence of consent or an extraordinary resolution, the court should not confirm the capital reduction. The company argued that article 7(B) only applied where there was a reduction of capital paid up on particular shares to a figure which exceeded zero. In other words, 'reduction' means something different from 'cancellation' or 'extinction'.

Held

The court declined to confirm the reduction. Article 7(B) had the effect that the proposed cancellation of the preference shares was a variation of rights attached to the preference shares and a class meeting was therefore required by article 6. As no such meeting had been held, the reduction of capital had not been carried out in accordance with the company's articles.

Millet LJ (considered s135 of the Companies Act 1985 and the authority of *Re Anglo-American Insurance Co Ltd* [1991] BCC 208, and continued):

'More compelling, in my judgment, is the particular context provided by article 7(B) itself. The 'reduction' of the capital paid up on shares of a particular class is made to require the consent of the holders of the class affected. That is obviously intended to be a protection for those shareholders. It is idle to speculate whether it was included in the articles at the insistence of those who applied to be issued with preference shares or at the instigation of the ordinary shareholders as an inducement to investors to apply for preference shares. That it was intended to protect them from some risk is undeniable. The question is: what was the risk against which the preference shareholders were to be protected? In my judgment, the conclusion is inescapable: it was to protect them from the risk which was identified by Lord Greene MR [in *Re Chatterley-Whitfield Collieries Ltd* [1948] 2 All ER 593 at p596E], that of being subjected, without their consent, to a premature repayment of their investment, in whole or in part, a risk which, absent such an article, is inherent in the shares themselves. The company's argument that, without their consent, it cannot reduce the capital paid up on their shares from £1 to 99 pence, or from £1 to one penny, but that it does not need their consent to reduce it to nothing, in my view makes a nonsense of the protection which has been afforded them. It would protect the preference shareholders from a partial repayment which would leave them with something, however large and however small, but not from a complete repayment which would leave them with nothing. Yet this is a fortiori. The suggestion that the preference shareholders were to be protected merely from the piecemeal repayment of their investment and not from its complete repayment outright appears to me to be fanciful.'

Commentary
This confirms the earlier decision of Ferris J in [1993] BCC 267.

White v *Bristol Aeroplane Co* [1953] Ch 65 Court of Appeal (Evershed MR, Denning and Romer LJJ)

Variation of class rights – increase in capital

Facts
The company had an issued share capital of £3,900,000 comprising of £600,000 5 per cent cumulative preference stock of £10 each and £3,300,000 of ordinary stock. It was proposed to increase the share capital by the issue of £660,000 preference shares of £1 each ranking pari passu with the existing preference stock and 2,640,000 shares of 10s each ranking pari passu with the existing ordinary stock. The new shares were to be issued to existing shareholders and paid for out of the company's reserve fund. A general meeting was summoned for the purpose of having the increase of capital authorised. The plaintiff sought an injunction to restrain the company from holding the general meeting or passing or acting on the resolution until a separate meeting of the holders of the preference stock had been held. At first instance Danckwerts J granted the injunction on the ground that the proposed increase in capital would affect the voting rights of the holders of the preference stock. On appeal:

Held
The increase in capital would not 'affect' the rights and privileges of the existing preference stockholders; it may affect the 'enjoyment' of the rights of the preference stockholders but this was not the same as matters affecting those rights themselves.

Evershed MR (his Lordship referred to the articles and, in particular, art 68 on which the case turned, which provided):

'... all or any of the rights or privileges attached to any class of shares forming part of the capital for the time being of the company may be affected, modified, varied, dealt with, or abrogated in any manner with the sanction of an extraordinary resolution passed at a separate meeting of the members of that class ...'

He then continued:

'... The question then is – and, indeed, I have already posed it – are the rights which I have already summarised "affected" by what is proposed? It is said in answer – and I think rightly said – no, they are not: they remain exactly as they were before; each one of the manifestations of the preference stockholders' privileges may be repeated without any change whatever after, as before, the proposed distribution. It is no doubt true that the enjoyment of, and the capacity to make effective, those rights is in a measure affected; for as I have already indicated, the existing preference stockholders will be in a less advantageous position on such occasions as entitle them to register their votes, whether at general meetings of the company or at separate meetings of their own class. But there is to my mind a distinction, and a sensible distinction, between an affecting of the rights and an affecting of the enjoyment of the rights, or of the stockholders' capacity to turn them to account ...'

Becoming a member – the share certificate

Bahia and San Francisco Railway Company Ltd, Re (1868) LR 3 QB 584 Court of Queen's Bench (Cockburn CJ, Blackburn, Mellor and Lush JJ)

Forged transfer of shares – appropriate remedy

Facts

Trittin, the registered holder of five shares in the company, left the share certificates in the hands of her broker and directed him to receive the dividends thereon. About a month later a transfer of these five shares, purporting to be made by Trittin, was made to Stocken and Goldner. The transfer and the certificates were left with the company secretary for registration and he wrote to Trittin notifying her that he had received the transfer from her. He received no reply and 10 days later removed her name from the register and placed those of Stocken and Goldner on the register as holders of these five shares. They were given share certificates for these shares. Subsequently Stocken and Goldner sold the five shares to one Bristowe, a stockbroker, and he transferred four to a Rev Burton and one to a Mrs Goodburn in pursuance to contracts made through the Stock Exchange. Subsequently it was discovered that the transfer to Stocken and Goldner was a forgery and the company was ordered to restore Trittin's name to the register under s35 CA 1862. The question then arose whether Rev Burton and Mrs Goodburn were entitled to these shares or equivalent shares in the company or whether they were entitled to damages from the company.

Held

The giving of the certificate by the company to Stocken and Goldner amounted to a statement by the company, intended by it to be acted upon by purchasers of shares in the market, that Stocken and Goldner were entitled to the shares and that Rev Burton and Mrs Goodburn, having acted on that statement, were entitled to recover from the company damages for the loss of the shares, damages to be the value of the shares at the time the company refused to recognise them as shareholders.

Cockburn, CJ:

> 'I am of opinion that our judgment must be for the claimants. If the facts are rightly understood, the case falls within the principle of *Pickard* v *Sears* 6 Ad & E 469 and *Freeman* v *Cooke* (1848) 2 Ex 654 The company are bound to keep a register of shareholders, and have power to issue certificates certifying that each individual shareholder named therein is a registered shareholder of the particular shares specified. This power of granting certificates is to give the shareholders the opportunity of more easily dealing with their shares in the market, and to afford facilities to them of selling their shares by at once showing a marketable title, and the effect of this facility is to make the shares of greater value. The power of giving certificates is, therefore, for the benefit of the company in general; and it is a declaration by the company to all the world that the person in whose name the certificate is made out, and to whom it is given, is a shareholder in the company, and it is given by the company with the intention that it shall be so used by the person to whom it is given, and acted upon in the sale and transfer of shares. It is stated in this case that the claimants acted bona fide, and did all that is required of purchasers of shares; they paid the value of the shares in money on having a transfer of the shares executed to them, and on the production of the certificates which were handed to them. It turned out that the transferors had in fact no shares, and that the company ought not to have registered them as shareholders or given them certificates, the transfer to them being a forgery. That brings the case within the principle of the decision in *Pickard* v *Sears* , as explained by the case of *Freeman* v *Cooke* , that, if you make a representation with the intention that it shall be acted upon by another, and he does so, you are estopped from denying the truth of what you represent to be the fact.

The only remaining question is, what is the redress to which the claimants are entitled? In whatever form of action they might shape their claim, and there can be no doubt that an action is maintainable, the measure of damages would be the same. They are entitled to be placed in the same position as if the shares, which they purchased owing to the company's representation, had in fact been good shares, and had been transferred to them, and the company had refused to put them on the register, and the measure of damages would be the market price of the shares at that time; if no market price at that time, then a jury would have to say what was a reasonable compensation for the loss of the shares.'

Mackley's Case (1875) 1 Ch D 247 Chancery Division (Malins V-C)

A subscriber to the memorandum will not become a member if all of the shares are allotted to other persons

Facts

A slate company was formed in 1863 and Mr Mackley subscribed the memorandum for 50 shares of £10 each on being told that a close friend of his was to be a director. This was untrue. On discovering this Mr Mackley requested that his name be removed from the company. He took no part in the management of the company and the whole of the share capital was allotted to other persons. There were no shares left which could be put in his name, his name was not on the register of members, nor did he pay any deposits or calls on any shares. Mr Mackley died in 1869 appointing his widow as his executrix. The company went into liquidation in 1874 and Mrs Mackley was placed on the list of contributories as Mr Mackley's executrix in respect of the 50shares for which he subscribed. She took out a summons to have her name removed.

Held

This should be done.

Malins, V-C:

'... Now it has occurred to me that when it appeared that there were no shares which Mr Mackley could have had if he had wanted them, the company were not in a position to say that they would continue to hold him liable for the shares for which he had signed.

It is true that this is a new case, but though the decision of no judge has been actually given upon facts like the present, it is evident that the opinion of the Lords Justices in *Evans's Case* (1867) 2 Ch 427 would have accorded with the view I have now taken if the point had arisen in that case. In that case Mr Evans had subscribed the memorandum of association of the company for ten shares, and had for a short time acted as a director. Afterwards other directors were appointed, and he never had anything more to do with the company. No shares were ever allotted to him. But, though all the shares were in the first instance allotted to other persons, it appeared that the allotment of some of them had never been confirmed in the manner required by the articles of association, and consequently there were in fact shares which might have been allotted to Mr Evans. The Lord Justice Turner, in giving judgment, says: "If indeed all the shares had been allotted to others, a question might have arisen; but 4,000 shares only were allotted subject to confirmation, and this never took place; therefore there are still 4,000 shares not allotted, and, for the shares in respect of which he must be considered allottee, he must be placed upon the list."

That remark exactly fits the present case. The Lord Justice Lord Cairns also says: "It is said that the shares which Mr Evans would have had, were allotted to other people, but it seems that the allotment was not final, and that there were left at all times shares sufficient to answer the right of Mr Evans." Can anything be more clear than that if there had been no shares he would have been relieved from liability?

In the present case no one has been deceived. It cannot be said that any creditor has given credit to the company because Mr Mackley subscribed the memorandum of association in 1863. And there is no equity on the part of any contributory. If the shareholders intended to look to Mr Mackley, they should not have allotted the shares to other persons. I am of opinion that this is an unjust demand as regards both creditors and contributories ...'

Ottos Kopje Diamond Mines Ltd, Re [1893] 1 Ch 618 Court of Appeal (Lindley, Bowen and A L Smith LJJ)

Forged share transfers

Facts

Goode, a member of the London Stock Exchange, purchased 4,300 shares at 2s 6d each in the company from a jobber. The jobber gave Goode a transfer and a share certificate sealed with the seal of the company. Goode executed the transfer and sent it with the certificate to the company for registration but the company refused to register him. It transpired that a former secretary of the company had made fraudulent transfers of shares in the company, had falsified the share register, and had, by means of fraud, induced two of the directors to affix the seal of the company to the certificate upon the faith of which Goode had paid his money. The fraud was discovered the day before Goode bought his shares. Goode applied to have the register rectified and his name inserted plus damages or, alternatively, damages by reason of the company's inability to register him as a shareholder. Stirling J ordered damages in Goode's favour, these to be assessed. The company appealed.

Held

The share certificate was not a warranty of title which would permit Goode to maintain an action at common law for damages against the company. However, it was a representation by the company intended to be shown to a purchaser at the time of purchase which estopped the company from denying its truth as against that purchaser and the company must, therefore, treat him as having a good title. Since the company had refused to register Goode as transferee whose title they were estopped from denying, Goode had a good cause of action for damages for their refusal to register.

Bowen LJ:

'... It seems to me that the first step to make clear is that the giving of the certificate, although a representation to a possible transferee, does not amount to more than a representation by the company to such transferee, which was intended to be shown by him at the time of the sale; but as between the company and the transferee the mere representation would not, unless it was fraudulent, give rise to a cause of action at common law, unless there were either a duty on the part of the company towards the transferee, or a contract at common law to make the representation good. That was the decision in *Derry v Peek* (1889) LR 14 App Cas 337. If the transferee has a right of action upon the certificate, it could only be because it was an implied warranty created between the company and him upon which an action could be brought. There was no privity at all between the company and the transferee. Neither was there any implied warranty. It was said that the case of *In re The Bahia and San Francisco Railway Company* (1868) LR 3 BQ 584 shows that there was a cause of action in the nature of an implied warranty upon the certificate, or breach of warranty arising out of the stipulation. A certificate is not like a promissory note; it does not transfer a chose in action, it is only a representation of an implied contract. *In re The Bahia and San Francisco Railway Company* was in truth, an attempt, which was successful, to make the company liable in the absence of fraud upon the estoppel created by the certificate. The way in which the court made the company liable was this: They said that if the certificate had been intended to have been acted upon, it became a document the truth of which the company could not deny as against the person to whom it was intended to be shown; and, therefore, it precluded them as against such transferee from denying the truth of what it contained – they could not be in any better position than if the statement were true; but that only obliged the company to act as if the title were good. Until, therefore, the company do something which ought not to be done, or omit to do something which ought to be done, as between them and the true owner of the shares, no cause of action would arise. But when, in addition to the other facts of the case, you have the incapacity of the company to deny their liability you must look at all the circumstances, and consider whether, having regard to the truth of the statements contained in the certificate, true by reason of the estoppel, an action would not lie against the company. That is the true view of the case in *In re The Bahia and San Francisco Railway Company*; and, seeing that no cause of action arises upon the estoppel, the court must look for the cause upon the assumption that the company could not dispute the facts stated in the certificate. There must be a refusal by the company to do what it was bound to do, or a refusal by an officer of the company to do what that officer was bound to do. The refusal relied on by Mr Buckmaster was the refusal by the acting secretary on 6 April to take in or consider the transfer. Did he, or did he not, then refuse to do that which he ought to have done?

I fully agree with what Lord Justice Lindley has said, that the company must be entitled to some time, if they want it, to consider the documents which are brought to them. I know of no case where it has been held that a man is bound to act upon a document at the moment that it is presented to him, without being allowed time to consider it. I do not think that it was intended in *In re Cawley* (1889) 42 Ch D 209 to decide that a company was not entitled to time to consider a transfer; and in *The Societe Generale de Paris* v *Walker* (1885) LR 11 App Cas 20 Lord Blackburn held that they were entitled. It does not, however, follow that the directors did exercise the discretion given them by arts 17, 18 and 23. In a case which fell within those articles it would be hard to deny them an opportunity, before determining what they would do, of seeing documents of which they knew nothing; but in the present case the directors were not in that position. They had considered the case the day before, and when the secretary had the documents presented to him on the 6th, they did not want time. They had made up their minds already, so that the refusal of the secretary to take the documents was not because the directors wanted time to consider them, but because they had made up their minds not to accept them ...'

Sheffield Corporation v *Barclay* [1905] AC 392 House of Lords (Earl of Halsbury LC, Lords Davey and Robertson)

Forged share transfers

Facts
Timbrell and Honnywill were registered as joint owners of £2,800 worth of Sheffield Corporation $3\frac{1}{2}$per cent stock. Timbrell in fraud of Honnywill forged a transfer of the stock in order to secure a loan. A bank which lent the money sent the transfer to the corporation and demanded to be registered as the holders of the stock. The corporation registered the stock in the name of the bank and, afterwards, the bank transferred the stock to holders for value who were registered in due course and they established their title against the corporation, who were estopped from denying that those whom they had registered were the stockholders entitled. After Timbrell's death Honnywill discovered the forgery and compelled the corporation to rectify the register. The question arose whether the corporation had any cause of action against the bank who caused them to act on a forged transfer.

Held
The bank was bound to indemnify the corporation upon an implied warranty that the transfer was genuine.

Lord Halsbury LC:

'... Apart from any decision upon the question (it being taken for granted all the parties were honest), I should have thought that the bank was clearly liable. They have a private bargain with a customer. Upon his assurance they take a document from him as a security for a loan, which they assume to be genuine. I do not suggest that there was any negligence – perhaps business could not go on if people were suspecting forgery in every transaction – but their position was obviously very different from that of the corporation. The corporation is simply ministerial in registering a valid transfer and issuing fresh certificates. They cannot refuse to register, and though for their own sake they will not and ought not to register or to issue certificates to a person who is not really the holder of the stock, yet they have no machinery, and they cannot inquire into the transaction out of which the transfer arises. The bank, on the other hand, is at liberty to lend their money or not. They can make any amount of inquiries if they like. If they find that an intending borrower has a co-trustee, they may ask him or the co-trustee himself whether the co-trustee would have prevented the fraud. They take the risk of the transaction and lend the money. The security given happens to be in a form that requires registration to make it available, and the bank "demand", as, if genuine transfers are brought, they are entitled to do, that the stock shall be registered in their name or that of their nominees, and they are also entitled to have fresh certificates issued to themselves or nominees. This was done, and the corporation by acting on this "demand" have incurred a considerable loss.

As I have said, I think, that if it were res integra, I should think that the bank were liable; but I do think that it is not res integra, but that it is covered by authority. In *Dugdale* v *Lovering* (1875) LR 10 CP 196, Mr Cave, arguing for the plaintiff, put the proposition thus:

"It is a general principle of law when an act is done by one person at the request of another, which act is not in itself manifestly tortious to the knowledge of the person doing it, and such act turns out to be injurious to the rights of a third party, the person doing it is entitled to an indemnity from him who requested that it should be done."

This, though only the argument of counsel, was adopted and acted upon by the court, and I believe that it accurately expresses the law ...'

Lord Davey:

'... I think that the appellants have a statutory duty to register all valid transfers, and on the demand of the transferee to issue to him a fresh certificate of title to the stock comprised therein. But, of course, it is a breach of their duty and a wrong to the existing holders of stock for the appellants to remove their names and register the stock in the name of the supposed transferee if the latter has in fact no title to require the appellants to do so. And it makes no difference that the appellants were not aware of the invalidity of the transfer or could not with reasonable diligence have discovered it. I am further of opinion that where a person invested with a statutory or common law duty of a ministerial character is called upon to exercise that duty on the request, direction, or demand of another (it does not seem to me to matter which word you use), and without any default on his own part acts in a manner which is apparently legal, but is in fact illegal and a breach of the duty, and thereby incurs liability to third parties, there is implied by law a contract by the person making the request to keep indemnified the person having the duty against any liability which may result from such exercise of the supposed duty. And it makes no difference that the person making the request is not aware of the invalidity in his title to make the request ...'

Taylor v *Midland Railway Company* (1860) 28 Beav 287 Rolls Court (Sir John Romilly MR)

Forged share transfer

Facts

Taylor and Bright carried on business in partnership as corn merchants. Part of the partnership assets consisted of 236 Midland Railway Co shares, which in 1848 had been converted into £9,440 stock. The stock was registered in the joint names of Taylor and Bright even though Bright's interest in the partnership and the shares was very small. In 1852 Bright executed a deed of transfer to the stock and forged the name of Taylor thereon. He sold the shares and received the proceeds which he spent. The company transferred the stock into the name of the purchaser on the strength of the forged transfer. After Taylor's death in 1856 the forgery was discovered and his personal representatives brought this action against the company claiming that they were bound to replace the stock to the extent of Taylor's interest therein.

Held

The transfer by Bright was void since it was a forgery and the stock of which the personal representatives of Taylor were the true owners had to be treated as standing in their names in the company's books.

Romilly MR:

'... In the present case, the shares stood in the names of two gentlemen who were both the nominal and the real owners, and they could have made a perfectly good transfer of them, but a transfer was made in which the name of one of them was forged. I adopt the doctrine laid down in *Davis* v *The Bank of England* 2 Bing 403 that the deed by which the transfer was made was a mere nullity. It is exactly the same as if a transfer had been made with the name of Mr John Taylor in blank. Assuming the forgery to be proved, which it appears to be in this case, I am of opinion that the deed amounts to nothing ...

... I therefore am of opinion, assuming the transfer to be void, that this stock, of which the plaintiff has established that he is the owner, must be treated as so much stock now standing in the company's books in the names of the two trustees. It is exactly the same as if the company had been induced, by some fraudulent representations, to make a transfer of stock, in a case where no deed at all had been executed by the trustees. The company have made a nominal transfer of stock to another person, upon an instrument which amounted to nothing, and that stock must be treated as still in their books in the names of the trustees, and which the person beneficially entitled has a right to come here to get it transferred to him ...'

Transfer, transmission and sale of shares

Bede Shipping Company Limited, Re [1917] 1 Ch 123 Court of Appeal (Lord Cozens-Hardy MR, Warrington and Scrutton LJJ)

Directors' refusal to register a transfer of shares

Facts

Under art 24 of the company's articles the directors had power to refuse registration of a transfer of shares where '... in their opinion it was contrary to the interests of the company that the proposed transferee should be a member thereof'. After the death of one of the founders of the company a dispute arose amongst his three sons over the affairs of the company. One of the sons sold some of his shares to persons ouside the family and the directors (other sons) refused to register the transfers on the ground that 'it is contrary to the interests of a company such as this, which is really a family concern, that the shares should be transferred, singly or in small lots to outside persons having no interest in, or knowledge of, shipping'. The question arose whether the directors' refusal was justified.

Held

The refusal to register the transfers was not justified since the only ground in the articles for such refusal was based on matters personal to the proposed transferee and these were not the grounds in the present case.

Cozens-Hardy MR:

'... What is the position of a shareholder in a company such as this? He has a property in his shares, a property which he is at liberty to dispose of, subject only to any express restriction which may be found in the articles of association of the company. If, for instance, to take a common case, the articles provide that before transferring to a stranger the shares shall be offered on certain terms to other shareholders, a man coming into that company takes subject to that restriction, and he cannot transfer to a stranger without having first made an offer of the shares to the shareholders. So, if there was a condition which is not common, but I conceive, quite possible, that no transfer should be made to a married woman, that condition would, I think, be perfectly good. Subject to that right, the shareholder is at liberty to transfer a share as much as he is at liberty to sell a chair or table or any other property.

In the present case we are dealing with fully paid up shares where there is no question of escaping from liability to calls or anything of that kind. But it was at one time thought that where the directors had a power to object to a transfer that could not be exercised properly unless the directors stated the grounds of the decision at which they have arrived. In the case of *Ex parte Penney* (1873) 8 Ch App 446 it was decided by the Court of Appeal (James LJ and Mellish LJ) that it was not necessary for directors to assign reasons, but the court will presume that they did exercise their power honestly and rightly, unless it appears by the document itself or by a confession on their part or by some other circumstance that they have not done so. For instance, if it had been a case not under the Companies Act but an action, then, of course, the plaintiff would have to prove his case. So anyone coming under this rule must prove his case. In the case of *Ex parte Penney* that great judge Mellish LJ says:

"The directors have no right to say, 'We will force a particular shareholder to continue a shareholder, and we will allow him to transfer his shares at all'. That would be an abuse of their power. In the same way it would be an abuse of this power to object, on any ground not applying personally to the transferee, to say, for instance, that a particular shareholder should not transfer his shares till he had given security for the calls."

That lays down a principle which seems to me to be perfectly sound and a principle which has been followed, so far as I am aware, for at least 40 years, and I should be very sorry in any way to infringe upon it. The point which is taken by Mellish LJ is this: You may look and see personally who the transferee is. There may be personal objections to him; it may be because he is a quarrelsome person, it may be because he is an uncertain person, or it may be that he is acting in the interests of a rival company, or something of that kind. All those things are fairly included in the word "personal"; but to seek to say "We will not accept any transfer of a single share from a particular shareholder who holds a large number" is, it seems to me, an abuse of the power which was conferred by the clause in the articles ...'

Lyle & Scott Ltd v *Scott's Trustees* [1959] AC 763 House of Lords (Viscount Simonds, Lords Reid, Tucker, Keith and Somervell)

Transfer of shares – compliance with the procedure in the articles

Facts
Under art 9 of Lyle & Scott Ltd's articles it was provided that '...no registered shareholder of more than one per centum of the issued ordinary share capital of the company shall, without the consent of the directors, be entitled to transfer any ordinary share ... Any such ordinary shareholder who is desirous of transferring his ordinary shares shall inform the secretary in writing of the number of ordinary shares he desires to transfer ...' Scott's trustees, who had a large holding in the company, were approached by solicitors on behalf of a take-over bidder with an offer of £3 per £1 share and accepted together with some other shareholders. An agreement was entered into with the take-over bidder by which they bound themselves to vote as he desired. This gave him control of the company in the circumstances without registering the transfer of the shares. The company sought a declaration that Scott's trustees were bound to put into effect the terms of art 9 and an order directing them to do so.

Held

The act of Scott's trustees in agreeing to sell their shares and receiving the price therefor showed that they were 'desirous of transferring' their shares within the meaning of art 9. Therefore, they were bound to put into effect the terms of art 9.

Viscount Simonds:

'... The question is not whether what has been done is a breach of the first part of the article but whether it demonstrates with sufficient clearness that Scott's trustees are persons desirous of transferring their ordinary shares. It appears to me that there is no room for doubt that this is just what they are. Here I can proceed on their admissions. For, since it is the admitted fact that they entered into the agreement for sale of their shares and have received and retain the price, it follows that, whether or not they have yet done all that they ought as vendors to do, they hold the shares as trustees for the purchaser. They are bound to do everything that in them lies to perfect the title as the holder of the shares, but everything else they must do, and it is straining credulity too far to suppose that everything else would not already have been done, if it had not been hoped to gain some tactical advantage by delay. In my opinion, (it is not open to a shareholder, who has agreed to do a certain thing and is bound to do it, to deny that he is desirous of doing it). I wish to make it quite clear, for it goes to the root of the matter, that I regard Scott's trustees as desirous of transferring their ordinary shares unless and until their agreement with Mr Fraser has been abrogated. Of this at least one acid test would be the return by them of the price they have received.

Against this view it was urged that they were not desirous of transferring their shares within the meaning of the article because they had not a general desire but a particular desire to transfer only to Mr Fraser at a certain price. (This makes nonsense of the article, the purpose of which would be wholly defeated if it did not apply to a desire to transfer to a particular person, who might be the person whom the company particularly wished to exclude) ...'

Safeguard Industrial Investments Ltd v *National Westminster Bank Ltd* [1982] 1 WLR 589 Court of Appeal (Lawton, Oliver and Fox LJJ)

Transfer of shares – compliance with the procedure in articles

Facts

A testator, who held one-sixth of the issued shares in a private company, died leaving his shares by will to the children of A. A had a substantial holding in the company as had B and the testator effectively held the balance of power, together with the plaintiff who also had one-sixth of the shares. The bank was appointed as the testator's executor and was registered as a shareholder for that purpose. It maintained the status quo. On completion of administration of the testator's estate the bank informed the plaintiff that it intended to continue to hold the shares on trust for A's children unless directed to transfer them. The plaintiff was concerned not to lose the balance of power and therefore invoked a pre-emptive right in art 7(B) of the company's articles which provided that a member wishing to transfer his shares was required to give notice of the transfer to the company and to offer the shares to other members pro rata and could not transfer them to a non-member if a member was willing to purchase them at a fair value. Article 8, however, provided that a member could in any event transfer his shares to a close relative either inter vivos or on death. The plaintiff sought a declaration that the bank was bound to give notice under art 7(B) of the 'transfer' which occurred when the beneficial interest in the shares was vested in A's children on the bank completed administration of the testator's estate. Vinelott J held that the bank was not bound to give notice. On appeal

Held

The appeal would be dismissed since the bank was not a 'proposing transferor' under Art 7(B), it had not expressed any desire to transfer the shares and the testator's desire to transfer them to A's children could not be attributed to the bank. Further, the term transfer in Art 7(B) only referred to a transfer of the legal title in the shares and not, as here, transfers of equitable interests only.

Oliver LJ:

'The question then is: Is the bank a proposing transferor? It says that it neither has proposed nor does propose to transfer. Counsel for the plaintiff says that that does not matter, because the *Lyle & Scott* case shows that, where the legal position is such that a person other than the member can require an immediate transfer to himself, then the member becomes a proposing transferor. If, of course, that is the effect of the *Lyle & Scott* case, then we must clearly follow it, but I confess that, for my part, I should require the most compulsive guidance before I allowed myself to be led to a conclusion which is, as this is in my judgment, so starkly at variance with any semblance of reality.

What had happened in the *Lyle & Scott* case was that the members of the company had voluntarily entered into contracts with a stranger for the sale to him of their shares. Those contracts provided in terms that the vendors should deliver up their share certificates and sign the relative transfer deeds, when called on to do so, in exchange for the price ... (His Lordship then referred to the decision in *Lyle & Scott* and continued): ' ... Indeed the speeches of all their Lordships emphasise the importance of the agreement into which the respondents had voluntarily entered and which they were, even at the hearing, seeking to affirm. In my judgment, therefore, this court is not bound, or even persuasively urged, by that authority to the acceptance of counsel for the plaintiff's proposition and, authority apart, the proposition appears to me to be untenable.'

Smith and Fawcett Limited, Re [1942] 1 Ch 304 Court of Appeal (Lord Greene MR, Luxmoore LJ and Asquith J)

Refusal to register a transfer of shares

Facts
The company was incorporated in 1937 with a share capital of £25,000 being divided into 10,000 preference and 15,000 ordinary shares of £1 each. Only 8,002 ordinary shares were issued, 4,001 to Smith and 4,001 to Fawcett, both of whom were directors of the company. In art 10 of the company's articles, it was provided: 'The directors may at any time in their absolute and uncontrolled discretion refuse to register any transfer of shares'. On Fawcett's death his will provided that 2,000 of his shares were to go to his wife for life, remainder to his daughter and 2,001 shares to his son, the plaintiff, absolutely. The plaintiff was appointed executor and applied for registration of the shares in his name as executor. Smith refused to register all the shares, but offered to register 2,001 in the plaintiff's name and to buy 2,000 at a price to be fixed by him.

The plaintiff applied for the register to be rectified and all 4,001 shares registered in his name.

Held
Since art 10 gave the directors a wide power to refuse registration of a transfer and there was nothing to show that their refusal had been other than in the interests of the company the application would be dismissed.

Lord Greene MR:

'... The principles to be applied in cases where the articles of a company confer a discretion on directors with regard to the acceptance of transfers of shares are, for the present purposes, free from doubt. They must exercise their discretion bona fide in what they consider – not what a court may consider – is in the interests of the company, and not for any collateral purpose. They must have regard to those considerations, and those considerations only, which the articles on their true construction permit them to take into consideration, and in construing the relevant provisions in the articles it is the right to deal freely with his property and to transfer it to whomsoever he pleases. When it is said, as it has been said more than once, that regard must be had to this last consideration, it means, I apprehend, nothing more than that the shareholer has such a prima facie right, and that right is not to be cut down by uncertain language or doubtful implications. The right, if it is to be cut down, must be cut down with satisfactory clarity ...

... There is nothing, in my opinion, in principle or in authority to make it impossible to draft such a wide and comprehensive power to directors to refuse to transfer as to enable them to take into account any matter which they conceive to be in the interests of the company, and thereby to admit or not to admit a particular person and to allow or not to allow a particular transfer for reasons not personal to the transferee but bearing on the general interests of the company as a whole – such matters, for instance, as whether by their passing a particular transfer the transferee would obtain too great a weight in the councils of the company or might even perhaps obtain control. The question, therefore, simply is whether on the true construction of the particular article the directors are limited by anything except their bona fide view as to the interests of the company. In the present case the article is drafted in the widest possible terms, and I decline to write into that clear language any limitation other than a limitation, which is implicit by law, that a fiduciary power of this kind must be exercised bona fide in the interests of the company. Subject to that qualification, an article in this form appears to me to give the directors what it says, namely, an absolute and uncontrolled discretion ...'

Smith New Court Securities Ltd v Scrimgeour Vickers (Asset Management) Ltd and Another [1994] 1 WLR 1271 Court of Appeal (Nourse, Rose and Hoffmann LJJ)

Misrepresentation – sale of shares – measure of damages

Facts
The plaintiff, Smith New Court Securities Ltd (SNC), purchased 28,141,424 shares in a public company at 82.25p. SNC claimed it was induced to make the purchase by fraudulent misrepresentations made by Roberts, an employee of Citibank NA (Citibank). The representations were that SNC was in competition with other bidders for the shares, which was not true. The shares had been charged to Citibank as a form of security by an American company and they were sold to SNC by Scrimgeour Vickers (Asset Management) Ltd (SVAM), who were acting as broker for Citibank. Roberts was also an executive director of SVAM.

Chadwick J, the judge at first instance, held that SNC were entitled to recover damages because of the misrepresentation. He measured the damages on the difference between the price paid and the true value of the shares on date of purchase, which was 21 July 1989. He then went on to find that due to another fraud, which was unconnected and then undiscovered, the value of each share at that date was 44p. The difference between the purchase price (£23,146,321) and the value of the shares at 44p each (£12,382,226) was £10,764,005, and judgment was awarded for this amount.

Citibank appealed against this judgment.

Held
The appeal was successful. The correct measure of damages was the difference between the price paid (82.25p per share, amounting to £23,146,321) and the price which the shares would have fetched on the open market, in the absence of the misrepresentation, on 21 July 1989 (78p a share, amounting to £21,950,311). The damages were accordingly reduced to £1,196,010.

Nourse LJ:

'In our judgment, therefore, the correct measure of damages was the difference between 82.25p and the price which, absent the misrepresentation, the parcel of shares would have fetched on the open market on 21 July 1989. Mr Sumption submitted that, on the evidence accepted by the judge, that price was 82.25p a share. That was the price which SNC decided to bid before any representation had been made. But that submission is undermined by our finding that the 9.43 am representation was made and that the pricing meeting acted upon it. The judge found that, in the absence of a representation, SNC would have offered 78p for a bought deal. He thought that Citibank would not have accepted this price: it would have preferred to deal in-house with CSV. But there was no evidence that CSV would have offered a higher price. It too was wanting a bought deal. It follows that, in our view, 78p was the market price on the date in question. The loss flowing from the misrepresentation was therefore 4.25p a share and the damages must be reduced from £10,764,005 to £1,196,010, being the difference between the price (£23,146,321) and the value of the shares at 78p each (£21,950,311).'

Commentary
The measure of damages for fraudulent misrepresentation in this case was assessed by the difference between the price paid and the price the shares would have fetched had the market not known about the fraud. An argument was put forward that damages should be assessed on the basis of omniscience, ie that the market knew everything including the unconnected fraud. This was rejected by the Court of Appeal, however, on the basis that omniscience is an 'arbitrary and irrational assumption'.

Restrictions on issue and payment for share capital

Hilder v *Dexter* [1902] AC 474 House of Lords (Earl of Halsbury LC, Lords Davey, Robertson and Brampton)

Issue of shares at a premium

Facts
A mining company was formed in 1900 with a share capital of 200,000 £1 shares. In January 1901 the directors invited 14 persons of whom Hilder was one, to subscribe for 33,333 of these shares. Hilder was allotted 6,975 shares on terms which gave him an option to purchase a further share for each share allotted to him at part value within one year of allotment. In July 1901 the shares were selling for £2 17s 6d and Hilder gave notice that he wished to exercise the option. Another shareholder, Dexter, claimed an injunction on the ground that this was a device for paying commission out of capital and contrary to s8(2) CA 1900. At first instance Byrne J granted an injunction; the Court of Appeal affirmed his decision. On appeal to the House of Lords:

Held
Hilder was entitled to exercise the option. It did not involve a commission out of either shares or capital because the company was not parting with any portion of its capital since it was receiving par value for the shares.

Lord Davey:

'... The agument seems to me to be that the company, by engaging to allot shares at par to the shareholder at a future date, is applying or using its shares in such a manner as to give him a possible benefit at the expense of the company in this sense, that it foregoes the chance of issuing them at a premium. With regard to the latter point, it may or may not be at the expense of the company. I am not aware of any law which obliges a company to issue its shares above par because they are saleable at a premium in the market. It depends on the circumstances of each case, whether it will be prudent or even possible to do so, and it is a question for the directors to decide. But the point which, in my opinion, is alone material for the present purpose is that the benefit to the shareholder from being able to sell his shares at a premium is not obtained by him at the expense of the company's capital.'

Ooregum Gold Mining Company of India v *Roper* [1892] AC 125 House of Lords (Lord Halsbury LC, Lords Watson, Herschell, Macnaghten and Morris)

Issue of shares at a discount

Facts

The company was incorporated in 1880 with a share capital of 125,000 £1 ordinary shares all of which were allotted. The company was not very successful and a winding up order was obtained. This was stayed by the court when undertakings were given to introduce fresh capital into the company. In 1885 an extraordinary general meeting of the company resolved to issue 120,000 preference shares of £1 each, which were to be credited in the company's books as having 15s paid thereon and carrying a non-cumulative preferential dividend of 10 per cent, based on the nominal value. Thus, subscribers for preference shares only had to pay 5s per share. At the time these shares were issued the market value of the ordinary shares was only 2s 6d. In 1889 Roper purchased some ordinary shares in the company. He brought this action claiming that the issue of the preference shares at a discount was ultra vires the company. At the time the action was brought the preference shares stood at a premium on the Stock Exchange. At first instance, North J held that the issue of the shares at a discount was ultra vires the company. His decision was affirmed by the Court of Appeal. On appeal to the House of Lords:

Held

On the true construction of the Companies Acts 1862 and 1867 the issue of the preference shares at a discount was beyond the powers of the company and the holders of these shares were liable to pay the full amount unpaid on these shares.

Lord Macnaghten:

'My Lords, your Lordships are called upon to determine whether it is or is not competent for a company limited by shares to issue shares at a discount so as to relieve persons taking shares so issued from liability to pay up their amount in full. It was suggested that different considerations might apply to shares in the capital with which a company is originally registered and shares in additional capital created afterwards. But it seems to me to be perfectly clear that, for the present purpose, no distinction can be drawn between one portion of the capital of a company limited by shares and another.

The question turns upon the construction of the Companies Act 1862. The provisions of the Act are, I think, plain enough if one bears in mind the condition of things which existed before the principle of limited liability was introduced in 1855. Before that time there was no way known to the law by which persons trading in partnership could restrict their liability. They were liable to the uttermost farthing. At last the legislature intervened and authorised persons who proposed to trade in partnership to form themselves into a registered company with a declared capital and shares of a fixed amount, and then limited the liability of the partners as members of the company to the amount unpaid upon their shares.

But all this legislation proceeds on the footing of recognising and maintaining the liability of the individual members to the company until the prescribed limit is reached. The memorandum of association of a company limited by shares must contain "the amount of capital with which the company proposes to be registered divided into shares of a certain fixed amount". It must also contain "a declaration that the liability is defined in the memorandum itself. And so the declaration carries you back to the earlier part of the section, where you are told what is meant by "a company limited by shares". It is a company "formed on the principle of having the liability of its members limited to the amount unpaid upon their shares". That must mean that the liability of a member continues so long as anything remains unpaid upon his shares. Nothing but payment and payment in full, can put an end to the liability.

Plainer still and more explicit is the section headed "Liability of members". It begins by declaring that, in the event of a company formed under the Act being wound up, the measure of the liability of every present and past member is the amount required to satisfy all claims of creditors, to pay all the expenses of liquidation, and to adjust the claims of members inter se. Then come certain qualifications to which that liability is subject. One is, that in the case of a company limited by shares no contribution shall be required from any member exceeding the amount, if any, unpaid on the shares in respect of which he is liable as a present or past member.

To sum the matter up, I cannot, I think, do better than adopt the language Mr Buckley has used in speaking of the Limited Liability Acts. "The dominant and cardinal principle of these Acts," he says, "is that the investor shall purchase immunity from liability beyond a certain limit, on the terms that there shall be and remain a liability up to that limit". Whether this liability is one of "the conditions of the memorandum", within the meaning of that expression in the Act of 1862, as Lord Selborne seems to have thought (*Dent's Case* (1873) 8 Ch App 768), or a condition attached by the Act to a company limited by shares and of the essence of such a company, though it may not be found contained within the four corners of the memorandum, is a matter of little or no importance. In either view of the case it is plain that the condition is one which cannot be dispensed with by anything in the articles of association, or by any resolution of the company, or by any contract between the company and outsiders who have been invited to become members of the company and who do come in on the faith of such a contract ...'

Ossory Estates plc, Re [1988] BCLC 213 Chancery Division (Harman J)

Payment for shares – requirement of plcs to have non-cash assets valued

Facts
The applicant sold certain properties to Ossory for £3.5m, the consideration being £1.495m in cash and the allotment of 8m ordinary shares of 5p each at a premium of 17p. Contrary to s103 of the Companies Act 1985, no valuer's report was delivered at the time of allotment and it was not filed (because it did not exist) with the return of allotment. The applicant sought an order under s113(2) of the 1985 Act exempting it from liability under s103 of the same.

Held
The order would be granted.

Harman J:

'In this case, the purchaser has appeared before me and the evidence before me shows that the purchaser has in fact sold on substantial parts of the properties purchased under the contract ... at substantial profits. It has retained some of the properties, but it quite evidently, so far as the ones it has sold on, has undoubtedly received at least moneys or moneys' worth equal in value, and probably exceeding in value, the aggregate of the nominal value of the shares and any premium ... . The exemption order is from the failure to deal with the valuation provisions which are all in s108 of the 1985 Act. There is now available ... a valuation report by the auditors of the purchaser. The provisions of s108 are curious and arcane. They require a person, who is to be described as the valuer, to be entitled not to be the valuer, and to rely on some other valuer. They require the person to be independent but to be entitled to be the auditor of the company, as indeed in this case they are, and they require various curious provisions as to what must be stated in the valuation report. In my view, this valuation report is adequate for the purposes ... and I do not need to go through the details of s108 for the purpose of making the exemption order which I propose to make in this case. I am satisfied that it is indeed just and equitable that the vendor should be relieved from liability, and I am further satisfied that it is just and equitable that the vendor should not pay any interest in respect of properties which it sold, which the purchaser obtained, on the due dates, and where the whole consideration was produced at the correct time.'

Park Business Interiors Ltd v *Park* [1990] BCC 914 Court of Session (Lord Coulsfield)

Allotment of shares – consideration repayment of expenditure

Facts

The evidence established that the defender had incurred expenditure to approximately the value of the shares issued to him; that the company, with the agreement of all those interested, had accepted liability to repay that expenditure to the defender; and that it was in consideration of the release of that liability for reimbursement that the shares were issued to the defender. The question arose whether, on this view of the facts, the shares issued to the defender could be said to have been issued without adequate consideration or without proper attention being paid to the adequacy of the consideration.

Held

This was not the case.

Lord Coulsfield:

'It is clear that the directors of a company are not entitled to agree to issue shares for no consideration or at a discount and that, if they purport to do so, the allottee remains liable to contribute, up to the nominal value of the shares, when called on to do so. It is, however, also clear that directors are entitled to allot shares as fully paid for a consideration other than cash. If they do so, the particulars required by s88 of the Companies Act 1985 must be registered. In deciding whether or not to allot shares for such a consideration, the directors owe a fiduciary duty to apply their minds to the adequacy of the consideration. If, however, there is a valid contract bona fide entered into, the court will not, in general, investigate the adequacy of the consideration, provided that it is not merely colourable or manifestly inadequate (see eg *Ooregum Gold Mining Co of India Ltd* v *Roper* [1892] AC 125 at pp136-137; *Re Wragg Ltd* [1987] 1 Ch 796). The consideration for the allotment of shares may be the discharge of a debt due by the company to the allottee. In that case, however, the debt must be one presently due by the company ...

Those cases were, however, decided under s25 of the Companies Act 1862, which required that the allottee should pay for shares "in cash", unless a written contract had been filed *before* the issue of the shares. In the cases cited, there had been no prior written contract and the question therefore was whether the discharge of a debt by accord and satisfaction could be treated as equivalent to a cash payment (*Ooregum Gold Mining Co* per Lord Halsbury LC at p129). Section 88 of the Companies Act 1985 does not require either a prior written contract or payment in cash and, in consequence, the earlier authorities are of limited assistance in dealing with the present case. It was agreed by counsel that a company may, by agreement after incorporation, render itself liable to reimburse expenses incurred by a promoter in the setting up of the company or in preparation for establishing its business ...

I think that it is clearly correct that a company is not liable to pay for pre-incorporation expenses unless it agrees to accept the liability after incorporation. However, in so far as the authorities suggest that a past consideration, such as services previously rendered, will not entitle a company to make such an agreement, they appear to be based on the general requirement of consideration in the English law of contract. Hence it is suggested in *Pennington's Company Law* (5th ed p608) that the company execute a deed under seal where the consideration is a past one. There does not seem to be any authority to the effect that a Scottish company cannot simply contract in Scotland to remunerate or reimburse a person who has rendered services in setting up the company and its business, provided the agreement is made after incorporation and is bona fide made. It would normally be expected that there would be a minute or other similar record of the company's agreement, but the absence of a minute is not fatal if the agreement can be proved without it ...

Applying that view of the law to the facts of the present case, it appears to me that the pursuers' case fails. Although there was no formal minute of the company recording that it accepted liability for the defender's expenditure, it seems to me that, in substance, the company did accept that liability. The transaction was entered into quite openly, under legal advice, and vouchers for the defender's expenditure were there to be checked. The amount of the expenditure vouched at the meeting was sufficient to satisfy the amount due in respect of the shares and there is nothing to indicate that the defender and his co-director failed to consider adequately the sufficiency of the amount or the nature of the transaction. It therefore follows that the pursuers have not established that the allotment of shares to the defender was made without consideration or without sufficient assessment of the amount of the consideration.'

Wragg Ltd, Re [1897] 1 Ch 796 Court of Appeal (Lindley, A L Smith and Rigby LJJ)

Issue of shares at a discount

Facts
Wragg and Martin were in partnership in an omnibus and coach business in Whitechapel. They decided to convert their business into a private company in 1894. The company was duly registered with a nominal capital of £20,000 being 2,000 shares of £10 each. They sold their business to the company for £46,300, this being paid as to £7,000 in cash, by the issue of the 20,000 shares to Wragg and Martin and by various debentures and mortgages. Not long afterwards the company went into liquidation and the liquidator took out a summons for misfeasance against Wragg and Martin. In support of this summons, the liquidator put in evidence which showed that the business was worth much less than the company paid for it at the date it was sold to the company.

Held
A company can buy property at any price it thinks fit and pay for it in fully paid up shares and the transaction will be binding upon its creditors provided the company has acted in it honestly and not colourably. As the liquidator was unable to show that the sale of the business to the company was colourable or a sham the summons was dismissed.

Lindley LJ:

'... That shares cannot be issued at a discount was finally settled in the case of the *Ooregum Gold Mining Co of India* v *Roper* [1892] AC 125, the judgments in which are strongly relied upon by the appellant in this case. It has, however, never yet been decided that a limited company cannot buy property or pay for services at any price it thinks proper, and pay for them in fully paid-up shares. Provided a limited company does so honestly and not colourably, and provided that it has not been so imposed upon as to be entitled to be relieved from its bargain, it appears to be settled by *Pell's Case* (1869) LR 5 Ch App 11 and the others to which I have referred, of which *Anderson's Case* (1868) 7 Ch D 75 is the most striking, that agreements by limited companies to pay for property or services in paid-up shares are valid and binding on the companies and their creditors. The Legislature in 1867 appears to me to have distinctly recognised such to be the law, but to have required in order to make such agreements binding that they shall be registered before the shares are issued.

There is certainly no decision yet which is opposed to the above statement of the law. The observations in *In re Addlestone Linoleum Co* (1887) 37 Ch D 191, *In re Almada and Tirito Co* (1888) 38 Ch D 415, *Lee* v *Neuchatel Asphalte Co* (1889) 41 Ch D 1, and *Ooregum Gold Mining Co of India* v *Roper*, relied upon by the appellant in this case, fall far short of deciding that the value of the property or services paid for in shares can be inquired into or is material in any case in which the sale is not impeached. These and other cases decided upon the Act of 1867 show (i) that since that Act, as before, shares must be paid for in money or money's worth; (ii) that since that Act, as before, they may be paid for in money's worth; (iii) that since the Act payment in money's worth can only be effectually made pursuant to a properly registered contract; (iv) that, even if there is such a contract, shares cannot be issued at a discount; (v) that if a company owes a person £100, the company cannot by paying him £200 in shares of that nominal amount discharge him, even by a registered contract, from his obligation as a shareholder to pay up the other £100 in respect of those shares. That would be issuing shares at a discount. The difference between such a transaction and paying for property or services in shares at a price put upon them by a vendor and agreed to by the company may not always be very apparent in practice. But the two transactions are essentially different, and whilst the one is ultra vires the other is intra vires. It is not law that persons cannot sell property to a limited company for fully paid-up shares and make a profit by the transaction. We must not allow ourselves to be misled by talking of value. The value paid to the company is measured by the price at which the company agrees to buy what it thinks it worth its while to acquire. Whilst the transaction is unimpeached, this is the only value to be considered ...'

Restrictions on a company purchasing and holding its own shares

Acatos and Hutchinson plc v *Watson* (1994) The Times 30 December Chancery Division (Lightman J)

Section 143 Companies Act 1985 – whether a company had purchased its own shares

Facts
Acatos and Hutchinson plc (AH), wanted to purchase the entire issued share capital of Acatos Ltd (A). A's sole asset was a substantial shareholding in AH. The agreement had been negotiated at arm's length and the independent directors of AH had been separately advised, by solicitors and accountants, that the transaction was in the best interests of AH and its shareholders. The question that the court had to decide was whether the transaction was in breach of the rule in *Trevor* v *Whitworth* (1877) 12 AC 409 and s143 Companies Act 1985, which prohibits a company from acquiring its own shares.

Held
The rule in *Trevor* v *Whitworth* and s143 Companies Act 1985 did not prevent AH from purchasing the entire share capital of A. Lightman J observed that under the rule in *Trevor* v *Whitworth,* AH could not have purchased the shareholding in AH held by A. The issue was whether the rule could be side-stepped by purchasing instead the issued share capital of A, which would have the same economic consequences. The defendant argued that the veil of incorporation should be lifted to treat AH as acquiring its own shares, and this would prevent the rule and s143 being circumvented.

After referring to three Australian authorities which supported the plaintiff's case, Lightman J decided that the transaction was valid. If a takeover of a target company was prohibited when it held shares in the bidding company, this would provide the target company with a good defence. Lightman J said that it was plain that the rule did not have this remarkable and far-reaching effect. Section 23 of the Companies Act 1985 put the matter beyond question, for this expressly allowed A, after the acquisition, to keep its shareholding in AH. (Under s23, A's voting rights are suspended during the ownership.) Finally, his Lordship added that due to the potential for abuse, the court would look carefully at the transaction to see if the directors of the acquiring company had fulfilled their fiduciary duties to safeguard the interests of shareholders and creditors.

Castiglione's Will Trusts, Re [1958] 1 Ch 549 Chancery Division (Danckwerts J)

Who can hold shares in a company?

Facts

By his will the testator left 1,000 shares in trust for his son for life and on his death to divide the shares between his children who survived him. He then directed that should his son die without lawful issue that the shares were to be transferred to Castiglione Erskine & Co Ltd. The 1,000 shares were shares in that company and on the death of the testator's son in 1956 the question arose as to how the shares were to be dealt with.

Held

A company could not be a member of itself and therefore it could not hold its own shares. However, there could be a trust for the company under which the shares were registered in the names of nominees who held on trust for the company.

Danckwerts, J:

'... It seems to me that it is quite plain that a company cannot hold its own shares because it cannot be a member, but it does not necessarily follow from that that it may not have a benificial interest arising from the shares in some way or other. It appears to me quite plain from the decision of Romer J in *Kirby* v *Wilkins* [1929] 2 CH 444 that there can be a trust under which certain powers on the share register of the company may hold the shares upon trust for the company beneficially ...'

Trevor v *Whitworth* (1887) 12 App Cas 409 House of Lords (Lords Herschell, Watson, Fitzgerald and Macnaghten)

Prohibition on a company purchasing its own shares

Facts

A company formed in 1865 to carry on the business of flannel manufacturers had, inter alia, articles which permitted it to purchase its own shares. These provided: art 179 'Any share may be purchased by the company from any person willing to sell it, and at such price, not exceeding the then marketable value thereof, as the board think reasonable.' Article 181 'Shares so purchased may at the discretion of the board be sold or disposed of by them or be absolutely extinguished as they may deem most advantageous for the company.' The memorandum was 'silent on the issue'. In 1880 the executors of Whitworth, a shareholder in the company, agreed to sell his 533 shares to the company for £3,305 with the price being paid over three years. The company went into liquidation in 1884 and at that time the executors of Whitworth were still owed £2,873 for the shares and they claimed this sum in the liquidation. The liquidators took out a summons to determine whether the claim ought to be allowed. The Vice Chancellor of the County Palatine of Lancaster refused to allow the claim. On appeal to the Court of Appeal his decision was reversed. On appeal to the House of Lords:

Held

The purchase by a company of its own shares was beyond its powers; the claim of Whitworth's executors must fail.

Lord Herschell:

'... I pass now to the main question in this case, which is one of great and general importance – whether the company had power to purchase the shares. The result of the judgment in the court below is certainly somewhat startling. The creditors of the company which is being wound up, who have a right to look to the paid-up capital as the fund out of which their debts are to be discharged, find coming into competition with them persons who, in respect only of their having been and having ceased to be shareholders in the company, claim that the company shall pay to them a part of that capital. The memorandum of association, it is admitted, does not authorise the purchase by the company of its own shares. It states as the objects for which the company is established the acquiring certain manufacturing businesses, and the undertaking and carrying on the businesses so acquired, and any other business and transaction which the company consider to be in any way auxiliary thereto, or proper to be carried on in connection therewith. It cannot be questioned, since *Ashbury Railway Carriage and Iron Co* v *Riche* (1875) LR 7 HL 653, that a company cannot employ its funds for the purpose of any transactions which do not come within the objects specified in the memorandum, and that a company cannot by its articles of association extend its power in this respect. These propositions are not, and could not be, impeached in the judgments of the Court of Appeal, but it is said to be settled by authority that, although a company could not under such a memorandum as the present by articles authorise a trafficking in its own shares, it might authorise the board to buy its shares "whenever they thought it desirable for the purposes of the company," or "in cases where it was incidental to the legitimate objects of the company that it should do so". The former is Cotton LJ's expression, the latter that of Bowen LJ.

I will first consider the question apart from authority, and then examine the decisions relied on. The Companies Act 1862, required (s8) that in the case of a company where the liability of the shareholders is limited, the memorandum shall contain the amount of the capital with which the company proposes to be registered, divided into shares of a certain fixed amount, and provided (s12) that such a company may increase its capital and divide it into shares of larger amount than the existing shares, or convert its paid-up shares into stock, but that, "save as aforesaid no alteration shall be made by any company in the conditions contained in its memorandum of association". What is the meaning of the distinction thus drawn between a company without limit on the liability of its members and a company where the liability is limited, but, in the latter case, to assure to those dealing with the company that the whole of the subscribed capital, unless diminished by expenditure upon the objects defined by the memorandum, shall remain available for the discharge of its liabilities? The capital may, no doubt, be diminished by expenditure upon and reasonably incidental to all the objects specified. A part of it may be lost in carrying on the business operations authorised. Of this all persons trusting the company are aware, and take the risk. But I think they have a right to rely, and were intended by the legislature to have a right to rely, on the capital remaining undiminished by any expenditure outside these limits, or by the return of any part of it to the shareholders. Experience appears to have shown that circumstances might occur in which a reduction of the capital would be expedient. Accordingly, by the Companies Act 1867, provision was made enabling a company under strictly defined conditions to reduce its capital. Nothing can be stronger than these carefully-worded provisions to show how inconsistent with the very constitution of a joint stock company, with limited liability, the right to reduce its capital was considered to be.

Let me now invite your Lordships' attention to the facts of the present case. The company had purchased, prior to the date of the liquidation, no less than 4,142 of its own shares – that is to say, considerably more than a fourth of the paid-up capital of the company had been either paid, or contracted to be paid, to shareholders, in consideration only of their ceasing to be so. I am quite unable to see how this expenditure was incurred in respect of or as incidental to any of the objects specified in the memorandum. And, if not, I have difficulty in seeing how it can be justified. If the claim under consideration can be supported, the result would seem to be that the whole of the shareholders, with the exception of those holding seven individual shares, might now be claiming payment of the sums paid upon their shares as against the creditors, who had a right to look to the moneys subscribed as the source out of which the company's liabilities to them were to be met. And the stringent precautions to prevent the reduction of the capital of a limited company, without due notice and judicial sanction, would be idle if the company might purchase its own shares wholesale and so effect the desired result. I do not think it was disputed that a company could not enter upon such a transaction for the purpose of reducing its capital, but it was suggested that it might do so if that were not the object, but it was considered for some other reason desirable in the interest of the company to do so. To the creditor whose interests, I think, ss8 and 12 of the Companies Act 1867, were intended to protect, it makes no difference what the object of the purchase is. The result to him is the same. The shareholders receive back the moneys subscribed, and there passes into their pockets what before existed in the form of cash in the coffers of the company, or of buildings, machinery, or stock available to meet the demands of the creditors.

What was the reason which induced the company in the present case to purchase its shares? If it was that they might sell them again, this would be a trafficking in the shares, and clearly unauthorised. If it was to retain them, this would be to my mind an indirect method of reducing the capital of the company. The only suggestion of another motive (and it seems to me to be a suggestion unsupported by proof) is that this was intended to be a family company, and that the directors wanted to keep the shares as much as possible in the hands of those who were partners, or who were interested in the old firm, or of those persons whom the directors thought they would like to be among this small number of shareholders. I cannot think that the employment of the company's money in the purchase of shares for any such purpose was legitimate. The business of the company was that of manufacturers of flannel. In what sense was the expenditure of the company's money in this way incidental to the carrying on of such a business, or how could it secure the end of enabling the business to be more profitably or satisfactorily carried on? I can quite understand that the directors of a company may sometimes desire that the shareholders should not be numerous, and that they should be persons likely to leave them with a free hand to carry on their operations. But I think it would be most dangerous to countenance the view that, for reasons such as these, they could legitimately spend the moneys of the company to any extent they pleased in the purchase of its shares. No doubt, if certain shareholders are disposed to hamper the proceedings of the company, and are willing to sell their shares, they may be bought out; but this must be done by persons, existing shareholders or others, who can be induced to purchase the shares, and not out of the funds of the company.

It is urged that the views I have expressed are inconsistent with the forfeiture and surrender of shares in a company. I do not think so.

The forfeiture of shares is distinctly recognised by the Companies Act, and by the articles contained in the schedule, which, in the absence of other provisions, regulate the management of a limited liability company. It does not involve any payment by the company and it presumably exonerates from future liability those who have shown themselves unable to contribute what is due from them to the capital of the company. Surrender no doubt stands on a different footing. But it also does not involve any payment out of the funds of the company. If the surrender were made in consideration of any such payment it would be neither more nor less than a sale, and open to the same objections. If it were accepted in a case when the company were in a position to forfeit the shares, the transaction would seem to me perfectly valid. There may be other cases in which a surrender would be legitimate. As to these I would repeat what was said by Sir George Jessel, MR in *Re Dronfield Silkstone Coal Co* (1880) 17 Ch D 76

> "It is not for me to say what the limits of surrender are which are allowable by the Act ... because each case as it arises must be decided upon its own merits.""

Commentary

Section 8 CA 1862 is now s2(5)(a) Companies Act 1985, for s12 CA 1862 see now s121 Companies Act 1985, and for reduction of capital see ss135-141 Companies Act 1985.

Restrictions on a company giving financial assistance in the acquisition of its own shares

Arab Bank plc v *Mercantile Holdings Ltd and Another* [1994] 2 WLR 307 Chancery Division (Millett J)

Section 151 CA 1985 – whether foreign company had given financial assistance for the purchase of shares

Facts

The Arab Bank plc agreed to lend £15.4m to S Ltd to enable it to acquire the entire share capital of Q Ltd. Mercantile Holdings Ltd was the wholly owned subsidiary of Q Ltd and owned some leasehold property in London, which it charged to the Arab Bank plc as security for loan to S Ltd. Q Ltd and S Ltd were English registered companies, but Mercantile Holdings Ltd was incorporated in Gibraltar. The Arab Bank plc wished to realise its security by selling the London property but Mercantile Holdings Ltd claimed the security was void as it infringed the financial assistance rules in s151 CA 1985.

Held

Section 151 does not cover the giving of financial assistance by a foreign subsidiary of an English parent company for the purchase of the parent company's shares. The security given by Mercantile Holdings Ltd was valid.

Millet J:

'*Section 151 of the Act of 1985*
Section 54 of the Act was repealed and replaced by ss43 to 44 of the Companies Act 1981, which have in turn been re-enacted in similar terms by ss151 to 158 of the Act of 1985. The language of s54 of the Act of 1948 has been completely recast. The whole perspective of the section has been altered. The prohibition is still directed to the assisting company. But the section no longer starts with the assisting company and prohibits it from giving financial assistance for the purchase of its own shares or shares in its holding company. Instead, it starts with the company whose shares are to be acquired ("the target company") and prohibits it or "any of its subsidiaries" from giving financial assistance for the purchase of its own shares.

It is difficult to believe that this change, which is primarily one of style, was intended to make any alteration in the substantive law, particularly when the opening words of s153 refer back to s151 as if it were still cast in the old form; and in an entirely domestic situation it does not do so. But because of the statutory definitions of "company" (which prima facie means an English company) and "subsidiary" (which does not) it appears to have made at least one change and may have made two. Formerly, the assisting company had to be "a company", ie an English company; but the target company did not: it was sufficient if it was the assisting company's holding company. Now, however, it is the target company which has to be "a company"; the assisting company does not: it is sufficient if it is one of the target company's subsidiaries. The new requirement that the target company must be "a company" means that the giving of financial assistance by the English subsidiary of a foreign parent company for the acquisition of shares in that company appears to be no longer prohibited. on the other hand, the removal of the former requirement that the assisting company must be "a company", coupled with the use of the words "any of its subsidiaries" instead of "any of its subsidiary companies" in place of the cumbersome and ungainly phrase "where the company is a subsidiary company", if taken literally, extends the prohibition for the first time to the case where the prohibited act, ie the giving of financial assistance, is committed by a foreign company.

Does the mere giving of financial assistance by the subsidiary ipso facto also constitute the giving of such assistance by the parent company?
In my judgment the answer is plainly "No". The prohibition is, and always has been, directed to the assisting company, not to its parent company. If the giving of financial assistance by a subsidiary for the acquisition of shares in its holding company necessarily also constituted the giving of financial assistance by the holding company, s73 of the Act of 1947 would not have been necessary. Moreover, ss153 to 158 of the Act of 1985 are clearly predicated on the assumption that it is the conduct of the subsidiary alone which needs statutory authorisation.

This is not to say that the giving of financial assistance by the subsidiary may not involve unlawful conduct on the part of the parent. If the acts of the subsidiary are in breach of s151, the conduct of the parent in procuring them will constitute an offence. And even if the section does not apply to foreign subsidiaries, the hiving down of an asset by an English company to such a subsidiary in order to enable it to be made available to finance a contemplated acquisition of shares of the English company would clearly contravene the section: it would constitute the indirect provision of financial assistance by the English company.

Does s151 of the Act of 1985 make it unlawful for a foreign subsidiary of an English parent company to give financial assistance for the purpose of the acquisition of shares of its parent company?
Read literally and with the assistance of the statutory definition of 'subsidiary', s51 clearly purports to make it unlawful for a foreign subsidiary of an English parent company to give financial assistance for the purpose of the acquisition of shares of its parent company. The result, however, is to give the section an extraterritorial effect contrary to the general principles of private international law; for the capacity of a corporation, the regulation of its affairs, the maintenance of its capital and the protection of its creditors and shareholders are generally recognised to be matters for the law of the place of incorporation. But there have been many cases in which the words of a statute have been given a more limited meaning than they are capable of bearing where there is a proper ground for concluding that this was the intention of Parliament: see, for example, *Drummond* v *Collins* [1915] AC 1011, 1017; *Astor* v *Perry* [1935] AC 398, 417; *Inland Revenue Commissioners* v *Collco Dealings Ltd* [1962] AC1; and In *re International Tin Council* [1987] Ch 419, 450; [1989] Ch 309, 329 CA. The consideration that the more limited meaning is necessary in order to avoid the creation of a jurisdiction wider than that generally recognised by international law has often been recognised as such a ground.

The defendants submit that a literal construction is necessary in order effectively to deal with the mischief which it is the object of the section to prevent. That mischief, it is submitted, is by means of the forbidden assistance to circumvent the rule which forbids an English company from distributing its assets to shareholders otherwise than by the lawful distribution of profits, reduction of capital or distribution of surplus assets on a winding up. Subsidiaries are included in the prohibition since the distribution of its assets to the shareholders in its holding company is tantamount to a distribution of the assets of the holding company itself. The same consideration applies whether the subsidiary is incorporated in Great Britain or abroad. If foreign subsidiaries were outside the prohibition, the defendants submit, a coach and horses could be driven through the section by the simple expedient of taking the precaution of always interposing a wholly owned foreign subsidiary between a company and its assets.

I am not impressed by the "coach and horses" argument. As I have already observed, the hiving down of the assets by an English company to a foreign subsidiary in order that they may be available for the purpose of assisting in the financing of a contemplated purchase of the parent company's own shares would, in my judgment, constitute the indirect provision of financial assistance by the parent company: while the presence of ss155 to 158 of the Act of 185 makes it unnecessary to interpose a foreign subsidiary in advance as a matter of routine forward strategic planning. Bearing in mind that the provision of financial assistance for the purchase will almost invariably be at the request and instigation of the purchaser rather than the target company, and that it can easily and lawfully be provided where this can be done without prejudice to the interests of creditors and minority shareholders, the interposition of a foreign subsidiary where no purchase was yet in contemplation would seem to require a combination of legal acumen, foresight and dishonesty which is most unusual.

Nor am I satisfied that the mischief which the section is designed to prevent is the extraction of the assets of the target company rather than those of its subsidiary. This was not the case before 1981, when the prohibition was limited to English subsidiaries even when the target company was an English company. The defendants submit that if the mischief sought to be prevented was the extraction of assets from the subsidiary, then the section would have prohibited an English subsidiary of a foreign parent company from giving financial assistance for the purchase of shares of the parent company. This would be a formidable argument if I were persuaded that the failure to cover this case, covered in the Act of 1948, was deliberate; but I am not. The primary class of persons which the section was designed to protect must, in my judgment, be the creditors of the assisting company; and they are equally prejudiced by the extraction of its assets for the purpose of financing the acquisition of shares in its parent company whether that parent company is English or foreign. I can see no possible reason or justification for excluding such a case from the prohibition and, if this was indeed the result of the recasting of the statutory language in 1981, I think that it must have been inadvertent.

Whether the section is intended primarily for the protection of the creditors of the assisting company or for the protection of the creditors of its parent company, however, it is directed to the conduct of the assisting company. Where that company is a subsidiary, it is directed to the subsidiary, not to its parent company. The section operates by regulating the conduct of the subsidiary and depriving it of the capacity to enter into transactions of the kind specified. The capacity of a corporation, the regulation of its conduct, the maintenance of its capital, and the protection of its creditors and shareholders are all matters for the law of the place of its incorporation, not the law of the place of incorporation of its parent company.

Conclusion

I have reached the firm conclusion that "any of its subsidiaries" in s151 must be construed as limited to those subsidiaries which are subsidiary companies, that is to say, English companies. My reasons for this conclusion are as follows. (i) The recasting of the language of the section, and in particular the change from "subsidiary company" to "any of its subsidiaries," was almost certainly a matter of style and not intended to make a substantive change in the law. (ii) There is a presumption that, in the absence of a contrary intention express or implied, United Kingdom legislation does not apply to foreign persons or corporations outside the United Kingdom whose acts are performed outside the United Kingdom. Some limitation of the general words of s151 is necessary in order to avoid imputing to Parliament an intention to create an exorbitant jurisdiction which is contrary to generally accepted principles of international law. (iii) In relation the maintenance of the capital of a corporation and the protection of its creditors and shareholders the place where its assets are depleted or put at risk by the giving of the forbidden assistance is irrelevant. To limit the section to the giving of the forbidden assistance in the United Kingdom, as the defendants contend, would be misdirected legislation which would be wholly inadequate to protect the creditors of the subsidiary and would still be at variance with generally accepted principles of international law. (iv) Section 151 is directed at the assisting company. It renders particular acts on the part of the assisting company unlawful. Whether the section is intended primarily for the protection of the creditors of the assisting company or for the protection of creditors of its parent company, where the assisting company is a subsidiary the section is directed at the subsidiary and not at the parent company. It operates by regulating the conduct of the subsidiary and depriving it of the capacity to enter into transactions of the kind specified. (v) The capacity of a corporation, the regulation of its conduct, the maintenance of its capital and the protection of its creditors and shareholders are all matters of the law of the place of its incorporation, not the law of the place of incorporation of its parent company. (vi) Section 54 of the Act of 1948, which the Acts of 1981 and 1985 replaced, did not prohibit a foreign subsidiary from providing financial assistance for the acquisition of shares in its parent company. (vii) Section 151 does not prohibit a partly-owned foreign subsidiary from providing financial assistance for the purchase of its own shares. (viii) The penalties for contravention of s151 do not extend to foreign subsidiaries or their officers. (ix) A number of the more important exemptions in s153 do not apply to a foreign subsidiary, which could not take advantage of the relaxation of s151 provided by ss155 to 158. One would expect the exemptions and relaxations to be co-extensive with the prohibition. (x) If s151 applies to foreign subsidiaries, such a subsidiary may be prevented from entering into a transaction which is lawful under the law of its incorporation, not only where that law is less stringent than our own, but even where it is in similar or even identical terms to our own. That cannot have been the intention of Parliament.

In my judgment s151 does not prohibit a foreign subsidiary of an English parent company from giving financial assistance for the acquisition of shares in its parent company and I will so declare. I will also make a declaration under para 1 of the originating summons that the power of sale has arisen and is now exercisable.'

Belmont Finance v Williams Furniture (No 2) [1980] 1 All ER 393 Court of Appeal (Buckley, Goff and Waller LJJ)

Contravention of the financial assistance rules

Facts

Williams Furniture owned all the shares in a company called "City" which in turn owned all the shares in Belmont. The chairman of all three companies was one James. In 1963 Col Lipert who controlled Williams Furniture and who then was the chairman of City wished to dispose of Belmont, and Grosscurth and his associates wished to buy it so that they could use its assets to finance property development carried on by other companies owned by them. It was eventually agreed that Grosscurth would pay for Belmont by selling the shares in one of his companies, Maximum, to Belmont for £500,000 and in return pay City £489,000 for Belmont. Williams Furniture guaranteed that City would perform its obligations and Grosscurth undertook to ensure that certain profits would be earned by Maximum. The negotiations for the sale of Belmont were at arm's length between Grosscurth and James but neither James, City or Belmont sought or obtained independent advice on the transaction. The parties had doubts as to whether the scheme would by-pass s54 (now s151 CA 1985) and sought and obtained counsel's opinion which concluded that it was not in breach of s54. The scheme was duly implemented, but later Belmont went into liquidation with debts of over £176,000. The receiver of Belmont obtained an independent valuation of Maximum as at October 1963 and this showed it was worth only £60,000 and not £500,000. This action was begun by the receiver on behalf of Belmont against Williams Furniture, City, Grosscurth and others claiming (a) that the £500,000 valuation of Maximum had been fixed so as to enable Grosscurth and his associates to use Belmont's money to purchase its own shares contrary to s54; (b) that all the defendants had conspired to breach s54 and (c) that they were liable as constructive trustees. At the trial Foster J accepted that Williams Furniture and City genuinely believed the purchase of Maximum at £500,000 was a good deal and dismissed the claim on the ground that the whole transaction was bona fide. Belmont appealed.

Held

1. The scheme was a commercial transaction in its own right because it was part of a scheme the purpose of which was to put Grosscurth and his associates in funds to acquire the shares in Belmont and it did not enable Belmont to acquire anything it needed for its business.
2. Because Williams Furniture and City genuinely believed the purchase of Maximum was a good deal they could not be held liable as constructive trustees on the ground that they knowingly participated in a dishonest and fraudulent design. But City was, however, liable as a constructive trustee of the £489,000 it received on the sale of Belmont's shares since that money had been misapplied under s54.

Buckley LJ:

'... The first question for consideration is whether the agreement did contravene s54 of the 1948 Act. Only if the answer to that question is affirmative does the question whether the defendants or any of them are guilty of conspiracy arise, for it is the illegality of the agreement, if it be illegal, which constitutes the common intention of the parties to enter into the agreement a conspiracy at law.

There is little judicial authority on the section. In *Re VGM Holdings* this court had to consider whether under the section in the form in which it stood in the Companies Act 1929, which did not contain the word "subscription", the section covered a case where money which a company had provided had been used to assist a subscription for the company's own shares. Lord Greene MR said:

"There could, I think be no doubt that, if that question were answered in favour of the liquidator, the £15,980 was provided by the company by way of financial assistance, because whether a company provides the money by way of gift or by way of loan or by buying assets from the person who is purchasing the shares at a fraudulent overvalue, all those transactions, it seems to me, would fall within the phrase 'financial assistance.'"

The transaction there in question was a fraudulent one. VGM Holdings Ltd bought all the share capital of Century, which was worthless, from Vanbergen for £8,301 and Vanbergen used the money to pay a call on shares which he held in VGM. The court, however, held that the transaction did not involve a purchase of VGM shares and so was not within the section. In reliance on the reference by Lord Greene MR to a purchase at a fraudulent overvalue, it was suggested to us that the section does not apply to any case in which the company which is alleged to have given financial assistance got fair value for its money. I think that Lord Greene MR must be understood to have been speaking in the context of the facts of the case before him and not to have intended to attempt to put any limit on the scope of the section ...

... Foster J treated as a proposition of law, accepted by counsel for Belmont, that a company does not give financial assistance in connection with a purchase of its own shares within the meaning of s54 by reason only of its simultaneous entry into a bona fide commercial transaction as a result of which it parts with money or money's worth, which in turn is used to finance the purchase of its own shares. He went on to find that the negotiations in the present case were at arm's length and that on the one side Mr James genuinely believed that to buy the capital of Maximum for £500,000 was a good commercial proposition for Belmont and on the other side Mr Copeland honestly believed that in October 1963 the value of the capital of Maximum with Mr Grosscurth's guarantee of Maximum's profits under cl 13(h) of the agreement secured on Rentahome's share capital was not less than £500,000. On these findings he reached the conclusion that the agreement was a bona fide commercial transaction, on which ground he dismissed the action.

This reasoning assumes, as I understand it, that if the transaction under consideration is genuinely regarded by the parties as a sound commercial transaction negotiated at arm's length and capable of justification on purely commercial grounds, it cannot offend against s54. This is, I think, a broader proposition than the proposition which the judge treated as having been accepted by counsel for Belmont. If A Ltd buys from B a chattel or a commodity, like a ship or merchandise, which A Ltd genuinely wants to acquire for its own purpose, and does so having no other purpose in view, the fact that B thereafter employs the proceeds of the sale in buying shares in A Ltd should not, I would suppose, be held to offend against the section; but the position may be different if A Ltd makes the purchase in order to put B in funds to buy shares in A Ltd. If A Ltd buys something from B without regard to its own commecial interests, the sole purpose of the transaction being to put B in funds to acquire shares in A Ltd, this would, in my opinion, clearly contravene the section, even if the price paid was a fair price for what is bought, and a fortiori that would be so if the sale to A Ltd was at an inflated price. The sole purpose would be to enable (ie to assist) B to pay for the shares. If A Ltd buys something from B at a fair price, which A Ltd could readily realise on a resale if it wished to do so, but the purpose, or one of the purposes, of the transaction is to put B in funds to acquire shares of A Ltd, the fact that the price was fair might not, I think, prevent the transaction from contravening the section, if it would otherwise do so, though A Ltd could very probably recover no damages in civil proceedings, for it would have suffered no damage. If the transaction is of a kind which A Ltd could in its own commercial interests legitimately enter into, and the transaction is genuinely entered into by A Ltd in its own commercial interests and not merely as a means of assisting B financially to buy shares of A Ltd, the circumstance that A Ltd enters into the transaction with B, partly with the object of putting B in funds to acquire its own shares or with the knowledge of B's intended use of the proceeds of sale, might, I think, involve no contravention of the section, but I do not wish to express a concluded opinion on that point.

The reasoning of the judge's judgment appears to me, with deference to him, to overlook the word "only" in the suggested proposition of law ...'

Brady v *Brady* [1988] 2 WLR 1308 House of Lords (Lord Keith of Kinkel, Lord Havers, Lord Templeman, Lord Griffiths and Lord Oliver of Aylmerton)

Financial assistance for the purchase of a company's own shares

Facts

Brothers Jack and Bob carried on business through T Brady and Sons Ltd (Brady) (road haulage) and a number of subsidiary companies, one of which was Thomsons Soft Drinks Ltd (Thomsons) (manufacture and distribution of drinks) and another Athersmith Bros Ltd (Athersmith) (haulage depot). Brady's objects stated that it could 'dispose of the whole or any part of the business … for such consideration as the company may think fit'. A quarrel between Jack and Bob resulted in a management deadlock with neither brother in a position to buy out the other. In order to save Brady from liquidation, it was agreed that the business be divided equally between the brothers, Jack taking the haulage business and Bob the drinks with any necessary cash adjustment. It was decided that Brady should be kept in existence and be under Jack's control and that the drinks business be hived off to a new company to be controlled by Bob, with any necessary asset adjustment. There was a shortfall between the value of the drinks business compared with the haulage. To give effect to the new arrangement Ovalshield Ltd (Ovalshield) was incorporated with Jack and Bob holding the subscribers' shares. Bob and Jack had been majority shareholders in Furness Transport Ltd (Furness): Bob transferred his shares to Jack. Bob and Jack also owned equally all the shares in Marsh's Sass Ltd (Sass): Jack transferred to Bob all his shares in this company. Two further companies were incorporated: Motoreal and Activista. Motoreal would hold the haulage group (Brady and subsidiaries) and Activista the drinks (Thomsons), subject to adjustment of assets to ensure equality. Ovalshield would then go into voluntary liquidation and the liquidator would, with the consent of corporators, distribute the shares in Motoreal in specie to a company called Superlanes controlled by Jack (which would also acquire his shares in Furness). The shares in Activista would be likewise distributed in specie to a company called Swancircle controlled by Bob (which would also acquire Bob's shares in Sass). After a number of steps involving increases in capital, capitalisation of profits and issues of renounceable letters of allotment, at the head of the group was Ovalshield, whose shares were owned by Bob, Jack and Tanda (a private company owned equally by Robert (son of Jack's brother) and John (Bob's other son). Beneath Ovalshield were two sub-groups, one headed by Motoreal containing the haulage business represented by Brady and its subsidiaries and the other headed by Activista containing the soft-drinks business represented by Thomsons. The equalisation value required to produce an equality between the two groups was represented by the loan stock now constituting a debt owed by Motoreal to Activista.

The separation of the two businesses was thus effectively accomplished. Bob resigned as a director of all the companies in the Motoreal group, whose directors were now Jack and Robert, and Jack resigned from Thomsons and Sass. In preparation for the voluntary winding up of Ovalshield a statutory declaration of solvency was made and filed. The one outstanding link was the Motoreal loan stock and it was envisaged and agreed at this stage that the indebtedness of Motoreal to Activista in respect of the loan stock would be discharged by the transfer from the Motoreal group (that is, effectively, from Brady and its subsidiaries) to the Activista group of assets equal to the value of that stock, which would then be redeemed. However, adjustments to figures were necessary before the scheme could be finally completed. Agreement could not be reached so Jack and Robert sued for specific performance. There were before the judge substantially only two points for decision:

1. Was the proposed transfer of assets from Brady to Activista ultra vires, as being outside Brady's corporate objects or a misfeasance on the part of the directors or in fraud of Brady's creditors?
2. If not, was the transaction one which, inasmuch as it would involve the provision to Motoreal by Brady of financial assistance in reducing the liability incurred by Motoreal for the purchase of Brady's shares, was rendered unlawful by the provisions of s151 of the Companies Act 1985?

The judge granted specific performance and the Court of Appeal reversed his decision on appeal to the House of Lords.

Held
The appeal would be allowed, subject to the case being remitted for the trial of further defences raised by Bob.

Lord Oliver of Aylmerton:

As to the first question, the broad contention ... was that such a transfer was not covered by any of Brady's objects, inasmuch as it was, on analysis, a gratuitous transfer and that it would in any event constitute an illegal reduction of capital ... As to the second question, it was and is common ground that the scheme propounded does indeed constitute the provision of financial assistance by Brady in connection with the purchase of its own shares. The only question was whether the appellants could rely on the provisions of s153 of the 1985 Act which disapply the prohibition in s151 in certain defined circumstances. It was the appellants' contention that what was proposed was something which was to be done bona fide in the interests of Brady and that Brady's principal purpose in carrying out the transaction was not simply that of reducing Motoreal's liability incurred in the purchase of the Brady shares but was merely an incidental part of the larger purpose of preserving Brady as a corporate entity from a pending and otherwise inevitable liquidation. As to this, the judge made the following important finding of fact:

"The plaintiffs' evidence was shorter than it would otherwise have been, but I am satisfied from it that in 1983 the continued existence of Brady was in serious jeopardy due to the management deadlock which I have described, caused by the family dispute, and that an equal division of the assets of the group in such a way as to give each brother a viable business was the only way to avoid liquidation, leading to a break up. This was accepted by (counsel) on behalf of the defendants, but he says that the method used to effect the division was illegal and that the end does not justify the means."

He expressed his conclusion thus:

"I find in this case the principal purpose of the giving of the financial assistance was not to reduce or discharge any liability incurred by any person for the purpose of the acquisition of the shares, but was incidental to the large purpose of the scheme of arrangement and was given in good faith. Accordingly, it is not, in my judgment, forbidden by s42 of the Companies Act 1981 [now s151 of the 1985 Act]. The result must therefore be that the defence of illegality, the only defence on which the defendants have relied, in my judgment, fails."

Accordingly, he made a decree of specific performance in the appellants' favour ...

My Lords, the arguments before your Lordships have followed the same course as those before the judge and the Court of Appeal and I will approach them in the same order. On the issue of whether the proposed transfers of assets by Brady and Athersmith are ultra vires and therefore void on that ground, the first essential is to consider the express objects of these companies as contained in their respective memoranda of association ...

My Lords, there can, on the face of it, be no question but that the transfers were intended, as between the various companies concerned, not to be gratuitous, for it was inherent in the scheme as proposed that the transfer of assets which were to be applied in discharging Motoreal's indebtedness to Activista on the loan stock was to be made only on the terms of the creation of an equivalent indebtedness from Motoreal to Brady or Athersmith as the case may be ...

The question whether the proposed transfers of assets are ultra vires Brady and Athersmith can perhaps best be tested by postulating the following successive questions. First, does the express object enabling the company to dispose of its assets for such consideration as it thinks fit authorise a transfer in consideration of the promise of the transferee or of a third party to pay to the company the value of the assets transferred? The answer to that question must clearly be in the affirmative. Second, is this express subject to some implied limitation excluding from the range of possible transferees or promisors either a company within the same group or a company which is the parent company of the transferor company? There can be no rational justification for any such implication and counsel for the respondents has not contended that there is. Third, if a promise of a parent or associated company is, in principle, an acceptable consideration, does it cease to be so because the promisor has, at the date of the promise, no other assets than the shares which it holds in the promisee? For my part, I can see no reason why, purely as a matter of the vires of the transferor company, it should do so, though of course there may be very good reasons for saying, according to the circumstances, that to enter into a contract on these terms may be ill-advised. But that, at any rate at this stage of the inquiry, is not the question ...

The argument that the transfer in the instant case constitutes a gift by Brady to Bob seems to me to ignore entirely the corporate existence of the companies in the Ovalshield group, of which Motoreal and Activista still form part. At the present stage, we are concerned only with the argument that the transfer will be ultra vires Brady and Athersmith and not with its wisdom or propriety as an exercise of the directors' powers, which is an entirely different question. Leaving aside other objects, both Brady and Athersmith have among their objects a corporate purpose enabling them to dispose of assets for consideration and, as was pointed out by the judge, the adequacy of the consideration is a matter on which the directors have to form a judgment. But the fact that it may be only barely equal in value to what is disposed of that it may prove, in certain circumstances, to be irrecoverable in whole or in part, does not turn the transaction into a transaction for which there is no consideration or render it otherwise ultra vires. The proposed transfers are, in my judgment, clearly ones which are authorised by Brady's and Athersmith's corporate objects and are therefore intra vires, there being no suggestion whatever of fraud or ill-faith.

Then it is said that, even if the transaction proposed is intra vires Brady and Athersmith, to carry it into effect will be a misfeasance on the part of the directors of those two companies which will render it either illegal or at least capable of being set aside. For my part I have been unable to see why this should be thought to be so ...

The suggestion therefore that the final implementation of the scheme will constitute a misfeasance on the part of the directors comes down finally to this, that the directors will themselves benefit from the scheme and therefore have an interest which conflicts with their duty to the company. But the answer to this is that the transaction is one carried out, as was conceded before the judge, not only with the knowledge and assent of all the shareholders but with their active co-operation and at their instigation. For my part, I am satisfied that [this ground of objection is not made out]. Nor equally do I consider that, quite apart from the approval of the shareholders, the transaction can be legitimately attacked on the ground that, in exercising their powers, the directors failed to take into account the interests of the company. The company was threatened with the total termination and extinction of its business unless the management deadlock could be resolved and this was an essential step in the breaking of the deadlock which it was quite clearly in the interests of the company, its shareholders and its employees (numbering, it seems, some 120 persons) to complete.

My Lords, it follows from what I have said that if the appellants' claim is to be successfully resisted at all, in can only be only on the ground that the transaction proposed infringes the provisions of s151 of the 1985 Act ...

The acquisition of the Brady shares by Motoreal has already taken place and has given rise to the issue of the loan stock to Activista. The proposed transfer therefore falls within the provisions of subs (2) and it is not in dispute that it does indeed constitute the provision of assistance by Brady to reduce Motoreal's liability incurred in the course of that acquisition. The appellants, however, rely on the provisions of s153(2) ...

My Lords, I have found myself unable to share the views of the majority of the Court of Appeal with regard to para (b) [of s151(2)]. The words "in good faith in the interests of the company" form, I think, a single composite expression and postulate a requirement that those responsible for procuring the company to provide the assistance act in the genuine belief that it is being done in the company's interest. In the circumstances of this case, where failure to implement the final stage of the scheme for the division of the two sides of Brady's business is likely to lead back to the very management deadlock that it was designed to avoid and the probable liquidation of Brady as a result, the proposed transfer is not only something which is properly capable of being perceived by Brady's directors as calculated to advance Brady's corporate and commercial interests and the interests of its employees but is indeed, viewed objectively, in the company's interest. The corporators who sanctioned the transactions clearly considered that it was in their interests and in the interests of the company's business that it should continue in being under proper management unhampered by insoluble differences between the directors and I am not sure that I understand why Nourse LJ considered that there was no evidence that the interests of the company's creditors had been considered and that this was fatal to the proposal ...

As it was, when the matter came before the court, there was clear evidence that the interests of creditors not only were not jeopardised by the proposal but that, in the view of the company's auditors their position would, indeed, be improved in the long term once the reorganisation was completed. I do not, therefore, for my part, entertain any doubt that para (b) is satisfied or, since we are in fact looking at something which has not yet occurred, that it is at least capable of being satisfied.

Where I part company both from the trial judge and from the Court of Appeal is on the question of whether para (a) [of s151(2)] can, on any reasonable construction of the subsection, be said to have been satisfied ...

Now of course in the instant case the reason why the reorganisation was conceived in the first place was the damage being occasioned to the company and its shareholders by reason of the management deadlock, and the deadlock was the reason for the decision that the business should be split in two, so that the two branches could be conducted independently. What prompted the particular method adopted for carrying out the split was commercial desirability of keeping Brady in being as a corporate entity. That involved, in effect, Jack buying out Bob's interest in Brady and it was, presumably, the fact that he did not have free funds to do this from his own resources that dictated that Brady's own assets should be used for the purpose. No doubt the acquisition of control by Jack was considered, at any rate by Jack and Robert, who were and are Brady's directors, to be beneficial to Brady. Indeed, your Lordships have been told that the business has thriven under independent management. But this is merely the result, and no doubt the intended result, of Jack's assumption of control and however one analyses the transaction the only purpose that can be discerned in the redemption of loan stock is the payment in tangible form of the price payable to enable the Brady shares to be acquired and ultimately vested in Jack or a company controlled by him. The scheme of reorganisation was framed and designed to give Jack and Robert control of Brady for the best of reasons, but to say that the "larger purpose" of Brady's financial assistance is to be found in the scheme of reorganisation itself is to say only that the larger purpose was the acquisition of the Brady shares on their behalf. For my part, I do not think that a larger purpose can be found in the benefits considered to be likely to flow or the disadvantages considered to be likely to be avoided by the acquisition which it was the purpose of the assistance to facilitate. The acquisition was not a mere incident of the scheme devised to break the deadlock. It was the essence of the scheme itself and the object which the scheme set out to achieve. In my judgment, therefore, s153(2)(a) is not satisfied and if the matter rested there the appeal ought to fall on that ground.

That is a conclusion which I reach with a measure of regret, for the bargain between the appellants and the respondents was freely negotiated and the respondents' attempt to resile from it is not immediately attractive. It is, however, a conclusion which makes it necessary to consider two additional points which the appellants have sought leave to raise in their written case, neither of which was raised either at the trial or in the Court of Appeal but each of which, it is claimed, would be sufficient to dispose of any objection to specific performance based on s151 ... Although ... I was much troubled by the argument of counsel for the respondents in the course of the hearing I should, for my part, have been content to permit the new points to be raised without imposing any condition save for an appropriate order as to costs.

I understand, however, that the majority of your Lordships take the contrary view and are prepared to entertain the new arguments only on terms that the respondents be afforded the opportunity, if they desire it, to reinstate some or all of the defences which they abandoned before the judge ...

I turn therefore to consider the new contentions. Both start from a proposition which must, I think, be correct as a matter of law. It is simply this, that where an agreement can be performed in alternative ways, one lawful and one unlawful, it is to be presumed that the parties intend to carry it out in the lawful and not the unlawful manner ... Thus the transfer contemplated could, at the time of the agreement, be perfectly lawfully made in this way. This is incontestible but the short answer to it is that it was not what was agreed between the parties and that it involves the consequence that, in the absence of a fresh Revenue clearance, which, it is common ground, has not been obtained , the individual shareholders in Ovalshield will suffer tax on the dividends. It is unnecessary, therefore, to consider this point further.

The second point, however, is a much more formidable one and, for my part, I can see no answer to it nor has counsel for the respondents suggested any. It is simply this, that since all the companies concerned are private companies the transaction can be perfectly lawfully carried out in the manner contemplated without any departure from the agreed terms. There is no reason to believe that sufficient distributable profits to cover the proposed transfers either [were] or are now unavailable in Brady. In that situation, the directors of Brady (who, of course, are individually parties to the agreement of which specific performance is sought) are and have at all material times been able to ensure that the scheme of reorganisation can be lawfully carried out precisely in the manner agreed without any infringement of the provisions of s151. This can quite simply be done by operating the provisions of ss155, 156 and 158 of the 1985 Act, which have the effect of disapplying the provisions of s151. This is a matter which lies entirely in their hands and which does not involve the respondents in doing or concurring in the doing of anything which they have not agreed to do.

It is unnecessary, for present purposes, to set out the statutory provisions in full. In summary they provide that, where financial assistance is provided by a private company in connection with the acquisition of its shares or the shares of its parent company (being also a private company) the prohibition in s151 can be disapplied in certain circumstances by the adoption of the statutory procedure prescribed in ss156, 157 and 158. These provisions apply only if either the assets of the company providing the assistance are not reduced by the provision of assistance or if the assistance is provided out of distributable profits (see s155(2)). Provision is made for the rendering of assistance to be approved by special resolution (which may be cancelled by the court on application by a dissentient minority) but this does not apply where the company giving the assistance is (as each of Brady and Athersmith is) the wholly-owned subsidiary of the company to which assistance is given. All that is required to avoid the prohibitions contained in s151 is that the directors of the company giving the assistance (in this case the directors of both Brady and Athersmith) shall make a statutory declaration in a prescribed form to the effect that there is no ground on which, immediately following the giving of the assistance, it could be found to be unable to pay its debts and that it will be able to pay its debts as they fall due during the year immediately following that date (see s156(2)). There has also be annexed to the statutory declaration a report by the auditors stating that, after due inquiry, they are not aware of anything to indicate that the opinion expressed by the directors in the declaration is unreasonable (see s156(4)). These documents have to be delivered to the Registrar of Companies within 15 days after the making of the declaration and the assistance must be given, if given at all, within eight weeks from the date on which the declaration is made (see s158).

There can, in my judgment, be no doubt that, in the absence of some startling change in the financial position of either Brady or Athersmith since the date of the last accounts, the conditions specified in s155(2) are fulfilled. Whilst the proposed transfer will have the effect of reducing the net worth of Motoreal, since although the amount of its liabilities will remain unchanged the underlying assets will be reduced by the value of the assets transferred out of the Motoreal group, the net assets of Brady and Athersmith as opposed to those of the Motoreal group remain unchanged. I have already pointed out that there is, for instance, no reason to doubt the ability of Motoreal to pay its prospective indebtedness to Athersmith, if required, which would justify treating the debt as not worth its face value. The same applies to Brady, but, even if it did not and even if the debt fell to be treated as worth less that its face value or should prove to be irrecoverable in toto, the amount of Brady's distributable accumulated profits is ample to cover the value of the Brady assets to be transferred. Compliance with the remaining provisions of ss155, 156 and 158 rests, therefore, entirely in the hands of Jack and Robert and assuming that the company's auditors are able to make the report required by s156(4) there can be no impediment to reliance on these provisions. The evidence before the judge of Mr Lewis of Binder Hamlyn, who were then Brady's auditors, clearly indicates that such a report could properly have been given both at the date of the agreement and at the date of the trial and there is no reason to doubt that it can still be given. If this is right, then there appears to be, and, indeed, always to have been, a complete answer to the suggestion that the agreement is rendered unlawful by s151 of the 1985 Act and therefore incapable of specific performance, though clearly any decree of specific performance would have to contain appropriate conditions or undertakings to ensure that the provisions of ss156 and 158 are complied with. Subject to this, therefore, I would allow the appeal but only on the terms previously indicated.'

Royal Brunei Airlines Sdn Bhd v *Tan Kok Ming* [1995] BCC 899 Privy Council (Lords Goff, Ackner, Nicholls, Steyn and Sir Christopher May)

Breach of trust – knowing assistance by a third party

Facts

The plaintiff airline appointed Borneo Leisure Travel Sdn Bhd ('BLT') to be its agent to sell passenger and cargo transportation in 1986. Tan was the managing director and principal shareholder of BLT. The agency agreement was in writing and it incorporated the International Air Transport Association Regulations, which provided that all monies collected by the agent (BLT) were the property of the carrier (the airline). In addition it provided that the monies were to be held on trust by the agent for the carrier. BLT did not open a separate bank account for the airline's money and paid it into its own current account for use in the ordinary course of its business. BLT was required to pay monies owed to the airline within 30 days, but fell into arrears. The airline terminated the agreement in 1992 and sued Tan for the money owed. Although Tan was not a party to the agency agreement, he had signed it on behalf of BLT.

The Court of Appeal of Brunei Darussalam refused to hold Tan liable as constructive trustee on the basis that he had knowingly assisted BLT's breach of trust. The Court of Appeal felt that Tan's liability depended on a dishonest and fraudulent design on the part of the trustee, BLT, and this had not been made out. The airline appealed.

Held

The appeal was allowed and Tan was liable to pay the airline damages for being an accessory to BLT's breach of trust. It was sufficient that the accessory was dishonest, and was not reliant on the trustee also being dishonest. The breach of trust was committed by BLT when it failed to keep the airline's money separate from its own and Tan assisted in this. Both BLT and Tan were dishonest as Tan was BLT's directing mind and will.

Lord Nicholls:

> *'The accessory liability principle*
> Drawing the threads together, their Lordships' overall conclusion is that dishonesty is a necessary ingredient of accessory liability. It is also a sufficient ingredient. A liability in equity to make good resulting loss attaches to a person who dishonestly procures or assists in a breach of trust or fiduciary obligation. It is not necessary that, in addition, the trustee or fiduciary was acting dishonestly, although this will usually be so where the third party who is assisting him is acting dishonestly. "Knowingly" is better avoided as a defining ingredient of the principle, and in the context of this principle the *Baden* scale of knowledge is best forgotten.

> *Conclusion*
> From this statement of the principle it follows that this appeal suceeds. The money paid to BLT on the sale of tickets for Royal Brunei Airlines was held by BLT upon trust for the airline. This trust, on its face, conferred no power on BLT to use the money in the conduct of its business. The trust gave no authority to BLT to relieve its cash flow problems by utilising for this purpose the rolling 30-day credit afforded by the airline. Thus BLT committed a breach of trust by using the money instead of simply deducting its commission and holding the money intact until it paid the airline. Mr Tan accepted that he knowingly assisted in that breach of trust. In other words, he caused or permitted his company to apply the money in a way he knew was not authorised by the trust of which the company was trustee. Set out in these terms, Mr Tan's conduct was dishonest. By the same token, and for good measure, BLT also acted dishonestly. Mr Tan was the company, and his state of mind is to be imputed to the company.

> The Court of Appeal held that it was not established that BLT was guilty of fraud or dishonesty in relation to the amounts it held for the airline. Their Lordships understand that by this the Court of Appeal

meant that it was not established that Mr Tan intended to defraud the airline. Mr Tan hoped, maybe expected, to be able to pay the airline, but the money was lost in the ordinary course of poorly-run business with heavy overhead expenses. These facts are beside the point. Mr Tan had no right to employ the money in the business at all. That was the breach of trust. The company's inability to pay the airline was the consequence of that breach of trust.

The Court of Appeal observed that it would have been unrealistic to expect BLT to keep the money in a separate bank account and not use any of the money in the conduct of the business, particularly as BLT was also the ticketing agent for a number of other airlines. Their Lordships express no view on this, or on what the parties are to be taken to have intended would happen in practice when the company's current bank account was overdrawn. It is possible that in certain circumstances these points might sustain an argument that, although there was a failure to pay, there was no breach of trust. They do not arise in this case because of Mr Tan's acceptance that there was a breach of trust.

Their Lordships will report their advice to His Majesty The Sultan and Yang Di-Pertuan that this appeal would be allowed, the order of the Court of Appeal set aside, and the order of the Chief Justice restored. The respondent must pay the appellant's costs before their Lordships' board and before the Court of Appeal.'

Selangor United Rubber Estates Ltd v *Cradock (No 3)* [1968] 1 WLR 1555
Chancery Division (Ungoed-Thomas J)

Financial assistance rules – liability as constructive trustee

Facts
In 1957/58 Selangor had about £235,800 in liquid assets after selling its rubber plantations in Malaysia. Cradock employed a banking company Contanglo, to make an offer on his behalf to acquire the company's stock. In April 1958 about 79 per cent of the stockholders had accepted Cradock's offer and the amount payable for the stock, plus expenses, was £195,000. Cradock did not have much money and he devised a scheme to use the assets of Selangor to pay for the controlling stockholding he had acquired. The scheme took the form of two transactions. In the first a board meeting of Selangor was convened in April 1958 and it was resolved that Selangor's account at the National Bank, in which there was £232,500 should be transferred to the Oxford Street branch of the District Bank. Cradock had a personal account at this branch of the District Bank. It was also resolved that Selangor would lend the £232,500 in this account to a company called Woodstock at 8 per cent pa. A cheque was signed by the directors of Selangor, who were Cradock's puppets, in favour of Woodstock. A director of Woodstock endorsed the cheque over to Cradock and the District Bank, whose representatives had been present at the meeting, credited Cradock's account with £232,500 and debited Selangor's account by the same amount. Cradock used some of the money to pay Contanglo for the shares; the stockholders were paid off and the stock transferred to a nominee company for Cradock. In 1961 Selangor was compulsorily wound up. There was a Board of Trade investigation into the company's affairs and in 1964 this action was begun by the Board of Trade seeking declarations that the directors of Selangor, Cradock, Contanglo, Woodstock and the District Bank were jointly and severally liable to replace the moneys of the company which had been misapplied under s54 CA 1948 (now s151 CA 1985).

Held
(Inter alia) the transactions were in breach of s54 and the directors of Selangor were in breach of trust in the circumstances. As for Contanglo, Woodstock and the District Bank they were liable as constructive trustees since they had assisted the directors of Selangor, who were trustees of its assets, with knowledge, in a dishonest and fraudulent design. The knowledge in such a case was knowledge of the circumstances

which would indicate to an honest, reasonable man that a dishonest and fraudulent design was being committed or would put him on inquiry.

Restrictions on reducing a company's capital

Holders Investment Trust Ltd, Re [1971] 1 WLR 583 Chancery Division (Megarry J)

Refusal by court to confirm a reduction of capital

Facts
The company was incorporated in 1933 and had an authorised share capital of £2,275,000. A petition was presented to the court to confirm a reduction of capital to be effected by cancelling 1,250,000 5 per cent cumulative redeemable preference shares of £1 each, redeemable at par on 31 July, 1971 and allotting to the holders of the same nominal amount of 6 per cent unsecured loan stock 1985 – 90. The preference shares were fully paid up and had priority to repayment in a winding-up but no further rights to participate in the profits or assets. The reduction had been authorised by a resolution of the company and a separate class meeting was carried because 90 per cent of the preference shares were held by trustees who also held 52 per cent of the ordinary shares. The petition for confirmation was opposed on two grounds; (i) that the preference shareholders who voted in favour of the resolution at the class meeting did so in their own interests and not in the interests of the preference shareholders as a whole and (ii) the reduction was not, in any event, fair because the 6 per cent unsecured loan stock was not adequate recompense for 5 per cent loan stock which was soon repayable especially since repayment was postponed to some unspecified date in between 1985 and 1990.

Held
The petition would be dismissed since the evidence showed that the trustees who voted in favour of the reduction had not applied their minds to the interests of the class as a whole but only considered their own interests. Further those supporting the petition had failed to discharge the burden of proof on them to show that the reduction was fair.

Megarry J:

'In the *British America* case ([1927] AC 369) Viscount Haldane, in speaking for a strong Board of the Judicial Committee, referred to:

"… a general principle, which is applicable to all authorities conferred on majorities of classes enabling them to bind minorities; namely, that the power given must be exercised for the purpose of benefiting the class as a whole, and not merely individual members only."

The matter may, I think, be put in the way in which Scrutton, LJ, put it in the *Shuttleworth* case (2) where the question was the benefit of the company rather than of a particular class of members. Adapting his language, I have to see whether the majority was honestly endeavouring to decide and act for the benefit of the class as a whole, rather than with a view to the interests of some of the class and against that of others. This is a decision that in this case I have to make on affidavit evidence; there has been no cross-examination or other viva voce evidence before me.

I pause here to point the obvious. Without guidance from those skilled in these matters many members of a class may fail to realise what they should bear in mind when deciding how to vote at a class meeting. The beneficial owner of shares may well concentrate on his own personal interests; even though he regards the proposal per se as one to be rejected, collateral matters affecting other interests of his may lead him to vote in favour of the resolution. Trustees, too, are under a fiduciary duty to do the best they properly can for their beneficiaries. A proposal which, in isolation, is contrary to the interests of those owning the shares affected may nevertheless be beneficial to the beneficiaries by reason of the improved prospects that the proposal will confer on other shares in the company which the trustees hold on the same trusts: and that, in essence, is what is in issue here. As I have mentioned, of the £1,250,000 preference shares in question, almost 90 per cent are vested in the supporting trustees, who also own some 52 per cent of the ordinary stock and shares ...'

... From first to last I can see no evidence that the trustees ever applied their minds to what, under company law, was the right question, or that they ever had the bona fide belief that is requisite for an effectual sanction of the reduction. Accordingly, in my judgment, there has been no effectual sanction for the modification of class rights ...'

Northern Engineering Industries plc, Re [1993] BCC 267 Chancery Division (Companies Court) (Ferris J)

Reduction of capital – variation of class rights

Facts

The company was seeking the court's approval of a reduction of capital, which involved paying off the preference shares and cancelling them. The reduction was opposed by a preference shareholder.

The company's articles provided in art 7(B) that, 'The rights attached to any shares shall be deemed to be varied by a reduction of the capital paid up on such shares ...'. Article 6 required such a variation to be consented to by the preference shareholders or by an extraordinary resolution passed at a separate meeting of the preference shareholders.

The preference shareholders argued that in the absence of consent or an extraordinary resolution, the court should not confirm the capital reduction. The company argued that art 7(B) only applied where there was a reduction of capital paid up on particular shares to a figure which exceeded zero. In other words 'reduction' means something different from 'cancellation' or 'extinction'.

Held

The court declined to confirm the reduction. Article 7(B) had the effect that the proposed cancellation of the preference shares was a variation of the rights attached to the preference shares and a class meeting was therefore required by art 6. As no such meeting had been held, the reduction of capital had not been carried out in accordance with the company's articles.

Poole v *National Bank of China* [1907] AC 229 House of Lords (Lord Loreburn LC, Lords Macnaghten, Robertson and Atkinson)

Reduction of capital – variation of class rights

Facts

The bank was incorporated with a share capital of £1,000,000 divided into 750 founders' shares of £1 each and 99,925 shares of £10 each. All the founders' shares were issued and fully paid and 40,453 ordinary shares were issued on which £8 per share had been paid. Because of falls in the Hong Kong dollar the bank's funds and profits were seriously affected and in 1904 it was proposed to reduce the capital to £699,475 being 99,925 ordinary shares of £7 each by writing off £3 per share on the ordinary shares and repaying the holders of founders' shares the sum of £1 per share as and when profits permitted this. The scheme was submitted for approval by the court but was opposed by the holders of 44 £1 founders' shares. Farwell J confirmed the reduction and the Court of Appeal affirmed his decision. On appeal:

Held

The reduction was fair and the appeal should be dismissed.

Lord Macnaghten:

'... In the present case creditors are not concerned at all. The reduction does not involve the diminution of any liability in respect of unpaid capital or the payment to any shareholder of any paid-up capital. The only questions, therefore, to be considered are these: 1. Ought the court to refuse its sanction to the reduction out of regard to the interests of those members of the public who may be induced to take shares in the company? 2. Is the reduction fair and equitable as between the different classes of shareholders?

Now the directors gave the shareholders the fullest information as to the reasons for the reduction and the causes which led them to propose it. All this is explained in the petition. It has not been suggested that the proposed reduction is open to any objection on public grounds. The question, therefore, must be this: Is it fair as between different classes of shareholders? The only objection put forward is made on the part of an insignificant number of holders of founders' shares. These are two individuals who hold five founders' shares each, and there is a public company holding 34 founders' shares. The directors, in their circular to the shareholders, stated that these shares were of no commercial value. That is not denied. It is proposed to pay the dissentient shareholders the par value of their shares out of profits, and to extinguish the founders' shares, because their continued existence would render it difficult, if not impossible, for the company to raise further capital. The dissentient shareholders do not demand, and never have demanded, better pecuniary terms, but they insist on retaining their holdings, which in all reasonable probability can never bring any profit to them, and may be detrimental to the company ...'

Westburn Sugar Refineries Ltd, ex parte [1951] AC 625 House of Lords (Lords Porter, Normand, Oaksey, Reid and Radcliffe)

Confirmation of reduction of capital by court

Facts

The company was incorporated in 1897 with a share capital of £609,000 being 609,000 shares of £1 each which had been converted into stock. The company was threatened with nationalisation of its assets and, through an investment company it formed, a scheme was devised for the reduction of the company's capital, which involved transferring to the shareholders assets the value of which could possibly exceed the amount by which the share capital was reduced. When the scheme was presented to the court for confirmation it was refused on the ground that it was an attempt to milk the company of its capital before nationalisation. On appeal:

Held

The reduction should be confirmed since if it was unobjectionable on other grounds the fact that it has an ulterior motive was not a sufficient reason for the court withholding its sanction.

Lord Radcliffe:

'... My Lords, I do not think that the contingency of nationalisation has any relevance to the public policy that the Courts of Justice should support. If the reduction is objectionable on other grounds, it will not become the more acceptable because it may have been proposed in view of a pending measure of nationalisation: conversely, the threat of nationalisation cannot render improper what is otherwise unobjectionable. I pass, therefore, to the second, and, indeed, the main, reason which weighed with the learned judge. In his view it was essential for the company, which showed by its petition that the ground of the proposed reduction was that the share capital to be returned was in excess of its wants, to demonstrate to the court by how much its capital was in fact surplus; and, since the evidence presented to the court was deficient in this respect, a material fact had not been made out. Whether this conclusion would on any view have justified a dismissal of the petition, rather than its remitter for further inquiry, I do not think it necessary to discuss; for I think that the conclusion itself is based on a misunderstanding.

I cannot find any good reason why the court should be concerned to know what is the extent by which the company's capital is surplus to its requirements. If by that phrase, itself susceptible of ambiguity, is meant the extent by which the whole of the company's assets, at the best contemporary valuation that can be placed upon them, exceed what is required for the future conduct of its business, precise information on this would do nothing to aid the task of the court. For it would throw no light on the sole thing which is here in question, how much of the paid-up share capital is to be returned as being surplus. Nor do I think that evidence of this kind is usually required in cases of this sort. In truth this, which is the real question, answers itself by the company's own resolution. When a company has come to employ in its business, as this company has, a volume of assets very much greater in value than the amount of its paid-up share capital, there is no obvious answer to the question how much of that capital it needs for future trading. It is a domestic matter, which the shareholders and their managers must decide among themselves, how much of the paid-up share capital the company can dispense with for the future. If the amount that they have decided upon works no injustice to creditors or to shareholders, I see no purpose which can be served by the court's insisting upon a precise figure of the company's wants or the striking of an exact balance between that figure and the total available resources in hand ...'

Prudential Assurance Co Ltd v *Chatterley-Whitfield Collieries Ltd* [1949] AC 512
House of Lords (Viscount Maugham, Lords Simons, Normand and Morton)

Reduction of capital – capital returned to preference shareholders

Facts
The company was incorporated in 1891, with a share capital of £400,000 which was divided into 20,000 preference shares of £10 each and 20,000 ordinary shares of £10 each. All the shares had been issued and fully paid. Under art 7 of the articles it was provided that the preference shareholders had a right to a fixed cumulative dividend of 6 per cent pa upon the amount paid up thereon and, in the event of the winding up of the company, to repayment of capital together with any arrears of dividend down to the date of repayment in priority to the claims of the holders of ordinary shares but no other right to participate in the assets of the company. In 1947 the company's colliery was nationalised and it became entitled to compensation therefor. The company had been very prosperous in the years before nationalisation and built-up a substantial reserve fund. It did not intend to go into liquidation but, instead, to mine coal in Northern Ireland if prospecting there was successful or, alternatively, dig clay and manufacture drainpipes and the like. In the circumstances, the company's capital was in excess of its needs and in October 1947 a resolution was passed to reduce its capital by returning to the preference shareholders all the capital paid on their shares. The petition for confirmation of the reduction was opposed by some preference shareholders. At first instance the petition was dismissed; the Court of Appeal reversed this decision. On appeal

Held
In the circumstances the reduction ought to be confirmed since it was fair and equitable because the preference shareholders would not have been entitled to anything more in liquidation than they were to receive in the reduction.

Lord Simonds:

'... I can see no reason for thinking that a claim by preference shareholders to be repaid more than the nominal amount of their capital has any substance in it. Counsel for the appellants, being asked to indicate the sort of adjustment that the preference shareholders might fairly claim, suggested that they might get

£12 for every £10 of capital upon their submitting to be paid off. As I said in the recent appeal from the Court of Session, I should not wish to prejudice any similar claim that may come before a statutory tribunal. But I see no slightest justification for such a claim. Of the two elements that have to be considered, "rights of priority" and "relative expectations of income yield", the first is fully satisfied in favour of the preference shareholders by the repayment of their capital in full before any payment is make to the ordinary shareholders; the second is more difficult to evaluate, but it is surely the ordinary shareholders whose position has been prejudiced by the expropriation of the company's property. The preference shareholders may or may not eventually find a 6 per cent investment for their money: probably they will not. But it is in the highest degree unlikely that the ordinary shareholders will receive an income commensurate with what they might reasonably have expected, if the Act had not been passed. It is therefore, to put it at the lowest, so unlikely that the preference shareholders can get anything more than the full amount of their capital returned to them, that the court should not depart from its well-known and familiar practice in dealing with a petition to confirm a reduction of capital. This practice would, as I have already pointed out, lead to a confirmation of the reduction proposed in this case.

I am of opinion, therefore, that this appeal should be dismissed with costs.'

In the Court of Appeal, Lord Greene MR said:

'... In respect of the loss of the coal mining business, under nationalisation the position is this ... the company will eventually become entitled to compensation ... it may be expected that the company will not receive this, its compensation, until after the expiration of a considerable period, running perhaps into several years. In the meanwhile the company is faced with the following situation. Its principal business is gone and it is proposing to embark upon certain new activities which may or may not turn out to be successful. So long as it was possessed of its colliery, it clearly required all of its capital in the business – there was no question of its having surplus capital to its requirements. The reduced form of its activities is however such that it has a great deal more capital than it requires and it is not unimportant to observe that it finds itself in this position quite apart from any compensation which it may receive when the share of the compensation is ultimately determined and paid. The repayment may be paid without recourse to the compensation.

What is a company in this situation to do? The business answer does not admit of doubt, particularly where the substantial part of the capital consists of preference shares bearing a higher rate of dividend than the company is reasonably likely to earn in the future. It would do what this company seeks to do, ie reduce its capital by paying off as much of the preference capital as it can afford out of its surplus. A company which satisfies its capital requirement by issuing preference shares only does so where satisfied that the new capital will earn at least the promised rate of dividend. A company which has issued preference shares carrying a higher rate of dividend and finds its business so curtailed that it has a capital surplus to its requirements and sees the likelihood or at any rate the possibility that its preference capital would not earn its keep would be guilty of financial ineptitude if it did not take steps to reduce its capital ...

The position of the company itself as an economic entity must be considered and nothing can be more destructive of a company's financial equilibrium than to carry the burden of capital which it does not need bearing a high rate of dividend which it cannot earn. In a company so situated the ordinary shareholders will be unfairly treated vis-a-vis the preference shareholders and the company may well fall into a situation where the preferential dividends fall into arrears irretrievably ...'

Saltdean Estate, Re [1968] 1 WLR 1844 Chancery Division (Buckley J)

Reduction of capital – preference shares repaid in full

Facts
The company was incorporated in 1926 and from 1932 its share capital was £12,500 divided into 20,000 preference shares of 10s each and 50,000 ordinary shares of 1s each. The company invested in land and

other real estate and this business proved to be very profitable and despite the payment of very large dividends on a regular basis it had, in 1968, a revenue reserve of £324,924. In July 1968 a special resolution was passed to reduce the capital of the company to £2,500 being 50,000 ordinary shares of 1s each. The preference shares were to be repaid in full with a premium of 5s per share. Some of the preference shareholders opposed the reduction on the ground, inter alia, that it was unfair and inequitable. Even with paying the preference shareholders in full with the 5s premium only £15,000 was needed from the revenue reserves so that the balance would go to the ordinary shareholders. If, however, the revenue reserve was distributed by way of dividend the preferred shareholders would receive £162,500. Under the articles the preference shareholders were, in the event of winding up, only entitled to priority in repayment of their capital and nothing further.

Held

The reduction was in accordance with the rights of the preferred shareholders in winding up and even though there was no prospect of winding up but every prospect of continued large profits the reduction was not unfair or inequitable.

Buckley J:

'... Unless this reduction can be shown to be unfair to the preferred shareholders on other grounds, it is in accordance with the right and liability to prior repayment of capital attached to their shares. The liability to prior repayment on a reduction of capital, corresponding to their right to prior return of capital in a winding up, is a liability of a kind which Lord Greene MR, in the passage I have referred to, said that anyone has only himself to blame if he does not know it. It is part of the bargain between the shareholders and forms an integral part of the definition or delimitation of the bundle of rights which make up the preferred share. Giving effect to it does not involve the variation or abrogation of any right attached to such a share ...

... The opponents of the petition say that notwithstanding this and notwithstanding that in a winding up the first capital to be repaid would be that paid-up on the preferred shares; the proposed reduction of capital is unfair to the preferred shareholders and should not be confirmed by the court. They say, as seems to be the case, that there is no present prospect of the company being wound up; that it can be regarded as certain that there will continue to be large distributions of profits in which, if the preferred shares were still to exist, the holders of them would participate equally with the ordinary shareholders; and that it is unfair that this right should be bought out at the price of no more than 15s for a 10s share.

On the other hand, the evidence indicates that during 1966 and 1967 six separate sales of small numbers of preferred shares were negotiated at arm's length at 11s a share. This may not be of great significance, for one does not know the circumstances of these sales, but this price, I think, indicates an appreciation on the part of the vendors of their vulnerability in the event of either a winding up or a reduction of capital.

It is true that the preferred shareholders, if they were to act unanimously, could block a special resolution, but a large number of preferred shares are held by the holder or holders of ordinary shares and a special resolution has, in fact, been passed to effect the proposed reduction of capital. It has not been suggested that the majority acted oppressively in this respect.

The fact is that every holder of preferred shares of the company has always been at risk that his hope of participating in undrawn or future profits of the company might be frustrated at any time by a liquidation of the company or a reduction of its capital properly resolved upon by a sufficient majority of his fellow members. This vulnerability is, and has always been, a characteristic of the preferred shares. Now that the event has occurred, none of the preferred shareholders can, in my judgment, assert that the resulting state of affairs is unfair to him ...'

7 Debentures

Nature of fixed and floating charges

Cimex Tissues Ltd, Re [1994] BCC 626 Chancery Division (Mr S J Burnton QC sitting as a deputy High Court judge)

Whether a charge over plant and machinery was fixed

Facts

The company's business was that of manufacturing toilet rolls. A debenture charged, 'by way of fixed charge', plant and machinery specified in a valuation annexed to the debenture. The machinery was used in the manufacturing process and was not of a type to be sold or replaced very often. The liquidator sought a determination whether the charge over the machinery was fixed or floating. The preferential creditors were claiming that it was a floating charge, in which case they would be paid off first out of the proceeds of the sale. The debenture-holder claimed that it was fixed, in which case he would be entitled to the proceeds at the expense of the preferential creditors.

Clause 3.2 of the debenture provided that the company would not 'without the previous consent in writing of the lender ... sell, mortgage or otherwise deal with the charged property otherwise than for the purpose of getting in and realising them in the ordinary course of, and for the purpose of, carrying on its trading business'. This, according to the preferential creditors, made the charge a floating charge, for it gave the company liberty to deal with the charged assets in the ordinary course of business, without obtaining the prior consent of the lender. Such a liberty is inconsistent with a fixed charge. The debenture-holder rejected this interpretation, but said that even if the charge did give such a liberty, it was not necessarily inconsistent with the creation of fixed charge.

Held

On its true construction, the debenture created a fixed charge.

1. The words 'getting in and realising' in clause 3.2 were inappropriate and inapplicable to the charged property due to its nature. The words were more appropriate to book debts. They were thought to be wholly inappropriate to the manufacturing equipment of a company. The clause did not therefore give the company power to deal with the charged property.
2. The words 'trading business' in clause 3.2 were construed as referring to the sale of stock and this was to be contrasted with the manufacturing business of the company. The clause gave no relevant power to the company, as the sale of capital manufacturing equipment could not be said to be 'in the ordinary course of its trading business'.
3. Where the chargor is given a licence to deal with the property this does not, in itself, lead to the conclusion that the charge is floating; however it would be if the licence to deal was extensive. On the facts, if clause 3.2 was construed as giving the chargor the right to sell the property without the lender's consent, the charge over the machinery was still a fixed one.

The decision of the case rests entirely upon the construction of the charge. The following extract concerns the difficult question of whether a liberty to sell in the ordinary course of business is necessarily inconsistent with a fixed charge.

Mr S J Burnton QC:

'The authorities on floating charges to which I have been referred do not lead me to conclude that, in the case of a charge over specific manufacturing machinery, a liberty for the chargor to deal to some extent with that machinery without the consent of the chargee is necessarily inconsistent with the creation of a fixed charge. I see no reason why, if the facts of *Holroyd* v *Marshall* were to recur today, in the case of a company, it could not be held that the charge created was a fixed charge.

In the present case, on any basis the company was prohibited from creating any charge over the secured property by virtue of cl 3.5 of the debenture. At most, the licence conferred implicitly by cl 3.2:1.2 entitled it to sell parts of the charged machinery "in the ordinary course of, and for the purpose of carrying on its trading business". If I assume that "trading" adds nothing to "business", this licence is scarcely different from that of the chargor in *Holroyd* v *Marshall,* except that in that case, substitute machinery had to be brought within the scope of the charge. I do not consider that that difference is sufficient to require me to find that the charge created by the debenture in the present case was, contrary to its description, and notwithstanding that only specific assets were charged, a floating charge. The difference relates to the commercial sense of the transaction from the point of view of the chargee, rather than the legal classification of the charge created. In this connection, I must say that I should be reluctant to be compelled to conclude, in the case of a charge on specific manufacturing equipment of a manufacturing company, that the unequivocal words of cl 2.1, explicitly referring to a fixed charge, could be overridden by what is in the present debenture a highly ambiguous and uncertain provision for sale in cl 3.2.

It follows that if I had concluded that cl 3.2:1.2 of the debenture had conferred a licence on the company without the subsequent consent of the chargee to sell parts of the specific manufacturing machinery constituting the charged property "in the ordinary course of, and for the purpose of carrying on its business", I should nonetheless have found that the charge created was a fixed charge.'

Commentary

This case is also interesting for it highlights the importance of having a well drafted debenture and one which is appropriate to the borrower's type of business. The debenture in this case was criticised as being 'defective', and the judge identified the debenture as deriving from the precedent at p145 of the *Encyclopaedia of Forms and Precedents* (5th edn). This contained a precedent for a debenture to secure bank lending. It was wholly inappropriate as the business of the company was that of a toilet roll manufacturer!

Hi-Fi Equipment (Cabinets) Ltd, Re [1988] BCLC 65 Chancery Division (Harman J)

Whether machinery was covered by a fixed charge

Facts

To enable it to carry on its business of manufacturing cabinets, the company possessed machinery which was free standing and attached to the floor only by its own weight. The company had executed a debenture in favour of its bank which provided in cl 3(c) that the company charged 'by way of first fixed charge all future freehold and leasehold property of the company together with all buildings fixtures (including trade fixtures) and fixed plant and machinery from time to time thereon' and in cl 3(d) that it charged 'by way of a first floating charge all the other undertaking and assets of the company whatsoever and wheresoever both present and future'. Receivers having been appointed by the bank, the question arose as to whether the machinery was covered by cl 3(c) ('fixed plant and machinery') so that the bank took the proceeds of sale in priority to preferential creditors.

Held

It was not so covered.

Harman J:

'It is said, and I think rightly, that there is no direct decision in England on the meaning of the phrase "fixed plant and machinery" in a debenture in the context of a clause where fixtures, including trade fixtures, are separately specified. One would, prima facie, expect a skilled draftsman (as I have said, this document must be by the hand of a skilled draftsman) to use different words to mean different classes or types of assets; here, in cl 3(c), he has expressly used the phrase "fixtures (including trade fixtures)", as defining one class of assets and has gone on to refer to "and fixed plant and machinery" as a separate class. Clause 3(c) is unhappy in that it mixes up tangibles and intangibles and purports to deal with some but not others of the normal intangibles of a company ...

However, to my mind the phrase "fixed plant and machinery" is a phrase so well known, both in commercial and in legal terms, as a composite phrase, what in German would be a portmanteau word all combined together, that one cannot properly divorce the word "machinery" from the words "fixed plant". The imposition of the word "and" in the clause before the words "fixed plant" so that it reads "buildings", in effect comma, "fixtures (including trade fixtures) and" points to my mind to there being three classes and not four classes of goods in this phrase and that the second "and" between the words "fixed plant and machinery" is merely the hyphening together of the composite phrase "fixed plant and machinery".

It is not a matter, I think, which can be elucidated by logical argument. It is a question of the impression of the use of the English language on somebody accustomed to reading such sorts of phrase and, to my mind, the words here in the context of a charge on items on freehold or leasehold property must be interpreted so that "machinery" by itself was not intended to be included. After all, if "machinery" by itself were intended to be included, that phrase would apply to mobile machinery as well as static. Whether mobile machinery is on or off some property of the company must obviously vary from time to time as it is moved or driven about. In my judgment, the phrase "fixed plant and machinery" means, as I say, a single item and the word "fixed" governs both parts of it. I find that to be the natural reading of a phrase where one is referring to something on property; one would expect it to refer in this context of a fixed charge to static items as I think.

It would be to my mind extremely surprising if a large forklift truck, which I think is undoubtedly a piece of machinery, were to be within the fixed charge upon the property of the company because, amongst other things, it would mean that the company would have no right to sell that forklift truck when it came to the end of its normal useful life in three or five years and replace it with another without the express consent of the mortgagee bank. Such a conclusion seems to me highly improbable and I would expect normal mobile machinery of that sort to be within the floating charge but not within the fixed charge in any ordinary contemplation of a debenture of this sort.

The apposition of the words "fixtures (including trade fixtures)" and the phrase, which I hold to be one composite phrase, "fixed plant and machinery" is, I accept, not a happy one. It is conceded that in this case the machinery was not "fixtures", whether trade or any other sort of fixture.'

New Bullas Trading Ltd, Re [1994] BCC 38 Court of Appeal (Nourse and Russell LJJ and Scott Baker J)

Whether charge over book debts created fixed or floating charge

Facts

The company granted a debenture to 3i plc which, in condition 12, created a fixed charge over the company's book and other debts owing to the company. The provision stated that such money was to be paid into a specified bank account and was to be dealt with according to any directions given by the debenture holder. In the absence of such directions, the money was to be released from the fixed charge and made subject to the floating charge also made under the same debenture. No directions were ever given. Administrative receivers were appointed and the issue on appeal was whether the charge over book debts as created was a fixed or floating charge. If it was floating, the preferential creditors would be paid in priority to the debenture holder. If, on the other hand, it was fixed the preferential creditors would be paid after the debenture holder's claims had been satisfied. There were not enough assets to satisfy both sets of creditors.

Held

While the book debts were uncollected they were subject to a fixed charge, but on realisation, and in the absence of a direction by the debenture holder on how to deal with them, they became subject to a floating charge.

Nourse LJ said that the parties to a debenture can, subject to public policy considerations, make whatever contract they wish and can create a fixed charge over future book debts. Whether they have done so depends upon the intention of the parties but the label they give the charge will be inconclusive if other terms of the debenture are inconsistent with it. His decision was made based on the declared intention of the parties in condition 12.

Siebe Gorman & Co v *Barclays Bank* [1979] 2 Lloyd's Rep 142 Chancery Division (Slade J)

Whether charge over book debts created fixed or floating charge

Facts

The plaintiff company were manufacturers and suppliers of safety equipment. They supplied such equipment to a firm known as RHM McDonald Ltd on credit. In 1972 McDonald was in financial difficulty and owed the plaintiff company over £10,000. Payment of this was demanded and this demand being unsatisfied, a writ was issued. In order to settle this claim and also to continue trading McDonald's assigned to the plaintiff company several bills of exchange and a letter of credit and paid £1,500 in cash. The plaintiff company gave notice of their assignment to Barclays Bank, McDonald's bankers and the holders of the bills of exchange and letter of credit. In October 1972 a compulsory winding-up order was made against McDonalds. The plaintiff company claimed, inter alia, that they were entitled to the value of the bills of exchange and the sums the bank had collected on some of these. The bank contested this and claimed that under the terms of a debenture executed in their favour in 1971 by McDonalds, the existence but not the details of which the plaintiffs were aware, that it had a first fixed charge upon the bills of exchange. Under cl 3(d) of the debenture McDonald's charge in favour of the Bank 'by way of first fixed charge all book debts and other debts, now and from time to time due or owing to the company.' The debenture further provided under cl 5(c): 'During the continuance of this security the company ... (c) shall pay into the company's account with the bank all monies which it may receive in respect of the book debts and other debts hereby charged and shall not without the prior consent of the bank in writing purport to charge or assign the same in favour of any other person and shall if called upon to do so by the bank execute a legal assignment of such book debts and other debts to the bank.'

Held

1. On the facts of the case the bills of exchange were book debts within the meaning of cl 3(d).
2. A mortgagor could in law grant a fixed charge over future book debts which attached to these as soon as they were received. This had the effect of preventing the mortgagor disposing of these without having obtained the mortgagee's prior consent even before the mortgagee had taken steps to enforce its security.

3. In the present case the debenture gave the bank a specific charge over the book debts (ie the bills of exchange).
4. Since cl 5(c) had the effect of preventing McDonald's dealing with their equity of redemption in the book debts and this, being something which the plaintiff company would not expect to find in the debenture, they had neither actual or constructive notice of cl 5(c). Accordingly, since the plaintiff company's assignment was not a charge and, therefore, not registrable under s95 CA 1948 they took priority in the circumstances of the case.

Slade J:

'... Before the decision of the House of Lords in *Tailby* v *Official Receiver* (1888) 13 App Cas 523, there was some doubt whether there could be an effective assignment of future book debts, because it was thought that an assignment in such terms might be so indefinite and uncertain that the courts could not give effect to it. Any such doubts, however, were removed by this decision, which shows that it is undoubtedly competent for anyone to whom book debts may accrue in the future to create for good consideration an equitable charge upon those book debts, which will attach to them as soon as they come into existence.

This much was common ground between the parties in the present case. Mr Phillips, however, on behalf of Siebe Gorman, strongly contended that, notwithstanding the wording of cl 3(d) of the debenture, referring to a first fixed charge on – "all book debts ... now and from time to time due or owing to the company ..." the charge on the relevant bills could not be and was not more than a floating charge. He referred to the often cited passage from the judgment of Romer LJ in *Re Yorkshire Woolcombers Association Ltd* [1903] 2 CH 284 at p295:

"I certainly think that if a charge has the three characteristics that I am about to mention it is a floating charge. (i) If it is a charge on a class of assets of a company present and future; (ii) if that class is one which in the ordinary course of business of the company would be changing from time to time; and (iii) if you find that, until some future step is taken by or on behalf of those interested in the charge, the company may carry on business in the ordinary way as far as concerns the particular class of assets I am dealing with."

The charge on the book debts represented by the relevant bills in the present case clearly possesses the first two of these three characteristics. The dispute arises in regard to the third. The provisions of cl 5(c) of the debenture obliged the debtor, even before the bank had taken any steps to enforce its security, to pay into the debtor's account with the bank all moneys which it might receive in respect of the relevant bills and not without prior consent of the bank in writing to purport to charge or assign the same in favour of any other person. Notwithstanding these provisions, Mr Phillips, on behalf of Siebe Gorman, submitted that it was plain in the context of the debenture that R H McDonald Ltd was intended, until the bank took steps to enforce its security, to be free to continue trading and to use the proceeds of its future book debts, including the relevant bills for the purpose of trading. He submitted that there were a number of forms of dealing with future book debts which were not precluded by the terms of cl 5(c), for example, dealings by way of barter, exchange or set-off, and that the sub-clause necessarily implied that the debtor had the right to deal with future book debts, save as thereby expressly precluded. He emphasised that, while according to the terms of cl 5(c) all the proceeds of future book debts would in the first instance have to go into the debtor's account with the bank, it must have been contemplated that R H McDonald Ltd would then be free immediately to draw out all those moneys for the ordinary purposes of its business, at least if such account was for the time being in credit.

In regard to the latter point, if I had accepted the premise that R H McDonald Ltd would have had the unrestricted right to deal with the proceeds of any of the relevant book debts paid into its account, so long as that account remained in credit, I would have been inclined to accept the conclusion that the charge on such book debts could be no more than a floating charge. I refer to the respective definitions of a floating charge and a specific charge given by Lord Macnaghten in *Illingworth* v *Houldsworth* [1904] AC 355 at p358.:

"A specific charge, I think, is one that without more fastens on ascertained and definite property or property capable of being ascertained and defined; a floating charge, on the other hand, is ambulatory and shifting in its nature, hovering over and so to speak floating with the property which it is intended to affect until some event occurs or some act is done which causes it to settle and fasten on the subject of the charge within its reach and grasp."

If the debenture on its true construction had given the bank no rights whatsoever, at a time when the account of R H McDonald Ltd was in credit, to prevent the company from spending in the ordinary course of business all or any of the proceeds of the book debts paid into the account, I would have been inclined to regard the charge, for all the wording of the debenture, as doing no more than "hovering over and so to speak floating with" the book debts, within the words of Lord Macnaghten. Such, I would conceive, is the effect of a charge on future book debts in the form usually employed. Commonly it is intended, by both creditor and debtor, that the debtor shall have the free disposal of the proceeds of future book debts which may come into his hands, so long as the creditor takes no steps to enforce his security, or the charge has not otherwise crystallised. In my judgment, however, it is perfectly possibly in law for a mortgagor, by way of continuing security for future advances, to grant to a mortgagee a charge on future book debts in a form which creates in equity a specific charge on the proceeds of such debts as soon as they are received and consequently prevents the mortgagor from disposing of the unencumbered title to the subject matter of such charge without the mortgagee's consent, even before the mortgagee has taken steps to enforce its security: (compare *Evans, Coleman & Evans Ltd* v *Nelson RA Construction* (1958) 16 DLR 123). This in my judgment was the effect of the debenture in the present case. I see no reason why the court should not give effect to the intention of the parties, as stated in cl 3(d), that the charge should be a first fixed charge on book debts. I do not accept the argument that the provisions of cl 5(c) negative the existence of a specific charge. All that they do, in my judgment, is to reinforce the specific charge given by cl 3. The mere fact that there may exist certain forms of dealing with book debts which are not specifically prohibited by cl 5(c) does not in my judgment turn the specific charge into a floating charge.

This conclusion that the charge is a specific charge involves the further conclusion that during the continuance of the security, the bank would have the right, if it chose, to assert its lien under the charge on the proceeds of the book debts, even at a time when the particular account into which they were paid was temporarily in credit. However, I see nothing surprising in this conclusion, bearing in mind that the charge afforded continuing security to the bank not only in respect of any indebtedness on that particular account but also in respect of any other indebtedness of R H McDonald Ltd to the bank. The bank's lien would, after all, continue only during the subsistence of the debenture, which the debtor would at all times have the right to redeem.'

Yorkshire Woolcombers Association Limited, Re [1903] 2 Ch 284 Court of Appeal (Vaughan Williams, Romer and Cozens-Hardy LJJ)

Characteristics of a floating charge

Facts
The company had an overdraft of £59,000 with its bankers which was guaranteed by the directors of the association and others. The guarantors wished to be relieved of this liability and pressed the company to discharge its indebtedness to the bank. The company was unable to do this and instead it gave the guarantors an assignment of all 'the book and other debts owing to the association, and also all ... the book and other debts which may at any time during the continuance of this security become owing to the association'. The assignment was made to a trustee for the benefit of the guarantors and he was given power to appoint a receiver, power he exercised a month later. This action was concerned with the enforcement of the security. The question arose whether the security was in the nature of a 'floating charge', a phrase used in s14 of the Companies Act 1900 and void for non-registration thereunder.

Held

The charge was a 'floating charge'.

Romer LJ:

'... I certainly do not intend to attempt to give an exact definition of the term 'floating charge' nor am I prepared to say that there will not be a floating charge within the meaning of the Act, which does not contain all the three characteristics that I am about to mention, but I certainly think that if a charge has the three characteristics that I am about to mention it is a floating charge. (i) If it is a charge on a class of assets of a company present and future; (ii) if that class is one which, in the ordinary course of the business of the company, would be changing from time to time; and (iii) if you find that by the charge it is contemplated that, until some future step is taken by or on behalf of those interested in the charge, the company may carry on its business in the ordinary way as far as concerns the particular class of assets I am dealing with.

In the present case those three characteristics do in my opinion distinguish the charge we have to consider. In the first place, the charge is one upon all the debts of the company, present and future, not even limiting them (though I do not think it makes any difference) to the trade debts, present and future. In the second place, it obviously contemplates a class of asset which, in the ordinary course of the life of the company, must continually, and, of necessity, change; and, thirdly, in the present case, if I look at the deed which created the charge here, to my mind it is clearly contemplated that until some step is taken by or on behalf of those who are to have the benefit of the charge, the company would be able to receive the debts due to the company in its ordinary course of business, and to deal with them for the ordinary purposes of the business ...'

Commentary

The Court of Appeal decision in this case was affirmed by the House of Lords in *Illingworth* v *Houldsworth* [1904] AC 355. In a short speech Lord Macnaghten contrasted a floating charge with a specific charge. He said:

'I should have thought that there was not much difficulty in defining what a floating charge is in contrast to what is called a specific charge. A specific charge, I think, is one which without more fastens on ascertained and definite property or property capable of being ascertained and defined; a floating charge, on the other hand is ambulatory and shifting in its nature, hovering over and so to speak, floating with the property which it is intended to affect until some event occurs or some act is done which causes it to settle and fasten on the subject of the charge within its reach and grasp ...'

Crystallisation of floating charges

Brightlife Ltd, Re [1986] 2 WLR 197 Chancery Division (Hoffmann J)

Automatic crystallisation of floating charges

Facts

Brightlife ('the company') gave N Ltd a charge over its book debts 'by way of first specific charge' and a floating charge over all its other property. The charge prevented the company dealing with book and other debts other than in the course of collecting or realising them and gave N Ltd the right, in specified circumstances, to serve a notice on the company converting the floating charge into a fixed charge. In December 1984 N Ltd served notice purporting to convert the floating charge into a fixed charge. Shortly afterwards the company was wound up owing £200,000 to N Ltd and £70,000 in unpaid VAT. The assets totalled £40,000, including £18,000 in book debts and £19,000 in a bank account. The

Customs and Excise claimed that N Ltd's charge was still floating despite the notice and that the VAT took priority as a preferential debt. N Ltd claimed priority on the ground that it had a fixed charge over the book debts and the balance in the bank or, alternatively, on the ground that the notice served by it prior to winding up converted all its floating charges into fixed charges.

Held

1. 'Book debts' did not cover cash at the bank so that this was not covered by the charge over 'book debts'.
2. The charge expressed to be a 'first specific charge' over book debts was in fact a floating charge as it related to fluctuating assets and under it the company was still free to deal with the moneys by collecting and paying them into the bank account.
3. Parties could stipulate in a floating charge that it crystallised on the giving of notice. The notice given by N Ltd had effectively crystallised its charge making it a fixed charge and, thus, giving N Ltd priority.

Hoffmann J

'... I come next to the alternative submission for [N Ltd], namely that the floating charge was converted into a fixed charge before the resolution for winding-up ... Mr Sheldon relies upon the notice ... as having crystallised the floating charge over all the assets before winding up ... The argument Mr Mummery actually advanced before me was ... that the events of crystallisation were fixed by law and not by agreement of the parties. Those events were (i) winding up, (ii) appointment of a receiver, and (iii) ceasing to carry on business. These three events and only these three would cause crystallisation notwithstanding any agreement to the contrary. Their common features were that in each case the business of the company would cease, or at any rate cease to be conducted by the directors.

Mr Mummery referred to a number of cases in support of this submission. First there were cases in which it was held that crystallisation had taken place on one or other of the three events notwithstanding the absence of an express provision to that effect. For example, in *In re Crompton & Co Ltd* [1914] 1 Ch 954 Warrington J held that a floating charge crystallised on a winding up for the purposes of reconstruction notwithstanding that event being excluded from a clause containing the events of default which made the loan immediately repayable. At p964 Warrington J described winding up as an event "which by law independently of stipulation would make the debenture realisable". It must be observed that Warrington J said "independently of stipulation" and not "notwithstanding any stipulation to the contrary". In a later passage he said, at p965: "the parties ... have not provided as a matter of bargaining that, notwithstanding the general law, the other events shall not crystallise the security."

In my judgment, when Warrington J said that crystallisation on winding up was a matter of general law, he meant only that such a consequence was an implied term of a floating charge in the sense described by Lord Tucker in *Lister* v *Romford Ice and Cold Storage Co Ltd* [1957] AC 555 when he said, at p594:

"Some contractual terms may be implied by general rules of law. These general rules, some of which are now statutory, for example, Sale of Goods Act, Bills of Exchange Act etc, derive in the main from the common law by which they have become attached in the course of time to certain classes of contractual relationships, for example, landlord and tenant, innkeeper and guest, contracts of guarantee and contracts of personal service."

The existence of such rules of law by which terms are implied in a floating charge is not inconsistent with the transaction being wholly consensual and the implied terms liable to exclusion by contrary agreement.

Secondly, Mr Mummery relied upon a number of cases in which courts have rejected a submission that an event of default, not being one of his three, has caused an automatic crystallisation. The most famous of these is the decision of the House of Lords in *Governments Stock and Other Securities Investment Co Ltd* v *Manila Railway Co Ltd* [1897] AC 81. Mr Mummery said that these cases showed that such events could not as a matter of law cause crystallisation.

In my view, however, the speeches in the *Manila Railway* case make it clear that the House of Lords regarded the question as being one of construction alone. They give rise to a plain inference that a sufficiently explicit provision for automatic crystallisation on default would have been given effect. It is true that the commercial inconvenience of automatic crystallisation gives rise to a strong presumption that it was not intended by the parties. Very clear language will be required. But that does not mean that it is excluded by a rule of law.

The nearest any judge in this country has come to asserting such a rule of law is in *Edward Nelson & Co Ltd v Faber & Co* [1903] 2 KB 367 where Joyce J, after citing various judicial descriptions of the standard characteristics of a floating charge, said, at p376:

> "It follows, I think, from these and other cases that such a debenture as this in the present case does not cease to be a floating security ... until the company has been wound up, or stops business, or a receiver has been appointed at the instance of the debenture-holders ..."

Taken by itself, that remark may appear to lend support to Mr Mummery's tripartite rule of law. But I think that a fair reading of the whole judgment shows that Joyce J also accepted that his enumeration was subject to contrary agreement.

Thirdly, Mr Mummery cited several authoritative statements of the standard characteristics of a floating charge, particularly those of Lord Macnaghten in the *Manila Railway* case and *Illingworth v Houldsworth* [1904] AC 355 and Romer LJ in the latter case in the Court of Appeal, *In re Yorkshire Woolcombers Association Ltd* [1903] 2 Ch 284. For example, in the *Manila Railway* case Lord Macnaghten said that it was of the essence of a floating charge that it remained dormant "until the undertaking charged ceases to be a going concern, or until the person in whose favour the charge is created intervenes". Mr Mummery said that this formulation appeared to rule out automatic crystallisation without any act on the part of the debenture-holder. To this Mr Sheldon replied that he was not asserting automatic crystallisation: both of the notices upon which he relied were acts of intervention by the party entitled to the charge.

There is force in this answer but in my judgment there is a more fundamental objection to the use Mr Mummery seeks to make of the authorities. In *Illingworth v Houldsworth* Lord Macnaghten was at pains to point out that he had not attempted in the *Manila Railway* case to propound a 'definition' of a floating charge. He had only offered a 'description'. In making this distinction, it seems to me that what Lord Macnaghten had in mind was that a floating charge, like many other legal concepts, was not susceptible of being defined by the enumeration of an exhaustive set of necessary and sufficient conditions. All that can be done is to enumerate its standard characteristics. It does not follow that the absence of one or more of those features or the presence of others will prevent the charge from being categorised as 'floating'. There are bound to be penumbral cases in which it may be difficult to say whether the degree or deviation from the standard case is enough to make it inappropriate to use such a term. But the rights and duties which the law may or may not categorise as a floating charge are wholly derived from the agreement of the parties, supplemented by the terms implied by law. It seems to me fallacious to argue that once the parties have agreed on some terms which are thought sufficient to identify the transaction as a floating charge, they are then precluded from agreeing to any other terms which are not present in the standard case.

Fourthly, Mr Mummery said that the courts should take a lead from Parliament, which in the Preferential Payments in Bankruptcy Amendment Act 1897 and subsequent company legislation apparently assumed that it need provide for only two possible events of crystallisation, namely the appointment of a receiver and a winding up. Even on Mr Mummery's own submission this means that Parliament failed to consider his third event, cessation of business. It is true that *In re Woodroffes (Musical) Instruments Ltd* [1986] Ch 366 was the first case in which a court expressly decided that cessation of business had crystallised a floating charge. But, as Nourse J pointed out, this had been generally assumed for about a century. Furthermore, if Parliament is to provide any guidance, it is of some interest that s7(1)(iv) of the Agricultural Credits Act 1928 creates a statutory floating charge which can be crystallised without appointment of a receiver or winding up by a notice not dissimilar from that given under cl 3(B) in this case. I therefore do not think that I can draw any inferences about the nature of a floating charge from the way in which it has been treated in legislation.

Fifthly, Mr Mummery said that public policy required restrictions upon what the parties could stipulate as crystallising events. A winding up or the appointment of a receiver would have to be noted on the register. But a notice under cl 3(B) need not be registered and a provision for automatic crystallisation might take effect without the knowledge of either the company or the debenture-holder. The result might be prejudicial to third parties who gave credit to the company.

Considerations of this kind impressed Berger J in the Canadian case of *Reg in right of British Columbia* v *Consolidated Churchill Copper Corporation Ltd* (1978) 5 WWR 652 where the concept of 'self-generating crystallisation' was rejected.

I do not think that it is open to the courts to restrict the contractual freedom of parties to a floating charge on such grounds. The floating charge was invented by Victorian lawyers to enable manufacturing and trading companies to raise loan capital on debentures. It could offer the security of a charge over the whole of the company's undertaking without inhibiting its ability to trade. But the mirror image of these advantages was the potential prejudice to the general body of creditors, who might know nothing of the floating charge but find that all the company's assets, including the very goods which they had just delivered on credit, had been swept up by the debenture-holder. The public interest requires a balancing of the advantages to the economy of facilitating the borrowing of money against the possibility of injustice to unsecured creditors. These arguments for and against the floating charge are matters for Parliament rather than the courts and have been the subject of public debate in and out of Parliament for more than a century.

Parliament has responded, first, by restricting the rights of the holder of a floating charge and secondly, by requiring public notice of the existence and enforcement of the charge. For example, priority was given to preferential debts in 1897 and the Companies Act 1907 invalidated floating charges created within three months before the commencement of the winding up. This period has since been extended and is now one year. The registration of floating and other charges was introduced by the Companies Act 1900. The Companies Act 1907 required registration of the appointment of a receiver and the Companies Act 1927 required notice of such appointment to be given on the company's letters and invoices.

These limited and pragmatic interventions by the legislature make it in my judgment wholly inappropriate for the courts to impose additional restrictive rules on grounds of public policy. It is certainly not for a judge of first instance to proclaim a new head of public policy which no appellate court has even hinted at before. I would therefore respectfully prefer the decision of the New Zealand Supreme Court in *In re Manurewa Transport Ltd* [1971] NZLR 909, recognising the validity of a provision for automatic crystallisation, to the contrary dicta in the Canadian case I have cited. For present purposes, however, it is not necessary to decide any questions about automatic crystallisation. The notices under clauses 3(B) and 13 constitute intervention by the debenture-holder and there is in my judgment no conceptual reason why they should not crystallise the floating charge if the terms of the charge upon their true construction have this effect ...'

ELS Ltd, Re [1994] 3 WLR 616 Chancery Division (Ferris J)

Crystallisation of floating charge – whether this prevented a local authority from levying distress to recover business rates

Facts
ELS Ltd carried on the business of retailing furniture from premises within the areas of two local authorities, which were responsible for collecting non-domestic rates. On 15 October 1990, the company granted the National Westminster Bank Ltd a debenture, secured by a floating charge. Pursuant to the terms of the debenture, on 14 February 1992 the bank appointed joint administrators which had the effect of crystallising the floating charge. The question the court had to decide was whether a local authority having a power of distress, in order to recover business rates, can exercise that power over the goods of a company which are subject to a floating charge after that charge has crystallised.

Held

The crystallisation of the bank's floating charge over the company's property completed the assignment of that property to the bank. The result was that the goods of the company could no longer be considered as the property of the company. The two local authorities could not therefore exercise their right under statute (reg 14 of the Non-Domestic Rating (Collection and Enforcement) (Local Lists) Regulations 1989) to levy distress over the goods of the company, by appointing bailiffs to seize the goods. They were not the company's goods to seize.

Ferris J:

'I therefore answer the question posed by paragraph 1 of the originating summons by declaring that the crystallisation of the bank's floating charge in this case completed the assignment of the goods of ELS effected by the floating charge contained in the debenture dated 15 October 1990, with the consequence that such goods were thereafter no longer the goods of ELS for the purpose of regulation 14 of the Regulations of 1989. So expressed the declaration relates to this particular case rather than following the generalised proposition put forward in the originating summons, but, in my view, that is as far as I ought to go.'

Evans v *Rival Granite Quarries Limited* [1910] 2 KB 979 Court of Appeal (Vaughan Williams, Fletcher-Moulton and Buckley LJJ)

Automatic crystallisation of floating charges

Facts

The plaintiff brought proceedings in the county court to recover the rent of a cottage leased by him to the defendant company and, eventually, recovered judgment for over £86. This judgment was not satisfied and he therefore obtained a garnishee order nisi over the bank account of the defendant company. A debenture holder of the defendant company who had a charge over the undertaking of the defendant company opposed an application by the plaintiff that the garnishee order be made absolute on the ground that he had priority over the plaintiff, as holder of the debenture, to the money in the bank account. There was no dispute that the debenture covered the whole of the company's property. The question was whether the mere existence of the debenture, without the holder's taking any step by way of acting upon it to appoint a receiver, to take possession of the assets, gave him a security interest which took priority over the plaintiff.

Held

A debenture in the form of a floating charge does not affect any particular assets until some event occurs which causes it to crystallise into a fixed security. Neither a demand for payment by the debenture holder nor a notice by him to the company's bank claiming the money in the company's bank balance were acts causing the charge to crystallise. Therefore, the plaintiff was entitled to a garnishee order absolute since the debenture holder had no interest in the bank account which would give him priority.

Buckley LJ:

'... This court is as much bound as the court below by the decisions in *Re Standard Manufacturing Co* [1891] 1 Ch 627 and *Re Opera Ltd* [1891] 3 Ch 260. Effect must be given to those decisions, and none the less because they involve consequences which, as I indicated, I deplore. The result of those cases is that, as between an execution creditor and a debenture-holder who possesses a floating charge, the execution creditor takes subject to the equity of the debenture-holder. The point of the present case lies in determining what that equity is. Mr Shearman's contention that the execution creditor takes subject to the equitable charge is not in my opinion right; the true view is that he takes subject to such equitable rights as an equitable charge of this kind confers.

The nature of a floating security has been discussed and described in *Re Florence Land and Public Works Co* (1878) 10 Ch D 530, *Simultaneous Colour Printing Syndicate* v *Foweraker* [1901] 1 KB 771, *Government Stocks Investment Co* v *Manila Ry Co* [1897] AC 81, *Illingworth* v *Houldsworth* [1904] AC 355, and other cases. The outcome of the decisions may be thus summarised. A floating security is not a future security; it is a present security, which presently affects all the assets of the company expressed to be included in it. On the other hand, it is not a specific security; the holder cannot affirm that the assets are specifically mortgaged to him. The assets are mortgaged in such a way that the mortgagor can deal with them without the concurrence of the mortgagee. A floating security is not a specific mortgage of the assets, plus a licence to the mortgagor to dispose of them in the course of his business, but is a floating mortgage applying to every item comprised in the security, but not specifically affecting any item until some event occurs or some act on the part of the mortgagee is done which causes it to crystallise into a fixed security. Mr Shearman argued that it was competent to the mortgagee to intervene at any moment and to say that he withdrew the licence as regards any particular item. That is not in my opinion the nature of the security; it is a mortgage presently affecting all the items expressed to be included in it, but not specifically affecting any item till the happening of the event which causes the security to crystallise as regards all the items. The crystallisation may be brought about in various ways. A receiver may be appointed, or the company may go into liquidation and a liquidator be appointed, or any event may happen which is defined as bringing to an end the licence of the company to carry on business. There is no case in which it has been affirmed that a mortgagee of this description may at any moment forbid the company to sell a particular piece of property or may take it himself and keep it, and leave the licence to carry on the business subsisting as regards everything else. This would be inconsistent with the real bargain between the parties, which is that the mortgagee gives authority to the company to use all its property until the licence to carry on business comes to an end. It is impossble to evolve from the contractual relation between a company and its debenture-holders the proposition for instance that the latter may serve a notice on the company's bankers with regard to the honouring of the company's cheques and still say that, although he had stopped payment of the company's cheques he was not interfering with the carrying on of the company's business. Such a contention would be inconsistent with the true relation between the parties.

When the cases cited on behalf of the debenture-holder are examined, there is apparent in all of them some circumstance by reason of which the freedom of the company to carry on business has come to an end. The first is *Davey & Co* v *Williamson* [1898] 2 QB 194. I have no fault to find with the decision. In that case the debentures were a security for money payable at a date which had not arrived, and the trust deed contained an authority to the company to carry on its business until the happening of one or more of certain events upon which the security became enforceable; one of those events was the suing out of an execution against the property of the company, and that event had happened; it resulted, therefore, that the authority of the company to carry on business was at an end, and it could no longer deal with the property comprised in the security as though the security were not in existence. The floating charge had become a specific security on all the assets of the company; it was specific as between the execution creditor and the debenture-holders, and the latter succeeded in their claim to the goods ...

... In the result there is nothing to prevent us from affirming the following proposition: notwithstanding the law laid down in *Re Standard Manufacturing Co* and in *Re Opera Ltd*, that the execution creditor takes subject to the equity of the debenture-holders, no equity arises in a debenture-holder, whose security is a floating charge, from his merely giving notice to seize a particular asset of the company; he must do something to turn his security from a floating charge into a fixed charge. The cases of *Re Standard Manufacturing Co* and *Re Opera Ltd* are, of course, binding upon us, but they do not in any way conflict with our decision. Our judgment must be in favour of the appellant.'

Manurewa Transport, Re [1971] NZLR 909 Supreme Court of New Zealand (Speight J)

Automatic crystallisation of floating charges

Facts

The company had a carrying business in which it employed a number of lorries. The company issued a debenture in 1968 to secure a loan of $8,000 by way of a floating charge. An annex to the debenture provided as follows:

'13. The moneys hereby secured shall immediately become due and payable and the charge hereby created shall immediately attach and become affixed:

(i) If the company mortgages charges or encumbers or attempts to mortgage charge or encumber any of its property or assets contrary to the provisions hereof without the prior written consent of the lender.'

In 1969 a Commer lorry belonging to the company was placed in the hands of a garage firm for repairs. The company owed the garage money on account and the repair bill was $2,500. The garage refused to allow the company to remove the lorry until it obtained security for the money due to it by the company. As a result, in September 1969, a chattel mortgage was duly made in favour of the garage. The consent of the debenture-holder was not obtained in accordance with cl 13. The question arose, inter alia, whether the floating charge had crystallised automatically by reason of the failure to observe cl 13.

Held

The floating charge crystallised automatically on the company mortgaging or attempting to mortgage the lorry.

Speight J:

'... However, there is another ground which in my view defeats Gills' security and that is that this floating charge had in fact crystallised prior to the completion and certainly prior to the registration of Gills' instrument by way of security. Most textbook writers, with the exception of Professor Pennington in his 1967 textbook *Company Law*, says that crystallisation does not take place until the debenture-holders intervene. In my respectful view this is erroneous and is so shown by an examination of the case which is usually quoted as authority for the proposition, namely *Evans v Rival Granite Quarries Ltd* [1910] 2 KB 979. Passages to the effect mentioned, namely that the debenture-holder must intervene, may be found in the judgment of Vaughan Williams LJ and Fletcher-Moulton LJ. But it will be seen by an examination of the debenture which is set out in full in the report, that it was a much simpler document than the one I am here concerned with. In addition the question of crystallisation then only arose in relation to a demand by the debenture-holder for payment which was not an act which under the terms of the debenture there crystallised it. I find authority for the view I take that crystallisation may, in certain circumstances, be self-generated, or at least, debtor-generated, from the judgment of Buckley, LJ at p1000. There the learned Lord Justice reviewed a number of cases which had been cited on behalf of the debenture-holders, and in particular, he approved *Davey & Co v Williamson & Sons* [1894] QB 194. Because of the terms of the debenture in that case, the suing out of an execution by a third party against the property of the company was one of the conditions expressed to crystallise the debenture and Buckley LJ says:

"One of those events was the suing out of an execution against the property of the company, and that event had happened; it resulted, therefore, that the authority of the company to carry on business was at an end, and it could no longer deal with the property comprised in the security as though the security were not in existence. The floating charge had become a specific security on all the assets of the company; it was specific as between the execution creditor and the debenture-holders, and the latter succeeded in their claim to the goods."

Now if one turns to that authority, it will be found that Lord Russell CJ delivering the judgment of himself and Mathew J dealt with an argument that crystallisation had not taken place in respect of a debenture because the debenture-holders had not taken the step of appointing a receiver. But the debenture had provided that part of the charge should be a floating charge and that the company could carry on its business until the happening of one or more of certain events upon which the security thereby constituted became enforceable. Execution had been attempted by a third party and this was sufficient reason in the judgment of the Lord Chief Justice to say that the charge had crystallised and the debenture-holder had priority over the execution creditor. ...'

Permanent House (Holdings) Ltd, Re (1989) 5 BCC 151 Chancery Division (Hoffmann J)

Whether a credit balance in a bank account was a fixed or floating charge – automatic crystallisation

Facts
This was an application for directions by the receiver of Permanent House (Holdings) the company who was appointed in 1981 under a debenture. By assignment the debenture and the debt which it secured had come to be vested in a Dutch company – Pakhoed BV Permanent Houses – the company, owed them £692,424. They also owed £26,000 to the Customs and Excise. The debenture contained a fixed charge over book debts and other debts, and a floating charge over the company's 'other undertakings and assets' and provided that on the occurrence of various events including a demand for payment, the floating charge would crystallise. The receiver held £486,166, which included a sum of £68,565 which stood to the credit of the company in a bank account.

The questions on the receiver's application were:

i)   whether the money in the bank account was subject to the fixed or floating charge;
ii) whether, if subject to the floating charge, that charge crystallised before appointment of the receiver; ie on making the unsatisfied demand for payment; and
iii) whether, if the charge had crystallised, the Customs & Excise were nevertheless entitled to be paid by the receiver in priority to Pakhoed pursuant to s196 Companies Act 1985 (as originally enacted: it was substituted by s439(1) of the Insolvency Act 1986).

Held
i)   The credit balance at the bank was not a 'book debt or other debt' within the meaning of the debenture, and was, therefore, not subject to the fixed, but only to the floating charge.
ii) The making of the demand for repayment was an event of default as defined in the debenture which caused the floating charge to crystallise in accordance with the terms of the debenture. If the language was sufficiently clear, there was no reason why the parties should not agree that any specified event should cause the charge to crystallise.
iii) Section 196 required that the charge over the assets in question should still be floating at the moment when the receiver was appointed; the assets in question were secured by a charge which at the date of appointment of the receiver subsisted as a fixed charge, and the operation of s196 was excluded.

Commentary
Point (iii), s196, applies to receivers appointed before the Insolvency Act 1986 came into force – 29 December 1986.

The Queen v *Consolidated Churchill Copper Corp Ltd* (1979) 90 DLR (3d) 357
(British Columbia Supreme Court)

Automatic crystallisation of floating charge

Facts

The dispute was over priority to royalties payable under the Mineral Royalties Act 1974 (BC). The province of British Columbia claimed a lien on the royalties under the Act and this attached on 15 April, 1975. Debenture-holders of the mine paying the royalties claimed their security had crystallised before that date giving them priority by reason of a clause in the debenture providing that it was 'enforceable' on default and such default having occurred sometime between April 1972 and April 1975, the charge had crystallised then. At p365 Berger J referred to *Re Manurewa Transport Ltd* and said:

'... Speight J relied upon what was said by Buckley LJ in the *Evans* case at p1000. But what Buckley LJ there said was dicta. All that had to be decided in that case was whether the debenture-holder could intervene so as to prevent the money in the company's bank account being paid to the execution creditor. I have already indicated that the ratio of the judgment was that the debenture-holder could not allow the company to carry on business and yet prevent the execution creditor attaching the company's bank balance. That is what Buckley LJ said in summing up his judgment on the main issue at p1002:

"In the result there is nothing to prevent us from affirming the following proposition: notwithstanding the law laid down in *In re Standard Manufacturing Co* [1891] 1 Ch 627 and *In re Opera Ltd* [1891] 3 Ch 260 that the execution creditor takes subject to the equity of the debenture-holders, no equity arises in a debenture-holder, whose security is a floating charge, from his merely giving notice to seize a particular asset of the company; he must do something to turn his security from a floating into a fixed charge."

Vaughan Williams LJ in the *Evans* case, said at pp989-90:

"In point of fact, the position of the debenture-holder when opposing the application to make the garnishee order absolute may be described in two ways. First, it may be said that the debenture-holder, though he has in no way interrupted the licence, that is the jus, of the company to carry on their business, wishes to interfere with their mode of dealing with a particular debt; in other words, the debenture-holder is willing that the company should continue to carry on its business, but wishes to arrogate to himself the right to prevent a particular debt from being paid; he says it should not be paid because it would not be a voluntary payment, but would be made under the order of the court just as much as where a sheriff puts in execution on a judgment. In my opinion nothing has happened in the present case to prevent the execution creditor from obtaining a garnishee order absolute, for although it may be that tomorrow there will be a receiver, at present there is nothing of the sort.'

Vaughan Williams LJ went on, at p990:

"I have dealt with the position which the debenture-holder takes up when he seeks to intervene in the affairs of the company without interrupting their licence to carry on their business. The other view put forward by the debenture-holder, if right, would lead to this result: that, although he had nothing more than an ordinary debenture and the company was in fact carrying on business, an execution levied upon the company's goods and chattels might without more be at once made void at the mere option of the debenture-holder. The result of this would be an absolute immunity of the company from executions, if the debenture-holder so chose."

Fletcher-Moulton LJ also said that intervention was necessary. He referred to the passage from the judgment of Lord Macnaghten in the *Manila Railway Co* case that I cited earlier, and then said at p993:

"Mere default on the part of the company does not change the character of the security; the debenture-holder must actually intervene."

It was only Buckley LJ who took the view (in obiter) that a floating charge might crystallise without intervention.

The question before the court in the *Evans* case was fundamentally the same question as in the case at bar. Can a debenture-holder allow the company to carry on business and yet insist, when another creditor (here the Province) makes a claim, that the floating charge has already crystallised? Brameda is seeking to undermine the footings upon which the law relating to debentures has been erected: you may terminate the company's licence to carry on business, or you may not. But you cannot seek to do both at the same time.

Of course this business of analysing and dissecting these early judgments can be taken too far. I have referred to what Lord Macnaghten said in the *Manila Railway* case. Yet in *Illingworth* v *Houldsworth* [1904] AC 355 he said at p358:

"A specific charge, I think, is one that without more fastens on ascertained and definite property or property capable of being ascertained and defined; a floating charge on the other hand, is ambulatory and shifting in its nature, hovering over and so to speak floating with the property which it is intended to affect until some event occurs or some act is done which causes it to settle and fasten on the subject of the charge within its reach and grasp."

It may be said that the words "until some event occurs or some act is done" are consistent with the argument in support of self-generating crystallisation. But no authority has gone as far as Brameda urges the court to go in the case at bar. In *Davey & Co* v *Williamson & Sons Ltd* [1898] 2 QB 154 which Speight J cited in the *Manurewa* case, supra, the debenture provided that the floating charge crystallised if an execution were made, and in the *Manurewa* case itself it provided that the floating charge crystallised if an attempt were made to mortgage any of the assets covered by the debenture, the latter being a usual clause, according to Yorston and Brown, *Company Law*, 3rd ed at p240. Neither case is authority for the proposition that crystallisation occurs on default of payment. In fact, in *Edward Nelson & Co Ltd* v *Faber & Co* [1903] 2 KB 367 this very argument was advanced in a case where the debenture provided that from and after default the debenture was to become enforceable (see p375). Joyce J held that (at pp376-7):

"... such a debenture as this ... does not cease to be a floating security ... until the company has been wound-up, or stops business, or a receiver has been appointed at the instance of the debenture-holders and it follows that, even after the interest payable on such debentures has been in arrears for the time specified, the company can deal with the property in the ordinary course of business until the company has been wound up, or stops business, or a receiver has been appointed."

Gower, *Modern Company Law*, supra, cites *Nelson & Co* v *Faber & Co* and the *Evans* case and concludes, at p421:

"Default alone will not suffice to crystallise the charge, the debenture-holders must intervene to determine the licence to the company to deal with the property, normally by appointing a receiver or by applying to the court to do so."

But there has been no judgment rendered on the question in Canada. The matter is one of first impression. So policy considerations should be placed on the scales. These considerations weigh heavily against the adoption of the notion of self-generating crystallisation. In the case at bar there were numerous acts of default, going back to 1972. Brameda did not, until 14 April, 1975, take the position that the floating charge had crystallised. If in truth it had crystallised back in 1972, when Brameda acquired the banks' interest in the debenture, Brameda did not treat the company thereafter as if its licence to carry on business was at an end. Brameda sought to have it both ways: to attain priority over the Province's lien without putting Churchill into receivership. This shows the parlous state of affairs which would result if the concept of self-generating crystallisation were to be adopted. The requirements for filing by a receiver under the Companies Act would be rendered a dead letter. The company would not know where it stood: neither would the company's creditors. How is anyone to know the true state of affairs between the debenture-holder and the company unless there is an unequivocal act of intervention? How can it be said that the default by the company terminated its licence to carry on business when in fact it was allowed by Brameda to carry on business for three years thereafter? If the argument were sound, the debenture-holder would be able to arrange the affairs of the company in such a way as to render it immune from executions. The debenture-holder would have all the advantages of allowing the company to continue in business, and all of the advantages of intervening at one and the same time, to the prejudice of all other creditors. This contention was rejected in the *Evans* case: see Vaughan Williams LJ at pp989-90, and Fletcher-Moulton LJ at p995.

It is my view that neither in the older cases, nor in the recent cases, nor in the exigencies of policy, is there any justification for the adoption of a concept of self-generating crystallisation. If there is any practical scope for such a theory it does not extend to a case where the conduct of the debenture-holder is inconsistent with the assertion of any such claim ...'

Priorities between charges

Automatic Bottlemakers Ltd, Re [1926] Ch 412 Court of Appeal (Lord Hanworth MR, Warrington and Sargant LJJ)

Priority between floating charges

Facts

The company was involved in the manufacture of bottles and glass ware, as its name indicates. In January 1925 it issued a series of debentures for £50,000 secured by way of a floating charge on the undertaking and property of the company. Under cl 6 of the charge a proviso stipulated:

'... the company is not to be at liberty, save as hereinafter provided, or except in accordance with the provisions of these presents, to create any mortgage or charge on such assets ranking pari passu with, or in priority to the charge hereby created.'

Clause 7 of the charge then went on to provide:

'The company shall be at liberty to create such mortgages charges or incumbrances as the company shall think proper upon such property, and for such amounts and purposes as are next hereinafter mentioned...(c) By the deposit of any dock warrants, bills of lading or other similar commercial documents, or upon any raw materials or finished or partly finished products and stock for the purpose of raising moneys in the ordinary course of the business of the company.'

In August 1925 the company issued a debenture for the benefit of its bankers to secure the sum of £12,000. This debenture was expressed to be issued in pursuance of cl 7 of the January 1925 debenture and secured by way of a first floating charge on the dock warrants and bills of lading of the company. Shortly after the issue of the second debenture a receiver was appointed of the company. The question then arose whether the company had power to issue the second debenture in view of the restrictions imposed on it by clauses 6 and 7 of the January 1925 debenture.

Held

The August 1925 debenture was valid and, in the circumstances, it took priority because the January 1925 debenture on its true construction reserved to the company power to create a floating charge over the assets referred to in cl 7 thereof which could rank in priority to or pari passu with the January 1925 charge. Further, the creation of a floating charge over specific assets was not inconsistent with the existence of an earlier general floating charge.

Warrington LJ:

'... I now turn to the construction of the deed. It is, of course, well settled that by creating a charge on its assets generally by way of floating security the company are not, in the absence of any stipulation to the contrary, prohibited from creating specific charges on specific portions of their assets in the ordinary course of business, as otherwise they would be prevented from effectually carrying on that business, the carrying on of which was contemplated by the parties to the security. Clauses 6 and 7 of the trust deed have the effect of excluding this rule of law so far as mortgages or charges are concerned except as provided by cl 7, and thus to allow, and allow only, in priority to, or pari passu with, the debenture, charges created in accordance with such provisions. I now turn to the material words of the clause. It gives liberty to the company to create such mortgages, charges, or incumbrances as the company shall think proper upon such property and for such amounts and purposes as are next thereinafter mentioned, but not for any greater amounts or for any other purpose; and then provided, by sub-cl 7(c), that the permitted charge may be effected by deposit of commercial documents or upon any raw materials or partly finished products or stock for the purpose of raising money in the ordinary course of the business of the company. In my opinion the true effect of this provision is that the form and nature of the charge is by the force of the expression "such charges as the company shall think proper" left to be determined by the company, the subject-matter of the charge and the purposes for which the money is raised being determined by the provisions of the clause. In the present case the subject-matter of the charge is raw materials, finished or partly finished products, and stock, and its purpose that of raising money in the ordinary course of the business of the company. It seems to me, therefore, that it is clearly within the clause unless some good reason is given for excluding it. The only reason suggested, other than the one I have disposed of, is that it is a floating security. With all respect to the learned Vice-Chancellor, I cannot see the force of this objection. The authority given to the company, except as to subject-matter, amount, and purpose, is unlimited, and I can find no good reason, in the absence of express words to that effect, to limit it in the way suggested. It is true that the commercial documents cannot be made the subject of a floating security because they have to be actually deposited but I cannot see why, by construction, the same disability should extend to the other subject-matters which are in themselves exempt from it.

It has, indeed, been contended that the true meaning of the clause is to authorise only such securities as, but for the general prohibition contained in cl 6, would have been allowed under the general rules relating to floating securities, and it is further contended that no floating security, although on a portion only of the assets, would be allowed. The answer is, in my opinion, first, that there is no reason to be found in the expressions used for any such limitation of the company's authority, and to act on the assumption that the parties so intended would be to act on a mere guess. The parties had excluded the general rule so far as charges are concerned and were making a special bargain. To interpret this we must simply ascertain the meaning of the words used, and as to this I have already expressed my opinion.

But in my judgment there is no authority for the proposition that no floating charge, though on a part only of the assets, would be allowed under the general law, and I am not prepared so to hold without authority. The only authority on which the respondents rely is *Re Benjamin Cope & Sons Ltd, Marshall v The Co* [1914] 1 Ch 800 but in that case the subsequent charge was a charge of the same nature and over the same property as the original charge; that is to say, a floating security on the whole undertaking and assets of the company, and what the learned judge determined was that such a charge, comprising, as it did, the identical property covered by the original charge, was not authorised by a provision in the trust deed authorising the company, in the course of its business and for the purpose of carrying on the same, to deal with its property as it might think fit, and in particular to sell and mortgage the same or any part thereof. I think the learned judge makes it quite clear that it was the fact that the charge in question covered the whole of the property included in the original charge, which, in his opinion, prevented it from ranking pari passu with the latter; see particularly the passage ((1914) 1 Ch at p807) beginning;

"and, generally speaking, it would, in my view, be as incompatible with the company's bargain with the first debenture-holders to put their debentures behind or on the same footing as subsequent debentures giving a charge of the same character as if the debentures had constituted a specific charge and it were then attempted to create a subsequent specific charge ranking pari passu with them or in priority to them."

'He is comparing one pair of charges with another pair and saying they were on the same footing in respect of the point in question. There would be no point in this comparison unless the property comprised in each of the first pair were identical with each other, as it certainly is in the case of the second pair.

On the whole I am of opinion that the appeal should be allowed ...'

Sargant LJ:

'... Great stress has, however, been laid for the respondents on a decision of my own as a judge of first instance in *Re Benjamin Cope & Sons Ltd, Marshall* v *The Co* and it has been urged that this case decides that a general floating charge is necessarily incompatible with the subsequent creation under a special charging power of a floating charge to rank in priority to or pari passu with the earlier floating charge. I have examined that decision with great care, and have no reason to think it was wrong, particularly in view of the fact that it appears to be in accord with an earlier decision of Vaughan Williams J in *Smith* v *English and Scottish Mercantile Investment Trust Ltd* [1896] WN 86, and not to have been questioned since. But the facts in that case were very different. There the original charge was on the whole undertaking and property for the time being of the company, and the reservation of a power to mortgage was in quite general terms; and it was held that such a power could not have been intended to authorise a competing charge upon the entirety of the property comprised in the earlier charge. Here the reservation of the power to mortgage is precise and specific in its terms, and extends only to certain particular classes of the property of the company ...'

Benjamin Cope & Sons Limited, Re [1914] 1 Ch 800 Chancery Division (Sargant J)

Priority between floating charges

Facts
In 1894 the company created a series of debentures for £2,000 which were secured by a floating charge on the company's undertaking, present and future. These debentures were expressed to rank pari passu as between themselves and the debenture, by cl 7, permitted the company to deal with its property in any way it thought fit or mortgage or sell it in the course of its business. In 1904 the company issued a second series of debentures which were similar to the first debentures but it was stated in cl 6 of these debentures that 'all of such debentures of this and the first series shall rank pari passu without regard to the date thereof.' Two holders of debentures of the first series brought an action to enforce their security. The question arose as to the priority between the first series and the second series.

Held
The second series did not rank pari passu with the first series, they ranked after them.

Sargant J:

'... All the debentures of the first series and 14 of the second series are outstanding, and the Master has certified that the 14 rank pari passu with the debentures of the first series.

Whether this decision is right or wrong depends on the answers given to two questions, namely, (i) whether in general a company has power to create a second floating charge ranking pari passu with a floating charge; and (ii) whether in this particular case the words of the first debentures are sufficient to alter the general rule ...

... it has been generally recognised that a floating security can be displaced by a specific legal or equitable mortgage. But does it follow that it can be displaced by a subsequent floating charge in the absence of words in the first charge authorising such displacement? Nothing in the reported cases has carried the matter so far, and in so laying down the law I should, I believe, be acting contrary to all professional and commercial views on the subject – and it must be remembered that these debentures are commercial instruments.

If the above view is true in the case of an ordinary floating charge, is there anything in the present case which prevents me from saying that the debentures of the first series are entitled to priority? I am not sure that the words here used are not more strongly in favour of the first debenture-holders than those of the forms ordinarily in use. The word "mortgage" apparently in contradistinction to the word 'charge' is used in both cl 5 and cl 7 of the debentures of the first series, and in the latter clause the mortgages and other dealings allowed to be made by the company must be "in the course of its business or for the purpose of carrying on the same". That was the sole object of the power, and I do not think that this second issue of debentures giving a floating charge fairly comes within clause 7.

There are other indications in favour of the contention on behalf of the first debenture-holders. The fact that the first debentures constitute a series which is limited to £2,000 is destructive of the suggestion that any future debentures giving a floating charge can be put before or made to rank pari passu with, the debentures of the first series. And, generally speaking, it would in my view, be incompatable with the company's bargain with the first debenture-holders to put their debentures behind or on the same footing as subsequent debentures giving a charge of the same character as if the debentures had constituted a specific charge and it were then attempted to create a subsequent specific charge ranking pari passi with them or in priority to them.

I hold therefore, that the first debentures have priority over the second debentures.'

Castell & Brown Limited, Re [1898] 1 Ch 315 Chancery Division (Romer J)

Creation of fixed charge having priority over an earlier floating charge

Facts
In 1885 the company issued debentures securing loans of £28,000 on all its property, both present and future. The debentures also provided that the company was 'not to be at liberty to create any mortgage or charges upon its freehold and leasehold hereditaments in priority to the said debenture'. The title deeds of the company's freehold and leasehold assets were left in its possession despite the charge and its terms. In 1892 the company needed to extend its overdraft to carry on business and its bankers agreed to do so taking the title deeds of some of the company's property as security. Further, loan facilities were extended in 1895 on the security of the same title deeds. In 1896 the debenture-holders began an action to enforce their security because of arrears in interest due to them. The bank was unaware of the debentures until it received notice of judgment in favour of the debenture-holders. There then arose a dispute as to who had priority as between the debenture-holders and the bank.

Held
The bank had priority since it had not been guilty of negligence and also because the title deeds had been left with the company by the debenture-holders enabling the company to deal with the property as if it were unencumbered.

Romer J:

'This is a question of priority between two equitable incumbrances. The debentures are prior in date, but the Union Bank, at the time of its charges, had no notice express or implied, of the prior incumbrance and having obtained possession of the title deeds, claims priority under the circumstances of the case. If the equities of two incumbrancers are in other respects equal, then of course priority depends upon the dates of the charges. But the question is whether under the circumstances of this case the bank has not the better equity so as to entitle it to priority. Now as between equitable incumbrancers in determining priority, the possession of the deeds has always been treated as a circumstance of great importance …

… In the first place, I cannot hold that there was any negligence on the part of the bank. When making its advances to Castell & Brown Limited (which I will hereafter call the company), it found the company in possession of the deeds in question, and apparently able, as unincumbered owner, to charge the property. The company purported as such unincumbered owner to give a charge to the bank, and I think the bank was, under the circumstances, entitled to rely upon obtaining a charge free from incumbrance. It is suggested on behalf of the debenture-holders that the bank ought to have made some special inquiries of the company. But it is not suggested that the bank wilfully abstained from making inquiries, and as the bank had no reason to suppose that the company was not fully able to give a valid first charge, and found the company in possession of the deeds, which showed no incumbrance, I think the bank was not bound to make any special inquiry. It is said on behalf of the debenture-holders that it is so common for companies to issue debentures that the bank ought to have assumed there were some in this case, or at any rate to have specially inquired about debentures. But every company does not issue debentures, and, moreover, every debenture does not charge all property of the company, and certainly not property the title deeds of which are left with the company. It might just as well be said, because it is common for private individuals to mortgage their properties, that a person asked to make advances to a borrower, who appears to be unincumbered owner and has the deeds showing him to be such owner, is bound to assume that the borrower has previously mortgaged, or to make special inquiries of him on the footing that he has previously mortgaged. Such a contention appears to me unreasonable. I therefore hold that there was no negligence on the part of the bank.

And I now look to see how it was that the company retained possession of the deeds notwithstanding the issue of the debentures. The reason appears to me obvious. The debentures were only intended to give what is called a floating charge, that is to say, it was intended, notwithstanding the debentures, that the company should have power, so long as it was a going concern, to deal with its property as absolute owner. And I infer it was on this account that the company was allowed to, and did, retain possession of the deeds. In other words, the debenture holders, notwithstanding their charge, and indeed by its very terms, authorised their mortgagor, the company, to deal with its property as if it had not been incumbered, and left with their mortgagor the deeds in order to enable the company to act as owner. It is true that having given this general authority to the company, the debentures purported to put a certain special restriction on its exercise. By the first condition it was provided, that though the charge was to be a floating security, the company was not to be at liberty to create any mortgage or charge upon its freehold and leasehold hereditaments in priority to the debentures. This restriction was no doubt quite valid as a private arrangment between the company and the debenture-holders. But can the debenture-holders, under the circumstances, set it up as against the bank taking its security without notice? I think not. I take it to be established that if a first mortgagee, even though he has the legal estate, authorises the mortgagor to retain the deeds in order that the mortgagor may thereby, as ostensible owner of the property, be able to deal with it though only to a limited extent, yet if the mortgagor takes advantage of the deeds so left with him to deal with the property to an extent beyond what was authorised, then the mortgagee cannot set up his charge as against an incumbrancer for value without notice, who claims under the unauthorised dealing and relied on the deeds and the apparent ability of the owner to deal with the property free from incumbrances ... In my opinion, therefore, the bank has a stronger equity than the debenture-holders and is entitled to priority.'

English and Scottish Mercantile Investment Company v *Brunton* [1892] 2 QB 700
Court of Appeal (Lord Esher MR, Bowen and Kay LJJ)

Restriction in a debenture prohibiting the creation of later charges having priority

Facts
The Electrical Engineering Corporation issued 200 first mortgage debentures of £100 each in February 1891 in pursuance of its powers to borrow. The company charged all its undertaking and property, both present and future, to secure the debentures and a clause in the debentures provided:

'The debentures of the said series are all to rank pari passu as a first charge on the property hereby charged, without any preference or priority one over another; and the charge hereby created is to be a floating security, but so that the corporation is not to be at liberty to create any mortgage or charge in priority to the said debentures.'

Shortly after the issue of the debentures the corporation needed a short term loan for the purposes of its business and obtained £1,400 from the plaintiffs secured by a mortgage of moneys due under a policy of insurance on the company's premises at West Drayton which had been damaged by fire. The solicitor instructed by the plaintiffs to act on their behalf in drawing up the mortgage inquired whether the insurance moneys were already charged under any other deed. Both the insurance company and the corporation's managing director replied in the negative. However, the latter informed the solicitor of the existence of the debentures but not their terms. The solicitor did not ask to see these and was in any event unaware that a debenture could be drawn containing a restrictive clause. In April 1891 the corporation went into voluntary liquidation and a dispute arose as to who was entitled to the moneys due under the insurance policy. At first instance Charles J gave judgment for the plaintiffs. The debenture holders appealed on the ground that the plaintiffs' solicitor had constructive notice of the contents of the debentures in the circumstances.

Held
The plaintiffs did not have constructive notice and the appeal therefore failed.

Lord Esher MR:

'In this case the question is whether the plaintiffs are entitled to the full benefit of the mortgage which they have taken. At the time they took it, through the managing director of the Electrical Engineering Corporation Limited, there were in existence debentures issued by the company, and there were things stated in those debentures which, if the plaintiffs had known, would have prevented them in equity from saying that their mortgage could be enforced in priority to the debentures. If they had known what was in the debentures they would, in equity, have taken the mortgage with notice of prior charges on the subject-matter of it. It is admitted that the plaintiffs did not in fact know that there was that in the debentures which would prevent them, in equity, from having the full benefit of the mortgage which they took; but it is said that they had what in equity is termed "constructive notice" of what was in the debentures. The doctrine of constructive notice is wholly equitable; it is not known to the common law ...

... In *Allen v Seckham* 11 Ch D 790 I pointed out that the doctrine is a dangerous one. It is contrary to the truth. It is wholly founded on the assumption that a man does not know the facts; and yet it is said that constructively he does know them. Now, what is the case here? We are not to deal with any question of constructive notice of a deed which affects the title to real property. It is, therefore, not necessary to say how the doctrine should be applied to such a case. We have to apply it to a case of a mortgage of a debt given by a company under powers contained in their articles of association, and who also had a right by their constitution to issue debentures. The mortgagees knew that the company had power to issue debentures, and that they had in fact issued some, but that is all that they did know. Under these circumstances their solicitor asked a question of the managing director of the company, with whom he was negotiating about taking the mortgage. It is clear to my mind that what he wanted to know, and what he was really asking, was whether there was anything in the debentures which had been issued to interfere with the validity of the mortgage he proposed to take from the company. It is equally clear to my mind that the person of whom he asked the question knew that was what he wanted to know; but answered so as to deceive him. The managing director wanted to effect the mortgage for his company, and he gave an answer which put the mortgagee's solicitor off further inquiry, and led him to believe that there was nothing in the debentures which would affect the mortgage. Now, we have to apply to these facts the doctrine of constructive notice ...

... in *Patman v Harland* (1881) 17 Ch D 353 Sir George Jessel MR dealt with the proposition, and pointed out the application of it, thus:

"Constructive notice of a deed is constructive notice of its contents, subject to what I am going to say presently ... When you know of a deed it is no answer to be told that it does not prejudicially affect the title, as if it does affect the title you are bound by its contents."

There he is talking of being told of a deed which does necessarily affect the property; but he goes on:

"There is a class of cases, of which I think *Jones* v *Smith* 1 Ph 244 is the most notorious, where a purchaser was told of a deed which might or might not affect the title and was told at the same time that it did not affect the title. Supposing you are buying land off a married man, as in *Jones* v *Smith* , and you are told at the same time that there is a marriage settlement, but the deed does not affect the land in question, you have no constructive notice of its contents, because although you know there is a settlement you are told it does not affect the land. If every marriage settlement necessarily affected all a man's land, then you would have constructive notice, but as a settlement may not relate to this land at all, or only some other portions of it, the mere fact of your having heard of a settlement does not give you constructive notice of its contents, if you are told at the same time it does not affect the land."

... The distinction which the Master of the Rolls draws is clearly between deeds which, in the sense I have stated, obviously must affect the property, and deeds which may or may not, in the sense I have stated, affect it. If the case is brought within the first category and a person is told that the deed does affect the property, he must look at the deed, and if he does not look at it, he will be taken to have constructive notice of its contents. If the case is brought within the second category, and the person is told that the deed does not affect the property, he may take that statement and cannot be held to have constructive notice of its contents. That reduces the question in the present case to this: Were the debentures ... instruments of such a nature as might or might not affect the transaction with respect to the mortgage which was given? ... the question here, in my opinion, is, were the debentures such as would necessarily affect the plaintiff's title to the mortgage or were they such as might or might not affect it? We were told that debentures which would not affect a subsequent mortgage of the company's property at all were exceptional; but I do not find that in the evidence. There are certainly a class of debentures issued by companies which would not affect the mortgage at all. The first class of debentures stated in the evidence given in the court below would not; (ie those which simply acknowledge the debt under seal) those in the second class would not affect the title to this mortgage, (ie an instrument which charges the property of the company with repayment) and those in the third class are the only ones which would so affect this title (ie an instrument which charges the property of the company with repayment and restricts the company from giving any prior charges). I therefore think that Charles J was right in saying that the notice which the plaintiff had was only notice of documents which might or might not affect their title to the mortgage. I have a strong opinion that, even if the false statement that the debentures did not affect the plaintiff's title to the mortgage had never been made, the doctrine of constructive notice would not have applied. It is not, however, necessary to decide that question now; and I do not decide it ...'

Griffiths v *Yorkshire Bank plc* [1994] 1 WLR 1427 Chancery Division (Morritt J)

Priority of fixed and floating charges

Facts

Skainmead Ltd ('the company') granted the Yorkshire Bank plc ('the bank') a debenture secured by a fixed and floating charge on 13 January 1977.

A second debenture of 12 August 1985 was granted by the company to APH Industries Ltd (APH) to secure a loan made to the company. This was also secured by a fixed and floating charge.

On 23 June 1986 APH demanded sums due to it under the 1985 debenture, amounting to £64,000. At the same time it also served a notice on the company under clause 5(1) of the debenture. This provided that:

'The lender may at any time by notice in writing to the company convert the said floating charge into a specific charge as regards any assets specified in the notice which the lender shall consider to be in danger of being seized or sold under any form of distress execution diligence or other process levied or threatened and may appoint a receiver thereof.'

In its notice, the company specified all stock in trade and book debts as being converted to a specific fixed charge.

Earlier that same day, on 23 June, the bank had demanded £91,500 owed to it by the company and on 24 June appointed receivers. The company continued to trade under the control of the receivers until 9 July 1986.

The assets subject to the 1977 floating charge realised £99,500. The question for the court to decide was whether the notice served by APH under the 1985 debenture converting the floating charge to a fixed charge gave priority to APH. If it did then APH would receive its £64,000 in full, the remaining £35,500 would be paid to the preferential creditors and the bank would get nothing. If APH did not get priority, then the preferential creditors would be paid off in full, the bank would receive the balance in part payment of its debt, and APH would get nothing.

Held

APH did obtain priority and they were therefore entitled to be paid first out of the £99,500 realised from the assets subject to the 1977 floating charge.

Morritt J:

'I can express my conclusions in accordance with what I understand to be the basic principles applicable to questions concerning the priorities of fixed and floating charges relatively shortly. (1) It was inherent in the floating charge granted by the 1977 debenture that the company might subsequently confer proprietary interests on others in assets subject to the floating charge to rank prior to the bank's. A subsequent charge would constitute a breach of contract but would not be invalid. (2) The floating charge granted by the 1985 debenture was inherently capable of being converted into a fixed charge by service of the notice prescribed by clause 5(1). (3) By service of the notice on 23 June 1986 APH crystallised its floating charge over stock and book debts into a fixed charge having priority over the floating charge contained in the 1977 debenture. (4) Such priority was not lost when, the following day, the floating charge in the 1977 debenture crystallised on the appointment of the receivers for there was no agreement as to priority requiring that result. (5) APH as the first (and by then the fixed chargee) was entitled to the stock and book debts as security for its debt. (6) Section 196(2) of the Companies Act 1985 did not on its true construction apply to the 1985 debenture or require APH to pay the preferential creditors. (7) In the circumstances that APH, not the bank, was entitled to the proceeds of realisation, the fact that the receivers realised the book debts and stock, rather than leaving it to APH, is immaterial because the plaintiffs were not entitled to do so as receivers appointed under the 1977 debenture. Consequently section 196(2) imposed no duty on them.'

Commentary

Re Portbase Clothing Ltd [1933] Ch 388 distinguished.

Monolithic Building Co Ltd, Re [1915] 1 Ch 643 Court of Appeal (Lord Cozens-Hardy MR, Phillimore LJ and Joyce J)

For a charge to have priority it must be registered

Facts

The company purchased some land in Hertfordshire and shortly afterwards executed a mortgage over it to secure an advance of £500 from the plaintiff. Due to a mistake as to the effect of what became s395 Companies Act 1985 (a new s395 was substituted by s93 of the Companies Act 1989) the charge was not registered within the statutory period since it was believed this provision did not apply to mortgages of land. Subsequently, two mortgage debentures were executed by the company and secured on the same property, both of these were registered. One of these mortgage debentures was executed in favour of one Jenkins, the managing director of the company, who knew of the plaintiff's mortgage as he had witnessed the execution of it. No case of fraud was made against Jenkins. The question arose as to whether the plaintiff could take priority over the subsequent charges after having registered her charge having obtained leave to register it out of time 'without prejudice to the rights of the parties prior to the time such mortgage was actually registered'. It was argued that the section (now s395) did not apply in cases where a second chargee actually knew of an earlier charge. Alternatively, it was argued that Jenkins was a trustee for the plaintiff.

Held

The plaintiff had lost her priority since the section declared that an unregistered charge was void against any creditor. The words of the section were too clear to be construed as saying that an unregistered mortgage must be void against any creditor of the company except where he has had notice of the existence of that prior unregistered charge.

Phillimore LJ:

'... It is suggested here that the defendant Jenkins' knowledge of the mortgage precludes him from insisting upon his rights as a registered holder of debentures. I answer in the terms of *Edwards* v *Edwards* (1876) 2 Ch D 291, which has been already quoted by the Master of the Rolls, but which I must just briefly read because I am not going to put any other answer in my own language: "The mortgagee says to the execution creditor, 'You are not prejudiced, for you knew of my security'. The execution creditor replies, 'I knew that you had a security, but you knew the law as well as I'". I omit the next words, because they have already been cited. "Both parties stood on their legal rights – neither of them was misleading the other." That is this case upon the facts as found ...'

... What principles does the plaintiff in the present case contend for? There are only two ways in which this matter can be put. The first is, the object of the registration is to prevent people advancing money or puchasing in the dark. It is in order that people who do not know shall not be affected by a prior assurance. If they do know, the mischief disappears, and therefore, although there is no such phrase in the Act, it does apply to such cases. The other is quite a different principle. The other makes the subsequent incumbrancer trustee for the first incumbrancer, and that is really the view in *Le Neve* v *Le Neve* (1748) 3 Atk 646, which Lord Hardwicke puts upon dolus malus and what he calls (quoting from the civil law) "machinationem ad circumeniendum" and in the particular case – and I do not say his authority would go further, or that it has been quoted as going further there was that very thing. If B knows of an incumbrance on Black Acre already effected in favour of A, he may take a second incumbrance without intending to destroy A's incumbrance; when he takes it thinking that there will not be sufficient for both he may effect registration of his incumbrance knowing that the other has not been registered, with a view to getting as much advantage as he can. There is no fraud in that. He is standing on his legal rights. But if A has a conveyance of the whole property, and B takes a second conveyance of the whole property knowing that A's is not registered, and promptly registers, then his endeavour from the beginning has been to destroy that which he knows was an honest transaction though not protected by law. It is the same, of course, if, knowing that A has a conveyance of the whole property, he takes a mortgage which partially affects A, or if, A having a mortgage, B takes a conveyance which will defeat A's mortgage, and that is what happened in *Le Neve* v *Le Neve*. It was not that the registration was effected in order to gain an advantage. It was that the whole inception of the transaction was to create an assurance which would defeat what the party intending to benefit by it knew was really an honest transaction. In that case, I assume that the manner in which the matter would be worked out would be by making the second person trustee of his advantages in favour of the first, at any rate as to third persons coming later, but, if that is not the case, then all that can be said is that the second person is postponed to the first because he is taken to have known of the first all along. The way of working out an administration of the assets if there was a liquidation, and if there were other creditors in, would be, it seems to me, difficult in both those cases, and extremely difficult in the case where, as in this case, there was no fraud at all.

On all these grounds it seems to me that the best thing is to go to the plain words of the statute. This document as against any creditor is void. The defendant here is a creditor, and therefore as against him it is as if it did not exist. Let us not import any consideration which may be applicable, or which it might be desirable to make applicable, where there is dolus malus, but which in any other case certainly neither are applicable, nor should be made applicable. Therefore I agree that this appeal should be allowed.'

Effect of crystallisation on priorities

Biggerstaff v *Rowatt's Wharf Limited* [1896] 2 Ch 93 Court of Appeal (Lindley, Lopes and Kay LJJ)

Crystallisation and the setting off of company debts

Facts
Rowatt's Wharf was established in 1892 and in 1893 it issued debentures secured by way of a floating charge over all its property goodwill, etc present and future. In November 1893 Harvey, Brand & Co purchased from Rowatt's Wharf 7,000 barrels at 3s 6d each and paid for them. Only 2,784 of the barrels were delivered by October 1894 when Harvey, Brand & Co discovered that Rowatt's Wharf did not have enough barrels to complete their contract. Meetings took place at which it was evident that Rowatt's Wharf was in financial difficulty. Harvey, Brand & Co agreed to help since they had large quantities of oil stored at the wharf which was used in the course of their business and they could not afford to see the wharf closed. In return for this assistance Harvey, Brand & Co were issued £25,000 of debenture stock. Shortly afterwards a receiver and manager of Rowatt's Wharf was appointed in a debenture-holder's action. At the date the receiver was appointed Harvey, Brand & Co owed Rowatt's Wharf storage charges for oil and other goods deposited by them at the wharf. They claimed a right to set-off the money owed to them for the barrels and lent to give financial assistance against what they owed to Rowatt's Wharf in storage charges. At first instance North J refused to allow the set-off on the ground that the claim in respect of the barrels was for an unliquidated sum while Rowatt's Wharf's claim for rent was for a liquidated sum. On appeal:

Held
The claim in respect of the barrels was for a liquidated sum as there was a total failure of consideration. Thus, Harvey, Brand & Co could set-off this claim against what was due to them from the company.

Kay LJ:

'Then it was urged that this claim could not be asserted against the debenture-holders, who had a charge on all the property of the company, inasmuch as Harvey, Brand & Co knew of the debentures. It is true that as against an assignee there can be no set-off of a debt accrued after the person claiming set-off has notice of the assignment. But does that apply to debentures such as these? Counsel hesitated to go so far as that, but said that there was no right of set-off, as no action had been brought in which it could have been asserted before 30 October, 1894. I think this is not so. I think that if at the time of the assignment there was an inchoate right to set-off it can be asserted after the assignment, for the assignment is subject to the rights then in existence. The question is whether the assignment took place at the issue of the debentures or the appointment of a receiver. The debentures contain provisions the effect of which is that the company is at liberty to go on with its business as if the debentures did not exist, until possession is taken under them. From that time the company cannot deal with its assets as against the title of the debenture-holders; up to that time it can deal with them in every legitimate way of business. Therefore the date to be regarded is the time of taking possession. A conclusion that set-off could not arise during the period before taking possession would be injurious to the debenture-holders, for it would hamper the company in carrying on its business, and so injure the debenture-holders, whose interest is that the company should carry on a prosperous business. There was an inchoate right of set-off at the time when the receiver was appointed; and that, and not the time of issuing the debentures, is the time to be looked to. The debentures must be regarded as incomplete assignments which do not become complete until the time when the receiver is appointed.'

George Barker (Transport) Ltd v *Eynon* [1974] 1 WLR 462 Court of Appeal (Edmund-Davies and Stamp LJJ, Sir Gorden Willmer)

Priority between a debenture-holder and a carrier having a lien over goods

Facts

The plaintiffs, a firm of road hauliers, had regular business with Alderley Meats (UK) Ltd (the company) by which they collected meat from the docks and delivered it to the company's customers. All orders from the company were accepted by the plaintiffs subject to Conditions of Carriage of the Road Haulage Association of which cl 13 provided:

'General lien. The carrier shall have a general lien against the owner of any goods for any moneys whatsoever due from such owner to the carrier. If any lien is not satisfied within a reasonable time the carrier may at his absolute discretion sell the goods as agents for the owner and apply the proceeds towards the moneys due and the expenses of sale ...'

The company's bankers held a debenture secured by way of a floating charge over all the company's assets. This charge contained a restrictive clause prohibiting the creation of other charges ranking pari passu or in priority to the bank's charge.

On 23 August, 1971 the company gave the plaintiffs an order to collect meat from the Port of London and deliver it to Gravesend. The consignment was comprised of 649 cartons and 333 of these were delivered on 25 August. On 31 August the bank appointed the defendant as receiver of the company. The plaintiffs heard of this on 2 September and refused to deliver the other 316 cartons claiming a lien on them for transport charges of £3,233 owed to them by the company, in accordance with cl 13. The plaintiffs sought a declaration that they were entitled to exercise the lien in these circumstances. Mocatta J refused the declaration. On appeal:

Held

The plaintiffs were entitled to exercise their lien in priority to the debenture-holders. The receiver had not repudiated the contract of carriage and the receiver or debenture-holder as assignee of the meat could not be in any better position than the company in taking this assignment which was subject to the right of lien already given to the plaintiffs.

Stamp, LJ:

'... Shorn of the arguments supporting it, the receiver's contention before this court was that this is a case of priorities. The lien was a possessory lien which did not come into existence until the carriers were in possession of the goods. Before the carriers came into possession of the goods the charge in favour of the debenture holder crystallised by the effect of the appointment of the receiver. The goods had become the subject of an equitable assignment to the debenture holder and the lien could not come into existence as against the debenture holder.

These submissions are not, in my judgment, well founded. What is in law described under the convenient label of a "lien" is in relation to a carrier the right to hold the goods which have been carried in respect of the costs of the carriage or, as in this case, the contractual right to hold the goods which have been carried in respect of the debt for the carriage and in the respect of the debts of the same character previously contracted. The duty of the carriers here was to carry the goods and deliver them, or they might say after they had carried them, "We will hold these goods in exercise of the right to do so conferred by the contract of carriage until we have been paid," and they might say, "Moreover, we will, unless we are paid within a reasonable time, in exercise of our right under the contract, sell the goods and pay ourselves out of the proceeds. These are the terms on which we carried the goods." In my judgment, these rights did not arise or come into existence at the time the carriers took possession of the goods. Nor clearly did they become exercisable at that time. The rights were rights created by the contract which became exercisable at the moment of time when the goods had been carried. The rights which were conferred on the carriers by condition 13 of the contract are conveniently and accurately described as a "lien", but you do not by so describing them alter their character. They are conveniently described as "a possessory lien", because it is only if the carriers have possession that they can be exercised. But to say that a lien, because it is so described, does not come into existence until possession is assumed is to reason falsely. Contractual rights come into existence at the time of the contract creating them notwithstanding that they may not be exercisable except on the happening of a future event. Here the fact of obtaining possession of the goods was a preliminary to the exercise of the right claimed, but still the rights were not exercisable until the carriers had carried the goods. The contractual "lien" to which the carriers were entitled under the contract was not a legal "thing" or "chose in action" arising by the effect of possession, but no more than a description of the bundle of rights belonging to the carriers under condition 13 and which the company had contracted they should have.

There was nothing remarkable about the contract. It was simply a contract for the carriage of goods incorporating the Conditions of Carriage of the Road Haulage Association. It was, in my judgment, clearly a contract into which, so long as the charge created by the debenture was a floating charge, the company could, consistently with the terms of the debenture, have properly entered. It was, as I have indicated, a contract which was not determined by the effect of the appointment of the receiver. The receiver might, so I will assume, have repudiated it before the carriers started the journey, so preventing the carriers obtaining possession of the goods and carrying out their obligations under it. He did not do so. How then could the receiver or the debenture holder as assignee of the goods and of the rights of the company under the contract be in any better position than would the company have been to insist at the end of the journey that the goods be handed over without making the payments for which condition 13 provided? In my judgment, counsel for the plaintiffs was right in his contention that the assignments to the company brought about by the appointment of the receiver were subject to the rights already given by the company to other persons under ordinary trading contracts. As against the company, the carriers on arriving at the door of the consignees at Gravesend could have withheld the goods against payment and, in my judgment, the debenture-holder as assignee from the company can be in no better position. The debenture-holder as assignee of the company's rights under the contract can be in no better position than any other assignee of the company's rights under the contract ...'

N W Robbie & Co Ltd v *Witney Warehouse Co Ltd* [1963] 1 WLR 1324 Court of Appeal (Sellers, Donovan and Russell LJJ)

Crystallisation and the right to set-off debts

Facts
In January 1960 Robbie granted its bankers a debenture imposing, inter alia, a floating charge on its

undertaking, to secure an overdraft. In July 1961 the bank appointed a receiver and manager under the debenture and the floating charge accordingly crystallised. Prior to crystallisation Robbie owed English Spinners Ltd a trading debt of £852. The receiver carried on Robbie's business and in doing so sold and delivered goods to Witney in the sum of £1,346. English Spinners Ltd and Witney were subsidiaries of the same parent company. English Spinners assigned the debt of £852 owed to them by Robbie to Witney and gave due notice of this. When Robbie sued Witney for the £1,346, Witney claimed to set-off against this the £852 debt assigned to them. At first instance Widgery J permitted the set-off. On appeal:

Held (Donovan LJ dissenting)
The set-off would not be permitted because there was not that mutuality between the debts to permit this.

Russell LJ:

'... By force of the debenture charge an equitable charge attached in favour of the debenture-holder ... on the ... debts constituting the total of £1,346 6s 1d as they came into existence on delivery of goods to the defendant after such appointment. These choses in action belonging to the plaintiffs became thus assigned in equity to the debenture-holder, at times when the defendants had no cross-claim of any kind against the plaintiffs and consequently no rights of set-off. Before the defendants acquitted by assignment this cross-claim the defendants must be fixed with knowledge of this equitable assignment to the debenture-holder (by way of charge) of the debt owed by the defendants to the plaintiffs. A debtor cannot set-off his claim against X against a claim by X against him which the debtor knows has been assigned by X to Y before the debtor acquired a right of set-off. Just as an assignee of a chose in action takes subject to an already existing right of set-off, so a debtor with no existing right of set-off cannot assert set-off of a cross-claim which he first acquires after he has notice of the assignment of the claim against him ...'

... Applying these considerations to the present case, at the time when the defendant first acquired the claim for £852 18s 4d the choses in action sought to be enforced against the defendants had been assigned to the debenture-holder by way of charge, but the claim for £852 18s 4d in no way involved the debenture-holder. There was consequently at the first moment of assertion of set-off no identity between the persons beneficially interested in the claim and the person against whom the cross-claim existed. There was, therefore, not that pre-requisite of set-off, mutuality, to use a word, which though perhaps not very exact, was made by Parliament philologically acceptable in the statutes of set-off (2 Geo 2 c 22 (1728)). It was sought to counter this conclusion by reference to the case in this court of *Bennett* v *White* [1910] 2 KB 643. In that case A sued B in debt, and B having obtained an assignment from C of a debt owed to C by A was held entitled to set if off. It was said by Lord Cozens-Hardy MR ([1910] 2 KB at p646):

"The assignee has a full and absolute right to say that the debt is his debt for all purposes including the purposes of the statutes of set-off. The debt is for all purposes in the same position as if it had been the original debt of the assignee":

and he said ([1910] 2 KB at p647) that they must treat the case exactly the same as if it had been under the statutes of set-off "a case in which the defendant had at the time when he was sued a debt originally due to him from the plaintiff himself." But to apply that language as decisive of the present totally different case would be quite mistaken. It is to be taken as referring to the circumstances then before the court, which involved no beneficial interests other than those of A and B, and not to circumstances never then in mind. It was never there said that the assignment was retrospective in its operation for all purposes, so as to enable acquisition of a cross-debt to circumvent and destroy the known rights of an equitable assignee of the plaintiffs' claim. That language could equally be cited, and with as little justification, as establishing the proposition that a sale by X of all debts accruing due to him in 1962 would embrace a debt due in 1962 to Y and assigned in 1963 to X.

I conclude, therefore, that there is in this particular case no right of set-off because there is no "mutuality" in beneficial interest. The claimant is primarily the debenture-holder: the cross-claim is against the company (the plaintiffs) alone, and is indeed one which in its origin could not be met and was not entitled to be met until the debenture-holder had been paid off in full.

If set-off is to be considered as only a procedural matter to avoid the mere pro and the mere contra in different actions, they do not exist here. If set-off is to be considered as a system designed to keep a debtor to X out of prison when in truth he is not a debtor to X at all when his financial relationship with X is fully investigated (which was the original purpose of the statutes of set-off), then the present circumstances are not such as are related to the purposes of that system ...'

Rother Iron Works Ltd v *Canterbury Precision Engineers* [1974] QB 1 Court of Appeal (Russell, Cairns and Stamp LJJ)

Crystallisation and the right to set off debts

Facts
The plaintiff company executed a floating charge over all its assets, present and future in 1971 in favour of its bank to secure loans. The plaintiff company and the defendants traded with each other. On 4 October, 1971 the plaintiff company owed the defendants £124 for goods sold and delivered. Shortly after 4 October the defendants contracted to buy goods worth £158 from the plaintiff company. But before this contract could be carried out the bank, on 21 October, appointed a receiver and manager causing its floating charge to crystallise. The goods pursuant to the contract were delivered to the defendants on 3 November. The defendants claimed they were entitled to set-off the £124 due to them under the previous contract against their £158 debt to the plaintiff company. The county court judge allowed the set-off. On appeal:

Held
The crystallisation of the floating charge did not operate to alter the rights between the parties. The claim sought to be set-off accrued before crystallisation and the contract against which set-off was claimed came into existence before crystallisation. The effect of crystallisation was that the rights under the contract were assigned to the chargee who could be in no better position than the company.

Russell LJ:

'... Now we are not concerned in the present case with a situation in which the cross-claim sought to be set off either arose or first came to the hands of the defendants after the crystallisation of the charge. Nor are we concerned with a claim made by a receiver against the defendants arising out of a contract made by the receiver subsequent to his appointment; for it is clear that the delivery of the goods was pursuant to the contract made by the plaintiff company before the appointment. Nor are there here any special considerations that might arise from a winding-up of the plaintiff company. The facts are simply as stated.

In our judgment the argument for the defendants is to be preferred. It is true that the right of the plaintiff company to sue for the debt due from the company was embraced, when it arose, by the debenture charge. But if this was because the chose in action consisting of the rights under the contract became subject to the charge on the appointment of the receiver, then the debenture-holder could not be in a better position to assert those rights than had been the assignor plaintiff company. And if the obligation of the defendant company to pay £159 be regarded as a chose in action on its own it never in our view came into existence except subject to a right to set off the £124 as in effect payment in advance. That which became subject to the debenture charge was not £159, but the net claim sustainable by the plaintiff company of £35 ...'

Registration of charges

Braemar Investments Ltd, Re [1988] 3 WLR 596 Chancery Division (Hoffman J)

Extension of time for registration

Facts
A bank lent money to a company and the loan was to be secured by a charge on the company's property. The bank asked the company's solicitors to register the charge; although they assured the bank several times that they were taking the necessary steps, they failed to do so. On discovering this, the bank the next working day, applied under s404 of the Companies Act 1985 for an extension of time for registration. The application was successful and the registrar's order, in usual form, contained a proviso protecting any rights acquired in the charged property between the date of the creation of the charge and its actual registration and it also gave liberty to the company or any unsecured creditor to apply to the court to have the order discharged within 56 days of a voluntary winding up becoming effective on or before 3 December 1986. A resolution to wind up the company was passed on 2 December and the liquidator applied to have the registrar's order discharged.

Held
His application would be dismissed.

Hoffmann J:

> 'In my judgment, this motion is similar to an application to discharge an ex parte order. It is a rehearing and a fresh exercise of the discretion on the whole of the material before the court. The judge is not confined to the evidence before the registrar or the grounds on which he founded his decision. Counsel for the liquidator said that the result would be to allow an applicant to put forward what was in substance a new application after the date of the liquidation. But I think that is an inevitable consequence of making the order first and leaving for later consideration the question of whether it should have been made. It would be wrong for the court at the subsequent hearing to shut its eyes to facts of which evidence is available or grounds on which the order could properly have been made.
>
> On the basis that this was to be treated as a rehearing, counsel for the liquidator submitted that on two grounds the order should be discharged. First, he said that, even now, the evidence did not justify a finding that the omission to register was due to inadvertence ... This may be true, but the jurisdiction may be exercised not only when the omission was due to inadvertence. In *Re MIG Trust Ltd* [1933] Ch 542 at 560 Lord Hanworth MR, after reciting the terms of the section, said:
>
>> "It seems to me quite clear that the Legislature did intend by those very wide terms not to give a restricted opportunity to repair an omission but to give the widest possible discretion to the court in circumstances which need not show that the omission was accidental or due to inadvertence but which would be sufficient on other grounds to make it just and equitable to grant relief."
>
> These last words suggest that the underlying guide to the exercise of the discretion is whether for any reason, whether specified in the section or not, it would be just and equitable to grant relief. I consider that in this case it would ...
>
> Counsel for the liquidator's second ground was that by the time of the registrar's order the company was crippled by ... two Mareva injunctions and plainly no longer a going concern. Although the proprietary interests of the unsecured creditors in its property had not yet technically crystallised, it was inevitable that they would. Liquidation was imminent ...
>
> As a matter of strict law an application to extend time is not too late if the registration can be effected before the liquidation actually commences. The court may as a matter of discretion on particular facts decide that it is too late at an earlier date, but the overriding question must be whether it would be just

and equitable to grant leave. On the facts of this case I think that the [bank] through no fault of their own, were only just in time. But they were, nevertheless, in time. When the application was made liquidation may well have appeared to be a likely short-term outcome ... Unlike the *Resinoid* [1983] Ch 132 case, no notice of a meeting of creditors had been sent out and it certainly could not be said that it was only the prospect of forthcoming liquidation which had alerted the [bank] to the necessity for an extension of time.

Taking all circumstances into account, therefore, I do not think that the imminence of liquidation was a ground on which the application should have been refused and the motion is therefore dismissed.'

Esberger & Son Ltd v *Capital & Counties Bank* [1913] 2 Ch 336 Chancery Division (Sargant J)

Charge to be registered within 21 days of execution

Facts
In September 1910 the company, needing an overdraft, deposited with the defendant bank the title deeds of land it owned in Lincolnshire, together with a sealed but undated memorandum of charge to secure further advances, which were from time to time to be subsequently made by the bank. On 14 June, 1911 the manager filled in that date on the memorandum and on 3 July, 1911 the memorandum was for the first time registered with the Registrar of Companies. In September 1911 the company went into voluntary winding-up. The liquidator demanded delivery of the deeds from the bank which refused them. The liquidator brought this action claiming that there was no charge on the deeds on the ground that the undated instrument was void for want of registration and the insertion of the date and registration did not change the fact that it was not registered within 21 days from its creation. The bank contended that the date of creation of the charge was when the money was advanced on it so for this reason it was within the time limits and not void.

Held
The date of the creation of a mortgage or charge by a company is the date on which the instrument of mortgage or charge is executed and not the date when money is subsequently advanced on it. The charge was void since it had not been registered within 21 days of its creation.

Sargant J:

'... In my opinion, from the time when the deed was in fact executed and handed to the bank, namely, 17 September, 1910, the bank had a complete and valid operative charge upon the property for the amount purporting to be secured by the deed.

But the argument in favour of the bank for the purpose of rebutting that prima facie result is twofold. In the first place Mr Romer says that a charge is not created within the meaning of the Companies (Consolidation) Act, s93, unless and until there is some money secured by it; that is to say, that if a document is dated on a certain day, and is to secure future advances, and then future advances are not made until a later date, the date of the creation of the charge is the date when the future advances are made and when, therefore, the document becomes an effective document to secure actual money, and is not the date when the actual charge was executed. Now looking at the terms of s95, I do not think that that is the true effect of the section. It has been said that the section is one which it is difficult to construe; but where there is in fact an instrument creating or evidencing a mortgage or charge – and that is the only case I need deal with – I feel clear that on the true meaning of that section the date of the creation of the mortgage or charge is the date when that instrument was executed and is not the date when any money is subsequently advanced, so as to make an effective charge for the amount of that money. There is authority for that view of the section in two cases, *In re Spiral Globe Ltd* (*No 2*) [1902] 2 CH 209, before Joyce J and *In re New London and Suburban Omnibus Co* [1908] 1 Ch 621, before Neville J ...

... That disposes of the main argument put forward by Mr Romer; but he has also put forward a subsidiary argument which is hardly distinguishable from his main argument and is to this effect. He says that although this document may be bad as to some part of the advances which are secured, still, as regards any advances which were in fact made within the 21 days before the actual registration and remain owing, there at any rate, there is nothing to avoid the effect of the document. As it happens, if that argument were to prevail, the bank would get home as to the whole of their effective claim, because on the figure it appears that something like £600 or £700 was advanced by the bank within the 21 days of the date of the registration and the whole amount realised by the property is only, as I have said, something like £340. But I cannot accept that argument. If that were so, it would seem to follow that there was a succession of dates which were the relevant dates. Here you have a document which is executed for the purpose of securing, not only sums which are due at that time, but any sums that may become owing in the future. It would be impossible, I think, to say that the creation of the charge was at one date as regards the sums that were then owing, and at another date as regards sums which became owing in the future. Such a construction would render the working of s93 of the Act exceedingly difficult, and, although that ought not to cause me to come to a conclusion which is contrary to the language of the section, I think it is something that may be taken into account in construing that language. The section is providing for the keeping of a register, which is to show what moneys are owing by the company on certain securities, so that creditors may have some notion of how far the property of the company is unencumbered; and the natural date and the workable date in respect of any one particular instrument must, I think, be the date on which the instrument is executed, and not the series of dates on which various sums of money may from time to time become due. The words in the first part of the section are "mortgage or charge created", and the subsequent words "unless the prescribed particulars of the mortgage or charge, together with the instrument (if any) by which the mortgage or charge is created or evidenced, are delivered to or received by the Registrar of Companies for registraton in manner required by this Act within 21 days", seem to me to point to one definite period of time from which the 21 days must be or can be readily calculated by the registrar.

In my opinion, therefore, there has been a failure to comply with the provisions of the section as regards this mortgage or charge, and the consequence is that, so far as any security is created by it, it is void as against the liquidator, and the liquidator is entitled to succeed in this action and to have paid to him, accordingly, for distribution the net proceeds of the sale of this land.'

George Inglefield Limited, Re [1933] Ch 1 Court of Appeal (Lord Hanworth MR, Lawrence and Romer LJJ)

Registration of agreements was not required

Facts

A company which carried on business as retailers of furniture and drapery goods went into liquidation in 1931 with substantial debts. A major portion of the company's business had been carried out by means of hire purchase transactions and for this purpose the company had entered into agreements with a finance company. The hire purchase transactions were carried out using printed forms supplied by the finance company which purchased the goods from the company together with the benefit of the hire purchase agreements. The terms of purchase were that the company assigned absolutely the goods and the hire purchase agreement and was paid in instalments by a series of bills of exchange. The assignment to the finance company was not to be notified to the hirer unless he should default. The liquidator of the company alleged that the assignments were not absolute, but by way of charge of book debts and were void for non-registration.

Held

The agreements were on their true construction in the form of an out-and-out sale and the assignments made thereunder did not require registration.

Romer LJ:

'... The only question that we have to determine is whether, looking at the matter as one of substance, and not of form, the discount company has financed the dealers in this case by means of a transaction of mortgage and charge, or by means of a transaction of sale; because, of course, financing can be done in either the one way or the other, and to point out that it is a transaction of financing throws no light upon the question that we have to determine.

It appears to me that the matter admits of a very short answer, if one bears in mind the essential differences that exist between a transaction of sale and a transaction of mortgage or charge. In a transaction of sale the vendor is not entitled to get back the subject-matter of the sale by returning to the purchaser the money that has passed between them. In the case of a mortgage or charge, the mortgagor is entitled, until he has been foreclosed, to get back the subject-matter of the mortgage or charge by returning to the mortgagee the money that has passed between them. The second essential difference is that if the mortgagee realises the subject-matter of the mortgage for a sum more than sufficient to repay him, with interest and the costs, the money that has passed between him and the mortgagor he has to account to the mortgagor for the surplus. If the purchaser sells the subject-matter of the purchase, and realises a profit, of course he has not got to account to the vendor for the profit. Thirdly, if the mortgagee realises the mortgage property for a sum that is insufficient to repay him the money that he has paid to the mortgagor, together with interest and costs, then the mortgagee is entitled to recover from the mortgagor the balance of the money, either because there is a covenant by the mortgagor to repay the money advanced by the mortgagee, or because of the existence of the simple contract debt which is created by the mere fact of the advance having been made. If the purchaser were to resell the purchased property at a price which was insufficient to recoup him the money that he paid to the vendor, of course would not be entitled to recover the balance from the vendor.

In this case the subject-matter of the mortgage or charge, or of the sale and purchase, whichever it be, is certain furniture subject to, and with the benefit of, the hiring agreements. If one considers the documents, which I do not intend to go through again, in relation to the three matters that I have mentioned, it will be found that in every one of those three respects the documents bear the attributes of a sale and purchase, and not the attributes of a mortgage or charge.

For these reasons, with great respect to the learned judge, I have come to the conclusion in this case that the financing has been done by a sale and purchase, and not by a mortgage or charge, and, accordingly, that it is not invalidated by non-registration by reason of s95 of the Companies Act.'

Kent & Sussex Sawmills Limited, Re [1947] Ch 177 Chancery Division (Wynn-Parry J)

Security void for non-registration

Facts

The company obtained a contract in 1944 to supply the Ministry of Fuel and Power with 30,000 tons of cut logs. The company asked its bankers for overdraft facilities to enable it to carry out the contract. The bank agreed to the overdraft on condition that a letter was sent to the Ministry on the following terms: 'With reference to the above contract we hereby authorise you to remit all moneys due thereunder to this company's (bankers) whose receipt shall be your sufficient discharge. These instructions are to be regarded as irrevocable unless the bank should consent to their cancellation in writing ...' The Ministry acknowledged the letter and followed the instructions. The company obtained further contracts from the Ministry and also obtained further overdraft facilities from the bank on the same terms. In 1946 the company went into liquidation. It was owed £30,000 under the contracts with the Ministry and had an overdraft with the bank of over £83,000. The liquidator contended that the letters did not amount to an absolute assignment of the moneys due to the company but, rather, charges on book debts which were void for non-registration.

Held

The letters were assignments by way of security for the overdraft and, consequently, were void for non-registration.

Wynn-Parry J:

'It is clear from the authorities that it is the duty of the court to come to a conclusion on what is the substance of the matter and for the sake of convenience I shall test this matter by reference solely to the language of the letter of 18 September, 1944. On behalf of the liquidator, Mr Strangman as his first point submitted that the proper conclusion is that in this letter there can be found no assignment at all, in which case cadit quaestio. In support of that argument he referred to the case of *Bell* v *The London and North-Western Railway Co* (1852) 15 Beav 548. In that case, a railway contractor gave his bankers a letter directing the railway company to pass the cheques which might become due to him "to his account with the bank" and it was held that that was not an equitable assignment, but that it would have been if it had directed the cheques to be passed to the banker. In his judgment, Lord Romilly MR said:

"The words of this letter are these: 'You will oblige by passing the cheques that may become due on my contract No 1, of the Rugby and Stamford Railway, into the National Provincial Bank of England' ... I should have thought than an effectual assignment of all that might become due to Thomas Burton under that contract had been made to the bank; but this order directs it to be paid to the account of Thomas Burton, not therefore, as it appears to me, doing more than constituting the bank to be Thomas Burton's agents for the receipt of the money."

If the letter of 18 September, 1944, had stopped at the end of the first paragraph, then, in my view, it would have followed that this case was completely covered by what was said by Lord Romilly in *Bell* v *London and North Western Railway Co*. I have to consider the effect on this aspect of the matter of the second paragraph, which opens with these words: "These instructions are to be regarded as irrevocable unless the said bank should consent to their cancellation in writing". I think that the effect of those words on the matter is really as submitted by Mr Buckley for the bank, because, as he points out, it appears from the paragraph in *Bell* v *London and North Western Railway Co* that the Master of the Rolls arrived at the conclusion which he did in view of the circumstance that, as he said,

"An order of that description would always be revocable by the person giving it, but not so an order to pay to the third person absolutely."

Effect must be given to those words and in my judgment the proper way of construing this letter, looking at it as a whole, is to bear in mind and never to lose sight of the circumstance that the relationship of the two parties in question, the company and the bank, was that of borrower and lender and that this letter was brought into existence in connexion with a proposed transaction of borrowing by the company and lending by the bank. So regarded, I think, the opening words of the second paragraph fall naturally into the picture and they must be regarded as having been introduced for the protection of the bank. But once that is admitted, it throws light upon the whole of the letter and serves to underline what is obviously equally the intention of the first paragraph, namely, to provide protection for the bank. It therefore appears to me that the result of that is to take this case out of *Bell* v *London and North Western Railway Co* and to lead to the conclusion that I must treat this letter as amounting to an equitable assignment.

That, however, does not conclude the matter because I have then to investigate the question whether that assignment on its true construction is an out-and-out assignment of the whole of the benefit accruing or to accrue to the company under the contract or whether it is no more than an assignment by way of security. Here, again, I think the truth is to be found by bearing in mind the relationship between the parties. Prima facie, at any rate when one has to look at a document brought into existence between a borrower and a lender in connection with a transaction of borrowing and lending, one must approach the consideration of that document with the expectation of discovering that the document is intended to be given by the borrower to the lender in order to secure repayment of a proposed indebtedness of the borrower to the lender.

Mr Buckley for the bank, however, has submitted, in a very attractive argument, that the true view of this matter, particularly when one regards the effect of payments made to a bank on behalf of a customer, is that this letter amounts to a sale by the company to the bank of the whole of the company's interest in the moneys due or to become due under a contract. He points out that the ultimate test of whether this can be said to amount to a security is that one must be able to discover on the fact of the letter, either in express words or by necessary implication, an equity of redemption in the company and that, properly read, this letter discloses neither expressly nor by implication any such equity of redemption. As I say, I approach this matter more in the expectation of finding that the parties have brought into existence a document consistent with their relations of borrower and lender, rather than finding that notwithstanding those relations they brought into existence a document in which their relationship changed to that of vendor and purchaser. In my judgment, by implication an equity of redemption is to be discovered in the language of the second paragraph. I can see no commercial business reason for the introduction of those words: "These instructions are to be regarded as irrevocable unless the said bank should consent to their cancellation" except upon the basis that the parties did deliberately contemplate that circumstances might arise in which it might become desirable that a cancellation of the instructions should be given by the bank; but the existence of that previous paragraph appears to me to operate strongly to lead to the conclusion that there was nothing in the nature of a sale. One is entitled to test the matter by looking at the situation in September, 1944, unembarrassed by what has happened since and to consider what possibilities were open. Suppose that in fact through one source or another the company's account had become in credit with the bank, is it to be supposed that the parties ever contemplated that notwithstanding that circumstance it should remain entirely a matter for the bank to determine whether it should give its consent to the cancellation of these instructions so that if it did not give that consent then for the rest of the period over which the contract had to be worked out, the payments still had to be paid into the company's account at the bank; so that whatever might have been the change in the friendly relations between the company and its bankers, it would have been compelled to maintain that account with the bank until the contract had been worked out? I recoil from coming to such a conclusion. In my view, if the company's account had come into credit the company would then have been entitled, in the true view of this letter, to require the bank to give the necessary instructions to the Ministry. The Ministry is in no way concerned with the position as between the bank and the company and as between those two parties I can see no ground either at law or in equity, on which the bank could have resisted a request or a requirement by the company to cancel the instructions. That at once shows that there is discoverable in this latter paragraph a true equity of redemption. I think the matter is if anything underlined by the other half of the sentence which is to the effect that the instructions are intended to cover any extension of the contract in excess of 30,000 tons if that should occur.'

National Provincial and Union Bank of England v *Charnley* [1924] 1 KB 431
Court of Appeal (Bankes, Scrutton and Atkin LJJ)

Conclusiveness of the certificate of registration

Facts
A company created a charge over leasehold property and certain movable chattels in order to secure payment of its overdraft at the plaintiff bank. The charge stated that the company 'demised' to the bank the leasehold property with all the movable 'plant used in or about the premises' for a term of about 996 years. The charge was submitted for registration with particulars, which stated that it was a mortgage of the leasehold premises; no mention was made of the chattels. The registrar entered this description in

the register – no mention was made of the chattels. Subsequently a judgment creditor of the company sought to execute judgment against the chattels on the footing that there was no charge against them. The bank claimed the chattels under their mortgage. The question arose whether there was an effective charge on the chattels.

Held

On the true construction of the document, a charge was created notwithstanding the use of the word 'demise'. Since the certificate of registration identified the instrument of charge and stated that the mortgage or charge thereby created had been duly registered it must be taken as certifying due registration of all the charges created by the instrument including that of the chattels even though the register by omitting them was not only defective but misleading.

Bankes LJ:

'But then it was contended that even if, apart from the provisions of the Companies (Consolidation) Act 1908, the document of 16 July 1921 gave the bank a valid floating charge over the chattels, including the motor vans, it was void by reason of non-compliance with the requirements of s93 of that Act ...'

... But where a mortgage or charge is created by an instrument, it seems to me quite impossible to treat that mortgage or charge otherwise than as one indivisible transaction, even though it covers several different items and different kinds of property, because it is evidenced by one instrument and one instrument only, and it is to that mortgage or charge so created by one indivisible instrument that the section, when requiring performance of the conditions necessary to prevent its avoidance, refers. Those conditions are that the prescribed particulars and the instrument by which the charge is created shall be delivered to the registrar within 21 days. It is not disputed, as I understand it, that the object of the legislature in requiring delivery to the registrar of the instrument as well as the particulars is to enable him to form an independent judgment in reference to what he ought to put on the register before he in fact registers it, and if he is entitled to do that, being only human, he may make a mistake, and if he makes a mistake and enters on the register something different from what the particulars really justify, the unfortunate person carrying in those particulars will, according to Mr Haydon, find himself possessed of a void instrument, because the register, which, as I understand Mr Haydon's argument, is the conclusive document, does not contain true particulars of the instrument. I agree with the judgments in *In re Yolland, Husson and Birkett Ltd* [1908] 1 Ch 152 to which we have been referred, as to the object of the statute. I think the object is to protect the grantee of the charge, and, as between him and the general body of creditors or prospective creditors, the registrar is appointed as the tribunal to decide what shall be put upon the register, and when it has been put there his certificate to that effect is conclusive evidence that all the requirements of the section have been complied with. One of those requirements, as I have already said, is that the prescribed particulars must be delivered, and we have been referred to the Statutory Rules and Orders, 1909, which contain the prescribed form of particulars, Form 47 ...

... It is quite true that there is an omission, because the property mortgaged or charged included chattels as well as land and fixtures; but when once the registrar has given his certificate that the registration was complete, and that the mortgage or charge was created by an instrument, identifying it, in my opinion you have to go to the instrument to see what was actually charged, there being nothing in the statute which says that when once registration has taken place the register shall be the evidence of the extent of the charge. All that the statute requires is satisfaction on the part of the appointed official that the preliminaries have been complied with, and, when once he certifies that, the parties are entitled to ask the court to say that what it has to look at in order to determine their rights is the instrument creating the mortgage or charge. For these reasons I think the view taken by the learned judge was right, and that this appeal should be dismissed ...'

Scrutton LJ:

'One of the reasons for that provision as to the conclusiveness of the certificate is that the person whose duty it is to register the charge is the company (subs 7), the party giving it, not the party to whom it is given. The company may give such charges to a large number of debenture-holders, who do not see the particulars, and very likely are not in a position to examine the register. The object of the certificate in that case is to prevent the debenture-holders' security from being upset if it turns out that the company or the registrar has made a mistake as to what has been put on the register. I am bound to say that the language of the statute is rather puzzling.' (Then he quotes): "'Every mortgage or charge created by the company ... shall be void unless the prescribed particulars of the mortgage or charge ... are delivered ... to the registrar ... within 21 days."' (He went on): 'That makes the avoidance depend on the neglect to send in the particulars. The neglect to register the charge will not make it void. Then when the registrar has got the particulars and the instrument creating the charge, he is to enter in the register, not the particulars delivered by the company, but the date of the instrument and its description, the amount secured, short particulars of the property mortgaged or charged, and the names of the mortgagees or persons entitled to the charge. So that there is a possibility, first of the company making an error in delivering the particulars, and secondly of the registrar making an error either in omitting to enter something specified in the particulars, or in misunderstanding the instrument of charge delivered to him with the particulars; and for that reason one can well understand a clause being put in in favour of the grantees of the charge, who are not the persons whose duty it is to deliver the particulars, that if the registrar gives a certificate that all is in order that certificate shall be conclusive evidence that the requirements as to registration have been complied with. The result of the legislation as it appears to me is that if the document sent in for registration does contain a charge on particular property, even if the company sending it in has misstated that charge, or the registrar considering it judicially has misunderstood it, when once the certificate has been given the grantees are safe. Though one can see that this may cause great hardship to a person who gives credit to the company in reliance on a defective register, one can also see that equal hardship would be caused to secured creditors if their security was to be upset for reasons connected with the action of persons over whom they had no control. For these reasons I take the view which was taken in *In re Yolland, Husson and Birkett Ltd* and *Cunard Steamship Co* v *Hopwood* [1908] 2 Ch 564, that the giving of the certificate by the registrar is conclusive that the document creating the charge was properly registered, even if in fact it was not properly registered. I do not know how the difficulty arose in this case. It looks as if somebody was very careless on behalf of the bank, and also as if somebody was very careless in the registrar's office.'

Commentary
See s401 of the Companies Act 1985 as substituted by s96 of the Companies Act 1989.

Paul & Frank Ltd v *Discount Bank (Overseas) Ltd* [1967] Ch 348 Chancery Division (Pennycuick J)

An assignment of an insurance policy was not a book debt and did not require registration

Facts
The plaintiff company exported furs to a Belgian company and had an insurance policy with the Export Credit Guarantee Department (ECGD) which covered the plaintiff in case the Belgian company should become insolvent. The plaintiff sent a letter back to the ECGD instructing it to pay over to the defendant bank any moneys which might fall due under the policy. This was an equitable assignment of the benefit of the policy. The Belgian company became insolvent and this had the effect of putting the plaintiff in financial difficulty and it too had to be wound up compulsorily. The liquidator of the plaintiff contended that the assignment of the benefit of the policy was a charge on a book debt and invalid because it had not been registered under s95(2)(e) CA 1948 (this became s396(1)(e) CA 1985 and a new s396 is substituted by s93 of the Companies Act 1989). He sought a declaration to this effect.

Held

'Book debts' in s95(2)(e) meant debts which in the ordinary course of business would be entered in the well-kept books of a company. Since an ECGD policy would not normally be entered in the books of a company the charge was not registrable and accordingly it was valid.

Pennycuick J:

'I turn now to s95 of the Companies Act, 1948. That section, so far as now material, runs as follows: '(His Lordship read s95(1) and (2)(e) and continued): 'It is not suggested that any of the other paragraphs in subsection (2) are material.

Looking at the matter for a moment apart from authority, I do not think that in ordinary speech one would describe as a "book debt" the right under a contingency contract before the contingency happens. By "contingency contract" in this connection I mean contracts of insurance, guarantee, indemnity and the like. However, this point is not free from authority, and I have been referred to two cases as to what is meant by a "book debt".

The first case is *Shipley* v *Marshall* (1863) 14 CBNS 566 where the four members of the Common Pleas Divisional Court gave judgments as to the meaning of the word "book debt"; I will quote a few sentences from those judgments. Erle CJ says:

"By 'book debts', the legislature doubtless intended to describe debts in some way connected with the trade of the bankrupt; and I am inclined to give the term a wider range. But is is enough to say that this was a debt connected with and growing out of the plaintiff's trade."

He finally said:

"To constitute the debt a 'book debt', it cannot to my mind be necessary that the transaction should be entered in a book."

Williams J said:

"This, it is said, can only mean debts which are actually entered in some book kept by the bankrupt in the course of his trade. I cannot, however, accede to that construction. I think the meaning of the statute is, that the assignees shall dispose of all debts due to the bankrupt in respect of which entries could be made in the ordinary course of his business: otherwise, a debt by accident omitted to be entered would not pass by the assignment. But the difficulty which I feel in this case, is to arrive at the conclusion that this is a debt arising out of a transaction which in the ordinary course of the bankrupt's business would find its way as an entry into any of the trade books."

The other case is *Independent Automatic Sales Ltd* v *Knowles and Foster* [1962] 1 WLR 974 where Buckley J had to deal with a deposit on certain hire-purchase agreements. He said:

"So far as I am aware, no more precise definition of the meaning of the term 'book debts' has ever been attempted judicially, and I shall not attempt one. *Shipley* v *Marshall*, I think, establishes that, if it can be said of a debt arising in the course of a business and due or growing due to the proprietor of that business that such a debt would or could in the ordinary course of such a business be entered in well-kept books relating to that business, that debt can properly be called a book debt whether it is in fact entered in the books of the business or not."

There are small verbal differences in the way in which this situation is expressed by the various judges. I do not, however, read Buckley J as intending either to differ from the members of the Common Pleas Divisional Court or as regarding them as having put different definitions on the expression. A certain difficulty is caused by the use of the words "would or could". It will be remembered that Williams J uses the two words in successive sentences. Byles J says: "They must be such debts as are", and Buckley J says "would or could". I think, however, that bearing in mind the context and the use of the following words "in the course of such a business", and the reference to "well-kept books", Buckley J is intending to apply what may be called a practical rather than a theoretical test, the test being: is the practice in well-kept books to enter the debt in question in the ordinary course of business? If there is any difference between the way in which it is put by the various judges, I would accept myself the way in which Byles J put it, that they must be such debts as are commonly entered in books. I will refer again to the judgment of Buckley J on another point.

I return now to the present case. On the accountancy evidence, it is common ground that the ECG policy would not, in practice, be entered as a book debt at the date of the letter of authority. I have found that the ECG policy would not, in practice, be entered as a book debt before the admission of liability and the ascertainment of the amount; and I have further found that it would not, as a matter of practice, be entered as a book debt even after the admission of liability and the ascertainment of the amount ...'

R v Registrar of Companies, ex parte Central Bank of India [1986] 1 All ER 105
Court of Appeal (Lawton, Slade and Dillon LJJ)

Conclusiveness of the certificate of registration

Facts
A bank granted documentary credits to the company which imposed an obligation on the company to grant additional security when required. On 9 February 1984 the bank called for additional security from the company by a letter of demand and on 10 February issued a writ for specific performance on the execution of a debenture set out in the letter. On 29 February the bank submitted to the registrar of Companies a photocopy of the instrument creating the debenture alleged to have been created by the letter of demand. However, Form 47, prescribed by the Companies (Forms) Regulations 1983, which accompanied the application for registration, was defective as it did not contain the particulars prescribed by s95 Companies Act 1948 (which became s395 of the 1985 Act: s395 has now been substituted by s93 of the Companies Act 1989), ie the documents creating the charge and the assets included in it. Further, the photocopy forwarded was insufficient as s95 required the original to be sent. Form 47 was returned by the registrar for completion and it was resubmitted to him on 29 March. In May 1984 the resubmitted Form 47 was returned by the registrar on the ground that the charge was unregistrable. But, after taking legal advice the charge was eventually registered with effect from 29 February 1984. Meanwhile, on 2 March an unsecured creditor of the company presented a petition for its compulsory winding-up. The registrar was unaware of this at the time of registration and the company was unaware that the charge had been registered. The company was eventually ordered to be wound up on 7 November 1984; it was massively insolvent and some unsecured creditors applied for an order of certiorari to quash the registrar's decision to register the charge on the ground that he had no jurisdiction to register a charge by considering particulars delivered out of time. Consequently, judicial review of the registrar's decision was available, it was argued. At first instance, Mervyn Davies J upheld these claims. On appeal:

Held
The effect of s98(2) Companies Act 1948 (which became s401(2) CA 1985 and has now been substituted by s96 of the CA 1989) was to preclude the court from going into the question whether a charge registered by the registrar did in fact comply with the requirements of s95 (now s395 CA 1985). This was because the section stated that the issue of the certificate was 'conclusive' evidence that the requirements of s95 had been satisfied. Therefore judicial review of the registrar's decision to register was not available even if the registrar had made an error of fact or law or mixed fact or law in his decision to register.

Slade LJ:

'It is obvious that the registrar in carrying out the function entrusted to him by Parliament of determining whether the requirements of Part III of the 1948 Act (now Part XII of the 1985 Act) as to registration have been complied with in any given case, will have to ask himself a number of questions. The questions will, no doubt, be primarily ones of fact, but may well include incidental questions of law, or mixed fact and law. Simply, for example, in a case where the facts are more complicated than usual, he may be faced with a question of mixed fact and law in determining what is the true date of the creation of the charge. Yet it will be his duty to answer the question as best he can for the purpose of determining whether or not the charge is eligible for registration. Parliament has clearly intended that he should answer it, whether or not it involves a point of mixed fact and law. Furthermore (and this is the crucial point for the purpose of the present case) the legislature in enacting s98(2), has, in my opinion, evinced a clear intention that no one (except the Attorney-General: see below) should be entitled to adduce evidence for the purpose of attacking the correctness of the registrar's answer once it has been incorporated in a s98 certificate. In the face of the "conclusive evidence" provisions of s98(2), I am driven to the conclusion ... that ss95 and 98 on their true construction confer on the registrar the power to decide finally and conclusively, all ancillary questions, whether they be questions of fact or law, or mixed fact and law, which fall to be decided in determining whether the requirements of Part III of the 1948 Act as to registration have been complied with in any given case. Even the clearest evidence that he had come to a wrong conclusion in answering any of these questions would not entitle anyone (except the Attorney-General: see below) to claim that he acted beyond his powers, since s98(2) would preclude the court from considering such evidence. If these conclusions are correct, it must follow that, even if the registrar erroneously registers a charge which should not have been registered and gives a consequent s98 certificate, such error may be incapable of correction. However, lest it be thought that this position may give rise to undue hardship or injustice, I would draw attention to two points. The first is the limited nature of the effect of a registration and a consequent s98 certificate. It does not operate to confer validity on a charge which is invalid for reasons other than lack of registration. All it does is to give a chargee who has a valid charge protection against the statutory invalidation of that charge against a liquidator and creditors of the company which would occur by virtue of s95(1) if the company were to go into liquidation and the charge were unregistered. As soon as the charge has in fact been registered, whether or not correctly, persons considering advancing money to the company will have notice of its existence and can make further inquiries if they wish. Even if a charge has been incorrectly registered (eg because the prescribed particulars were delivered out of time) I think there are likely to be very few, if any, creditors who could, on the subsequent liquidation of the company, show that they had suffered any substantial injustice as a result of this erroneous registration. The legislature, no doubt, had in mind the limited effect of a registration in providing for this certificate to be conclusive.

Second ... s98(2) of the 1948 Act does not bind the Crown, so that there might be nothing to prevent the Attorney-General from intervening, if he saw fit, by way of an application for judicial review – in what he considered to be an appropriae case, where the evidence was available to show that the registrar had erred in the exercise of his functions as to registration. There is, therefore, in my opinion, no question of the registrar being wholly beyond the reach of the law.

Two special cases may arise on which I wish to express no concluded opinion in this present judgment, because it is not necessary to do so. The first is the hypothetical case where a purported certificate given by the registrar under s98(2) discloses an error on the face of it. It may well be that even the protection afforded by s98(2) would not operate in that situation. The second special situation may arise where the certificate had been obtained by fraud. Even in that case a direct attack on the certificate would, at least prima facie, be ruled out by s98(2) ... though it might well be that the court would act in personam against the fraudulent party, so as to prevent him taking advantage of the fraudulently obtained certificate ... and furthermore, a creditor personally damaged by the fraud might be able to take proceedings for damages ...'

Watson v Duff, Morgan & Vermont Holdings [1974] 1 WLR 450 Chancery Division (Templeman J)

Late registration of charges

Facts

On 22 January, 1971, the company created two debentures secured by floating charges. One was in favour of a Dr Watson to secure a loan of £10,000, the other in favour of Duff, Morgan and Vermont for £5,000; the latter was expressed to 'rank immediately after' the former. Duff, Morgan & Vermont's charge was registered on 28 January, 1971 but, by an oversight, Dr Watson's charge was not. In October 1971, Dr Watson applied under s101 CA 1948 (which became s404 CA 1985 and a new s404 is substituted by s99 of the Companies Act 1989) for time to be extended for registration of his charge and an order was made but 'without prejudice to the rights of any parties acquired prior to the time when the said debenture is to be actually registered'. This order was made on 28 October and gave Dr Watson 14 days to register. On the same day that the order was made Duff, Morgan & Vermont appointed a receiver. Dr Watson appointed a receiver on 8 November and the following day the company went into liquidation. The question arose as to who had priority.

Held

Dr Watson had priority since Duff, Morgan & Vermont acquired their rights on creation and not on registration as it was created expressly subject to Dr Watson's charge.

Templeman, J:

'Although the first debenture became void under s95 on 12 February, 1971, the effect of the order dated 28 October, 1971 extending the time for registration under s101, followed by registration within that extended time, on 5 November, 1971, was to constitute the first debenture valid ad initio, for in the words of Romer LJ in *Re Ehrmann Brothers Ltd* [1906] 2 Ch 697:

"... if the time is extended and registration is made within the extended time, then the debentures would be constituted a valid charge ab initio subject only to such conditions as might be imposed by a judge giving the extended time."

In the words of Vaughan Williams, LJ in the same case, the effect of s101 is "to place the debenture-holders in the same position as they would have been in if they had registered in due time", subject, in the present case, to the fact that the order under s101 was expressly made without prejudice to the rights of any party acquired prior to the time when the said debenture shall be actually registered. The claim that the second debenture has achieved priority over the plaintiff's first debenture depends on whether the defendants, as second debenture-holders, or their receiver, "acquired rights" within the meaning of the order under s101 made on 28 October, 1971. The inclusion in an order under s101 of a provision saving rights acquired before actual registration has been common form since the decision in *Re Joplin Brewery Co Ltd* [1902] 1 Ch 79. Such a provision should not in the absence of dealings or other relevant circumstances be made so as to affect the priorities inter se of registered and unregistered debentures intended to rank pari passu; see, for example, *Re I C Johnson & Co Ltd* [1902] 2 Ch 101 where a special provision was inserted in the order to preserve the position.

The object of the usual provision saving rights acquired before actual registration is, in the words of Vaughan Williams LJ in *Re Ehrmann Brothers Ltd* :

"... to protect intervening rights, rights which intervene between the time, the end of the 21 days within which the statute requires registration, and the time of registration under the order for extension of the time."

The rights intended to be preserved are, said Cozens-Hardy LJ in the same case –

"rights acquired against the property of the company or affecting the property of the company intervening between the expiration of the 21 days and the extended time allowed by the order."

It follows that unsecured creditors with no charge on the property of the company do not qualify for the purposes of the common-form provision in an order under s101 as parties possessing rights acquired: see, for example, *Re Ehrmann Brothers Ltd* and *Re MIG Trust Ltd* [1933] Ch 542.

If, however, before registration the company has gone into liquidation the rights and duties of the liquidator to distribute all the assets of the company between its creditors is a right acquired against the company's property and is protected by the proviso: see *Re Spiral Globe Ltd* [1902] 1 Ch 396 approved in *Re Ehrmann Brothers Ltd* .

In the present case the first argument put forward by counsel for the defendants was that the proviso to the order dated 28 October, 1971, extending the time for registration of the first debenture, but without prejudice to the rights of any party acquired prior to actual registration, made the plaintiff's first debenture, when registered, subject to the rights acquired by the defendants under the second debenture. But from the authorities which I have already cited – and in particular from *Re Ehrmann Brothers Ltd* it appears that the rights acquired by the defendants under the second debenture do not fall within the proviso to the order because the defendants' rights were acquired on the date the second debenture was executed, and were not acquired during the period which elapsed while the first debenture was void, that is to say, they were not acquired during the period between the expiration of 21 days after the execution of the first debenture and the date of actual registration of the first debenture.

Counsel's second argument is that the defendants acquired rights which gave the second debenture priority over the first debenture when, at the end of 21 days after the execution of both debentures, the first debenture was unregistered and void, and the second debenture was registered and valid.

In my judgment the mere expiration of the 21 day period did not confer any rights on the defendants, although it is true that if they had thereafter exercised their powers of sale, they could, for example, have conferred rights on a purchaser free from the first debenture …

… Counsel for the defendants' third argument was that the defendants, or their receiver, acquired rights when the receiver was appointed on 28 October, 1971, the date when the court extended the time for registration of the first debenture, but before the first debenture was actually registered on 5 November, 1971. The rights acquired by the defendants, or their receiver, at the date of the appointment of the receiver conferred, submits counsel, permanent priority on the second debenture over the first debenture.

Very properly, no reliance was, in the circumstances, placed on any action taken by the receiver after his appointment when the priority of the two debentures was in dispute and there was correspondence between the parties. The submission was that the stroke of the pen which appointed the receiver crystallised the floating charge created by the second debenture, and hey presto conferred on the defendants, or their receiver, rights which were not at that time subject to the first debenture, and which had the effect of conferring permanent priority on the second debenture over the first debenture.

In my judgment when the defendants appointed a receiver they did not thereby acquire rights but exercised a power which had been acquired when the debenture was executed. The exercise of this power did not alter any rights. It is true that the floating charge was crystallised by the appointment but no new rights were acquired. The debenture itself created an equitable charge on the assets of the company in favour of the defendants, and a licence to the company to deal with those assets in the ordinary course of business. The appointment of the receiver revoked the licence to the company to deal with its assets in the ordinary course of business, and placed the receiver in a position to exercise powers which had been created by the debenture under which he was appointed.

This case, as I have said, does not concern any exercise by the receiver of his powers, and the consequences of such an exercise, but his appointment, which in itself was only machinery to enforce the rights of the defendants acquired under their debenture. No rights were in my judgment acquired by the mere appointment of the receiver.

Alternatively, in my judgment, the reference in the proviso to the order dated 28 October 1971, extending the time for registration of the first debenture, to "the rights of any parties acquired prior to the time when the said debenture is to be actually registered" cannot have been intended to include the rights acquired by the defendants, or their receiver …'

… In any future similar unfortunate case consideration may possibly be given, when application is made for an order under s101 extending the time for registration, to the inclusion of an express provision confirming that a second debenture remains subordinate to a first debenture. A similar course was, as I have said, adopted in *Re I C Johnson & Co Ltd*, where it was desirable to emphasise that the rights of debentures ranking pari passu at creation were not intended to be affected by the proviso. But even in the absence of such an express provision, I decline to be driven to stand priorities on their head.'

Floating charges and s245 Insolvency Act 1986

Destone Fabrics Limited, Re [1941] 1 Ch 319 Chancery Division (Simonds J)

Insolvency – validity of floating charge

Facts
In 1940 the company was insolvent but it nevertheless issued a debenture to one Zimmerman by a floating charge on its assets and undertaking to secure a loan of £900. The £900 was paid into the company's bank account and on the same day £350 was paid to A and £350 to B for director's fees due to them and £200 was paid to D, being the amount guaranteed by him in respect of the company's overdraft. Six months after the date of issue of the debenture, the company was compulsorily wound-up. The liquidator sought a declaration that the debenture was invalid on the ground that it was issued to enable certain creditors to be paid and leave Zimmerman with a charge which would render other creditors unable to share in the assets.

Held
Since the object of the charge was to provide cash for other creditors it was not valid because under (s322 CA 1948) there was no cash bona fide 'paid to the company at the time of or subsequently to the creation of, and in consideration of the charge'.

Simonds J:

'... What are the facts? I have the minutes of the board meeting of 1 April, 1940, the date on which the debenture was issued, although in fact the money was not paid into the bank until 12 April. It was reported to the meeting that Zimmerman had offered to lend the company £900 on the security of a debenture to carry interest at 5 per cent per annum, and it was resolved that that offer be accepted. The company's solicitor was instructed to prepare the debenture and the debenture was produced and sealed in the presence of two directors and the secretary. It is to be remembered that, at this time, the company was hopelessly insolvent and the directors must have been well aware of that fact. They must have been aware, further, that the company could not be put on its legs merely by the provision of £900 whereby to pay off certain of its creditors. It could only be put on its legs by a substantial sum of working capital being obtained and from nothing short of this could it derive any advantage. It follows that the purpose of this debenture was nothing more than a contrivance by which the debenture holder himself or the person for whom he was trustee and the directors might have a sum of money provided which would not in any way benefit the company, but which would largely benefit them, placing them in a better position than the other unsecured creditors of the company ...

... I find it impossible to believe that the purpose of this transaction was anything else but, by the issue of this security, to procure the payment to certain directors of the sums due to them in preference to other creditors of the company, and payment also to Davis who was himself advancing the money on the security of the debenture.

The ultimate test in such cases may well be whether the transaction is to be regarded as one intended bona fide for the benefit of the company, or whether it is intended merely to provide certain moneys for the benefit of certain creditors of the company to the prejudice of other creditors of the company ...'

Commentary
See now s245 of the Insolvency Act 1986.

F and E Stanton Limited, Re [1929] 1 Ch 180 Chancery Division (Maugham J)

Insolvency – validity of the floating charge

Facts
In late 1925 two debenture-holders in the company agreed to advance money to it on the security of their debentures. The company was slow to issue the debentures and the debenture-holders, although making the advances agreed, continually pressed for them. Fifty-four days elapsed after the first advance and five days after the last advance before the issue of the debentures on 20 January, 1926. The company which had always been in financial difficulty went into liquidation on 25 January, 1926. However, when the debenture-holders made most of their advances they were unaware that the company was on the verge of liquidation. The question arose whether the debentures were valid under (s322 CA 1948) on the ground that the advances were made 'at the time of the creation of the charge'.

Held
The debentures were valid; the payments were made at the time of 'the creation of the charge'.

Maugham J:

'Now I have to apply the law. On the law I have the assistance of several cases of considerable value. The first is the well known case in *In re Columbian Fireproofing Co* [1910] 1 Ch 758. That is a decision of Neville J, which was approved by the Court of Appeal without qualification [1910] 2 Ch 120. The decision amounts to this: That in each case where a question arises under (s322), where cash has been paid to the company at the time of the creation of the debentures, it is a question of fact, under all the circumstances of the case, whether the sum paid before the issue of the debentures was cash paid to the company at the time of the creation of the security. The word "time" is held by Neville J and by the Court of Appeal to be in that connection an indefinite word, and it was held that: "A payment made on account of the consideration for the security, in anticipation of its creation and in reliance on a promise to execute it, although made some days before its execution, is made at the time of its creation within the meaning of the section". I have not a doubt here, as I have already said, that the payments were made on account of the consideration and in anticipation of its creation and in reliance on a promise to execute, and the real difficulty is whether the lapse of time which took place between that promise and between the payments made in reliance on that promise and the actual date of the issue of the debentures is so long that I ought to hold that the exception in the section does not apply. In that matter I have two other cases which seem to help me to some extent. One is an Irish case of *In re Olderfleet Shipbuilding Co* (1865) 6 B & S 314, and the other is an unreported case of *In re Nathan Hope & Son Ltd*, where the judgment of Romer J was delivered on 5 June, 1924. I have had the advantage of reading a shorthand note of the judgment in that case. In both of those cases there was a substantial delay between the dates of the payment in reliance on the promise to issue debentures and the date upon which the debentures were secured, and, in fact, in the case before Romer J there was a delay of not less than 67 days after the first advance and 15 days after the last advance, before the issue of the debentures. In the present case the delay is serious, but not so serious as that. There were 54 days after the first advance and five days after the last advance before the issue of the debentures.

Now I am myself strongly of opinion that the exception in (s322) in regard to cash advances at the time will not avail the debenture-holder if the delay in the issue of the debenture is one which he has himself procured or suggested, or if the delay is one in which he has in any true sense acquiesced. I am not thinking of a delay such as would ordinarily be necessary for the passing of the resolution and the consideration of the form of the debenture and its actual execution, because the four or five days necessary in most cases to do those things is clearly not a delay which, according to the authority of the first case I have mentioned, the *Columbian Fireproofing* case, would be sufficient to invalidate the debentures if the cash had been or was being paid. But I think a delay greater than that requires explanation. In the present case I think there is sufficient explanation in the circumstances which I have mentioned ...'

Matthew Ellis Limited, Re [1933] 1 Ch 458 Court of Appeal (Lord Hanworth MR, Slesser and Romer LJJ)

Insolvency whether money advanced was paid at the time of the charge

Facts

In 1932 the company was in financial difficulty and insolvent. The chairman, who was also a partner in a firm which supplied much of the stock and goods for the company's locksmith business, had hopes of turning the company's fortunes around and agreed to advance £3,000 on condition that a debt of £1,954 owed to the partnership by the company was discharged. The £3,000 was advanced on the security of a debenture dated March 1932 on condition the £1,954 be paid out of it. In July 1932 an order was made that the company be compulsorily wound-up. The liquidator contended that the debenture was invalid as to the £1,954 as this had been applied in payment of an antecedent debt and was not 'cash paid to the company' within (s322 CA 1948). On appeal

Held

The total sum of £3,000 was 'cash paid to the company at the time of ... the charge' and was valid.

Romer LJ:

'... I can see no justification for excepting from the words "cash paid" in the section payments of cash made conditionally as to their mode of application. Astbury J in *In re Hayman, Christy & Lilly Ltd* [1917] 1 Ch 283, excepted from those words cash payments as to which a condition of any kind is imposed by the lender. Eve J has given what in my opinion appears to be conclusive reasons for not adopting that construction. He has, however, himself, as I read his judgment, excluded from the words any payments of cash made upon the condition that the cash shall be applied in discharge of an existing liability of the company. For myself, I am unable to impose any such restriction upon the words of the section. Where, therefore, a man advances money to a company on the security of a debenture on the terms that the money so advanced is to be applied by the company in discharge of one of its existing liabilities or in the acquisition of some asset which the company does not at the moment possess, the money paid by the lender does not in my opinion cease to be cash paid to the company merely by reason of the imposition of that condition. There are, of course, certain considerations for the issue of a debenture which plainly do not amount to payments in cash. Where, for instance, an existing creditor of a company takes a debenture from the company to secure the amount of his debt on the terms that he shall not immediately press for payment of his debt, or where he takes a debenture for the amount of his debt on the terms that the debt itself is to be extinguished, obviously no cash passes from the debenture-holder to the company. If in such a case he goes through the form of drawing a cheque in favour of the company for the amount of his debt on the terms that the company shall forthwith itself hand to him in exchange a cheque for the same amount, there has in form been a payment in cash. But in such a case there has not been a payment in cash if one looks at the substance and not at the form, and in considering whether there has been a payment in cash ... it is always the question of substance that must be regarded and not the question of form. Parker J had a case to decide under the section in *In re Orleans Motor Co* [1911] 2 Ch 241. In that case directors of a company who had guaranteed the company's overdraft were being pressed by the bank, as indeed was the company, for repayment of the overdraft. £1,500 was the amount that the bank required to be paid. The company was liable for it as principal debtor and the directors were liable for it as guarantors. The company being unable to pay, the obvious thing would have been for the guarantors to pay the £1,500, in which case they would have been unsecured creditors of the company for that amount. Instead of that, they went through the form of handing three cheques for £500 to the company on the terms that the company should hand those cheques over to the bank and issue debentures for the amount to them, and they then said that they had paid cash to the company. Parker J was not misled by such a transparent subterfuge, and held that there had not in fact been any cash paid. The directors had not parted with any cash to the company and never intended to part with any cash to it. The company never received any cash from the directors and never contemplated receiving any cash from them. All that had happened was that the directors had, using the company as a conduit pipe, paid £1,500 cash to the bank. Of course, that debenture was invalidated by the section.

In the present case, if I am right, all that has to be considered is whether as a matter of substance – looking at the substance and not at the form – Mr Tipper paid cash to the company. I can well understand that, if it had transpired that the two persons to whom Mr Tipper refers as his partners were made figures holding no real interest in the partnership, and that the partnership was only another name for Mr Tipper himself, it might have been held that as regards the sum of £1,954 paid over to the partners there was no payment in case to the company. But there is no such evidence; indeed, the evidence strongly suggests to my mind that these other two partners were real persons with a live interest in the partnership firm negotiating on its behalf. The fact is that Mr Tipper, the debenture-holder, has parted with £1,954 in cash out of his private estate, and that that cash has been handed over by the company to the firm of which indeed Mr Tipper is a partner, but of which he is not the only partner, and in which he does not hold the only interest or even a controlling interest so far as I know. Why in those circumstances it should be said that this was merely a subterfuge to make it appear there had been a payment in cash when there was in fact no payment in cash I do not know. The circumstances appear to me to point strongly in favour of the conclusion that here there was in truth and in fact, in substance and not merely in form, a payment of cash by Mr Tipper to the company.'

Commentary
See now s245(3)(a) of the Insolvency Act 1986.

Power v *Sharp Investments Ltd and Another* [1993] BCC 609 Court of Appeal (Ralph Gibson and Nolan LJJ and Sir Christopher Slade)

Section 245 of the Insolvency Act – avoidance of floating charges

Facts
Shoe Lace Ltd sold shoes by retail and by mail order. Eighty per cent of its share capital was held by Sharp Investments Ltd. In March 1990 the directors resolved to obtain further financial support from Sharp in return for a debenture secured by fixed and floating charges. Between 3 April and 16 July 1990, Sharp advanced a total of £436,000 to the company. The debenture though was not executed until 24 July 1990.

A winding-up petition was presented in September 1990. Before the winding-up order was granted the company sold all its assets and the proceeds were passed to Sharp as a debenture-holder.

The main issue in this case was whether the advances made by Sharp between April and July were made 'at the same time as' the creation of the floating charge within the meaning of s245(2)(a) of the Insolvency Act 1986. If the answer to this question was no, then the charge would be invalid and Sharp would have to account for the proceeds to the liquidator.

Hoffmann J applied a test of whether a businessman would say that the payments would have been made at the same time as the execution of the debenture. He concluded that no businessman would, having regard to the time limits imposed by the Insolvency Act and Companies Act, consider that the payments were made at the same time as the execution of the charge. Sharp appealed.

Held

The Court of Appeal refused to follow its earlier approach to such cases as illustrated by *Re Columbian Fireproofing Co Ltd* [1910] 2 Ch 120. This approach was that if the payment was made on account of, and in consideration for, the floating charge, then even if the payment was made some days before the execution of the charge, it was treated as having been made 'at the same time as' the floating charge.

A unanimous Court of Appeal however adopted a much stricter approach to s245(2)(a). Giving the leading judgment, Sir Christopher Slade took the view that the section would not be satisfied if, 'the making of the advance precedes the formal execution of the debenture by any time whatsoever, unless the interval is so short that it can be regarded as de minimis – for example a coffee break.'

To apply a different construction to the section would mean that unsecured creditors who had given credit between April and July would be disadvantaged because they would have given credit without realising the existence of the floating charge as it was not registered until 13 August 1990. The prudent course of action is for the lender not to lend until the charge has actually been executed. The appeal was dismissed.

Reservation of title clauses

Armour v Thyssen Edelstahlwerke AG [1990] 3 WLR 810 House of Lords (Lord Keith of Kinkel, Lord Griffiths, Lord Oliver of Aylmerton, Lord Goff of Chieveley and Lord Jauncey of Tullichettle)

Reservation of property clause

Facts

The appellants, a German company, sold and supplied steel strip to Carron Co Ltd, a Scottish company, and the contract provided, inter alia, that the property in the goods would not pass to the purchaser until all debts due from the purchaser to the vendor had been paid. Under powers contained in a floating charge, the respondents were appointed receivers of Carron before payment had been made for the steel strip: they maintained that Carron was the owner of the goods and that they (the receivers) were entitled to take possession of the goods and sell them. The Scottish courts shares this view and the appeal was against those decisions.

Held

The appeal would be allowed as the appellants had not created a right of security over the steel strip. The reservation of property clause was simply one of the conditions of a genuine sale and s62(4) of the Sale of Goods Act 1979 therefore did not apply.

Lord Jauncey of Tullichettle:

'I consider that the courts below were in error in failing to appreciate the true nature of the transaction between the parties. A right in security is a right over property given by a debtor to a creditor whereby the latter in the event of the debtor's failure, acquires priority over the property against the general body of creditors of the debtor. It is of the essence of a right in security that the debtor possesses in relation to the property a right which he can transfer to the creditor, which right must be re-transferred to him on payment of the debt. The Second Division took the view that [the contract] amounted to an ineffective attempt to create a right of security over moveables without the transfer of possession thereof. This conclusion presupposed that Carron were in a position to transfer the title to the steel to the appellants, this being the only right available to them to transfer so long as they retained possession.

My Lords, in terms of the contract of sale Carron never acquired title to the steel. They acquired possession thereof on delivery but would only have acquired dominium in and hence title to it on fulfilment of the conditions in [the contract]. It follows that they never acquired any right under the contract, other than a right of possession, which they were in a position to transfer in security to the appellants. The contract of sale did not attempt to create a right in security in favour of the appellants, rather did it operate to transfer possession and dominium in two stages. Until the conditions of [the contract] were satisfied dominium remained in the appellants.'

Clough Mill Ltd v *Martin* [1985] 1 WLR 111 Court of Appeal (Donaldson MR, Oliver and Goff LJJ)

Reservation of title clauses – whether registration required

Facts

Clough Mill supplied a company known as Heatherdale Fabrics Ltd with yarn for use in the manufacture of fabrics. Four contracts for the supply of yarn were entered into between Clough Mill and Heatherdale between December 1979 and March 1980. Each of the contracts incorporated Clough Mill's standard conditions of sale which included a condition, condition 12, as to the passing of title. This condition provided: (i) that the ownership of the yarn was to remain in Clough Mill who reserved the right to dispose of the yarn until payment in full for all the yarn had been received or until such time as Heatherdale sold the yarn to its customers under a bona fide sale; (ii) if payment became overdue in whole or in part Clough Mill could resell the yarn and enter Heatherdale's premises for that purpose; (iii) payment would become immediately due if there was any act or proceeding involving Heatherdale's insolvency; (iv) if any of the yarn was incorporated in, or used as material for other goods before payment, the property in the whole of such goods was to be with Clough Mill until payment. Heatherdale became insolvent and a receiver was appointed by the company's debenture-holders on 11 March 1980. At the time of the receiver's appointment much of the yarn was unpaid for and/or unused. The receiver refused to allow Clough Mill to repossess the unused yarn in accordance with the terms of the contract of supply on the ground that condition 12 created a charge in favour of Clough Mill, which was void for non-registration under s95 of the Companies Act 1948 (which became s395 of the Companies Act 1985 and has now been substituted by s93 of the 1989 Act). The receiver permitted the yarn to be used in the manufacturing process. Clough Mill sued the receiver for damages for wrongfully depriving them of the yarn and for converting it to his own use. The receiver argued that the powers in the contract given to Heatherdale to mix the yarn with other materials and to sell it was inconsistent with unqualified ownership remaining with the buyers. A purpose of condition 12 was to provide security for payment of the purchase price and in this respect it created a charge which was void for non-registration. At first instance the judge accepted the receiver's contentions. On appeal

Held

The true effect of the contract was that title in the yarn remained in Clough Mill after delivery to Heatherdale, until it was paid for or resold by Heatherdale to their customers. The purpose of this retention of title, which was acceptable under s19(1) of the Sale of Goods Act 1979, was to provide Clough Mill with security. However, this security was not in the nature of a charge registrable under s95 of the Companies Act 1948 because at all times Clough Mill retained legal title in the yarn and Heatherdale never had any such title in the yarn so as to enable them to confer a charge in favour of Clough Mill.

Robert Goff LJ (his Lordship dealt first with the effect of a clause in a contract which retains title only in goods not yet paid for):

'... the submission of Mr Henry as to the nature of the appellants' retention of title under the first sentence of the condition was extremely simple. Under the Sale of Goods Act 1979 a seller of goods is fully entitled, after delivery of goods to the buyer, to retain title in the goods until he has been paid: see s19(1) of that Act. That is precisely what the appellants have done by condition 12. The appellants' title did not derive from the contract; on the contrary, it was simply retained by them, though under the contract power was conferred on the buyers both to sell the goods and to use them in manufacturing other goods. As the buyers never acquired any title to the unused yarn in question, they could not charge the yarn to the appellants. So the appellants were, quite simply, the owners of the yarn; and there was no question of there being any charge on the yarn in their favour, which was void if unregistered.

This attractively simple approach was challenged by Mr Blackburne. He submitted, first of all, that, if the first sentence of condition 12 is read literally, as Mr Henry suggested it should be read, the buyers can only have had possession of the yarn in a fiduciary capacity, whether as bailees or fiduciary agents. But, he said, the power conferred on the buyers under the contract, not merely to sell the material but also to mix it with other materials in the manufacture of goods, was inconsistent with the existence of any fiduciary capacity in the buyers, or indeed with the appellants' unqualified ownership of the yarn. In support of this submission, he relied in particular on a proposition derived from the judgment of Slade J in *Re Bond Worth Ltd* [1980] Ch 228 when he said:

"... where an alleged trustee has the right to mix tangible assets or moneys with his own other assets or moneys and to deal with them as he pleases, this is incompatible with the existence of a *presently* subsisting fiduciary relationship in regard to such particular assets or moneys." (Slade J's emphasis).

Now this is a submission which I am unable to accept. In every case, we have to look at the relevant documents and other communications which have passed between the parties, and to consider them in the light of the relevant surrounding circumstances, in order to ascertain the rights and duties of the parties inter se, always paying particular regard to the practical effect of any conclusion concerning the nature of those rights and duties. In performing this task, concepts such as bailment and fiduciary duty must not be allowed to be our masters, but must rather be regarded as the tools of our trade. I for my part can see nothing objectionable in an agreement between parties under which A, the owner of the goods, gives possession of those goods to B, at the same time conferring on B a power of sale and a power to consume the goods in manufacture, though A will remain the owner of the goods until they are either sold or consumed. I do not see why the relationship between A and B, pending sale or consumption, should not be the relationship of bailor and bailee, even though A has no right to trace the property in his goods into the proceeds of sale. If that is what the parties have agreed should happen, I can see no reason why the law should not give effect to that intention. I am happy to find that both Staughton and Peter Gibson JJ have adopted a similar approach in the recently reported cases of *Hendy Lennox (Industrial Engineers) Ltd* v *Grahame Puttick Ltd* [1984] 1 WLR 485 and *Re Andrabell Ltd* [1984] 3 All ER 407 ...'

His Lordship then concluded:

'... I recognise that, on the view which I have formed of the retention of title in the first sentence of condition 12 in this case, its effect is very similar to that of a charge on goods created by the buyer in favour of the seller. But the simple fact is that under the first sentence of the condition the buyer does not in fact confer a charge on his goods in favour of the seller; on the contrary, the seller retains his title in his goods, for the purpose of providing himself with security. I can see no reason in law why a seller of goods should not adopt this course, and, if the relevant contractual term is effective to achieve that result, I can see no reason why the law should not give effect to it in accordance with its terms. We were treated in argument to what I understand to be the common form appeal to the merits in cases of this kind describing the unfortunate plight of suppliers of goods to manufacturers who, if in a poor financial position, are kept going by the suppliers for the benefit of debenture-holders, usually banks, and counsel for the receiver describing the difficulties of liquidators grappling with incomprehensible Romalpa clauses. I sympathise with both; though I am tempted to observe that the mechanism of the floating charge, on which secured creditors are content to rely, is perhaps as much open to criticism as the mechanism of the retention of title clause, at which they now express their dismay. Be that as it may, my conclusion in the present case derives not from sympathy, but from an analysis of the clause.

For these reasons, I find myself reaching a different conclusion from the judge as to the meaning and effect of condition 12. I would allow the appeal.'

Tatung (UK) Ltd v *Galex Telesure Ltd & Others* (1989) 5 BCC 325 Queen's Bench Division (Phillips J)

Reservation of title clause – whether void for non-registration

Facts

The plaintiff company manufactured and supplied televisions and other electrical goods. The first three defendants (companies in the same group as the plaintiff) were in receivership: the remaining defendants were the receivers of those companies. The plaintiffs had supplied the first three defendants with goods under a contract which contained a retention of title clause. The defendants had hired out these goods and the plaintiffs claimed that they were entitled to the proceeds of hire in satisfaction of the debts owed to them by the defendants. The question for the court, therefore, was whether the interest of the plaintiffs in the debts constituted either a charge on book debts or a floating charge which had to be registered under s95. If it did then it would be void for non-registration. If it did not, then the plaintiffs could receive sums in satisfaction of the debts owed to them by the defendants in priority to the debenture-holders, who appointed the receivers.

Held

1. On the wording of the conditions of sale, the plaintiffs' interest in the hire debts was clearly defeasible upon payment of what the defendant companies owed to the plaintiff and therefore was an interest by way of security.
2. The conditions made express provision for the interest that the plaintiff was to have in the proceeds of dealing with the goods. The source of the plaintiffs' rights was therefore the contractual agreement and not the equitable principles which might be applied in the absence of such an agreement. The *Romalpa* case (*Aluminium Industrie Vaassen BV* v *Romalpa Aluminium Ltd* [1976] 1 WLR 676) was distinguished on this point.
3. The plaintiffs' interest was created by the defendant companies. The charge was directly created by the agreement, to which the defendant companies were party, that the plaintiff should have the specified interest in the proceeds of dealing with the property.
4. Section 95 clearly requires registration of charges over future property of a company, notwithstanding the effect of the creation of a charge might be that, when the property vested, it was already encumbered by the charge. Provided the charge was created by the company, s95 applied.

Phillips J:

'... In so far as the question of whether or not the plaintiffs' interest is a charge depends upon whether it arose under the principle in *Re Hallett's Estate* (1880) 13 Ch D 696 or out of the agreement between the parties. I rule in favour of the latter alternative. In *Romalpa* the retention of title clause dealt expressly with the basis upon which the purchasers held the foil prior to resale, but did not deal expressly with the proceeds of sale – ave for one provision in respect of mixed goods which was not held to be of critical relevance. In those circumstances the Court of Appeal held the plaintiffs' rights in respect of the proceeds of sale were derived automatically as a consequence of their interest in the goods prior to resale – under the principle in *Re Hallett's Estate*.

In the present case, however, the contracts made express provision for the interest that the plaintiffs were to have in the proceeds of dealing with the goods. In those circumstances I consider that the source of the plaintiffs' rights was the contractual agreement between the parties and equitable principles that might have applied in the absence of such agreement.

... I have already held that the nature of the interest conferred upon the plaintiffs under the agreement was by way of security. The legal title in the debts unquestionably vested in the defendants. The plaintiffs' equitable interest in those debts was in my judgment a charge on those debts within the meaning of s95.'

Weldtech Equipment Ltd, Re [1991] BCC 16 High Court (Hoffmann J)

Reservation of title clause – book debts – failure to register

Facts

A German company supplied goods to an English company which had gone into liquidation. A reservation of title clause, governed by German law, in the standard conditions of sale of the German company purported to assign the book debts to the German company, but this charge had not been registered under s395 of the Companies Act 1985.

Held

The clause was therefore void against the liquidator. Hoffmann J said that it was clear that s395 of the 1985 Act applied to all charges created by companies registered in England, whatever might be the proper law of the instrument which created the charge. The liquidator, however, had correctly regarded the clause as effective to preserve the title of the German company to the goods still physically in the company's possession.

Administrative receivers

Appointment by the court

London Pressed Hinge Company Limited, Re [1905] 1 Ch 576 Chancery Division (Buckley J)

Appointment by court where judgment creditor intended to execute judgment

Facts

The plaintiff held debentures in the company by way of floating security on the undertaking and all property, present and future, of the company. All interest had been paid on the debentures and none of the events causing the principal to be repayable had occurred. However, a trade creditor of the company issued a writ claiming £109 from the company for goods supplied. There was no defence and judgment was entered against the company. The trade creditor intended to issue execution. The plaintiff sought the appointment of a receiver because the company was so loaded with debentures that its profits were barely sufficient to keep down the interest and, accordingly, the execution by the trade creditor would result in injury to the plaintiff's security by reducing its value.

Held

As the security was in danger a receiver would be appointed.

Buckley J:

'The cases are numerous in which the undertaking of a limited company is so loaded with debentures that the profits are barely sufficient, or perhaps not sufficient, to keep down the debenture interest, and that, if the company is wound up, there is nothing for anyone but the debenture-holders. In short, the facts often are that the undertaking is substantially carried on only for the benefit of the debenture-holders who have a floating security over it. In this state of facts money is lent or goods consigned to the company in respect of which a debt accrues to a creditor, and so long as the security floats, as it is termed, and no receiver is appointed, the creditor has a possibility or expectation of being paid by the company, for as between the company and the debenture-holders, the former may pay in the ordinary course of business. But directly a receiver is appointed, this expectation of the creditor is intercepted. He may have lent his money, or consigned his goods, to the company last week; but if he has the audacity to ask payment and to enforce his legal remedies to obtain it, the debenture-holder obtains a receiver in a proceeding to which the execution creditor is not a party, and thus closes the door against him, taking his money or his goods as part of the security, and leaving the creditor who supplied the money or the goods to go unpaid. I regret to be driven to the conclusion that, as the law stands, those are the rights of the debenture-holder entitled to a floating charge.

It was decided in the Court of Appeal in *In re Standard Manufacturing Co* [1891] 1 Ch 627 that an execution creditor takes subject to all equities, and that the sheriff cannot by seizing get rid of the rights of debenture-holders to which the property was subject when in the hands of the debtor company. The Court of Appeal in *In re Opera Ltd* [1891] 3 Ch 260 stated that the decision in *In re Standard Manufacturing Co* was a clear decision that the execution creditor takes subject to the equity of the debenture-holders. From this decision it has resulted that, in interpleader, that is to say, even in a case where no receiver has been appointed, the execution creditor can have no more than the benefit of the equity of redemption, and that the rights of debenture holders prevail over his rights; *Davey & Co v Williamson & Sons* [1898] 2 QB 194; *Simultaneous Colour Printing Syndicate v Foweraker* [1901] 1 KB 771; *Duck v Tower Galvanising Co* [1901] 2 KB 314. This being the law, the fact is that the appointment of a receiver does not, as between the execution creditor and the debenture-holder, disappoint the execution creditor of anything which would otherwise be his right. From those authorities it results that the creditor never had any right as between himself and the debenture-holder to enforce payment in priority to the debenture-holder. If he availed himself of his legal right to judgment and execution the debenture-holder could intercept his execution. In fact the unfortunate creditor had no right enforceable by legal process in cases where the equity of redemption was of no value, notwithstanding the fact that his money or his goods had gone to increase the property included in the security. His right to look for payment from the company rested only upon the expectation that the debenture-holder would not put an end to the company's authority to pay the creditor in the ordinary course of business. The authorities seem to me to involve that the creditor has no right to complain because steps are taken to put an end to the authority thus given by the debenture-holders to their mortgagor.

The appointment of a receiver at the instance of an equitable incumbrance, at any rate where there is nothing presently payable to him, is no doubt a matter of discretion: *Thorn v Nine Reefs Ltd* 67 LT 93. But if the execution creditor's rights are not affected except as above stated by the appointment of a receiver there exist so far as I see, no grounds why the court should exercise its discretion against the appointment of a receiver by reason of any considerations arising as between the execution creditor and the debenture-holder. The only relevant consideration would seem to be whether, as between the company and the debenture-holder, it is just and convenient that the company's authority to dispose of its assets in the ordinary course of business should be stopped. As between those parties it would seem reasonable that the authority should be stopped if its continuance would injure the debenture-holder. A legal mortgagee may take possession simply because he chooses. In so doing he accepts the responsibility of a mortgagee in possession. An equitable mortgagee must show good reason why the court should at his instance take possession by its receiver. Lord Chelmsford in *Wildy v Mid-Hants Ry Co* 16 WR 409 held that danger to the security by anticipated acts of an execution creditor is good reason. Jeopardy of the security thus becomes relevant. The mere fact of consent by the mortgagor would not be enough. This probably explains the fact that in both the more recent cases in which a receiver has been appointed on the rounds of jeopardy – *McMahon* v *North Kent Ironworks Co* [1891] 2 Ch 148; *Edwards* v *Standard Rolling Stock Syndicate* [1893] 1 Ch 574 – the question of jeopardy was treated as material, although the company appeared and consented. But for this consideration, the fact that jeopardy was treated as material might be thought to tend to some extent in the direction in which I desire to find authority; but the implication even if it exists, seems to me inconsistent with the express decisions. I am unable upon the authorities to find anything to enable me to put a stop to what I feel to be an injustice. It is an injustice arising from the nature as defined by the authorities of a floating security. The mischief arises from the fact that the law allows a charge upon all future property. The subject, however, is one which I think, urgently requires attention ...'

Newdigate Colliery Limited, Re [1912] 1 Ch 468 Court of Appeal (Cozens-Hardy MR, Fletcher Moulton and Buckley LJJ)

A court-appointed receiver is not allowed to cause the company to breach its contracts if this would injure the company's goodwill

Facts
The company owned a working colliery in Warwickshire, and in connection with its business had entered into contracts for the sale of coal over various periods. One of the contracts was for the sale of coal until the end of December 1912. On 8 January, 1912 a debenture-holders' action was commenced because interest on the debentures was in arrears and on 20 January, 1912 an interlocutory order was made for the appointment of a receiver and manager. On 24 January, 1912 the receiver and manager took out a summons asking that he might be at liberty to disregard the contracts for the sale of coal, including that for the sale of coal until December, 1912 on the ground that these would exhaust the total output of the colliery which could now be sold at higher prices because of steep rises in the value of coal.

Held
It was the duty of a receiver and manager of the property and undertaking of a company to preserve both the goodwill and assets of the company. Thus, a failure to honour the contracts would be to disregard this duty as it would reflect on the goodwill of the company.

Buckley J:

'... The receiver and manager is a person who under an order of the court has been put in a position of duty and responsibility as regards the management and carrying on of this business, and has standing behind him – I do not know what word to use that will not create a misapprehension, but I will call them "constituents" – the persons to whom he is responsible in the matter, namely the mortgagees and the mortgagor, being the persons entitled respectively to the mortgage and the equity of redemption. If we were to accede to the application which is made to us, and to allow the receiver and manager to sell the coal at an enhanced price, the result would be that the enhanced price would fall within the security of the mortgagees and they would have the benefit of it; but on the other hand, there would be created in favour of the persons who had originally contracted to purchase the coal a right to damages against the mortgagor, the company, with the result that there would be large sums of damages owing. Thus, while the increased value of the coal would be thrown into the security for the benefit of the mortgagees, the surplus assets of the mortgagor, whatever they might be, would be affected in the sense that they would be subject to claims not only presented by the unsecured creditors, but also by persons who had thus become entitled to damages for breach of contract. A receiver and manager owes a duty to two classes of persons. The order asked for would have the effect of allowing him to do an act which would benefit one class to the injury of the other. It has been truly said that in the case of a legal mortgage the legal mortgagee can take possession if he choose of the mortgaged property, and being in possession can say, "I have nothing to do with the mortgagor's contracts, I shall deal with this property as seems to me most to my advantage." No doubt that would be so, but he would be a legal mortgagee in possession, with both the advantages and disadvantages of that position. This appellant is not in that position. He is an equitable mortgagee who has obtained an order of the court under which its officer takes possession of assets in which the mortgagee and mortgagor are both interested, with the duty and responsibility of dealing with them fairly in the interests of both parties. It seems to me that an order of the kind we are asked to make would be an order in the interest of one of these parties in disregard of the interest of the other.

Then it has been argued, and it is true, that primarily and principally the duty of the receiver is to have regard to what will benefit the mortgaged property and nothing besides the mortgaged property; this property goes to the mortgagee first, and the owner of the equity of redemption afterwards; and it is said that so far as the mortgaged property is concerned the order asked for will increase its value because the coal now in the bowels of the earth will be sold at an enhanced price. That is no doubt true, but the security of the mortgage is on the undertaking and all the property present and future, including the uncalled capital, of this company. So that the property for which the receiver and manager is responsible includes this business and undertaking, and it is his duty to do, and our business to see that he does, everything reasonable and right for the protection of the property as an undertaking for the benefit of all the persons interested in it. The order asked for is an order directing the receiver and manager to disregard the interests of one of his constituents, the mortgagor, in order to benefit another of his constituents, namely, the mortgagee. It seems to me that such an order is necessarily wrong ...'

New York Taxicab Company Limited, Re [1913] 1 Ch 1 Chancery Division (Swinfen-Eady J)

Refusal by court to appoint receiver

Facts

The company owned a fleet of taxicabs and a leasehold of a garage for them in New York. About 1910 all these assets were transferred to an American company in which the company owned all the shares in order to avoid difficulties with local laws. In July 1910 debentures were issued by the company secured on its undertaking including the taxicabs and the garage. In 1910 the insurers of the company's taxicabs failed, forcing them to meet claims out of their own resources. There was stiff competition and a strike all of which caused the company to suffer heavy losses. To enable the company to continue trading the taxicabs were sold to another company in return for shares in that company and the garage underlet. In addition a debenture-holders' meeting passed a resolution postponing payment of a debenture interest for two years and sanctioning a charge of $30,000 on the rent of the garage in priority to the debentures. The plaintiff, a debenture-holder, asked the court to appoint a receiver as the company's assets were now insufficient to satisfy the claims of the debenture-holders.

Held

The mere fact that the security was inadequate was insufficient reason for appointing a receiver on the grounds of 'jeopardy'.

Swinfen Eady J:

'... The real ground of the plaintiff's application, is that his security appears to be insufficient to pay the principal or interest of the debentures ... In these circumstances the plaintiff alleges that his security is in jeopardy. But is there, in fact, any jeopardy as to require the interference of the court? The assets are in no danger of being seized. No creditor is pressing or threatening proceedings ... The company is not in any pecuniary difficulty. No doubt it cannot pay the debenture interest in full yet and will not be able to do so for some considerable time. But it is always open to a meeting of debenture-holders to give further time for payment. The assets are not in jeopardy in the sense that there is any risk of their being seized or taken to pay claims not really prior to the claims of the debenture-holders. The company is a going concern ... The security is not yet enforceable according to its tenor, and the fact that if now realised it would be wholly insufficient to pay the principal and interest in full is not a sufficient reason for appointing a receiver on the ground of jeopardy ...'

Moss Steamship Co v *Whinney* [1912] AC 254 House of Lords (Lord Loreburn LC, the Earl of Halsbury, Lords Ashbourne, Atkinson, Shaw and Mersey)

A court-appointed receiver is not an agent of the company

Facts

Messrs Ind, Coope & Co had for many years shipped beer to Malta on vessels owned by the Moss Steamship Co. The beer was shipped under bills of lading which provided that Moss should have a lien over the beer, not only for the freight applicable to the cargo, but for all freights unpaid by Ind, Coope & Co. The company became embarrassed in its affairs and on 5 January, 1909 Whinney was appointed receiver and manager in a debenture-holder's action. On 13 January, 1909 Whinney gave an order to Moss for the shipping of a cargo of beer; the order was signed 'Arthur F Whinney, Receiver and Manager'. Moss shipped the beer and made out the bill of lading in the usual terms viz the lien. At the time of this shipment Moss were owed £171 for freight upon earlier contracts from Ind, Coope & Co. They claimed a lien on the beer for this sum and the £56 due on shipment of the beer under Whinney's order.

Whinney claimed that Moss were only entitled to a lien for the £56 and not the £171 on the beer he shipped as receiver.

Held

(Lords Shaw and Mersey dissenting) the shipment of beer by Whinney was a transaction in which he, as receiver, was personally liable. As the transaction was with him and not with Ind Coope & Co, Moss could not have a lien in respect of the £171 against him.

The Earl of Halsbury:

'... A great many joint-stock companies obtain their capital, or a considerable part of it, by the issue of debentures, and one form of securing debenture-holders in their rights is a well-known form of application to the Court of Chancery, which practically removes the conduct and guidance of the undertaking from the directors appointed by the company, and places it in the hands of a manager and receiver, who thereupon absolutely supersedes the company itself, so that the company becomes incapable of making any contract on behalf of the company or exercising any control over any part of any property or assets of the company ...'

... But once a receiver and manager is appointed things are changed, and every man of business would know, and ought to know, that the only person with whom he could contract safely would be the manager appointed by the Court of Chancery ...'

Lord Atkinson:

'... The appointment of a receiver and manager over the assets and business of a company does not dissolve or annihilate the company, any more than the taking possession by the mortgagee of fee land let to tenants annihilates the mortgagor. Both continue to exist; but it does entirely supersede the company in the conduct of its business, deprives it of all power to enter into contracts in relation to that business, or to sell, pledge, or otherwise dispose of the property put into the possession or under the control of the receiver and manager. Its powers in these respects are entirely in abeyance ... The very words "receiver and manager" convey, according to the above mentioned authority, that Whinney was not an agent of the company, but that he was managing their affairs under the order of the court, and that all their powers were in abeyance ...'

Appointment by debenture-holder

American Express International Banking Corporation v Hurley [1985] 3 All ER 564 Queen's Bench Division (Mann J)

Negligence of a receiver

Facts
The defendant was a director of a company in the business of providing sound and lighting equipment for pop concerts. In 1978 the bank asked for security for overdraft facilities given to the company and was given a floating charge over the company's sound and light equipment, its only assets valued at over £191,000. The defendant gave a personal guarantee in support, in addition. In 1981 the bank appointed a receiver under the terms of the floating charge. In February 1982 the company was put into liquidation but the receiver continued to act as such following instructions and directions from the bank and in October 1983 he sold the sound and lighting equipment for £34,500. The defendant received a demand from the bank thereafter calling upon him to pay over £52,000 on his personal guarantee. The defendant claimed that the receiver was negligent in that he sold the equipment for too little and without taking specialist advice as to its value – which was found to be about £60,000. Further, he claimed that the bank was liable for the receiver's negligence since his taking instructions from the bank after February 1982 made him the agent of the bank.

Held
The receiver was negligent and, in the circumstances, he had become the agent of the bank.

Mann J:

'... A receiver appointed under the common form of charge here employed acts as the agent of the mortgagor. If the mortgagor is put into liquidation then the agency terminates. See *Gosling v Gaskell*; [1897] AC 575. If the receiver continues to act he does not automatically become the agent of the mortgagee. See *Re Wood* [1941] 1 Ch 112 but he may become so if the mortgagee treats him as such. In this case I find that after the liquidation on 18 February 1982 the bank constituted the receiver its agent. Lord Meston (counsel for the bank) did not seriously contend to the contrary. He could not do so. There was constant communication between the bank and the receiver and the latter sought the former's approval to such actions as he proposed to take ...'

The judge then considered the claim in negligence and stated:

'... I propose to proceed on the basis that the following propositions represent the law. (i) The mortgagee when selling mortgaged property is under a duty to a guarantor of the mortgagor's debt to take reasonable care in all the circumstances of the case to obtain the true market value of that property. (ii) A receiver is under a like duty. (iii) The mortgagee is not responsible for what a receiver does whilst he is the mortgagor's agent unless the mortgagee directs or interferes with the receiver's activities. (iv) The mortgagee is responsible for what a receiver does whilst he is the mortgagee's agent and acting as such

...

... The receiver knew of the guarantee, and was provided with the valuation which had been given to the bank. The receiver sought advice of a firm of valuers who were specialists in the realisation of the assets of insolvent undertakings .... The firm said they were not qualified to value the equipment which was of a special nature and that the receiver would have to rely on people in the trade of the equipment for advice ... The equipment was not advertised for sale. The receiver did not seek advice. The receiver did not seek out prospective purchasers whose identity might have been discovered in publications ... In my judgment the receiver did not take reasonable care in all the circumstances of the case to obtain the true market value of the equipment. He had in his hands equipment which he knew had been valued at £191,323 and which he knew was of a specialist nature ... In my judgment the failure to take reasonable care is manifest in these forms: (i) a failure to take specialist advice from a person in the popular music industry; (ii) a failure to advertise in publications concerning the popular music industry. The receiver is liable in negligence to the guarantor ...'

B Johnson & Co (Builders), Re [1955] Ch 634 Court of Appeal (Evershed MR, Jenkins and Parker LJJ)

An administrative receiver is not an officer of the company to which s212 of the Insolvency Act 1986 can apply

Facts
The company, which was incorporated in 1940 to carry on the business of builders and contractors, had since its inception loans from a bank which were secured by a floating charge. In 1947 the company owed the bank £29,000 and the bank appointed a receiver in August 1947 under the terms of its debenture. The receiver went into possession and proceeded to realise the company's assets. In doing this the receiver halted all work on 29 houses in the process of being built. In 1949 a liquidator was appointed and the receiver discharged. The applicant, who had been chairman and manager of the company, issued a summons seeking an order that the conduct of the receiver and the liquidator be investigated under s333 CA 1948 (now s212 of the Insolvency Act 1986) and claimed that the sale of the uncompleted houses resulted in loss to the company and alleged that the receiver and liquidator each had been negligent.

Held
Since the receiver was not an 'officer' of the company within the definition of 'officer' in s455 CA 1948 (now s744 CA 1985) nor a manager of the company for the purposes of s333 of the Companies Act 1948 (now s212 of the Insolvency Act 1986) its provisions did not apply to him. Instead the receiver was managing the company's affairs on behalf of the debenture holder in order to obtain the realisation of the security rather than on behalf of the company.

Jenkins LJ:

'... A receiver and manager for debenture-holders is a person appointed by the debenture-holders to whom the company has given powers of management pursuant to the contract of loan constituted by the debenture and as a condition of obtaining the loan, to enable him to preserve and realise the assets comprised in the security for the benefit of the debenture-holders. The company gets the loan on terms that the lenders shall be entitled, for the purpose of making their security effective, to appoint a receiver with powers of sale and of management pending sale, and with full discretion as to the exercise and mode of exercising those powers. The primary duty of the receiver is to the debenture-holders and not to the company. He is receiver and manager of the property of the company for the debenture-holders, not manager of the company. The company is entitled to any surplus of assets remaining after the debenture debt has been discharged, and is entitled to proper accounts. The whole purpose of the receiver and manager's appointment would obviously be stultified if the company could claim that a receiver and manager owes it any duty comparable to the duty owed to a company by its own directors or managers.

In determining whether a receiver and manager for the debenture-holders of a company has broken any duty owed by him to the company, regard must be had to the fact that he is a receiver and manager – ie a receiver, with ancillary powers of management – for the debenture-holders, and not simply a person appointed to manage the company's affairs for the benefit of the company. A receiver without powers of management would, I apprehend, clearly be outside s333, and it is difficult to see why superadded powers of managing the property comprised in the security should bring him within it.

The duties of a receiver and manager for debenture-holders are widely different from those of a manager of the company. He is under no obligation to carry on the company's business at the expense of the debenture-holders. Therefore he commits no breach of duty to the company by refusing to do so, even though his discontinuance of the business may be detrimental from the company's point of view. Again, his power of sale is, in effect, that of a mortgagee, and he therefore commits no breach of duty to the company by a bona fide sale, even though he might have obtained a higher price and even though, from the point of view of the company, as distinct from the debenture-holders, the terms might be regarded as disadvantageous.

In a word, in the absence of fraud or mala fides (of which there is not the faintest suggestion here), the company cannot complain of any act of omission of the receiver and manager, provided that he does nothing that he is not empowered to do and omits nothing that he is enjoined to do by the terms of his appointment. If the company conceives that it has any claim against the receiver and manager for breach of some duty owed by him to the company, the issue is not whether the receiver and manager has done or omitted to do anything which it would be wrongful in a manager of a company to do or omit, but whether he has exceeded or abused or wrongfully omitted to use the special powers and discretions vested in him pursuant to the contract of loan constituted by the debenture for the special purpose of enabling the assets comprised in the debenture-holders' security to be preserved and realised. That seems to me to be an issue wholly outside the scope of s333 ...'

Hand v *Blow* [1901] 2 Ch 721 Court of Appeal (Rigby, Collins and Romer LJJ)

Claim by a company landlord against a receiver for rent arrears

Facts

A company which had four leasehold shops in the Edgware Road, which it used in its drapery business, got into financial difficulties. The company had given debentures secured on the leasehold premises and, eventually, a receiver was appointed by the trustees of the debenture. The receiver went into possession of the demised premises and carried on the company's business there from the end of August 1899. In February 1900 the landlord served notice on the company to make good dilapidations in the premises under the terms of the lease but this was never complied with. On 20 March, 1900 the receiver sold all the company's stock-in-trade and all its goods under a court order. On 25 March a quarter's rent was due in advance. This was not paid. The landlord brought these proceedings claiming the value of the dilapidation and for leave to distrain for the quarter's rent. When the landlord realised all the company's goods had been sold off the summons was amended claiming the rent due out of the proceeds of sale in the receiver's hands or out of any other moneys in the receiver's hands.

Held

The landlord could not claim the rent due out of the moneys in the receiver's hands since the appointment was in right of the mortgagee. It did not matter that the receiver was in possession of the premises because there was no privity of estate between him and the landlord.

Romer LJ:

'... If you have a company or person whose estate is being dealt with or administered by the court, and a liquidator or receiver appointed by the court has occupied or used premises that are part of the estate, then, as to rent and other outgoings payable to the landlord or other parties in respect of the premises for that occupation or user and for which the company or person whose estate is being dealt with or administered is liable, the court will see that such rent and other outgoings are paid out of the assets got in by the liquidator or receiver. But that principle does not and cannot apply to cases as between mortgagor and mortgagee when the mortgaged premises are leasehold demised or agreed to be demised by the mortgagor to the mortgagee, or charged by the mortgagor in favour of the mortgagee in such a way that the mortgagee is not liable to pay rent or other outgoings either to the mortgagor or to the mortgagor's landlord. In such a case the liquidator or receiver is appointed in right of the mortgagee. The court is not administering the mortgagor's estate; it is only dealing with the mortgaged property, and the mortgaged property, it is to be borne in mind, involves in itself ex hypothesi no liability to the landlord whatever. It must be remembered that in such a case, a case as between mortgagee and mortgagor, the latter remains liable to rent, even if the mortgagee is in possession; and the mortgagee on going into possession, even though remaining in possession and paying no rent, does not become liable, in respect of such occupation, to the landlord for rent.

Is the matter changed by the mortgagee getting a receiver appointed? Not at all. The appointment of a receiver does not take away from the mortgagor his primary liability. The mortgagor remains liable, not the mortgagee, nor the receiver, nor the mortgaged property. The landlord has no claim as against the mortgagee or the receiver, or the mortgaged property during the occupation by the receiver. Of course, in a case where the landlord, by reason of his not being paid or of his covenants not being complied with, has a right to complain and to re-enter, he can apply, notwithstanding the appointment of a receiver, and obtain leave from the court to re-enter, and so take away from the receiver his right of occupation; and he can also, in a proper case, get leave to distrain: but the mere appointment of a receiver does not of itself, in my opinion, give the landlord any special rights, and has never, so far as I know, been held to do so.

There is no authority whatever in support of the proposition that in such a case as I have indicated, a case between an ordinary mortgagee of leaseholds by sub-demise and an ordinary mortgagor of such leaseholds, where a receiver has been appointed in an ordinary action by the mortgagee to enforce his security, the landlord can apply to have his rent paid out of the assets coming to the hands of the receiver during his occupation. For the reasons I have stated, that would be contrary to principle. As to the argument that there is something in the nature of honesty and common justice requiring the court to interfere, that is only a plea ad misericordiam which cannot be supported by any legal or equitable right …'

Inland Revenue Commissioners v *Goldblatt* [1972] Ch 498 Chancery Division (Goff J)

Administrative receiver in breach of statutory duty to pay preferential creditors

Facts

In 1959 a company gave its bankers a debenture to secure its overdraft. This created a fixed charge on certain leasehold property, fixtures and plant and machinery of the company and a floating charge on the undertaking and all other assets of the company, present and future. In 1960 when the company owed the bank £25,000 it cleared off the overdraft and transferred the debenture to another debenture-holder. In 1961 the debenture-holder appointed a receiver and manager who took possession of the company's assets and collected over £6,000 in moneys due to the company. Two months after the receiver was appointed the debenture-holder revoked his appointment and asked him to deliver up all moneys and goods to the company and agreed to indemnify him against all liabilities. Subsequently the debenture-holder entered into an agreement with the directors of the company under which the company assigned all its assets to the debenture-holder in full satisfaction of all claims under the debentures. Neither the receiver nor debenture-holder troubled to pay the preferential creditors who included the Revenue, who were owed £9,707. In July 1961 a company winding-up order was made in respect of the company. The preferential creditors claimed that the receiver and debenture-holder were in breach of statutory duty under s94(1) CA 1948 (which became s196(2) Companies Act 1985 and has now been substituted by s439(1) of the Insolvency Act 1986) in failing to pay preferential debts in the circumstances and that the debenture-holder was liable for breach of trust.

Held
The receiver was in breach of his statutory duty under s94(1) CA 1948 in failing to pay the preferential creditors in priority to the other creditors. The debenture-holder in arrogating the assets to himself with notice of the preferential creditor's claim was, thereby, a party to that breach of statutory duty.

Goff J:

'... It is clear on the authority of *Woods* v *Winskill* [1913] 2 Ch 303 that a preferential creditor who is injured by a breach of this duty has a claim for damages against the receiver. Astbury J, quoting Vaughan Williams LJ, there said, at p309:

"In *Groves* v *Lord Wimborne* [1898] 2 QB 402 Vaughan-Williams LJ says 'It cannot be doubted that, where a statute provides for the performance by certain persons of a particular duty, and someone belonging to a class of persons for whose benefit and protection the statute imposes the duty is injured by failure to perform it, prima facie, and if there be nothing to the contrary, an action by the person so injured will lie against the person who has so failed to perform the duty.'"

See also *Pulsford* v *Devenish* [1903] 2 Ch 265.

Nevertheless Mr Oliver Smith argues that the receiver is not liable. He submits that s94 of the Companies Act 1948 deals only with priority of debts and that, on the authority of *Woods* v *Winskill, In re Clyncorrwg Colliery Co* [1926] Ch 951 and *Westminster Corporation* v *Haste* [1950] Ch 422 the only duty the receiver had was to pay the preferential debts of which he had notice in priority to any other debt, whether secured by the debentures or not, and that, he says, does not touch this case where the receiver did not pay any of the debts.

Further, or perhaps alternatively, Mr Oliver Smith submits that when the receiver was removed his title wholly ceased and, therefore, he was entitled and bound to account to the company. He says he had no option.

I cannot accept these arguments. In *Westminster* v *Haste* Danckwerts J, said:

"To my mind that is not simply a negative provision which means that the receiver is protected if he simply does not pay the debenture-holders; it is a provision which requires him to pay the preferential creditors out of any assets coming to the hands of him as receiver. Therefore, it seems to me that, if he has had any assets out of which this payment could have been made, he is under a liability in tort to the plaintiffs."

I accept that, and, in my judgment it concludes this case as against the receiver in favour of the plaintiff ...'

Duties of an administrative receiver

Downsview Nominees Ltd v First City Corporation [1993] 2 WLR 86 Privy Council (Lord Templeman, Lord Lane, Lord Goff of Chieveley, Lord Mustill and Lord Slynn of Hadley)

Duties of a receiver and manager

Facts
Glen Eden Motors Ltd (GEM') carried on the business of new and used car dealers. The principal

shareholder and manager of GEM was P. In 1975 it issued a first debeture ('the Westpac debenture') to secure the sum of $230,000 in priority to a second debenture ('the FCC debenture'). The second debenture was granted in 1986 to First City Corporation Ltd, the first plaintiff. Both debentures contained fixed and floating charges over the property of GEM and also contained a power for the debenture-holder to appoint a receiver and manager. In 1987 the monies secured by the second debenture became due and payable and the first plaintiff appointed two chartered accountants to become the receivers and managers of GEM. P was removed as manager of GEM and he then consulted the second defendant, Mr Russell, who controlled the first defendant company, Downsview Nominees Ltd. As a result of this consultation, the Westpac debenture was assigned to the first defendant and the second defendant, Mr Russell, became the receiver and manager under that debenture. Mr Russell took over the assets and management of GEM and declared his intention to trade GEM out of its defficulties. P was also restored to his former management position. Four days after the assignment of the Westpac debenture, the plaintiff, First City Corporation Ltd, wrote to the first defendant, Downsview Nominees Ltd, expressing concern at the intention to trade out of the difficulties of GEM as they felt that this would result in damage to the shareholders of GEM and also to itself as subsequent debenture-holder. Because of their concerns, First City Corporation Ltd offered to buy the Westpac debenture for a price equivalent to all amounts secured and outstanding on it. This offer was refused and the company continued to trade, during which time substantial losses were incurred and no interest or principal was paid on the Westpac or FCC debentures. Later, the court ordered Downsview Nominees Ltd to transfer the Westpac debenture to First City Corporation Ltd and Mr Russell ceased to be the receiver. The plaintiffs then brought this action and an award of damages was made against both defendants on the basis of negligence. The defendants appealed to the Privy Council.

Held

A receiver and manager owes no general duty in negligence to subsequent encumbrancers or the mortgagor but equity imposes specific duties including the duty to exercise their powers in good faith. The receivership of Mr Russell had been conducted by him in bad faith and for improper purposes and there had been a breach of duty in failing to transfer the Westpac debenture when requested by First City Corporation. The measure of damages for breach of a receiver's equitable duties was the same as that which would have been awarded if liability was based in negligence.

Lord Templeman:

'The duties owed by a receiver and manager do not compel him to adopt any particular course of action, by selling the whole or part of the mortgaged property or by carrying on the business of the company or by exercising any other power and discretions vested in him. But since a mortgage is only security for a debt, a receiver and manager commits a breach of his duty if he abuses his powers by exercising them otherwise than "for the special purpose of enabling the assets comprised in the debenture-holders' security to be preserved and realised" for the benefit of the debenture-holder. In the present case the evidence of the second defendant himself and the clear emphatic findings of Gault J [1989] 3 NZLR 710, 749, which have already been cited, show that the second defendant accepted appointment and acted as receiver and manager

"not for the purpose of enforcing the security under the Westpac debenture but for the purpse of preventing the enforcement by the plaintiff of the [FCC] debenture."

This and other findings to similar effect establish that, ab initio and throughout his receivership, the second defendant did not exercise his powers for proper purposes. He was at all times in breach of the duty, which was pleaded against him, to exercise his powers in good faith for proper purposes.

Gault J rested his judgmemt not on breach of a duty to act in good faith for proper purposes but on negligence. He said, at pp744, 747:

"On an application of negligence principles, a receiver owes a duty to the debenture-holders to take reasonable care in dealing with the assets of the company ... [The first defendant's] position is merely a specific example of the duty a mortgagee has to subsequent chargeholders to exercise its powers with reasonable care ..."

Richardson J delivering the judgment of the Court of Appeal [1990] 3 NZLR 265, 278-280, agreed that duties of care in negligence as defined by Gault J were owed by the second defendant as receiver and manager and by the first defendant as first debenture-holder to the plaintiffs as second debenture-holders. Richardson J agreed that the second defendant was in breach of his duty but, differing from Gault J, held that the first defendant had committed no breach.

The general duty of care said to be owed by a mortgagee to subsequent encumbrancers and the mortgagor in negligence is inconsistent with the right of the mortgagee and the duties which the courts applying equitable principles have imposed on the mortgagee. If a mortgagee enters into possession he is liable to account for rent on the basis of wilful default; he must keep mortgage repair; he is liable for waste. Those duties were imposed to ensure that a mortgagee is diligent in discharging his mortgage and returning the property to the mortgagor. If a mortgagee exercises his power of sale in good faith for the purpose of protecting his security, he is not liable to the mortgagor even though he might have obtained a higher price and even though the terms might be regarded as disadvantageous to the mortgagor. *Cuckmere Brick Co Ltd* v *Mutual Finance Ltd* [1971] Ch 949 is Court of Appeal authority for the proposition that, if the mortgagee decides to sell, he must take reasonable care to obtain a proper price, but is no authority for any wider proposition. A receiver exercising his power of sale also owes the same specific duties as the mortgagee. But that apart, the general duty of a receiver and manager appointed by a debenture-holder, as defined by Jenkins LJ in *In Re B Johnson & Co (Builders) Ltd* [1955] Ch 634, 661, leaves no room for the imposition of a general duty to use reasonable care in dealing with the assets of the company. The duties imposed by equity on a mortgagee and on a receiver and manager would be quite unnecessary if there existed a general duty in negligence to take reasonable care in the exercise of powers and to take reasonable care in dealing with the assets of the mortgagor company.

Richardson J appreciated the contradictions and inconsistencies between the duties of a receiver and manager as set forth by Jenkins LJ in *In Re B Johnson & Co (Builders) Ltd* based on historical equitable principles and the suggested additional or alternative duty of care based on negligence. Richardson J said [1990] 3 NZLR 265, 276:

"The existence, nature and extent of the receiver's duty of care must be measured in relation to the primary objective of the receivership which is to enforce the security by recouping the moneys which it secures from the income or assets of the company subject to the security, and for that purpose by exercising incidental powers of management, and when recoupment is complete to hand the remaining property back to the control of the company."

'Their Lordships consider that it is not possible to measure a duty of care in relation to a primary objective which is quite inconsistent with that duty of care.

There is a great difference between managing a company for the benefit of a debenture holder and managing a company for the benefit of a debenture-holder and managing a company for the benefit of shareholders. If the debenture-holder is dissatisfied with the policy or performance of his appointed receiver and manager, the appointment can be revoked. A dissatisfied second debenture-holder may require the prior debenture to be assigned to him or may put the company into liquidation. A dissatisfied company may raise the money to pay off a debenture-holder or put the company into liquidation. But if a receiver and manager decides at his discretion to manage and is allowed to manage and does manage in good faith with the object of preserving and realising the assets for the benefit of the debenture-holder, he is subject to no further or greater liability.

In the United Kingdom the possible harsh consequences to a company of a receivership may be averted by an administration order under the Insolvency Act 1986. Such an order may be made if the company is or is likely to become insolvent and if the order will be likely to achieve, inter alia, the survival of the company or any part of its undertaking as a going concern. A petition for an administration order may be presented by the company or the directors or by a creditor. The order appoints an administrator to manage the affairs of the company with powers of sale and automatically prevents a receiver from acting and prevents a creditor from enforcing any security without the consent of the administrator or the leave of the court. The administrator may be removed if the company's affairs are managed by him in a way "which is unfairly prejudicial to the interests" of the company's creditors or members: s27. Similar legislation is in force in the United States. In the absence of any such legislation, the only limitations on the exercise of power by a receiver and manager are the requirements to act in good faith for the purpose of preserving and realising the assets for the benefit of the debenture-holder.

The House of Lords has warned against the danger of extending the ambit of negligence so as to supplant or supplement other torts, contractual obligations, statutory duties or equitable rules in relation to every kind of damage including economic loss: see *CBS Songs Ltd* v *Amstrad Consumer Electronics Plc* [1988] AC 1013, 1059: *Caparo Industries Plc* v *Dickman* [1990] 2 AC 605 and *Murphy* v *Brentwood District Council* [1991] 1 AC 398. If the defined equitable duties attaching to mortgagees and to receivers and managers appointed by debenture-holders are replaced or supplemented by a liability in negligence the result will be confusion and injustice. A receiver and manager liable in negligence will be tempted to sell assets as speedily as possible for the purpose of repaying the mortgage debt, a decision which, whether negligent or not, does not expose him to a suit for damages but may be disadvantageous to the company. A receiver who is brave enough to manage will run the risk of being sued if the financial position of the company deteriorates, whether that deterioration be due to imperfect knowledge or bad advice or insufficient time or other circumstances. There will always be expert witnesses ready to testify with the benefit of hindsight that they would have acted differently and fared better.

A receiver and manager is appointed when the mortgagor company is in financial difficulties. He may know nothing of the trade carried on by the mortgagor company and nothing about the individual affairs of the company. He is dependent on information furnished by the directors and managers who must bear some responsibility for the financial difficulties of the company. Richardson J in the present case [1990] 3 NZLR 265, 284, in discussing the ambit of s189 of the Companies Act 1955, said:

"There is a further justification for maintaining that clear distinction between the acts of the manager of the company and the acts of the receiver and manager of its property. The company has vicarious responsibility for the acts of the manager and in the exercise of those functions as manager the manager is not personally liable to other parties except for misfeasance. In contrast the receiver is personally liable on any contract entered into by him in the performance of his functions, except in so far as the contract otherwise provides (s345(2)). In policy terms it may be considered entirely appropriate to confine the external sanction under s189(1)(c) to officers of the company, leaving errant receivers and managers to their personal liability in respect of contracts, and recognising too that in the ordinary course poorly performing receivers are not likely to be given further assignments by debenture-holders of other companies."

Similar considerations apply to the first defendant. A mortgagee owes a general duty to subsequent encumbrancers and to the mortgagor to use his powers for the sole purpose of securing repayments of the moneys owing under his mortgage and a duty to act in good faith. He also owes the specific duties which equity has imposed on him in the exercise of his powers to go into possession and his powers of sale. It may well be that a mortgagee who appoints a receiver and manager, knowing that the receiver and manager intends to exercise his powers for the purpose of frustrating the activities of the second mortgagee or for some other improper purpose or who fails to revoke the appointment of a receiver and manager when the mortgagee knows that the receiver and manager is abusing his powers, may himself be guilty of bad faith but in the present case this possibility need not be explored.

The liability of the second defendant in the present case is firmly based not on negligence but on the breach of duty. There was overwhelming evidence that the receivership of the second defendant was inspired by him for improper purposes and carried on in bad faith, ultimately verging on fraud. The liability of the first defendant does not arise under negligence but as a result of the first defendant's breach of duty in failing to transfer the Westpac debenture to the first plaintiff at the end of March 1987. It is well settled that the mortgagor and all persons having any interest in the property subject to the mortgage or liable to pay the mortgage debt can redeem. It is now conceded that the first plaintiff was entitled to require the first defendant to assign the Westpac debenture to the first plaintiff on payment of all moneys due to the first defendant under the Westpac debenture. On 27 March 1987 the first plaintiff offered to purchase the Westpac debenture and to pay the first defendant all that was owing to it. It was faintly argued that the first defendant was entitled to refuse the offer because at a later stage it reasonably believed, so it was said, albeit wrongly, that the FCC debenture was void for non-registration. There is nothing in this point. The reason given by the second defendant on behalf of the first defendant for the refusal of the first defendant to assign the Westpac debenture to the first plaintiff as a subsequent charge-holder was that "we do not know of any right of assignment which subsequent charge-holders have in respect of an earlier charge". The second defendant is now older and first defendant is now wiser.

The first defendant was from the end of March 1987 in breach of its duty to assign the Westpac debenture to the first plaintiff. If that debenture had been assigned, the second defendant would have ceased to be the receiver and manager and none of the avoidable losses caused by the second defendant would have been sustained.

Gault J [1989] 3 NZLR 710, 758-759, decided that the damages payable by the first and second defendants were

> "the difference between the loss that would have been incurred had the first receivership of Messrs Chatfield and Chilcott been allowed to proceed unimpeded, and the loss actually incurred as it has emerged following the second receivership by those two accountants."

Gault J found that the second defendant accepted appointment as a receiver and manager for an improper purpose, namely the purpose of disrupting the receivership under the FCC debenture and for the purpose of preventing the enforcement of the FCC debenture. He was therefore in breach of his duty from 23 March 1987 onwards. The measure of damages decided by Gault J applies to this breach of duty just as it would have applied if the second defendant had been liable in negligence. The breach of duty of the first defendant in refusing to assign the Westpac debenture following the letter dated 27 March 1987 can be dated from the end of March. There was no difference in the position of the company between 23 March 1987 when the second defendant was appointed receiver and manager and the date when the first defendant received the letter dated 27 March and should have agreed to assign the Westpac debenture and withdraw the second defendant. Accordingly the first defendant, by committing a breach of duty in not accepting the offer of the first plaintiff to take an assignment of the Westpac debenture, is liable with the second defendant for the difference between the loss that would have been incurred, had the first receivership of Messrs Chilcott and Chatfield been allowed to proceed unimpeded, and the loss actually incurred as it emerged following the second receivership by those two accountants. The first plaintiff accepted that if the first receivership had continued it would not have been possible to get in all the assets of the company until 31 August 1987. Gault J [1989] 3 NZLR 710, 762, after hearing expert evidence, concluded that 31 August 1987 was

> "the date by which substantially all funds available from the disposal of assets would have been paid over to [the first plaintiff] the debenture-holder."

'Gault J also found that $898,461 was the amount that would have been recovered by the FCC debenture holder at 31 August 1987. After making adjustments for interest, the amount received by the first plaintiff and other matters not in dispute, judgment was entered for $554,566.33.

The Court of Appeal held [1990] 3 NZLR 265, 284, that Gault J lacked jurisdiction under s189 of the Companies Act 1955 to prohibit the second defendant from acting as a director or promoter or being concerned in the management of the company. Their Lordships agree for the reasons given by Richardson J.

In the result their Lordships are of the opinion that the appeal ought to be dismissed and the cross-appeal allowed and that the orders made by Gault J against the first and second defendants should be restored, save that the order against the second defendant under s189 of the Companies Act 1955 should be quashed. The costs of the plaintiffs in the courts below and the costs of the appeal and cross-appeal before the board should be paid by the first and second defendants subject to the conditions imposed by the board and accepted by the plaintiffs when, on 17 June 1992, the board granted leave for arguments to be advanced which had not been raised before the Court of Appeal. Those conditions were set forth in a letter dated 18 June 1992 addressed to the parties by the Registrar of the Judicial Committee. Their Lordships will humbly advise Her Majesty to order accordingly.'

Standard Chartered Bank v *Walker* [1982] 1 WLR 1410 Court of Appeal (Lord Denning MR, Watkins and Fox LJJ)

Administrative receiver – duty of care

Facts
The bank had a debenture secured by both fixed and floating charges over the assets of a company of which Walker and his wife were the only directors and shareholders. The company was in the business of trading in metal presses and moulding machines. The overdrafts to the company were also personally guaranteed by Walker and his wife to the extent of £75,000. In 1978 the company's business was hit by a worldwide slump in trade and the overdraft soared. The Walkers considered that the company could trade its way out of its difficulties but in November 1980 the bank appointed a receiver. The receiver instructed auctioneers to sell the company's stock. The auctioneer valued the company's stock at £90,000 and held an auction in February 1981 after some advertising. The auction was held on a very cold day, few buyers turned up and the stock only realised £42,864. The costs of realisation were over £42,000 and there was nothing to pay the receiver, the £37,000 owed to preferential creditors or the £88,000 owed to the bank. The bank called on the Walkers to honour their guarantee in full. When they failed to do so a writ was issued and followed by summary judgment for £75,000. The Walkers appealed against this claiming that the sale had been at a gross undervalue and that if reasonable care had been taken it would have realised much more and the amount due on the guarantee reduced.

Held
The appeal would be allowed since a receiver owed a duty of care both to the company and a guarantor of the company's liability to exercise reasonable care in obtaining the best possible price in the realisation of the company's assets.

Lord Denning MR:

'We have had much discussion on the law. So far as mortgages are concerned the law is set out in *Cuckmere Brick Co Ltd* v *Mutual Finance Ltd* [1971] Ch 949. If a mortgagee enters into possession and realises a mortgaged property, it is his duty to use reasonable care to obtain the best possible price which the circumstances of the case permit. He owes this duty not only to himself (to clear off as much of the debt as he can) but also to the mortgagor so as to reduce the balance owing as much as possible, and also to the guarantor so that he is made liable for as little as possible on the guarantee. This duty is only a particular application of the general duty of care to your neighbour which was stated by Lord Atkin in *Donoghue* v *Stevenson* [1932] AC 562) and applied in many cases since: see *Home Office* v *Dorset Yacht Co Ltd* [1970] AC 1004 and *Anns* v *Merton London Borough* [1978] AC 728 The mortgagor and the guarantor are clearly in very close "proximity" to those who conduct the sale. The duty of care is owing to them, if not to the general body of creditors of the mortgagor. There are several dicta to the effect that the mortgagee can choose his own time for the sale, but I do not think this means that he can sell at the worst possible time. It is at least arguable that, in choosing the time, he must exercise a reasonable degree of care.

So far as the receiver is concerned, the law is well stated by Rigby LJ, in *Gosling* v *Gaskell* [1896] 1 QB 669 a dissenting judgment which was approved by the House of Lords. The receiver is the agent of the company, not of the debenture-holder, the bank. He owes a duty to use reasonable care to obtain the best possible price which the circumstances of the case permit. He owes this duty not only to the company (of which he is the agent) to clear off as much of its indebtedness to the bank as possible, but he also owes a duty to the guarantor, because the guarantor is liable only to the same extent as the company. The more the overdraft is reduced, the better for the guarantor. It may be that the receiver can choose the time of sale within a considerable margin, but he should, I think, exercise a reasonable degree of care about it. The debenture-holder, the bank, is not responsible for what the receiver does except in so far as it gives him directions or interferes with his conduct of the realisation. If it does so, then it too is under a duty to use reasonable care towards the company and the guarantor.

If it should appear that the mortgagee or the receiver have not used reasonable care to realise the assets to the best advantage, then the mortgagor, the company, and the guarantor are entitled in equity to an allowance. They should be given credit for the amount which the sale should have realised if reasonable care had been used. Their indebtedness is to be reduced accordingly.

The only doubt on those propositions is cast by two cases at first instance. The first is *Barclays Bank Ltd v Thienel* [1978] 247 EG 385. It is only reported in the Estates Gazette, but we have been provided with a transcript of the judgment. That was a case of a mortgagee. The amount realised was only £6,500 to meet a debt of £11,000. The allegation on the part of the guarantor was that the sale was at a gross undervalue, and that there had been a want of care in the realisation. Thesiger J said that the guarantor could not rely on that want of care because of a very wide clause in the form of guarantee. But it seems to me that, if a clause in a guarantee makes the guarantor liable for a larger sum than the mortgagor, the clause is unenforceable. The guarantor is only under a secondary obligation to guarantee the debt of the principal debtor. if the principal debtor's debt is reduced for good reason, equally the guarantor's obligation is reduced. If there is a term in the contract to the contrary, it should be rejected as being repugnant or unreasonable: see *Gillespie Bros & Co Ltd* v *Roy Bowles Transport Ltd* [1973] AB 400 and the cases cited therein. But nowadays we do not have to look at those cases. The Unfair Contract Terms Act 1977 applies to this contract. The terms of a contract are only good in so far as they are fair and reasonable. So I would reject Thesiger J's reliance on the contract.

The second case is *Latchford* v *Beirne* [1981] 3 All ER 705. That was a case of a receiver. A debenture-holder had put in a receiver. The receiver sold the property. Again the guarantor sought to say that there had been want of reasonable care in the disposal of the assets. Milmo J went so far as to say that there was no duty of care towards the guarantor. He said that there was no duty of care towards the creditor. He treated the guarantor as though he was simply a creditor. I cannot agree with that either. Clearly the guarantor's lability is dependent on the company's. He is in a very special position. The amount of his liability depends entirely on the amount that the stock realises when sold with proper care. To my mind he is well within the test of "proximity". The receiver owes a duty not only to the company, but to the guarantor, to exercise reasonable care in the disposal of the assets. I say nothing about creditors. We are not concerned with them today.

Neither counsel before us sought to support the decisions in those two cases. In so far as those decisions hold that guarantor is liable for a larger amount than the principal debtor they are erroneous and should not be followed ...'

Examinations by administrative receivers under s236(2) Insolvency Act 1986

Levitt (Jeffrey S) Ltd, Re [1992] 2 WLR 975 High Court (Vinelott J)

Receiver's examination – privilege against self-incrimination

Facts

A bank, which had a debenture over all the company's assets, appointed administrative receivers. As they (the receivers) had been unable to interview Levitt, one of the company's directors, they were granted an order under s236(2) of the Insolvency Act 1986 for his examination. Levitt refused to answer any questions, relying on the privilege against self-incrimination.

Held

Levitt was under an overriding statutory duty to assist the receivers and to answer their questions.

Vinelott J:

'The Insolvency Acts 1985 and 1986 were the outcome of an overall review of the insolvency legislation, individual and corporate, which followed the report of the Cork committee. The authors of the report (having observed in para 1734 that insolvency proceedings have –

"never been treated in English law as an exclusively private matter between a debtor and his creditors, the community itself has always been recognised as having important interests in them,"

an observation which I should observe is not confined to individual insolvency) went on to explain the public disquiet that had been expressed to the committee about the apparent inability of the law to deal adequately with dishonesty or malpractice on the part of bankrupts or company directors, and suggested means, including the reappraisal of the law relating to insolvent trading and the disqualification of delinquent directors, by which these defects could be remedied. The question whether a respondent to an inquiry under s236 can rely on the privilege against self-incrimination cannot in my judgment be answered by comparing the language used in s236 and the language used in s268 or in other statutes. The provisions of the Insolvency Act and cognate legislation must be looked at as a whole to ascertain the purpose of an examination under s236, and whether that purpose necessarily involves the abrogation of the privilege. To answer that question the court must ask whether the person whom it sought to examine owes a duty to furnish the information sought and whether there is any public interest in ensuring that the inquiry is carried out thoroughly and expeditiously.

If s236 is read in the context of ss234 and 235 I do not myself see that there can be any doubt as to the answers to those questions. Section 234(1) defines an "office-holder" as "the administrator, the administrative receiver, the liquidator or the provisional liquidator, as the case may be". The office-holder, if a private individual, must be a qualified insolvency practitioner registered with the Department of Trade. Section 235(2) ... clearly imposes on those persons a duty to give any information which the office-holder may reasonably require, and sub-s(5) makes a failure to comply without reasonable excuse an offence punishable by a fine ...

If there were any doubt whether a person who is required to give the office-holder information and who is brought before the court by a summons under s236 to be examined on oath can refuse to answer questions on the ground of self-incrimination, that doubt is in my judgment removed by the Company Directors Disqualification Act 1986. The provisions of that Act and the provisions relating to public and private examinations are alike derived from the Insolvency Act 1985 and must clearly be read as part of a single statutory scheme. Under s7 of the Company Directors Disqualification Act the Secretary of State has power, if it appears to him that it is expedient in the public interest that a disqualification order should be made against any person, either to apply for a disqualification order or, in the case of a company which is being wound up by the court, to direct the Official Receiver to do so. Section 7(3) imposes on the office-holder, in the case of a company which is being wound up or is subject to an administration order or if an administrative receiver has been appointed, the duty of reporting to the Secretary of State if it appears to him that the conditions set out in s6(1), which would give the court jurisdiction to make a disqualification order, are satisfied. It would clearly be wrong that inquiries by an office-holder which might reveal matters which would be required to be reported to the Secretary of State should be frustrated or hampered because a director or shadow director of the company refused to furnish information or to answer questions on the ground of self-incrimination. Under s7(2) an application for a disqualification order must be made within two years after the commencement of an insolvent winding up or the making of an administration order or the appointment of an administrative receiver, whichever first happens, and the feared criminal proceedings might well not be completed within that period. It is precisely those cases, involving serious misconduct calling for an application for a disqualification order for the protection of the public, in which the privilege against self-incrimination is most likely to be invoked. The fact that a director owes a duty to co-operate with the office-holder is also recognised by para 10(g) of Sch 1 to the Company Directors Disqualification Act, where one of the matters for determining the unfitness of a director is identified as "s235 (duty to co-operate with liquidator, etc)".

In my judgment therefore Mr Levitt is not entitled in answering questions in the examination before the registrar to decline to answer them on the ground that the answer might tend to incriminate him.'

Commentary

Approved in *Bishopsgate Investment Management Ltd* v *Maxwell* [1992] 2 WLR 991. (this case appears on page 365 of the casebook). This case concerned the same provisions but was between a liquidator and a director, and not a director and administrative receiver as in the *Levitt* case.

8   Meetings

Shareholders' meetings

BML Group Ltd v *Harman and Another* [1994] 1 WLR 893 Court of Appeal (Dillon, Leggatt and Henry LJJ)

Section 371 of the Companies Act 1985 – power of court to order meeting

Facts
The share structure of BML Group Ltd consisted of A and B ordinary shares. H and M held between them 260,000 A shares. The other three members of the company were B and L, who each owned 25,000 A shares and SB who owned 190,000 B shares. There was a shareholders' agreement between them that a shareholders' meeting would not have a quorum unless a B shareholder was present. At a shareholders' meeting on 3 August 1993 B, L and SB voted to remove H and M as directors. Accountants were also instructed to investigate allegations of financial irregularities against them. H and M then applied to the court under s371 CA 1985 for an order that a meeting be held so that B and L could be removed as directors.

Held
The court would not exercise its powers under s371 where this would override the class rights of the B shareholder. Dillon LJ said that B could use his class rights not only to protect himself but also his allies on the board of directors. It was not right to use s371 to bypass those rights. The court refused to order that a meeting be called.

Dillon LJ:

'For present purposes I do not regard it as the function of the court to intervene in these sort of proceedings by requiring various cross undertakings to achieve the conduct of the business of the company on sensible terms. That is for the parties' advisers to achieve. It is not for the court to make a new shareholders' agreement between the parties and impose it on them. Beyond that, however, I am of the view that the judge has not given sufficient weight to the situation of the s459 petition and the allegations there. He has misdirected himself. Much more, it is not right, in my view, to invoke s371 to override class rights attached to a class of shares which have been deliberately – in this case by the shareholders' agreement – imposed for the protection of the holders of those shares, although they are a minority. It is not the case that the overriding position is that the majority shareholders must prevail on everything. Class rights have to be respected and I regard the right of Mr Blumenthal, as the holder of the B shares, to be present in the quorum as a class right for his protection which is not to be overridden by this machinery. I would therefore allow this appeal.'

Commentary
Re El Sombrero Ltd [1958] 3 WLR 349 distinguished. See *Re Opera Photographic Ltd*, below.

British Union for the Abolition of Vivisection, Re (1995) The Times 3 March Chancery division (Rimer J)

Section 371 Companies Act 1985 – power of court to order meeting

Facts
The British Union for the Abolition of Vivisection ('BUAV') was a company incorporated in 1929. Its main object was 'to oppose vivisection absolutely and entirely and without attempts at compromise of any kind.' Its articles of association provided that all votes at annual and extraordinary general meetings were to be cast in person and that proxies were not allowed. At an extraordinary general meeting of the company, held in November 1995, there was a serious disturbance, caused by opposing factions within the BUAV. The police were called and no orderly business was able to be conducted.

Eight executive members of the BUAV applied to the court for an order under s371 Companies Act (CA) 1985, which provides that: 'If for any reason it is impracticable to call a meeting of a company … the court may … order a meeting to be called, held and conducted in any manner the court thinks fit.' The applicants sought an order that a meeting should be convened to propose a resolution to abolish the requirement of personal attendance at general meetings for voting purposes and that personal attendance at this meeting also be dispensed with.

Held
The order was granted. His Lordship had no doubt that the behaviour of the extremist minority at the November meeting caused the majority of BUAV members to be genuinely frightened. Referring to *Re El Sombrero Ltd* [1958] Ch 900, and the special and unusual circumstances of the case, Rimer J felt that s371 was satisfied so that he could give the directions sought for the calling and conduct of a meeting to consider the introduction of proxy voting.

Rimer J went on to direct the convening of a meeting consisting solely of the committee members of the BUAV. All of the members were to be allowed a postal vote on the proposed resolution, but only the committee members could attend and vote in person. The applicants thought that some members of the committee were the ringleaders of the extremist minority, but it was not thought that they would resort to violence at such a small meeting. The police were also to be notified of the meeting.

Allowing only 13 of the 9,000 members of the BUAV to attend a meeting and allowing all of the members to vote by post was contrary to the BUAV's constitution, but His Lordship still felt able to make the order under s371 in the terms sought by the applicants.

Duomatic Ltd, Re [1969] 2 Ch 365 Chancery Division (Buckley J)

Informal agreement of all shareholders does not require the holding of a meeting

Facts
The company was incorporated in 1960 to carry on the business of selling washing machines and its first directors were Messrs Elvins, Hanley and East. The company had 100 ordinary shares and 80,000 non-voting redeemable preference shares all of £1. All the ordinary shares were issued, 76 to Elvins, 22 to Hanley and two to East. In May 1963 Hanley transferred his 22 shares to Elvin and ceased to be a director of the company. In April 1964 several representatives of a finance company became members of the board since they were financing the company's hire-purchase business. In July 1964 Elvins transferred 96 out of his 98 shares to these representatives. At this time the company was not in a healthy position and Elvins was asked to accept a lower rate of remuneration of £60 per week. However, the company's fortunes did not improve and it went into liquidation in October 1964. The liquidator brought

this action against Elvins claiming, inter alia, the repayment of remuneration totalling £21,348 received by Elvins in the financial years ending: 30 April, 1963 (£10,151); 30 April, 1964 (£9,000); 1 May, 1964 to October 1964 (£2,197). It was claimed that Elvins was not entitled to this under the memorandum or articles because the articles provided that the remuneration of the directors shall from time to time be determined by the company in general meeting and no resolutions had ever been passed authorising directors' remuneration in this period. It was argued that the payments were justified since at the relevant times there had been informal agreement between all the members that the payments should be made or all the relevant shareholders had approved them.

Held

1. As to the £10,151 paid in the year ending 30 April, 1963 Elvin could retain this because he and East were the only shareholders who had approved the accounts for that period and this informal agreement to approve was as binding as a resolution of a general meeting of the company.
2. As to the £9,000 paid in the year ending 30 April, 1964 since no accounts had ever been drawn up for this period or agreed, there was no informal agreement to approve these. However, Elvins would be excused repayment as he had acted honestly and reasonably and ought fairly to be excused under s448 CA 1948 (now s727 CA 1985).
3. As to the £2,197 paid between May and October 1964 such of this as was within the agreed £60 per week drawings of Elvin could be retained since he received it with the consent of all the voting shareholders at that time.

Buckley J:

'It is common ground that none of the sums which I have mentioned were authorised by any resolution of the company in general meeting, nor were they authorised by any resolution of any formally constituted board meeting; but it is said on behalf of Mr Elvins that the payments were made with the full knowledge and consent of all the holders of voting shares in the company at the relevant times, and he contends that in those circumstances the absence of a formal resolution by the company in duly convened meeting of the company is irrelevant. Alternatively he relies on the provisions of s448 of the Companies Act 1948, which empowers the court to grant relief in certain cases where an officer of the company has acted honestly and reasonably and where, having regard to all the circumstances, he ought fairly to be excused.

In support of the first part of his argument counsel for Mr Elvins has relied on two authorities. The first was *Re Express Engineering Works Ltd* [1920] 1 Ch 466. There three persons formed a private company in which they were the sole shareholders, and they sold to it for £15,000, which was in fact secured by debentures of the company, property which they had, a few days before, acquired for £7,000. The contract for sale to the company and the issue of debentures was carried out at a meeting of the five individuals, who thereupon appointed themselves directors of the company. That meeting was described in the books of the company as a board meeting. The articles forbade any director to vote in respect of any contract or arrangement in which he might be interested; and in a winding-up if the company the liquidator claimed that the issue of the debentures was invalid. In the Court of Appeal it was held, there being no suggestion of fraud, that the company was bound in a matter intra vires by the unanimous agreement of its members.

Warrington LJ said:

"It was competent to them (the five corporators of the company) to waive all formalities as regards notice of meetings, etc and to resolve themselves into a meeting of shareholders and unanimously pass the resolution in question. Inasmuch as they could not in one capacity effectually do what was required but could do it in another, it is to be assumed that as businessmen they would act in the capacity in which they had power to act. In my judgment they must be held to have acted as shareholders and not as directors, and the transaction must be treated as good as if every formality had been carried out."

Younger LJ said:

"... I agree with the view that when all the shareholders of a company are present at a meeting that becomes a general meeting and there is no necessity for any further formality to be observed to make it so. In my opinion the true view is that if you have all the shareholders present, then all the requirements in connection with a meeting of the company are observed, and every competent resolution passed for which no further formality is required by statute becomes binding on the company."

In that case there were no non-voting shares, but counsel for Mr Elvins contends that the presence of the non-voting shares in the present case does not matter. If he can establish that those who were entitled to attend and vote at general meetings of the company in fact agreed to all or any of these payments then he says that that is tantamount to a resolution passed at a general meeting of the company, and that the agreement of those persons is binding on the company.

In *Parker and Cooper Ltd* v *Reading* [1926] Ch 975 the second case relied on by counsel for Mr Elvins, the directors of a company had created a debenture and proceedings were commenced to establish that the debenture and the resolution which authorised its issue and the appointment of a certain receiver under it were invalid. The case was tried by Astbury J who referred to *Re Express Engineering Works Ltd* and to *Re George Newman & Co* [1895] 1 Ch 674 and himself expressed this view:

"Now the view I take of both these decisions is that where the transaction is intra vires and honest, and especially if it is for the benefit of the company, it cannot be upset if the assent of all the corporators is given to it. I do not think it matters in the least whether that assent is given at different times or simultaneously."

So that the effect of his judgment was to carry the position a little further than it had been carried in the *Express Engineering Works* case, for Astbury J expressed the view that it was immaterial that the assent of the corporators was obtained at different times, and that it was not necessary that there should be a meeting of them all at which they gave their consent to the particular transaction sought to be upheld. In that case also, as in the *Express Engineering Works* case, no question arose about the position of any shareholders whose shares conferred no right of attending or voting at general meetings of the company.

The evidence in the present case, I think, establishes that Mr Elvins and Mr East both approved the accounts of the company for the year ending 30 April, 1963 and they signed a copy of those accounts; and the evidence is that that was done on an occasion when they met together with the auditor of the company ... and at a time when Mr Elvins and Mr East were the only two directors of the company, and the only shareholders in the company were Mr Elvins and Mr East and the preference shareholder. No attempt has been made to show that the preference shareholder ever knew anything about the remuneration of the directors or their drawings or about any of the matters with which I am concerned; and it follows of course, that no attempt has been made to show that the preference shareholder agreed to any of those matters ... It seems to me that if it had occurred to Mr Elvins and Mr East, at the time when they were considering the accounts, to take the formal step of constituting themselves a general meeting of the company and passing a formal resolution approving the payment of directors' salaries, that would have made the position of the directors – that is to say, Mr Elvins and Mr Hanley – who received the remuneration, secure, and nobody could thereafter have disputed their right to retain their remuneration. The fact that they did not take that formal step but that they nevertheless did apply their minds to the question of whether the drawings by Mr Elvins and Mr Hanley should be approved, as being on account of remuneration payable to them as directors, seems to me to lead to the conclusion that I ought to regard their consent as being tantamount to a resolution of a general meeting of the company. In other words, I proceed on the basis that where it can be shown that all shareholders who have a right to attend and vote at a general meeting of the company assent to some matter which a general meeting of the company could carry into effect, that assent is as binding as a resolution in general meeting would be. The preference shareholder having shares which conferred on him no right to receive notice of or attend and vote at a general meeting of the company could be in no worse position if the matter were dealt with informally by agreement between all the shareholders having voting rights than he would be if the shareholders met together in a duly constituted general meeting.

Accordingly, it seems to me that the evidence that I have heard leads to the conclusion that the drawings by Mr Elvins and Mr Hanley during the accounting year ending 30 April, 1963, which are covered by the item of directors' salaries £15,661 1s 8d in the profit and loss account, cannot now be disturbed ...'

Kaye v Croydon Tramways Co [1898] 1 Ch 358 Court of Appeal (Lindley MR, Rigby and Vaughan-Williams LJJ)

Content of notice calling a meeting

Facts
The Croydon Tramways Co entered into a provisional agreement in 1897 for the sale of its undertaking to another company. Under the terms of the agreement a substantial sum was to be paid to the company for the undertaking and the directors of the company were to receive compensation for loss of office. The agreeent was subject to the approval of the Croydon company's shareholders and a general meeting was convened by the directors. The notice of the meeting and a circular relating to the matter did not mention the compensation which was to be paid to the directors. The plaintiff, a shareholder in the company, made enquiries and discovered the full terms of the agreement. At the meeting the compensation was not referred to and a resolution approving the agreement was passed by a large majority, despite the plaintiff's objections. The plaintiff issued a writ claiming an injunction to restrain the directors from carrying the agreement into effect.

Held
The notice did not fairly disclose the purpose for which the meeting was convened by omitting to refer to the compensation payable to the directors.

Lindley MR:

'... Now comes the question – to my mind a difficult question – whether, in ordinary fairness of language, one can say that this notice does, to use the words of the Companies Clauses Act, "specify the purpose for which the meeting is called". On behalf of the company it is argued that it does – that the purpose is to confirm the agreement. That, no doubt, is true by the card, but, in my opinion, this notice has been most artfully framed to mislead the shareholders. It is a tricky notice, and it is to my mind playing with words to tell shareholders that they are convened for the purpose of considering a contract for the sale of their undertaking, and to conceal from them that a large portion of that purchase-money is not to be paid to the vendors who sell that undertaking. I am perfectly alive to the danger of putting into notices, especially notices of advertisement, more than the Act of Parliament requires, and I agree that all the Act of Parliament requires is that the purpose shall be stated. But it must be stated fairly; it must not be stated so as to mislead; and one of the main purposes of this agreement, so far as the directors care about it, is that they shall get a large sum of money without disclosing the fact to their shareholders. I do not think that this notice discloses the purpose for which the meeting is convened. It is not a notice disclosing that purpose fairly, and in a sense not to mislead those to whom it is addressed. It follows that, although in my judgment this contract is one which the companies can lawfully enter into, it is a contract which the selling company has not yet adopted – that is to say, the resolution which was passed under this notice is not one which is binding upon absent or dissenting shareholders ...'

Moorgate Mercantile Holdings Ltd, Re [1980] 1 WLR 227 Chancery Division (Slade J)

The notice calling EGM was inaccurate

Facts

The company had power under its articles to reduce its share premium account. On 2 April 1979 the company secretary sent out a notice to the members informing them of a special resolution which was to be proposed at an EGM to be held on 26 April to the effect that 'the share premium account of the company amounting to £1,356,900.84p be cancelled'. At the meeting on 26 April it was discovered that the share premium account actually had £321.17p credited to it in March 1979 and that this had been overlooked. The resolution was altered to read: 'That the share premium account of the company amounting to £1,356,900.84p be reduced to £321.17p.' This resolution was passed unanimously by the members present. The company then sought the confirmation of the court to reduce the share premium account.

Held

Despite the fact that no creditor or shareholder appeared in order to oppose the reduction, it would not be confirmed as the notice sent to the shareholders on 2 April was inaccurate.

Slade J:

(His Lordship referred to s141 of the Companies Act 1948 (now s378 CA 1985, as amended) and stated the facts and continued):

'... In these circumstances, did the notices of 2 April 1979 give notice within the meaning of s141(2), specifying the intention to propose a resolution which was in the event actually passed?

In the absence of authority, I would have thought that the answer to this short question of statutory construction was manifestly: No. The notices of 2 April, 1979 specified the intention to propose one resolution; the resolution passed at the meeting on 26 April, 1979 was another, different resolution. Furthermore, the difference was not one merely of form but also of substance, albeit of slight substance, inasmuch as one provided for the entire cancellation of the company's share premium account, while the other provided merely for its reduction, albeit by almost the entirety thereof.

The terms of s141(2) at least if read in isolation and in the absence of authority seem to me to require that if a special resolution passed at a meeting of members is to be valid, it must be the same resolution as that which the requisite notice has specified the intention to propose. As I have already indicated, the phrase "the resolution" appearing in the later words of the subsection clearly refers back to and echoes the phrase "a resolution" appearing at the beginning of the subsection. I can see strong arguments for contending that a resolution passed at a meeting may properly be regarded as the resolution (that is, the same resolution as that) referred to in the preceding notice, if the only differences between the two are merely clerical or grammatical; ... if, however, there are any differences whatsoever of substance between the two, I would not in the absence of authority have regarded the later resolution which was actually passed as having been preceded by proper notice for the purpose of s141(2).' (His Lordship considered the cases, including *Re Bridport Old Brewery* (1867) LR 2 Ch App 191 and *Tiessen v Henderson*, above, and found that they did not affect the situation, and went on to lay down several propositions).

1. If a notice of the intention to propose a special resolution is to be a valid notice for the purpose of s141(2) it must identify the intended resolution by specifying either the text or the entire substance of the resolution which it is intended to propose.
2. If a special resolution is to be validly passed in accordance with s141(2) the resolution as passed must be the same resolution as that identified in the preceding notice.
3. A resolution as passed can properly be regarded as the resolution identified in the preceding notice even though (i) it departs in some respects from the text of a resolution set out in such notice (for example by correcting grammatical or clerical errors which can be corrected as a matter of construction, or by reducing the words to more formal language) or (ii) it is reduced into the form of a new text, which was not included in the notice, provided only in either case there is no departure whatever from the substance.

4. However, in deciding whether there is complete identity between the substance of a resolution as passed and the substance of an intended resolution as notified there is no room for the court to apply the de minimis principle ... The substance must be identical ...'

Opera Photographic Ltd, Re [1989] 1 WLR 634 Chancery Division (Morritt J)

Section 371 of the Companies Act 1985 – power of the court to order a meeting

Facts

A court order under s371 was granted, to convene a meeting of the company at which one member constituted a quorum for the purpose of considering and if thought fit passing a resolution for the removal of the second respondent as a director.

In a classic situation, 51 shares had been issued to the applicant, a director, and 49 to the only other director. The quorum for the meetings was two. The directors fell out and the applicant requisitioned the company to convene a meeting for the purpose of considering a resolution for the second director, but the latter declined to attend. A stalemate situation arose leading to the applicant seeking an order under s371.

Held

That the applicant, as the holder of 51 per cent of the issued shares, had a statutory right to remove the second director, and if no order was made the deadlock would continue. Also, that the provisions relating to a quorum could not be regarded as conferring on the second director a power of veto; and accordingly, the order was granted.

Division of power between the board and the general meeting

Automatic Self-Cleansing Filter Syndicate v *Cuninghame* [1906] 2 Ch 34 Court of Appeal (Collins MR and Cozens-Hardy LJ)

Whether the general meeting can interfere with the management of a company

Facts

The company was incorporated in 1896 to acquire certain inventions relating to the filtration, treatment, purification and storage of liquids and to sell its undertaking for such consideration as it might deem fit to another company having similar objects. By the articles the general management and control of the company was vested in the directors and, in particular, the directors were empowered to sell or otherwise deal with any property of the company on such terms as they might think fit. At a general meeting of the company a resolution was passed by a simple majority of the shareholders for the sale of the company's assets on certain terms to a company formed for the purpose of acquiring them, and directing the directors to carry the sale into effect. The directors refused to comply with the resolution since they considered the contract was not in the best interests of the company. The shareholders sought an order that the directors be directed to carry the contract into effect. Warrington J refused to make such an order. On appeal:

Held

On the construction of the articles the directors could not be compelled to comply with the resolution.

Collins MR: (after referring to the articles)

'... the directors have absolute power to do all things other than those that are expressly required to be done by the company; and then comes the limitation on their general authority; "subject to such regulations as may from time to time be made by extraordinary resolution". Therefore, if it is desired to alter the powers of the directors that must be done, not by a resolution carried by a majority at an ordinary meeting of the company, but by an extraordinary resolution. In these circumstances it seems to me that it is not competent for the majority of the shareholders at an ordinary meeting to affect or alter the mandate originally given to the directors, by the articles of association.

It has been suggested that this is a mere question of principal and agent, and that it would be an absurd thing if a principal in appointing an agent should in effect appoint a dictator who is to manage him instead of his managing the agent. I think that that analogy does not strictly apply to this case. No doubt for some purposes directors are agents. For whom are they agents? You have, no doubt, in theory and law one equity, the company, which might be a principal, but you have to go behind that when you look to the particular position of directors. It is by the consensus of all the individuals in the company that these directors become agents and hold their rights as agents. It is not fair to say that a majority at a meeting is for the purposes of this case the principal so as to alter the mandate of the agent. The minority also must be taken into account. There are provisions by which the minority may be over-borne, but that can only be done by special machinery in the shape of special resolutions. Short of that the mandate which must be obeyed is not that of the majority – it is that of the whole entity made up of all the shareholders. If the mandate of the directors is to be altered, it can only be under the machinery of the memorandum and articles themselves. I do not think I need to say more' ...

Barron v Potter [1914] 1 Ch 895 Chancery Division (Warrington J)

Default powers of the general meeting

Facts

In 1914 there were only two directors of the British Seagumite Company Ltd, Mr Potter, the chairman and managing director, and Canon Barron. They were not on speaking terms. On 9 February Canon Barron sent out a notice convening an extraordinary general meeting for the purpose of removing Potter as managing director and appointing a new managing director. On 21 February Potter sent out a notice convening a board meeting for 24 February which Canon Barron did not receive. On 23 February Potter met Canon Barron when he arrived by train at Paddington Station and purported to call a board meeting on the platform to appoint three additional directors. He proposed the new directors formally and asked Canon Barron 'Do you agree or object?' to which he replied: 'I object and I object to saying anything to you at all.' Potter then said: 'In my capacity as chairman I give my casting vote in their favour and declare them duly elected' and finally concluded: 'That is all I want to say, thank you. Good day.' On 24 February Canon Barron came to the company's offices for the purpose of attending the extraordinary general meeting he had convened. Potter met him before the meeting and stated again the proposed appointment of additional directors. Canon Barron disregarded this and Potter voted and declared them elected. The extraordinary meeting of the company was then held and a resolution to remove Potter was put to the meeting and carried on a show of hands. Potter demanded a poll, stating he would fix a time and place. Then Potter left, and thus in default of a chairman, Canon Barron put a second resolution appointing a new managing director and two other directors and this was carried. Potter claimed this was illegal since the power to appoint additional directors lay with the directors under the company's articles and not with the shareholders. Canon Barron issued a writ claiming an injunction to restrain the persons appointed by Potter at the alleged board meeting from acting as directors and a declaration that their appointment was invalid. Potter issued a writ in a cross-action claiming that the appointment of directors by the general meeting was invalid. Potter admitted at the trial that the meeting at Paddington was not a valid board meeting.

Held
The purported board meeting on 24 February was ineffective since Potter knew all along that Canon Barron would not attend such a meeting and in any event a casual meeting could not be converted into a board meeting against the will of one of the parties. The appointment of directors by the general meeting was valid since the board was deadlocked and since the directors were unable or unwilling to exercise their powers of appointment of directors, these powers fell to be exercised by the general meeting.

Warrington J:

'... The question is whether certain additional directors appointed at a general meeting of the company were validly appointed or whether certain additional directors were validly appointed at a directors' meeting, in which case the resolution of the company in general meeting would be invalid ...'

... Mr Potter originally insisted that what took place on the platform of Paddington Station was a directors' meeting at which a sufficient proposal was made for the appointment of the three persons named as additional directors, and that if Canon Barron did not vote it was competent to Mr Potter to vote and carry the resolution, or if Canon Barron did vote, then it was competent for Mr Potter to carry it by his own casting vote. It is not, however, now contended that what took place on that occasion was a valid appointment of the additional directors, but it is contended that what took place the next day immediately before the general meeting did amount to a valid appointment. I will first refer to the articles of association under which the company is substantially governed by table A, cl 85 of which provides that "the directors shall have power at any time, and from time to time, to appoint a person as additional director ..." and cl 87 gives power to the directors to regulate their business as they think fit and gives the chairman a second or casting vote in case of equality. Another article provides that the quorum of directors, unless otherwise fixed by the directors, shall be two ...

... What then took place is said to have been a directors' meeting at which a valid appointment was made of the three additional directors proposed by Mr Potter. The answer, in my opinion, is that there was no directors' meeting at all for the reason that Canon Barron to the knowledge of Mr Potter insisted all along that he would not attend any directors' meeting with Mr Potter or discuss the affairs of the company with him, and it is not enough that one of two directors should say: "This is a directors' meeting" while the other says it is not. Of course if directors are willing to hold a meeting they may do so under any circumstances, but one of them cannot be made to attend the board or to convert a casual meeting into a board meeting, and in the present case I do not see how the meeting in question can be treated as a board meeting. In my opinion therefore the true conclusion is that there was no board meeting, but that Canon Barron came with the deliberate intention of not attending a board meeting. If he had received the notice sent to him by Mr Potter summoning him to a board meeting different considerations might have arisen, but he had not received it and came with the fixed intention of not attending any such meeting. There was therefore no board meeting at which Canon Barron was present. Mr Potter was alone present, so that there was no quorum, and I must hold that the three additional directors named by him were not validly appointed.

The question then arises, was the resolution passed at the general meeting of the company a valid appointment? The argument against the validity of the appointment is that the articles of association of the company gave to the board of directors the power of appointing additional directors, that the company has accordingly surrendered the power, and that the directors alone can exercise it. It is true that the general point was so decided by Eve J in *Blair Open Hearth Furnace Co v Reigart* (1883) 25 Ch D 320, and I am not concerned to say that in ordinary cases where there is a board ready and willing to act it would be competent for the company to override the power conferred on the directors by the articles except by way of special resolution for the purpose of altering the articles. But the case which I have to deal with is a different one. For practical purposes there is no board of directors at all. The only directors are two persons, one of whom refuses to act with the other, and the question is, what is to be done under these circumstances? On this point I think that I can usefully refer to the judgment of the Court of Appeal in *Isle of Wight Ry Co* v *Tahourdin* (1913) 108 LT 665, not for the sake of the decision, which depended on the fact that it was a case under the Companies Clauses Consolidation Act, 1845, but for the sake of the observations of Cotton and Fry LJJ upon the effect of a deadlock such as arose in the present case.

'Cotton LJ says:

"Then it is said that there is no power in the meeting of shareholders to elect new directors, for that under the 89th section the power would be in the remaining directors. The remaining directors would no doubt have that power if there was a quorum left. But suppose the meeting were to remove so many directors that a quorum was not left, there being no board which could act, there would be no power of filling up the board so as to enable it to work. In my opinion that is utterly wrong. A power is given by the 89th section to the remaining directors 'if they think proper so to do' to elect persons to fill up the vacancies. I do not see how it is possible for a non-existent body to think proper to fill up vacancies. In such a case a general meeting duly summoned for the purpose must have power to elect a new board so as not to let the business of the company be at a deadlock."

Fry LJ says this:

"Then with regard to the objection that a general meeting cannot elect directors to fill up vacancies, it appears to me that a general meeting would at any rate have that power in the event of all the directors being removed. In my judgment it is quite impossible to read the 89th section as the only section relating to the filling up of vacancies in the office of directors. That applies only where there are remaining directors and those remaining directors think proper to exercise their power. That does not, in my judgment, deprive the general meeting of the power to elect directors, where there are no directors, or where the directors do not think fit to exercise their powers."

Those observations express a principle which seems to me to be as applicable to the case of a limited company incorporated under the Companies (Consolidation) Act, 1908, as to a case falling under the Companies Clauses Consolidation Act, 1845, and moreover to be a principle founded on plain common sense. If directors having certain powers are unable or unwilling to exercise them – are in fact a non-existent body for the purpose – there must be some power in the company to do itself that which under other circumstances would be otherwise done. The directors in the present case being unwilling to appoint additional directors under the power conferred on them by the articles, in my opinion, the company in general meeting has power to make the appointment ...'

Breckland Group Holdings Ltd v *London & Suffolk Properties Ltd* [1989] 4 BCC 542 Chancery Division (Harman J)

Whether a shareholder can commence litigation in the name of the company

Facts

The plaintiffs, BGH Ltd, held 49 per cent of the shares in LSP Ltd. BGH Ltd sought an injunction restraining C, who held the other 51 per cent of the shares in LSP Ltd, from continuing an action in the name of LSP Ltd. There was a shareholder agreement between them that C could appoint two non-executive directors and BGH Ltd one director. The agreement also provided that the institution of legal proceedings required the supporting vote of one C director and the BGH Ltd director, thus ensuring that the 49 per cent and 51 per cent shareholder representatives were in favour of the action.

Held

The action was improperly commenced. Harman J took into account the shareholders' agreement and also the company's management article in art 80 of table A 1948. The commencement of the action by the 51 per cent shareholder was in breach of the agreement and this could not be cured by the action being adopted by the general meeting by an ordinary resolution. The general meeting is not competent to interfere with matters which have been properly entrusted to the board. Harman J said: 'Art 80 confides the management of the business to the directors and in such a case it is not for the general meeting to interfere.'

Commentary

There was a minority view which supported the proposition that it was possible for the general meeting to interfere with the management of a company which had given the board of directors the powers of management by art 80 table A 1948. This, it was argued, could be done by an ordinary resolution. This view can probably no longer stand in the light of Harman's decision.

Gramophone & Typewriter Ltd v *Stanley* [1908] 2 KB 89 Court of Appeal (Cozans-Hardy MR and Fletcher-Moulton, Buckley LJJ)

Tax liability – parent and subsidiary – powers of management as between the shareholders and directors

Facts

This case was concerned with the liability of an English company to pay tax on dividends from its wholly owned German subsidiary. The Crown argued that the profits of the German subsidiary should be treated as the profits of the English company while the latter argued it was only liable to pay tax on dividends it actually received from the German subsidiary. The arguments put forward by the Crown and rejected by the court, were that the German company was a sham and that it was an agent of the English company.

Held

The profits of the German company were not to be regarded as those of the English parent company. A wholly owned subsidiary is not, without more, to be treated as an agent.

Buckley LJ:

'Further, it is urged that the English company, as owning all the shares, can control the German company in the sense that the German company must do all that the English company directs. In my opinion this again is a misapprehension. This court decided not long ago in *Automatic Self-Cleansing Filter Syndicate Co* v *Cuninghame* that even a resolution of a numerical majority at a general meeting of the company cannot impose its will on the directors when the articles have confided to them the control of the company's affairs. The directors are not servants to obey directions given by the shareholders as individuals; they are not agents appointed by and bound to serve the shareholders as their principals, they are persons who may by the regulations be entrusted with the control of the business, and if so entrusted they can be dispossessed from that control only by the statutory majority which can alter the articles. Directors are not, I think, bound to comply with the directions even of all the corporators acting as individuals; of course, the corporators have it in their power by proper resolutions, which would generally be special resolutions, to remove directors who do not act as they desire, but this in no way answers the question here to be considered, which is whether the corporators are engaged in carrying on the business of the corporation. In my opinion, they are not. To say that they are involves a complete confusion of ideas ...'

Grant v *United Kingdom Switchbank Railway Co* (1888) 40 Ch D 135 Court of Appeal (Cotton, Lindley and Bowen LJJ)

Whether the general meeting could prevent the sale of part of the company's undertaking

Facts

The objects of the company were to acquire and sell patents relating to railways. Its articles authorised the sale of part of its undertaking to any other company but contained a proviso prohibiting any director from voting on a contract in which he was interested. The directors of the company entered into a contract for the sale of part of the undertaking to the defendant company of which all of them, save one, were also directors. At a general meeting of the company called to consider a resolution to approve and adopt the agreement the resolution was passed as an ordinary resolution. No grounds were stated as to why the meeting was necessary. The plaintiff, a shareholder in the company, claimed an injunction to restrain the company from carrying the contract into effect. Chitty J refused the injunction. On appeal:

Held

The resolution of the general meeting was not invalidated by the fact that the notice convening it did not suggest any reason why the contract could not be carried into effect without the sanction of a general meeting.

Cotton LJ:

'It was urged for the appellant that the directors could not, being interested, make a contract which would bind their company, and that a general meeting could not, by a mere ordinary resolution, affirm that contract, for that this would be an alteration of the articles, which could only be effected by a special resolution. This is a mistake. The ratifying of a particular contract which had been entered into by the directors without authority, and so making it an act of the company, is quite a different thing from altering the articles. To give the directors power to do things in future which the articles did not authorise them to do, would be an alteration of the articles, but it is no alteration of the articles to ratify a contract which has been made without authority.

It was urged that the contract was a nullity, and could not be ratified. That is not the case. There was a contract entered into on behalf of the company, though it was one which could not be enforced against the company. Article 100 prevented the directors from binding the company by the contract, but there was nothing in it to prevent the company from entering into such a contract. Two passages in *Irvine* v *Union Bank of Australia* (1877) 2 App Cas 366 were referred to. Being in the same judgment, they must be taken together and they appear to me to express what I have said – that power to do future acts cannot be given to directors without altering the articles, but that a ratification of an unauthorised act of the directors only requires the sanction of an ordinary resolution of a general meeting, if the act is within the powers of the company ...'

John Shaw & Sons (Salford) Ltd v *Shaw* [1935] 2 KB 113 Court of Appeal (Greer, Slesser and Roche LJJ)

Whether a general meeting could discontinue legal proceedings against certain directors

Facts

The company was a family company of which Peter, John and Percy Shaw were the principal shareholders and also directors together with two other relatives. Peter, John and Percy Shaw, in breach of their duty as directors, wrongfully used for their own purposes substantial sums of money belonging to the company in an attempt to conceal their true income from the tax authorities. Percy Shaw came to an arrangement with the company about repaying these monies but, only after doing so, discovered the breaches of trust by Peter and John Shaw and took proceedings against them to account for the monies they owed. These proceedings were settled on terms which provided, inter alia, that two independent directors were to be appointed together with a third person as permanent directors and the Shaws were to be ordinary directors. Further, Peter, John and Percy Shaw were to have no right to vote in relation to matters concerning the debts due to them and the articles altered to provide for this. Disputes arose over the meaning of the terms of the settlement and the three permanent directors held a meeting to which none of the ordinary directors was summoned and passed resolutions instructing the company's solicitors to issue proceedings to enforce payment of the debts due from Peter and John Shaw. Before the action came on for hearing an EGM was held by which the Shaws as principal shareholders attempted to compel the directors to discontinue the actions. One of the contentions at the trial was that the permanent directors had no authority to commence the action on behalf of the company and, as they were not the company, judgment could not be given in their favour.

Held

The proceedings were authorised (per Greer LJ – because in the circumstances the effect of the articles was to vest control over the financial affairs of the company and all powers of management in the permanent directors) (per Roche LJ – the objection should have been taken by interlocutory motion on summons and not at the trial) (per Slesser LJ – the ordinary directors should have been summoned to the meeting and it was, therefore, improperly called).

Greer, LJ:

'... Article 86a restricts the rights and duties of the three brothers, and prohibits them as directors from dealing on behalf of the company with any of the debts due from them under the terms of settlement. It has the same effect as it would have had if it had said: "the directors other than the three brothers shall alone have power on behalf of the company to control the conduct of the company with regard to such debts, and the sole right to deal with them." Article 86a alone would not have had the effect of excluding the two additional directors, John Bryan Shaw and James Fitzgerald Fern, from control over or from dealing with these debts, but art 87 has a wider effect than 86a. This article applies to all the ordinary directors, and not only restricts their rights at directors' meetings to vote in respect of, but it also provides that they shall have no control over the financial affairs of the company, and that they shall only have such rights of voting and such control over the management as may from time to time be conferred upon them by the permanent directors. The effect of this article is the same as it would have been if it had provided that the power of control over the financial affairs of the company, and all powers of management of the affairs of the company, except such as might from time to time be conferred upon the ordinary directors by the permanent directors, should be vested in the three permanent directors alone ...

... In my judgment, on 23 March, 1934, when the permanent directors decided to instruct the company's solicitors to bring these actions on behalf of the company, they had power under the articles to do so. The power was not in the board of directors, but in the permanent directors. The ordinary directors were not entitled to any say on the question, which was the only one considered at the meeting. If they had been summoned and had come to the meeting they could have been directed by the permanent directors to retire and could not have refused ...

... I am, therefore, of opinion that the learned judge was right in refusing to dismiss the action on the plea that it was commenced without the authority of the plaintiff company. I think the judge was also right in refusing to give effect to the resolution of the meeting of the shareholders requiring the chairman to instruct the company's solicitors not to proceed further with the action. A company is an entity distinct alike from its shareholders and its directors. Some of its powers may, according to its articles, be exercised by directors; certain other powers may be reserved for the shareholders in general meeting. If powers of management are vested in the directors, they and they alone can exercise these powers. The only way in which the general body of the shareholders can control the exercise of the powers vested by the articles in the directors is by altering their articles, or, if opportunity arises under the articles, by refusing to re-elect the directors of whose actions they disapprove. They cannot themselves usurp the powers which by the articles are vested in the directors any more than the directors can usurp the powers vested by the articles in the general body of shareholders. The law on this subject is, I think, accurately stated in *Buckley on Companies* (11th ed) at p723 as the effect of the decisions there mentioned ...'

Slesser LJ:

'As to the third ground of want of authority, that the shareholders instructed the directors to discontinue the action on 30 April, 1934; if the permanent directors had power under the articles to bring the action, I do not see how the shareholders could interfere with that power, otherwise than by altering the articles, which they have not proposed to do. This would seem to be the effect of the decision of the House of Lords in *Quin and Axtens* v *Salmon Ltd*, though the decision of Neville J in *Marshall's Valve Gear Co Ltd* v *Manning Wardle & Co* is difficult to reconcile with that case. However, I do not think it necessary in the present circumstances to decide the point finally, but I incline to the view that art 95 in matters within the powers of the permanent directors would require an alteration of the regulations by special resolution to prevent this action continuing; that is to say, that Lord Loreburn's dictum in *Quin and Axten's* case is correct, that the words "regulation" and "article" in the articles in that case, which were substantially similar to the present art 95, mean the same thing ...'

Marshall's Valve Gear Co Ltd v *Manning, Wardle & Co Ltd* [1909] 1 Ch 267
Chancery Division (Neville J)

Company management – minority view – majority shareholder allowed to bring an action in the name of the company

Facts
Marshall's was incorporated in 1904 to acquire and work a patent for improving valve gears in locomotives and engines. Under art 55 of the Articles it was provided: 'the business of the company shall be managed by the directors, who may ... exercise all such powers of the company as are not by the foregoing Act (CA 1862), or by these articles, required to be exercised by the company in general meeting.' The first directors of the company were Marshall, whose patents the company acquired, and three others, and they held nearly all of the company's issued share capital. Marshall held a majority of the shares but not a three-fourths majority of the votes. A dispute arose at the board between Marshall and the other three directors, who were interested in a patent vested in Manning. Marshall was advised that the Manning patent infringed his patent. Marshall therefore brought an action in the name of the company against Manning. The three directors sought an injunction to strike out the action on the ground that the name of the company had been used without authority.

Held
The claim would be dismissed because on the true construction of art 55 the majority of shareholders had a right to control the actions of the directors in the matter.

Neville J:

'... Mr Marshall has commenced an action in the name of the company for the purpose of restraining an alleged infringement on the part of the owners of the new patent, and the other directors come to the court and ask to have the writ in that action taken off the file on the ground that the action was commenced without the authority of the company. It is admitted that the calling of a meeting of shareholders to ascertain the wishes of the company would be useless because the position of the voting power is perfectly well understood. It is divided between the persons concerned, and undoubtedly the managing director, who has commenced this action, would have the majority of votes at a general meeting, and, therefore, if it is right that effect should be given to the wishes of the majority of the company in the present case, it is admitted that no object is to be gained by calling a meeting, because the result of that meeting is a foregone conclusion. Under those circumstances ought the court to direct the removal of the writ? Prior to the decision in *Automatic Self-Cleansing Filter Syndicate Co v Cuninghame* [1906] 2 Ch 34 the matter, I think, would have presented little difficulty, because I think in several cases, and certainly in *Pender v Lushington* (1877) 6 Ch D 70 and *Duckett v Gover* (1877) 6 Ch D 82, the principle has been acted upon that in the absence of any contract to the contrary the majority of the shareholders in a company have the ultimate control of its affairs, and are entitled to decide whether or not an action in the name of the company shall proceed. I think that that principle was recognised also by the Court of Appeal in the case of *Harben v Phillips* (1883) 23 Ch D 14, and, I take it that prior to the decision in the case of *Automatic Self-Cleansing Filter Syndicate Co v Cuninghame* the law was established to the effect that the majority of the shareholders, in the absence of a contract to the contrary, had the ultimate control of the affairs of the company and could assert their rights in general meeting. Now the question arises whether the decision in the case of *Automatic Self-Cleansing Filter Syndicate Co v Cuninghame* is a decision to the contrary. To my mind it is quite clear that the decision itself in that case is not in the least inconsistent with any of the decisions that preceded it, because in the case of *Automatic Self-Cleansing Filter Syndicate Co v Cuninghame* the terms of the articles were that the directors should have the entire management of the affairs of the company subject to regulations "not being inconsistent with these presents as may from time to time be made by extraordinary resolution". In that case the directors had before them the consideration of a proposed sale of the assets on certain terms. They considered that those terms were not beneficial to the company. The majority of the shareholders in general meeting came to a different conclusion and sought to control the management of the directors in conformity with the views of a bare majority, but the contract between the shareholders in that case had been to the direct effect that the management of the directors should not be controlled except upon the passing of an extraordinary resolution. Inasmuch as there was no extraordinary resolution in that case the court, it seems to me, could have come to no other conclusion than that at which they did arrive. I think that the head-note quite accurately sets out the effect of the decision: "Held, upon the construction of the articles, that the directors could not be compelled to comply with the resolution". There are among the observations which fell from one or more of the learned judges who decided that case propositions which, if I understand them correctly, I think extend beyond any of the decisions in the former cases, and, if I may say so very respectfully, appear to me to be inconsistent with the law as it stood at the time when the case of *Automatic Self-Cleansing Filter Syndicate Co v Cuninghame* was decided. Perhaps I have not correctly interpreted those observations. They are in any case dicta not binding upon me. I am, of course, bound by the decision at which the court arrived, and which, as I said before, seems to me in complete conformity with the law as I understand it. If I am right in this conclusion, it is obvious, I think, that I ought not to interfere with the progress of the present action, because it is brought with the approval of the majority of the shareholders in the company, and, upon the decisions which I have referred to, they are the persons who are entitled to say aye or no, whether the litigation shall proceed. In the present case there is no difficulty about the articles of association, because there is no unusual contract between the members of the company with regard to the powers of the directors.'

9 Directors

Appointment

Craven-Ellis* v *Canons Ltd [1936] 2 KB 403 Court of Appeal (Greer, Greene LJJ and Talbot J)

Remuneration of directors – quantum meruit

Facts
The plaintiff, an estate agent, agreed with the directors of the defendant, a property development company, to provide the company with his skills and experience as an estate agent. The company itself was newly formed and by its articles the directors were required to have a share qualification and ceased to be directors if the qualification was not satisfied within two months of appointment. At first the company received and accepted services rendered by the plaintiff without any express agreement. Subsequently, the directors executed an agreement, under the seal of the company, appointing the plaintiff as managing director. At the time this agreement was exercised none of the directors had taken up their share qualification and, therefore, had ceased to be directors. The plaintiff rendered the services provided for in the agreement. The company refused to pay him either under the agreement or on a quantum meruit for technical reasons. Goddard J dismissed the plaintiff's claim. On appeal:

Held
Even though the plaintiff had carried out the work under an agreement which was void he was, nevertheless, entitled to a quantum meruit.

Greer LJ:

'... I think the plaintiff is entitled to succeed. The contract, having been made by directors who had no authority to make it with one of themselves who had notice of their want of authority, was not binding on either party. It was, in fact, a nullity, and presents no obstacle to the implied promise to pay on a quantum meruit basis which arises from the performance of the services and the implied acceptance of the same by the company ...

... In my judgment, the obligation to pay reasonable remuneration for the work done when there is no binding contract between the parties is imposed by a rule of law, and not by an inference of fact arising from the acceptance of the services or goods. It is one of the cases referred to in the books on contracts as obligations arising quasi ex contractu, of which a well known instance is a claim based on money had and received.'

Guinness plc* v *Saunders [1990] 2 AC 663 House of Lords (Lords Brandon, Templeman, Griffiths and Goff)

Remuneration of a director

Facts

The facts of this case appear on page 294.

Held

Mr Thomas Ward's appeal against the Court of Appeal's decision that he should repay £5.2m to Guinness was dismissed on the ground that the payment, by a committee of directors, including Ward, was unauthorised by the company's articles. The House of Lords also refused to allow Ward to keep the payment on the basis of a quantum meruit or under s727 CA 1985 on the ground that he acted both honestly and reasonably.

Lord Templeman:

'... Thus Mr Ward admits receipt of £5.2m from Guinness and pleads an agreement by Guinness that he should be paid this sum for his advice and services in connection with the bid. Mr Ward admits that payment was not authorised by the board of directors of Guinness.

The articles of association of Guinness provide:

"Remuneration of directors. 90. The board shall fix the annual remuneration of the directors provided that without the consent of the company in general meeting such remuneration (excluding any special remuneration payable under article 91 and article 92) shall not exceed the sum of £100,000 per annum ... 91. The board may, in addition to the remuneration to any director who serves on any committee or who devotes special attention to the business of the company or who otherwise performs services which in the opinion of the board are outside the scope of the ordinary duties of a director. Such special remuneration may be made payable to such director in addition to or in substitution for his ordinary remuneration as a director, and may be made payable by a lump sum or by way of salary, or commission or participation in profits, or by any or all of those modes or otherwise as the board may determine."

Articles 90 and 91 of the articles of association of Guinness depart from the table A articles recommended by statute, which reserve to a company in general meeting the right to determine the remuneration of the directors of the company. But by art 90 the annual remuneration which the directors may award themselves is limited and by art 91 special remuneration for an individual director can only be auhorised by the board. A committee, which may consist of only two or, as in the present case, three members, however honest and conscientious, cannot assess impartially the value of its work or the value of the contribution of its individual members. A director may, as a condition of accepting appointment to a committee, or after he has accepted appointment, seek the agreement of the board to authorise payment for special work envisaged or carried out. The shareholders of Guinness run the risk that the board may be too generous to an individual director at the expense of the shareholders but the shareholders have, by art 91, chosen to run this risk and can protect themselves by the number quality and impartiality of the members of the board who will consider whether an individual director deserves special reward. Under art 91 the shareholders of Guinness do not run the risk that a committee may value its own work and the contribution of its own members. Article 91 authorises the board, and only the board, to grant special remuneration. It was submitted that art 2 alters the plain meaning of art 91. In art 2 there are a number of definitions each of which is expressed to apply "if not inconsistent with the subject or context." The expression "the board" is defined as

"The directors of the company for the time being (or a quorum of such directors assembled at a meeting of directors duly convened) or any committee authorised by the board to act on its behalf."

The result of applying the art 2 definition to art 91, it is said, is that a committee may grant special remuneration to any director who serves on a committee or devotes special attention to the business of the company or who otherwise performs services which in the opinion of the committee are outside the scope of the ordinary duties of a director. In my opinion the subject and context of art 91 are inconsistent with the expression "the board" in art 91 meaning anything except the board. Article 91 draws a contrast between the board and a committee of the board. The board is expressly authorised to grant special remuneration to any director who serves on *any* committee. It cannot have been intended that any committee should be able to grant special remuneration to any director, whether a member of the committee or not. The board must compare the work of an individual director with the ordinary duties of a director. The board must decide whether special remuneration shall be paid in addition to or in substitution for the annual remuneration determined by the board under art 90. These decisions could only be made by the board surveying the work and remuneration of each and every director. Article 91 also provides for the board to decide whether special remuneration should take the form of participation in profits; the article could not intend that a committee should be able to determine whether profits should accrue to the shareholders' funds or be paid out to an individual director. The rumuneration of directors concerns all the members of the board and all the shareholders of Guinness. Article 2 does not operate to produce a result which is inconsistent with the language, the subject and the context of art 91. Only the board possessed power to award £5.2m to Mr Ward ...

Mr Lords, the short answer to a quantum meruit claim based on an implied contract by Guinness to pay reasonable remuneration for services rendered is that there can be no contract by Guinness to pay special remuneration for the services of a director unless that contract is entered into by the board pursuant to art 91. The short answer to the claim for an equitable allowance is the equitable principle which forbids a trustee to make a profit out of his trust unless the trust instrument, in this case the articles of association of Guinness, so provides. The law cannot and equity will not amend the articles of Guinness. The court is not entitled to usurp the functions conferred on the board by the articles ...

Mr Ward requested the committee to pay him and received from the committee out of moneys belonging to Guinness the sum of £5.2m as a reward for his advice and services as a director. Mr Ward had no right to remuneration without the authority of the board. Thus the claim by Guinness for repayment is unanswerable. If Mr Ward acted honestly and reasonably and ought fairly to be excused for receiving £5.2m without the authority of the board, he cannot be excused from paying it back. By invoking s727 as a defence to the claim by Guinness for repayment, Mr Ward seeks an order of the court which would entitle him to remuneration without the authority of the board. The order would be a breach of the articles which protect shareholders and govern directors and would be a breach of the principles of equity to which I have already referred.

I would dismiss this appeal.'

Removal of a director

Bushell v *Faith* [1970] AC 1099 House of Lords (Lords Reid, Morris, Guest, Upjohn and Donovan)

Removal of a director – weighted votes in the articles

Facts
The company was formed in 1960 with an issued share capital of 300 fully paid up shares of £1 each. The shares were held as to 100 shares each by a brother and two sisters, Mr Faith, a Mrs Bushell and Dr Kathleen Bayne respectively. For various reasons Mr Faith's conduct as a director of the company displeased his sisters who requisitioned a general meeting at which an ordinary resolution was proposed for his removal as a director. The resolution was passed on a show of hands with the two sisters voting in favour and Mr Faith against. Mr Faith demanded a poll. Under the company's articles each share carried one vote in a poll but if the poll was in relation to a resolution to remove any of the directors from office it was provided by special art 9 of the articles that any shares held by the director affected by such a resolution carried the right to three votes per share. Thus, on a poll the resolution was rejected by 300 votes to 200 votes. The two sisters sought a declaration that Mr Faith had been removed from office and argued that special art 9 was void since it defeated the object and purpose of s184 CA 1948

(now s303 CA 1985). Ungoed-Thomas J granted the declaration but on appeal by Mr Faith the Court of Appeal allowed his appeal. On appeal to the House of Lords:

Held

Special art 9 was valid and did not conflict with s184 since all that s184 was intended to do was to make an ordinary resolution sufficient to remove a director and to override articles which provides that a director could only be removed on an extraordinary or a special resolution.

Lord Donovan:

'My Lords, the issue here is the true construction of s184 of the Companies Act, 1948: and I approach it with no conception of what the legislature wanted to achieve by the section other than such as can reasonably be deduced from its language.

Clearly it was intended to alter the method by which a director of a company could be removed while still in office. It enacts that this can be done by the company by ordinary resolution. Furthermore, it may be achieved notwithstanding anything in the company's articles, or in any agreement between the company and the director.

Accordingly any case (and one knows there were many) where the articles prescribed that a director should be removable during his period of office only by a special resolution or an extraordinary resolution, each of which necessitated inter alia a three to one majority of those present and voting at the meeting, is overriden by s184. A simple majority of the votes will now suffice; an ordinary resolution being, in my opinion, a resolution capable of being carried by such a majority. Similarly any agreement, whether evidenced by the articles or otherwise, that a director shall be a director for life or for some fixed period is now also over-reached.

The field over which s184 operates is thus extensive for it includes, admittedly, all companies with a quotation on the Stock Exchange.

It is now contended, however, that it does something more; namely, that it provides in effect that when the ordinary resolution proposing the removal of the director is put to the meeting each shareholder present shall have one vote per share and no more: and that any provision in the articles providng that any shareholder shall, in relation to this resolution, have "weighted" votes attached to his shares, is also nullified by s184. A provision for such "weighting" of votes which applies generally, that is as part of the normal pattern of voting, is accepted by the appellant as unobjectionable: but an article such as the one here under consideration which is special to a resolution seeking the removal of a director falls foul of s184 and is overridden by it.

Why should this be? The section does not say so, as it easily could. And those who drafted it and enacted it certainly would have included among their numbers many who were familiar with the phenomenon of articles of association carrying "weighted votes". It must therefore have been plain at the outset that unless some special provision were made, the mere direction that an ordinary resolution would do in order to remove a director would leave the section at risk of being made inoperative in the way that has been done here. Yet no such provision was made, and in this Parliament followed its practice of leaving to companies and their shareholders liberty to allocate voting rights as they pleased.

When, therefore, it is said that a decision in favour of the respondent in this case would defeat the purpose of the section and make a mockery of it, it is being assumed that Parliament intended to cover every possible case and block up every loophole. I see no warrant for any such assumption. A very large part of the relevant field is in fact covered and covered effectively. And there may be good reasons why Parliament should leave some companies with freedom of manoeuvre in this particular matter. There are many small companies which are conducted in practice as though they were little more than partnerships, particularly family companies running a family business; and it is, unfortunately, sometimes necessary to provide some safeguard against family quarrels having their repercussions in the boardroom. I am not, of course, saying that this is such a case: I merely seek to repel the argument that unless the section is construed in the way the appellant wants, it has become "inept" and "frustrated".

I would dismiss the appeal.'

Disqualification

Carecraft Construction Co Ltd, Re [1994] 1 WLR 172 Chancery Division (Ferris J)

Section 6 Company Directors Disqualification Act 1986 – adoption of a summary procedure

Facts

W and H were directors of five building construction companies all of which went into liquidation between 1986 and 1988. W looked after the building side of the business and H the financial side, as he was a chartered accountant. H discovered that no proper accounts had been kept and that the companies had failed to file annual returns. H took legal advice and the company was put into liquidation. Both directors accepted that they were unfit to be concerned with the management of the company and the court was asked to deal with disqualification on the basis of a summary procedure without the need for a full hearing.

Held

It was appropriate to deal with disqualification in this way and both directors were disqualified for the minimum period of two years under s6 CDDA 1986.

Ferris J:

'... I was asked to follow a procedure which has not hitherto been adopted in cases of this kind. What was proposed can be summarised as follows. (i) There was presented to me a schedule of agreed facts. These were, in substance, the facts which I have already stated. (ii) It was stated on behalf of Mr Wilson and Mr Hayes that, on the footing that I was prepared to deal with the matter as proposed, they accepted that I would be likely to find that their conduct as directors of CDC, CPHS, CG and CRC, made them unfit to be concerned in the management of a company. The result of my so finding would be that I would be obliged to make a disqualification order for the minimum period of two years in the case of each of them. (iii) On this footing the Official Receiver stated through counsel that he did not think it necessary to press me to decide the various issues about which there was no agreement. Moreover he accepted that, even if I were to find in his favour on most or all of these issues, such findings would not raise the case against either Mr Wilson or Mr Hayes into a different bracket of seriousness. Although such findings, if made, might cause me to make a disqualification order for longer than the minimum period, the Official Receiver was content, in all the circumstances, including the mitigation advanced on behalf of Mr Wilson and Mr Hayes, not to submit that the case is one in which more than the minimum period of disqualification ought to be imposed. (iv) On the same footing it was not submitted on behalf of Mr Wilson and Mr Hayes that no disqualification order at all should be made. Counsel for Mr Wilson and Mr Hayes did, however, make submissions to me to the effect that the period of disqualification should be no longer than two years. These submissions were both as to the seriousness of the conduct of Mr Wilson and Mr Hayes, as appearing from the agreed facts, and as to various features of mitigation based upon those facts and upon evidence not going directly to the conduct complained of. (v) It was common ground between the parties that if I were unwilling to proceed on the basis I have summarised at paragraphs (i) to (iv) and to make a disqualification order for two years only, I should make no further decision but should give procedural directions with a view to the applications coming before another judge for a full hearing.

It appears to me that these proposals raised three issues: first, whether the court has jurisdiction to proceed in this way, without requiring a full hearing; second, if the court has such jurisdiction, whether the present cases are appropriate to be dealt with in accordance with it; and third whether, in all the circumstances, I can be satisfied both that a disqualification order has to be made and that it should be for no longer than two years. After hearing argument I came to the conclusion that each of these questions is to be answered in the affirmative.

Has the court jurisdiction to proceed in the way proposed?
... In disqualification proceedings, therefore, there is no scope for the parties to reach an agreement in a consent order. The court itself has to be satisfied, after having regard to the prescribed matters and other facts which appear to be material, that the respondent is unfit to be concerned in the management or a company; and the court itself must decide the period of disqualification if it decides to made a disqualification order.

Does it follow from this that the court ought to insist on a fully contested hearing in every case under the Act of 1986? Pragmatically it would seem that the answer ought to be in the negative. It would be unrealistic for the court to disregard any admission which one party may make in respect of factual contentions advanced by the opposite party. Moreover in practical terms the court has no means to control the way in which either party conducts its case, whether in respect of the scope and definition of the charges made or disputed or in respect of the evidence which is presented in order to support or rebut the charges.

It was suggested in argument that a number of analogous situations exist in which a court, while needing to be satisfied of certain matters and to exercise its own discretion, has been able, in appropriate cases, to dispense with a full hearing.

The most obvious of these, perhaps, is where an accused person pleads guilty in a criminal case. The whole purpose of the time honoured and thoroughly entrenched practice of requiring an accused person to plead guilty or not guilty at the time of arraignment is to decide whether or not there is to be a trial. If there is a plea of guilty to a particular charge there is no need for a trial on that charge and the court proceeds to deal with sentence. Presumably the rationale of this is that, at the initial stage, what the court needs to know is whether the accused person is guilty or not and an admission, in the form of an unequivocal plea of guilty, is unambiguous evidence of guilt. It may be said that unfitness has a qualitative aspect to it which is not, I think, usually present in criminal charges. Moreover difficulty raised in criminal cases where there is a plea of guilty and the court needs to know, in order to assess the seriousness of the offence for purposes of sentence, which of two or more positive versions of the facts of the offence is to be accepted. The problem is discussed in *Archbold, Criminal Pleading Evidence & Practice*, 44th ed, (1992), vol 1, at pp669-673, paras 5-41 to 5-47. In some cases the court will require evidence to be called to deal with the matter: see *Reg v Newton* (1982) 77 Cr App R 13.

... A third analogy comes from the field of competition law. Under s21 of the Restrictive Trade Practices Act 1956 (now s10 of the Restrictive Practices Act 1976) a restriction accepted in pursuance of an agreement of a particular kind was deemed to be contrary to the public interest, and thus void and susceptible to injunctive relief, unless the court was satisfied of any one or more of specified sets of circumstances. In *In re Net Book Agreement, 1957* (1962) LR 3 RP 246, certain restrictions in an agreement between members of the Publishers' Association were held, after a hearing lasting more than 20 days, not to be contrary to the public interest on the ground that the court was satisfied of various of the specified circumstances in relation to each restriction. In *In re Net Book Agreement, 1957, (No 2)* (1964) LR 4 RP 484, another agreement containing virtually identical restrictions but made between different parties, came before the court. A procedure was followed under which (i) the Registrar of Restrictive Trading Agreements did not deliver an answer in response to the statement of case of those who were concerned to uphold the restrictions; (ii) evidence in support of the restrictions was given by a short affidavit verifying the statement of case and deposing to a few other relevant matters, on which the deponent was not cross-examined; and (iii) the matter was heard summarily, the registrar making no submissions against the making of the declaration which was asked for. In acceding to this procedure Mocatta J, giving the decision of the court, said, at p489:

> "Clearly the view of the registrar is important and we give much weight to it, but the court cannot rely exclusively on his view before it can be satisfied that the restrictions in the ... agreement are not contrary to the public interest."

After reading the affidavit the court made the declaration asked for, thus implicitly, if not expressly, indicating that it was satisfied of the relevant matters. A similar procedure was, to my knowledge, later followed in respect of substantially the same restrictions under the Resale Prices Act 1964: see *Halsbury's Laws of England*, 4th ed, vol 47 (1984), p 208, para 240, note 10.

This, I think, is a fairly close analogy. The Restrictive Trade Practices Act 1956, like its successors, was passed to protect the public interest against anti-competitive agreements and it required the court to be satisfied of particular matters. The approach adopted by the Restrictive Practices Court shows how the court may be satisfied of those matters without requiring a full trial and without requiring the parties to contest every point. The fact that in *In re Net Book Agreement, 1957 (No 2)* the relevant matters had already been established in other proceedings does not, in my judgment, qualify the effect of the decision so far as jurisdiction is concerned. It merely resulted in it being easy for the court to be satisfied of the relevant matters by evidence which was little more than formal ...

Are the present cases appropriate to be dealt with in accordance with the summary procedure?
I am satisfied that the evidence establishes all the facts which I have previously narrated as being undisputed, agreed or facts which the respondents are content for me to assume. This is so even in respect of facts which the respondents might have wished to challenge at a full hearing. I take the view that, in the absence of such a challenge, I am entitled to accept the evidence which supports these facts at its face value, and I do accept it.

I am satisfied also that, on the basis of these facts, the conduct of Mr Wilson and Mr Hayes as directors of the companies which I have mentioned makes then unfit to be concerned in the management of a company. I refer in particular to the failure to file annual returns and accounts; the failure to keep adequate financial and other records; the consequential failure to appreciate the true financial position of Carecraft until just before it went into liquidation; the failure to cause Carecraft to make returns in respect of PAYE and national insurance; and the non-payment of Crown debts in contrast to the payment of suppliers and wages, which is indicative of a tendency to pay creditors who were pressing for payment, or were in a position to exert pressure for payment, and to use the money due to other creditors as additional working capital. I have not attempted to arrange these factors in order of importance. ...

Am I satisfied both that a disqualification order must be made in each case and that it shall be for no longer than two years?
The finding of unfitness which I have made means that a disqualification order must be made for at least two years. As I have indicated, my starting point, subject to mitigation, was disqualification for three years in each case.

On behalf of Mr Wilson, Miss Skekerdemian asked me to take account of his youth and background. He left school at the age of 16. He is a builder, with no qualifications. He had no experience of running a limited company when he incorporated Carecraft at the age of 25. There is no suggestion that he acted dishonestly or for his own benefit. His remuneration from Carecraft was modest, beginning at £3,500 in 1984-85 and rising to only a little over £10,000 in 1986-87. He received no remuneration from any of the other companies. He lent substantial sums to the companies all of which have been lost. He has also had to pay over £10,000 under his bank guarantee. He should be given credit for what is, in effect, a plea of guilty. The fact that this application has been hanging over his head for an unusually long time, largely due to the "10 days' notice" required under s16(1), which was attributable to an error or delay in the office of the Secretary of State, should also be taken into account. Miss Skekerdemian also asked me to accept as an explanation of the want of financial records, although no an exoneration from responsibility for it, the fact that Mr Wilson had delegated reponsibility for these to Mr Hayes. I found that all these factors, except perhaps the last, carried some weight. In all the circumstances I took the view that the period of disqualification in respect of Mr Wilson should be two years.

On behalf of Mr Hayes, Mr Kaye pointed out that he too is young, having been born in 1956, and without any real experience as a company director or any experience at all as a builder. He became director on a part-time basis and was faced with a situation in which inadequate records had been kept. In order to remedy this he became a full time director after about nine months and, within the next seven months, brought the companies books up to date, despite various difficulties, including a lack of input and assistance from Mr Wilson. When he realised the true position of the companies he called in expert assistance and, since the liquidation, he has co-operated fully with the Official Receiver. He received little benefit from the companies while they were trading, and he has had to pay £30,000 under his guarantee. He will also have to pay at least some of the costs of these proceedings. He is a chartered accountant, so that the stigma of a finding of unfitness will be considerable, regardless of the period of disqualification. He may be further penalised in disciplinary proceedings brought by his professional body. Like Mr Wilson he should be given credit for a guilty plea and the fact that these proceedings have been pending for a long time should be taken into account.

I found that all these points of mitigation carried some weight. In the case of Mr Hayes too, I took the view that the period of disqualification should be two years.'

Churchill Hotel (Plymouth) Ltd, Re [1988] BCLC 341 Chancery Division (Peter Gibson J)

Refusal to make a disqualification order

Facts

This was an application for a disqualification order under s300 of the Companies Act 1985: the respondent had been the sole or controlling director of four companies. Save only for an initial profitable development by one of them, all four companies had traded unprofitably throughout the whole of their trading lives. All had negligible amounts of capital. Two had borrowed heavily and carried on trading in the expectation or hope that the capital appreciation of certain properties would eventually enable them to pay off creditors. Two had carried on trading unprofitably without owning the capital assets to which their trading was related (they were owned by associated companies). All had gone into liquidation owing substantial amounts to creditors, in particular to the Crown, notably in respect of PAYE tax, which had to some time prior to the companies' ceasing trading been deducted from wages but not paid over to the Revenue and which had therefore, as the respondent knew or ought to have known, been used improperly to finance the continued trading of the companies. Each of the companies had failed to comply with administrative obligations imposed on directors by the Companies Acts. On the other hand, the respondent was now a director of eight successful companies depending almost entirely on his expertise and experience.

Held

A disqualification order would not be made.

Peter Gibson J:

'As I see it, the court has no jurisdiction to make a disqualification order unless three conditions are satisfied. The first two are that it should appear to the court that the respondent is or was a director of the companies specified in paras (a) and (b) respectively of the subsection (300(1) of the 1985 Act). The third condition is that it should appear to the court that the respondent's conduct as director of any of those companies makes him unfit to be concerned in the management of a company. The subsection requires the court to look only to that conduct in deciding whether that makes him unfit. If all three conditions are satisfied then the court may make a disqualification order. Thus the court, in the exercise of that discretion, is not obliged to make a disqualification order; it will have regard to all matters which bear on the question whether it is appropriate, at the date when the court is considering its decision, to disqualify the director, including matters such as the respondent's directorship of other companies, whether the respondent appears to have learned his lesson from his experiences with the companies that went into liquidation and the consequences for others if a disqualification order were made. Such considerations can lead the court to make no disqualification order, notwithstanding that the third condition is satisfied ... I accept that these proceedings do have serious consequences for the respondent. The rules of natural justice require that the respondent should know the allegations made against him and have a proper opportunity to answer them. But the rules of natural justice are flexible in their adaptation to particular circumstances and so long as the respondent has a proper opportunity to know and answer the allegations before the court reaches any decision on them, I do not see that fairness requires anything further. These are civil, not criminal, proceedings ...

However, this is not a case where the respondent has been guilty of any dishonesty, nor is it a case where a director, having failed with one company, has promptly started the same business up again with another company. I do not regard it as among the most serious of cases. Nevertheless, having regard to the fact that there are no less than four companies which have gone into liquidation leaving substantial debts unpaid and virtually no assets and that complaints can, in my view, justifiably be made of the respondent's conduct as director of such companies, I reach the conclusion that the third condition of s300(1) is satisfied and that his conduct as director of those companies makes him unfit to be concerned with the management of a company.

Should the court, in the exercise of its discretion, make a disqualification order? On the one hand there is the conclusion to which I have just referred, based solely on the respondent's conduct as a director of the four companies, which strongly points to an order for disqualification being made ... On the other hand the respondent has put before me a number of facts, in particular relating to other companies of which he is a director ...

A plea that a disqualification order will cause undue hardship may often fail to win the sympathy of the court because it is always open to a man to carry on business otherwise than through the medium of a limited liability company. But in this case, on the unchallenged evidence, very substantial business is being done through the medium of other companies of which the respondent is a director, and it is not unreasonable that this volume of work should be conducted through limited liability companies. The respondent relies further on the evidence that he has not taken steps to ensure that annual returns and accounts are filed on time in the future. His accountant has confirmed that his companies are now up-to-date in this regard ...

The respondent has apologised for his defaults and expressed regret for the failure of the four companies. In all the circumstances, I have reached the conclusion that I should take an exceptional course in this case and that I should not make a disqualification order. But the respondent has only by the narrowest margin escaped disqualification. I trust that he has truly learned his lesson.'

Commentary
Section 300 of the Companies Act 1985 was repealed by the Insolvency Act 1985: see now the Company Directors Disqualification Act 1986.

Gibson Davies Ltd, Re [1995] BCC 11 Chancery Division (Companies Court) (Sir Mervyn Davies)

Company Directors Disqualification Act 1986 s17 – whether the appellant could be given leave to act as a director

Facts
The director was disqualified in his absence on 22 March 1993 for a period of five years. His conduct while a director of Gibson Davies & Co Ltd (GDC) amounted to unfitness. The conduct relied on involved:

1. the granting of a preference contrary to s239 Insolvency Act 1986;
2. continuing to trade after distraint had been levied by the Inland Revenue, thereby eroding the position of creditors;
3. the raising of misleading invoices;

4. paying undue remuneration at a time when the company's losses were increasing; and

5. failure to file audited accounts.

The director then applied, pursuant to s17 CDDA 1986, to be allowed to act as a director of a company called Congratulations Franchising Ltd (CFL), whose main business was the selling of wedding presents contained in the company's catalogue. The appellant had set up a similar business, called Congratulations Ltd, in Ireland which was successful. He now wanted to carry on the same business in England through CFL, and be a director of the company. His application was a dismissed and he now appealed against that decision.

Held

The appeal was successful and leave to allow the appellant to act as a director was granted. Sir Mervyn Davies was satisfied that there was a need to make such an order and that the public would remain adequately protected, by virtue of the safeguards offered by the appellant.

Sir Mervyn Davies:

'Since I am of the view that there is need for the making of an order, one goes on to consider whether, if an order is made, there will be adequate protection for the public. The appellant offered the following safeguards:

(1) no cheque or financial agreement on behalf of the company be signed or executed by the appellant alone;

(2) any director's loan owed by the company to the appellant shall not be repaid unless all creditors of the company are paid first;

(3) the appellant shall not be granted or accept any security over the company assets;

(4) the appellant's total emoluments from the company shall not exceed £380 per week or such greater sum as shall hereafter be agreed in writing by the Secretary of State, such consent not to be unreasonably refused;

(5) the appellant shall procure the company to file annual returns and accounts at Companies House within the time limits set out in the *Companies Act* 1985;

(6) the appellant will procure the company to complete the implementation of the accounting controls as set out by Mr Heer of Robson Rhodes [the company's chartered accountants] in his affidavit sworn on 3 February 1994;

(7) the appellant will procure the company to prepare monthly management accounts and submit the said accounts to Robson Rhodes or to the company's auditors for the time being;

(8) Robson Rhodes, or the company's auditors for the time being, shall be instructed to report to the board of directors in writing any matters of concern relating to the management or financial control of the company and in default of prompt and appropriate action by the directors of the company will bring these matters to the attention of the Secretary of State's solicitors;

(9) in the event that the company seeks to change the identity of its auditors the appellant will procure the company only to instruct auditors who are willing to accept and act upon the obligations set out above;

(10) the appellant will take no step as a shareholder or director of Congratulations Ltd (ie the Irish company) which would in any way impede, direct or control the activities of the company.

The first nine of those safeguards were offered before Judge Gosling [the judge at first instance] in written form. The tenth safeguard was discussed but never precisely formulated. The accounting controls referred to in item (6) are: (a) all cheques over £2,500 to be signed by more than one director; (b) all cheques below £2,500 to be signed by both Mr Davies [the appellant director] and the company's financial controller, Mrs Richards; (c) monthly management accounts to be reviewed by Robson Rhodes; (d) the company to complete the implementation of the internal accounting control recommended by Robson Rhodes; (e) Robson Rhodes to accept an obligation to bring to the attention of the directors in writing any matters of concern relating to the management or financial control of the company and in default of prompt and appropriate action by the directors to bring these matters to the attention of the applicant's solicitors.

I am of the opinion that the appellant ought to be allowed to act as a director of Franchising by an order which incorporates the safeguards set out above. Accordingly, I allow the appeal and make such an order as I have mentioned.'

Commentary
This is the first case based on an appeal under s17 CDDA 1986.

Grayan Building Services Ltd (In Liquidation), Re [1995] 3 WLR 1 Court of Appeal (Neill, Hoffmann and Henry LJJ)
Appeal against a refusal to make a disqualification order

Facts
In disqualification proceedings brought against two directors under s6 Company Directors Disqualification Act 1986, Arden J found the following allegations were proved:

1. failure to keep proper accounting records;
2. failure to file audited accounts on time;
3. preferential payments to creditors had been made contrary to s239 Insolvency Act 1986;
4. trading while insolvent.

In respect of the preference payments, their Lordships felt that as the liquidator had used other remedies against the directors, which had made them realise the effects of the payments, this conduct no longer made them unfit. Despite serious shortcomings, their conduct did not make them unfit so as to be disqualified. The Secretary of State for Trade and Industry appealed.

Held
The appeal was allowed. Hoffmann LJ felt that a disqualification order for two years was required. Disqualification for unfitness under s6 was mandatory. It is not permissible to argue that the subsequent conduct of the director shows that he has now seen the error of his ways, so that this should be taken into account when deciding whether or not to disqualify him.

Hoffmann LJ:

'Mr Bannister [counsel for the first defendant] submitted that this required the court to be satisfied that the defendant was at the time of the hearing a person who, for the future protection of the public, should not be allowed to concern himself in the management of a company. For this purpose the court could look at any evidence which showed that despite the defendant's shortcomings in the past, he was unlikely to offend again.

I do not agree. It is true that the subsection uses the present tense "makes" but I agree with Peter Gibson J in *In re Bath Glass Ltd* [1988] BCLC 329, 332 that this means only that the court has to make the decision on the evidence put forward at the hearing. In that case the judge, rightly in my view, rejected the submission that the court could consider conduct "other than conduct as a director of the insolvent company or other companies relied upon by the [official receiver] to obtain a disqualification order." The court is concerned solely with the conduct specified by the Secretary of State or official receiver under rule 3(3) of the Insolvent Companies (Disqualification of Unfit Directors) Proceedings Rules 1987. It must decide whether that conduct, viewed cumulatively and taking into account any extenuating circumstances, has fallen below the standards of probity and competence appropriate for persons fit to be directors of companies.

In my view the construction for which Mr Bannister contends is not consistent with the court having a *duty* to disqualify a director whose conduct has shown him to be unfit. If the court always had to be satisfied at the hearing that the protection of the public required a period of disqualification, there would be no need to make disqualification mandatory. Even if the court had a discretion, it would not, having formed the view that disqualification was necessary in the public interest, be acting judicially if it did not make a disqualification order. The purpose of making disqualification mandatory was to ensure that everyone whose conduct had fallen below the appropriate standard was disqualified for at least two years, whether in the individual case the court thought that this was necessary in the public interest or not. Parliament has decided that it is occasionally necessary to disqualify a company director to encourage the others. Or as Sir Donald Nicholls V-C said in *In re Swift 736 Ltd* [1993] BCLC 896, 899:

> "Those who make use of limited liability must do so with a proper sense of responsibility. The directors' disqualification procedure is an important sanction introduced by Parliament to raise standards in this regard."

If this should be thought too harsh a view, it must be remembered that a disqualified director can always apply for leave under section 17 and the question of whether he has shown himself unlikely to offend again will obviously be highly material to whether he is granted leave or not. It may also be relevant by way of mitigation on the length of disqualification although I note that the guidelines in *In re Sevenoaks Stationers (Retail) Ltd* [1991] Ch 164 are solely by reference to the seriousness of the conduct in question.'

Moorgate Metals Ltd, Re [1995] BCC 143 Chancery Division (Warner J)

Whether respondent was a de facto or shadow director

Facts

The case concerned disqualification proceedings against two directors, R and H. The company's business was that of a metal merchant, reselling container loads of scrap metal. One issue in the case was whether R was a de facto director. He was not formally appointed as a director as he was an undischarged bankrupt. However, R controlled the company's entire trading operation.

Held

R was a de facto director.

Warner J:

> **'The case against Mr Rawlinson**
> As regards Mr Rawlinson the first question is whether he was a director of Moorgate within the meaning of that expression in s6(1) of the Act. In his affidavit Mr Rawlinson contended that he was not. He pointed to the absence from the Act of any express mention of a de facto director and he referred to the definition of a shadow director in s22(5) of the Act. He said that his position was that of metal trader of the company; that every trading company on the Metal Exchange employed a metal trading expert like himself; and that the majority of such employees were not directors. He accepted that he 'controlled the company's entire trading operation', but said that that was because of his professional expertise.
>
> Mr Davis-White referred me to a number of authorities on the matter, namely *Re Lo-Line Electric Motors Ltd* (1988) 4 BCC 415, *Re Tasbian Ltd (No 3)* [1991] BCC 435 and [1992] BCC 358, *Re Cargo Agency Ltd* [1992] BCC 388, and *Re Hydrodan (Corby) Ltd* [1994] BCC 161. It appears to me clear from those authorities:

(1) that the word 'director' in s6(1) includes a 'de facto director'; and

(2) that for this purpose a de facto director is a person who in fact acts as a director, though not appointed as such.

Some of the expressions used by Millett J in the *Hydrodan* case could be construed as meaning that, for a person to be held to have been a de facto director, the label 'director' must have been attached to him. But I am sure that Millett J did not mean that. He was concerned to distinguish between a de facto director and a shadow director, the latter being a person in accordance with whose directions or instructions the directors of a company (whether de jure or de facto) are accustomed to act.

I have come to the conclusion that Mr Rawlinson was a de factor director of Moorgate. I have already mentioned many of the facts that have led me to that conclusion: the fact that Moorgate came into existence as a result of Mr Rawlinson inviting Mr Huhtala to join him in a business that he was minded to set up; the fact that Mr Rawlinson and Mr Huhtala shared the responsibilities of managing the company and that Mr Rawlinson was in sole charge of the company's trading with no limit on the extent of the commitments that he could enter into on behalf of the company; and the fact that Mr Rawlinson and Mr Huhtala received equal remuneration. (Mr Huhtala had the additional benefit of motor cars but the purchase of company cars for both Mr Huhtala and Mr Rawlinson was authorised at the board meeting on 4 July 1989. I was not told why none was in fact purchased for Mr Rawlinson.) Other factors support the conclusion. Mr Huhtala told me that he consulted Mr Rawlinson on all important decisions, including the appointment of bankers, the appointment of solicitors, the appointment of Mr Robertson's firm as accountants and the investment in CIP. Indeed it is clear (as I have mentioned) that Mr Robertson thought Mr Rawlinson was acting as if he were a director of the company and in his letter to the official receiver of 11 December 1989 Mr Robertson said "We were instructed by both Mr Huhtala and Mr Rawlinson …" When the company's main bank account was moved from Barclays Bank to Commerzbank, although Mr Huhtala was named in the mandate as the sole signatory on the account, Commerzbank were informed that both Mr Rawlinson (who was described as "chief executive") and Mr Huhtala (who was named second and described as "managing director") had authority to give instructions over the telephone to effect payment orders. Lastly, there is in evidence a promotional brochure published by Moorgate which repeatedly refers to Mr Rawlinson (there described as "senior trader") and Mr Huhtala (described as "managing director") as "partners". Again Mr Rawlinson is named first. The overall picture conveyed by the evidence is of Mr Huhtala and Mr Rawlinson as equals, running the company between them, and not of Mr Rawlinson being Mr Huhtala's subordinate in any way. In my view Mr Rawlinson was a director in all but name.

Having reached that conclusion I need not advert to the question whether Mr Rawlinson could be regarded as having been a shadow director of Moorgate.'

Commentary

Whether or not a person is fulfilling the functions of a director can be a difficult question to answer. The judgement of Warner J contains a number of useful factors which his Lordship relied on to decide that the overall picture was that R was a director. Once again the court stressed that the label attached to a director is not conclusive. Simply calling someone a director, or vice versa, will not necessarily decide the issue.

Pamstock Ltd, Re [1994] BCC 264 Chancery Division (Vinelott J)

Company Directors Disqualification Act 1986 s6 – whether director who was the provider of venture capital was unfit

Facts

The respondent director, I, specialised in assisting small, and often newly formed, companies by providing financial advice and obtaining outside finance. The new companies were often formed under the Business Enterprise Scheme and I, as the provider of venture capital, was often required to accept a directorship. The official receiver complained about the conduct of I in relation to ten companies over a 15-year period. In relation to Pamstock Ltd, the allegations by the official receiver against I were that:

1. He had allowed the company to trade whilst insolvent.
2. He failed to give sufficient attention to the financial affairs of the company, in particular, by allowing cheques to be tendered in the knowledge that they would not be met.
3. He failed to ensure the proper filing of annual accounts and returns.

Pamstock Ltd was undercapitalised and was reliant on bank borrowing and borrowing from the participators to finance its trade. As well as making losses in every year, Crown debts, such as unpaid VAT and PAYE deductions, increased each year and by the end of its life, these debts financed the company to a large extent.

Held

I's conduct as a director of Pamstock Ltd amounted to unfitness and he was disqualified for a period of two years. I was not found to be unfit in relation to the other companies, despite allegations of trading whilst insolvent and failing to submit annual returns. Despite the fact that he had not been concerned in the affairs of any company that had become insolvent since 1987–88, the court had to take into account past conduct, even if it was now satisfied that the director was now behaving responsibly.

Vinelott J:

'I accept that this is not the case of a director who has taken large remuneration or who has obtained other benefits from a company at the expense of creditors. The respondent obtained no benefit beyond the use of a flat for the purposes of the company's business and of course he suffered financially to a greater extent than the creditors even if taken as a whole. However the question is not whether there was culpable misconduct in the sense that he benefited himself at the expense of the creditors. The failure of Pamstock with substantial debts which could only be met if and to the extent that the respondent personally honoured them came about in part because he failed to put into place an adequate system of management and, when the company was clearly running into difficulty, allowed it to continue to trade beyond the point at which trading should have ceased. To that extent the respondent in my judgment fell short of the standard of conduct which is today expected of a director of a company which enjoys the privilege of limited liability. In this context the failure to file accounts and returns promptly is also a serious default. Creditors (including, in this case, the Crown) may be prejudiced if accounts which would have shown that a company's assets exceed its liabilities and that it is continuing to trade at a loss and is dependent upon the continued support of its participators are not filed.

I reach this conclusion with regret. I have had the advantage of seeing the respondent give oral evidence when he was skillfully cross-examined by Mr Chivers. There is no evidence that the respondent has been involved in the affairs of any company which has ended in an insolvent winding-up since 1987–88. He told me and I accept that in recent years he has made a practice of ensuring that a chartered accountant is appointed secretary of all companies with which he is concerned and is instructed to ensure that annual accounts and returns are promptly filed. The respondent seemed to me (so far as I can judge from the evidence before me) to be a man who today is capable of discharging his duties as a director, honestly and diligently. His failures in relation to Pamstock came at a time when his time was fully occupied with the affairs of other companies and when he was under considerable financial pressure. However, I cannot, I think, be sure that these difficulties wholly excuse the respondent's serious misconduct in relation to Pamstock.

Nor can it be said that his subsequent conduct justifies the conclusion that his past misconduct should be overlooked upon the ground that there is no reason today for saying that a disqualification order is needed for the protection of the public. A disqualification order must to some extent express the view of the court as to the seriousness of past misconduct. As I observed at the beginning of this judgment, a disqualification order is likely to have a disproportionately severe effect on him. Apart from the stigma of a disqualification order it will be difficult and may be impossible for him to continue in his career as the provider of venture capital and as a professional non-executive director if he must seek leave before accepting any appointment. However, as Mr Collings expressed it, under the legislation as it now stands, I am required to have tunnel vision and to consider whether in relation to Pamstock the respondent's conduct fell short of the minimum standard which the court today requires to be observed by the director of a company which enjoys the privilege of limited liability, and if it does, to impose a disqualification order for a minimum of two years. I have reached the conclusion after anxious consideration and some hesitation that in the circumstances I am bound to make a disqualification order. In the circumstances of this case I think I am justified for making the order for the minimum period of two years.'

Commentary

Vinelott J took the opportunity in this case to question whether it was right that a director should have to face a mandatory disqualification order under s6, where the conduct complained of was some years ago and where the court was now satisfied that the director was behaving responsibly. He urged those currently reviewing the operation of the Company Directors Disqualification Act 1986 to consider whether this is necessary. His Lordship also criticised the practice of the official receiver to include in the evidence every matter which could be the possible subject of complaint. Some matters, which do not amount to serious failures, would be better put before the court in the form of a schedule.

Rex Williams Leisure plc (In Administration), Re [1994] 3 WLR 745 Court of Appeal (Russell, Staughton and Hoffmann LJJ)

Company Directors Disqualification Act 1986 s8 – disqualification after investigation of a company – procedural points

Facts

The respondent directors were the boxing promoter, Mr Frank Warren, and a solicitor, Mr Peter Sealey. They were both directors of the company whose principal business was the supply of business machines. The company agreed to buy from Mr Warren shares which he owned in another company for £2m. The purchase did not go ahead, but £200,000 was paid to him by the company, which Mr Sealey authorised. The money was not repaid at the time Rex Williams Leisure plc went into administration in April 1990.

An investigation of the company took place under s447 Companies Act 1985 and the inspectors concluded that the money had simply been extracted from the company in breach of the directors' fiduciary duties. The result was that the Secretary of State applied for a disqualification order under s8 Company Directors Disqualification Act 1986. He then filed his affidavit evidence against the directors in accordance with the Insolvent Companies (Disqualification of Unfit Directors) Proceedings Rules 1987 (SI 1987 No 2023). The next step would have been for the directors to file their affidavit evidence in reply. However, at this stage they sought the following relief:

1. An order striking out the summons seeking the disqualification orders on the ground that it was an abuse of process to hear the application while civil proceedings to recover the £200,000 were still pending.
2. A declaration that the directors were entitled to give evidence or call witnesses at the hearing, without first having filed affidavit evidence.
3. An order striking out those parts of the affidavit evidence filed on behalf of the Secretary of State, which included statements made by persons other than the directors themselves. Such statements, they argued, amounted to hearsay.

The judge refused the relief sought and the defendants appealed.

Held

The appeal was dismissed. The relief in (1) was dismissed as it was felt that it would be absurd to hold up the Secretary of State's application to disqualify directors indefinitely by other proceedings over which he has no control. The relief in (2) was dismissed on the ground that the words in the 1987 Rules were to be interpreted as meaning that the evidence that the director wishes the court to take into account must first be filed on affidavit. The hearsay relief sought in (3) was also dismissed on the basis that it was impliedly admissible in proceedings under the Company Directors Disqualification Act 1986.

Staughton LJ:

'I agree that this appeal should be dismissed. Of the two points which seem to me to be most significant, the first is whether the Insolvent Companies (Disqualification of Unfit Directors) Proceedings Rules 1987 are ultra vires. It is said that they are, if and to the extent that they do not allow a respondent to call evidence unless he has filed an affidavit of the proposed witness. That is said to conflict with s16(1) of the Company Directors Disqualification Act 1986, which provides that the person against whom an order is sought "may appear and himself give evidence or call witnesses".

The Act of 1986 contemplates in s21, although somewhat indirectly, that rules may be made. In my judgment, it enables rules to deal with how evidence shall be given and witnesses called; and in particular it permits a requirement that affidavits shall first be filed. This is essentially a rule as to how the right conferred by s16(1) shall be exercised, and not a derogation from that right.

The second point that has troubled me concerns hearsay evidence. RSC O.41, r.5 provides that, subject to a number of exceptions which do not apply in the present case, "an affidavit may contain only such facts as the deponent is able of his own knowledge to prove".

How then can the Secretary of State be entitled to use affidavits of information and belief in disqualification proceedings? As Hoffmann LJ has shown, this stems from an implied statutory provision as to the use of hearsay as evidence, or at any rate as provisional evidence until it is challenged. That doctrine is now of respectable antiquity, having been established between 1967 and 1975. I would for my part have hesitated to accept it when first propounded. But as it has existed for a substantial period of time, during which relevant statutory provisions have been replaced and re-enacted or amended, I would not now alter it.'

Seagull Manufacturing Co Ltd, Re (In Liquidation) (No 2) [1994] 2 WLR 453
Chancery Division (Mary Arden QC sitting as a deputy High Court judge)

Company Directors Disqualification Act 1986 – service of proceedings outside the jurisdiction

Facts

Seagull Manufacturing Co Ltd was in liquidation. Its director, Slinn, was a British subject resident in the Channel Islands. He sought a declaration, inter alia, that disqualification proceedings served upon him pursuant to s6 of the Company Directors Disqualification Act 1986 (on the grounds of unfitness), were improperly served on him as the court had no jurisdiction, since at all material times he was resident and domiciled in the Channel Islands.

Held

That, in the circumstances, the court did have jurisdiction over the director even though he resided outside England.

Mary Arden QC:

'In the present case, the positions taken by counsel in their submission on jurisdiction have been widely different. Mr Teverson, for Mr Slinn, while reserving, he said, the right to argue elsewhere that the Company Directors Disqualification Act 1986 applied only to directors present within the jurisdiction, submitted before me that the limitation which ought fairly to be implied into the Company Directors Disqualification Act 1986 is that the activities which it is said rendered him unfit to be a director should either take place in the jurisdiction or be directed from abroad. Thus, the activities of a director would only be relevant to the extent that they had some effect here. Mr Davis, on the other hand, submitted that s6(1) applied to any person, that is to a British subject or a foreigner, irrespective of their presence here at the time the activities took place.

Section 6 of the Company Directors Disqualification Act 1986 contains no express statement of any jurisdictional requirement. Indeed, on its face it applies to any person and to any conduct. However, when it is analysed in a manner similar to that undertaken in *In re Paramount Airways Ltd* [1993] Ch 223 it is, in my judgment, clear that it too has no jurisdictional limitation as a matter of plain implication. The word "company" in s6(1) includes any company which may be wound up under the Act: see s22(2). In this way companies incorporated in other jurisdictions are included: see s220 and 221 of the Insolvency Act 1986. In the case of foreign companies the likelihood is that some of the directors will not be persons resident here, or even foreigners present here, when the conduct relied upon as rendering them unfit takes place. Accordingly, in my judgment, Parliament must be presumed to have been legislating not simply for British subjects and foreigners who happened to be here at the relevant time, but also for other foreigners who were out of the jurisdiction at the critical time. Likewise, in relation to conduct, s6(1) contains no territorial restriction. Accordingly, the court must ask what is the conduct in respect of which Parliament must have been presumed to have been legislating?

There are two factors which, in my judgment, indicate that the conduct in question in s6(1) need not be conduct which occurred within the jurisdiction. The first such factor is the definition of "company" to which I have already referred. This includes foreign companies and the acts of the directors of those companies are likely to have taken place abroad, and Parliament must have been presumed to have been legislating with that in mind. Secondly, in these days of modern communications a person may conduct himself as a director in such a way as to affect persons within the jurisdiction without himself ever entering the jurisdiction. Again, in my judgment, Parliament must be presumed to have been legislating with this in mind and, accordingly, by plain implication to be taken to have been referring to conduct wherever committed.

Were there a distinction in s6(1) between foreigners based on presence, the results would be anomalous. For example, proceeding could be brought under that section against a director who from his office in London had caused a company to do acts in a foreign country which had no effect on the British public. Yet, on the other hand, a director who was a citizen of another country and who conducted the company's business here from abroad could not be proceeded against under s6(1) since his activities would be outside the scope of s6. In my judgment, Parliament cannot have intended those anomalous results. They are significant because as Dillon LJ, with whom Butler-Sloss and Staughton LJJ agreed, said in *In re Sevenoaks Stationers (Retail) Ltd* [1991] Ch 164, 176, in a passage to which Mr Teverson referred me:

"It is beyond dispute that the purpose of s6 is to protect the public, and in particular potential creditors of companies, from losing money through companies becoming insolvent when the directors of those companies are people unfit to be concerned in the management of a company."

Accordingly, as a matter of construction, I prefer Mr Davis' approach to that of Mr Teverson. Moreover, it seems to me that Mr Teverson's construction would lead to anomalous results. It would mean that disqualification proceedings could not be brought against a foreign director whose activities, which had been exclusively conducted abroad, had shown him to be unfit to be a director even though he might seek to expand his activities and to act as a director in England.

... In the circumstances, I decline to make the declaration sought.'

Commentary

In earlier proceedings the court had to decide whether Mr Slinn could be served with proceedings s◌ that he could be ordered to attend for public examination by the Official Receiver, in London, pursuan to s133 1A 1986.

Seagull Manufacturing Co Ltd, Re (1993) The Times 8 February Court of Appeal (Lloyd, Hirst LJJ and Peter Gibson J)

Public examination of director – court's jurisdiction

Facts

The company was being compulsorily wound up and its director, Mr Slinn, a British subject, now lived in Alderney, Channel Islands. In the view of the Official Receiver the affairs of the company could not be duly wound up without the public examination of Mr Slinn in order to establish his conduct of the affairs of the company and the application of its assets. The Official Receiver maintained that the court had jurisdiction to order the public examination of Mr Slinn since upon its true construction s133 of the Insolvency Act 1986 empowered the court to order the attendance of a British subject who was or had been an officer of a company registered in England and Wales being wound up by the court notwithstanding his residence abroad.

Held

This was the case as s133 of the 1986 Act, on its true construction, plainly implied that it applied to all who fell within a class of persons specified in s133(1), whether they were British subjects or not and whether they were within the jurisdiction of the English court or not at the relevant time. Hirst LJ explained that an examination under s133 was to enable the Official Receiver to investigate, inter alia, the causes of a company's business failure for which the officer was or might be partly responsible. That official investigation was of great public importance and it would be frustrated if the appellant's contention was right that the company official was immune from public examination if he happened to be abroad, or if the company had been defrauded and he had fled the jurisdiction. Those were not fanciful illustrations. Therefore all officers as described in s133(1), whether inside or outside the jurisdiction, were within its legislative grasp, and there were no territorial limitations.

Secretary of State for Trade and Industry v *Bannister* [1995] BCC 1027 Court of Appeal (Glidewell and Morritt LJJ and Sir John May)

Court does have power to suspend a disqualification order pending appeal

Facts

A director was disqualified for a five-year period under s6 Company Directors Disqualification Act (CDDA) 1986. His application to the judge for a stay of execution pending appeal against the order was refused. The director appealed.

Held

The director was unsuccessful. The Court of Appeal does have jurisdiction to suspend a disqualification order pending appeal. However, the normal relief which should be requested is leave to act as a director, under s17 CDDA 1986, unless the case is exceptional, which this case was not. The prospects of the director's appeal being successful were slim, and it is appropriate to ask what level of public protection will be lost pending the appeal.

Glidewell LJ:

> 'Despite the persuasive argument advanced on behalf of the Secretary of State, I also am clearly of the opinion that the High Court and the Court of Appeal have an inherent power to grant a stay of an order disqualifying a person from acting as a company director. Nevertheless I wish to emphasise that this power should only be exercised in exceptional circumstances. In most cases, the provisions of s17 of the Act

entitling the person subject to a disqualification order to apply for leave to act, pending appeal, as a director of a specified company is sufficient to ensure that no unjust hardship is caused. Moreover, this course has the advantage that the grant of such leave may be subject to conditions, which should ensure leave is only granted if the court is satisfied that the company has proper financial advice and control. If, therefore, the court is minded to exercise discretion in favour of the disqualified director at all, in the great majority of cases an application under s17 will be the appropriate course to enable it to do so.'

Commentary

No view was expressed on whether a county court judge could suspend an order pending appeal.

Sevenoaks Stationers (Retail) Ltd, Re [1990] BCC 765; [1990] 3 WLR 1165 Court of Appeal (Dillon, Butler-Sloss and Staughton LJJ)

Disqualification of directors – guidelines

Facts

A director of a company which had become insolvent and gone into liquidation had been disqualified, under s6 of the Company Directors Disqualification Act 1986, for seven years. On appeal, he contended that this period was too long.

Held

In all the circumstances, the period of disqualification would be reduced to five years. It was a paramount requirement that the director should know the charges that he had to meet; here, the judge had found further allegations established which had not been included in the Official Receiver's report. Further, the non-payment by a company of sums due to the Crown in respect of PAYE, national insurance contributions and value added tax, collectively known as Crown debts, was not automatically to be regarded as evidence of unfitness of the directors: here, the director had not 'ripped off' the public and pocketed the proceeds. On the other hand, there had here been incompetence or negligence in a very marked degree and, contrary to the suggestion of Sir Nicolas Browne-Wilkinson V-C in *Re Lo-Line Electric Motors Ltd* [1988] Ch 477, it was not necessary for incompetence to be 'total'.

Dillon LJ:

'The main point ... on this appeal was ... that the period of seven years' suspension imposed by the judge was too long. In that regard this appeal has an importance beyond its own facts, since it is the first appeal against a disqualification order which has come to this court.

Counsel ... took the view that the disqualification order was an order made by the judge in his discretion with which an appellate court could only interfere on the grounds set out in *G v G* [1985] 1 WLR 647 or *Hadmor Productions Ltd v Hamilton* [1983] 1 AC 191.

I do not, however, wholly share that view in this particular case because guidelines have not yet been laid down, and fairness requires that there should be a degree of similarity between the periods of disqualification imposed by different judges or different courts for similar offences. Of course no two cases are entirely similar and it is fundamental that every case must be decided on its own facts and circumstances. But I found certain statistics produced by the Official Receiver somewhat disturbing, viz in 1989, of 115 disqualification orders made in the High Court under s6, only one, that against Mr Cruddas, imposed disqualification for more than five years, whereas of 123 such orders made in county courts 18 involved disqualification for more than five years, and in the first six months of 1990 of 79 disqualification orders made in the High Court under s6 only four imposed disqualification for more than five years whereas of 96 such orders made in county courts again 18 imposed disqualification for more than five years.

Under s6 the court having jurisdiction to make a disqualification order is, where the company is in compulsory liquidation, the court by which the company is being wound up. That is likely to depend, under s117 of the Insolvency Act 1986, on where the petitioning creditor found it most convenient to present the petition for winding up. It seems surprising if it were the case that the applications for disqualification orders under s6 made in the High Court should have been in significantly less serious cases than those made in the county courts.

I would for my part indorse the division of the potential 15-year disqualification period into three brackets ..., viz: (i) the top bracket of disqualification for periods over ten years should be reserved for particularly serious cases – these may include cases where a director who has already had one period of disqualification imposed on him falls to be disqualified yet again; (ii) the minimum bracket of two to five years' disqualification should be applied where, though disqualification is mandatory, the case is, relatively, not very serious and (iii) the middle bracket of disqualification for from six to ten years should apply for serious cases which do not merit the top bracket.'

T & D Services (Timber Preservation & Damp Proofing Contractors) Ltd, Re [1990] BCC 592 High Court (Vinelott J)

Disqualification of director – length

Facts
The respondent had been a director of four companies which had ended in insolvent liquidation, in three of the cases before the Company Directors Disqualification Act 1986 came into force. He was now managing director of South Place Investments Ltd and the Official Receiver sought his disqualification under the 1986 Act.

Held
In all the circumstances, the respondent would be disqualified for ten years. In relation to T & D alone, he had, amongst other things, bought a property from the company at a gross undervalue and his application of a local authority grant had been grossly improper.

Vinelott J:

'The conduct of the respondent in relation to T & D alone shows a serious want of probity such as to compel the conclusion that he is wholly unfit to be concerned in the management of a company. However, in deciding what is the appropriate period for an order under s6(1), I must also have regard to his conduct in relation to other companies ...

This is a serious case – the most serious that has yet come before me. The respondent manipulated the affairs of T & D for his own benefit and to the detriment of creditors and induced the local authority to advance public moneys to a company which was not entitled to receive them and which he knew would not be in a position to repay them. All these companies (and in particular T & D) were financed by the retention of moneys due to the Crown, much of which was allowed to build up over a long period of time. The affairs of all these companies were conducted without regard to a director's duty to see that proper books of account are kept and that returns are promptly made to the Companies Registry.

However, the respondent asks that the court should have regard to the effect which a disqualification order will have upon the future of the company now known as South Place Investment Ltd and its employees. It is said that this company is now profitable and expanding and is an important employer in the locality in which it operates – the Thames Valley. The respondent estimates that the workforce has expanded from 11 at the end of 1986 to 30 today and that the company now has a turnover of £1.2m a year. He claims that if he were to cease to be a director the business of this company would disintegrate. The only other director, Mr Ramsey, is a carpenter with no business experience. He, the respondent, has established a close relationship of trust and confidence with the company's suppliers – Dutch and German companies whom, he says, would be unlikely to deal with any other director. If the company were to cease to trade, employees thrown out of work would find it difficult to find other employment – in particular those employed at the company's premises in Henley-on-Thames, and their specialist skills would be wasted.

I need hardly say that I am reluctant to take any step that might imperil the livelihood of innocent employees. However, even if I thought that a disqualification order would have this result it would still be my duty to make the order: in my judgment, it is impossible on the evidence that I have seen to avoid the conclusion that the respondent has shown himself unfit to be concerned in the management of a company and a disqualification order for two years is therefore mandatory. I should, however say that I am by no means satisfied that the position of this company is as secure, or that its prospects are as hopeful, as is represented by the respondent.

The Official Receiver has pointed out that the accounts for the year to 31 December 1987 (which are the most recent audited accounts – they were filed on 29 March 1989) show a loss on current trading for the years to 31 December 1985 and 31 December 1986 and a deficit of current assets over current liabilities of £200,000. The capital and reserves amount to £18,000 which is a very small capital base for a company with a turnover of £1.2m. Moreover, during the period covered by these accounts, the company's Crown debts increased from just under £9,000 to just under £28,000. Bearing in mind the history of the other companies with which the respondent has been concerned, the future of this company must be regarded as uncertain. If the business is capable of being successfully run others may be found who will be willing to undertake the responsibility for it. The employees could then face the future with greater confidence. As to the relationship with the Dutch and German suppliers, if those who take over the control of the company take the view that the respondent's relationship with them is important to the company's future, the respondent can be employed in a capacity which will enable him to continue to deal with them on behalf of the company and, if necessary, an application can be made to the court to modify the terms of the disqualification order to enable that to be done.

In view of the respondent's present position, I shall defer the operation of the order for two weeks to give him an opportunity of deciding whether the company could continue to trade under new management with or without his assistance in dealing with Dutch and German suppliers. I will hear an application for an extension of this period or for an order permitting him to act in a specified and subordinate position at short notice during that period. Subject to that the disqualification will be for a period of ten years from today.'

Wimbledon Village Restaurant Ltd, Re; Secretary of State for Trade and Industry v *Thomson and Others* [1994] BCC 753 Chancery Division (Michael Hart QC sitting as a deputy High Court judge)

Company Directors Disqualification Act s6 – court refused to find that two executive directors and one non-executive director were unfit

Facts

The business of Wimbledon Village Restaurant Ltd (WVR) was that of a restaurant proprietor. It carried on business from March 1985 to late September 1989. It went into creditors' voluntary liquidation in November 1989 with debts of £327,356. The respondent directors were Mrs Woods ('W') and two brothers, Graham and Ian Thomson ('G' and 'I'). The management of the company was left to G and I. W was a non-executive director and held her directorship to protect her position as the unlimited guarantor of the company's overdraft. The allegations made against the directors, by the Secretary of State for Trade and Industry, were that:

1. Since February 1989 the directors knew or ought to have known that the company was trading whilst insolvent.

2. They had improperly used the company's bank account by issuing cheques which they knew or ought to have known would not be honoured.
3. They had failed to co-operate in the liquidation.
4. They failed to file annual accounts for the year ending 31 March 1988.
5. On one occasion there was a failure to file an annual return.

Held

In relation to allegation (1), the judge felt that I and G had not paid sufficient regard to the interests of creditors. Allegations (2) and (3) were not proved, while (4) and (5) were proved. Bearing in mind some special factors of the case, all three directors were found not to be unfit. The special factors referred to were:

1. With hindsight, the then economic climate was encouraging a degree of false optimism within the business community. It was also a climate which suffered from unpredictable instabilities, such as a rise in minimum lending rates from 7.55 per cent in May 1988 to 14 per cent in May 1989.
2. The brothers believed that if the matters came to a head, they could sell the lease of the company's premises for £300,000. It was commercial misjudgment not to obtain a formal valuation of the lease, but an understandable one, given the explosion of commercial property prices in Wimbledon at that time.
3. The breakdown of the relationship between the two brothers, rather than incompetence, explained their failure to deal with the company's worsening situation.
4. The nature of the business made it difficult to say whether a bad period of trading was any more than a seasonal downturn. The true picture was blurred by a change in management, which in itself could be evidence that the directors had a genuine belief that the business was still viable.
5. The company had an unusual degree of accountancy experience, via the Thomson family, and their mute presence may have explained why professional advice was not sought earlier.
6. Neither G nor I prolonged the life of the company with any view to personal advantage.

Michael Hart QC:

'These factors mitigate, though they do not excuse, the deficiencies in the conduct of WVR to which I have referred. I have to decide in each case whether Ian's and Graham's acts and omissions were in 1988 and 1989 such as to demonstrate their unfitness now to be concerned in the management of a company. The Act requires me to consider whether the unfitness then displayed makes them unfit now to be so concerned: see *Re Bath Glass Ltd* [1988] 4 BCC 130 at p132 per Peter Gibson J. The law rightly exacts high standards of those who claim the privilege of trading with limited liability. Those standards are particularly appropriate where, as here, the adventure was fraught with risk from the outset. In my judgment the lapses from those standards in the case of both Ian and Graham demonstrated a failure to appreciate their responsibilities, and I have found that this failure did in the event damage trade creditors of the business. To that extent they may be said to have been shown to have been unfit to be concerned in the management of a company. It is not, however, every past impropriety which should lead to a conclusion that the director responsible is unfit. Having regard to what seem to me to have been the peculiar combination of family and commercial circumstances in which they found themselves in relation to WVR, I find myself left with a significant measure of doubt as to whether the lapses properly attributable to either of them were sufficiently serious as to compel a finding that either is now unfit to be concerned in the management of a company. That doubt is sufficiently strong to make me conclude that the correct course is to resolve it in their favour.

I turn now to the position of Mrs Woods. This has given me some difficulty. Mrs Woods played no role whatsoever as a director of WVR following the Diga takeover. The Thomsons appeared to her, as indeed they were, to be experienced in the relevant catering skills and to have available to them within their family all relevant accountancy and business skills. They were men of some personal worth. Her agreement with them was that they would be wholly responsible for the running of the business, she retaining a directorship simply as a means of being able to protect her own position as the unlimited guarantor of the company overdraft. In those circumstances, she neither asserted nor accepted any wider responsibility. In taking that attitude, she seems to me wholly to have misconceived her duties as the director of a limited liability company. She seems to have been completely unaware of the wider responsibilities owed by her to the company and its creditors. This attitude (or lack of one) in relation to WVR certainly points in the direction of her being unfit to be concerned in the management of a company. I do not, however, think that the mere fact that she had this attitude drives me inexorably to the conclusion that she is so unfit. I must measure her actual responsibility in relation to the allegations which I have found proved. Given the division of responsibilities on the board, while she must bear some responsibility for not having ascertained the state of the audit of the 1988 accounts, I have no doubt that Ian would have advised her after February 1989 that this matter was well in hand. Equally I have no doubt that until August 1989, the noises she had heard from Ian about the business were on the whole reassuring. I should add that her ability to take a more active interest was in any case compromised at the material time by her own domestic pressures: she had an adolescent daughter and a husband with Parkinson's disease to care for. She alone of the directors has in the event suffered financially, having found herself at the end of the day liable to the bank in the sum of some £140,000. I would also add that the allegations made against her appear to have been made and maintained by Mr Rose in the wholly mistaken belief that she was occupied full-time at the restaurant as 'a meeter and greeter'. In all the circumstances, while her failure to appreciate that she had duties as a director beyond those that she owed to herself was regrettable, and while I accept the argument that, had she appreciated the fact, events might have taken a different course, I do not find her misconduct in relation to WVR to have been so serious as to justify my finding her to be unfit to be concerned in the management of a company.'

Re Working Project Ltd; Re Fosterdown Ltd; Re Davies Flooring (Southern) Ltd
[1995] BCC 197 Chancery Division (Carnworth J)

Whether disqualification proceedings were possible after the companies had gone into liquidation

Facts
All three companies had gone into liquidation and disqualification proceedings had been commenced in the County Court against various directors under the unfitness ground in s6 CDDA 1986. The questions that Carnworth J had to decide was whether the court had lost jurisdiction to disqualify when the winding up of a company had been concluded. If it did, the second question was when was winding up concluded for this purpose.

Held
1. Disqualification proceedings already commenced in the County Court did not have to be aborted simply because the liquidator had completed his task.
2. The right to commence disqualification proceedings in the County Court ended when the winding up had been concluded
3. In relation to Fosterdown, proceedings were commenced only after the liquidator had lodged his final return, but before dissolution. The proceedings were allowed to continue because the winding up process does not end until dissolution of the company.

Carnworth J:

'It would be patently absurd if disqualification proceedings, validly commenced in the county court, were at risk of being aborted at any time (even in the middle of the hearing, or after judgment has been reserved), simply because the liquidator has completed his work. No one has suggested any sensible legislative purpose for such a rule. There is no reason why the continuing jurisdiction of the county court in the disqualification proceedings should depend on the speed with which the liquidator is able to progress the winding up. The disadvantages of such a rule (in terms of cost, uncertainty and delay) are obvious.

The only substantial argument in favour of that approach is that it accords with a literal reading of s6. Under subsection (1) it is the "court" which must make the disqualification order. On a strict reading of subs 3(a) and (b), the county court remains "the court" as defined only so long as the company "is being wound up". Accordingly, it is said, once the winding up has been completed, the county court ceases to have jurisdiction to make the disqualification order – whatever stage the proceedings have then reached.

It is, however, permissible to modify a literal reading, where it produces absurdity, and a reasonable alternative is available (see Cross, *Statutory Interpretation* (7th edn. 1990), p47). This is such a case. Where, as here, a section defines a particular court for the purposes of proceedings under that section, the correct inference, in my view, will normally be that the definition is directed to the *commencement* of proceedings. In the absence of express provision, Parliament can be assumed to have intended proceedings properly commenced in a particular tribunal to be carried to a conclusion in that tribunal. In subs 6(3), therefore, the words "for the purpose of the commencement of proceedings" should be regarded as implicit. On this view, provided the respective county courts had jurisdiction at the time of the commencement of proceedings, they were, and are, empowered to carry them to conclusion; and I so hold. It follows that the order made against Mr Hollington's client was validly made.'

His Lordship then considered, and rejected, another submission by counsel for the Secretary of State for Trade and Industry and the Official Receiver and continued:

'The other main question only arises in the case of *Fosterdown,* where the disqualification proceedings were commenced after the registration of the liquidator's final return, but before dissolution. At which point was the "winding up" complete – or, more precisely, at which point did the company cease to be a company "being wound up"?

It seems to me that the winding up is complete when the company is finally dissolved, and not before. The expression "winding up" naturally refers to the whole statutory process designed to secure the completion of the company's affairs, the distribution of its assets, and its final quietus. That process does not end until dissolution.'

Commentary

This is an important judgement on the disqualification jurisdiction of the County Court. If the court had held that jurisdiction to disqualify was lost when the liquidator had completed his task, this would have the unintentional effect of sabotaging a significant number of disqualification cases. Where the liquidation of a company is complete, by the dissolution of the company, then the right to commence proceedings in the County Court is lost. Here the solution is to commence proceedings in the High Court.

R v *Young* [1990] BCC 549 Court of Appeal (Farquharson LJ, Tudor Evans and Brooke JJ)

Disqualification of director – appeal

Facts

The appellant had pleaded guilty to a charge of managing a company as an undischarged bankrupt and on 8 November 1989 he had been conditionally discharged for three years and ordered to pay £400 towards the costs of the prosecution. In addition, he had been disqualified for two years under s2 of the Company Directors Disqualification Act 1986. The offence had been committed between January 1984 and June 1985 and he had been discharged from bankruptcy in 1986. He appealed against the disqualification order.

Held

The appeal would be allowed and the order quashed.

Brooke J:

'In passing sentence the judge referred to the very long time which had elapsed since these offences had been committed. He said that there was no evidence of a deliberate abuse of the system. It was not a case where somebody was exploiting limited liability in a cynical way with a disregard to proper responsibility or exploiting it because he was so stupid or ignorant that he was quite incapable of appreciating what had happened, thereby causing large losses by incompetence.

The judge could find no evidence of any attempt to defraud or of any dishonesty. In those circumstances, although, as he said, the offence of managing a company as an undischarged bankrupt was a serious offence, he considered that he could treat the case as wholly exceptional. In these circumstances, he made the orders for conditional discharge and costs ... So far as the disqualification was concerned, he said this:

"I take the view that this is a case in which, although there should be a disqualification, it should be a short one. I take the view that as a mark of the deliberation of your conduct, but weighing the other factors that I have been referred to in mitigation, it would seem to me that a disqualification for a period of two years would be appropriate, and that I order disqualifying you under the appropriate section of the Companies Act."

In written grounds of appeal it was submitted that this disqualification was wrong in principle or excessive. It was said that the appellant was not guilty of any dishonesty or fraudulent misconduct. He was not found unfit to act as a company director, and the judge had expressly made a finding that the badges of unfitness to which Harman J referred in the case of *Re Douglas Construction Services Ltd & Anor* (1988) 4 BCC 553 at p557 were absent in this case ...

This court is of the view that, all other things being equal, there was nothing wrong with the sentence of two years' disqualification on the facts of this case. It was a serious offence, as the judge said, and the prohibition by Parliament on undischarged bankrupts taking part in the management of a company is a serious prohibition. If undischarged bankrupts do get involved in management of a company, they must expect to be disqualified when the matter is brought before a court.

On the other hand, there are two features of this case which temper the court's approach to the proper penalty. The first is that the company ... went into liquidation in the early summer of 1985. During 1986 the appellant was discharged from bankruptcy. Early in 1987 the enquiries were made on behalf of the Department of Trade and Industry ... This is another case in which for unexplained reasons (it may very well be for lack of resources in the Department) a quite intolerable delay has occurred before the matter comes before a court, and a court is inevitably in a difficult position in knowing how to do justice in contemplating a period of disqualification as a director when a defendant has, as this appellant unquestionably had had, a very good three-and-a-half year record of successful business from the time that his bankruptcy was lifted.

If that was the only particular matter in this case, it is unlikely, despite the court's concern, that it would be minded to change the order of disqualification. But on the other hand ... the judge decided that on the facts of this case that it was an exceptional case which warranted the making of a conditional discharge. This court has considerable difficulty with the conclusion that the judge arrived at in this matter, especially as he said in his sentencing remarks that he regarded this as a serious offence. However, there is no appeal against that conditional discharge. It appears to the court that as the order for disqualification under s2 of the Act is unquestionably a punishment, it would be quite inappropriate for a punishment of this kind to be linked with a conditional discharge in a case under the Companies Act in which the sentencing court thought that a punishment was inexpedient.

It is for this reason and this reason only that in the quite exceptional circumstances of this case the court is of the view that the sentence of disqualification cannot stand and it must therefore be quashed.'

Directors' duty of skill, attention and care

City Equitable Fire Insurance Co Ltd, Re [1925] Ch 407 Chancery Division (Romer J)

Common law duty of skill, attention and care

Facts

The company was formed in 1908 as an insurance company. In 1922 an order was made for winding-up the company. An investigation into the affairs of the company showed that there was a shortage of about £1,200,000 in the company's funds. The liquidator brought these proceedings against the directors for misfeasance, negligence, breach of trust and breach of duty. The allegations of negligence included, inter alia, making bad investments with the company's monies; allowing the managing director, who had become bankrupt, to borrow over £110,000; allowing £350,000 to remain in the hands of the company's brokers, which became lost, and lending £9,329 to the chairman, who was adjudicated bankrupt and convicted of fraud, which was lost. It was not disputed that the directors sued in this action, had acted anything other than honestly throughout. Under art 150 of the company's articles it was provided that none of the directors were answerable for the acts, receipts, neglects or defaults of the other directors or the loss of company monies unless the same should happen through their own wilful neglect or default. The directors were held not liable and, in reference to the law as to a director's duty of skill, attention and care.

Romer J said:

'It has sometimes been said that directors are trustees. If this means no more than that directors in the performance of their duties stand in a fiduciary relationship to the company, the statement is true enough. But if the statement is meant to be an indication by way of analogy of what those duties are, it appears to me to be wholly misleading. I can see but little resemblance between the duties of a director and the duties of a trustee of a will or of a marriage settlement. It is indeed impossible to describe the duty of directors in general terms, whether by way of analogy or otherwise. The position of a director of a company carrying on a small retail business is very different from that of a director of a railway company. The duties of a bank director may differ widely from those of an insurance director, and the duties of a director of one insurance company may differ from those of a director of another. In one company, for instance, matters may normally be attended to by the manager or other members of the staff that in another company are attended to by the directors themselves. The larger the business carried on by the company the more numerous, and the more important, the matters that must of necessity be left to the managers, the accountants and the rest of the staff. The manner in which the work of the company is to be distributed between the board or directors and the staff is in truth a business matter to be decided on business lines. To use the words of Lord Macnaghten in *Dovey* v *Cory* [1901] AC 477:

"I do not think it desirable for any tribunal to do that which Parliament has abstained from doing – that is, to formulate precise rules for the guidance or embarrassment of businessmen in the conduct of business affairs. There never has been, and I think there never will be, much difficulty in dealing with any particular case on its own facts and circumstances: and, speaking for myself, I rather doubt the wisdom of attempting to do more."

In order, therefore, to ascertain the duties that a person appointed to the board of an established company undertakes to perform, it is necessary to consider not only the nature of the company's business, but also the manner in which the work of the company is in fact distributed between the directors and the other officials of the company, provided always that this distribution is a reasonable one in the circumstances, and is not inconsistent with any express provisions of the articles of association. In discharging the duties of his position thus ascertained a director must, of course, act honestly; but he must also exercise some degree of both skill and diligence. To the question of what is the particular degree of skill and diligence required of him, the authorities do not, I think give any very clear answer. It has been laid down that so long as a director acts honestly he cannot be made responsible in damages unless guilty of gross or culpable negligence in a business sense ...

... If, therefore, a director is only liable for gross or culpable negligence, this means that he does not owe a duty to his company, to take all possible care. It is some degree of care less than that. The care that he is bound to take has been described by Neville J in the case referred to above as "reasonable care" to be measured by the care an ordinary man might be expected to take in the circumstances on his own behalf. In saying this Neville J was only following what was laid down in *Overend & Gurney Co v Gibb* (1869) LR 4 Ch App 460 as being the proper test to apply, namely:

> "Whether or not the directors exceeded the powers entrusted to them, or whether if they did not so exceed their powers they were cognisant of circumstances of such a character, so plain, so manifest, and so simple of appreciation, that no men with any ordinary degree of prudence, acting on their own behalf, would have entered into such a transaction as they entered into?"

There are, in addition, one or two other general propositions that seem to be warranted by the reported cases: (i) A director need not exhibit in the performance of his duties a greater degree of skill than may reasonably be expected from a person of his knowledge and experience. A director of a life insurance company, for instance, does not guarantee that he has the skill of an actuary or of a physician. In the words of Lindley MR:

> "If directors act within their powers, if they act with such care as is reasonably to be expected from them, having regard to their knowledge and experience, and if they act honestly for the benefit of the company they represent, they discharge both their equitable as well as their legal duty to the company."

See *Lagunas Nitrate Co v Lagunas Syndicate* [1899] 2 Ch 392. It is perhaps only another way of stating the same proposition to say that directors are not liable for mere errors of judgment. (ii) A director is not bound to give continuous attention to the affairs of his company. His duties are of an intermittent nature to be performed at periodical board meetings, and at meetings of any committee of the board upon which he happens to be placed. He is not, however, bound to attend all such meetings, though he ought to attend whenever, in the circumtances, he is reasonably able to do so. (iii) In respect of all duties that, having regard to the exigencies of business, and the articles of association, may properly be left to some other official, a director is, in the absence of grounds for suspicion, justified in trusting that official to perform such duties honestly. In the judgment of the Court of Appeal in *In re National Bank of Wales Ltd* [1892] 2 Ch 100 the following passage occurs in relation to a director who had been deceived by the manager, and managing director, as to matters within their own particular sphere of activity:

> "Was it his duty to test the accuracy or completeness of what he was told by the general manager and the managing director? This is a question on which opinions may differ, but we are not prepared to say that he failed in his legal duty. Business cannot be carried out upon principles of distrust. Men in responsible positions must be trusted by those above them, as well as by those below them, until there is reason to distrust them. We agree that care and prudence do not involve distrust; but for a director acting honestly himself to be held legally liable for negligence, in trusting the officers under him not to conceal from him what they ought to report to him, appears to us to be laying too heavy a burden on honest business men."

That case went to the House of Lords, and is reported there under the name of *Dovey v Cory*. Lord Davey, in the course of his speech to the House, made the following observations:

> "I think the respondent was bound to give his attention to and exercise his judgment as a man of business on the matters which were brought before the board of the meetings which he attended, and it is not proved that he did not do so. But I think he was entitled to rely upon the judgment, information and advice, of the chairman and general manager, as to whose integrity, skill and competence he had no reason for suspicion. I agree with what was said by Sir George Jessel in *Hallmark's Case* (1878) 9 Ch D 329, and by Chitty, J in *In re Denham & Co* (1884) 25 Ch D 752, that directors are not bound to examine entries in the company's books. It was the duty of the general manager and (possibly) of the chairman to go carefully through the returns from the branches, and to bring before the board any matter requiring their

consideration; but the respondent was not, in my opinion, guilty of negligence in not examining them for himself, notwithstanding that they were laid on the table on the board for reference."'

D'Jan of London Ltd, Re [1993] BCC 646 Chancery Division (Hoffmann LJ sitting as an additional judge of the Chancery Division)

Director's negligence – relief from liability under s727 of the Companies Act 1985

Facts

D, a director of the company, signed an insurance proposal form without reading it. The form was filled in by D's broker. An answer given to one of the questions on the form was incorrect and the insurance company rightly repudiated liability for a fire at the company's premises in which stock worth some £174,000 was lost. The company became insolvent and the liquidator bought this action under s212 of the Insolvency Act 1986 alleging D was negligent.

Held

In failing to read the form D was negligent. However, he had acted honestly and reasonably and ought therefore to be partly relieved from liability by the court under s727 of the Companies Act 1985.

Hoffmann LJ said that directors need not always read the whole of every document they sign. But this was an extremely simple document asking few questions which D was the best person to answer. Relying on the *Multinational Gas Case* [1983] Ch 258, it was argued on behalf of D that as he held 99 of 100 shares issued and his wife the other one, he must be taken to have authorised the wrong answer in the proposal because he signed it himself. Hoffmann LJ answered this by stating that the *Multinational* principle, 'requires that the shareholders should have, whether formally or informally, mandated or ratified the act in question. It is not enough that they probably would have ratified if they had known or thought about it before the liquidation removed their power to do so.'

Hoffmann LJ went on to state that D owed a duty of care to the company as a separate entity which did not vary according to the number of shares he owned. That said, in applying s727 the economic realities could be taken into account in that D was a 99 per cent shareholder. When the form was signed the company was solvent and the only persons whose interest he was putting at risk in failing to read the form were himself and his wife.

The court concluded that D had acted honestly and reasonably and that his liability to compensate the company should be limited to the amount of any unpaid dividends to which he would otherwise be entitled to receive from the liquidator as an unsecured creditor of the company.

Directors' fiduciary duty

Bishopsgate Investment Management Ltd (in liquidation) v *Maxwell* [1993] BCC 120 Court of Appeal (Ralph Gibson, Leggatt and Hoffmann LJJ)

Misappropriation in breach of fiduciary duty

Facts

BIM Ltd was the trustee of a number of pension schemes for employees of companies controlled by the late Mr Robert Maxwell. After his death it was discovered that some £428 million held on behalf of the pension funds had been wrongfully lent or misappropriated for the benefit of Mr Maxwell's other companies. The company was unable to meet its liabilities and was compulsorily wound up on 4 March 1992.

The defendant Ian Maxwell (IM) was a director of BIM Ltd. He took no interest whatever in the management of the company. He attended a few meetings and paid little attention to business when he did. He said he trusted and relied upon the other directors.

One particular transaction involved the transfer of shares in a publicly quoted company which were owned by BIM Ltd. These shares were transferred for a nil consideration to RMG plc of which IM was also a director. He co-signed the transfer as a director under the signature of his brother, Kevin. At the same time, as a director of RMG plc, he signed blank transfers to enable RMG plc to pledge the shares to a bank to secure advances which were used to fund Mr Robert Maxwell's private interests.

In the High Court Chadwick J considered that IM was under a duty to consider and understand why the stock was being transferred to RMG plc and to satisfy himself that the transfers were in the interests of the company.

Summary judgment in respect of this transaction was obtained and IM ordered to make an interim payment of £500,000. IM appealed.

Held

Hoffmann LJ made it clear that it was no excuse for IM to argue that he signed the transfers because he was following the lead of his brother. IM was in breach of his fiduciary duty, 'because he gave away the company's assets for no consideration to a private company of which he was a director. This was prima facie abuse of his powers as a director for an improper purpose ...'.

It was argued on IM's behalf that his breaches of duty did not cause the loss, because if IM *had* asked about the propriety of the transfers, he would have been given an apparently plausible explanation or someone else would have been found to sign instead. To this argument Hoffmann LJ replied:

In the case of breach of the fiduciary duty ... the cause of action is constituted not by failure to make enquiries but simply by the improper transfer of the shares to Robert Maxwell Group plc. Even if Mr Maxwell had made enquiries and received reassuring answers from other directors whom he was reasonably entitled to trust, he would not have escaped liability for a transfer which was in fact for a purpose outside the powers entrusted to the board.'

Ralph Gibson LJ also took the same view. Signing the transfers constituted misapplication of the company's property and it did not matter the directors acted honestly. No attempt had been made to show that the transactions were even arguably for the benefit of the company.

The appeal was dismissed.

Canadian Aero Service Ltd v *O'Malley* (1973) 40 DLR (3d) 371 Supreme Court of Canada (Martland, Judson, Ritchie, Spence and Laskin JJ)

Fiduciary duties – conflict of interest – diversion of company contract

Facts

O'Malley and two other persons had been senior managerial officers in the plaintiff company which was in the business of topographical mapping and geophysical exploraton. All had worked for the company for a long time and O'Malley became president. In 1961 the company came under the control of a US corporation. The US corporation placed limitations on the authority of O'Malley and the others, and limited the scope of their independent action. They became dissatisfied and also feared loss of their position if the company failed to get contracts. Consequently they decided to form their own company to carry on a similar business, Terra Surveys Ltd. Terra obtained a contract for topographical mapping and aerial photographing in Guyana. O'Malley had been attempting to obtain this contract for the plaintiff company up until July 1966 and having reached the final stages in negotiations managed to divert the contract to Terra through his influence in August 1966.

Held
Diverting the contract was a breach of their fiduciary duty. Damages were awarded to the plaintiff.

Laskin J:

'... I do not think it matters whether O'Malley and Zarzycki were properly appointed as directors of Canaero or whether they did or did not act as directors. What is not in doubt is that they acted respectively as president and executive vice-president of Canaero for about two years prior to their resignations. To paraphrase the findings of the trial judge in this respect, they acted in those positions and their remuneration and responsibilities verified their status as senior offices of Canaero. They were "top management" and not mere employees whose duty to their employer, unless enlarged by contract, consisted only of respect for trade secrets and for confidentiality of customer lists. Theirs was a larger and more exacting duty which, unless modified by statute or by contract (and there is nothing of this sort here), was similar to that owed to a corporate employer by its directors ...

O'Malley and Zarzycki stood in a fiduciary relationship to Canaero which in its generality betokens loyalty, good faith and avoidance of a conflict of duty and self-interest. Descending from the generality the fiduciary relationship goes at least this far: a director or a senior officer like O'Malley or Zarzycki is precluded from obtaining for himself either secretly or without the approval of the company (which would have to be properly manifested on a full disclosure of the facts), any property or business advantage either belonging to the company or for which it has been negotiating; and especially is this so where the director or officer is a participant in the negotiations on behalf of the company.

An examination of the case law in this court and in the courts of other jurisdiction on the fiduciary duties of directors and other senior officers shows the pervasiveness of a strict ethic in this area of the law. In my opinion, this ethic disqualifies a director or senior officer from usurping for himself or diverting to another person or company with whom or with which he is associated a maturing business opportunity which his company is actively pursuing; he is also precluded from so acting even after his resignation where the resignation may fairly be said to have been prompted or influenced by a wish to acquire for himself the opportunity sought by the company, or where it was his position with the company rather than a fresh initiative that led him to the opportunity that he later acquired ...'

Duckwari plc v *Offerventure Ltd* [1995] BCC 89 Court of Appeal (Neill, Beldam and Millet LJJ)

Substantial property transaction within ss320 and 322 CA 1985

Facts
C was a director of both D plc and O Ltd. C and his wife were the only shareholders of O Ltd, which agreed to purchase a freehold property worth £495,000. C then wrote to a fellow director of D plc and offered to let D plc take over the benefit of the contract from O Ltd, so that D plc would purchase the property. The contract was later completed with D plc paying the £495,000 purchase price to the vendor and reimbursing the deposit of £49,500 to O Ltd. After completion, D plc alleged that the property was worth substantially less than this amount and argued that the arrangement was a substantial property transaction within s320 CA 1985 and sought to avoid the transaction.

Held
The court of Appeal agreed with D plc, that the arrangement was a substantial property transaction. D plc had acquired a non-cash asset from C, via his company, O Ltd. It was accepted that O Ltd was connected with C for the purposes of the substantial property transaction provisions in ss320 and 322 CA 1985.

Millet LJ:

'It remains necessary only to consider an argument which was advanced and rejected by the judge below and which has been repeated before us on behalf of Duckwari, namely, that the value of the non-cash asset acquired by Duckwari from Offerventure was £495,000. It was submitted that the reality of the matter was that it was acquiring the property or the right to buy the property and that the purchase price of £495,000 was payable in its entirety to or to the direction of Offerventure, so that even the £445,500 which was paid to the vendor was only paid to the vendor because Offerventure so directed. That is true, but we are concerned with the identification and valuation of the asset which moved in the other direction; and the problem is that, although it is true that the property itself passed from the vendor to Duckwari only because Offerventure directed the vendor to transfer the property to Duckwari and therefore moved from the vendor through Offerventure to the purchaser, the fact remains that the vendor had his own independent valuable proprietary right in the property, namely the unpaid vendor's lien. That had to be discharged by Duckwari by payment direct to the vendor (that was worth £445,500) and that figure must be deducted from the value of the property acquired from Offerventure. In my judgment, there were two assets being acquired by Duckwari. One was the asset acquired from Offerventure, viz the right to call on completion for the conveyance on discharging Offerventure's obligations to the vendor and paying Offerventure £49,500; and the other was the extinction of the vendors' unpaid lien by discharging Offerventure's obligation to pay the balance of the purchase money due to the vendor.

Duckwari has pointed to the capricious results which appear to follow from this analysis because it makes the question whether a transaction needs to be approved by the company in general meeting depend upon the amount, if any, of the deposit rather than the value of the property being acquired by the company.

If this is an anomaly it results from a combination of the facts (1) that cash assets and liabilities are excluded from the computation and (2) that Parliament has seen fit, for obvious reasons, to exclude the operation of the section where the transaction is not of substantial value. I do not think that it is possible in isolation to consider whether this analysis does lead to capricious results without considering the consequences of an infringement of the section.

These proceedings have been brought by Duckwari in order to enforce the indemnity provided for s322(3). Duckwari's object is to seek to recover from the appellants the amount of the loss which has resulted from the fall in market values since the date of the transaction. Whether Duckwari would succeed in that endeavour will depend upon the question whether the loss or damage resulting from the arrangement or transaction referred to in s322(3)(b) is to be measured by the difference between the value of the property at the date of the transaction and the purchase price (which in this case was nil) or is to be measured by the purchase price and the value of the property at some other and later date. That is a question which still remains for decision, and I express no opinion at all upon it. But it must not be assumed from anything that I have said in the course of this judgment that I take any view on that one way or the other.'

Guinness plc v *Saunders* [1988] 1 WLR 863 Court of Appeal (Fox, Glidewell LJJ and Sir Frederick Lawton)

Fiduciary duty – accounting for profits – s317 of the Companies Act 1985 disclosure of interest – s727 of the Companies Act 1985 whether directors

Facts
Ward was a director of Guinness when it launched a takeover bid for Distillers plc: Ward and two other directors formed a committee of the board for the purpose of conducting the bid. Marketing and Acquisition Consultants Ltd, a Jersey company controlled by Ward, submitted to Guinness an invoice for £5.2m for services rendered in connection with the bid and this sum was duly paid. Ward admitted that the payment was received for and on his behalf, but he claimed that it was made pursuant to an oral agreement between Guinness and himself. Guinness denied this and contended that, even if such an agreement had been concluded, it was in breach of Ward's fiduciary duty as a director in that it had not been disclosed to the Guinness directors as required by s317 of the Companies Act 1985 or the company's articles of association. Guinness sought the recovery of the £5.2m.

Held

They were entitled to succeed.

Fox LJ:

'Are Guinness entitled to judgment?

In relation to this question it is necessary first of all to consider the effect of s317 of the 1985 Act.

In my opinion, it imposes an obligation to make a disclosure to a meeting of the full board of directors duly convened. Section 317(1) requires a disclosure to "a meeting of the directors". These words, it seems to me, cannot be satisfied by a disclosure to a sub-committee of the directors. It is simply not what the subsection says. Nothing in the articles can alter that. Section 317(1) is a statutory requirement and its provisions are mandatory. In fact, in my view, nothing in the articles seeks to alter it ...

It is said, as I understand it, on behalf of Mr Ward, that disclosure to the full board would be an absurdity because the board, or at any rate the executive committee of the board for the purpose of the bid, knew about the payment. Assuming it were true that all the members of the board knew about the payment, that does not alter the fact that the requirement of the statute that there be a disclosure to "a meeting of the directors of the company" (which is a wholly different thing from knowledge by individuals and involves the opportunity for positive consideration of the matter by the board as a body) was not complied with.

I conclude, therefore, that the statute required disclosure to a duly convened meeting of the full board of Guinness. There was, it is admitted, no such disclosure. Mr Ward, therefore, acted in breach of duty in receiving the £5.2m.

The next question is what are the consequences of the breach of duty? I deal first with a contention advanced by Mr Ward regarding art 100. It is said that art 100 is concerned to give a director certain exemptions from the duties which are imposed on him to account for profits which he obtains from the company. Thus, it is said that art 100(D) expressly permits a director to act in a professional capacity and provides that he shall be entitled to retain remuneration for professional services as if he were not a director.

I do not think that is correct. A director is in a fiduciary position. A person in a fiduciary position is not permitted to obtain a profit from his position except with the consent of his beneficiaries or other persons to whom he owes the duty. In the case of a director the consent required is that of the members in general meeting. That is inconvenient in relation to the day-to-day running of a business. It has, therefore, become the practice to relax the general rule by special provisions in the articles. The purpose of s317(1) is not to destroy the power to relax the general rule by the articles, but to impose a binding safeguard on that power.

In my opinion, a provision such as art 100(D) must be read in the light of s317(1) to which it is always subject, and, for that matter, to art 100(A), which gives effect or, perhaps more accurately, draws attention to the statute. The interest of a director under any contract to which art 100(C) or (D) applies must be disclosed in accordance with s317(1).

Accordingly, I conclude that Mr Ward plainly acted in breach of duty in failing to disclose his interest in the agreement to a meeting of the directors. The consequence, in my opinion, is that stated by Lord Denning MR in *Hely-Hutchinson v Brayhead Ltd* [1968] 1 QB 549 (which was concerned with a breach by a director of the statutory predecessor of s317, namely s199 of the Companies Act 1948) where he said:

> "It seems to me that when a director fails to disclose his interest, the effect is the same as non-disclosure in contracts uberrimae fidei, or non-disclosure by a promoter who sells to the company property in which he is interested ... Non-disclosure does not render the contract void or a nullity. It renders the contract voidable at the instance of the company and makes the director accountable for any secret profit which he has made."

Lord Wilberforce and Lord Pearson also accepted that such a contract is voidable at the instance of the company ... It seems to me that consistently with these views s317(1) must be regarded as imposing a duty which has consequences in the civil law in addition to the penalty of a fine; in addition a civil law duty arises, it seems to me, under art 100(A). It is not in doubt that, if the agreement ever existed, Guinness has exercised its right to avoid it (at the latest by the institution of the present proceedings) and did so within due time, there is no issue as to delay. Prima facie, therefore, it seems to me that Guinness is entitled to judgment for the £5.2m.

Has Mr Ward valid defences?

Mr Ward advances a number of objections under the claim for judgment. He says, first, that he has completed his obligations under the agreement (ie to render services) and that accordingly restitutio in integrum is now impossible and Guinness cannot claim the return of the money consideration. The argument is not well founded. This is not a case of rescission of a partly performed contract because of breach of contract. It is the case of a fiduciary who, in plain disregard of his duty to the company, has improperly received the company's money and has thereby become a constructive trustee of that money. It is said that Mr Ward received a good title to the money initially since the agreement was not void but voidable. I do not think that Mr Ward ever had a good title to the money. The money was the absolute property of Guinness which was received by him in breach of his fiduciary duty and his title to it was imperfect from the first since Guinness could avoid the agreement. Mr Ward was, in my view, a constructive trustee of the money as soon as he received it. The basis of the constructive trust was the combination of three factors, namely a fiduciary relationship, a breach of a duty arising in respect of that fiduciary relationship and the receipt, in breach of duty, of property belonging to the person to which such duty was owed.

Second, it is said that, assuming that Mr Ward was otherwise liable to repay the £5.2m, he is entitled at law to a quantum meruit or (under the principle of *Boardman v Phipps* [1967] 2 AC 46) to an allowance in equity for services which he had given to the company. Let it be assumed for the present purposes that Mr Ward might have a claim under either of these heads. Since any such claim is unquantified, any set-off would have to be equitable. Lord Denning MR in *Federal Commerce and Navigation Co Ltd v Molema Alpha Inc, The Nanfri, The Benfri, The Lorfri* [1978] QB 927 said, in relation to equitable set-off:

"... it is not every cross-claim which can be deducted. It is only cross-claims that arise out of the same transaction or are closely connected with it. And it is only cross-claims which go directly to impeach the plaintiff's demands, that is, so closely connected with his demands that it would be manifestly unjust to allow him to enforce payment without taking into account the cross-claim."

Do the cross-claims in this case impeach Guinness's title to receive the money claimed? I agree ... that they do not. As I have already indicated, Mr Ward received the £5.2m as a constructive trustee for Guinness. No doubt the constructive trust would have determined if Guinness had ratified the agreement or had delayed for too long in avoiding it. But those circumstances apart, it seems to me that, from the first, Mr Ward held the money as a constructive trustee for Guinness. The existence of some cross-claim for a quantum meruit or allowance did not impeach or determine the trust. It continues to subsist. In that respect cases such as *Boardman v Phipps* and *O'Sullivan v Management Agency and Music Ltd* [1985] QB 428 differ from the present case in that they were not concerned with claims for the recovery of property belonging to the plaintiff and wrongly retained by the defendant. In *Boardman v Phipps* the defendants had misused for their own benefit an opportunity (which belonged to the trust) to make a profit. They had not received trust property. In *O'Sullivan* the action was for an account of profits which the defendant had made for itself in the course of managing O'Sullivan who was a singer. There was no receipt of his property except some copyrights which were ordered to be returned ...

Further, in my opinion, the respective claims of Guinness and Mr Ward cannot be truly described as arising out of the same transaction. Guinness's claim does not depend on the agreement at all. It is simply a claim to its own money improperly received by Mr Ward. In that respect there were no mutual dealings between them because the agreement was never disclosed to the board as required by the statute.

Lastly, Mr Ward claims that he is entitled to relief under s727 of the 1985 Act. That section, in the manner of the statutory relief provisions for trustees, confers on the court power to relieve a director from liability for breach of duty if he has acted honestly and reasonably and in all the circumstances ought fairly to be excused. Whether a director who, in breach of his fiduciary duty, is wrongfully in possession of the company's property is within the provisions of s727 at all I need not consider. What Mr Ward claims, in effect, is that he be compensated for his services in connection with the bid. That, however ... is exactly the basis on which he claims payment by way of quantum meruit or equitable compensation. But, if his claim under either of these heads succeeds, he will not need relief under s727 and, if it fails, he will have failed to disclose any grounds for relief under s727. Accordingly, it does not avail Mr Ward to invoke s727. He could not succeed under that section.

In general, I am not disposed to give any encouragement to the idea that a director who has succeeded in getting his hands on the company's money in reliance on a contract which, in breach of duty, he failed to disclose under the provisions of s317(1) should be allowed to retain the money while he litigates claims for a quantum meruit or an allowance in equity for his services or alleged services. Such a result, it seems to me, would make inroads on the policy of the statute.'

Commentary
An appeal against this decision ([1990] 2 AC 663) was dismissed on other grounds by the House of Lords see page 246.

Hogg v *Cramphorn Ltd* [1967] Ch 254 Chancery Division (Buckley J)

Fiduciary duty – whether directors' powers exercised for a proper purpose – issue of shares

Facts
The company was incorporated in 1896 and carried on the business of corn and seed merchants. It was a public company but not quoted on the Stock Exchange. In March 1963 the issued capital of the company was £136,000 being 96,000 £1 preference shares of which 90,293 were issued and 40,000 £1 ordinary shares of which 35,888 were issued. The company was in a healthy financial position but, if anything, its capital was under utilised. The directors and their friends held 37,000 of the 126,181 issued shares. All shares carried one vote at company meetings. In March 1963 an offer was made to Col Cramphorn by a Mr Baxter to buy the whole of the issued share capital in the company. Mr Baxter did not have any experience of the company's business and Col Cramphorn considered that a take-over by Mr Baxter would unsettle the company's staff and would not be in its interests. To ensure that Mr Baxter's bid did not succeed a scheme was devised under which the company entered into a trust deed for its employees and allotted to the trustees 5,707 unissued preference shares on the condition that they have 10 votes per share on a poll. Mr Baxter later discovered what happened through circulars he received when he purchased 50 shares in the company with the assistance of a friend. He brought this action claiming, inter alia, that the issue of the 5,707 shares to the trustees was void and of no effect.

Held
Since the power to issue shares was a fiduciary power and had been exercised for improper purposes, ie to prevent Mr Baxter's take-over bid, the issue of the 5,707 shares was liable to be set aside. It was irrelevant that the issue was made bona fide in the belief that it was in the best interests of the company.

Buckley J:

'I now turn to what has been the main matter of debate in this case, which is whether the allotment of the 5,707 shares was an improper use by the directors of their discretionary and fiduciary power under art10 to decide to whom these unissued shares would be allotted. Mr Instone has submitted that the allotment was made with the primary object of preventing Mr Baxter from obtaining control of the company and ousting the then existing board of directors and that the allotment was accordingly a breach of the directors' fiduciary duties and should be set aside on the authority of *Piercy* v *S Mills & Co Ltd* (1). In this connection, I should, I think, ignore the fact that the directors were incompetent to attach to the shares the spcial voting rights which they purported to attach to them.

It is common ground that the scheme of which this allotment formed part was formulated to meet the threat, as the directors regarded it, of Mr Baxter's offer. The trust deed would not have come into existence, nor would the 5,707 shares have been issued as they were, but for Mr Baxter's bid and the threat that it constituted to the established management of the company. It is also common ground that the directors were not actuated by any unworthy motives of personal advantage, but acted as they did in an honest belief that they were doing what was for the good of the company. Their honour is not in the least impugned, but it is said that the means which they adopted to attain their end were such as they could not properly adopt.

I am satisfied that Mr Baxter's offer, when it became known to the company's staff, had an unsettling effect upon them. I am also satisfied that the directors and the trustees of the trust deed genuinely considered that to give the staff through the trustees a sizeable, though indirect, voice in the affairs of the company would benefit both the staff and the company. I am sure that Colonel Cramphorn and also probably his fellow directors firmly believed that to keep the management of the company's affairs in the hands of the existing board would be more advantageous to the shareholders, the company's staff and its customers than if it were committed to a board selected by Mr Baxter. The steps which the board took were intended not only to ensure that if Mr Baxter succeeded in obtaining a shareholding which, as matters stood, would have been a controlling shareholding, he should not secure control of the company, but also, and perhaps primarily, to discourage Mr Baxter from proceeding with his bid at all ...

... Accepting as I do that the board acted in good faith and that they believed that the establishment of a trust would benefit the company, and that avoidance of the acquisition of control by Mr Baxter would also benefit the company, I must still remember that an essential element of the scheme, and indeed its primary purpose, was to ensure control of the company by the directors and those whom they could confidently regard as their supporters. Was such a manipulation of the voting position a legitimate act on the part of the directors? ...'

His Lordship then referred to *Punt v Symonds & Co Ltd* [1903] 2 Ch 506; *Piercy v S Mills & Co Ltd* [1920] 1 Ch 177; and *Fraser v Whalley* (1864) 2 H & M 10 and concluded as follows:

'... These considerations lead me to the conclusion that the issue of the 5,707 shares, with the special voting rights which the directors purported to attach to them, could not be justified by the view that the directors genuinely believed that it would benefit the company if they could command a majority of the votes in general meetings. The fact that, as I have held, the directors were mistaken in thinking that they could attach to these shares more than one vote each is irrelevant. The power to issue shares was a fiduciary power and if, as I think, it was exercised for an improper motive, the issue of these shares is liable to be set aside ...'

Howard Smith Ltd v *Ampol Petroleum* [1974] AC 821 Privy Council (Lords Wilberforce, Diplock, Simon, Cross and Kilbrandon)

Fiduciary duty – whether directors' powers exercised for a proper purpose

Facts
Millers' Ltd was at the centre of a take-over battle. Ampol Ltd and an associated company, Bulkships Ltd, between them held 55 per cent of Millers' Ltd's shares. The other 45 per cent was held by outside shareholders. In June 1972 Ampol Ltd made an offer to purchase all the issued shares in Millers' Ltd for $2.27. The board recommended this to be rejected as too low. Millers' Ltd had two oil tankers under contruction and the management did not want these to pass into the hands of Ampol Ltd. A scheme was devised to avoid this by Howard Smith Ltd, a company favoured by the management, making an offer to buy Millers' Ltd's shares in toto, and Howard Smith Ltd therefore made an offer of $2.50 per share. However, Ampol Ltd and Bulkships Ltd said they had decided to reject any offer for their shares 'whether from Howard Smith Ltd or from any other source.' This made it useless for Howard Smith Ltd to proceed

since they could not obtain control. A new scheme was evolved. Under this a calculation was made as to how much capital Millers' Ltd needed to finance the building of the tankers. This worked out at $10,000,000. Thus, 4,500,000 shares were issued to Howard Smith Ltd by Millers' Ltd at $1.30 per share giving them a sufficient holding to make a successful offer to the other shareholders and put Ampol Ltd and Bulkheads Ltd in a minority position. Ampol Ltd challenged the validity of the issue of the shares. At the trial Street J found that the directors had not been motivated by personal gain or advantage, or a desire to retain their positions on the board, that Millers' Ltd needed capital, but that the primary purpose of the allotment to Howard Smith Ltd was to eliminate the control held by Ampol Ltd. He held that the issue of the shares was an improper exercise of the directors' powers and set it aside. Howard Smith Ltd appealed.

Held
The appeal would be dismissed because the directors had improperly exercised their power to issue shares primarily to destroy one majority shareholding and to create a new majority shareholding.

Lord Wilberforce:

'The directors, in deciding to issue shares, forming part of Millers' unissued capital, to Howard Smith, acted under cl 8 of the company's articles of association. This provides, subject to certain qualifications which have not been invoked, that the shares shall be under the control of the directors, who may allot or otherwise dispose of the same to such persons on such terms and conditions and either at a premium or otherwise and at such time as the directors may think fit. Thus, intra vires though the issue may have been, the directors' power under this article is a fiduciary power: and it remains the case that an exercise of such power though formally valid, may be attacked on the ground that it was not exercised for the purpose for which it was granted. It is at this point that the contentions of the parties diverge. The extreme argument on one side is that, for validity, what is required is bona fide exercise of the power in the interests of the company: that once it is found that the directors were not motivated by self-interest – ie by a desire to retain their control of the company or their positions on the board – the matter is concluded in their favour and that the court will not inquire into the validity of their reasons for making the issue. All decided cases, it was submitted, where an exercise of such a power as this had been found invalid, are cases where directors are found to have acted through self-interest of this kind.

On the other side, the main argument is that the purpose for which the power is conferred is to enable capital to be raised for the company, and that once it is found that the issue was not made for that purpose, invalidity follows ...

... In their Lordships' opinion neither of the extreme positions can be maintained. It can be accepted, as one would only expect, that the majority of cases in which issues of shares are challenged in the courts are cases in which the vitiating element is the self-interest of the directors, or at least the purpose of the directors to preserve their own control of the management ...

... But it does not follow from this, as the appellants assert, that the absence of any element of self-interest is enough to make an issue valid. Self-interest is only one, though no doubt the commonest, instance of improper motive: and, before one can say that a fiduciary power has been exercised for the purpose for which it was conferred, a wider investigation may have to be made. This is recognised in several well-known statements of law ...

... On the other hand, taking the respondents' contention, it is, in their Lordships' opinion, too narrow an approach to say that the only valid purpose for which shares may be issued is to raise capital for the company. The discretion is not in terms limited in this way: the law should not impose such a limitation on directors' powers. To define in advance exact limits beyond which directors must not pass is, in their Lordships' view, impossible. This clearly cannot be done by enumeration, since the variety of situations facing directors of different types of company in different situations cannot be anticipated. No more, in their Lordships' view, can this be done by the use of a phrase – such as "bona fide in the interest of the company as a whole," or "for some corporate purpose". Such phrases, if they do anything more than restate the general principle applicable to fiduciary powers, at best serve, negatively, to exclude from the area of validity cases improperly favouring one section of the shareholders against another. Of such cases it has been said:

> "The question which arises is sometimes not a question of the interest of the company at all, but a question of what is fair as between different classes of shareholders. Where such a case arises some other test than that of the 'interests of the company' must be applied ..." (*Mills* v *Mills*, 60 CLR, 150, 164, per Latham CJ).

In their Lordships' opinion it is necessary to start with a consideration of the power whose exercise is in question, in this case a power to issue shares. Having ascertained, on a fair view, the nature of this power, and having defined as can best be done in the light of modern conditions the, or some, limits within which it may be exercised, it is then necessary for the court, if a particular exercise of it is challenged, to examine the substantial purpose for which it was exercised, and to reach a conclusion whether that purpose was proper or not. In doing so it will necessarily give credit to the bona fide opinion of the directors, if such is found to exist, and will respect their judgment as to matters of management; having done this, the ultimate conclusion has to be as to the side of a fairly broad line on which the case falls ...

... The main stream of authority, in their Lordships' opinion, supports this approach. In *Punt* v *Symons & Co Ltd* [1903] 2 Ch 506 Byrne J expressly accepts that there may be reasons other than to raise capital for which shares may be issued. In the High Court case of *Harlowe's Nominees Pty Ltd* v *Woodside (Lakes Entrance) Oil Co NL* (1968) 121 CLR 483, an issue of shares was made to a large oil company in order, as was found, to secure the financial stability of the company. This was upheld as being within the power although it had the effect of defeating the attempt of the plaintiff to secure control by buying up the company's shares. The joint judgment of Barwick CJ, McTiernan J and Kitto J contains this passage, at p493:

> "The principle is that although primarily the power is given to enable capital to be raised when required for the purposes of the company, there may be occasions when the directors may fairly and properly issue shares for other reasons, so long as those reasons relate to a purpose of benefiting the company as a whole, as distinguished from a purpose, for example, of maintaining control of the company in the hands of the directors themselves or their friends. An inquiry as to whether additional capital was presently required is often most relevant to the ultimate question upon which the validity or invalidity of the issue depends; but that ultimate question must always be whether in truth the issue was made honestly in the interests of the company. Directors in whom are vested the right and the duty of deciding where the company's interests lie and how they are to be served may be concerned with a wide range of practical considerations, and their judgment, if exercised in good faith and not for irrelevant purposes, is not open to review in the courts. Thus in the present case it is not a matter for judicial concern, if it be the fact, that the allotment to Burmah would frustrate the ambitions of someone who was buying up shares as opportunity offered with a view to obtaining increased influence on the control of the company, or even that the directors realised that the allotment would have that result and found it agreeable to their personal wishes ...'

Their Lordships were referred to the recent judgment of Berger J in the Supreme Court of British Columbia, in *Teck Corporation Ltd* v *Millar* (1972) 33 DLR (3d) 288. This was concerned with the affairs of Afton Mines Ltd in which Teck Corporation Ltd, a resource conglomerate, had acquired a majority shareholding. Teck was indicating an intention to replace the board of directors of Afton with its own nominees with a view to causing Afton to enter into an agreement (called an 'ultimate deal') with itself for the exploitation by Teck of valuable mineral rights owned by Afton. Before this could be done, and in order to prevent it, the directors of Afton concluded an exploitation agreement with another company, Canex. One of its provisions, as is apparently common in this type of agreement in Canada, provided for the issue to Canex of a large number of shares in Afton, thus displacing Teck's majority. Berger J found at p328:

> "Their (the directors') purpose was to obtain the best agreement they could while ... still in control. Their purpose was in that sense to defeat Teck. But, not to defeat Teck's attempt to obtain control; rather it was to foreclose Teck's opportunity of obtaining for itself the ultimate deal. That was ... no improper purpose."

His decision upholding the agreement with Canex on this basis appears to be in line with the English and Australian authorities to which reference has been made ...'

Industrial Development Consultants Ltd v *Cooley* [1972] 1 WLR 443 Birmingham Assize (Roskill J)

Fiduciary duty – conflict of interest – use of corporate information

Facts

Cooley worked as chief architect to the West Midlands Gas Board until 1967 when he took up an offer to become managing director of IDC who were in the business of offering construction services to large industrial enterprises, including those of architects, engineers and project managers. One of the aims behind Cooley's appointment was that he could help IDC to obtain new business in the public sector. In 1968 Cooley approached the Eastern Gas Board about designing and constructing new depots for them. In 1969 the Eastern Gas Board approached Cooley in a private capacity about this work and from conversations Cooley realised he stood a good chance of obtaining this work for his own benefit if he could be released quickly from his obligations with IDC. Cooley represented to IDC that he was ill and in this way obtained a release from his contract. This was, in fact, an untrue representation. He then formed his own business and obtained the scheme for designing and constructing new depots which he had pursued for IDC. When IDC discovered this they issued a writ against Cooley seeking a declaration that he was a trustee for them of all contracts made with the Eastern Gas Board and an account of all fees and remuneration payable under these contracts.

Held

Cooley was in a fiduciary relationship to IDC as their managing director and he had allowed that duty and his own interests to conflict when he received information about the Eastern Gas Board project and used that for his own benefit. As managing director he had a duty to pass on information he received to IDC. He was liable to account to IDC.

Roskill J:

'The first matter that has to be considered is whether or not the defendant was in a fiduciary relationship with his principals, the plaintiffs. Mr Davies argued that he was not because he received this information which was communicated to him privately. With respect, I think that argument is wrong. The defendant had one capacity and one capacity only in which he was carrying on business at that time. That capacity was as managing director of the plaintiffs. Information which came to him while he was managing director and which was of concern to the plaintiffs and was relevant for the plaintiffs to know, was information which it was his duty to pass on the the plaintiffs because between himself and the plaintiffs a fiduciary relationship existed.

It seems to me plain that throughout the whole of May, June and July 1969 the defendant was in a fiduciary relationship with the plaintiffs. From the time he embarked upon his course of dealing with Eastern Gas Board, irrespective of anything which he did or he said to Mr Hicks, he embarked upon a deliberate policy and course of conduct which put his personal interests as a potential contracting party with the Eastern Gas Board in direct conflict with his pre-existing and continuing duty as managing director of the plaintiffs. That is something which for over 200 years the courts have forbidden. The principle goes back far beyond the cases cited to me from the last century. The well-known case of *Keech* v *Sandford* (1726) Sel Cas Ch 261 is perhaps one of the most striking illustrations of this rule ...

... Therefore, I feel impelled to the conclusion that when the defendant embarked on this course of conduct of getting information on 13 June, using that information and preparing those documents over the weekend of 14/15 June, and sending them off on 17 June, he was guilty of putting himself into the position in which his duty to his employers, the plaintiffs, and his own private interests conflicted and conflicted grievously. There being the fiduciary relationship I have described, it seems to me plain that it was his duty once he got this information to pass it to his employers and not to guard it for his own personal purposes and profit. He put himself into the position when his duty and his interests conflicted. As Lord Upjohn put it in *Phipps* v *Boardman* [1967] 2 AC 46: "It is only at this stage that any question of accountability arises".

Does accountability arise? It is said: "Well, even if there were that conflict of duty and interest, nonetheless, this was a contract with a third party in which the plaintiffs never could have had any interest because they would have never got it." That argument has been forcefully put before me by Mr Davies.

The remarkable position then arises that if one applies the equitable doctrine upon which the plaintiffs rely to oblige the defendant to account, they will receive a benefit which, on Mr Smettom's evidence at least, it is unlikely that would have got for themselves had the defendant complied with his duty to them. On the other hand, if the defendant is not required to account he will have made a large profit, as a result of having deliberately put himself into a position in which his duty to the plaintiffs who were employing him and his personal interests conflicted ...

... Therefore, if the plaintiffs succeed they will get a profit which they probably would not have got for themselves had the defendant fulfilled his duty. If the defendant is allowed to keep that profit he will have got something which he was able to get solely by reason of his breach of fiduciary duty to the plaintiffs.

When one looks at the way the cases have gone over the centuries it is plain that the question whether or not the benefit would have been obtained but for the breach of trust has always been treated as irrelevant. I mentioned *Keech* v *Sandford* a few moments ago and this fact will also be found emphasised if one looks at some of the speeches in *Regal (Hastings) Ltd* v *Gulliver* [1942] 1 All ER 378, though it is true, as was pointed out to me, that if one looks at some of the language used in the speeches in *Regal* such phrases as "he must account for any benefit which he obtains in the course of and owing to his directorship" will be found.

In one sense the benefit in this case did not arise because of the defendant's directorship; indeed, the defendant would not have got this work had he remained a director. However, one must, as Lord Upjohn pointed out in *Phipps* v *Boardman* look at the passages in the speeches in *Regal* having regard to the facts of that case to which those passages and those statement were directed. I think Mr Brown was right when he said that it is the basic principle which matters. It is an over-riding principle of equity that a man must not be allowed to put himself in a position in which his fiduciary duty and his interests conflict. ...'

Joint Receivers and Managers of Niltan Carson Ltd v *Hawthorne* [1988] BCLC 298 (Hodgson J)

Fiduciary duty – profits – substantial property transaction

Facts

A company (later called Niltan Carson Ltd) was formed by Mr Nelson and its directors and shareholders included Mr Nelson, Mrs Hawthorne and their son Vaughan. The company bought a hotel which Mrs Hawthorne ran; the family lived there. The hotel did not prosper and Mrs Hawthorne, a teacher, conceived the idea of using the premises as a community home for children in the care of local authorities. She made it clear to Mr Nelson, the company's managing director, that she would run the home herself, independently of the company. Mr Nelson agreed to this and they and Vaughan agreed that there should be a letting of the premises to Mrs Hawthorne's daughter Nilou as her nominee and that Mrs Hawthorne should pay the company £1,500 a month rent for a periodic monthly tenancy. Various disputes arose which fell to be determined in the proceedings.

Held

1. Although there was no written memorandum or note of the agreement to satisfy s40(1) of the Law of Property Act 1925, Mr Nelson had agreed on behalf of the company to grant the tenancy, the contract had been partly performed and it was therefore enforceable.
2. As Mr Nelson had failed to produce any evidence of the value of the lease, no breach of s48 of the Companies Act 1980 (see now s320 of the Companies Act 1985) had been established.
3. The contract was not voidable on general equitable principles as the company's articles provided that a director could retain any profit made from a transaction with the company and that such a contract was not liable to be avoided.
4. Mrs Hawthorne had not acted in breach of her fiduciary duty to the company.
5. Mrs Hawthorne was entitled to the local authority fees and they did not form part of the company's assets, subject to a charge given by the company under which debenture-holders had appointed receivers and managers.

Hodgson J:

'None of Mr Nelson's many submissions have any merit whatsover, but perhaps the least meritorious is his contention that the agreement to grant a lease which he made on behalf of the company in April 1983 is one on which no action can be brought, because there is no memorandum or note in writing, contrary to s40(1) of the Law of Property Act 1925. The contract was made between the managing director, who was the father of the majority shareholder, with another director, who was the mother of the majority shareholder, and with the approval of the majority shareholder who was also a director. It would be astonishing if anyone would think it necessary that such a contract should be reduced to writing or need a note or memorandum to make it enforceable.

However, s40(1) does not, of course, in terms affect the law relating to part performance, and I am satisfied that there was, in this case, part performance ...

I now turn to consider s48 of the 1980 Act. Mr Nelson's main contention has throughout been that the contract ... was illegal because it contravened s48 ... Mr Nelson submits that the value of this lease exceeds 10 per cent of the net assets of £50,000, but has adduced no evidence as to what the value of the lease was or how the value of such a lease is calculated. Nor has he produced any accounts of the company although, certainly in 1981, there were such accounts. It seems to me clear that anyone who alleges that a non-cash asset exceeds the requisite value has to prove that fact. I have no idea how a monthly periodic lease is valued. No premium was agreed to be paid, and the obligation to pay the rent of £1,500 per month would presumably appear in Mrs Hawthorne's business accounts as a debt item. I cannot imagine that anyone could value a lease of this nature at over £50,000, and I have no idea whether its value, which I know not anyway, exceeds 10 per cent of the net assets. Mr Nelson seeks to invoke s48(2)(b) but he cannot, I think, do that in the absence of evidence as to the latest accounts and evidence as to the value of the lease.

In the absence of any evidence as to value it is, I think, impossible to hold that the April agreement contravenes the section ...

Of the main submissions made on the Chancery issue part of this case, that only leaves Mr Nelson's contention that the agreement of April was contrary to the equitable principle laid down in *Aberdeen Rly Co* v *Blaikie Bros* (1854) 1 Macq 461 and he has bombarded me with authority which, he submits, shows that Mrs Hawthorne was in breach of her fiduciary duty to the company in acting as she did.

So far as the *Aberdeen Rly Co case* was concerned, Mr Nelson seemed to have completely overlooked the waiver clause in reg 84(3) of the table A of the 1948 Act, which had been incorporated into the articles of association of the company. So far as relevant, that regulation reads:

"... no director ... shall be disqualified by his office from contracting with the company ... as vendor, purchaser or otherwise, nor shall any such contract ... be liable to be avoided, nor shall any director so contracting ... be liable to account to the company for any profit realised by any such contract or arrangement by reason of such director holding that office or of the fiduciary relation thereby established."

There was, therefore, nothing ex facie illegal with the contract made in April. Mr Nelson also cited case after case, all designed to show that Mrs Hawthorne had acted in breach of her fiduciary duty. In every case there was an element of unconscionable behaviour, secret profit, deception or non-disclosure, and none seemed to me to be in any way relevant to what happened in this case. I think it is really plain that, on my findings of fact, and I reach them all without doubt or hesitation, there can be no possible suggestion that Mrs Hawthorne was, at any time, in breach of her fiduciary duties. The company did not want to run the home (as was the case in *Peso Silver Mines Ltd* v *Cropper* (1966) 58 DLR (2d) 1; it was only too happy for Mrs Hawthorne to take the risk and, if she could, make the profit, and everyone was very happy with the arrangement until Mr Nelson's volte face. I do not propose to burden this already lengthy judgment with a detailed examination of all the cases cited to me by Mr Nelson. Every one of them seemed to me to be based on fact situations miles away from the affairs of this family company, and quite irrelevant to them.

Finally, I should say that, in my view, Mrs Hawthorne would, if necessary, be entitled to rely on a promissory estoppel. She certainly substantially altered her position, and expended time, effort and money in reliance on the promise made to her on behalf of the company by Mr Nelson. In the Chancery issue, Mr Nelson seeks equitable remedies; to do that he must come with clean hands, and that he cannot do for the remedies he seeks would result in his promise being broken, his promise, I add, being made on behalf of the company ...

I turn then to consider the interpleader issues ... I do so on the basis that the contracts entered into with the boroughs by Mrs Hawthorne were made on her own personal behalf, and that there was nothing unlawful or in breach of any fiduciary duty she owed to the company in her so doing. The company never had any interest or rights over any money received as fees from the boroughs. They at all times belonged to Mrs Hawthorne in her personal capacity. Therefore, when ... the floating charge crystallised by the appointment of receivers and managers, the company had no claim to or rights over the moneys due from, or paid into court by, the boroughs. Accordingly, the money formed no part of the assets of the company and, therefore, on crystallisation there was nothing on which the charge could settle.'

Commentary

Section 40 of the Law of Property Act 1925 was repealed by the Law Reform (Miscellaneous Provisions) Act 1989.

Lee Panavision Ltd v *Lee Lighting Ltd* [1991] BCC 620 Court of Appeal (Dillon, Stocker LJJ and Sir David Croom-Johnson)

Directors' resolution unconstitutional

Facts
Panavision had been appointed managing agent of Lighting with exclusive control of its business. Westward Communications plc, the beneficial owner of all of Lighting's issued shares, gave notice to terminate the management agreement and that it would replace Lighting's directors. Before the notice of termination expired, Lighting's present directors resolved that Lighting should enter into a second management agreement with Panavision. In the circumstances, was this within their powers, however much they might have thought it was in that company's interest, as well as Panavision's, to thwart the intentions of the 100 per cent shareholders?

Held
It was not. As Dillon LJ explained, it was unconstitutional for the directors, knowing that the shareholders were proposing as soon as they could to exercise their constitutional right to appoint new directors, to take all managerial powers away from such new directors by committing Lighting to the second management

agreement. His Lordship recalled that it was well established that directors could not use their powers to perpetuate their or their friends' control of their company (see *Piercy* v *S Mills & Co Ltd* [1920] 1 Ch 77) and that in *Howard Smith Ltd* v *Ampol Petroleum Ltd* [1974] AC 821, 834 Lord Wilberforce had said that where the self-interest of directors was involved, they were not permitted to assert that their action was bona fide thought to be in the interest of the company.

Neptune (Vehicle Washing Equipment) Ltd v *Fitzgerald* [1995] BCC 474 Chancery Division (Lightman J)

Directors' duties – self dealing by a director – whether a sole director had to comply with s317

Facts
The defendant was the sole director of the plaintiff company. A majority shareholding was acquired in the plaintiff by a holding company who appointed Phillips to represent its interests. His involvement in the plaintiff company became so great that the defendant felt that his services were no longer required. He therefore passed resolutions as sole to terminate his service contract, under which he acted as the plaintiff's managing director, and also to award himself over £100,000 compensation. He then retired as a director. The plaintiff, under a new director, sought recovery of the money. Awarding himself compensation in this way amounted to self-dealing. Article 13 of the company's articles of association allowed self-dealing by directors, but required the director to comply with s317 (CA) 1985 and disclose his interest in the contract to the board of directors. This raised a preliminary point whether a sole director had to comply with s317 and, if so, how.

Held
A sole director must comply with s317. He should hold a meeting with himself and make a disclosure to himself which should be recorded in the minutes, otherwise it might be difficult for a court to accept that the declaration had been made. If another person is present, such as the company secretary, then the declaration has to be read out loud and, again, recorded.

Lightman J:

'In the context of legislation which specifically authorises sole directorships and where Table A provides for a committee of one, the legislature cannot have intended by use of the word "meeting" in s317 to exclude from its ambit and the achievement of the statutory object sole directors, and I so hold. This conclusion is reinforced by the consideration that the concept of the holding of a directors' meeting in case of a sole directorship is familiar to company lawyers.

Two different situations may arise. The sole director may hold a meeting attended by himself alone or he may hold a meeting attended by someone else, normally the company secretary. When holding the meeting on his own, he must still make the declaration to himself and have the statutory pause for thought, though it may be that the declaration does not have to be out loud, and he must record that he made the declaration in the minutes. The court may well find it difficult to accept that the declaration has been made if it is not so recorded. If the meeting is attended by anyone else, the declaration must be made out loud and in the hearing of those attending, and again should be recorded. In this case, if it is proved that the declaration was made, the fact that the minutes do not record the making of the declaration will not preclude proof of its making. In either situation the language of the section must be given full effect: there must be a declaration of the interest.

In the present case, the meeting at which the resolutions were passed was attended by the defendant as sole director and by the company secretary. The minute makes no reference to any such declaration being made, but that is not conclusive. There is a substantial issue between the parties which I cannot resolve on the affidavit evidence before me whether the necessary declaration was made. I must therefore leave over this issue to the trial as also the vexed question of law (which will only arise if the declaration was not made) whether this failure is fatal to any defence to the plaintiff's claim for recovery on grounds of self-dealing. The trial judge will in this event have to decide whether (in accordance with orthodox doctrine) the rule of equity gives the plaintiff an absolute right to recovery or whether today the rule is more flexible and the court has some residual discretion, at least if there is "a mere technical non-declaration" of an interest shared by or known to all the directors: consider *Lee Panavision Ltd* v *Lee Lighting Ltd* [1991] BCC 620 at p637 and *Runciman* v *Walter Runciman plc* [1993] BCC 223 at p233.'

Peso Silver Mines Ltd v *Cropper* (1966) 58 DLR (2d) 1 Supreme Court of Canada (Cartwright, Martland, Judson, Ritchie and Hall JJ)

Fiduciary duty – whether a director can take benefit of corporate opportunity after it has been bona fide rejected by board

Facts

Cropper was managing director of Peso which was involved in the exploration and development of mineral claims. In 1960 Peso had a large number of claims upon which it was doing field work and its financial resources were strained because of this. Further claims were offered to Peso but it neither needed nor wanted them at this time. In 1962 certain claims which were highly speculative in nature were offered to Peso. The board considered these and rejected them. At this time it was usual for Peso to be offered two or three mining properties per week and the board's decision was bona fide in the interests of the company. Cropper was persuaded by several persons to join in forming a company to take up the claim rejected by the board and he informed the Peso board of these matters. However, Peso demanded that he should turn his interest over to Peso and when he refused they dismissed him and sued him for an account on the ground that he had breached his fiduciary duty to Peso. Cropper counterclaimed for damages for wrongful dismissal.

Held

Although Cropper had been in a fiduciary relationship to Peso when it was first offered the claims in 1962, he was not in a fiduciary relationship when the offer to acquire the properties was made to him through the companies he helped form. Therefore, he had not obtained the claims by reason of the fact that he was a director of Peso. Further, the offer made to Peso did not contain any confidential information to which Cropper had access and the subsequent offer was made to him as a member of the public.

Cartwright J:

'... On the facts of the case at bar I find it impossible to say that the respondents obtained the interests he holds in Cross Bow and Mayo by reason of the fact that he was a director of the appellant and in the course of the execution of that office.

When Dickson, at Dr Alio's suggestion, offered the claims to the appellant, it was the duty of the respondent as director to take part in the decision of the board as to whether that offer should be accepted or rejected. At that point he stood in a fiduciary relationship to the appellant. There are affirmative findings of fact that he and his co-directors acted in good faith, solely in the interests of the appellant and with sound business reasons for rejecting the offer. There is no suggestion in the evidence that the offer to the appellant was accompanied by any confidential information unavailable to any prospective purchaser or that the respondent directors had access to any such information by reason of his office. When, later, Dr Alio approached the respondent it was not in his capacity as a director of the appellant, but as an individual member of the public whom Dr Alio was seeking to interest as a co-adventurer ...'

Piercy v S Mills & Co Ltd [1920] 1 Ch 77 Chancery Division (Peterson J)

Fiduciary duty – issue of shares – whether for a proper purpose

Facts

The company had an issued share capital of 4,252 shares. The plaintiff was appointed a temporary manager in the company and the directors did not consider him suitable for the position. However, the plaintiff had a majority of shares (2,146) and he wished to be a director but the directors considered he was not a fit person to be a director of the company. The plaintiff gave the directors notice requiring them to call a general meeting at which he proposed resolutions for, inter alia, the removal of the existing directors and their replacement by himself and his brothers. Before the meeting took place the directors met and issued further shares in the company to themselves and a friend so that they could retain control. The plaintiff's resolutions were defeated at the meeting but he purchased further shares and attained a majority again. He then requisitioned the directors to call another meeting and, again, the directors allotted more shares to themselves to keep control. When the plaintiff discovered the further allotment he brought this action to determine whether the directors' actions were legitimate.

Held

A power to issue shares in a limited company for the purpose of enabling them to raise capital when required for the purpose of the company was a fiduciary power to be exercised by them bona fide for the benefit of the company. When the company was in no need of further capital the directors were not entitled to use this power to retain themselves in control or to defeat the wishes of an existing majority of shareholders.

Peterson, J:

'... The question is whether the directors were justified in acting as they did, or whether their conduct was a breach of the fiduciary powers which they possessed under the articles. What they did in fact was to override the wishes of the holders of the majority of the shares of the company for the time being by the issue of fresh shares issued solely for that purpose. There are two cases to which my attention has been called. One is *Fraser v Whalley* (1864) 2 HCM & M 10, in which there are some observations which are in point, though I agree that the case had points of difference from the present case. The learned judge in that case came to the conclusion that the directors were not justified in using their powers for a purpose which had once been authorised but which had come to an end. In the course of the argument the Vice-Chancellor remarked:

"No doubt both sides think their views the best for the company. But have you a right to force your views upon the majority of the shareholders by the exercise of a power of this kind?"

In his judgment the Vice-Chancellor said:

"I cannot look upon these directors otherwise than as trustees for a public company, and I must judge of the propriety of their conduct in this matter on the ordinary principle applicable to cases of trustee and cestui que trust ... But ... the point is reduced to this – the directors are informed that at the next general meeting they are likely to be removed; and therefore, on the very verge of a general meeting, they, without giving notice to anyone, with this indecent haste and scramble which is shown by the times at which the meetings were held, resolve that shares are, on the faith of this obsolete power entrusted to them for a different purpose, to be issued for the very purpose of controlling the ensuing general meeting. I have no doubt that the court will interfere to prevent so gross a breach of trust. I say nothing on the question whether the policy advocated by the directors, or that which I am told is to be pursued by Savin, is the more for the interest of the company. That is a matter wholly for the shareholders ... If the directors can clandestinely, and at the last moment, use a stale resolution for the express purpose of preventing the free action of the shareholders, this court will take care that, when the company cannot interfere, the court will do so."

It was said that the real point of that case was that the directors were using what the Vice-Chancellor calls a stale resolution, but I think the real substance of his judgment is that the directors were not entitled to issue shares for the express purpose of preventing the free action of the shareholders. In *Punt* v *Symons & Co* [1903] 2 Ch 506 the question was again somewhat similar to that in the present case. Byrne J in a reserved judgment, after dealing with the first point, which is immaterial for the present purpose, says this:

> "I now come to the last and most important point. It is argued on the evidence that but for the issue by the directors of the shares under their powers as directors, and, therefore, in their fiduciary character under the general power to issue shares, it would have been impossible to pass the resolution proposed; and that the shares were not issued bona fide, but with the sole object and intention of creating voting power to carry out the proposed alteration in the articles."

The shares, he says, were not issued bona fide for the general advantage of the company, but they were issued with the immediate object of controlling the holders of the greater number of shares in the company, and of obtaining the necessary statutory majority for passing a special resolution. Then he continues:

> "A power of the kind exercised by the directors in this case, is one which must be exercised for the benefit of the company: primarily it is given them for the purpose of enabling them to raise capital when required for the purposes of the company. ... When I find a limited issue of shares to persons who are obviously meant and intended to secure the necessary statutory majority in a particular interest, I do not think that is a fair and bona fide exercise of the power."

The basis of both cases is, as I understand, that directors are not entitled to use their powers of issuing shares merely for the purpose of maintaining their control or the control of themselves and their friends over the affairs of the company, or merely for the purpose of defeating the wishes of the existing majority of shareholders. That is, however, exactly what has happened in the present case. With the merits of the dispute as between the directors and the plaintiff I have no concern whatever. The plaintiff and his friends held a majority of the shares of the company, and they were entitled, so long as that majority remained, to have their views prevail in accordance with the regulations of the company; and it was not, in my opinion, open to the directors, for the purpose of converting a minority into a majority, and solely for the purpose of defeating the wishes of the existing majority, to issue the shares which are in dispute in the present action ...'

Regal (Hastings) Ltd v *Gulliver* [1942] 1 All ER 378 House of Lords (Viscount Sankey, Lords Russell, MacMillan, Wright and Porter)

Fiduciary duty – accountability for profits

Facts
Regal was incorporated in 1933 and owned and managed, very successfully, a cinema in Hastings called the Regal. In 1935 the directors of Regal formed a scheme to acquire leases of two other cinemas and then to sell their own cinema together with the leasehold interest in the two cinemas they proposed to acquire. A subsidiary company was formed to acquire the leases, it had a share capital of 5,000 £1 shares. The leases were offered to the subsidiary but the landlord insisted that the directors guarantee the rent unless the paid up capital of the subsidiary was £5,000. The purpose of the scheme had been that Regal should own all the shares in the subsidiary but it was unable to purchase more than £2,000 of the shares. Therefore, the directors, not wanting to give the guarantee made the following arrangement: Regal would purchase 2,000 shares, the chairman found buyers of 500 shares, each of the four directors would take 500 shares and the company solicitor, Garton, would take 500 shares. The scheme to sell the three cinemas fell through and a new scheme was devised under which the buyer would buy the shares in Regal and the subsidiary from the individual shareholders. This scheme was successful and as a result the 3,000 shares in the subsidiary held otherwise than by Regal were sold for £3 16s 1d per share, ie a profit of £2

16s 1d. A new board of directors took over in Regal and they launched this action to recover from Regal's five former directors and the company solicitor the profit they made on the shares.

Held

The directors, other than the chairman, had in the circumstances made a profit out of their fiduciary position to the company and were liable to repay the profit they made. The chairman was not liable to repay the profit on the shares he found purchasers for since he did not take them beneficially and the purchasers were not in a fiduciary relationship to the company. The solicitor was not liable to repay the profit as he did not stand in a fiduciary relationship to the company.

Lord Russell:

'... The rule of equity which insists on those, who by use of a fiduciary position make a profit, being liable to account for that profit, in no way depends on fraud, or absence of bona fides; or upon such questions or considerations as whether the profit would or should otherwise have gone to the plaintiff, or whether the profiteer was under a duty to obtain the source of the profit for the plaintiff, or whether he took a risk or acted as he did for the benefit of the plaintiff, or whether the plaintiff has in fact been damaged or benefited by his action. The liability arises from the mere fact of a profit having, in the stated circumstances, been made. The profiteer, however honest and well-intentioned, cannot escape the risk of being called upon to account ...

... Let me now consider whether the essential matters, which the plaintiff must prove, have been established in the present case. As to the profit being in fact made there can be no doubt. The shares were acquired at par and were sold three weeks later at a profit of £2 16s 1d per share. Did such of the first five respondents as acquired these very profitable shares acquire them by reason and in course of their office of directors of Regal? In my opinion, when the facts are examined and appreciated, the answer can only be that they did. The actual allotment no doubt had to be made by themselves and Garton (or some of them) in their capacity as directors of Amalgamated; but this was merely an executive act, necessitated by the alteration of the scheme for the acquisition of the lease of the two cinemas for the sole benefit of Regal and its shareholders through Regal's shareholding in Amalgamated. That scheme could only be altered by or with the consent of the Regal board. Consider what in fact took place on 2 October 1935. The position immediately before that day is stated in Garton's letter of 26 September, 1925. The directors were willing to guarantee the rent until the subscribed capital of Amalgamated reached £5,000. Regal was to control Amalgamated and own the whole of its share capital, with the consequence that the Regal shareholders would receive their proportion of the sale price of the two new cinemas. The respondents then meet on 2 October 1935. They have before them an offer to purchase the Regal cinema for £77,500, and the lease of the two cinemas for £15,000. The offer is accepted. The draft lease is approved and a resolution for its sealing is passed in anticipation of completion in five days. Some of those present, however, shy at giving guarantees, and accordingly the scheme is changed by the Regal directors in a vital respect. It is agreed that a guarantee shall be avoided by the six respondents bringing the subscribed capital up to £5,000. I will consider the evidence and the minute in a moment. The result of this change of scheme (which only the Regal directors could bring about) may not have been appreciated by them at the time; but its effect upon their company and its shareholders was striking. In the first place, Regal would no longer control Amalgamated, or own the whole of its share capital. The action of its directors had deprived it (acting through its shareholders in general meeting) of the power to acquire the shares. In the second place, the Regal shareholders would only receive a largely reduced proportion of the sale price of the two cinemas. The Regal directors and Garton would receive the moneys of which the Regal shareholders were thus deprived ...

... My Lords, I have no hesitation in coming to the conclusion, upon the facts of this case, that these shares, when acquired by the directors, were acquired by reason, and only by reason of the fact that they were directors of Regal, and in the course of their execution of that office ...'

His Lordship then reviewed several cases and continued:

'... In the result, I am of opinion that the directors standing in a fiduciary relationship to Regal in regard to the exercise of their powers as directors, and having obtained these shares by reason and only by reason of the fact that they were directors of Regal and in the course of the execution of that office, are accountable for the profits which they have made out of them. The equitable rule laid down in *Keech* v *Sandford* (1726) Sel Cas Ch 61 and *Ex p James* (1803) 8 Ves 337, and similar authorities applies to them in full force. It was contended that these cases were distinguishable by reason of the fact that it was impossible for Regal to get the shares owing to lack of funds, and that the directors in taking the shares were really acting as members of the public. I cannot accept this agument. It was impossible for the cestui que trust in *Keech* v *Sandford* to obtain the lease, nevertheless the trustee was accountable. The suggestion that the directors were applying simply as members of the public is a travesty of the facts. They could, had they wished, have protected themselves by a resolution (either antecedent or subsequent) of the Regal shareholders in general meeting. In default of such approval, the liability to account must remain. The result is that, in my opinion, each of the respondents Bobby, Griffiths, Bassett and Bentley is liable to account for the profit which he made on the sale of his 500 shares in Amalgamated.

The case of the respondent Gulliver, however, requires some further consideration, for he has raised a separate and distinct answer to the claim. He says: "I never promised to subscribe for shares in Amalgamated. I never did so subscribe. I only promised to find others who would be willing to subscribe. I only found others who did subscribe. The shares were theirs. They were never mine. They received the profit. I received none of it." If these are the true facts, his answer seems complete. The evidence in my opinion establishes his contention. Throughout his evidence Gulliver insisted that he only promised to find £500, not to subscribe it himself ...

There remains to consider the case of Garton. He stands on a different footing from the other respondents in that he was not a director of Regal. He was Regal's legal adviser; but, in my opinion, he has a short but effective answer to the plaintiff's claim. He was requested by the Regal directors to apply for 500 shares. They arranged that they themselves should each be responsible for £500 of the Amalgamated capital, and they appealed, by their chairman, to Garton to subscribe the balance of £500 which was required to make up the £3,000. In law his action, which has resulted in a profit, was taken at the request of Regal, and I know of no principle or authority which would justify a decision that a solicitor must account for profit resulting from a transaction which he has entered into on his own behalf, not merely with the consent, but at the request of his client.'

Teck Corporation v *Millar* (1973) 33 DLR (3d) 288 British Columbia Supreme Court (Berger J)

Whether directors had acted bona fide in the best interests of the company

Facts

Afton Mines Ltd purchased the options on mining claims near Kamloops, British Columbia, in 1964 since its directors felt there was a copper ore body there. Afton lacked the financial resources and, to some extent, the facilities to carry on drilling and development of the property and in 1965 attempted to interest major mining companies in the property. These attempts were not very successful and further money for drilling had to be obtained by underwriting the company's shares. In September 1971 drilling results were encouraging and interest was aroused in Afton. Millar, the president of the company, was besieged by major mining companies seeking to obtain a deal. Two companies who were interested were Placer and Teck. Afton's directors preferred Placer since they had a better record of success in developing mines and had considerable experience and good personnel. On the other hand, Teck had a poor record in bringing mines into production, especially in British Columbia. However, Afton conducted negotiations with both companies in order to obtain the best possible deal, but finally decided to contract with Placer. During the negotiations Teck attempted an alternative move, namely, to attempt to purchase the shares in Afton. Millar and his co-directors were offered $4 per share but refused, Placer was only offering $3 per share. Teck then went into the open market and began to purchase Afton's shares and by May 1972 had acquired over 50 per cent of Afton's shares and advised Afton's directors accordingly. Teck then asked for its nominees to be placed on Afton's board and requistioned a general meeting to achieve this. Millar replied by formally entering into a contract with a subsidiary of Placer granting the subsidiary exclusive rights to develop the copper reserves. This contract was signed a few days after Afton became aware of Teck's 50 per cent plus holding and apart from granting development rights the subsidiary was given an option to acquire 30 per cent of Afton's voting shares. Consequently, Teck's take-over bid was undermined and in order to prevent the contract being implemented Teck brought this action claiming that Millar and his co-directors had abused their fiduciary powers in depriving Teck of the fruits of its victory.

Held

1. The directors had, in entering the contract with Placer, acted in what they honestly believed to be the best interest of the shareholders as a whole and not in their own interests since they considered that a take-over by Teck would be adverse to the company's interest in developing the mines.
2. Where directors on reasonable grounds and in good faith believed that a take-over of the company was likely to cause substantial damage to the company's interest they were entitled to use their powers to protect the company and they were not to be restrained from issuing shares or criticised for doing so for this purpose.

Berger J:

'... My own view is that the directors ought to be allowed to consider who is seeking control and why. If they believe that there will be substantial damage to the company's interests if the company is taken over, then the exercise of their powers to defeat those seeking a majority will not necessarily be categorised as improper.

I do not think that it is sound to limit the directors' exercise of their powers to the extent required by *Hogg* v *Cramphorn et al* [1967] Ch 254. But the limits of their authority must be clearly defined. It would be altogether a mistake if the law, in seeking to adapt itself to the reality of corporate struggles, were to allow the directors any opportunity of achieving an advantage for themselves at the expense of the shareholders. The thrust of companies legislation has brought us a long way since *Percival* v *Wright* [1902] 2 Ch 421.

If the directors have the right to consider the consequences of a takeover, and to exercise their powers to meet it, if they do so bona fide in the interest of the company, how is the court to determine their purpose? In every case the directors will insist that their whole purpose was to serve the company's interest. And no doubt in most cases it will not be difficult for the directors to persuade themselves that it is in the company's best interests that they should remain in office. Something more than a mere assertion of good faith is required.

How can the court go about determining whether the directors have abused their powers in a given case? How are the court to know, in an appropriate case, that the directors were genuinely concerned about the company and not merely pursuing their own selfish interests? Well, a similar task has been attempted in cases of conspiracy to injure. There the question is whether the primary object of those alleged to have acted in combination is to promote their own interests or to damage the interests of others: *Crofter Hand Woven Harris Tweed Co Ltd* v *Veitch* [1942] AC 435.

I think the courts should apply the general rule in this way: The directors must act in good faith. Then there must be reasonable grounds for their belief. If they say that they believe there will be substantial damage to the company's interests, then there must be reasonable grounds for that belief. If there are not, that will justify a finding that the directors were actuated by an improper purpose.

A similar test has been adopted in English law in another context. In *Shuttleworth* v *Cox Bros & Co*

(Maidenhead) Ltd et al [1927] 2 KB 9 a decision of the English Court of Appeal, the question was whether a company's articles were being changed bona fide for the benefit of the company ...' (His Lordship then referred to the judgment of Scrutton LJ and considered supporting US authorities.)

... Counsel then goes on to say that *Hogg* v *Cramphorn* lays it down that an allotment of shares and any transaction connected with it made for the purpose of defeating an attempt to secure a majority is improper, even if the directors genuinely consider that it would be deleterious to the company if those seeking a majority were to obtain control.

This, it seems to me, raises an issue of profound importance in company law. Lord Greene expressed the general rule in this way in *Re Smith & Fawcett Ltd* [1942] Ch 304 at 306:

> "They (the directors) must exercise their discretion bona fide in what they consider – not what a court may consider – to be in the interests of the company, and not for any collateral purpose."

Yet, if *Hogg* v *Cramphorn* is right, directors may not allot shares to frustrate an attempt to obtain control of the company, even if they believe that it is in the best interests of the company to do so. This is inconsistent with the law as laid down in *Re Smith & Fawcett*. How can it be said that directors have the right to consider the interests of the company, and to exercise their powers accordingly, but that there is an exception when it comes to the power to issue shares, and that in the exercise of such power the directors cannot in any circumstances issue shares to defeat an attempt to gain control of the company? It seems to me that this is what *Hogg* v *Cramphorn* says. If the general rule is to be infringed here, will it not be infringed elsewhere? If the directors, even when they believe they are serving the best interests of the company, cannot issue shares to defeat an attempt to obtain control, then presumably they cannot exercise any other of their powers to defeat the claims of the majority or, for that matter, to deprive the majority of the advantages of control. I do not think that the power to issue shares can be segregated on the basis that the rule in *Hogg* v *Cramphorn* applies only in a case of an allotment of shares ...'

Thornby v *Goldberg* (1965) 112 CLR 597 High Court of Australia (McTiernan, Kitto, Menzies, Windeyer and Owen JJ)

Whether directors had fettered their discretion in exercising their powers

Facts
An agreement was made between a group of persons called the 'O' Group and another group of persons, the 'G' Group, to reorganise a company in which the members of the 'O' Group held all the share capital and to demolish a building that the company owned in Sydney and redevelop the site. By the terms of the agreement, the directors of the company, who were members of the 'O' Group, bound themselves to do certain things in the reorganisation of the company and redevelopment of the building site. One of the issues in the case was whether the directors of a company could bind their discretion in this way.

Held
The court rejected the argument on the ground that the time when the discretion was to be exercised was now rather than later so that there was no question of the discretion being fettered.

Kitto J:

'... The argument for illegality postulates that since the discretionary powers of the directors are fiduciary in the sense that the exercise of them is required to be in good faith for the benefit of the company as a whole, an agreement is contrary to the policy of the law and void if thereby the directors purport to fetter their discretion ... There are many kinds of transactions in which the proper time for the exercise of the directors' discretion is the time of the negotiation of a contract and not the time at which the contract is to be performed. A sale of land is a familiar example. Where all the members of the company desire to enter as a group into a transaction such as that in the present case the transaction being one which requires action by the board of directors to decide whether their proposed action will be in the interests of the company as a whole is the time when the transaction is being entered into and not the time when their action under it is required. If at the former time they are bona fide of the opinion that it is in the interests of the company that the transaction should be entered into and carried into effect I see no reason why they should not bind themselves to do whatever under the transaction is to be done by the board. In my opinion the defendant's contention that the agreement is void for illegality should be rejected.

W & M Roith Ltd, Re [1967] 1 WLR 432 Chancery Division (Plowman J)

Whether directors had acted bona fide for the benefit of the company – provision of pension

Facts
The company was incorporated in 1934 and Mr Roith was a director of it from then until his death in 1959. All the shares were owned by Mr and Mrs Roith and two relations. In 1957 Mr Roith was in poor health and wished to make provision for his wife. In 1958 the company entered into a new service agreement with him that he should be its managing director and a director for life at such salary as should be agreed from time to time. The company also covenanted to pay Mrs Roith a pension of £1,040 pa for life in the event of Mr Roith's death in office. Mr Roith died in 1959 and at that time the company was prosperous. In 1963 the company went into voluntary liquidation. Mr Roith's executors put in a proof of debt in respect of the pension for £10,400 which the liquidators rejected. The executors took out a summons seeking to have the liquidators' decision reversed.

Held
The proof had been rightly rejected since the whole purpose of Mr Roith entering the service agreement in 1958 was to benefit his widow, by way of a pension, and not the company. The agreement was not bona fide for the benefit of the company.

Commentary
Re Lee Behrens and Co Ltd [1932] 2 Ch 46 applied.

Welfab Engineers Ltd, Re [1990] BCC 600 High Court (Hoffmann J)

Directors – sale of company's assets

Facts
In late 1982 the company was trading at a loss and it was being pressed by the bank to reduce its borrowing. Its principal asset was its freehold premises, valued earlier that year at £145,000. Although two other offers had been made, in March 1983 the directors decided to sell the premises, equipment and work in progress for £110,000 the purchaser having agreed to take over the entire work force, including the directors. £103,000 went to repay the bank as debenture-holder, leaving very little for other creditors when the company was wound up three months later. On the hearing of a misfeasance summons, the liquidators alleged, inter alia, that the directors had acted improperly because they had given priority to job preservation and that, had they advertised the property, they may have obtained a higher price for it.

Held
The summons would be dismissed as the directors had not been in breach of duty, even if the sale had been at minimal undervalue. Hoffmann J said that, in judging the propriety of the directors' actions,

they should be compared with the alternatives of receivership or liquidation, in accordance with recent developments in insolvency law intended to encourage trying to save the business, rather than destroy it. An honest attempt to save the business should not be judged by a stricter standard, particularly against the background of pressures which must have been imposed on directors by widespread unemployment and industrial devastation in the Midlands at the time. The directors were completely honest and believed in good faith that they were entitled to enter into the deal. In any case, they had acted honestly and reasonably and ought fairly to be excused from liability under s727 of the Companies Act 1985.

Relieving directors from breach of duty

Cook v Deeks (1916) 1 AC 554 Privy Council (Lord Buckmaster LC)

Breach of duty – satisfaction

Facts
The Toronto Construction Co was formed in 1905 in order to tender for contracts for the construction of railway lines for the Canadian Pacific Railway Co. The directors and shareholders in the company were G S Deeks, C M Deeks, Cook and Hinds and each held a quarter of the shares, with the exception of four shares held by Mrs G S Deeks to bring the number of members up to five to fulfil statutory requirements. The Toronto company was very successful in tendering for contracts with the Canadian Pacific Railway. In 1911 the Deekses and Hinds fell out with Cook and decided they could not longer continue in business with him. Subsequently, a large contract came up for tender from the Canadian Pacific Railway and the Deekses and Hinds used the Toronto company's facilities to obtain it. They then formed another company, the Dominion Construction Co and it took over the contract. Cook protested and issued a writ. The Deekses and Hinds called a meeting of the Toronto company to consider the question of its voluntary liquidation. Subsequently a resolution was passed to this effect plus resolutions to sell assets of the Toronto company to the Dominion company and to declare that the Toronto company had no interest in the contract. As the Deekses and Hinds held three-quarters of the voting shares they were able to outvote Cook on all these resolutions. Cook claimed a declaration that the contract was held by the Deekses, Hinds and the Dominion company as trustees for the Toronto company.

Held
The benefit of the contract belonged to the Toronto company and it must be accounted for. The purported ratification that the Toronto company had no interest in the contract was a fraud on the minority and ineffective.

Lord Buckmaster LC:

'... There remains the more difficult consideration of whether this position can be made regular by resolutions of the company controlled by the votes of these three defendants. The Supreme Court have given this matter the most careful consideration, but their Lordships are unable to agree with the conclusion which they reached. In their Lordships' opinion the Supreme Court has insufficiently recognised the distinction beetween two classes of case, and has applied the principles applicable to the case of a director selling to his company property which was in equity as well as at law his own, and which he could dispose of as he thought fit, to the case of a director dealing with property which, though his own at law, in equity belonged to his company. *North-West Transportation Co v Beatty* (1887) 12 App Cas 589 and *Burland v Earle* [1902] AC 83 both belonged to the former class. In each, directors had sold to the company property in which the company had no interest at law or in equity. If the company claimed any interest by reason of the transaction, it could only be by affirming the sale, in which case such sale, though initially voidable, would be validated by subsequent ratification. If the company refused to affirm the sale the transaction would be set aside, and the parties restored to their former position, the directors getting the property and the company receiving back the purchase price. There would be no middle course. The company could not insist on retaining the property while paying less than the price agreed. This would be for the court to make a new contract between the parties. It would be quite another thing if the director had originally acquired the property which he sold to his company under circumstances which made it in equity the property of the company. The distinction to which their Lordships have drawn attention is expressly recognised by Lord Davey in *Burland* v *Earle* and is the foundation of the judgment in *North-West Transportation Co* v *Beatty Estates Ltd* v *Marler* (1913) 114 TL 640292.

If, as their Lordships find on the facts, the contract in question was entered into under such circumstances that the directors could not retain the benefit of it for themselves, then it belonged in equity to the company, and ought to have been dealt with as an asset of the company. Even supposing it be not ultra vires of a company to make a present to its directors, it appears quite certain that directors holding a majority of votes would not be permitted to make a present to themselves. This would be to allow a majority to oppress the minority. To such circumstances *North-West Transportation Co* v *Beatty* and *Burland* v *Earle* have no application. In the same way, if directors have acquired for themselves property or rights which they must be regarded as holding on behalf of the company, a resolution that the rights of the company should be disregarded in the matter would amount to forfeiting the interest and property of the minority of shareholders in favour of the majority, and that by the votes of those who are interested in securing the property for themselves. Such use of voting power has never been sanctioned by the courts, and, indeed, was expressly disapproved in *Menier* v *Hooper's Telegraph Works* (1874) LR 9 Ch 250.
...'

Customs and Excise Commissioners v *Hedon Alpha Ltd* [1981] QB 818 Court of Appeal (Stephenson, Ackner and Griffiths LJJ)

Breach of duty – s727 of the Companies Act 1985 – whether directors had acted honestly and reasonably

Facts
The company carried on the business of an off course bookmaker. Between April 1978 and May 1979 the company failed to pay general betting duty on bets made with it; this amounted to over £18,000. As a result of the company's failure to pay the Customs and Excise brought proceedings under s2(2) of the Betting and Gaming Duties Act 1972 to recover the duty from the directors. This provision rendered the directors of the company jointly and severally liable for the duty if the company failed to pay. Gough, a director, entered a defence against the claim under s448 CA 1948 (now s727 CA 1985). The trial judge held that s448 did not apply in the circumstances. On appeal:

Held
Section 448 did not apply to civil claims brought against a director of a company by a stranger; it was limited to claims brought by the company or on behalf of the company against the director. In any event s448 could not apply to the present case since in the present 'proceeding ... for default' it was the company and not the director who was in default. The director was liable under s2(2) only if the company was in default.

Stephenson LJ:

'There is a surprising absence of authority (1) on the meaning of default in s448 and (2) on the extent of its applicaton on the section. As to (2) ... Pennington's *Company Law* 4th Ed 1979 p548 states:

"Relief can be given against any of the criminal penalties imposed by the Companies Acts 1948 and 1976 but not it would appear against civil liability to anyone other than the company, and so apparently no relief may be given in the rare cases where a member of the company has a personal right to sue the directors."

I agree with the judge below in preferring counsel for the Commissioners' submissions and construction of the statutes ... I would hold that s448 is inapplicable to the Commissioners' claim because it is inapplicable to any claim by third parties to enforce any liability except a director's liability to his company or his director's duties under the Companies Acts.

Wide and general though the words in s448 are, read in their context they do not allow an officer or auditor of a company to escape relief in "any" legal proceedings which may be brought against him in his capacity as an officer or auditor of the company by the rest of the world. If Parliament had wished to provide a director, whom it exceptionally makes liable to discharge a company liability, with the protection of s448 or some other protection, it would, in my judgment, have done so by express words. That Parliament had not done in s2 of the 1972 Act and it is that Act and not the 1948 Act which governs the appellant's liability for betting duty and imposes on him an absolute liability irrespective of knowlege or any personal default. But I also agree that if s448 did apply to claims by third parties, the Commissioners' claim is not a proceeding for default, since s2(2) of the 1972 Act gives the right to recover the debt against a director who is not in breach of any duty except a duty to pay on demand which he would not owe had it not been placed on him by the 1972 Act. If there was any duty, it was the company's ...'

Duomatic Ltd, Re [1969] 2 Ch 365 Chancery Division (Buckley J)

Breach of duty – s727 of the Companies Act 1985 – whether director had acted honestly and reasonably – compensation paid to a director

Facts
The facts of this case are set out in Chapter 8.1 above. For present purposes the question was whether a director of a company in liquidation (Elvins) acted in a manner which would bring him within the provisions of s448 (now s727) when he paid £4,000 as compensation to get rid of a fellow director who was frequently intoxicated, indiscreet with regard to company secrets and who had no security of tenure.

Held
Section 727 of the Companies Act could not be relied on as Elvins had not acted reasonably by taking legal advice.

Buckley J:

'Section 448 enables the court to grant relief where three circumstances are shown to exist. First of all, the position must be such that the person to be excused is shown to have acted honestly. Secondly, he must be shown to have acted reasonably. And thirdly, it must be shown that, having regard to all the circumstances of the case, he ought fairly to be excused. Let me say at once that nobody has impugned Mr Elvins' honesty in respect of any of these matters, and having seen him in the witness box I should be the last to do so. I therefore proceed on the footing that both in respect of the £4,000 and in respect of his drawings in the year to 30 April, 1964, he acted honestly. Did he act reasonably in those respects, and are the circumstances such that he ought to be excused?

Now as regards the £4,000 paid to Mr Hanley, Mr Hanley was not in a strong position to stipulate for any compensation for loss of office. He had no contract of service, he had no security of tenure of his seat on the board, his conduct during the 12 months or so preceding his departure from the board appears, from the evidence, to have been such as to merit very little consideration from the point of view of remuneration for his services during that period. He had been constantly in default in the performance of his duties and had been causing his co-directors a great deal of trouble, and his conduct seems to have been likely to have caused the company considerable damage. Nevertheless, in respect of the last 12 months or so of his service as a director of the company he received remuneration of the order of £5,000, and there really was no ground at all on which he could claim any compensation for loss of office as a director of the company. On the other hand I think it is very probable that Mr Elvins and Mr East were justified in their view that he could have made himself a considerable nuisance to the company had he chosen to do so after he had ceased to be a director. It never seems to have occurred to Mr Elvins or to Mr East that it would be desirable to obtain any professional advice as to what Mr Hanley's position was, what the strength of his bargaining position was. They obtained no legal advice and no professional advice of any other kind, except so far as they had advice from their accountant and auditor, Mr Preston ...

... In my judgment a director of a company dealing with a matter of this kind who does not seek any legal advice at all but elects to deal with the matters himself without a proper exploration of the considerations which contribute, or ought to contribute, to a decision as to what should be done on the company's behalf, cannot be said to act reasonably. In my judgment, Mr Elvins did not act reasonably in this respect. He failed to take those steps which, as a director of the company, he should have taken before making the bargain which he made with Mr Hanley. It may be that, after considering legal advice, and any other advice that he might have sought, he still would have thought it desirable to pay Mr Hanley something to get rid of him with as little friction as possible, but it does not follow that the sum which he would have paid him would have been £4,000. But the question I have to ask myself is whether, in acting in the way in which he did, Mr Elvins acted reasonably. I do not think he was acting in the way in which a man of affairs dealing with his own affairs with reasonable care and circumspection could reasonably be expected to act in such a case, for I think that any such imaginary character would take pains to find out all the relevant circumstances, many of which in this case depended on some knowledge of the law and ought to have encouraged Mr Elvins to seek the assistance of a legal adviser. Moreover, it was Mr Elvins' failure to seek legal advice that resulted in this payment being made in contravention of s191 of the Act of 1948 and constituted it an ultra vires payment which the company could not lawfully make. In these circumstances I do not think that the provisions of s448 avail Mr Elvins in respect of this sum ...'

Movitex Ltd v *Bulfield* [1988] BCLC 104 Chancery Division (Vinelott J)

Breach of duty – whether provision in articles could exclude or modify the self-dealing rule

Facts

In 1969 the plaintiff company Movitex contracted to buy certain freehold premises for the purpose of its business: Bulfield, Perry and Dawes were at that time Movitex's directors. As Movitex was financially unable to complete the purchase, on behalf of the board Bulfield arranged for the property to be conveyed to City Road Securities Ltd (CRS), a company set up by Bulfield and Perry of which they were the directors and shareholders. CRS completed the purchase and leased the property to Movitex (the first transaction). In 1974, when Bulfield, Perry and Thayer were the Movitex directors, it executed a mortgage and further charge of the leasehold interest in favour of Harper Investments Ltd (Harper) (the second transaction). Most of the Harper shares were held by trustees of settlements created by Perry, some by Perry personally, and Bulfield was a Harper director. The benefit of the mortgage and charge in favour of Harper was transferred to CRS. Movitex's art 99 modified the self-dealing rule and provided that a director could be interested in a contract with his company provided he made full disclosure of his interest. Where a director was so interested he could not vote on the matter or be counted towards the quorum. However, art 100 provided that these latter prohibitions did not apply to 'any contract or dealing ... with a corporation where (his) sole interest is that he is a director or other officer, member or creditor thereof.' Movitex sought to have the first transaction set aside on the ground, inter alia, that it constituted a breach of the self-dealing rule: it also sought to have the second transaction set aside on the ground that it had not been authorised by the company or that it had been authorised by a board to which proper disclosure of the interest of Bulfield and Perry in Harper had not been made.

Held

The first transaction would not be set aside. As to the second, the further charge would be set aside but the mortgage would not.

Vinelott J:

'I turn, therefore, to the questions of law which have been argued. Counsel for Movitex submitted that even if the first transaction was carried out in accordance with the agreement in principle and with the authority of Mr Dawes, Movitex is entitled none the less to have the transaction set aside on the ground that it constituted a breach of the rule which it will be convenient, following the example of Sir Robert Megarry V-C in *Tito* v *Waddell (No 2)* [1977] Ch 106 to describe as "the self-dealing rule", that no person who owes a fiduciary duty to another will be allowed to enter into a transaction in which he has a personal interest that may conflict with that duty or which may give rise to a conflict between a fiduciary duty to one and a fiduciary duty to another person.

Two questions arise. The first is whether this rule is modified in a material respect by the articles of association of Movitex. The second is whether, if the self-dealing rule is modified by the articles of Movitex, the modification is nullified by s205 of the Companies Act 1948 ... The true principle is that if a director places himself in a position in which his duty to the company conflicts with his personal interest or his duty to another, the court will intervene to set aside the transaction without inquiring whether there was any breach of the director's duty to the company. That is an over-riding principle of equity. The shareholders of the company, in formulating the articles, can exclude or modify the application of this principle. In doing so they do not exempt the director from or from the consequences of a breach of a duty owed to the company ... In the instant case Mr Perry and Mr Bulfield as directors of Movitex owed a statutory duty of disclosure under s199 of the 1948 Act and a duty of disclosure under art 99. Moreover, it is common ground that as directors of Movitex they owed a duty to promote the interests of Movitex and, where the interests of Movitex conflicted with their own, to prefer the interests of Movitex. Any purported modification of either duty would infringe s205.

The remaining question is whether in relation to the first transaction Mr Bulfield or Mr Perry was in breach of either of these duties. As regards the first of these duties, the duty "to declare the nature of his interest" must, I think, impose on a director the duty to disclose full information as to the nature of any transaction which it is proposed to enter into. The disclosure must be such that the other director or directors can see what his interest is and how far it goes ... No material information was withheld. Movitex could not afford to buy the ... property. Mr Perry and Mr Bulfield could. The question is whether, given that they alone could purchase the property and make it available to Movitex, they did so on terms which were fair to Movitex. I have no doubt that they did ...

Then it is said in the statement of claim that the seal of Movitex was affixed to the mortgage without the authority of the board. That claim in my judgment ... fails. Lastly, it is said in the statement of claim that the execution of the mortgage was a breach of Mr Perry's and Mr Bulfield's fiduciary duties to Movitex. In so far as the allegation is that the mortgage was not entered into in good faith for the benefit of Movitex, this claim is in my judgment wholly misconceived ...

The effect of non-disclosure of Mr Bulfield's and Mr Perry's interests in Harper (assuming in favour of Movitex that their interests were not disclosed) would be that neither could rely on art 100 as a defence to a claim that the transaction was in breach of the self-dealing rule. Where there is a breach of the self-dealing rule, the transaction is liable to be set aside on the application of the beneficiary and in an appropriate case the court may direct an account of any profit made by the fiduciary or award equitable compensation. Non-disclosure by itself cannot found an action for damages. In the instant case ... the only possible remedy would be to set aside the transaction. Neither Mr Bulfield nor Mr Perry directly or through Harper made any profit. Apart from non-disclosure the transaction was a perfectly proper one and, indeed, beneficial to Movitex. It is not suggested that the rate of interest was excessive; indeed no claim is made for recoupment of interest already paid. But it is elementary law that a transaction cannot be set aside unless restitutio in integrum is possible. So if a transaction is one of loan, it will only be set aside on payment of the sum advanced with any interest allowed by the court ... Once it is accepted, as I think it must be, that the rate of interest charged was fair, it follows that the mortgage cannot be set aside unless Movitex is willing to repay the mortgage debt with the arrears of unpaid interest. And that, of course, is all that CRS (as the person presently entitled to the benefit of the mortgage) seeks to obtain by enforcing the mortgage.'

His Lordship reviewed the facts as to the creation of the further charge and found that the charge had been created without the authority of the board of Movitex. It followed that Harper acquired no rights under the charge and CRS as assignee could be in no better a position and therefore CRS was an unsecured creditor of the company.

Commentary
Section 199 of the Companies Act 1948 is now s310 of the Companies Act 1985.

North-West Transportation Co v *Beatty* (1887) 12 App Cas 589 Privy Council (Lord Hobhouse, Sir Barnes Peacock, Sir Richard Baggallay and Sir Richard Couch)
Breach of duty – ratification – whether directors can vote

Facts
The company needed a boat and its directors entered into a contract with Beatty, who was one of the directors, to purchase one from him. However, the articles contained no provisions allowing a director to contract with the company. The contract was therefore put to a general meeting for approval and a resolution affirming it was carried against the wishes of minority shareholders who were outvoted by Beatty, who held the majority of the shares in the company. The price to be paid for the boat was fair but a minority shareholder sought to have the agreement set aside.

Held
The resolution was valid and there had been no unfairness or impropriety since Beatty had only used his votes as a shareholder to pass the resolution as he was entitled to do.

Sir Richard Baggallay:

'... Unless some provision to the contrary is to be found in charter or other instrument by which the company is incorporated the resolution of the majority of the shareholders, duly convened, upon any question with which the company is competent to deal, is binding upon the majority, and consequently upon the company, and every shareholder shall have a perfect right to vote upon any such question, although he may have a personal interest in the subject matter opposed to, or different from, the general or particular interests of the company ...

The only unfairness or impropreity which, consistently with the admitted and established facts could be suggested, arises out of the fact that the defendant J H Beatty possessed a voting power as shareholder which enabled him, and those who thought with him, to adopt the byelaw and thereby either to ratify and adopt a voidable contract into which he, as a director and his co-directors had entered or to make a similar contract, which latter seems to have been what was intended to be done by the resolution passed ...

But the constitution of the company enabled the defendant Beatty to acquire this voting power; there was no limit upon the number of shares which a shareholder might hold and for every share so held he was entitled to a vote; the charter itself recognised the defendant as a holder of 200 shares, one third of the aggregate number; he had a perfect right to acquire further shares and to exercise his voting power in such a manner as to secure the election of directors whose views upon policy agreed with his own and to support those views at any shareholders' meetings ... To reject the votes of the defendants upon the adoption of the byelaw would be to give effect to the minority and to disregard those of the majority ...'

Insider dealing

An Inquiry under the Company Securities (Insider Dealing) Act 1985, Re [1988] 2
WLR 33 House of Lords (Lord Keith of Kinkel, Lord Roskill, Lord Griffiths, Lord
Oliver of Aylmerton and Lord Goff of Chieveley).

Insider dealing – investigation under s177 FSA – journalist's refusal to disclose source of
information to inspectors – contempt of court

Facts

Mr Jeremy Warner was a financial journalist and he wrote two articles, one in 'The Times' and the
other in 'The Independent'. In the first article, he accurately predicted the decision of a reference of a
take-over bid to the Monopolies and Mergers Commission. In the second article, he predicted that
another take-over bid would be referred to the Commission by the Director General of Fair Trading, Sir
Gordon Borrie. It was suspected that this price sensitive information was being leaked by someone in
the Office of Fair Trading, the Department of Trade and Industry or the Monopolies and Mergers
Commission, to people who were using it to deal on the Stock Exchange in the shares of the companies
concerned, contrary to the Company Securities (Insider Dealing) Act 1985. Inspectors were appointed
under s177 of the Financial Services Act 1986 and, although there was no suggestion that Mr Warner had
dealt as an insider, they naturally wanted to question him about the source of his information. It was felt
that his source was close to the leak. He refused to answer the questions put to him about his sources,
claiming that he had a reasonable excuse under s10 of the Contempt of Court Act 1981, allowing
journalists to keep their sources confidential. The inspectors argued that disclosure under s10 was not
reasonable as the information was needed '… for the prevention of … crime.'

Held

Mr Warner had to answer the questions put to him by the inspectors. He continued to refuse to answer
questions relating to his source and was fined £20,000 for contempt, which was actually paid by the
newspaper for whom he worked.

Lord Oliver of Aylmerton:

'My Lords, I have had the advantage of reading in draft a speech delivered by my noble and learned friend,
Lord Griffiths. I entirely agree that, for the reasons which he has given, s10 of the Contempt of Court
Act 1981 is not directly applicable to a reference to the court under s178 of the Financial Services Act
1986. I also agree, however, that, even though not directly applicable, s10 is indicative of a general
policy which should, on such a reference, be applied by way of analogy. Thus the essential question raised
by this appeal is whether, it being accepted that unless the information sought can be brought within one
or other of the exceptions mentioned in s10 Mr Warner has a reasonable excuse for declining to disclose
it, it is information which is "necessary … for the prevention of … crime". That is the question which
the judge before whom it arises can determine only in the context of the particular facts proved before him
and I share the doubt expressed by my noble and learned friend whether it is either possible or desirable
to seek to provide for him, by reference to other more or less synonymous adjectives, some absolute
yardstick by which the question is to be answered. Necessity is a relative concept and the degree of need
before an act or measure can be said to be "necessary" although not, clearly, a question which is to be
answered without reference to some objective standards, must in the end be and remain a matter of
judgment.
    Like my noble and learned friend, I have found myself unable to accept that the expression "prevention
of … crime" in s10 of the Act of 1981 is to be construed in the narrow sense for which Mr Kentridge has
contended. Clearly, in enacting s10, Parliament was enunciating a public policy for the protection of a

journalist's or author's sources of information. Equally clearly, in providing for exceptional circumstances in which that protection should be overridden, it did so on the footing that those exceptions would have some practical application. The narrow construction contended for would as it seems to me, largely deprive the exception of any useful content at all, for it is difficult to imagine circumstances in which a court or tribunal would be concerned to investigate a particular anticipated crime. The words must bear a wider meaning than that and must, I think, at least embrace the detection and prosecution of crimes which are shown to have been committed and where detection and prosecution could sensibly be said to act as a practical deterrent to future criminal conduct of a similar type. I do not, therefore, for my part doubt that a disclosure required to enable persons shown to have been engaged in a criminal activity to be identified and prosecuted is a disclosure required for "the prevention of ... crime". At the same time it has to be borne in mind that the protection against disclosure is not lightly to be cast aside and that the conditions required for its removal have to be positively established to the satisfaction of the court. If there is a danger that the exception may be deprived of any useful content by too narrow an interpretation of the requirements for its application, there is equally a danger of the protection itself being attenuated to an unacceptable degree if the need for positive establishment of those requirements is too lightly regarded. What has chiefly concerned me in the instant appeal is whether this onus has been sufficiently discharged by the evidence filed on behalf of the inspectors. I have to confess to having entertained doubts on this score during the course of the hearing, although a careful examination of that evidence in the context of the inquiry which the inspectors were required to undertake has finally convinced me that the onus has been discharged. In my judgment, however, it has only narrowly been discharged and I am concerned that it should not be thought that the protection afforded by the Act can be overcome merely by a ritualistic assertion on affidavit that particular information is required for the prevention of crime. Obviously the court will pay a proper regard to the views of those constituting the inquiring body, who in the nature of things, know better than anyone else the stage which their inquiries have reached and what is needful for their successful prosecution. But it cannot, in my judgment, and must not be thought to be sufficient simply to say that the inquiry upon which the body is engaged is one which has as its object the detection and prevention of crime and that, because a deponent says that certain information is required for the purpose of the inquiry, it therefore follows inexorably that the information is necessary for "the prevention of ... crime". The court must, in my judgment, be presented at least with sufficient material to enable it to exercise an independent judgment on the extent of the need.

If the evidence filed on behalf of the inspectors is open to the criticism that it could have been more specific about the results so far of the inquiries undertaken, one can, at the same time, see very good reasons why the inspectors, in an inquiry whose avowed purpose is to identify and report on criminal activity, should not wish to reveal in greater detail than is strictly requisite the course which their inquiries are taking. What the evidence does disclose is, first, that there is a ring of people who have dealt on the Stock Exchange using price-sensitive information derived from at least one servant of the Crown. Secondly, it is demonstrated that the dealings have been on a considerable scale. Thirdly, it is an irresistible inference that the Crown servant or servants responsible for providing the price-sensitive information has or have been acting in breach of a duty of confidence. Fourthly, the inference is well-nigh irresistible that unless both the source of the information and the persons engaged in the ring can be identified and stopped the course of criminal conduct involved in such dealings is likely to continue. Fifthly, it is beyond dispute that Mr Warner, without any suggestion of impropriety on his part, is the author of two articles in which unpublished information has been deployed with an accuracy which cannot reasonably be attributed to mere coincidence. That information clearly was, before its publication by Mr Warner, price-sensitive information and it can, initially, only have come from a Crown servant. Now obviously the precise purpose which will be served by the disclosure of the source of Mr Warner's information is not capable of being predicated with complete accuracy until the disclosure takes place, but I cannot for my part think that the evidence can properly be criticised as insufficient simply on that score. It may be that it will lead, whether by way of original inquiry or by way of confirmation, directly to the identification of a member of the ring or of the Crown servant or servants involved. It may be that it will lead to the identification of someone not at present even suspected as a member of the dealing ring or to the revelation of a second and at present unidentified ring of dealers. It may be entirely inconclusive or serve only for the purpose of elimination. None of these results appears to me, on analysis, to disqualify it as information "necessary ... for the prevention of ... crime", for, if the exception in s10 is to have any sensible operation, it cannot, in my judgment, be an essential characteristic of such information that the result to which it will lead should be capable of being predicated with precision before it is even known what the information is. For these reasons and for the reasons contained in the speech of my noble and learned friend, Lord Griffiths, I agree that the appeal should be dismissed.'

Attorney-General's Reference (No 1 of 1988) [1989] 2 WLR 729 House of Lords (Lord Keith of Kinkel, Lord Templeman, Lord Ackner, Lord Oliver of Aylmerton and Lord Lowry)

Insider dealing – whether a person had 'obtained' information within s1(3) Company Securities (Insider Dealing) Act 1985

Facts

At his trial the appellant was acquitted on two counts of insider dealing. He had been given a piece of price-sensitive information by an employee of a merchant bank with whom he had been dealing. The information related to a take-over bid and the appellant went on to buy some shares in the target company, despite being told by the bank's employee of the price-sensitive nature of the information. At his trial he was acquitted on the basis that the elements of the offence had not been made out by the prosecution, in that he had not 'obtained' the information within the meaning of s1(3) of the Company Securities (Insider Dealing) Act 1985. The trial judge was satisfied that the meaning of the word 'obtained' meant that the appellant had to have acquired the information by purpose or effort, and not by receiving the information passively, by been given it without asking for it. On his acquittal, the Attorney-General referred the matter to the Court of Appeal who, at the appellant's request, referred the matter to the House of Lords under s36 of the Criminal Justice Act 1972.

Held

Affirming the decision of the Court of Appeal, the meaning of the word 'obtain' could be wider than acquiring information actively, that is, by purpose or effort. A person who receives information without effort has obtained it within the meaning of the Act.

Lord Templeman:

'My Lords, by ss1(3), 1(4) and 8 of the Company Securities (Insider Dealing) Act 1985, a criminal offence is committed, subject to exceptions and conditions not here material, where "an individual has information which he knowingly obtained (directly or indirectly) from" a person connected with a company knowing that the information is confidential unpublished price-sensitive information in relation to those shares.

The appellant was informed by a merchant bank connected with a company that a take-over bid had been agreed and that this information was confidential. The appellant promptly purchased 6,000 shares in the company on the Stock Exchange and, following the announcement of the take-over, made a profit of £3,000. If a member of the police force, after studying the Act of 1985, had asked the appellant whether he had obtained information and, if so, from whom, a truthful appellant would have answered that he obtained information from the merchant bank. Yet when the appellant was tried for an offence under the Act, the trial judge held that the appellant had not obtained any information.

The argument is that, according to the dictionary, information is not "obtained" if the information is volunteered. The object of the Act was to prevent insider dealing. The appellant became an insider when he learned of the take-over agreement and he became an insider dealer when he bought 6,000 shares.

Parliament cannot have intended that a man who asks for information which he then misuses should be convicted of an offence while a man who, without asking, learns the same information which he also misuses should be acquitted.

In *Customs and Excise Commissioners* v *Top Ten Promotions Ltd* [1969] 1 WLR 1163 this House construed a taxing statute and reached a conclusion adverse to the taxpayer. Lord Upjohn said, at p1171:

> "It is highly dangerous, if not impossible, to attempt to place an accurate definition upon a word in common use; you can look up examples of its many uses if you want to in the Oxford Dictionary but that does not help on definition; in fact it probably only shows that the word normally defies definition. The task of the court in construing statutory language such as that which is before your Lordships is to look at the mischief at which the Act is directed and then, in that light, to consider whether as a matter of common sense and everyday usage the known, proved or admitted or properly inferred facts of the particular case bring the case within the ordinary meaning of the words used by Parliament."

My Lords, without troubling any dictionary, I am satisfied that the appellant obtained information which he made no effort to obtain and that his subsequent misuse of that information was in breach of the Act of 1985.'

Commentary

The new insider dealing regime is contained in Part V of the Criminal Justice Act 1993, which repeals the Company Securities (Insider Dealing) Act 1985. The new provisions do not require the insider to have 'obtained' the information. Instead the Act applies where an individual 'has' information, thus removing any uncertainty about whether this has to be by effort on the recipients part. It does not.

10 Minority Protection

The rule in *Foss* v *Harbottle* and minority protection

George Fischer (Great Britain) Ltd v *Multi-Construction Ltd* [1995] BCC 310
Court of Appeal (Glidewell and McCowan LJJ and Sir Christopher Kerr)

Damages for breach of contract – whether holding company could claim damages for losses incurred by its wholly owned subsidiary

Facts
George Fischer (Great Britain) Ltd ('Fischer') was a holding company and ran its business through a number of wholly owned subsidiaries. 'Castings' manufactured metal piping, 'Plastics' manufactured plastic piping, and 'Sales' was a marketing company. Fischer contracted with the defendants for the design and construction of a warehouse and distribution centre, which was to be occupied by Sales as a storage and distribution centre for the metal and plastic pipes.

The defendants sub-contracted with a third party, 'Dexion', for the design and installation of three cranes inside the warehouse. The cranes were supposed to be able to store the pipes and also retrieve them when an order was received. The cranes had a design defect and as a result Fischer incurred additional operating costs of £262,000, and lost sales amounting to £229,000. The subsidiaries were not a party to the contract and so could not sue and the issue in the Court of Appeal was whether Fischer, as a shareholder in the subsidiaries, could sue for losses incurred by those subsidiaries. Dexion relied on the case of *Prudential* v *Newman Industries Ltd & Others (No 2)* [1982] Ch 204, on the basis that it was the company that should be the proper plaintiff for the loss in value of its shares, and not the individual shareholder.

Held
The claim by Fischer was not too remote and a £1 loss to the subsidiary companies was treated as also being a £1 loss to Fischer. As a 100 per cent shareholder in each of the three subsidiaries, Fischer was entitled to claim damages representing losses which it indirectly suffered as a result of the diminution of the value of its shares in the subsidiaries, or for the loss of its profits resulting from the diminution in the subsidiaries' profits. *Prudential* v *Newman Industries* was distinguished.

Sir Michael Kerr:

'I also agree. The so-called rule in *Foss* v *Harbottle*, and its discussion in *Prudential* v *Newman*, were both concerned with situations in which the company in question had a right of action, or would have had such a right if the alleged wrong done to it – whether it be tort or breach of contract or both – were established. The effect of the rule is accordingly that, save in exceptional circumstances, it must be left to the company, ie effectively to the majority of its shareholders, to exercise the company's right of action.

In the present case, however, the position is the opposite. The plaintiff, the 100 per cent shareholder in its three subsidiaries, has an unquestionable – and indeed admitted – right of action for damages (at least nominal) for breach of contract. The companies, on the other hand, have no right of action. The only issues which arise are therefore concerned with the determination of the loss, if any, which the shareholder plaintiff has suffered as the result of the breach of contract, and whether damages may be recovered for it. That determination involves questions of evidence, foreseeability and remoteness which were decided by the judge in favour of the plaintiff on the facts and on which there can be no appeal in this case. It follows that the present case is quite unaffected both by *Foss* v *Harbottle* and *Prudential* v *Newman*. I would accordingly dismiss this appeal ...'

Nurcombe v *Nurcombe* [1985] 1 WLR 370 Court of Appeal (Lawton, Browne-Wilkinson LJJ and Sir Denys Buckley)

Derivative action – whether member came with 'clean hands'

Facts
The plaintiff and her ex-husband, the defendant, were the shareholders in an investment company. The plaintiff held one share and the defendant held 99 shares in the company. The plaintiff and the defendant were divorced in 1974 and thereafter the plaintiff began proceedings against the defendant for financial provision. In the course of these proceedings it became apparent that in 1976 the company had purchased some valuable development land and, as sole director of the company, the defendant had negotiated the sale of 13 acres of this land, to another company he owned, for £125,000 and, via that company, sold the same 13 acres to Tesco Stores for £500,000. It was thus clear that the defendant had breached his fiduciary duty to the company. Having become aware of these facts the plaintiff continued her proceedings for financial relief and in making an award of a lump sum in these proceedings the judge took into account the breach of fiduciary duty and resulting profit made by the defendant. After receiving two instalments of the lump sum the plaintiff started a minority shareholder's action against the defendant seeking to recover from him the profit he had made from his breach of fiduciary duty. Vinelott J dismissed the plaintiff's action on the ground that she, by continuing the proceedings for financial relief after becoming aware of the defendant's breach of fiduciary duty, had elected to treat the profit as belonging to the defendant and thus could not now allege that it belonged to the company. The plaintiff appealed on the ground that she had brought this action for the benefit of the company and thus her personal interest in the outcome of the action was irrelevant.

Held
The appeal would be dismissed because a minority shareholder's action in which the plaintiff sued on behalf of the company was a mere procedural device to ensure that justice was done for the benefit of the company against its miscreant controllers. As such the court was entitled to look at the plaintiff's conduct to see if the plaintiff was a proper person to bring the action. Further, the defendant in a minority shareholder's action was entitled to raise any defence which could have been raised if the plaintiff had brought the action personally. In the circumstances it would be inequitable to allow the plaintiff to continue the minority shareholder's action as she had been aware of the defendant's wrongful conduct before she accepted an award in the proceedings for financial relief and this award had taken the defendant's conduct into account.

Browne-Wilkinson LJ:

'In my judgment behaviour by the minority shareholder, which, in the eyes of equity, would render it unjust to allow a claim brought by the company at his instance to succeed, provides a defence to a minority shareholder's action. In practice this means that equitable defences which would have been open to the defendants in an action brought by the minority shareholder personally (if the cause of action had been vested in him) would also provide a defence to those defendants in a minority shareholder's action brought by him ...

... Since the wrong complained of is a wrong to the company, not to the shareholder, in the ordinary way the only competent plaintiff in an action to redress the wrong would be the company itself. But, where such a technicality would lead to manifest injustice, the courts of equity permitted a person interested to bring an action to enforce the company's claim. The case is analogous to that in which equity permits a beneficiary under a trust to sue as plaintiff to enforce a legal right vested in trustees (which right the trustees will not themselves enforce), the trustees being joined as defendants. Since the bringing of such an action requires the exercise of the equitable jurisdiction of the court on the grounds that the interests of justice require it, the court will not allow such an action to be used in an inequitable manner so as to produce an injustice. *Towers* v *African Tug Co* [1904] 1 Ch 558 shows that "all personal objections against the individual plaintiff" must be considered. It is for this reason that, in my judgment, a court of equity will not allow a minority shareholder to succeed in a minority shareholder's action where there are equitable defences which, as between the shareholder personally and the defendants, the defendants could properly rely on in equity, eg the duty to elect between conflicting rights, acquiescence or lack of the minority shareholders ...'

Prudential Assurance Co Ltd v *Newman Industries Ltd (No 2)* [1982] Ch 204 Court of Appeal (Cumming Bruce, Templeman and Brightman LJJ)

Derivative action – proper procedure

Facts
In 1975 Thomas Poole and Gladstone China Ltd (TPG) was in serious financial difficulties. It had borrowings of over £1 million much of these being repayable on 31 January, 1975. TPG was in effect an investment company with substantial shareholdings in several companies quoted on the Stock Exchange, including Newman in which it had a 25 per cent shareholding. Over 35 per cent of the issued shares in TPG were held by a company known as Strongpoint Ltd and all the shares in Strongpoint were owned by Bartlett and Laughton. Bartlett and Laughton were directors of both TPG and Newman and in the case of Newman, Bartlett was the chairman and chief executive, while Laughton was the vice-chairman. Bartlett also had a personal shareholding in Newman.

TPG's financial difficulties were largely the result of a decline in the value of its shareholdings on the Stock Exchange. In order to keep TPG afloat Bartlett and Laughton conceived a plan under which TPG would sell certain shareholdings to Newman for £216,000. These shareholdings were in fact only worth about £141,000. Accordingly, in January 1975 an agreement was entered into between TPG and Newman to this effect with Bartlett and Laughton acting on behalf of Newman without the authority or knowledge of the Newman board. The money received by TPG failed to alleviate its difficulties and Bartlett and Laughton decided to sell all TPG's assets, save its shareholding in Newman and another asset, to Newman. A document was put before Newman's board explaining the transaction; this document contained misleading information as to the valuation of the assets, which document had been drawn up by Bartlett. TPG's assets were valued at £325,000; this was a gross over valuation. By deceit Bartlett and Laughton persuaded Newman's board to accept the valuation and the transaction, with the exception of one director who objected. Thus, in June 1975 Newman agreed to adopt the transaction and pay £325,000 for TPG's assets and assume TPG's liabilities. However, under Stock Exchange regulations the agreement was conditional on approval by Newman's shareholders. A circular was sent to all Newman's shareholders to explain the transaction and it recommended that shareholders vote in favour of it. The circular was drafted by Newman's solicitors with the assistance of Bartlett and Laughton. A meeting to approve the transaction was convened for 8 July 1975 but this meeting was adjourned until 29 July until a report could be obtained from a merchant bank on the merits of the transaction. This report was not ready by 29 July but the general meeting nevertheless passed a resolution approving the transaction on 29 July. The resolution obtained a small majority only. The plaintiff who held 3.2 per cent of the ordinary shares in Newman brought an action against Bartlett Laughton and TPG seeking (i) by way of derivative claim, on behalf of itself and the other shareholders of Newman, except Bartlett and TPG, damages against Bartlett and Laughton for breach of fiduciary duty to Newman; (ii) by way of a direct personal claim, damages for conspiracy against Bartlett and Laughton and (iii) by way of a representative claim on behalf of Newman shareholders as at 29 July 1975, except Bartlett and TPG, declarations that the circular issued to the shareholders was tricky and misleading, and damages against Bartlett and Laughton for conspiracy. At the trial of the action Vinelott J held that there was a good cause of action in the personal and representative claims. However, the plaintiff wished to pursue the derivative claim but Bartlett contended that this was not possible because the defendants did not have voting control of Newman. Vinelott J permitted the derivative claim to proceed because there was no prospect of Newman bringing an action itself. Bartlett and Laughton appealed.

Held

The appeal would be allowed in part beause when a minority shareholder brought a derivative action, the question whether the company was controlled by alleged wrongdoers had to be determined first before allowing the derivative action to proceed. Thus, the judge erred in dismissing the defendant's application as to whether the plaintiff was entitled to bring a derivative action. But, since the action had been heard and determined and Newman intended to accept the order of the court in its favour, it was no longer appropriate to decide the question as to whether the plaintiff was entitled to bring a derivative action in the circumstances.

Cumming Bruce, Templeman and Brightman JJ:

'... A derivative action is an exception to the elementary principle that A cannot, as a general rule, bring an action against B to recover damages or secure other relief on behalf of C for an injury done by B to C. C is the proper plaintiff because C is the party injured, and therefore the person in whom the cause of action is vested. This is sometimes referred to as the rule in *Foss* v *Harbottle* (1843) 2 Hare 461 when applied to corporations, but it has a wider scope and is fundamental to any rational system of jurisprudence. The rule in *Foss* v *Harbottle* also embraces a related principle, that an individual shareholder cannot bring an action in the courts to complain of an irregularity (as distinct from an illegality) in the conduct of the company's internal affairs provided that the irregularity is one which can be cured by a vote of the company in general meeting. We are not concerned with this aspect of the rule.

The classic definition of the rule in *Foss* v *Harbottle* is stated in the judgment of Jenkins LJ in *Edwards* v *Halliwell* [1950] 2 All ER 1064 as follows. (i) The proper plaintiff in an action in respect of a wrong alleged to be done to a corporation is, prima facie, the corporation. (ii) Where the alleged wrong is a transaction which might be made binding on the corporation and on all its members by a simple majority of the members, no individual member of the corporation is allowed to maintain an action in respect of that matter because, if the majority confirms the transaction, there is no valid reason why the company should not sue. (iii) There is no room for the operation of the rule if the alleged wrong is ultra vires the corporation, because the majority of members cannot confirm the transaction. (iv) There is also no room for the operation of the rule if the transaction complained of could be validly done or sanctioned only by a special resolution or the like, because a simple majority cannot confirm a transaction which requires the concurrence of a greater majority. (v) There is an exception to the rule where what has been done amounts to fraud and the wrongdoers are themselves in control of the company. In this case the rule is relaxed in favour of the aggrieved minority, who are allowed to bring a minority shareholders' action on behalf of themselves and all others. The reason for this is that, if they were denied that right, their grievance could never reach the court because the wrongdoers themselves, being in control, would not allow the company to sue.

By their summons issued on 10 May 1979 Mr Bartlett and Mr Laughton invoked the rule in *Foss* v *Harbottle*. After some two and a half days of argument the judge (on 18 June 1979) dismissed the summons, not on the ground that the plaintiffs were entitled to bring a derivative action but on the ground that it was more convenient to decide that issue after the action has been tried. For reasons which we explain later we have no doubt whatever that that was a wrong decision ...

... We turn now to certain of the authorities, starting with *Foss* v *Harbottle*. This case was decided in 1843 by the Court of Chancery. It came before Wigram V-C on demurrer. The facts are narrated in that report at intimidatng length, and can be summarised as follows. The company concerned was the Victoria Park Co, which had been incorporated by Act of Parliament in 1837 to develop certain plots of land. There were eight promoters, Harbottle, Adshead, Byrom, Westhead, Bealey, Denison, Bunting and Lane. The directors were the first five of these gentlemen.

Lane was the architect and Bunting the solicitor. Foss and Turton were the complaining shareholders. They filed a bill on behalf of themselves and all other shareholders in the company (except the defendants) against the eight promoters, including the assignees of three of them who had become bankrupt. It was alleged that the plots had been bought by the company in pursuance of an arrangement fraudulently concocted between seven of the promoters to enable them to derive a personal benefit from the establishment of the company and the sale to it of the price at exorbitant prices. It was further alleged that –

"the Defendants concealed from the Plaintiffs ... the several fraudulent and improper acts of the ... Defendants, and the Plaintiffs ... had only recently ascertained the particulars thereof ... and they were unable to set forth the same more particularly, the Defendants having refused to make any discovery thereof, or to allow the Plaintiffs to inspect the books, accounts or papers of the company ... and that at (general meetings of the company) false and delusive statements respecting the circumstances and prospects of the company were made by the directors to the proprietors who attended such meetings, and the truth of the several fraudulent and improper acts and procedings therein complained of was not disclosed."

(See 2 Hare 461 at 478-480)

The bill charged that, in the circumstances, the defendants were jointly and severally liable to make good to the company the losses incurred in consequence of the wrongful and fraudulent acts and proceedings to which they were parties or privies. The defendants (except Byrom, who took no part) demurred to the bill of the ground that the corporation was not before the court, and that the defect could not be cured by making the corporation a defendant because the plaintiffs were not entitled to represent the corporation.

For the purposes of the application Wigram V-C made the assumption that the company was entitled, as matters then stood, to complain of the transactions mentioned in the bill. He continued (2 Hare 461 at 490-492)

"... the bill in this case is brought by two individual corporators, professedly on behalf of themselves and all the other members of the corporation, except those who committed the injuries complained of – the Plaintiffs assuming to themselves the right and power in the manner to sue on behalf of and represent the corporation itself. It was not, nor could it successfully be, argued that it was a matter of course for any individual members of a corporation thus to assume to themselves the right of suing in the name of the corporation. In law, the corporation, and the aggregate members of the cororation, are not the same thing for purposes like this; and the only question can be, whether the facts alleged in this case justify a departure from the rule which prima facie would require that the corporation should sue in its own name and in its corporate character, or in the name of some one whom the law has appointed to be its representative ... If a case should arise of injury to a corporation by some of its members, for which no adequate remedy remained, except that of a suit by individual corporators in their private characters, and asking in such character the protection of those rights to which in their corporate character they were entitled, I cannot but think that the principle so forcibly laid down by Lord Cottenham in *Wallworth* v *Holt* (1841) 4 My & Cr 619 and other cses, would apply, and the claims of justice would be found superior to any difficulties arising out of technical rules respecting the mode in which corporations are required to sue. But, on the other hand, it must not be without reasons of a very urgent character that established rules of law and practice are to be departed from, rules which, though in a sense technical, are founded on general principles of justice and convenience; and the question is whether a case is stated in this bill, entitling the Plaintiffs to sue in their private characters."

Wigram V-C then proceeded to answer this question in the negative, for the reasons indicated in the following extracts from his judgment (2 Hare 461 at 492-493):

"... the directors are made the governing body, subject to the superior control of the proprietors assembled in general meetings; and, as I understand the Act, the proprietors so assembled have power, due notice being given of the purposes of the meeting, to originate proceedings for any purpose within the scope of the company's powers, as well as to control the directors in any Acts which they may have originated ... The first ground of complaint is one which, though it might prima facie entitle the corporation to rescind the transactions complained of, does not absolutely and of necessity fall under the description of a void transaction. The corporation might elect to adopt those transactions, and hold the directors bound by them. In other words, the transactions admit of confirmation at the option of the corporation."

Wigram V-C then considered the second ground of complaint (which we need not deal with) and continued (2 Hare 461 at 493-495).

"... whilst the supreme governing body, the proprietors at a special general meeting assembled, retain the power of exercising the functions conferred upon them by the Act of Incorporaton, it cannot be competent to individual corporators to sue in the manner proposed by the Plaintiffs on the present record ... the majority of the proprietors at a special general meeting assembled, independently of any general rule of law upon the subject, by the very terms of the incorporation in the present case, has power to bind the whole body, and every individual corporator must be taken to have come into the corporation upon the terms of being liable to be so bound. How then can this Court act in a suit constituted as this is, if it is to be assumed, for the purposes of the argument, that the powers of the body of the proprietors are still in existence, and may lawfully be exercised for a purpose like that I have suggested? Whilst the Court may be declaring the acts complained of to be void at the suit of the present Plaintiffs, who in fact may be the only proprietors who disapprove of them, the governing body of proprietors may defeat the decree by lawfully resolving upon the confirmation of the very acts which are the subject of the suit. The very fact that the governing body of proprietors assembled at the special general meeting may so bind even a reluctant minority is decisive to show that the frame of this suit cannot be sustained whilst that body retains its functions. In order then that this suit may be sustained, it must be shown either that there is no such power as I have supposed remaining in the proprietors, or, at least, that all means have been resorted to and found ineffectual to set that body in motion: this latter point is nowhere suggested in the bill: there is no suggestion that an attempt has been made by any proprietor to set the body of proprietors in motion, or to procure a meeting to be convened for the purpose of revoking the acts complained of. The question then is whether this bill is so framed as of necessity to exclude the supposition that the supreme body of proprietors is now in a condition to confirm the transactions in question: or, if those transactions are to be impeached in a Court of Justice, whether the proprietors have not power to set the corporation in motion for the purpose of vindicating its own rights."

These questions were answered against the plaintiffs.

The next case which falls for consideration related to the fraudulent promotion of some worthless lead mines. There were in fact two actions. it is important to observe that in the first action there was a motion to strike out, but no such motion in the second action, which proceeded to trial. The first action is reported as *East Pant Du United Lead Mining Co Ltd* v *Merryweather* (1864) 2 Hem & M 254. It was alleged that Merryweather, a director of the company, acting in concert with one of his co-directors, Whitworth, had fraudulently sold the mines to the company for £4,000 cash, which they shared between themselves, and 600 shares, to be allotted to Merryweather. In June 1864 a bill was filed in the name of the company against Merryweather to set aside the sale. In August the defendant moved to strike out the bill by way of demurrer. The court adjourned the application in order to allow an opportunity for a general meeting to be held. The meeting was held in October. A resolution was proposed for adopting the proceedings and continuing the action. Whitworth proposed an amendment to stay the action and refer the dispute to arbitration. The amendment was put to the vote, and a poll was taken. Out of 668 votes cast 324 were against the stay and 344 were in favour of the stay, but of the latter 78 votes were cast by Merryweather and 28 votes by Whitworth; if Merryweather had not voted, the motion would have been supported by only 266 votes and would have been lost. It was argued by counsel for the company (2 Hem & M 254 at 257):

> "If a minority of a company were allowed to file a bill in the company's name, charging fraud against some of the majority and alleging that those persons were not to be considered as shareholders or entitled to vote, and thus endeavouring to turn their minority into a majority so as to acquire the right to use the name of the company, any company's affairs might be made the subject of litigation upon allegations of fraud which might be entirely false; and yet, as this could not be proved till the hearing, irremediable mischief might be done in the meantime."

Page Wood V-C acceded to the motion, expressing his reasons as follows (2 Hem & M 254 at 261):

> "Then comes the question, has the company now sanctioned the suit? To decide that it has done so would be to discard Mr Merryweather's votes, and to do that would in effect be to decide now on this application the question at issue in the suit. But if I assume, as upon this motion I must assume that Mr Merryweather was entitled to the 600 shares which he actually holds in the company, the further question occurs, has he a right to vote in respect of such shares upon a question in which he is personally interested? Now, as to the management of the company by the board, no director is entitled to vote as a director in respect of any contract in which he is interested; but the case is different when he acts as one of the whole body of shareholders. The shareholders of one company may have dealings with interests in other companies, and therefore it would be manifestly unfair to prevent an individual shareholder from voting as a shareholder in the affairs of the company. At a general meeting, therefore, Mr Merryweather's votes must be held to be good so long as he continues to hold his shares. Further than this the Court cannot be asked now to give an opinion, for to do so would be to decide the very question at issue in the cause."

A shareholder then began another action in December, suing on behalf of himself and all other shareholders (except Merryweather and Whitworth) against Merryweather, Whitworth and the company. This is reported as *Atwool* v *Merryweather* (1867) LR 5 Eq 464 at 468 in a footnote to *Clinch* v *Financial Corp* (1868) LR 5 Eq 450 at 464 and more fully in 37 LJ Ch 35. On this occasion the defendant did not move to strike out the bill. The action was fought to a finish. Page Wood V-C held, first, that the contract was a complete fraud and, second, that there was not such a defect in the constitution of the suit as would be fatal according to the authority of *Foss* v *Harbottle*. Page Wood V-C referred to the fact that there was plainly a majority of shareholders, independent of those implicated in the fraud, who supported the bill.

The principles which seem to emerge from these two cases are (i) that, if the defendant against whom fraud is alleged applies to strike out the action in limine, it will not be assumed that he was guilty of fraud so as to disentitle him from casting his votes at a general meeting against the action, but (ii) that, if the action is in fact fought to a conclusion, and the court finds the defendant guilty of fraud, it will in those circumstances discount the votes of those implicated in the fraud in reaching a conclusion whether the plaintiff is authorised to sue on the company's behalf. What the two cases leave open is the question of what circumstances the alleged delinquent, or the company, can leave the proceedings in limine.

Vinelott J placed considerable reliance on this case in widening the accepted exception to the rule in *Foss* v *Harbottle*. He said:

> "... *Atwool* v *Merryweather* shows that the court has jurisdiction to entertain a claim by a minority shareholder and to make an order in favour of the defendant company even where the other defendants, alone or together with the plaintiffs, do not have a majority of votes in general meeting and where the other shareholders are not parties. If that is so, then as I see it, the exception can only be found on a general jurisdiction of the court to make an order for recovery of property or damages in favour of a defendant company against co-defendants where the jurisdiction is invoked by a minority shareholder."

We doubt whether *Atwool* v *Merryweather* goes so far in support of the judge's conclusion. It was not a case in which the company or the delinquents sought to stop the action in limine. The action had been fought to a conclusion, the liability of the defendant directors had been established, and nothing therefore remained except for the company to reap the benefit of the judgment. The court could hardly deny the rights of the plaintiff to an order in favour of the company to give effect to its proved rights, in the face of a resolution which, excluding the votes of the proven fraudsters, was a majority resolution:

"... having it plainly before me that there was a majority of the shareholders, independent of those implicated in the fraud, supporting the bill, it would be idle to go through the circuitous course of saying that leave must be obtained to file a bill for the company, and pro forma have a totally different litigation."

(See Page Wood V-C in *Atwool* v *Merryweather*)

There is a clear distinction to be drawn between the application of the rule in *Foss* v *Harbottle* when it is sought to stay proceedings in limine and its application when nothing remains but to enforce a judgment in a derivative action which has been permitted to proceed.

A simple application of the first aspect of the rule in *Foss* v *Harbottle* is to be found in *Gray* v *Lewis* (1873) LR 8 Ch App 1035. The facts, shortly stated, were as follows. Charles Lafitte & Co Ltd (the company) was incorporated in December 1865 to purchase the right to extend to his country the business of Charles Lafitte & Co of Paris (the partnership). The plaintiff Gray subscribed for shares. The company never acquired anything from the partnership, and was ordered to be wound up in November 1866. Shortly thereafter Gray filed a bill on behalf of himself and all other shareholders in the company, against the company, its directors, its liquidator and the National Bank, alleging that the assets of the company had been misapplied by the National Bank and by the directors of the company, and seeking an order that the bank and the directors of the company might be declared liable to make "good to the shareholders of the company" the loss sustained "by the shareholders" Mallins V-C made a decree declaring that the bank and the directors were liable to replace the money, and directed that the amount found due should be paid into court. The National Bank, and Lewis and Henshaw, two of the directors, appealed. The appeal of the National Bank was compromised with the concurrence of the liquidator, on the basis (clearly unobjectionable) that the National Bank should discharge the debts of the company. The appeal by Lewis and Henshaw came before the Court of Appeal in Chancery, and was allowed. The reasons were put trenchantly by James LJ, with whom Mellish LJ agreed, in these words (at 1050-1051):

"The bill should not have been filed by a shareholder on behalf of himself and all other the (sic) shareholders. It is very important, in order to avoid oppressive litigation, to adhere to the rule laid down in *Mozley* v *Alston* (1847) 1 Ph 790 and *Foss* v *Harbottle*, which cases have always been considered as settling the law of this Court, that where there is a corporate body capable of filing a bill for itself to recover property either from its directors or officers, or from any other person, that corporate body is the proper Plaintiff, and the only proper Plaintiff. One object of incorporating bodies of this kind was, in my opinion, to avoid the multiplicity of suits which might have arisen where one shareholder was allowed to file a bill on behalf of himself and a great number of other shareholders. The shareholder who first filed a bill might dismiss it, and if he was a poor man the Defendant would be unable to obtain his costs, then another shareholder might file a bill and so on. It was also stated to us in the course of the argument that even after the Plaintiff had dismissed his bill against a particular Defendant a fresh bill might be filed against the Defendants so dismissed. Therefore there might be as many bills as there are shareholders multiplied into the number of Defendants. The result would be fearful, and I think the Defendant has a right to have the case made against him by the real body who are entitled to complain of what he has done. Now in this case I am of opinion that the only person – if you may call it a person – having a right to complain was the incorporated society called Charles Lafitte & Co. In its corporate character it was liable to be sued, and was entitled to sue; and if the company sued in its corporate character, the Defendant might allege a release or a compromise by the company in its corporate character – a defence which might not be open in a suit where a Plaintiff is suing on behalf of himself and other shareholders. I think it is of the utmost importance to maintain the rule laid down in *Mozley* v *Alston* and *Foss* v *Harbottle*, to which, as I understand, the only exception is where the corporate body has got into the hands of directors and of the majority, which directors and majority are using their powers for the purpose of doing something fraudulent against the minority, who are overwhelmed by them, as in *Atwool* v *Merryweather*, where Vice-Chancellor Wood, under those circumstances, sustained a bill by a shareholder on behalf of himself and others, and there it was after an attempt had been made to obtain a proper authority from the corporate body itself in public meeting assembled."

This case highlights what the rule in *Foss* v *Harbottle* is primarily concerned with, namely: is a plaintiff shareholder entitled to prosecute an action on behalf of the company for a wrong done to it, or ought the action to be struck out on the footing that it is for the company and not for a shareholder to sue? That is what *Foss* v *Harbottle* itself was about, and what the first *East Pant Du* case was about. The second *East Pant Du* case (*Atwool* v *Merryweather*) raised a related but different question, namely, if at the end of the day fraud is proved, are the circumstances such that the company is capable of condoning the fraud? Clearly not, if the fraud will only be confirmed by a majority by the use of the fraudsters' own voting power.'

Commentary
In *Smith* v *Croft (No 2)* [1988] Ch 114 Chancery Division, Knox J, appears to have created a further hurdle for minority shareholders in that even if one of the exceptions to the rule in *Foss* v *Harbottle* can be made out, it is then necessary to consider the majority within the minority principle. The plaintiffs will have no right to sue if the majority of shareholders who are independent of the defendants do not want to litigate.

Common law exceptions to the rule in *Foss* v *Harbottle*

Barrett v *Duckett & Others* [1995] BCC 362 Court of Appeal (Russell, Beldam and Peter Gibson LJJ)

Derivative action – whether winding up was a more appropriate remedy

Facts
B was a 50 per cent shareholder in Nightingale Travel Ltd ('Travel'). She complained that D, the other 50 per cent shareholder, together with his wife, had diverted assets belonging to Travel to another company which they owned. She also complained that they had paid themselves excessive remuneration and had taken cash from the company. As B was only a 50 per cent shareholder she was unable to commit the company to litigation to recover these amounts. Prior to the commencement of this action, D had presented a winding up petition on the grounds that Travel was insolvent and in deadlock. Because of this, D argued that a derivative action by B was not appropriate because there was an alternative remedy in the winding up proceedings – the liquidator could consider whether proceedings on Travel's behalf against D should be commenced. Additionally, D argued that B was unable to exercise an independent and unbiased judgment in the matter and this was shown by the fact that B had made no claim against her daughter. This was despite the fact that her daughter was a director and had allegedly benefited from the misappropriation of Travel's money.

The judge refused to strike out the derivative action brought by B and ordered that it was to be heard with the winding up petition. D and the other defendants appealed.

Held
The appeal was allowed and the action struck out. B had no more money to fund the action, but Travel did have just under £37,000. Peter Gibson LJ felt that an independent liquidator would be best placed to decide whether this money should be spent on litigating B's claims. Although B could not be certain that the liquidator would sue, this was not an answer to D's argument that there was an alternative

remedy. His Lordship was also convinced that B was not pursuing the action bona fide on behalf of the company. If she had been she would have also sued her daughter.

Peter Gibson LJ:

'I am left in no doubt that this is an action which should not be allowed to proceed. Hoffmann LJ in giving leave to appeal said:

"As a matter of common sense, it seems arguable that the parties should not be subjected to lengthy and costly proceedings exacerbated by family hostilities when an independent liquidator might decide that the action could be settled on reasonable terms."

I entirely agree with such argument. I hope that even now Mrs Barrett will agree to a voluntary winding up to save costs and that she will promptly give the liquidator the benefit of all the work that has been done in this case on her behalf to facilitate any proceedings which he may wish to pursue.

For these reasons I respectfully differ from the judge in his conclusions. I would allow the appeal and strike out this action.

Daniels v Daniels [1978] Ch 406 Chancery Division (Templeman J)

Fraud on the minority – negligence

Facts

The company, Ideal Homes (Coventry) Ltd had an authorised share capital of 3,000 £1 shares. Of these a total of 1,348 were held by the three plaintiffs in this action whilst the first two defendants who were husband and wife, held 1,651 shares. In October 1970 when the first two defendants were the only directors of the company they authorised the sale of certain land belonging to the company to the second defendant for £4,250. In 1974 the same land was resold by the second defendant for £120,000. The plaintiffs' statement of claim alleged that the sale to the second defendant was at an undervalue since the price paid was the probate value of the land at the time which, it was alleged, was customarily less than open market value. The first two defendants applied to have the action struck out as there was no allegation of fraud in the statement of claim and as such the plaintiffs could not continue the claim on behalf of the company under an exception to the rule in *Foss* v *Harbottle*.

Held

The application would be dismissed. There was no reason why the minority could not bring an action in the name of the company where the directors were using their powers, whether intentionally or unintentionally, fraudulently or negligently in a manner which benefited them at the expense of the company.

Templeman J:

'... Mr Richards says, and it is conceded, that the statement of claim in its present form does not allege fraud. Mr Blackburne says of course he is not alleging fraud because the plaintiffs do not really know what happened: all they know is what is set out in the statement of claim. There has been a sale at an undervalue and the second defendant has made a substantial profit, therefore fraud is not pleaded. But says Mr Blackburne, when the authorities are considered, "the rights of a minority" are not limited to cases of fraud; they extend to any breach of duty. As the plaintiffs cannot remedy the breach, save by a minority shareholder's action, they should be entitled to bring the action.

Foss v *Harbottle* ((1843) 2 Hare 461 was a case in which there was no oppression by a majority. The next case in point of time to which I was referred was *Atwool* v *Merryweather* (1867) LR 5 Eq 46 qn. The exception of fraud, in *Foss* v *Harbottle* was emphasised, the reason being, according to Page-Wood V-C:

> "If I were to hold that no bill could be filed by the shareholders to get rid of the transaction on the ground of the doctrine of *Foss* v *Harbottle*, it would be impossible to set aside a fraud committed by a director under such circumstances as the director obtaining so many shares by fraud would always be able to outvote everybody else."

That was a case described as "simple fraud". In the next case, *Clinch* v *Financial Corpn* (1869) LR 5 Eq 450 allegations were made of fraud and of acts which were said to be ultra vires. The charges of fraud were not sustained, but the minority shareholder was allowed to bring an action to restrain or correct an act which was ultra vires the company.

Then in *Turquand* v *Marshall* (1869) LR 5 Ch App 376 Lord Hatherley LC in dealing with a loan to one of the directors said:

> "There was no specific allegation of any impropriety in lending the money to him, nor was any specific relief prayed in this respect. It was within the powers of the deed to lend to a brother director, and however foolish the loan might have been, so long as it was within the powers of the directors, the Court could not inferfere and make them liable. They were intrusted with full powers of lending the money, and it was part of the business of the concern to trust people with money, and their trusting to an undue extent was not a matter with which they could be fixed, unless there was something more alleged, as, for instance, that it was done fraudulently and improperly and not merely by a default of judgment. Whatever may have been the amount lent to anybody, however ridiculous and absurd their conduct might seem, it was the misfortune of the company that they chose such unwise directors ..."

So that even a foolish and negligent loan to a director, if made in good faith and within the powers of the directors, does not enable a minority shareholder to recover in an action.

The next case, *Gray* v *Lewis* (1873) LR 8 Ch App 1035 is an instance of fraud creating an exception to the rule in *Foss* v *Harbottle* . For example, James LJ said:

> "I think it is of the utmost importance to maintain the rule laid down in *Mosley* v *Alston* (1847) 1 Ph 790 and *Foss* v *Harbottle* to which, as I understand, the only exception is where the corporate body has got into the hands of directors and of the majority, which directors and majority are using their power for the purpose of doing something fraudulent against the minority, who are overwhelmed by them ..."

In *Menier* v *Hooper's Telegraph Works* (1874) LR 9 Ch App 350 a minority shareholders' action was allowed where the majority intended to divide the assets of the company more or less between themselves to the exclusion of the minority. Mellish LJ said:

> "I am of the opinion that although it may be quite true that the shareholders of a company may vote as they please, and for the purpose of their own interests, yet that the majority of shareholders cannot sell the assets of the company and keep the consideration, but must allow the minority to have their share of any consideration which may come to them."

In *MacDougall* v *Gardiner* (1875) LR 20 Eq 383 although the actual decision was reversed, Malins V-C said that there had to be something at least bordering on fraud to found a minority shareholders' action.

In *Mason* v *Harris* (1879) 11 Ch D 97 Jessel MR, in an action to set aside a sale by a managing director to the company on the grounds of fraud, said:

> "As a general rule the company must sue in respect of a claim of this nature, but general rules have their exceptions, and one exception to the rule requiring the company to be plaintiff is, that where a fraud is committed by persons who can command a majority of votes, the minority can sue. The reason is plain, as unless such an exception were allowed it would be in the power of a majority to defraud the minority with impunity. If the majority were to make a fraudulent sale and put the money into their own pockets, would it be reasonable to say that the majority could confirm the sale."

In 1900 there was a case of rather wider import on which counsel for the plaintiffs relies, *Alexander* v *Automatic Telephone Co* [1900] 2 Ch 56. In that case directors issued shares and required some people who took up the shares to make payments in respect of those shares, but the directors did not themselves make payments on the shares which they had taken up. The headnote reads, in part:

"If directors require other applicants for shares to make payments on application and allotment, and issue their own shares for which they have been subscribed the memorandum without requiring any such payments to be made, and without disclosing to the other shareholders this difference beween their position and that of the directors, they commit a breach of duty, even though in so doing they act without fraud, and in the belief that they are doing nothing wrong."

A minority shareholders' action was allowed. Fraud was negatived and the basis for the action was given as "breach of duty". Lindley MR said:

"The directors, in fact, so managed matters as to place themselves in a better position as regards payment than the other shareholders, and they did so without informing the other shareholders of the fact. This, the plaintiffs contend, was a breach of duty on the part of the directors to those who applied for and took shares upon the faith that the directors were not obtaining advantages at their expense. It is no answer to the plaintiffs' case so put to appeal to the contracts alone, for the charge is that the directors were guilty of a breach of duty in procuring those contracts and in taking advantage of them so as to benefit themselves at the expense of the other shareholders."

Lindley MR further said:

"The Court of Chancery has always exacted from directors the observance of good faith towards their shareholders and towards those who take shares from the company and become co-adventurers with themselves and others who may join them. The maxim caveat emptor has no application to such cases, and directors who so use their powers as to obtain benefits for themselves at the expense of the shareholders, without informing them of the fact, cannot retain those benefits and must account for them to the company, so that all the shareholders may participate in them."

That was a case which falls within the first exception to *Foss* v *Harbottle*, in that the plaintiff shareholder could be said to be suing in respect of his individual rights as a shareholder to receive the same treatment as any other shareholder. But Lindley MR also considered the directors to be in breach of duty to the company:

"The breach of duty to the company consists in depriving it of the use of the money which the directors ought to have paid up sooner than they did. I cannot regard the case as one of mere internal management which, according to *Foss* v *Harbottle* and numerous other cases, the court leaves the shareholders to settle amongst themselves. It was ascertained and admitted at the trial that, when this action was commenced, the defendants held such a preponderance of shares that they could not be controlled by the other shareholders. Under these circumstances an action by some shareholders on behalf of themselves and the others against the defendants is in accordance with the authorities, and is unobjectionable in form."

That was a case intermingled with the individual grievances of the shareholders in respect of their own righs, but contemplated an exception to *Foss* v *Harbottle* going wider than fraud.

Shortly thereafter, in *Burland* v *Earle* [1902] AC 83 it was said that minority shareholders can sue in their own names, but must show that the acts complained of are either fraudulent or ultra vires. In particular, Lord Davey, who delivered the advice of the Judicial Committee said:

"It is an elementary principle of the law relating to joint stock companies that the court will not interfere with the internal management of companies acting within their powers and in fact has no jurisdiction to do so. Again, it is clear law that in order to redress a wrong done to the company or to recover moneys or damages alleged to be due to the company, the action should prima facie be brought by the company itself. These cardinal principles are laid down in the well-known cases of *Foss* v *Harbottle* and *Mozley* v *Alston* and in numerous later cases which it is unnecessary to cite. But an exception is made to the second rule, where the persons against whom the relief is sought themselves hold and control the majority of the shares in the company. In that case the courts allow the shareholders complaining to bring an action in their own names. This, however, is mere matter of procedure in order to give a remedy for a wrong which would otherwise escape redress, and it is obvious that in such an action the plaintiffs cannot have a larger right to relief than the company itself would have if it were plaintiff, and cannot complain of acts which are valid if done with the approval of the majority of the shareholders, or are capable of being confirmed by the majority. The cases in which the minority can maintain such an action are, therefore, confined to those in which the acts complained of are of a fraudulent character or beyond the powers of the company. A familiar example is where the majority are endeavouring directly or indirectly to appropriate to themselves money, property, or advantages which belong to the company, or in which the other shareholders are entitled to participate ..."

The decision in this case turned on the fact that those against whom allegations were made were not, in fact, in control of the company.

Then in 1916 minority shareholders were allowed to sue, although fraud in the true sense of the word was not sustained; fraud was pleaded but rejected. In *Cook* v *Deeks* [1916] 1 AC 554 directors obtained for themselves the benefit of a contract which might otherwise have gone to the company. Fraud was expressly negatived. Lord Buckmaster LC said:

"It is quite right to point out the importance of avoiding the establishment of rules as to directors' duties which would impose upon them burdens so heavy and responsibilities so great that men of good position would hesitate to accept the office. But, on the other hand, men who assume the complete control of a company's business must remember that they are not at liberty to sacrifice the interests which they are bound to protect, and, while ostensibly acting for the company, divert in their own favour business which should properly belong to the company they represent."

Counsel for the defendants said that was really a case of constructive fraud, but express fraud having been negatived, it seems to me that it established that an action will lie where, without fraud, directors in a majority, divert in their own favour business which should properly belong to the company they represent.

Then in 1956 there was a case on which counsel for the defendants very strongly relies and from which counsel for the plaintiffs asked me to differ. In *Pavlides* v *Jensen* [1956] Ch 565 it was alleged that directors had been guilty of gross negligence in selling a valuable asset of the company at a price greatly below its true market value, and it was alleged that the directors knew or well ought to have known that it was below market value. Danckwerts J struck out the statement of claim as disclosing no cause of action because no fraud was pleaded. The headnote says:

"... since the sale of the asset in question was not beyond the powers of the company, and since there was no allegation of fraud on the part of the directors or appropriation of the assets of the company by the majority shareholders in fraud of the minority, the action did not fall within the admitted exceptions to the rule in *Foss* v *Harbottle* ..."

Danckwerts J said:

"On the facts of the present case, the sale of the company's mine was not beyond the powers of the company, and it is not alleged to be ultra vires. There is no allegation of fraud on the part of the directors or appropriation of assets of the company by the majority shareholders in fraud of the minority. It was open to the company, on the resolution of a majority of the shareholders, to sell the mine at a price decided by the company in that manner, and it was open to the company by a vote of the majority to decide that, if the directors by their negligence or error of judgment had sold the company's mine at an undervalue, proceedings should not be taken by the company against the directors."

Counsel for the defendants relies very strongly on this decision as showing that, whatever the exceptions to *Foss* v *Harbottle* may be, mere gross negligence is not actionable, and he says all that is pleaded in the present case is gross negligence at the most. But in *Pavlides* v *Jensen* no benefits accrued to the directors. Counsel for the plaintiffs asks me to dissent from *Pavlides* v *Jensen* but the decision seems to me at the moment to be in line with the authorities, in what is a restricted exception to the rule in *Foss* v *Harbottle*.

In *Birch* v *Sullivan* [1957] 1 WLR 1247 the decision really went off on a point of pleading: moreover the learned judge was not satisfied that the dissenting shareholders could not put matters right by a meeting of the company. Finally I was referred to *Heyting* v *Dupont* [1963] 1 WLR 1192. But that was only an instance of the court refusing on its own initiative to hear an action begun by minority shareholders where the *Foss* v *Harbottle* exceptions did not come into play.

The authorities which deal with simple fraud on the one hand and gross negligence on the other do not cover the situation which arises where, without fraud, the directors and majority shareholders are guilty of a breach of duty which they owe to the company, and that breach of duty not only harms the company but benefits the directors. In that case it seems to me that different considerations apply. If minority shareholders can sue if there is fraud, I see no reason why they cannot sue where the action of the majority and the directors, though without fraud, confers some benefit on those directors and majority shareholders themselves. It would seem to me quite monstrous particularly as fraud is so hard to plead and difficult to prove, if the confines of the exception to *Foss* v *Harbottle* were drawn so narrowly that directors could make a profit out of their negligence. Lord Hatherley LC in *Turquand* v *Marshall* opined that shareholders must put up with foolish or unwise directors. Danckwerts J in *Pavlides* v *Jensen* accepted that the forebearance of shareholders extends to directors who are "an amiable set of lunatics". Examples, ancient and modern, abound. But to put up with foolish directors is one thing; to put up with directors who are so foolish that they make a profit of £115,000 odd at the expense of the company is something entirely different. The principle which may be gleaned from *Alexander* v *Automatic Telephone Co* (directors benefitting themselves) from *Cook* v *Deeks* (directors diverting business in their own favour) and from dicta in *Pavlides* v *Jensen* (directors appropriating assets of the company) is that a minority shareholder who has no other remedy may sue where directors use their powers intentionally or unintentionally, fraudulently or negligently in a manner which benefits themselves at the expense of the company. This principle is not contrary to *Turquand* v *Marshall* because in that case the powers of the directors were effectively wielded not by the director who benefited but by the majority of independent directors who were acting bona fide and did not benefit. I need not consider the wider proposition for which counsel for the plaintiffs against some formidable opposition from the authorities contends that any breach of duty may be made the subject of a minority shareholder's action ...'

Downs Wine Bar Ltd, Re [1990] BCLC 839 High Court (Harman J)

Whether claims for declarations should be struck out

Facts
The plaintiff shareholder and director by originating summons sought an order pursuant to s371 of the Companies Act 1985 that an extraordinary general meeting of the company be convened to consider a specific resolution (a proper use of the originating summons procedure) and, in paras 3 to 6, certain declarations. The first defendant, a co-director and holder of the other shares, moved to strike out para 3 of the summons and specified words elsewhere in it.

Held
The motion would be successful.

Harman J:

'During argument para 3 has been broken down into three sub-paragraphs, and although no such sub-paragraphs appear in the originating summons I think it is convenient to use them. Paragraph 3(a) reads:

"permitting, causing or procuring the company to make dispositions of its property and assets without the consent of his co-director."

That claim plainly cannot be a proper claim for the plaintiff to make against the first defendant in any proceedings concerning the 1985 Act. If there were some contract or shareholders' agreement or something of that sort between them he could sue on the agreement. Absent that, there is no cause of action at all for that matter. There is no rule of company law that a company can only dispose of assets or property with the consent of all or both directors.

Paragraph 3(b) reads:

"the company [has been caused] to make dispositions of its property for a collateral purpose."

The phrase is of the most general but, plainly, it includes such a matter as a disposition of the property of the company made in what the person making the disposition bona fide believes, on sensible grounds it may be, was in the interest of the company but which was also made for a purpose collateral to the benefit of the company, as was revealed in the Privy Council decision, mentioned but not specifically cited to me, in *Howard Smith Ltd v Ampol Petroleum Ltd* [1974] AC 821 That decision of the Privy Council, in the speech of Lord Wilberforce, shows that an act of a board of directors can be done perfectly bona fide, in the sense of honestly intending something and not seeking to line their own pocket or benefit their own friends, but can be for a collateral purpose and not within the power of the board. But no such claim has ever founded ... an action by one shareholder against the other in connection with the company purporting to be an action under the exception in *Foss v Harbottle* (1843) 2 Hare 461.

Paragraph 3(c) reads:

"[disposing] of ... property ... in circumstances where [the first defendant] was in a position where his duty to the company conflicted with his own self-interest ..."

That by itself tells one nothing. If he had a conflict of duty and interest and acted in accordance with his duty, then he would be acting perfectly properly. The sentence goes on, after "self-interest":

"was acting in breach of his fiduciary duty owed to the company."

The language ... is extremely ungrammatical, and I am far from clear what it is alleging. But it does appear to be alleging that there was a breach of fiduciary duty in disposing of property. That again might be a *Howard Smith Ltd v Ampol Petroleum Ltd*-type breach of duty. But it is entirely unclear what is alleged, and it is entirely unclear ... how it would be within the exception to the rule in *Foss v Harbottle*, which was so pithily and neatly set out in the decision in *Prudential Assurance Co Ltd v Newman Industries Ltd (No 2)* [1982] Ch 204 at 201–11 in the judgment of the court, where it specifically spells out the current understanding of the rule affirming the classic definition by Jenkins LJ in *Edwards v Halliwell* [1950] 2 All ER 1064. Those observations are, of course, binding on me and on the Court of Appeal, and are entirely in accordance with the principle as I have ever understood it.

That sets out, therefore, the requirement that the company must be the plaintiff, which it is not here, unless there is an allegation of something done which amounts to fraud and that the wrongdoers are in control of the company. No such allegations appear in para 3 of the originating summons. Paragraphs 4, 5 and 6 of the originating summons are entirely ancillary to para 3 ...

As it seems to me, counsel for the plaintiff ... has never managed to formulate any justification for this being a proper claim to be pleaded as a *Foss v Harbottle* claim. He accepted, as counsel did not when this matter was before me a fortnight ago, that if the matter is to be a *Foss v Harbottle* action then it must proceed by pleadings ...

Counsel for the plaintiff submits to me that an action within *Foss v Harbottle* is not an action within RSC Ord 5, r2(b) in which a claim is made based on an allegation of fraud. He submits that "fraud" there means an action for the tort of deceit, as it has been held to mean under RSC Ord 14, r1(2), and that "fraud" does not include oppression of a minority by wrongful acts of the majority, which is the equitable head of fraud which is the foundation for *Foss v Harbottle*. The observation in *Prudential Assurance Co Ltd v Newman Industries Ltd (No 2)* suggests that fraud is required but, in my view, counsel is correct on this and "fraud" in Ord 5, r2(b) does mean an action based on the tort of deceit and does not mean an action based on the exception to the rule in *Foss v Harbottle*.

However, that does not answer the point that, none the less, an action, as counsel for the plaintiff accepted, based on the exception to the rule in *Foss v Harbottle*, must be an action raising contentious issues of fact and can only be properly dealt with by pleadings. It seems to me that when I look at para 3 in the originating summons, which I tried to analyse earlier in this judgment, there is no allegation which can clearly be seen to be an allegation within the exception to the rule in *Foss v Harbottle* ...

The result must be that counsel for the plaintiff, observing that there would need to be some amendment but not coming here with any application to amend, is faced with a paragraph where large parts are not within the rule. A part, he says, may be within the rule but it is entirely unclear that it would be within the rule, and there would inevitably be a tortuous procedural tangle resulting from the attempt to combine within one proceeding two entirely differently constituted claims. The first claim for a meeting under s371 has nothing to do with the rule in *Foss* v *Harbottle* and is entirely appropriately brought on originating summons by [the] plaintiff, with [his co-director] and the company as defendants. The claim under para 3 and the subsequent paragraphs is not appropriately brought in that way, and cannot be brought at all unless it can be shown to be within the exception to the rule.

In my judgment, counsel for the first defendant in seeking to have paras 3 to 6 struck out is not simply making the plaintiff plead his case as the defendant wants, nor even as the court would wish. It must always be remembered that, if a plaintiff has a right to elect what form of proceedings he brings, the court, unless it is embarrassing, will not prevent him from so doing. But that right in the plaintiff to elect for his own preferred procedural route cannot apply when a claim is formulated which has no legal justification as formulated, which, in my view, para 3 of this originating summons at present has not. Thus, I reach the conclusion that paras 3 to 6 inclusive of the originating summons ought to be struck out as an abuse of process and, on that ground, the motion should succeed.

There will remain standing the claim to have a general meeting, and that can proceed perfectly properly and easily on its own terms. If the plaintiff wishes to bring an action within the exception to the rule, he is entirely at liberty to issue a writ for it. There will be no res judicata or other bar preventing him so doing, and we shall see how he then formulates what counsel for the plaintiff says would have to be amended forms of claim. In my view, that can be the only conclusion to which one comes, that the originating summons as it stands cannot be left and paras 3 to 6 must go.'

Edwards v *Halliwell* [1950] 2 All ER 1064 Court of Appeal (Evershed MR, Asquith and Jenkins LJJ)

Application of the rule in *Foss* v *Harbottle* where the articles require a special majority or procedure

Facts

The plaintiffs were members of the Cricklewood branch of the National Union of Vehicle Builders, a trade union. Under the rules of the union it was provided that the contributions of employed members were as set out in certain tables in the rules of the union. Rule 19 of the rules stated, as regards the contributions, 'no alteration to the same shall be made until a ballot vote of the members has been taken and a two-thirds majority obtained'. A meeting of delegates of the union was held in December 1943 and this meeting resolved to increase the contributions of employed members without any ballot. The plaintiffs claimed that the increases in the contributions were a nullity. Vaisey J gave judgment for the plaintiffs. The defendants appealed and contended that the matter was a mere irregularity concerning the internal management of the union and within the rule in *Foss* v *Harbottle*.

Held

The appeal would be dismissed since the invalid increases in the contributions were an invasion of the individual rights of membership of the plaintiffs.

Jenkins LJ:

'... There is a further exception which seems to me to touch this case directly. That is the exception noted by Romer J in *Cotter* v *National Union of Seamen* [1929] 2 Ch 58. He pointed out that the rule did not prevent an individual member from suing if the matter in respect of which he was suing was one which could validly be done or sanctioned, not by a simple majority of the members of the company or association, but only by some special majority, as, for instance, in the case of a limited company under the Companies Act, a special resolution duly passed as such. As Romer J pointed out, the reason for that exception is clear, because otherwise, if the rule were applied in its full rigour, a company which, by its directors, had broken its own regulations by doing something without a special resolution which could only be done validly by a special resolution could assert that it alone was the proper plaintiff in any consequent action and the effect would be to allow a company acting in breach of its articles to do de facto by ordinary resolution that which according to its own regulations could only be done by special resolution. That exception exactly fits the present case inasmuch as here the act complained of is something which could only have been validly done, not by a simple majority, but by a two-thirds majority obtained on a ballot vote. In my judgment, therefore, the reliance on the rule in *Foss* v *Harbottle* (1843) 2 Hare 461 in the present case may be regarded as misconceived on that ground alone.

I would go further. In my judgment, this is a case of a kind which is not even within the general ambit of the rule. This is not a case where what is complained of is a wrong done to the union, a matter in respect of which the cause of action would primarily and properly belong to the union. It is a case in which certain members of a trade union complain that the union, acting through the delegate meeting and the executive council in breach of the rules by which the union and every member of the union are bound, has invaded the individual rights of the complainant members, who are entitled to maintain themselves in full membership with all the rights and privileges appertaining to that status so long as they pay contributions in accordance with the tables of contributions as they stood before the purported alterations of 1943, unless and until the scale of contributions is validly altered by the prescribed majority obtained on a ballot vote. Those rights, these members claim, have been invaded. The gist of the case is that the personal and individual rights of membership of each of them have been invaded by a purported, but invalid, alteration of the tables of contributions. In those circumstances, it seems to me the rule in *Foss* v *Harbottle* has no application at all, for the individual members who are suing sue, not in the right of the union, but in their own right to protect from invasion their own individual rights as members.

I would be content so to hold as a matter of self-evident principle, but the matter is not free from authority. It will, I think, be enough for the present purposes if I refer, briefly, to a passage in the judgment of Sir George Jessel MR in *Pender* v *Lushington* (1877) 6 Ch D 70. There was a discussion in the course of the case whether the action was one which an individual shareholder could maintain and Sir George Jessel MR said:

> "But there is another ground on which the action may be maintained. This is an action by Mr Pender for himself. He is a member of the company, and whether he votes with the majority or the minority he is entitled to have his vote recorded – an individual right in respect of which he has a right to sue. That has nothing to do with the question like that raised in *Foss* v *Harbottle* and that line of cases. He has a right to say, 'Whether I vote in the majority or minority, you shall record my vote, as that is a right of property belonging to my interest in this company, and if you refuse to record my vote I will institute legal proceedings against you to compel you.' What is the answer to such an action? It seems to me it can be maintained as a matter or substance and that there is no technical difficulty in maintaining it."

In my judgment, precisely the same conclusions as are there expressed apply in the present case, and the rule in *Foss* v *Harbottle* affords no answer to the action. It was sought to show that this was not a matter affecting the individual rights of any particular member of the union because all were subject to the same alteration of the tables and, theefore, it was a matter which affected the general body of members as a whole. I do not agree. For one thing the contributions to be paid by any individual member would depend on the particular category of membership to which he belonged, but, for another thing and more important, it seems to me that, although all the members are liable to pay the subscriptions appropriate to their respective categories, the right of each member to maintain himself in membership by paying his subscription – that is to say, by paying whatever subscription appropriate to his case is validly fixed and for the time being in force under the rules – is an individual right of his own which he himself is entitled to protect by an action on his own behalf ...'

Estmanco (Kilner House) Ltd v *Greater London Council* [1982] 1 WLR 2 Chancery Division (Megarry V-C).

Fraud on the minority

Facts

The GLC owned a block of 60 flats in Lambeth in need of renovation. In 1980 it was decided that the flats should be sold off on 135 year leases at a low price taking into account the need for repairs. There was a strong demand for the flats and 12 were sold very quickly and contracts signed with purchasers for others. In July 1981 political control changed in the GLC and the new GLC decided to halt the sales of the flats and instead, rent them to homeless families. In October 1980 a company, Estmanco Ltd, had been formed to manage the flats. The company had an issued share capital of £3,000 divided into 60 £50 shares. Each flat was to have one share but all the voting rights attached to the shares were to be in the hands of the three GLC employees. There was a covenant between the company and the GLC that the GLC would use its best endeavours to sell the flats. In August 1981 the directors of the company issued proceedings to enforce this covenant considering the GLC's change in policy. But some days later an extraoridinary general meeting of the company was convened and resolutions were passed that the proceedings be discontinued. These resolutions were put forward and passed because the GLC had a voting monopoly until all the flats were sold. A Mrs Cope, one of the flat-owners, accordingly applied for the action to include her as plaintiff so that she might pursue a derivative action on behalf of the company. The GLC claimed Mrs Cope could not succeed in her application because, inter alia, she was not within any of the exceptions to the rule in *Foss* v *Harbottle* and as the GLC was not a director of the company it owed no fiduciary duty and was using its voting power in a way in which it was entitled to do; viz its own interests.

Held

Mrs Cope was entitled to bring a derivative action under the exception of fraud on the minority since this exception was not confined to fraud at common law but included abuse or misuse of powers. In the circumstances the GLC was abusing its majority position by attempting to change its policy without regard to how this affected the rights or property of the minority shareholders.

Megarry V-C:

'... If the rule in *Foss* v *Harbottle* had remained unqualified, the way would have been open to the majority to stultify any proceedings which were for the benefit of the minority and to the disadvantage of the majority. Accordingly, a number of exceptions from the rule have been established; and it is here that the difficulties begin. (For convenience, I use the words "exceptions" to embrace cases which are outside the true scope of the rule). It is far from clear just what the exceptions are, or what is the ambit of some of them.

I do not think that it can simply be said that there is an exception from the rule whenever the justice of the case requires it. There are some dicta which support such a view eg *Edwards* v *Halliwell* [1950] 2 All ER 1064, and this seems to have been part of the ratio in *Prudential Assurance Co Ltd* v *Newman Industries Ltd (No 2)* [1981] Ch 57. But in the Court of Appeal in the latter case, the court observed that this was "not a practical test", and I would respectfully concur. If it were the test, I feel no doubt that in this case the applicant would succeed.

Although the concept of injustice is not the test, I think that it is nevertheless a reason, and an important reason, for making exceptions from the rule; yet the reasons for an exception must not be confused with the exception itself. If the test were simply justice or injustce, this would mean different things to different men; and the courts have in fact proceeded by way of formulating, not always with great clarity, a number of individual exceptions. The subject has, indeed, been gradually developing: and unless the remedy introduced by the Companies Act 1980 s75 inhibits that development, no doubt one day the courts will distil from the exceptions some guiding principle that is wide enough to comprehend them all and yet narrow enough to be practicable and workable. It may be that the test may come to be whether an ordinary resolution of the shareholders could validly carry out or ratify the act in question; but I do not think that a motion in the long vacation is the time or place for a judge to attempt any far-reaching analysis of the exceptions, or any distillation of a guiding principle to be found in them.

Counsel's basic contention for the council was founded on the distinction between directors and shareholders. Directors of a company admittedly owe a fiduciary duty to the company, whereas shareholders do not. In this case the council owns shares in the company but is not a director of the company, and so owes no fiduciary duty to it. When voting, a shareholder may consult his own interests, and may use his voting power to protect himself from being sued by the company. Where the majority shareholders genuinely believe that it is in the best interests of the company as a whole that an action by the company should not be brought, that is decisive, unless no reasonable shareholder in their position could hold this belief. The self-interest in the council, though relevant, was not a determinative factor; and there was no separate category for the "expropriation" cases, ie where the company was being deprived of some of its property, whether a right of action or anything else. In support of these propositions counsel for the council relied on a variety of authorities, including *North-West Transportation Co Ltd* v *Beatty* (1877) 12 App Cas 589, *Allen* v *Gold Reefs of West Africa Ltd* [1900] 1 Ch 656, *Sidebottom* v *Kershow Leese & Co Ltd* [1920] 1 CH 254, *Shuttleworth* v *Cox Bros & Co (Maidenhead) Ltd* [1929] 2 KB 9, *Greenhalgh* v *Arderne Cinemas Ltd* [1951] Ch 286, *Pavlides* v *Jensen* [1956] Ch 565 and *Clemens* v *Clemens Bros Ltd* [1976] 2 All ER 286.

Now the question is how far authorities such as these on the validity of making alterations in the articles fit in with the rule in *Foss* v *Harbottle* and its exceptions. I do not think that counsel ever succeeded in anwering that question satisfactorily. Plainly there must be some limit to the power of the majority to pass resolutions which they believe to be in the best interests of the company and yet remain immune from interference by the courts. It may be in the best interests of the company to deprive the minority of some of their rights or some of their property, yet I do not think that this gives the majority an unrestricted right to do this, however unjust it may be, and however much it may harm shareholders whose rights as a class differ from those of the majority. If a case falls within one of the exceptions from *Foss* v *Harbottle*, I cannot see why the right of the minority to sue under that exception should be taken away from them merely because the majority of the company reasonably believe it to be in the best interests of the company this this should be done. This is particularly so if the exception from the rule falls under the rubric of "fraud on a minority". I accept, of course, that company discontinuing an action by the company against himself, as in *East Pant Du United Lead Mining Ltd* v *Merryweather* (1864) 2 Hem & M 254, but in that case there was no question of the discontinuance injuring one category of shareholders to the benefit of another.

It was on the firmly established exception of "fraud on a minority" that counsel for the applicant mainly relied. It does not seem to have yet become very clear exactly what the word "fraud" means in this context; but I think it is plainly wider than fraud at common law, in the sense of *Derry* v *Peek* (1889) 14 App Cas 337. In a valuable survey of the authorities, Templeman J recently came to the conclusion that this head permitted the minority to sue even though there had not been even an allegation of fraud: See *Daniels* v *Daniels* [1978] Ch 406. That was a case in which a husband and wife were the two directors of a company to sell to the wife land owned by the company and four years later she sold the land for over 28 times what she had paid for it. The judge refused to strike out the statement of claim of minority shareholders in *Foss* v *Harbottle* proceedings against the two directors and the company. The principle which he derived from the cases was that "a minority shareholder who has no other remedy may sue where directors use their powers, intentionally or unintentionally, fraudulently or negligently, in a manner which benefits themselves at the expense of the company". Apart from the benefit to themselves at the company's expense, the essence of the matter seems to be an abuse or misuse of power. "Fraud" in the phrase "fraud on a minority" seems to be being used as comprising not only fraud at common law but also fraud in the wider equitable sense of that term, as in the equitable concept of a fraud on a power.

Now of course *Daniels* v *Daniels* was a case on acts by directors as such, rather than by shareholders, and I do not forget this. At the same time it seems to me to be useful as preventing "fraud" from being read too narrowly. Suppose too, the decision to sell the land had been made not by the husband and wife qua directors, but by a resolution of the company carried by their votes: could it then be said that the minority could not sue? Is this exception from the rule in *Foss* v *Harbottle* open to easy evasion by directors who hold the majority of votes in general meeting if they take care to reach their decisions not by voting as directors but by voting as shareholders? I think not.

In considering whether there is a fraud on a minority in this case in the sense which this phrase has acquired, and whether counsel for the council has made good his main contention, certain matters seem plain enough. First, I do not think that it can reasonably be thought to be for the benefit of the company that the action should be discontinued. This is not a case of a trading company, seeking to make a profit. The company is a non-profit-making company, and so the test cannot be the financial benefit of the company. The company was formed for a particular purpose, namely to manage the block of flats under the control of the purchasers of the flats; and the covenant by the council with the company was part of the mechanism for securing this result. On the face of it I do not think that it can readily be said to be for the benefit of a company to stultify a substantial part of the purpose for which it was formed ...

... Second, it is very far from clear that the council, or any properly authorised organ of the council, ever adequately considered and decided what was for the company's benefit before voting at the extraordinary general meeting ...

... Third, the council does not appear to have considered the effect of its vote on the rights of purchasers qua shareholders. Counsel for the council emphasised more than once that the applicant's real complaint was not as a shareholder but as a purchaser of a flat. Instead of having as her neighbours the occupants of 59 other flats which had all been purchased on long lease, she would have only 11 flats occupied thus, and 48 occupied by tenants who would not have the stake in the block of flats which the purchase of long leases would have obtained. That, of course, is so; but it is not all. What she bought, inter alia, was a share which had no voting rights, but would have voting rights at a future point of time, namely, when all the other flats had been sold; and the due arrival of that time was secured, so it seemed, by cl 3(1) of the agreement, and recognised by recital (4) of the lease. Furthermore, when she obtained her voting rights, she and all the other purchasers of flats would be in control of the company, which would not only manage the block of flats as they collectively wished, but would also, as landlord, be able to enforce the terms of the leases against all the purchasers. The council's conclusion that it is in the best interests of the company that cl 3(1) of the agreement should not be enforced is a conclusion that it is in the best interests of the company (including the applicant as one of the corporators) that this state of affairs, so plainly intended by the documents, should never be reached; and there is not a shred of evidence to suggest that this was ever considered by the council ...

... As matters appear to me now, it seems clear enough that the council has throughout been actuated by its desire to put into effect its new housing policy, even though that plainly and admittedly involves the council in a breach of contract, in depriving the purchasers of flats and their rights as shareholders, and in destroying the scheme under which they were induced to buy their flats. That new housing policy may well be an entirely right and proper policy for the council to adopt for any block of flats where that can be done without committing flagrant breaches of contract; but it is a different matter where, as for this block, the policy cannot be carried out without committing such breaches. Furthermore, I find it impossible to give any real credence to the contention that the reason why the council voted in favour of discontinuing the action was that the council considered this to be in the best interests of the company. The council did this in order to suppress proceedings which stood in the way of carrying out their new housing policy regardless of breaches of contract and injuries to the existing purchasers of flats. As for whether it was reasonable to believe that it was in the best interests of the company not to sue, it must be remembered that the directors who had been appointed by the council, had decided to sue ...'

Statutory provisions in s459 CA 1985 and minority protection

Bird Precision Bellows Ltd, Re [1984] Ch 419 Chancery Division (Nourse J)

Unfairly prejudicial conduct – exclusion from management – valuation of shares

Facts

The company was incorporated in 1975 to carry on the business of manufacturing industrial bellows. It had an issued share capital of 30,000 £1 shares and the petitioners held 26 per cent of these between them whilst the respondents held the remaining 74 per cent of the issued share capital. The petitioners had been directors of the company until their removal from that office in April 1981. They alleged that as the company was a quasi-partnership and there had been an understanding from the date of incorporation that they would participate in the conduct of the company's affairs, their removal as directors wrongfully excluded them from the conduct of the company's business. Accordingly, the petitioners petitioned under s75 of the Companies Act 1980 (now s459(1) CA 1985) that the affairs of the company had been conducted in a manner unfairly prejudicial to them and sought an order under s75(4)(d) (now s461(2)(d) CA 1985) of the 1980 Act that the respondents purchase their shares. An order was made by Vinelott J in November 1981 that the respondents purchase the petitioners' shares. A question which now arose was the price that the respondents should pay for the shares.

Held

1. When an order was made by the court for the purchase of shares under s75(4)(d) of the Companies Act 1980 the price fixed by the court should be fair having regard to the facts of the particular case.
2. Where the shareholding was a minority shareholding in a small private company it was not necesssarily the case that the value of the shares should be fixed on a pro rata basis according to the value of the shares as a whole or that a discount should be made to reflect that fact that the shareholding was a minority shareholding. If the sale was being forced upon the petitioner because of the conduct of the majority and the shares had been acquired on the incorporation of a quasi-partnership company in which the petitioner expected to participate, the price should, as a general rule, be fixed on a pro rata basis. But, if the petitioner had conducted himself so as to deserve exclusion from the company's affairs, the price should be as a general rule, discounted as if he had elected to sell his shares. Since the petitioners had been wrongfully excluded from the company's affairs in this case the price should be fixed on a pro rata basis.

Nourse J:

'... I would expect that in a majority of cases where purchase orders are made under s75 in relation to quasi-partnerships the vendor is unwilling in the sense that the sale has been forced on him. Usually he will be a minority shareholder whose interests have been unfairly prejudiced by the manner in which the affairs of the company have been conducted by the majority. On the assumption that the unfair prejudice has made it no longer tolerable for him to retain his interest in the company, a sale of his shares will invariably be his only practical way out, short of a winding-up. In that kind of case it seems to me that it would not merely be unfair, but most unfair, that he should be bought but on the fictional basis applicable to a free election to sell his shares in accordance with the company's articles of association, or indeed any other basis which involved a discounted price. In my judgment the correct course would be to fix the price pro rata according to the value of the shares as a whole and without any discount, as being the only fair method of compensating an unwilling vendor of the equivalent of a partnership share. Equally, if the order provided, as it did in *Re Jermyn Street Turkish Baths Ltd* [1971] 1 WLR 1042, for the purchase of the shares of the deliquent majority, it would not merely not be fair, but most unfair, that they should receive a price which involved an element of premium.

Of the other, I would expect more rare, cases in which the court might make a purchase order in relation to a quasi-partnership, the arguments of Mr Jacob require me to mention one. Suppose the case of a minority shareholder whose interests have been unfairly prejudiced by the conduct of the majority, but who had nevertheless so acted as to deserve his exclusion from the company. It is difficult to see how such a case could arise in practice ... As will appear, Mr Jacob submitted that the petitioners did act in such a way as to deserve their exclusion from the company. He further submitted that it would be fair for them to be bought out on the basis which would be applicable if they had made a free election to sell their shares pursuant to the articles, ie at a discount ... I think that the further submission of Mr Jacob is correct ...

... Next, I must consider the example from the second category of cases in which, broadly speaking, shares in a small private company are acquired ... In the case of a shareholder who acquires shares from another at a price which is discounted because they represent a minority, it is to my mind self-evident that there cannot be any universal or even a general rule that he should be bought out under s75 on a more favourable basis, even in a case where his predecessor has been a quasi-partner in a quasi-partnership. He might himself have acquired the shares purely for investment and played no part in the affairs of the company. In that event it might well be fair, I do not know, that he should be bought out on the same basis as he himself had bought, even though his interests had been unfairly prejudiced in the meantime. A fortiori, there could be no universal or even a general rule in a case where the company had never been a quasi-partnership in the first place ...'

BSB Holdings Ltd, Re (1995) The Times 2 August Chancery Division (Arden J)

Section 459 Companies Act (CA) 1985 – petition failed – warning about s459 actions being used as a vehicle of oppression

Facts
The petitioner was London Merchant Securities plc ('LMS'), a member of BSB Holdings Ltd ('BSBH'). BSBH was incorporated in 1986 as a vehicle for a consortium, which had been successful in acquiring a franchise granted by the Independent Broadcasting Authority. At the time, a share capital of £625 million was anticipated. Delays and difficulties, however, led to the issue of £160 billion share capital and also a merger with BSkyB. The report does not detail the substance of the petition, but in essence LMS complained that it had been unfairly prejudiced by the financing of BSBH and also by the merger with BSkyB.

Held
The petition was dismissed. Arden J concluded that, on the facts, none of the petitioner's 14 allegations of unfair prejudice were justified. The importance of this decision though lies in her Ladyship's comments that, unless carefully controlled, s459 petitions could become a means of oppression. The proper workings of business and the investement of capital should not be inhibited by unfounded threats of action.

A Company, Re [1983] Ch 178 Chancery Division (Lord Grantchester QC)

Whether refusal to purchase shares or formulate a scheme of reconstruction was unfairly prejudicial conduct

Facts
A testator died leaving a substantial minority shareholding in a family company for the benefit of his two infant children. The company ran an advertising and commercial artists' business and had substantial assets, including liquid assets. It was proposed to apply part of the liquid assets in setting up a wine bar

and restaurant business in London. The executors of the testator's estate wished to apply the children's shareholding for their education and maintenance and considered this could be best done by selling the shareholding. However other members of the family were unwilling to purchase the shares and the company offered £112,000 for them whilst the executors wanted £175,000. The executors petitioned for relief under s75 Companies Act 1980 (now ss459(1) CA 1985) claiming that the company's failure to formulate a scheme of reconstruction under ss287 Companies Act 1948 (which became s582 CA 1985: see now ss110 and 111 of the Insolvency Act 1986) or to purchase the shares under ss46 and 47 Companies Act 1981 (now s162 CA 1985) was unfairly prejudicial conduct. Further, it was alleged that the setting-up in the wine bar and restaurant business was unfairly prejudicial as this would leave insufficient assets to purchase their shares.

Held

The petition would be struck out; neither of the matters complained of could amount to unfair prejudice.

Lord Grantchester QC:

'... Turning back to s76 of the 1980 Act, the section operates where "the affairs of the company are being or have been conducted in a manner which is unfairly prejudicial to the interests of some part of the members" ... To my mind, in passing s75 of the 1980 Act, Parliament did not intend to give a right of action to every shareholder who considered that some act or omission by his company resulted in unfair prejudice to himself. In argument, an example was advanced of a shareholder who objected to his company carrying out some operation on land adjoining his dwelling house, which resulted in that house falling in value. It is not difficult to envisage an act or omission on the part of a company rendering an asset of a shareholder, other than his shares, of lesser value. In my judgment s75 is to be construed as confined to "unfair prejudice" of a petitioner "qua member"; or, put in another way, the word "interests" in s75 is confined to "interests of the petitioner as a member". I do not consider that *Ebrahimi v Westbourne Galleries Ltd* [1972] 2 All ER 492, (1973) AC 360, which was a decision involving s210 in very different circumstances, requires a wider scope to be given to s75. The decision in that case was primarily concerned with the rights of a member to obtain a widing-up order on just and equitable grounds, and not on what constituted "oppression" for s210 purposes.

If the foregoing be correct, then what I have now to consider is whether or not the matters of which the petitioning executors complain in the petition and the evidence in support can amount to conduct of the affairs of the company "in a manner which is unfairly prejudicial to them" as shareholders. The matters of which complaint is made are: (i) the failure by the company and its management to propound a s287 scheme of reconstruction; (ii) the failure by the company and its management to propound a purchase scheme under ss46 and 47 of the 1981 Act; and (iii) the making of the proposal for the establishment of a wine bar and restaurant through the medium of a partly-owned subsidiary.

Let me take the first two together. The argument proceeds on this basis. The petitioning executors require cash for the benefit of the two infant children. They can obtain cash under a suitable scheme in respect of their shares. Therefore the failure to propound such a scheme is "unfairly prejudicial" to them as members. I do not accept that line of reasoning because I do not consider that a refusal to propound a scheme does affect or prejudice a member as a member. I take the view that under s287 of the 1948 Act and, to take a similar type of provision, s206 of the same Act, a member of a company has certain statutory rights if and when a scheme is proposed. In relation to an article empowering a reconstruction in terms similar to s287 aforesaid, a member has certain contractual rights as and when a scheme is proposed by analogy with s287. But to my mind, these rights and any concomitant interests only arise on and by virtue or by reason of the scheme. I do not accept that a member of a company has an interest "as a member" in a non-existent hypothetical scheme which could be proposed or in having such a scheme proposed for his benefit. It follows that I do not consider that a member can be affected or prejudiced, unfairly or otherwise, by a failure or omission or refusal to propose or propound such a scheme.

I take the view that similar reasoning applies to the complaint of the failure to propose a scheme of purchase under ss46 and 47 of the 1981 Act. To my mind, on an agreement being made for the purchase of shares by a company, contractual rights arise, subject to and with the benefit of the provisions of the two sections. In such a case, however, such rights, and any interests of the vendor shareholder, arise ex conractu and not qua member. Accordingly I have come to the conclusion that the sections do not create interests for members qua members, and that a refusal, failure or omission to proceed under the section before any agreement on price has been reached cannot be conducted "unfairly prejudicial" of the prospective vendors as members.

The first extract which I read from *Gore-Browne* seems to arrive at a similar solution, but by another route. It suggests that to constitute "unfair prejudice", the value or the quality of the shareholder's interest, ie his shares in a company limited by shares, must be adversely affected. Certainly the refusals or failure by the company to proceed in this case with a s287 scheme or a purchase under ss46 and 47, do not adversely affect the value of the shares of the petitioning executors; instead, the propounding of such a scheme or purchase would or might have brought about benefit to them.

I am therefore left with the third complaint, the fact that a proposal has been advanced for the establishment of a wine bar and restaurant in the company's premises through the medium of a subsidiary. The reasoning behind this complaint is that if the proposal proceeds, the liquid resources may then be insufficient to buy out the 1,844 shares of the petitioning executors. In my judgment, a decision of the directors or even the omission of the directors to come to a decision relating to the conduct of its business, may amount to conduct which comes within s75 of the 1980 Act, so as to be actionable by a member who is thereby unfairly prejudiced as a member. But I cannot accept that the foregoing extends to a consideration by directors of a company of proposals or suggestions similar to the one with which I am now concerned and at the stage at which the proposal or suggestion now stands. It is the duty of the directors to manage the business of the company, and to put its assets to the best use, or realise them to the best advantage for the benefit of the company as a whole. For such purposes they must duly consider all proposals and suggestions put forward. In my view, in relation to this aspect of the proceedings, I agree with Mr Hamilton that the petition now presented is premature. The wine bar proposal or suggestion may, or may not, be adopted but, if it is adopted, the petitioning executors accept, that the correct procedures will then be followed.

In the outcome I have accepted the submission that the petition cannot succeed. I do not consider that s75 was enacted so as to enable a "locked-in" minority shareholder to require the company to buy him out at a price which he considered adequately to reflect the value of the underlying assets referable to his shareholding, providing the company held sufficient resources so to do. I will order the petition to be removed from the file and struck out accordingly.'

Commentary
By virtue of schedule 19, para 11(a) to the Companies Act 1989, in s459(1) of the 1985 Act unfair prejudice may be 'to the interests of members generally or ... some part of its members'.

A Company (No 00789 of 1987), Re, ex parte Shooter [1990] BCLC 384 High Court (Harman J)

Unfairly prejudicial conduct – the calling of meetings

Facts
The company, which ran a football club, had, inter alia, held extraordinary general meetings without giving sufficient notice. At these meetings new shares had purportedly been created and the petitioner had subscribed for some of these shares and purchased others from members.

Held

The ineffective creation of new shares was conduct of the company's affairs which was unfairly prejudicial particularly to the interests of the petitioner and the court therefore had jurisdiction under s459 of the Companies Act 1985.

Harman J:

'The conduct of the extraordinary general meetings is, plainly, the conduct of the company's affairs. To hold an extraordinary general meeting to enable the company to raise money but, by reason of the deliberate (I am afraid), although not malicious, holding of the meeting on short notice resulting in the meeting being totally ineffective, must be prejudicial to the interests of members, and when it comes to [the petitioner], unfairly prejudicial particularly to his interests because he paid the company money, a substantial sum, for shares which did not exist. Further, he was led to pay money to others on the faith of the company's representation made by the issue of share certificates to them for shares which did not exist. Thus, as it seems to me, [the petitioner] has, plainly, been unfairly prejudiced by the conduct of the affairs of this company.

Thus I hold that I have jurisdiction under s459, and I then have to turn to s461(1) of the Act ... In my view, there is power here to make such orders as I consider will enable the company, for the future, to be properly run, and for its affairs to be under the conduct of somebody in whom shareholders generally can have confidence that the company will be properly conducted.'

Commentary

In s459(1) of the 1985 Act, for 'unfairly prejudicial to the interests of some part of the members' there is now substituted 'unfairly prejudicial to the interests of the members generally or of some part of its members': schedule 19, para 11(a), to the Companies Act 1989.

Estates Acquisition & Development Ltd, Re [1995] BCC 338 Chancery Division (Ferris and Warner JJ)

Section 459 Companies Act (CA) 1985 – petition dismissed – petitioner had no legitimate expectations beyond the articles and the Companies Acts – costs could be enforced against the petitioner by way of a charge over her shares

Facts

The petitioner held just under 12 per cent of the shares in the company and was also a director. She commenced an action under s459 and complained of:

1. a derisory offer by another director and shareholder to buy her shares;
2. proposals to remove her as a director;
3. an alteration to the memorandum and articles of association;
4. failure to provide her with information to allow her to carry out her duties as a director, to assess whether the affairs of the company were being properly managed, and also to value her shares.

Held

The petition was dismissed by Ferris J. In later proceedings Warner J held a costs order against the petitioner could be enforced by a charging order over her shares in the company.

1. The offer to purchase the petitioner's shares was not capable of being treated as part of the conduct of the company's affairs. It was simply an offer to purchase her shares by a director who was acting on his own behalf.
2. Subject to special circumstances not present in this case, a shareholder who was also a director was

always at risk of being removed under s303 CA 1985. There were ample grounds to justify removal here. She had no qualities which made her particularly suited to be a director of this company. Although a director since 1979, she had never attended a directors' meeting and had shown no interest in the affairs of the company until about 1988.

3. General alterations to the objects clause and to the articles which reduced the quorum for both shareholders' and directors' meetings from five to two could also not be complained of, even though as one of five directors, the petitioner could have prevented a board meeting taking place prior to the alteration.

4. On the facts and considering the evidence, Ferris J felt that the petitioner had been provided with the requested management and shareholder information. Her demands for information were said to be insatiable and oppressive. In any event, the proper remedy would have been to order production of the missing information. The remedy sought by the petitioner, however, was the purchase of her shares by the majority.

Ferris J:

'Having dealt at some length, perhaps at undue length, with the individual component parts of Mrs Felton's [the petitioner] case I must now turn to the case which she seeks to make on the basis of these component parts taken in conjunction with each other. However, I find this a troublesome task because, although Mr Davies [counsel for the petitioner] made it clear throughout that he relied upon the matters pleaded as a whole rather then individually, I found it difficult to understand precisely what the whole is said to be beyond the sum of its component parts.

At one time I thought that Mrs Felton was trying to make good a case that the various acts or omissions which she alleges subsequent to June 1988 were part of a plan to bring pressure to bear upon her to accept Mr Scott's [one of the respondents] derisory offer for her shares. But such a case is not open on the pleadings and if pursued, which it was not, would face the difficulty that no offer, derisory or otherwise, was on the table for acceptance after the initial offer was made and rejected in June 1988. Mr Davies confined himself, as he must, to what is said in the pleadings which, so far as a general case going beyond the specific matters is concerned, seems to be limited to paras 24 and 28 of the petition, which I have already read. When I pressed Mr Davies to formulate the proposition which he advanced as defining the interests of Mrs Felton which had been unfairly prejudiced, he put it in this way:

"In a company of this sort, in which the rights and liabilities of members inter se are not absolutely governed by the memorandum and articles of association of the company, a member to whom an offer is made for the purchase of that member's minority shareholding, certainly if made by the person who is in control of the company, has a right to the provision of all information necessary to enable her to decide whether she is willing to be a vendor or prospective vendor of her shares. Her position as a prospective vendor is part of her position as a member of the company."

I have endeavoured to set out the proposition exactly as it was put by Mr Davies and I make no criticism of any linguistic inelegance which might have been avoided if it had been formulated otherwise than in the course of Mr Davies' oral submissions. The last sentence of the proposition, relating to the minority shareholder's position as a prospective vendor being part of her position as a member, is supported by the decision in the 1986 case of Hoffmann J [*Re A Company No 008699 of 1985* (1986) 2 BCC 99]. Mr Davies submitted that the rest of the proposition was also supported by the 1986 case, but this would only be so if that case established that a member has the right not to be unfairly prejudiced without the need to identify the prejudice with any separate interest of the member. As I have indicated, I reject the view that the 1986 case is authority for such a proposition.

Apart from this the submission runs into a number of other difficulties. Mr Davies did not put it forward as a proposition applicable to all companies but limited it to 'a company of this sort in which the rights and liabilities of members inter se are not absolutely governed by the memorandum and articles'. But, as Lord Wilberforce said in *Ebrahimi v Westbourne Galleries* [1973] AC 360 at p 379E, in most cases the basis of the association between members will be 'adequately and exhaustively' laid down in the articles and the superimposition of equitable considerations will require something more. There is nothing in the pleadings in this case, and there was nothing in the evidence, to indicate what is distinctive about this company or what it is that has the effect that the rights and liabilities of its members are not governed by the memorandum and articles of association of the company.

Beyond this, the proposition makes no allowance for the fact that, as I find, Mr Scott's offer was made in his personal capacity and not as part of the conduct of the company's affairs and was a once and for all offer which ceased to operate once it had been refused, as it was immediately after it was made. I cannot see how a single offer of this kind can trigger a right to have information which did not previously exist and which goes well beyond the usual rights that a member has to information about the company's affairs.

In any event, as I have held, the company has in the event provided Mrs Felton with a great deal of information, probably going well beyond what she would be entitled to even if Mr Davies's proposition were correct. While it is true that the management information has been provided during the course of the proceedings rather than before the presentation of the petition and it is also true that the provision of information at that stage is not by itself a bar to an otherwise well-founded petition based on the failure to provide information, I cannot accept that the failure to give effect to the right asserted in Mr Davies's proposition could lead to the remedy sought by Mrs Felton, namely the purchase of her shares. In other words, even if I were to accept Mr Davies's proposition, which I do not, and were also to accept that the failure to provide management information at an earlier stage constitutes unfair prejudice to Mrs Felton's interests as a member of the company, I do not see how this could, in the circumstances of the present case, lead to anything more than an order for the provision of the missing information which, for the reasons I have indicated, I regard as being unnecessary and inappropriate.

In the result I conclude that this petition must be dismissed. I add only this. The evidence indicates that prior to October 1988 the affairs of the company had been conducted with a degree of informality and a disregard for the provisions of the company's constitution which is unacceptable. Although the irregularities which have occurred do not, in my judgment, entitle Mrs Felton to the relief which she has sought on this petition, it must not be thought that the dismissal of the petition entitles those who control the company's affairs to revert to the old irregular ways.'

London School of Electronics, Re [1986] 1 Ch 211 Chancery Division (Nourse J)

Section 459 unfairly prejudicial conduct – valuation of petitioner's shares

Facts
The petitioner, L, held 250 out of the 1,000 shares issued by London School of Electronics Ltd ('LSE') and was also a director. The respondent was City Tutorial College Ltd ('CTC') whose two directors and major shareholders were also G and A. The remaining shares in LSE were owned by CTC. LSE provided courses in electronics and CTC ran a tutorial college in which the courses were taught. In 1983 L was removed as a director by the other directors, G and A, who alleged bad behaviour on the part of L. In addition he discovered that they had procured a new course to be run by CTC to the exclusion of LSE students. L told his students that he would not be teaching at LSE the next year but that he would be teaching for a new rival college which he had set up. In fact he took some 10 students of LSE with him to the new institution. L alleged unfairly prejudicial conduct by G and A because they had diverted students to CTC and had dismissed him as a director. He sought an order under s75 of the CA 1980 [now ss459-461 CA 1985] that CTC purchase his shares in LSE.

Held
The conduct was unfairly prejudicial and it did not matter that the petitioner did not come to court 'with clean hands'. The order for the purchase of the petitioner's shares was granted.

Nourse J:

'There are two main areas of dispute between parties. First, CTC contends that the petitioner is not entitled to any relief under s75 of the Companies Act 1980. Secondly, if he is, it is accepted that the petitioner should be bought out of CTC but there are disputes as to when and how his shares should be valued.

Mr Oliver, for CTC, relied on the fact that s210 of the Companies Act of 1948, which was the predecessor of s75, required, first, that to wind up the company would unfairly prejudice the members concerned but, secondly, that the facts would otherwise justify the making of a winding-up order on the just and equitable ground. Therefore, said Mr Oliver, the just and equitable test is imported into s75. He then relied on what was said by Lord Cross of Chelsea in relation to that test in *In re Westbourne Galleries Ltd* [1973] AC 360, 387G, and submitted that a petitioner under s75 must come to the court with clean hands. Although the practical consequences may often be the same, I do not share Mr Oliver's view of s75. I agree with Mr Instone, for the petitioner, that that section must be construed as it stands. The combined effect of subs (1) and (3) is to empower the court to make such order as it thinks fit for giving relief, if it is first satisfied that the affairs of the company are being or have been conducted in a manner which is unfairly prejudicial to the interests of some part of the members. the conduct of the petitioner may be material in a number of ways, of which the two most obvious are these. First, it may render the conduct on the other side, even if it is prejudicial, not unfair: cf: *In re R A Noble & Sons (Clothing) Ltd* [1983] BCLC 273. secondly, even if the conduct on the other side is both prejudicial and unfair, the petitioner's conduct may nevertheless affect the relief which the court thinks fit to grant under subs(3). In my view there is no independent or overriding requirement that it should be just and equitable to grant relief or that the petitioner should come to the court with clean hands.

Mr Oliver then submitted that on a view of the facts as a whole the affairs of the company were not conducted in a manner which was unfairly prejudicial to the interests of the petitioner as a member of the company. He relied in particular on the injury caused to the company by the petitioner, whilst still a director, in deliberately taking away a dozen or so students and enrolling them with LCEE. He also relied on the nine grounds of complaint specified in the letter of 17 June 1983, although it must be said that those matters were not much investigated in the evidence. Mr Oliver submitted that in all the circumstances the conduct of CTC, even if it was prejudicial, was not unfair.

While I have no doubt that during the academic year 1982-83 the petitioner proved himself to be difficult and unreliable, perhaps lazy, in the discharge of his teaching and related duties, there was in my view no adequate justification for the decision of CTC to transfer to itself students who had completed their first year of the BSc course in electronics and to register with itself all new students for that course. It was by then clear that the students doing the BSc course were, and would continue to be, the substantial source of the company's income and profits. It was no recompense to the company to be able to continue with the certificate and diploma courses. It was suggested in this court that CTC still intended to account to the company for a due proportion of the profits attributable to the BSc students, but that suggestion cannot stand with a fair reading of the minutes of the meeting on 3 June. They record that Mr Athanasiou sought to justify the proposal on the ground that the arrangement with Newport was due to his own initiative and the efforts of both Mr George and himself. They also record that Mr George stated, with the agreement of Mr Athanasiou and Mr Mukerjee, that there had been no co-operation from the petitioner and that he was partly responsible for the refusal of CPU to approve the BSc course. All this demonstrates that there had been a conscious and deliberate decision on the part of the CTC to effect the diversion and to maintain it. It was only when Mr George came to swear his affidavit in 1984, no doubt after advice from his then solicitor, that CTC agreed to treat all fees received in respect of its electronics students as accruing to the company. That was not what was said or intended on 3 June 1983. The petitioner clearly understood what was then intended. That was why he said that his relationship with the company had broken down.

In my judgment it was CTC's decision to appropriate the BSc students to itself which was the effective cause of the breakdown in the relationship of mutual confidence between the quasi-partners. Furthermore, that was clearly conduct on the part of CTC which was both unfair and prejudicial to the interests of the petitioner as a member of the company. It is possible, although I do not so decide, that CTC would have been entitled to relieve the petitioner of his teaching duties before June 1983. It is even possible, although it is much less likely, that CTC, had it gone through the appropriate formalities, could have properly removed the petitioner as a director of the company. But none of that is to say that CTC was entitled to take the extreme step of determining to deprive the petitioner of his 25 per cent interest in the profits attributable to the BSc students. Furthermore, I do not think that the petitioner's removal of a dozen or so students to LCEE in August and September can have any effect on the question of unfair prejudice. It was Mr Athanasiou and Mr George who had unfairly brought about the petitioner's departure from the company and his remaining a director was little more than a technicality. His removal of the students is certainly something which will have consequences later in the case. It did not in my view have the effect of rendering the prejudicial conduct no longer unfair.

In the circumstances I hold that the petitioner is entitled to an order under s75 requiring CTC to purchase his shares. That makes it necessary for me to go on and consider three further questions. First, at what date ought the shares to be valued? Secondly, ought the valuation to be made on the footing that the students who the petitioner removed to LCEE remained with the company or ought they to be left out of account? Thirdly, ought the price to be fixed pro rata according to the value of shares as a whole or ought it to be discounted on the ground that the petitioner's shares constitute a minority in number?

Both counsel urged me to hold that there is a general rule as to the date on which shares which are ordered to be purchased pursuant to s75 ought to be valued. Mr Instone submitted that the valuation ought usually to be made at the date of the order as being the only fair method of compensating an unwilling vendor of the equivalent of a partnership share. Mr Oliver, although I think with less enthusiasm for a general rule, submitted that the valuation ought usually to be made at the date of presentation of the petition or perhaps at the date when the unfair prejudice occurred. He said that the petition date is a natural starting point, because that is when the petitioner formally elects to buy or to be bought out. On the facts of the present case he submitted that the date ought to be 3 June 1983, because it was at the board meeting on that day that the unfair prejudice, as I have now held, occurred and at which, as it happened, the petitioner offered to sell his shares to CTC.

If there were to be such a thing as a general rule, I myself would think that the date of the order or the actual valuation would be more appropriate than the date of the presentation of the petition or the unfair prejudice. Prima facie an interest in a going concern ought to be valued at the date on which it is ordered to be purchased. But whatever the general rule might be it seems very probable that the overriding requirement that the valuation should be fair on the facts of the particular case would, by exceptions, reduce it to no rule at all. That that is so is already suggested by such authorities as there are on this question. In *Scottish Co-operative Wholesale Society Ltd* v *Meyer* [1959] AC 324 the shares were ordered to be purchased at the value which they would have had at the date of the petition if there had been no oppression. In *In re Jermyn Street Turkish Baths Ltd* [1970] 1 WLR 1194 the order of Pennycuick J discloses that the assets, undertaking and goodwill of the company were to be valued on an inquiry as at the date of the master's certificate. In *In re A Company (No 002567 of 1982)* [1983] 1 WLR 927 Vinelott J held that the shares of a petitioner who had unreasonably rejected previous fair offers to purchase them ought to be valued at the date of the valuation and not at the date when he had been excluded from participation in the affairs of the company. However, Vinelott J said that he could conceive of many cases where, in an application under s75, fairness would require that the valuation should relate back to an earlier date such as, in that case, the exclusion of the petitioner: see [1983] 1 WLR 927, 937D-E. That observation was approved by Mervyn Davies J in *In re O C (Transport) Services Ltd* [1984] BCLC 251, 258, where he held that the facts required the valuation to be made at a date earlier than the date of the petition, in fact at the date when the unfair prejudice had occurred. Finally, in *In re Bird Precision Bellows Ltd* [1984] Ch 419 the valuation was made as at the date of a consent order that the shares should be purchased at such price as the court should thereafter determine. That case is not of any real assistance on this point, because the date was no doubt implicit in the terms of the consent order.

In the present case I have held that the conduct which was unfairly prejudicial to the interests of the petitioner as a member of the company was CTC's decision to appropriate the BSc students to itself. Had that conduct not taken place the petitioner would effectively have become entitled to 25 per cent of the profits attributable to the BSc students. Since those profits would not have been earned until the academic year 1983-84, it would not in my view be fair to value the petitioner's shares as at 3 June 1983. He is at least entitled to have them valued at some date during the academic year 1983-84 and, since no other date has been suggested, the date of the presentation of the petition – 10 February 1984 – is as good as any other. Ought I to go further and order a valuation as at today's date or the actual date of valuation, ie at a date during the academic year 1984-85? It is not clear to me on the evidence whether there has been a significant increase in the number of BSc students this year. I suspect that there may have been. The more important point is that Mr Athanasiou and Mr George have now been able to acquire a greater academic standing for the course in this country. I find that that has been entirely due to their own efforts and owes nothing to the petitioner and, moreover, that it is unlikely that it would have been achieved if the petitioner had remained with the company. It would therefore be unfair to Mr Athanasiou and Mr George to order a valuation as at today's date. I shall direct that the petitioner's shares be valued as at 10 February 1984.

I am also in no doubt that the valuation ought to be made on the footing that the students which the petitioner removed to LCEE remained with the company. Mr Oliver's primary submission here was that the petitioner's continuing status as a director rendered him accountable to the company in a fiduciary capacity for any profits earned by LCEE in respect of those students. I do not dissent from that submission, but it seems to me that it would in any event be fair to treat those students as having remained with the company, since the whole object of the exercise is that the petitioner should be bought out on the footing that the unfair prejudice had never occurred, in which event both he and the students would have remained with the company.

Finally, it is clear that the price must be fixed pro rata according to the value of the shares as a whole and not discounted: see *In re Bird Precision Bellows Ltd* [1984] Ch 419. Mr Oliver argued that this was a case where the petitioner had made a constructive election to sever his connection with the company and thus to sell his shares, but that argument falls within the findings of fact which I have already made.

The parties are agreed that the valuation should be made out of court. Having now decided the outstanding questions in dispute, I hope that it will be possible for there to be an agreed order referring the matter to a valuer.'

Macro (Ipswich) Ltd and Another, Re [1994] BCC 781 Chancery Division (Arden J)

Unfairly prejudicial conduct – mismanagement

Facts

Mr Thompson (T) was the sole director and majority shareholder of two companies. The business of the companies was that of landlords of residential property and garages. In Companies Act 1985 s459 proceedings, the petitioners alleged various failures of management by T and they sought relief requiring T to purchase their shares.

The petitioners claimed that management by T was inadequate in that T:

1. Failed to attend to the companies' affairs while abroad during the winter period.
2. Between the mid-1930s to 1987 wasted money on building repairs and committed the companies to poor lettings.
3. From 1970 to 1988 received commissions from builders which he failed to account to the companies.
4. From 1970 to 1988 allowed employees to charge 'key money' for granting lettings of company properties.
5. Currently left the property management to an inexperienced person.

Held

There was unfairly prejudicial conduct. The mismanagement by T was serious enough to justify intervention by the court. T was ordered to purchase the petitioners' shares, but the judge declined to appoint an additional director as it was felt that this would make matters worse, rather than resolve the disputes between the parties.

Arden J:

> 'With respect to alleged mismanagement, the court does not interfere in questions of commercial judgment, such as would arise here if (for example) it were alleged that the companies should invest in commercial properties rather than residential properties. However, in cases where what is shown is mismanagement, rather than a difference of opinion on the desirability of particular commercial decisions, and the mismanagement is sufficiently serious to justify the intervention by the court, a remedy is available under s459.
>
> ... In view of Mr Thompson's control and personality, there has since the 1969 reconstruction been no realistic possibility of the appointment of alternative property managers. However, this is not a case where what happened was merely that quality of management turned out to be poor (cf *Re Elgindata Ltd* at pp994–1000). This is a case where there were specific acts of mismanagement by Thompsons, which Mr Thompson failed to prevent or rectify. Moreover, several of the acts of mismanagement which the plaintiffs have identified were repeated over many years, as for example in relation to the failure to inspect repairs. In my judgment, viewed overall, those acts (and Mr Thompson's failures to prevent or rectify them) are sufficiently significant and serious to justify intervention by the court under s461.'

Commentary

This decision is a significant extension of conduct which may fall within s459, but it should not come as too much of a surprise. The possibility of serious mismanagement, as opposed to poor management, amounting to unfair prejudicial conduct had been alluded to before in the mismanagement cases of s459. It was probably only a matter of time before such conduct was found to be sufficiently serious.

Nuneaton Borough AFC Ltd, Re (1989) 5 BCC 377 Court of Appeal (Fox, Ralph Gibson and Nicholls LJJ)

Unfair prejudicial conduct – locus standi – s22 of the Companies Act 1985

Facts

Mr Shooter, the Vice-Chairman of Nuneaton Borough AFC presented a petition, as a member of the company, under s459 of the Companies Act 1985, alleging unfairly prejudicial conduct. Section 22(2) of the Companies Act 1985 provides that a 'member' includes a person 'who agrees to become a member of the company, and whose name is entered in its register of members'. The conduct complained of included failure to answer 'pertinent inquiries regarding the conduct of the company's affairs', and the almost total failure to observe the most simplest of legal requirements in relation to the holding of general meetings and the conduct of directors' affairs. Mr Noel Kelly, the president of the club, applied to strike out the petition on the ground that Mr Shooter had no locus standi to present it. Mr Shooter, who had offered to subscribe for 10,000 £1 shares, was co-opted onto the board, and at a subsequent board of directors' meeting it was resolved to allot him the shares. He then paid over the £10,000 and was registered as a shareholder. The issue was, did Mr Shooter agree to become a member within s22 of the Companies Act 1985. Mr Kelly argued that he had not, because merely agreeing to become a member was not sufficient to come within s22(2): what was required was a contract between the company and Mr Shooter. Mr Michael Wheeler QC, sitting as a deputy chancery court judge, held that Mr Shooter did not have locus standi. He appealed.

Held

Mr Shooter was a member within s22(2) of the Companies Act 1985, and therefore he had locus standi to bring an action under s459. Fox LJ said that as a matter of the ordinary use of English he had agreed to become a member. Section 22 does not refer to any bilateral contract between the company and the person who has agreed to become a member. Therefore, no contract is required, consent by a person to become a member is enough. Both Fox and Nicholls LJJ identified a practical difficulty in applying a 'contract' interpretation to the word 'agrees' in s22. The difficulty is that where a person acquires shares from a transferor, the person does not, usually, enter into a contract with the company prior to being entered on its register of members. The appeal was allowed.

Quickdome Ltd, Re [1988] BCLC 370 Chancery Division (Mervyn Davies J)

Unfairly prejudicial conduct – who can sue?

Facts

The subscribers to the company's memorandum were its initial shareholders. Subsequently, they executed a transfer of their shares, but the transfers did not identify the intended transferees. When presenting a petition for winding up or for relief under s459 of the Companies Act 1985, Mrs O'Callaghan claimed that the company had been set up as a joint venture between her husband and a Mr Palmer and that it had been intended that the two subscriber shares be transferred to her and Mrs Palmer respectively as nominees for their husbands. Did Mrs O'Callaghan have any standing to seek either a winding-up order or s459 relief?

Held

She did not.

Mervyn Davies J:

'The persons who may apply to the court for the winding up of a company are specified in s124 of the Insolvency Act 1986 as being the company, or the directors, or a creditor or creditors, or a contributory or contributories. In this case the application is by Mrs O'Callaghan, and it is said that she is a contributory. Section 124(2) is material as respects an application by a contributory. The subsection reads:

"Except as mentioned below, a contributory is not entitled to present a winding-up petition unless either – a) the number of members is reduced below 2, or b) the shares in respect of which he is a contributory, or some of them, either were originally allotted to him, or have been held by him, and registered in his name, for at least 6 months during the 18 months before the commencement of the winding-up, or have devolved on him through the death of a former holder."

The words "except as mentioned below" do not apply here, nor do the words in subs(2)(a). As to subs(2)(b) no shares have ever been registered in Mrs O'Callaghan's name and there is no question of devolution. So Mrs O'Callaghan's standing to petition depends on her showing that the share she claims was "originally allotted" to her. An allotment of a share involves a transaction between a company and an intending shareholder: see *Re Florence Land and Public Works Co, Nicol's Case, Tufnell and Ponsonby's Case* (1885) 29 Ch D 421 where Chitty J says:

"What is termed 'allotment' is generally neither more nor less than the acceptance by the company of the offer to take shares."

See also *Re JN2 Ltd* [1977] 3 All ER 1104; [1978] 1 WLR 183.

In this case Mrs O'Callaghan does not suggest that the share she claims emerges from any transaction she had with the company. Her claim is that a subscriber share was to be transferred to her.

So, since Mrs O'Callaghan's claim is a claim to a share by transfer, I do not see how she can contend that any share was originally allotted to her …

I come now to the question of Mrs O'Callaghan's standing to present a petition for s459 relief. Section 459(1) provides that a member of the company may petition. Section 459(2) then provides:

"The provisions of this Part apply to a person who is not a member of a company but to whom shares in the company have been transferred or transmitted by operation of law, as though those provisions apply to a member of the company and references to a member or members are to be construed accordingly."

So it seems that a s459 petition may be presented not only by a member but also by a person to whom shares in the company have been transferred. Counsel for the petitioner did not contend that Mrs O'Callaghan was a member. She submitted that Mrs O'Callaghan was a person to whom a share in the company has been transferred. The argument was, as I understand, that the two subscribers had handed over signed transfers of the two issued shares of the company. The transfers are, as I have said, in blank as to the names of the intended transferees; but, said counsel, it was agreed between the Palmers and the O'Callaghans that one of the blank transfers should be completed in her name. Thus, so the argument goes, Mrs O'Callaghan has an equity to complete the share transfer by inserting her name as transferee.

Counsel said further that the share transfer need not be signed by Mrs O'Callaghan since the company has adopted table A, and art 23 read with s182(1)(b) of the 1985 Act provides that a transfer need not be signed by the transferee if a share is fully paid.

I am content to assume that, for that or any other reason, a transfer does not have to be signed by Mrs O'Callaghan. But that leaves the fact that the transfer relied on is in blank as to the name of the transferee.'

Supreme Travels Ltd v *Little Olympian Each-Ways Ltd and Others* [1994] BCC 947
Chancery Division (Lindsay J)

Whether the court could add a non-member as a respondent to a s459 action

Facts

ST Ltd was a preference shareholder in LOEW Ltd and presented a petition under s459 Companies Act 1985. The unfairly prejudicial conduct consisted of allegations that the directors of LOEW Ltd had sold the company's business and goodwill to another company, which they controlled, for a grossly inadequate consideration. The company was thereafter a mere shell and it ceased to trade.

In this action, the petitioners were now seeking to add another company, Owners Abroad Group plc (OAG), as additional respondents, even though it had never been a shareholder, director or an alleged wrongdoer in LOEW Ltd, whose affairs were said to have been conducted in a manner unfairly prejudicial to the interests of the petitioner. By adding OAG as a respondent, it would, along with the other respondents, be obliged to purchase the petitioners' shares, if this relief was eventually granted by the court.

Held

1. Relief could be sought against a non-member of the company.
2. A non-member would not be added, however, when the likelihood of relief sought being ordered against the non-member was so remote as to amount to an abuse of process. This was such a case, as no court would order OAG to purchase the petitioners' shares.
3. The court therefore refused to add OAG as an additional respondent.

Lindsay J (after reviewing the statutory provisions and authorities for guidance his Lordship continued):

'That concludes a look at the authorities cited to me. Whilst I would be very willing to follow a pattern that emerged from the earlier cases at first instance, I do not regard any clear pattern as having yet emerged, and I have certainly found nothing conclusive that suggests that the words of s459 and s461 should not be given their full effect. From the existing authorities cited it can be seen that in an appropriate case relief can be sought against a non-member other than the company itself, or against a person not involved in the acts complained of (at least if that person would be affected by the relief sought) and that a person against whom no relief is in terms sought cannot necessarily escape being a respondent, whilst, on other facts, it can be right to strike out a petition, even as against those whose acts are complained of, so long as no relief is sought against such a person.

This summary suggests to me that in point of jurisdiction the wide language of s459 and s461 is not to be cut down. Nonetheless, cases may arise where, notwithstanding that the claim cannot be clearly said to be outside that wide jurisdiction, the likelihood of the court's discretion being exercised so as to lead to relief against, or relief having any material effect upon, a given respondent can be seen to be so remote that the case can fairly be described as "perfectly hopeless", to use Hoffmann J's phrase, and hence that it would be abusive to require that respondent to remain as such or to be added as such. Is this such a case?'

After considering counsels' arguments for both sides, his Lordship felt:

'Although the court *could,* if it chose, make a buy-out order against OAG of the kind which the petitioner seeks, it is on the case put in the amended petition, even if wholly true, plain and obvious, in my judgment, that no court would make such an order. Had OAG been a respondent from the start it could, in my view, have successfully moved to have the buy-out provisions and its role as a respondent struck out. It not yet being a respondent, it would be an abuse of process were it to be required, against its will, to be a respondent obliged to resist relief which would in practice never be granted.'

Tottenham Hotspur plc, Re [1994] 1 BCLC 655 Chancery Division (Sir Donald Nicholls V-C)

Chief executive dismissed – remained as a director – whether unfairly prejudicial conduct

Facts
In June 1991, the football manager Terry Venables (V) and the entrepreneur Alan Sugar (S) held a 50/50 interest in Tottenham Hotspur plc (Tottenham). It was agreed that V should become the chief executive and that S would be the company's chairman. Later, in December 1991, as a result of a rights issue, both S and V acquired more shares, but due to S's deeper financial pocket, he was able to take up a further £3.85m shares, compared to V's £800,000. S's stake in the company now amounted to 48 per cent and V's to 23 per cent. S held his shares in Tottenham through his privately owned company Amshold Ltd, and V held his shares via Edennote plc, which he owned and controlled.

As a result of disagreements between them, S and V were unable to work together as chairman and chief executive. At a board meeting, it was resolved that V's service contract be terminated and as a result he ceased to be the chief executive.

Companies Act s459 proceedings were commenced by Edennote plc in which it argued that it had a legitimate expectation that V would participate in the management of the company on the basis of shared control existing in June 1991, notwithstanding the later change in the shareholdings of S and V as a result of the rights issue. Edennote plc sought an order that Amshold sell its shares to it and that Tottenham be restrained from acting on the board resolution to remove V and from ending V's service contract.

Held
Edennote did not have a legitimate expectation that V would participate in the management of the company. There was nothing to suggest that V's rights were regulated by anything other than the company's constitution and that the board had the normal right to hire and fire.

Sir Donald Nicholls V-C:

'But nothing was disclosed which would suggest to anybody that Mr Venables's rights in relation to his appointment as chief executive were regulated by anything other than the company's constitution and the formal legal documents. There was nothing to suggest that the board of directors did not have the normal right to 'hire and fire' the company's chief executive, or that there was an agreement or understanding that, if Mr Sugar and Mr Venables should fall out, they were nevertheless bound to continue to support each other indefinitely or even, as proposed in the draft second shareholders' agreement, which was never signed, that for five years Mr Sugar would exercise certain voting rights as Mr Venables might direct.

The case that, in those circumstances, Mr Venables and Edennote or other members nevertheless had an expectation which the court should now recognise and give effect to in the running of this public company is not an easy one.

I appreciate that Tottenham is a very special type of company. Its shareholders were attracted, not by commercial considerations, but by the wish to become more closely linked with and involved in the affairs of the club they support, often passionately. They are football enthusiasts. Even so, with the background of formal documents and published information, Mr Venables's case that he or his company Edennote has been unfairly prejudiced as a shareholder by the recent actions of Mr Sugar is fraught with difficulty.

This being so, I do not think it would be right or sensible for me to make an order having the effect of overriding the majority decision of the board and restoring to Mr Venables all or some of his functions as chief executive until the trial. To do so would, in all probability, merely be postponing the date on which *all* concerned must face up to the fact, that for better or worse, Mr Venables's appointment has been determined and face up to the consequences of that fact. By all concerned, I mean the directors of Tottenham, its shareholders, its staff, including above all its players, its season-ticket holders and thousands of supporters, as well as Mr Sugar and Mr Venables themselves. Whether Mr Venables's dismissal was in the best interests of Tottenham is not a matter for the court to decide. That is a matter for the Tottenham board to whom this decision is entrusted under the company's constitution, although it is a matter on which the shareholders can express their views to the board. I will not, therefore, make any order regulating the affairs of Tottenham pending the trial.'

Company investigations

R v Director of Serious Fraud Office, ex parte Smith [1992] 3 WLR 66 sub nom Smith v Director of Serious Fraud Office [1992] 3 All ER 456 House of Lords (Lord Templeman, Lord Bridge of Harwich, Lord Ackner, Lord Lowry and Lord Mustill)

Powers of investigation after person charged

Facts
The chairman of a company was charged with carrying on the business of a company with intent to defraud its creditors. After being charged he was duly cautioned but he elected to make no reply. Subsequently, the director of the Serious Fraud Office issued a notice under s2(2) of the Criminal Justice Act 1987 requiring the chairman to attend for interview and the question arose as to whether he could be compelled to answer the director's questions in relation to his alleged offence.

Held
He could be so compelled.

Lord Mustill:

'I conclude that as a matter of interpretation the powers of the director do not cease, as regards the questioning of the person under investigation when he is charged; that the principle of common sense, expressed in the maxim generalia specialibus non derogant, entails that the general provisions of code C [as to, inter alia, the questioning of persons by police officers, issued under s67 of the Police and Criminal Evidence Act 1984] yield to the particular provisions of the 1987 Act in cases to which that Act applies; and that neither history nor logic demands that any qualification of what Parliament has so clearly enacted ought to be implied ...

In the present case the only issue is whether there is something in the language of the Act, or by necessary implication, to show that the policy embodied in the Act should not be given effect as regards the questioning of a suspect who has been charged. [I am] of the opinion that there is not ...'

London United Investments plc, Re [1992] 2 WLR 850 Court of Appeal (Dillon, Mustill and Stuart-Smith LJJ)

Duty to answer inspector's questions

Facts

The Secretary of State having appointed inspectors, under s432(2) of the Companies Act 1985, to investigate a public company's affairs, the question arose as to whether a director of the company could invoke the common law privilege against self-incrimination and refuse to answer the inspectors' questions. No charges had been made against the director or anyone else in the company.

Held

The common law privilege had been impliedly removed by the relevant provisions of the 1985 Act and, in all the circumstances, the director's refusal to answer the questions had been unjustified.

Dillon LJ:

'We have ... to consider whether it is clear that the United Kingdom Parliament intended, when enacting Pt XIV of the 1985 Act, to take away a person's right to rely on the privilege against self-incrimination as a ground for refusing to answer questions put to him by inspectors ...

On these provisions [ss434, 436 and 452 of the 1985 Act], I reach without hesitation the conclusion that as (i) inspectors will in very many cases have been appointed where there are circumstances suggesting that there has been fraud in the conduct or management of a company's affairs, and (ii) persons questioned are bound to answer the inspectors' questions and (iii) the inspectors' report may lead the Secretary of State to petition for the winding up of the company or to bring civil proceedings in the company's name in the public interest, the privilege against self-incrimination is impliedly excluded and is not available to the person being questioned by the inspectors.

I note that a similar conclusion was reached by ... the Criminal Division of this court (Watkins LJ, Alliott and Cresswell JJ) in *R* v *Seelig* [1992] 1 WLR 148, approving statements of law by Henry J in the court below ...

I turn therefore now to the question of fairness. I have referred earlier in this judgment to the process of public examination, in the winding up of a company, under s270 of the Companies Act 1948 ... where there has been a further report by the Official Receiver stating that fraud has been committed by a promoter, director or other officer in relation to the company.

There is an entirely separate process whereby application can be made for a private, as opposed to public, examination of any officer or other person whom the court deems capable of giving information concerning the promotion, formation, trade, dealing, affairs or property of the company. This process ... is now covered by s236 of the Insolvency Act 1986.

In relation to this procedure of private examination it has long since been held that the court is concerned to ensure that the procedure is not exercised in a manner oppressive to the person to be examined ... The importance of avoiding oppression to the person to be examined is again emphasised in the most recent decision of this court on private examination of which I am aware, *Cloverbay Ltd* v *Bank of Credit and Commerce International SA* [1991] Ch 90 ...

It may be that the court has power under s463(2) of the 1985 Act, after inquiring into a case, to refuse to compel a person to answer, or to punish him for refusing to answer, questions if the court feels that the questioning, or further questioning is, in the circumstances and at the stage that the case has reached, oppressive and therefore unfair.

But that is not this case. If I am right that the privilege against self-incrimination is not available to [the director], the mere fact that the answers might incriminate him cannot be enough, by itself, to make it unfair that he should be required to answer the questions which the inspectors have so far put to him. But [the director] has nothing to add to that mere fact as a ground of unfairness. There is nothing to suggest that the inspectors are acting with [an] improper purpose …'

11   Liquidation

An alternative to winding up – administration – voluntary arrangements

Atlantic Computer Systems plc, Re [1992] 1 All ER 476; [1990] BCC 859 Court of Appeal (Neill, Nicholls and Staughton LJJ)

Administration – entitlement to computer rents

Facts
On the application of Atlantic Computer Services Group plc, the immediate parent of Atlantic Computer Systems plc (the company), an administration order had been made in respect of the company in order to achieve a more advantageous realisation of the company's assets than would be effected on a winding-up: see s8(3)(d) of the Insolvency Act 1986. The company had granted leases of computers and in two particular categories of leases the capital cost of acquiring the computers had been provided by a bank or other financial institution (the funders). In the first category the computer was owned by the funder and let to the company under a hire purchase agreement. The company in turn, and as had been intended by the funder, had then let the computer to the end user under a further lease (the sublease). In the second category the procedure had been similar save that the arrangement between the funder and the company had been a lease (a headlease) as distinct from a hire purchase agreement. The fundamental feature, common to both categories, was that the computers were the property of the funder. Up to June 8 the administrators had received from end users sums in excess of £1.7 million. Most end users had now stopped paying. As to the headleases (including hire purchase agreements between funders and the company), substantial payments had fallen due, and were continuing to fall due, from the company to the funders. However, since the date of the administration order no payments had been made by the administrators to the funders, in respect of headleases, and the administrators had declined to consent to the funders exercising their rights to terminate the headleases. The administrators had received and retained money payable under the subleases in respect of computer equipment which was the property of the funders. Were the administrators obliged, as the funders contended, to pay as expenses of the administration all the sums falling due under the headleases? Ferris J ((1990) The Times 21 June) answered this question in the affirmative: the administrators appealed.

Held
The appeal would be allowed. Nicholls LJ explained that the objectives of winding-up orders and administration orders were different and, therefore, that the approach adopted by the court when exercising its discretion under the two regimes was different. In the case of administrations, there was no room for the application of a rigid principle that, if land or goods in the company's possession under an existing lease or hire purchase agreement were used for the purposes of an administration, the continuing rent or hire charges would rank automatically as expenses of the administration and as such be payable ahead (so it would seem) of the pre-administration creditors; nor, even, for a principle that

361

leave to take proceedings would be granted as of course. Such rigid principles would be inconsistent with the flexibility Parliament must have intended should apply by giving the court a wide discretion.

Nicholls LJ added that, as between the funders and the company, the computer equipment remained in the company's possession for the purposes of s11(3)(c) of the 1986 Act and it followed that it could not be repossessed save with consent or leave. In all the circumstances, such leave would be granted.

Commentary
See also *Re Atlantic Computer Systems plc (No 2)* (1990) Financial Times 3 July.

Charnley Davies, Ltd [1990] BCC 605; [1988] BCLC 243 Chancery Division (Millet J)

Administration – s27 of the Insolvency Act 1986 – unfair prejuducial management by an administrator

Facts
This was an action commenced by petition by the creditors of the company pursuant to s27 of the Insolvency Act 1986 (unfairly prejudicial management by the administrator). The creditors claimed, inter alia, that the administrator had been negligent in selling the business as a going concern. They were seeking compensation for loss suffered by the company as a result of an alleged negligent undervalue of the company's assets by the administrator.

Held
The creditors' petition was dismissed because a claim of professional negligence, without more, against an administrator was insufficient to amount to unfairly prejudicial management.

Millett J:

'When the petitioners launched the present proceedings, they wrongly believed that Mr Richmond was managing the affairs of the company in a manner which disregarded their interests and those of the creditors generally. That was a perfectly proper complaint to bring under s27. Long before the case came to trial, however, it had become a simple action for professional negligence and nothing more. That, if established, would amount to misconduct; but it would neither constitute nor evidence unfairly prejudicial management. In my judgment it would be a misuse of language to describe an administrator who has managed the company's affairs fairly and impartially and with a proper regard for the interests of all the creditors (and members where necessary), conscientiously endeavouring to do his best for them, but who has through oversight or inadvertence fallen below the standards of a reasonably competent insolvency practitioner in the carrying out of some particular transaction, as having managed the affairs of the company in a manner which is unfairly prejudicial to the creditors.

In my judgment, the proper course to follow in the present case was to have the adminstration order discharged, the company put into compulsory liquidation, a person other than Mr Richmond appointed liquidator, and the claim brought against Mr Richmond by the liquidator under s212 of the Act. By persisting in their s27 petition the petitioners did not merely adopt the wrong procedure. They undertook the burden of establishing that the sale of the company's assets at an undervalue (whether or not due to negligence) was due to Mr Richmond's management of the company's affairs in a manner prejudicial to their interests. At the trial no attempt of any kind was made to establish this. In my judgment, it would have been a hopeless task.

I dismiss the petition.'

Powdrill & Another v *Watson & Another (Paramount Airways Ltd)* [1995] BCC 319 House of Lords (Lords Keith, Browne-Wilkinson, Mustill, Woolf and Lloyd)

Administration orders – whether administrators had 'adopted' contracts of employment

Facts

Administrators were appointed on 7 August 1989. In accordance with established practice, the administrators wrote to the company's employees on 14 August stating that they had not adopted their contracts of employment. The company carried on trading until 30 November 1989, when the business closed down and all the employees were dismissed. The administrators paid the employees their wages for the period of the administration, but two employees made additional claims, under s19(5) Insolvency Act (IA) 1986. The additional claims were:

1. unpaid holiday pay which had accrued prior to administration;
2. pay in lieu of two months' notice under their contracts of employment;
3. agreed loyalty bonuses;
4. pension contributions;
5. compensation for unfair dismissal.

The success of these claims depended upon whether the contracts of employment had been adopted by the administrators. If they had, then the claims had to be paid in priority to the administrators' remuneration and expenses.

The Court of Appeal held that despite the letter of 14 August, the contracts of employment had been adopted. On this point Dillon LJ said:

'And the mere assertion by an administrator or receiver that he is not adopting the contract is mere wind with no legal effect, because adoption is a matter not merely of words but of fact. Here all the facts point to the administrators having adopted the contracts.'

Accordingly, the employees were able to claim their accrued holiday pay, pay in lieu of notice and the pension contributions. The claims for the loyalty bonus and compensation for unfair dismissal failed, as they arose under statute rather than their contracts of employment. The administrators appealed.

Held

The appeal was dismissed but the order of the Court of Appeal was varied, in that liability in respect of the holiday pay entitlement was only in respect of holiday pay accruing after the administrators' appointment. By virtue of s19 IA 1986, a contract of employment was adopted if the employee continued in employment for more than 14 days after the appointment of the administrator. This cannot be avoided by the administrators informing the employees that they are not adopting their contracts.

Lord Browne-Wilkinson:

'*Summary*
I therefore reach the following conclusions:

(1) for the purposes of both s19 and s44 an employee's contract of employment is "adopted" if he is continued in employment for more than 14 days after the appointment of the administrator or receiver;
(2) it is not possible for an administrator or receiver to avoid this result or alter its consequences unilaterally by informing the employees that he is not adopting their contracts or only doing so on terms;
(3) in the case of both administration and receivership the consequence of adoption of contracts of employment is to give priority only to liabilities incurred by the administrator or receiver during his tenure of office.

I would therefore vary the order of the Court of Appeal in the *Paramount* case so as to declare that the sums in respect of holiday pay payable under cl.8(f) of the respondents' contracts of employment are only payable by the administrators in respect of months of employment after the appointment of the administrator. I would otherwise dismiss the appeal.'

Types of winding-up

A Company (No 003028 of 1987), Re [1988] BCLC 282 Chancery Division (Scott J)

Just and equitable winding up

Facts

Mr A and Mr E set up a joint venture company of which they were both directors. A shareholders agreement provided that Mr A would lend the company £200,000 interest free and enter into a service contract with it; it also stated that the agreement did not constitute a partnership between the parties. Mr A and Mr E became involved in a fracas at the company's premises and the police removed Mr A from them. Because of this assault, the directors purported to remove Mr A from office and to terminate his service contract with the company. Mr A commenced a Queen's Bench action alleging a repudiatory breach of his contract of service which he had accepted. Subsequently, he petitioned for the winding-up of the company on the ground that it was just and equitable that it should be wound up. The company sought to have the petition struck out.

Held

The company would be successful. Although a contingent creditor could present a petition under s122(1)(g) of the Insolvency Act 1986 and a petition under that provision was not precluded merely because the agreement stated that it did not constitute a partnership, in view of the Queen's Bench proceedings the petition served no valuable purpose.

Scott J:

'It follows from s124(1) of the 1986 Act that a contingent creditor has locus standi to present a petition to wind up. Prima facie I would have supposed that a contingent creditor had locus standi to present a petition to wind up on any of the s122 grounds. Whether, of course, a petition would succeed would depend on the underlying facts relied on by the petitioner as bringing the case within the chosen ground and justifying a winding-up order.

Counsel for the company, however, has submitted that a contingent creditor is not entitled to petition for winding up on the just and equitable ground ...

If a contingent creditor seeks to wind up on the just and equitable ground, the court would have to look very closely at what was alleged in support of the petition to see whether the contingent creditor did in fact have such an interest in the company as to make it proper to wind up on that ground. Ordinarily, the interest of a creditor is in obtaining repayment of his debt. If his debt is repayable and is not repaid, the creditor can apply to wind up on the ground that the company cannot pay its debts: para (f) of s122(1). If the petitioner were a contingent creditor, the debt would not be immediately repayable, and in order to obtain a winding-up order the contingent creditor would have to show something in the affairs of the company to justify the apprehension that when the time for repayment of the debt arrived, the company would be unable to repay, and that in those circumstances the company ought to be at once wound up. Current inability on the part of a company to pay its debts would not necessarily entitle a contingent creditor to succeed in a winding-up petition. The contingent creditor would, I think, be expected to show, not only and not necessarily a current inability by the company to pay its debts, but rather an inability to pay its debts at the time when the contingent debt became payable. A case of that character would, in my opinion, fall more clearly within para (g) than para (f) of s122(1).

Be that as it may, I can see no ground on authority or in principle for limiting the ability of a contingent creditor to present a petition to only some of the paragraphs contained in s122(1). A contingent creditor has, in my judgment, locus standi to present a petition. Whether the petition will succeed, whether the petition is an abuse of process, will depend on the underlying facts and not upon a lack of status to present the petition.

... counsel for the company submitted that it was not open to Mr A to invoke the just and equitable ground, as explained by Lord Wilberforce in his judgment in the *Westbourne Galleries* case [1973] AC 360, because Mr A could not contend that the present case was a quasi partnership case. Counsel relied on ... the shareholders' agreement ... It expressly excluded, it will be recalled, partnership between the parties to the agreement. But Mr A's case is in substance that there was a joint venture agreement between himself and Mr E incorporated eventually into the formal agreements ... and that his exclusion from management in circumstances where he is not himself to blame represents such a breach of the underlying obligations of trust and confidence accepted by the joint ventures towards one another as to entitle him under the just and equitable ground to invoke the jurisdiction of the court.

Again, in my view, the approach of counsel for the company is too narrow to be acceptable. A joint venturer is not, in my judgment, precluded from applying to wind up on the just and equitable ground simply because in the legal agreement between himself and his co-venturers partnership is expressly excluded. That may well be a feature, and perhaps an important feature, that the court must take into account in coming to a decision; but it does not, in my view, bar the making of a winding-up order if the underlying facts of the case taken as a whole justify the conclusion that it would be just and equitable to wind up the company.

The question that I must decide ... depends on the substance of the case for winding-up made by Mr A in his petition. I must ask myself whether, in view in particular of the Queen's Bench action, his petition is one which it is proper for him to bring and prosecute, or is one which has no real ground of success.

The implications of the Queen's Bench action are, in my view, all important. In the Queen's Bench action Mr A alleges repudiatory breach ... of the various agreements, including the shareholders agreement and the service agreement. Mr A has elected to accept those breaches as determining the agreements. If the contentions made by Mr A in his pleading in the Queen's Bench action are well founded and the action succeeds, he will obtain damages for breach of contract and an order for the repayment of the £200,000. The £200,000 will then either be repaid by the company, or will not be repaid by the company. If the money is repaid by the company, the basis on which Mr A petitions to wind up will be gone. If the winding-up were still pending, it would, in that event, have to be dismissed. Mr A would have no further interest. If there is an order for repayment of the £200,000 obtained by Mr A in the Queen's Bench action and the money is not repaid, he will then be in a position to present a petition to wind up. He will be an unpaid judgment creditor. He would be entitled ex debito justitiae to a winding-up order if the debt were not paid. Again, the current petition would serve no useful purpose at all.

I have reviewed the position if the Queen's Bench action which Mr A started ... succeeds. That will be the position if his allegations in the pleadings in that action are well founded.

What will be the position if that action fails? If the action fails in toto, because Mr E's version of the underlying facts is right and Mr A's is false, then as I see it the position will be thus. Mr A will, by his own manifestly unreasonable conduct in interrupting the proper conduct of the business of the company, have brought on himself his own dismissal. His dismissal would not have been wrongful. There is nothing suggested as a breach of the shareholders agreement other than his dismissal. He could not rely on his own misconduct in order to invite the court on the just and equitable ground to order the company to be wound up. In that event, the winding-up petition would I think be bound to fail with the Queen's Bench action.

Is there, I must ask myself, an intermediate position, in which the petition might serve some real valuable purpose? ... I do not think there is any reality in the intermediate position suggested by counsel for Mr A; that is to say, success by Mr A in challenging his dismissal, but failure by Mr A in asserting repudiation of the shareholders' agreement.

If that is so, what then, I must ask myself, is the point of the petition? Counsel for the company would answer that the point of the petition from Mr A's point of view was to bring unreasonable and improper pressure on the company ... It may be that that is a motive of Mr A's; I know not. But I must ask myself what other legitimate purpose the petition can serve. If Mr A succeeds in the Queen's Bench action, it can serve none. If he fails in the Queen's Bench action I think his petition is bound to fail; and for reasons which I have given, I cannot at the moment see any viable intermediate position.

This is an unusual application to strike out in that, on the view I take, if it had not been for the Queen's Bench action I think counsel for the company would have been in great difficulty in asserting that the position was one which was bound to fail. I think that a person in Mr A's position, part contingent creditor, part contingent shareholder, in substance co-venturer with risk capital at stake, is entitled to invoke the court's jurisdiction under the just and equitable ground if he has been wrongfully excluded from the management that he was intended to have. If it had not been for the Queen's Bench action, I think an application to strike out would have been doomed to failure. But there is the Queen's Bench action. Mr A started it, and is prosecuting it. He is entitled to do that. But he has in a real sense, I think, made an election in favour of the relief sought in that action. The implications of this election render improper the presentation and prosecution of the petition.

Accordingly, I have come to the conclusion that in the circumstances of this case the petition ought not to be allowed to stand, and I therefore propose to accede to the application and to order it to be removed from the file.'

A Company (No 0012209 of 1991), Re [1992] 1 WLR 351 High Court (Hoffmann J)

Creditor's petition – restraining by injunction

Facts

A dispute having arisen in relation to a contract for the refurbishment of an office building, the contractors proposed to present a petition for the winding-up of the employer company. The employer sought an injunction to restrain such presentation. It was accepted that the employer was solvent and capable of paying the debt on which the petition was to be founded.

Held

In all the circumstances, the injunction would be granted.

Hoffmann J:

'In order to say that [the contractors] are entitled to present a winding-up petition I must come to the conclusion that [the employer's] argument is either not put forward in good faith or that it has really no rational prospect of success. In my view it is not possible on the affidavit evidence to come to that conclusion. There is in my judgment a triable issue on that question ...

In addition to that the [employer] says that it has a cross-claim for damages arising out of the repudiation of the contract. It is, I think, fair to say that the grounds upon which it claims to have repudiated the contract are not stated with any degree of particularity in the evidence, and I do not think it is necessary for me to say what view I would have taken if that had been the sole ground relied upon. For present purposes, however, it is sufficient to say that there seems to me to be a bona fide dispute on substantial grounds ...

It does seem to me that a tendency has developed, possibly since the decision in *Cornhill Insurance plc* v *Improvement Services Ltd* [1986] 1 WLR 114, to present petitions against solvent companies as a way of putting pressure upon them to make payments of money which is bona fide disputed rather than to invoke the procedures which the rules provide for summary judgment. I do not for a moment wish to detract from anything which was said in the *Cornhill Insurance* case, which indeed followed earlier authority, to the effect that a refusal to pay an indisputable debt is evidence from which the inference may be drawn that the debtor is unable to pay. It was, however, a somewhat unusual case in which it was quite clear that the company in question had no grounds at all for its refusal. Equally it seems to me that if the court comes to the conclusion that a solvent company is not putting forward any defence in good faith and is merely seeking to take for itself credit which it is not allowed under the contract, then the court would not be inclined to restrain presentation of the petition. But, if, as in this case, it appears that the defence has a prospect of success and the company is solvent, then I think that the court should give the company the benefit of the doubt and not do anything which would encourage the use of the Companies Court as an alternative to the RSC Ord 14 procedure.

For those reasons the injunction will go. The basis upon which the injunction is granted is that the application is an abuse of the process of the court. I think that it should be made clear that abuse of the petition procedure in these circumstances is a high risk strategy, and consequently I think the appropriate order is that the [contractor] should pay the [employer's] costs on an indemnity basis.'

Ebrahimi v *Westbourne Galleries Ltd* [1973] AC 360 House of Lords (Lord Wilberforce, Viscount Dilhorne, Lords Pearson, Cross and Salmon)

Just and equitable winding up – quasi partnership

Facts
Since about 1945 Ebrahimi and one Nazar were in business as partners as dealers in Persian and other carpets. In 1958 a company was formed to take over the business and Ebrahimi and Nazar were the first directors and each held 500 shares of £1 each. Shortly afterwards Nazar's son joined the business and Ebrahimi and Nazar each transferred to him 100 shares, giving him a total of 200 shares, and he became a director. Thus the Nazars had a majority at general meetings. The company was profitable and all profits were distributed as directors' fees and no dividends were paid. In 1969 Ebrahimi and the Nazars had a disagreement and the latter voted to remove Ebrahimi from his directorship under s184 CA 1948 (now s303 CA 1985). Ebrahimi presented a petition for an order under s210 CA 148 (see now s459 CA 1985, as amended) that the Nazars should purchase his shares on such terms as the court should think fit or alternatively, for an order under s222(f) CA 1948 (now s122(1)(g) IA 1986) that it would be 'just and equitable' to wind-up the company. Plowman J refused to make an order under s210 but ordered that the company be wound-up under s222(f). The Nazars appealed; their appeal was allowed by the Court of Appeal. On appeal by Ebrahimi to the House of Lords:

Held
The company was formed on the basis of the relationship between Ebrahimi and Nazar, as partners, continuing so that each would be entitled to participate in the management of the business. Since Nazar had effectively repudiated this relationship and Ebrahimi was now excluded from the profits or unable to dispose of his share without the consent of the Nazars and, in this respect at their mercy, it was just and equitable that the company should be wound up.

Lord Wilberforce:

'... My Lords, the petition was brought under s222(f) of the Companies Act 1948, which enables a winding-up order to be made if "the court is of the opinion that it is just and equitable that the company should be wound-up". This power has existed in our company law in unaltered form since the first major Act, the Companies Act 1862. Indeed, it antedates that statute since it existed in the Joint Stock Companies Winding-Up Act 1848. For some 50 years, following a pronouncement by Lord Cottenham LC (*Ex parte Spackman* (1849) 1 Mac & G 170) in 1849, the words "just and equitable" were interpreted so as only to include matters ejusdem generis as the preceding clauses of the section, but there is now ample authority for discarding this limitation. There are two other restrictive interpretations which I mention to reject. First, there has been a tendency to create categories or headings under which cases must be brought if the clause is to apply. This is wrong. Illustrations may be used, but general words should remain general and not be reduced to the sum of particular instances. Secondly, it has been suggested, and urged upon us, that (assuming the petitioner is a shareholder and not a creditor) the words must be confined to such circumstances as affect him in his capacity as shareholder. I see no warrant for this either. No doubt, in order to present a petition, he must qualify as a shareholder, but I see no reason for preventing him from relying upon any circumstances of justice or equity which affect him in his relations with the company, or, in a case such as the present, with the other shareholders.

One other signpost is significant. The same words "just and equitable" appear in the Partnership Act 1892, s25, as a ground for dissolution of a partnership and no doubt the consideration which they reflect formed part of the common law of partnership before its codification. The importance of this is to provide a bridge between cases under s222(f) of the Act of 1948 and the principles of equity developed in relation to partnerships.

The winding-up order was made following a doctrine which has developed in the courts since the beginning of this century. As presented by the appellant, and in substance accepted by the learned judge, this was that in a case such as this the members of the company are in substance partners, or quasi-partners, and that a winding-up may be ordered if such facts are shown as could justify a dissolution of partnership between them. The common use of the words "just and equitable" in the company and partnership law supports this approach. Your Lordships were invited by the respondents' counsel to restate the principle on which this provision ought to be used; it has not previously been considered by this House. The main line of this submission was to suggest that too great a use of the partnership analogy had been made; that a limited company, however small, essentially differs from a partnership; that in the case of a company, the rights of its members are governed by the articles of association which have contractual force; that the court has no power or at least ought not to dispense parties from observing their contracts; that, in particular, when one member has been excluded from the directorate, or management, under powers expressly conferred by the Companies Act and the articles, an order for winding-up, whether on the partnership analogy or under the just and equitable provision, should not be made. Alternatively, it was argued that before the making of such an order could be considered the petitioner must show and prove that the exclusion was not made bona fide in the interests of the company ...'

His Lordship then reviewed the authorities, in particular *Symington* v *Symington* [1905] F 121; *Re Yenidje Tobacco* (see above); *Loch* v *John Blackwood* (see above); *Re Cuthbert Cooper & Sons* [1937] Ch 392; *Re Lundie Bros Ltd* [1965] 1 WLR 1051; *Re Expanded Plugs* [1966] 1 WLR 514; *Re K/9 Supplies (Guildford) Ltd* [1966] 1 WLR 1112; *Lewis* v *Haas* 1970 SLT (Notes) 67; and *Re Wondoflex Textils Pty Ltd* [1951] VLR 458 and continued:

'... My Lords, in my opinion these authorities represent a sound and rational development of the law which should be endorsed. The foundation of it all lies in the words "just and equitable" and, if there is any respect in which some of the cases may be open to criticism, it is that the courts may sometimes have been too timorous in giving them full force. The words are a recognition of the fact that a limited company is more than a mere legal entity, with a pesonality in law of its own; that there is room in company law for recognition of the fact that behind it, or amongst it, there are individuals with rights, expectations and obligations inter se which are not necessarily submerged in the company structure. That structure is defined by the Companies Act and by the articles of association by which shareholders agree to be bound. In most companies and in most contexts, this definition is sufficient and exhaustive, equally so whether the company is large or small. The "just and equitable" provision does not, as the respondents suggest, entitle one party to disregard the obligation he assumes by entering a company, nor the court to dispense him from it. It does, as equity always does, enable the court to subject the exercise of legal rights to equitable considerations; considerations, that is, of a personal character arising between one individual and another, which may make it unjust, or inequitable, to insist on legal rights, or to exercise them in a particular way.

It would be impossible, and wholly undesirable, to define the circumstances in which these considerations may arise. Certainly the fact that a company is a small one, or a private company, is not enough. There are very many of these where the association is a purely commercial one, of which it can safely be said that the basis of association is adequately and exhaustively laid down in the articles. The superimposition of equitable considerations requires something more, which typically may include one, or probably more, of the following elements: (i) an association formed or continued on the basis of a personal relationship, involving mutual confidence – this element will often be found where a pre-existing partnership has been converted into a limited company; (ii) an agreement, or understanding, that all, or some (for there may be "sleeping" members), of the shareholders shall participate in the conduct of the business; (iii) restriction upon the transfer of the members' interests in the company so that if confidence is lost, or one member is removed from management, he cannot take out his stake and go elsewhere.

It is these, and analogous, factors which may bring into play the just and equitable clause, and they do so directly, through the force of the words themselves. To refer, as so many of the cases do, to "quasi-partnerships" or "in substance partnerships" may be convenient but may also be confusing. It may be convenient because it is the law of partnership which has developed the conceptions of probity, good faith and mutual confidence, and the remedies where these are absent, which become relevant once such factors as I have mentioned are found to exist: the words "just and equitable" sum these up in the law of partnership itself. And in many, but not necessarily all, cases there has been a pre-existing partnership the obligations of which it is reasonable to suppose continue to underlie the new company structure. But the expressions may be confusing if they obscure, or deny, the fact that the parties (possibly former partners) are now co-members in a company, who have accepted, in law, new obligations. A company, however small, however domestic, is a company not a partnership or even a quasi-partnership and it is through the just and equitable clause that obligations, common to partnership relatons, may come in.

My Lords, this is an expulsion case, and I must briefly justify the application in such cases of the just and equitable clause. The question is, as always, whether it is equitable to allow one (or two) to make use of his legal rights to the prejudice of his associate(s). The law of companies recognises the right, in many ways, to remove a director from the board. Section 184 of the Companies Act 1948 confers this right upon the company in general meeting whatever the articles may say. Some articles may prescribe other methods: for example, a governing director may have the power to remove (compare *In re Wondoflex Textiles Pty Ltd* [1951] VLR 458. And quite apart from removal powers, there are normally provisions for retirement of directors by rotation so that their re-election can be opposed and defeated by a majority, or even by a casting vote. In all these ways a particular director-member may find himself no longer a director, through removal, or non-re-election: this situation he must normally accept, unless he undertakes the burden of proving fraud or mala fides. The just and equitable provision nevertheless comes to his assistance if he can point to, and prove, some special underlying obligation of his fellow member(s) in good faith, or confidence, that so long as the business continues he shall be entitled to management participation, an obligation so basic that, if broken, the conclusion must be that the association must be dissolved. And the principles on which he may do so are those worked out by the courts in partnership cases where there has been exclusion from management (see *Const* v *Harris* (1824) Turn & R 496) even where under the partnership agreement there is a power of expulsion (see *Blisste* v *Daniel* (1853) 10 Hare 493, *Lindley on Partnership*, 13th ed (1971), pp331, 595) …'

Emmadart Ltd, Re [1979] Ch 540 Chancery Division (Brightman J)

Compulsory winding up – who can petition

Facts

The company granted a bank a floating charge over all its undertaking and assets in 1973. In 1976 the bank appointed a receiver and manager under its debenture. It appears that the company was hopelessly insolvent. However, the company had a 25 year lease of a shop in King's Lynn at a rent of £4,000 pa. The shop had been unoccupied for 2 1/2 years as the receiver was unable to dispose of it. The rates on the shop were £3,000 pa. In order to gain exemption from the rates under r2 of the Rating (Exemption of Unoccupied Property) Regulations 1967 a winding-up petition was presented by the receiver. The question arose whether the receiver had authority to present the petition in the name of the company.

Held

The receiver, as the company's agent, had no power to present a petition for winding-up since his authority was co-terminous with that of the directors. The directors did not have authority under table A art 80 (now art 70 with amendments) to present a petition for winding-up as this amounted to a stoppage of the company and not its management. For directors to present such a petition it was necessary that they have the authority to do so under a special resolution by the shareholders or have the power to present such a petition conferred on them by the articles or by an ordinary resolution of the shareholders. None of these circumstances applied. However, the court would, nevertheless, permit a receiver to present a winding-up petition on the ground that it was incidental or conducive to his power to take possession of the company's assets and to protect them. In the circumstances the presentation of the petition would protect the company's assets and the court would exercise its discretion to make a winding-up order.

Brightman J:

'... The position, in my view, is this. It would be theoretically possible for the articles of association of a company to be drawn in terms which confer power on the board of directors to present a winding-up petition. But an article on the lines of art 80 of table A is not so drawn. The board of directors can resolve to present a petition in the name of the company if a special resolution has already been passed resolving that the company be wound-up by the court, because that is expressly covered by s222(a) of the 1948 Act (now s122(1)(b) IA 1986). The board can also properly act on an ordinary resolution of the shareholders conferring the requisite authority on the board provided that this does not contravene any provision in the articles.

I have been told that over the years a winding-up order has often been made on a petition presented by an insolvent company pursuant to a resolution of the board of directors and without reference to the shareholders. That would seem to be so. It is certainly so stated in the passage that I have read from Buckley on the Companies Acts. Despite the defect in the petition, any order so made will be fully valid and effective unless and until it is recalled. I express no view as to whether it would be competent for the court to recall an order so made. The practice which seems to have grown up, under which a board of directors of an insolvent company presents a petition in the name of the company where this seems to the board to be the sensible course, but without reference to the shareholders, is in my opinion wrong and ought no longer to be pursued, unless the articles confer the requisite authority, which art 80 of table A does not. What is stated in Buckley to be the law according to Irish authority is in my view equally the law in this country. I express this view with greater confidence on finding that it coincides with the conclusion expressed by Lord Cohen and Raymond Walton, when contributing the title Companies to the third edition of Halsbury's Laws of England, and by Walton J, when contributing this title to the fourth edition.

In the instant case the articles of association of the company incorporate art 80 of table A. There is no other article on which reliance can be placed. Accordingly counsel's first submission fails.

The authority of a receiver is not, however, co-terminous with the authority of the board of directors. The powers of the receiver stem from (i) the powers contained in the memorandum and articles of association of the company to create mortgages and charges, coupled with (ii) the particular powers which have been conferred on a duly appointed receiver pursuant to the due exercise of the company's borrowing powers. In the instant case the debenture has been regularly created, the receiver has been duly appointed and the powers which I have already read have been properly conferred on the receiver. The only question, therefore, is whether the presentation of the petition by the receiver in the name of the company is incidental or conducive to any of the matters or powers mentioned in cl 6(c) of the debenture. In my judgment the protection and preservation of the assets of the company in respect of which the receiver has been appointed, though not expressly mentioned in s109 of the Law of Property Act 1925 or in cl 6(c) of the debenture, are incidental to his possession of such assets. As the company is unable to pay its debts, and a winding-up order will have the effect of protecting the assets under the control of the receiver from depletion by a levy of rates in respect of vacant property, I am of the opinion that the receiver has the requisite authority by virtue of his appointment to present a petition in the name of the company, and the court has jurisdiction to make a winding-up order ex debito justitiae. The discretion of the court is all important. The petition has been brought to the attention of those who might be concerned to oppose it and the secretary of the company has been made a respondent and served. In the special circumstances I think it is right that I should exercise my discretion and make a winding-up order. This decision is in no way inconsistent with the observations of Shaw LJ, in *Newhart Developments Ltd* v *Co-Operative Commercial Bank Ltd* [1978] QB 814 at 819, when he said: "One has got to see what the function of the receiver is. It is not, of course, to wind-up the company." Those words were spoken in a wholly different context.'

Loch v *John Blackwood Ltd* [1924] AC 783 Privy Council (Lords Shaw, Phillimore and Carson)

Just and equitable winding up – lack of confidence in the management of the company's affairs

Facts

John Blackwood carried on an engineering business until his death in 1904 and by his will he left the business in trust for the benefit of various members of his family. In 1910 the trustees converted the business into a company and one McLaren, the husband of one of the beneficiaries entitled to half the income from the business, was made managing director and had voting control in the business. The company made considerable profits but other beneficiaries became dissatisfied with the conduct of the company. They presented a petition for winding-up which claimed (truthfully), inter alia, that general meetings were not held, no accounts and reports were being submitted and conditions as to audit in the articles were not being observed. They accordingly claimed that it was just and equitable to wind-up the company. There was suspicion that the reason for these failures was to keep the petitioners in ignorance so that they might sell their shares in the company to the McLarens at an undervalue.

Held

It was just and equitable that the company should be wound-up in the circumstances, regard being had to the fact that the company was practically a domestic and family concern.

Lord Shaw:

'... in a consideration of the justice and equity of pronouncing an order for winding-up. Such a consideration in their Lordships' view, might be to proceed upon a sound induction of all the facts of the case, and should not exclude, but should include circumstances which bear upon the problem of continuing or stopping courses of conduct which substantially impair those rights and protections to which shareholders, both under statute and contract, are entitled. It is undoubtedly true that at the foundation of applications for winding-up, on the "just and equitable" rule, there must lie a justifiable lack of confidence in the conduct and management of the company's affairs. But this lack of confidence must be grounded on conduct of the directors, not in regard to their private life or affairs, but in regard to the company's business. Furthermore the lack of confidence must spring not from dissatisfaction at being outvoted on the business affairs or on what is called the domestic policy of the company. On the other hand, wherever the lack of confidence is rested on a lack of probity in the conduct of the company's affairs, then the former is justified by the latter, and it is under the statute just and equitable that the company be wound up ...'

Martin Coulter Enterprises Ltd, Re [1988] BCLC 12 Chancery Division (Vinelott J)

Just and equitable winding up – striking out of the petition refusal

Facts
Incorporated in 1969 as a theatrical and literary agent, by 1982 the company had ceased to carry on business. In 1975 the company had taken an assignment of a lease containing an unqualified covenant against assignment. If the value of this lease, the largest of this company's fixed assets, was written down to nothing, it was hopelessly insolvent. The holder of 50 per cent of the company's shares sought a winding up order under s517(1)(d) of the Companies Act 1985 (the company had suspended business for more than one year; see now s122 of the Insolvency Act 1986) or on the just and equitable ground. An application was made to strike out the petition, it being contended that as this lease was unassignable it was of no value, the company was therefore insolvent and the position could not be pursued on the just and equitable ground as the petitioner could not demonstrate a tangible interest in the company's assets.

Held
The petition would not be struck out as there remained the possibility that the company would have a surplus to distribute in the winding-up.

Vinelott J:

'I have come to the conclusion that I ought not to strike out the petition on this ground. It is true that as a general rule a non-assignable lease has no market value and would not normally be included as an asset in the balance sheet. (See the observations of Lord Wilberforce in *Tucker* v *Granada Motorway Services Ltd* [1979] 1 WLR 683. But the rule is not a rule of law and it is not difficult to conceive of circumstances in which a non-assignable lease might have a value and even a value sufficiently well established for it to be included as an asset in the balance sheet of a company ... it would be wrong, it seems to me, to rule out altogether the possibility that the landlord might be willing to pay something for the surrender of the lease or that the liquidator might be able to negotiate a renewal or obtain the landlord's consent to an assignment for business use ... On balance, although, on the admitted facts, the claim that there should be surplus in a winding up comes very near to being obviously unsustainable, I do not think that I would be justified in striking out the petition at this stage. The power to strike out a proceeding on the ground that it is an abuse of the process of the court is founded on the principle that parties are not to be harassed by frivolous, vexatious or hopeless litigation.'

Stonegate Securities Ltd v *Gregory* [1980] Ch 576 Court of Appeal (Buckley, Goff LJJ and Sir David Cairns)

Compulsory winding up – injunction to prevent the presentation of the petition

Facts
The defendant served notice on the company in January 1979 under s223(a) CA 1948 (now s124(1) IA 1986, as amended) requiring it to pay him £33,000 within 21 days which was alleged to be due to him from the company. The £33,000 was the purchase price of certain shares bought by the company. The company disputed that the £33,000 was presently owed by it but, rather, claimed that it was contingent and, accordingly, issued a writ seeking an injunction to restrain the plaintiff from presenting a petition to wind-up the company on the basis of the alleged debt of £33,000. At the hearing of the motion the judge granted a stay for three weeks but held that the defendant was entitled to know whether the company had any assets. The company appealed against the order on the ground that there was a bona fide dispute as to whether any part of the £33,000 was presently due and that, in the circumstances, the defendant had no right to know what the company's assets were.

Held

The company was entitled to an injunction to prevent the defendant presenting a petition to wind-up without conditions because there was a bona fide dispute as to whether the debt was presently due and this relegated the defendant to the position of a contingent creditor.

Buckley LJ:

'Where a creditor petitions for the winding-up of a company, the proceedings will take one of two courses, depending on whether the petitioner is a creditor whose debt is presently due, or one whose debt is contingent or prospective by reason of the proviso in s224(1), proviso (c) (now s124(1) IA 1986, as amended). If the creditor petitions in respect of a debt which he claims to be presently due, and that claim is undisputed, the petition proceeds to hearing and adjudication in the normal way. But if the company in good faith and on substantial grounds disputes any liability in respect of the alleged debt, the petition will be dismissed or, if the matter is brought before a court before the petition is issued, its presentation will in normal circumstances be restrained. That is because a winding-up petition is not a legitimate means of seeking to enforce payment of a debt which is bona fide disputed.

Ungoed-Thomas J, put the matter thus in *Mann* v *Goldstein* [1968] 2 All ER 769 at 775:

"For my part, I would prefer to rest the jurisdiction directly on the comparatively simple propositions that a creditor's petition can only be presented by a creditor, that the winding-up jurisdiction is not for the purpose of deciding a disputed debt (that is, disputed on substantial and not insubstantial grounds) since, until a creditor is established as a creditor he is not entitled to present the petition and has no locus standi in the companies court; and that, therefore, to invoke the winding-up jurisdiction when the debt is disputed (that is, on substantial grounds) or after it has become clear that it is so disputed is an abuse of the process of the court."

'I gratefully adopt the whole of that statement, although I think it could equally well have ended at the reference to want of locus standi. In my opinion a petition founded on a debt which is disputed in good faith and on substantial grounds is demurrable for the reason that the petitioner is not a creditor of the company within the meaning of s224(1) at all, and the question whether he is or is not a creditor of the company is not appropriate for adjudication in winding-up proceedings.

The circumstances may, however, be such that the company adopts an intermediate position, denying that the debt is presently due but not denying that it will or may become due in the future, in other words, accepting it as a contingent or prospective debt. The present case is of the last-mentioned kind, and the present appeal involves a consideration of what is proper in such a case ...'

... So that situation is such that the defendant cannot petition to wind the company up on the basis that he is a debtor for a sum which is presently due, because that position is disputed in good faith and on substantial grounds; but he is competent to petition as a contingent creditor. As a petitioner in that capacity, however, he would have to comply with the requirements of s224(1) proviso (c) under which the burden rests with him of establishing a prima facie case for winding-up the company ...'

Yenidje Tobacco Co Ltd, Re [1916] 2 Ch 462 Court of Appeal (Lord Cozens-Hardy MR, Pickford and Warrington LJJ)

Just and equitable winding up – quasi partnership

Facts

Rothman and Weinberg decided to amalgamate their businesses and, accordingly, formed a company. The company had 'A' voting shares and each held an equal number. There was no provision in the articles for a casting vote and one director was to form a quorum. There was also a provision that all disputes between the directors over the factory manager of one of the businesses was referred to arbitration. Rothman refused to accept the decision of the arbitrator, he refused to allow the factory manager to work. As a result Rothman and Weinberg refused to speak to each other and directors' meetings became a farce; all communications between them had to be relayed through a third party. Weinberg petitioned under what is now s122(1)(g) Insolvency Act 1986 for the winding-up of the company. Rothman resisted.

Held

The company was in reality a partnership between Rothman and Weinberg and the same principles were to be applied as applied in a partnership. Since there was deadlock in the management of the company it was just and equitable in the circumstances that it should be wound-up.

Lord Cozens-Hardy, MR:

'... It is possible that it is not "just and equitable" (now s122(1)(g) of the Insolvency Act, 1986) that the state of things should not be allowed to continue, but that the court should intervene and say: "This is not what the parties contemplated by the arrangement which they entered into." They assumed, and it is the foundation of the whole of the agreement which was made, that the two would act as reasonable men with reasonable courtesy and reasonable conduct in every way towards each other, and that arbitration was only to deal with some particular dispute between the board which might be wanted to go to arbitration. Certainly the state of things that the only two directors will not speak to each other and no business can be conducted which deserves the name of business in the affairs of the company should not be allowed to continue.

I have treated this matter as a partnership. Under the Partnership Act, of course, the application for a dissolution would take the form of an action. This is not a partnership strictly, it is not a case in which it can be dissolved by action. But ought not the same principles precisely to apply to a case like this, where in substance, it is a partnership? It is a partnership taking the form or the guise of a private company, and it is a private company as to which there is no way to be found out of the state of things which now exists except by means of a compulsory order. It has been urged upon us that, although it is admitted that the "just and equitable" clause in s129 of the Companies (Consolidation) Act, 1908, which provides that a company may be wound-up by the court "if the court is of opinion that it is just and equitable that the company should be wound-up" is not to be read as being ejusdem generis with the preceding provisions of the section which afford certain specific grounds for winding-up (now s122(1)(g) of the Insolvency Act 1986, it has been held not to apply except where the substratum of the company has gone and there is a complete deadlock. Those are the two instances which are given. But I should be very sorry to suppose that they are strictly the limits of the "just and equitable" clause as found in the Companies (Consolidation) Act, 1908. I think that in a case like the present we are bound to say that circumstances which would justify the winding-up of a partnership by action are circumstances which should induce the court to exercise its jurisdiction under the "just and equitable" clause and to wind-up the company. Astbury J dealt with this case, as it seems to me, in a most satisfactory way. At the end of his judgment he said that he tried to suggest a solution. He suggested that the two shareholders should "continue for six months to see if they can get on better, or that they should appoint one or more additional directors to assist them in the business". But this neither would do. If ever there was a case of deadlock I think that it exists here. But, whether it exists or not, I think that the circumstances are such that we ought to apply, if necessary, the analogy of the partnership law, and to say that this company is now in a state which could not have been contemplated by the parties when the company was formed and ought to be terminated as soon as possible. We are told that the court ought not to interfere because the company is prosperous, making large profits, rather larger profits than before the dispute became so acute. I think one's knowledge from what one sees in the streets can quite account for that. The number of cigarettes that are sold is enormous, and we can take judicial notice of that in judging whether the business is much larger than it was before. Whether there would be such profits made in circumstances like this or not, it does not seem to me to remove the difficulty with exists, which is contrary to the good faith and essence of this, that the parties formed the scheme of a company managed by these two directors which should be worked amicably, and it would not justify the continuance of the state of things which we find here. In my opinion, the appeal fails and ought to be dismissed with costs.'

Effect of liquidation

Barn Crown Ltd, Re [1995] 1 WLR 147 Chancery Division (Judge Rich QC sitting as a High Court Judge)

Whether third party cheques paid into a company's bank account constituted a disposition of company property contrary to s127 IA 1986

Facts
After the commencement of the company's winding up, its bank collected third party cheques, amounting to £37,000 odd pounds, and credited the company's account with this amount. The liquidator applied for an order that the bank pay over to him this sum of money as it constituted a disposition of company property and was therefore void under s127 IA 1986.

Held
The application was dismissed. There was no disposition of the company's property.

Judge Rich QC:

'In collecting payment upon a cheque the bank credits the customer's account with the amount of the cheque. If the account is already in credit, no disposition of the property of the customer takes place in favour of the bank. The amount standing to the credit of a customer's account is increased in return for the surrender of the cheque, which becomes a voucher for payment. It is the drawer of the cheque whose property is disposed of. All that happens between the customer and the banker is an adjustment of entries in the statement recording the accounts between them.'

Commentary
If the company's bank account was overdrawn in this case, then there would have been a disposition of property within s127 IA 1986. There would also be a similar disposition of property each time money was paid out of the account.

Bowkett v *Fullers United Electric Works Ltd* [1923] 1 KB 160 Court of Appeal (Bankes and Scrutton LJJ, Eve J)

Whether a judgment creditor could levy execution after a petition for winding up had been presented

Facts
The company suffered severe losses because of a trade depression and was unable to meet its obligations. On 18 August 1920 a petition for winding-up was presented with a view to preparing a scheme for the reconstruction of the company under s108 CA 1908. On 28 August, 1920, the plaintiff brought an action against the company claiming £41 for goods sold and delivered, got judgment and was about to levy execution. The company took out a summons to stay further proceedings on the ground that a petition for winding-up had been presented.

Held

The execution ought to be stayed since there were no special circumstances which would allow the plaintiff to proceed. In fact, if he were permitted to do so he would obtain a preference over the general body of creditors.

Bankes LJ:

'... The general policy of the court is exercising this jurisdiction, when a petition has been presented which may result in a winding-up order or a scheme, is to secure that no creditor shall thenceforward gain priority over others of his class, and when an application is made to stay proceedings under s140 very exceptional circumstances must exist to justify the court in refusing to accede to the application, because if the plaintiff's action is not stayed he will get payment in full while if his action is stayed he will take his place properly among other creditors of his class. I cannot see any exceptional circumstances in the present case. To allow the plaintiff to proceed would be in effect, during the interval between the presentation of a petition and the working out of a scheme of arrangement, to allow certain creditors to help themselves out of the assets of the company in priority to some others in a less fortunate position. No doubt the court has a discretion whether it will stay a plaintiff's action, but it is against the policy of the court to exercise that discretion by allowing the plaintiff to proceed except in very special circumstances ...'

Clifton Place Garage Ltd, Re [1970] Ch 477 Court of Appeal (Harman, Sachs and Phillimore LJJ)

Section 127 of the Insolvency Act 1986 – disposition of company property after the commencement of winding up

Facts

A petition for the winding-up of the company was presented in November 1966 and the company's bankers froze its account thus leaving it with no means of carrying on any further trade. A debenture-holder in the company appointed a receiver and manager in December 1966. The receiver was given a misleadingly optimistic assessment of the company's position by its sole director and believed that the company's shares were a valuable asset which could only be realised for everybody's benefit by continuing to trade. A special bank account was opened and the company continued to trade. About £4,878 was paid out of the account and £4,024 paid from the receiver on the ground that it was a disposition of the company's property made after the commencement of winding-up and void under s227 (now s127 IA 1986). The receiver asked the court to validate the disposition. Megarry J affirmed a refusal by the registrar to do so. On appeal

Held

The appeal would be allowed; whether a disposition would be validated depended on the circumstances of each case and, in the present case, as the receiver had acted bona fide and the creditors suffered no detriment, it was just and equitable to validate the disposition, otherwise the creditors would be unjustly enriched at the expense of the receiver.

Sachs LJ:

'At the outset I too wish to make clear my respectful support of the approach to questions arising under s227 of the 1948 Act which was adopted by Vaisey J, in *Re Steane's (Bournemouth) Ltd* (1). In particular, I have in mind what he said at p25:

"... each case must be dealt with on its own facts and particular circumstances (special regard being had to the question of the good faith and honest intention of the persons concerned) ... the court is free to act according to the judge's opinion of what would be just and fair in each case."

Moreover, a little later, he went on, at p25:

"The legislature, by omitting to indicate any particular principles which should govern the exercise of the discretion vested in the court, must be deemed to have left it entirely at large, and controlled only by the general principles which apply to every kind of judicial discretion."

In assessing what is just and fair, it is, inter alia, necessary to strike some balance upon looking at what is fair vis-a-vis the applicant as well as what is fair vis-a-vis the creditors of the relevant company. In the present case, there is fortunately no dispute whatsoever but that the receiver's action was entirely bona fide. From that starting point, it seems right to examine two facets of this matter. First, and most importantly, is one that stems from the fact that the £4,024 at stake represents in substance money which would never have come into the hands of the company at all but for the advances, exceeding that sum, made by the receiver from moneys provided by the parent company. Moreover, those advances were made without putting the company's creditors to any apparent risk.

If the court acceded to the liquidator's contentions, the creditors would have the benefit of the major part of the £4,024 whilst in justice it should in the first place be allocated to reimburse so much as possible of the advances of £4,878 mentioned by Harman LJ – those being advances which would never have been obtained without it being assumed that the £4,024 would be available as a counterbalance. Of course, had the liquidator sought, and been able, to prove that the creditors suffered some detriment because of the arrangement under which the £4,024 came to be paid into a special account, then to the extent that any such detriment was established, different considerations would arise. But no attempt whatsoever was made by the liquidator to establish such a detriment. There is thus no evidence of any such detriment: and in the special circumstances of the present case the onus of so doing lay upon the liquidator. Indeed, the creditors have prima facie gained some £800. Moreover (and this is a point to which I shall return), it was at all material times unlikely that the creditors would suffer detriment and more likely that they would stand to make some advantage under the arrangement.

It is in those circumstances clearly fair and just that the court should make the order proposed by my Lord. Any other course would involve what Mr Heyman has described as an unjust enrichment of the creditors, and would impose an undeserved penalty on those who provided the £4,878 ...'

Commentary

As to s127 of the Insolvency Act 1986, see now ss164 and 175 of the Companies Act 1989.

Gray's Inn Construction Co Ltd, Re [1980] 1 WLR 711 Court of Appeal (Buckley, Goff LJJ and Sir David Cairns)

Section 127 of the Insolvency Act 1986 – disposition of company property after commencement of winding up

Facts

A creditor of the company presented a petition to have it wound-up on 3 August, 1972. At that date the company was trading at a loss and had an unsecured bank overdraft of £5,322. The bank did not become aware of the petition until 17 August. A compulsory winding-up order was made in respect of the company on 9 October. Between 3 August and 9 October the bank allowed the company to operate the account and never considered opening a separate account to avoid the payment of pre-liquidation debts. In this period over £25,000 was paid into the account and over £24,000 was paid out of it including £4,824, which was paid to creditors in respect of goods and services supplied prior to the commencement of the winding up. The liquidator applied for declarations (i) that the receipts into the account in this period were dispositions of the company's property which were void under s227 (now s127 IA 1986) and for payment of these amounts or (ii) that the amounts debited to the account were dispositions of the company's property which were void under s227 and an order for repayment of these. At the hearing the claim against the bank was limited to £5,000, this being the trading loss suffered by the company in the relevant period. Templeman J held that payments into the account did not fall within s227 and decided to exercise his discretion to validate payments out of it. The liquidator appealed. On appeal:

Held

Both the payments into and out of the accounts fell within s227 as dispositions of the company's property.

Buckley LJ:

'... It is a basic concept of our law governing the liquidation of insolvent estates, whether in bankruptcy or under the Companies Acts, that the free assets of the insolvent at the commencement of the liquidation shall be distributed rateably amongst the insolvent's unsecured creditors as at that date. In bankruptcy this is achieved by the relation of the trustee's title to the bankrupt's assets back to the commencement of the bankruptcy. In a company's compulsory winding-up it is achieved by s227. There may be occasions, however, when it would be beneficial, not only for the company but also for its unsecured creditors, that the company should be enabled to dispose of some of its property during the period after the petition has been presented but before a winding-up order has been made. An obvious example is if the company has an opportunity by acting speedily to dipose of some piece of property at an exceptionally good price. Many applications for validation under the section relate to specific transactions of this kind or analogous kinds. It may sometimes be beneficial to the company and its creditors that the company should be enabled to complete a particular contract or project, or to continue to carry on its business generally in its ordinary course with a view to a sale of the business as a going concern. In any such case the court has power under s227 to validate the particular transaction, or the completion of the particular contract or project, or the continuance of the company's business in its ordinary course, as the case may be.

In considering whether to make a validating order the court must always, in my opinion, do its best to ensure that the interests of the unsecured creditors will not be prejudiced. Where the application relates to a specific transaction this may be susceptible of positive proof. In a case of completion of a contract or project the proof may pehaps be less positive but nevertheless be cogent enough to satisfy the court that in the interests of the creditors the company should be enabled to proceed, or at any rate that proceeding in the manner proposed would not prejudice them in any respect. The desirability of the company being enabled to carry on its business generally is likely to be more speculative and will be likely to depend on whether a sale of the business as a going concern will probably be more beneficial than a break-up realisation of the company's assets. In each case, I think, the court must necessarily carry out a balancing exercise of the kind envisaged by Templeman, J in his judgment. Each case must depend on its own particular facts.

Since the policy of the law is to procure so far as practicable rateable payments of the unsecured creditors' claims, it is, in my opinion, clear that the court should not validate any transaction or series of transactions which might result in one or more pre-liquidation creditors being paid in full at the expense of other creditors, who will only receive a dividend, in the absence of special circumstances making such a course desirable in the interests of the unsecured creditors as a body. If for example it were in the interests of the creditors generally that the company's business should be carried on and this could only be achieved by paying for goods already supplied to the company when the petition is presented but not yet paid for, the court might think fit in the exercise of its discretion to validate payment for those goods.

Where a third party proposes to enter into a transaction with a company which is liable to be invalidated under s227, the third party can decline to do so until the company has obtained a validating order, or it might itself seek a validating order, or it can enter into the transaction in anticipation of the court making a retroactive validating order at a later date. In the present case the bank adopted the last course. A third party who does that takes the risk of the court refusing to make the order.

It may not always be feasible, or desirable, that a validating order should be sought before the transaction in question is carried out. The parties may be unaware at the time when the transaction is entered into that a petition has been presented; or the need for speedy action may be such as to preclude an anticipatory application; or the beneficial character of the transaction may be so obvious that there is no real prospect of a liquidator seeking to set it aside, so that an application to the court would waste time, money and effort. But in any case in which the transaction is carried out without an anticipatory validating order the disponee is at risk of the court declining to validate the transaction. It follows, in my view, that the parties when entering into the transaction, if they are aware that it is liable to be invalidated by the section, should have in mind the sort of considerations which would influence the court's decision.

A disposition carried out in good faith in the ordinary course of business at a time when the parties are unaware that a petition has been presented may, it seems, normally be validated by the court (see *Re Neath Harbour Smelting and Rolling Works* (1887) 56 LT 727 and *Re Liverpool Civil Service Associaton* (1874) LR 9 Ch App 511, unless there is any ground for thinking that the transaction may involve an attempt to prefer the disponee, in which case the transaction would probably not be validated. In a number of cases reference has been made to the relevance of the policy of ensuring rateable distribution of the assets: see *Re Civil Service and General Store Ltd* (1887) 57 LJ Ch 119; *Re Liverpool Civil Service Association* and *Re Leslie Engineers Co Ltd* [1976] 1 WLR 292. In the last mentioned case Oliver J said:

> "I think that in exercising discretion the court must keep in view the evident purpose of the section which, as Chitty J said in *Re Civil Service and General Store Ltd* , is to ensure that the creditors are paid pari passu."

But, although that policy might disincline the court to ratify any transaction which involved preferring a pre-liquidation creditor, it has no relevance to a transaction which is entirely post-liquidation, as for instance a sale of an asset at its full market value after presentation of a petition. Such a transaction involves no dissipation of the company's assets, for it does not reduce the value of those assets. It cannot harm the creditors and there would seem to be no reason why the court should not in the exercise of its discretion validate it. A fortiori the court would be inclined to validate a transaction which would increase, or has increased, the value of the company's assets, or which would preserve, or has preserved, the value of the company's assets from harm which would result from the company's business being paralysed (*Re Wiltshire Iron Co* (1868) LR 3 Ch App 433; *Re Park Ward & Co Ltd* [1926] Ch 828), where business of the company was eventually sold as a going concern presumably to the advantage of the creditors, and *Re Clifton Place Garage Ltd* [1970] Ch 477). In *Re A I Levy (Holdings) Ltd* [1964] Ch 19 the court validated a sale of a lease which was liable to forfeiture in the event of the tenant company being wound up, and also validated as part of the transaction, payment out of the proceeds of sale of arrears of rent which had accrued before the presentation of the petition for the compulsory liquidation of the company. If that case was rightly decided, as I trust that it was, the court can in appropriate circumstances validate payment in full of an unsecured pre-liquidation debt which constitutes a necessary part of unsecured creditors. But we have been referred to no case in which the court has validated payment in full of an unsecured pre-liquidation debt where there were no such special circumstances, and in my opinion it would not normally be right to do so, because such a payment would prefer the creditor whose debt is paid over the other creditors of equal degree.'

Transactions arising in liquidation

Wrongful and fraudulent trading

A Company (No 001418 of 1988), Re [1990] BCC 526 High Court (Judge Leonard Bromley QC)

Fraudulent trading

Facts
Having been incorporated in 1979, the company had last made a net profit before tax in 1983 and it had always shown an adverse net current assets/liabilities balance. The company had gone into creditors'

voluntary liquidation in June 1986 with an estimated deficiency for unsecured creditors of some £212,000, but in 1984, although its bank overdraft limit had been exceeded and it had fallen behind with payments for PAYE, NICs and VAT and to ordinary trade creditors, it had continued to pay significant sums by way of remuneration to the respondent, its chairman, managing director and majority shareholder. The liquidator alleged fraudulent trading contrary to s630 of the Companies Act 1985 (see now s213 of the Insolvency Act 1986).

Held

There had been fraudulent trading, as from 31 July 1984.

Judge Leonard Bromley QC:

'The principles were established by the Court of Appeal in *R v Grantham* [1984] QB 675, which Mr Hollington cited to me. In that decision the earlier authorities were reviewed. A finding that a person was knowingly party to the business of a company having been carried on with intent to defraud creditors may be made if the following two conditions are satisfied:

1. if that person realised at the time the debts were incurred that there was no reason for thinking that funds would be available to pay the debt in question when it became due or shortly thereafter (see p682D); and

2. there was actually dishonesty involving, according to current notions of fair trading among commercial men, real moral blame.

The intent to defraud is to be judged by its effect on the person who is the object of the conduct in question (see pp683E and 684F, applying *Welham v Director of Public Prosecutions* [1961] AC 103 per Lord Radcliffe, cited at p683 of *Grantham*). There appear to me to be two types, relevantly, of such object persons. There are those who choose to make the company their debtor, as ordinary trade suppliers, and those in whose favour liability from the company arises by the choice of the company, not their own; for example, the Revenue as to PAYE and national insurance contributions, and the Customs and Excise as to VAT. As to trade creditors the position is made clear in *Grantham* at p683E and 684F. There is intent to defraud within the meaning of the section if the person responsible was intending to deceive or actually deceiving a supplier that he would be paid at the stipulated time or shortly thereafter when the person so intending or deceiving knew perfectly well that there was no hope of that coming about.

As to non-choice creditors, there is no question of deceit. The intent to defraud in my views lies in continuing to incur the liability for tax or national insurance contributions or VAT when there is no honest belief that those liabilities will be discharged when they become due or shortly thereafter ...

As this stage I refer to a matter which has concerned me, and that is the risk of unfairness by the application of hindsight. For a person to be held knowingly party to carrying on a company's business with intent to defraud creditors requires findings and inferences as to the facts known to that person at the relevant times. At those times the business might either have succeeded or failed. The certainty that the business failed, which a creditors' liquidation affords, was not a fact known at the time the relevant business decisions were taken. In my judgment accordingly the risk of unfairness through hindsight needs to be borne in mind ...

I come to the directors' remuneration. In my judgment the amounts of remuneration were very high for a company in such a state. For the year ended 31 March 1983 the remuneration was £35,000. That was the year of the substantial profit and I see the case that that might well have been justified. However, the following year, to 31 March 1984, the remuneration package increased to £37,521. That was the year where there was a sharp swing to loss and a large adverse change in the net assets position. For the year ended 31 March 1985 the directors' remuneration total was £41,726 – even higher – and I ask rhetorically, what were the directors doing paying themselves these significant and increasing sums while the debts to the company's creditors mounted? ...

[The respondent] told me that he did not intend to defraud creditors and he did not know about fraudulent trading. I am satisfied that he was in full control of the company and had full knowledge of its affairs. He is an experienced businessman ... in my judgment within the principles I have referred to, from the end of July 1984 at least [the respondent] had no reason for thinking that the company could pay its debts as they fell due or shortly thereafter. There was in my judgment real moral blame according to current notions of fair trading in his procuring the company to continue to trade, ie within the meaning of the section, dishonesty. I accordingly determine that there was fraudulent trading and, as a convenient date for start, that it began on the 31 July 1984 ...

The question now arises as to the form of the relief. Having been helpfully taken through the authorities ... the following principles are in my view relevant on this application by a liquidator.

1. The declaration should specify responsibility for a definite sum and not be in general terms as, for example, to creditors whose debts were incurred after commencement of the fraudulent trading (see Re William C Leitch Bros Ltd [1932] 2 Ch 71 at pp77-79, per Maugham J).

2. The provision being applied is in the nature of a punitive provision (see the same case at p80). It follows that the declared sum may be or contain a punitive element as well as a compensatory element (see per Lord Denning MR in *Re Cyona Distributors Ltd* [1967] Ch 889, at p902).

3. The usual order on an application by a liquidator is that the sum for which the person concerned is declared to be personally liable ought to be dealt with as part of the general assets in the liquidation (see per Eve J in *Re William C Leitch Bros Ltd (No 2)* [1933] Ch 261, approved by Lord Denning in *Re Cyona Distributors Ltd* at p902).

4. So far as the sum for which the person in question is declared to be responsible is compensatory, then in my judgment it is more appropriate under this particular statutory provision to adopt the approach of Maugham J in the first *Leitch* case at p80, ie to limit the sum to the amount of the debts of the creditors proved to have been defrauded by the fraudulent trading.

[Counsel for the liquidator] urged me to adopt the formulation of Knox J in *Re Produce Marketing Consortium Ltd* (1989) 5 BCC 569, where his Lordship said at p597G:

> "Prima facie the appropriate amount that a director is declared to be liable to contribute is the amount by which the company's assets can be discerned to have been depleted by the director's conduct which caused the discretion under s214(1) to arise."

That is a reference to the Insolvency Act 1986. The preceding section of that, s213, is the re-enactment of s630 of the Companies Act 1985, with which I am concerned.

Knox J was, however, concerned with a different statutory provision and it is, I think, preferable to found myself on a direct nexus with the statutory language before me, particularly in the light of Maugham J's observations. (I add that there may not be a difference of principle and I am in no way dissenting from what Knox J said.) Where the context is fraudulent trading with intent to defraud creditors, there is a clear logic in asking what the creditors have lost as a result of the fraudulent trading. I agree ... that an adequate measure of the maximum compensatory element (I emphasise maximum) is the amount of the trading loss during the period of fraudulent trading ...

I am satisfied that there are elements in this case which point to a need for a considerable punitive element. Thus, first [the respondent] well knew from the years of [the company's bank's] concern expressed to him and the accounts that he was providing that he was trading dangerously. There were large excesses of current liabilities over the current assets which did not come down, and there were serious cash flow difficulties. Secondly, the fraudulent trading continued for a long period after 31 July 1984 for some 22 months, drawing more creditors into the net. Thirdly, the directors' remuneration was high in relation to a company in such a long-continued parlous financial state ...

I consider that a punitive element of £25,000 is appropriate. The total of the two sums of £131,420 and £25,000 is £156,420, and that is the amount as to which I propose to make a declaration.'

Farmizer (Products) Ltd, Re [1995] BCC 926 Chancery Division (Companies Court) (Blackburne J)

Wrongful trading – limitation period – whether there had been inordinate and inexcusable delay

Facts

The company went into liquidation on 12 October 1987 but the liquidators did not commence wrongful trading proceedings against the two directors, Mr and Mrs Gadd, until 13 April 1992. The claim came as a complete shock to the defendants as they had been given no warning of the proceedings. The case raised the following issues:

1. whether there is a limitation period for wrongful trading actions, and, if so, whether it had expired;
2. whether there had been inordinate and inexcusable delay by the liquidators;
3. whether any such delay had prejudiced the directors.

Held

The directors' application to have the wrongful trading action struck out was successful.

1. The limitation period was six years as laid down in s9(1) Limitation Act 1980, with time running from the date the company went into liquidation on 12 October 1987, and expiring six years later on 11 October 1993.
2. Delay in commencing proceedings will not be inordinate if commenced within the limitation period. But where, as in this case, the liquidators waited four and half years before starting proceedings, it was incumbent on the liquidators to prosecute their claim without further delay. His Lordship felt that this had not been the case and that the subsequent delay was both inordinate and inexcusable.
3. The liquidators' delay caused prejudice to the directors as it would affect the memories of the directors and others to recall events. A claim for business prejudice was not made out.

Blackburne J:

'In my view the ability of Mr Gadd, and to a lesser extent Mr Beirne [a partner in the company's accountants and auditors], and Mrs Chick [Mr Gadd's daughter], to recall the course of events during this period will be of significance to the outcome of the liquidators' claims. After the passage of so many years, this is likely to prove extremely difficult. The question is whether their ability to recall events has been made more difficult as a result of the 18 months or so of culpable delay on the liquidators' part in prosecuting this claim. I have come to the conclusion that it has, at any rate in the case of Mr Gadd. Loss of recollection is a progressive matter. A total of 18 months or so out of the period of up to nine years or so since the events occurred with which these proceedings are concerned is significant. In my judgment the Gadds have suffered something more than minimal additional prejudice as a result of the liquidators' delay since these proceedings were launched.'

On the business prejudice point, his Lordship said:

'The evidence before me filed on behalf of the Gadds refers, not surprisingly, to the enormous strain that this litigation has imposed on them including the threat of bankruptcy if the claim were to succeed. It is not suggested that the liquidators' inordinate and inexcusable delay in prosecuting the claim has forced the Gadds, or either of them, to defer making business decisions of one kind or another which might otherwise have been made. In these circumstances, paying heed to the words of caution uttered by Lord Griffiths in the *Chris Smaller* [1989] AC 1197 and *Eagil Trust* [1985] 3 All ER 119 cases, and notwithstanding the apparent approach of the Court of Appeal in *Moyneux* v *Bull* [unreported 7 May 1991 CA], I do not consider that the fact that the Gadds face a very substantial uninsured claim and that the existence of that claim has caused and continues to cause them much strain *of itself* constitutes prejudice of a kind to justify making a striking out order.'

If I am wrong in that conclusion then I would agree with Miss Harman [counsel for Mr Gadd] and Mr McFarland [counsel for Mrs Gadd] that the continued existence of so large a claim did cause the Gadds to suffer additional prejudice during the period of the liquidators' culpable delay.

In the result the Gadd's applications succeed and I shall make an order on each application striking out the liquidators' claims.'

Fleet Disposal Services Ltd, Re [1995] BCC 605 Chancery Division (Companies Court) (Lightman J)

Liquidation – whether proceeds held in a bank account were held on trust for the respondent

Facts

Fleet Disposal Services Ltd ('Fleet') sold cars as an agent for the respondent, 'Nortel'. The agreement between them required Fleet to pay to Nortel the proceeds of sale, less commission and agreed costs, five days after receipt by Fleet. Payments had to be made on separate cheques. Although the agreement did not require a separate account, all proceeds were in fact paid into and out of such an account, along with the proceeds of sale from cars sold belonging to other principals. When Fleet went into liquidation, Nortel claimed to be able to trace proceeds of sale amounting to £27,417 which was held in the account. The liquidator sought direction from the court on the matter.

Held

Nortel could claim the £27,417 on the basis of a trust relationship between the parties. This was the result of a proper construction of the agency agreement in the light of the surrounding circumstances and the intention of the parties.

Lightman J:

'**Law**

The question whether Nortel had a proprietary interest in the proceeds of sale of its cars on receipt of the same by the company is one of construction of the agency agreement in the light of the surrounding circumstances at the time when it was made, and these circumstances include the intentions of the parties express or to be inferred: see *Neste Oy* v *Lloyds Bank plc* [1983] 2 Ll Rep 658 at p663.

The intentions for this purpose are limited to intentions of the parties communicated to, or reasonably to be inferred by, each other, and do not extend to private uncommunicated intentions. Accordingly the established but uncommunicated intentions on the part of the company (and its advisers and the bank) that the company should be entitled to use the moneys in the agency account as its own free moneys is not relevant for this purpose, for it was never so stated nor reasonably to be inferred.

One surrounding circumstance was that the agency account existed; that all sale proceeds of cars sold as agent were paid into this account and all payments to principals were made out of this account; that this arrangement was intended to continue; and that this was communicated by the company to Nortel as (in the words of Mr Dicker, counsel for the liquidator) a selling point of the company as agent. For this purpose, I attach little (if any) importance to the designation of this account as "the agency account", for Mr Farrington did not attach importance to the name; indeed he was uncertain as to the name of the account. The importance is the existence of the separate designated account.

I turn second to the relationship between the parties. The company was Nortel's agent for sale. As it seems to me, notwithstanding "the general disinclination of the courts to see the intricacies and doctrines connected with trusts introduced into everyday commercial transactions" (see *Neste Oy* v *Lloyd Bank* [1983] 2 Lloyd's Rep 658 at p665), that is a relationship where, in respect of moneys received by the agent representing the proceeds of sale of the principals' property, the court is particularly ready to infer a trust: it is not readily to be inferred that the agent is intended to be able to finance his business out of the proceeds of sale of his principal's property: see eg *Re Cotten* (1913) 108 LT 310 and *Re Hallett's Estate* (1880) 13 ChD 696.

I turn third to the agency agreement. It contains no express term whether the proceeds of sale should be held as trustee or retained in a separate account. But there are indications of a trust relationship, or at least language consistent with it. Provision is made for "payment of sale proceeds five days after receipt of moneys" (a short period) and payment by separate cheques – language and provisions at least to some degree apposite to a trust and inapposite to a mere accounting relationship – certainly inapposite to a running account.

Taking these factors together, it seems to me that a trust relationship is appropriate to the commercial relationship which existed between these parties and I can see no unfair or undue consequences for the company or its unsecured creditors (consider *Lord Napier and Ettrick & Anor* v *Hunter & Ors* [1993] AC 713 at p744C–H). Indeed the company had the opportunity expressly to exclude any trust obligation when it drafted its standard contract and agreed the agency contract, for it had this matter very much in mind. Far from doing so, the selling point was made of the separate account and no disclaimer of any trust obligation was expressed.'

Gerald Cooper Chemicals, Re [1978] 1 Ch 262 Chancery Division (Templeman J)

Fraudulent trading – whether a single transaction suffices

Facts
Cooper formed a company with the object of making indigo for blue jeans. J Ltd and its two directors agreed to lend the company £150,000 to purchase and instal equipment in a factory. The agreement provided that the company would repay the money within three months and pay a further £1.35 million in another 12 months. The £150,000 was insufficient to enable the company to begin production and by July 1976 it was insolvent. Cooper attempted to keep the company afloat by obtaining advance orders for indigo and he obtained an order from H Ltd and obtained a payment of £12,698 in advance. On the same day as this was paid Cooper paid over the money to J Ltd and soon afterwards went into liquidation. H Ltd applied for a declaration that J Ltd and its directors were liable under s332 (now s213 IA 1986) in that they knew of the circumstances and were parties to the fraud (there was no point in suing the company as it was insolvent). J Ltd applied for an order to strike out the proceedings as vexatious and frivolous on the ground that a single transaction could not amount to 'carrying on a business with intent to defraud creditors' under s332.

Held
A single transaction could fall within s332 where it was a fraud on a creditor in the course of business since the company accepted the advance payment from H Ltd knowing at that time it could not supply the indigo and would not repay the money it had carried on its business with intent to defraud creditors. J Ltd was a party to this fraud since they accepted the money knowing of the circumstances in which it was obtained.

Templeman J:

'Counsel for the respondents submitted that one transaction cannot amount to the carrying on of a business with intent to defraud creditors. For this submission he relied on certain observations of Oliver J in *Re Murray Watson Ltd*. The learned judge said:

"(Section 332) is aimed at the carrying on of a business ... and not at the execution of individual transactions in the course of carrying on that business. I do not think that the words 'carried on' can be treated as synonymous with 'carried out', nor can I read the words 'any business' as synonymous with 'any transaction or dealing'. The director of a company dealing in second-hand motor cars who wilfully misrepresents the age and capabilities of a vehicle is, no doubt, a fraudulent rascal, but I do not think that he can be said to be carrying on the company's business for a fraudulent purpose, although no doubt he carried out a particular business transaction in a fraudulent manner ..."

... In the present case, the Cooper company was carrying on the business of selling indigo. In my judgment, they carried on that business with intent to defraud creditors if they accepted deposits knowing that they could not supply the indigo and were insolvent. They were carrying on business with intent to defraud creditors as soon as they accepted one deposit knowing that they could not supply the indigo and would not repay the deposit. It does not matter for the purposes of s332 that only creditor was defrauded, and by one transaction, provided that the transaction can properly be described as a fraud on a creditor perpetrated in the course of carrying on business. If the Cooper company had fraudulently supplied sub-standard indigo to Harrisons, the Cooper company would have committed a fraud on a customer, but by accepting a deposit knowing that they could not or would not supply indigo, and by using the deposit in a way which made it impossible for them to repay Harrisons, the Cooper company, in my judgment, committed a fraud on a creditor. If a mail order company advertises goods and solicits deposits with no intention of suppling the goods or of returning the money, and if 100 customers in response to the advertisement pay over £100,000, the business of the company is plainly being carried on with intent to defraud creditors of the company. If the company, as in the present case, solicits and obtains an advance of £100,000 from one customer, the situation is no different ...'

R v Grantham [1984] QB 675 Court of Appeal (Lord Lane CJ, Boreham and Stuart-Smith JJ)

Fraudulent trading – s213 of the Insolvency Act 1986

Facts
Grantham was convicted of fraudulent trading under s332 of the Companies Act 1948 in respect of his activities in the management of a company involved in the importing and marketing of potatotes and other root crops. The company was registered in March 1980 and traded from 29 May to 25 June 1980. In the trading period the company purchased potatoes from a supplier in France for which a payment of £88,000 was due. The company had no, or very little, capital and no overdraft facilities to enable it to pay for the potatoes and they were resold for £68,000 with commission being paid out of this sum to Grantham and others involved in the company, through other companies they controlled, for services in respect of marketing the potatoes. The supplier of the potatoes only received £19,668 towards the £88,000 owed to him. Grantham appealed against his conviction on the ground that the trial judges had misdirected the jury on the question of whether he was dishonest and had an intention to defraud. It was submitted that under s332 it was necessary for the prosecution to prove that at the time the debts were incurred he knew that there was no reasonable prospect of the creditors ever receiving payment of their debts.

Held
The appeal would be dismissed. It was not necessary under s332 for the prosecution to prove that there was no reasonable prospect of the creditors receiving payment. If a person took part in the management of a company and obtained credit for the company knowing that there was no reason for thinking that funds would become available to pay the debt when it fell due or shortly thereafter, he might be found guilty under s332.

Commentary
See now s213 of the Insolvency Act 1986.

Oasis Merchandising Services Ltd, Re [1995] BCC 911 Chancery Division (Robert Walker J)

Section 214 Insolvency Act (IA) 1986 – wrongful trading – liquidator assigned the 'fruits' of the action – was this champertous?

Facts

Only a liquidator can bring an action for wrongful trading, but in this case he was unwilling to bear the costs and expenses of such an action against the company's five directors. He therefore sold and assigned the 'fruits' of the action to London Wall Litigation Claims Ltd ('London'). Under the agreement London was to finance the action and was entitled to any contributions ordered against the directors should the liquidator be successful. The directors applied to have the wrongful trading action against them struck out on the grounds that the liquidator's agreement with London was champertous and an abuse of process.

Held

The action was stayed. Assignment of the 'fruits' of a wrongful trading claim was not within the liquidator's powers as it was not property capable of assignment within the meaning of para 4, Schedule 6 of the Insolvency Act 1986. As such it was champertous. His Lordship also felt that a s214 claim should not be regarded as ordinary commercial litigation. It had a potential public and penal element and a loss of control of the litigation by the liquidator could be objected to.

Robert Walker J:

> 'Mr Wright [counsel for London Wall] then went on to submit that where a liquidator makes an outright legal assignment of the entirety of a cause of action, he loses any vestige of control over the future conduct of the litigation; whereas under an equitable assignment of fruits of litigation, his loss of control is not complete. Partial loss of control must, he submitted, be less objectionable than complete loss of control. In the present case there is, it seems to me, a short answer to this point, that is that a claim under s214 is simply incapable of outright legal assignment – it can only be made and pursued by a liquidator – and that even a partial loss of control is objectionable where the claim has a public or penal element. So my view on the office of liquidator point – in the context of s214 – strongly reinforces my conclusion on the property point.'

Patrick & Lyon Ltd, Re [1933] Ch 786 Chancery Division (Maugham J)

Section 213 of the Insolvency Act 1986 – fraudulent trading

Facts

The company had never made a trading profit. About six months before it was voluntarily wound up a debenture was issued to the respondent to secure a loan of £400 by him to the company. Around the same time debts owed to the respondent by the company were repaid by the company. The respondent had once been a director of the company but did not hold that office when these events took place. The liquidator alleged that the respondent should be liable without limitation, for any or all of the company's debts since he had been a party to carrying on the company's business with intent to defraud creditors. Maugham, J dismissed the liquidator's summons and on the terms 'intent to defraud' and 'fraudulent purpose', now in s213 IA 1986 (formerly s332 CA 1948), he said:

Held

The liquidator's summons was dismissed.

Maugham J:

'Without repeating anything which my brother Eve has said or I have said in either of those cases, I will express the opinion that the words "defraud" and "fraudulent purpose" where they appear in the section in question, are words which connote actual dishonesty involving, according to current notions of fair trading among commercial men, real moral blame. No judge, I think, has ever been willing to define "fraud", and I am attempting no definition. I am merely stating what, in my opinion, must be one of the elements of the words as used in this section. In my opinion it is not used in the same sense as that in which the word "fraud" is used in s320 of the Act. There, following the example set by s44 of the Bankruptcy Act, 1914, and by s92 of the Bankruptcy Act, 1869, both of which deal with the avoidance of fraudulent preferences, the Legislature has thought fit to state that certain acts are to be deemed a fraudulent preference and to be invalid accordingly. A fraudulent preference within the meaning of the Companies Act, 1948, or the Bankruptcy Act, 1914, whether in the case of a company or of an individual, possibly may not involve moral blame at all. For example, there may be discrimination between creditors, irrespective of pressure, on grounds with which most people would sympathise. Again, there is nothing in the language of s322 of the Companies Act, 1929 (which enables a floating charge created within 12 months of a winding-up to be attacked in certain circumstances), to indicate that the Legislature took the view that the creation of such a charge when the company is insolvent is fraudulent, however blameworthy it may be. That appears from the fact that the right to attack such a floating charge is limited to cases where the company goes into liquidation within 12 months of the creation of it. Coming to the present case, I think that in exercising jurisdiction under s332 the court, however little it may approve of the conduct of the director who is being attacked, is bound to consider whether he has been guilty of a dishonest fraud, and it is hardly necessary for me to point out that the onus is upon the person who seeks to make good the charge, whether he be the official receiver, or the liquidator, or a creditor, or a contributory …'

Produce Marketing Consortium Ltd, Re (1989) 5 BCC 569 Chancery Division (Knox J)

Section 214 Insolvency Act 1986 – wrongful trading

Facts

The company acted as agents in connection with the importation of fruit from Spain. It had traded successfully for many years since its incorporation in 1964, but in October 1987 it went into liquidation owing £317,694. During its drift towards liquidation, the company continually exceeded its agreed overdraft, liabilities exceeded assets, its bankers returned cheques unpaid, accounts were prepared and delivered late, trade creditors were not paid and the auditors warned the directors of the possibility of a finding of fraudulent trading. The Liquidator wrote to the two directors, Mr David and Mr Murphy, in 1988 asking why they had traded while the company was insolvent. Mr David replied that the directors realised that insolvency was inevitable on receipt of the accounts in February 1987, and that they continued to trade until October only to realise the perishable stock in the company's cold store. The liquidator sought a declaration from the court that the two directors were liable to make a contribution to the assets of the company under the wrongful trading provisions in s214 IA 1986.

Held

The two directors had traded wrongfully and they were ordered to make a contribution of £75,000

Knox J:

'The Insolvency Act 1986 now has two separate provisions: s213 dealing with fraudulent trading – to which the passages which I have quoted from the judgments of Maugham J and Buckley J no doubt are still applicable – and s214 which deals with what the side-note calls "wrongful trading". It is evident that

Parliament intended to widen the scope of the legislation under which directors who trade on when the company is insolvent may, in appropriate circumstances, be required to make a contribution to the assets of the company which, in practical terms, means its creditors.

Two steps in particular were taken in the legislative enlargement of the court's jurisdiction. First, the requirement for an intent to defraud and fraudulent purposes was not retained as an essential, and with it goes the need for what Maugham J called "actual dishonesty involving real moral blame". I pause here to observe that at no stage before me has it been suggested that either Mr David or Mr Murphy fell into this category.

The second enlargement is that the test to be applied by the court has become one under which the director in question is to be judged by the standards of what can be expected of a person fulfilling his functions, and showing reasonable diligence in doing so. I accept Mr Teverson's submission in this connection, that the requirement to have regard to the functions to be carried out by the director in question, in relation to the company in question, involves having regard to the particular company and its business. It follows that the general knowledge, skill and experience postulated will be much less extensive in a small company in a modest way of business, with simple accounting procedures and equipment, than it will be in a large company with sophisticated procedures.

Nevertheless, certain minimum standards are to be assumed and attained. Notably there is an obligation laid on companies to cause accounting records to be kept which are such as to disclose with reasonable accuracy at any time the financial position of the company at that time (Companies Act 1985 s221(1) and (2)(a)). In addition directors are required to prepare a profit and loss account for each financial year and a balance sheet as at the end of it (Companies Act 1985 s227(1) and (3)). Directors are also required, in respect of each financial year, to lay before the company in general meeting copies of the accounts of the company for that year and to deliver to the registrar of companies a copy of those accounts, in the case of a private company, within ten months after the end of the relevant accounting reference period (Companies Act 1985 s241(1) and (3) and s242(1) and (2)(a)).

As I have already mentioned, Mr Halls gave evidence that the accounting records of PMC were adequate for the purposes of its business. The preparation of account was woefully late, more especially in relation to those dealing with the year ending 30 September 1985, which should have been laid and delivered by the end of July 1986.

The knowledge to be imputed in testing whether or not directors knew or ought to have concluded that there was no reasonable prospect of the company avoiding insolvent liquidation is not limited to the documentary material actually available at the given time. This appears from s214(4) which includes a reference to facts which a director of a company ought not only to know but those which he ought to ascertain, a word which does not appear in s214(2)(b). In my judgment this indicates that there is to be included by way of factual information not only what was actually there but what, given reasonable diligence and an appropriate level of general knowledge, skill and experience, was ascertainable. This leads me to the conclusion in this case that I should assume, for the purposes of applying the test in s214(2), that the financial results for the year ending 30 September 1985 were known at the end of July 1986 at least to the extent of the size of the deficiency of assets over liabilities.

Mr David and Mr Murphy, although they did not have the accounts in their hands until January 1987, did, I find, know that the previous trading year had been a very bad one. They had a close and intimate knowledge of the business and they had a shrewd idea whether the turnover was up or down. In fact it was badly down in that year to £526,459 and although I have no doubt that they did not know in July 1986 that it was that precise figure, I have no doubt that they had a good rough idea of what it was and in particular that it was well down on the previous year. A major drop in turnover meant almost as night follows day that there was a substantial loss incurred, as indeed there was. That, in turn, meant again, as surely as night following day, a substantial increase in the deficit of assets over liabilities.

That deals with their actual knowledge but, in addition, I have to have regard to what they have to be treated as having known or ascertained, and that includes the actual deficit of assets over liabilities of £132,870. This was £80,000 over Mr David's personal guarantee. It was a deficit that, for an indefinite period in the future, could not be made good, even if the optimistic prognostications of level of turnover estimated by Mr David and Mr Murphy were achieved. They later estimated, when they visited the bank on 16 February 1987, a turnover of £1.6m. If one assumes half as much again, at £2.4m., the gross income of the company would only have risen to £84,000 and the overheads were accepted as being not less than £65,000. That gives a notional profit of £19,000 per annum. If one takes the figure of £1.6m, overheads of £65,000 would not have been covered.

Mr Teverson was not able to advance any particular calculation as constituting a basis for concluding that there was a prospect of insolvent liquidation being avoided. He is not to be criticised for that for, in my judgment, there was none available. Once the loss in the year ending 30 September 1985 was incurred PMC was in irreversible decline, assuming (as I must) that the directors had no plans for altering the company's business and proposed to go on drawing the level of reasonable remuneration that they were currently receiving.

It was stated by Mr David that the persons and companies with whom PMC did business were in the main long established trading partners. In fact that could not be said of Ramona which was, by July 1986, a very important creditor. But even if one disregards that aspect, it would not be right to assume that even old established trading partners will wait indefinitely to have their debts paid. Nor, in my judgment, do the facts that the bank was throughout willing to continue its facilities and that Mr Tough, although expressing the grave warnings that he did when the accounts for the years ending 30 September 1985 and 1986 were available to him, was willing to accompany Mr David and Mr Murphy to the bank in February 1987 to see if further facilities would be granted, detract from the conclusion I have reached that Mr David and Mr Murphy ought to have concluded, at the end of July 1986 that there was no reasonable prospect that PMC would avoid going into insolvent liquidation. The bank was secured by Mr David's guarantee, if not to any significant extent by the other securities which it took, and Mr Tough's attitude was never more than one of doubt and caution.

The next question which arises is whether there is a case under s214(3) for saying that after the end of July 1986 the respondents took every step with a view to minimising the potential loss to the creditors of PMC as, assuming them to have known that there was no reasonable prospect of PMC avoiding insolvent liquidation, they ought to have taken. This clearly has to be answered 'No', since they went on trading for another year.

Mr Teverson gallantly attempted to establish that – assuming that the first time when the respondents ought to have concluded that there was no such reasonable prospect was February 1987 when they actually signed the preceding two year's accounts – their decision to trade on so as to realise the fruit in cold store to the best advantage satisfied the requirement of s214(3). I would not have accepted that submission in any event because the continued trading was far from limited to the realisation of the fruit in cold store, and Ramona were not told, as they should have been, what the true financial picture was so as to be given the opportunity of deciding for themselves what to do. But this is academic because that submission, even if correct in relation to February 1987, quite plainly was untenable in relation to the end of July 1986.

I am therefore driven to the conclusion that the court's discretion arises under s214(1). Upon the nature of that discretion there were conflicting submissions made to me. Mr Teverson submitted that the court's discretion is entirely at large, and he pointed to no less than three sets of words indicating the existence of a wide discretion: the court *may* declare that that person is to be liable to make *such* contribution (*if any*) to the company's assets as the court thinks *proper*. He also submitted that the provision is both compensatory and penal in character. He referred me to *Re William C Leitch Bros Ltd* at pp79-80, where Maugham J said of s275 of the Companies Act 1929:

"I am inclined to take the view that s275 is in the nature of a punitive provision, and that where the court makes such a declaration in relation to "all or any of the debts or other liabilities of the company", it is in the discretion of the court to make an order without limiting the order to the amount of the debts of those creditors proved to have been defrauded by the acts of the director in question, though no doubt the order would in general be so limited."

However, Mr Teverson also submitted that the amount which the court concluded had been lost as a result of the wrongful trading should provide a ceiling for the figure which the court declared should be contributed to the company's assets, which is of course the exact opposite of what Maugham J said in that regard. He also relied upon the provisions of s214(3) which prevent the exercise of the discretion under subs (1) in any case where, to put it briefly, the director has done everything possible to minimise loss to creditors, and suggested that it would be inequitable for a director who has just failed to escape scot-free under the provision because he had only done nearly but not quite everything to that end, to be treated on a par with a director who had done nothing to minimise loss to creditors.

Miss Arden, for the liquidator, submitted that s214 of the Insolvency Act 1986 gave a purely civil remedy, unlike the predecessors of s213 of that Act, such as s275 of the Companies Act 1929 and s332 of the Companies Act 1948 which combined the civil and criminal. More significantly, for my purpose, she submitted that s214 was compensatory rather than penal. What is ordered to be contributed goes to increase the company's assets for the benefit of the general body of creditors. On that basis she submitted that the proper measure was the reduction in the net assets which could be identified as caused by the wrongful activities of the persons ordered to contribute. This jurisdiction, it was submitted, is an enhanced version of the right which any company would have to sue its directors for breach of duty; enhanced in the sense that the standard of knowledge, skill and experience required is made objective.

On this analysis, once the circumstances required for the exercise of discretion under s214(1) are shown to exist, she submitted that the situation was analogous to that obtaining where a tort such as negligence was shown to have been committed, in that quantum was a matter of causation and not culpability. The discretion given to the court was to enable allowance to be made for questions of causation and also to avoid unjust results such as unwarranted windfalls for creditors. Thus in *Liquidator of West Mercia Safetywear Ltd* v *Dodds & Anor* (1988) 4 BCC 30, at p33 Dillon LJ said of s333 of the Companies Act 1948:

"The section in question, however, s333 of the Companies Act 1948, provides that the court may order the delinquent director to repay or restore the money, with interest at such a rate as the court thinks fit, or to contribute such sum to the assets of the company by way of compensation in respect of the misapplication as the court thinks fit. The court has a discretion over the matter of relief, and it is permissible for the delinquent director to submit that the wind should be tempered because, for instance, full repayment would produce a windfall to third parties, or, alternatively, because it would involve money going round in a circle or passing through the hands of someone else whose position is equally tainted."

In my judgment the jurisdiction under s214 is primarily compensatory rather than penal. Prima facie the appropriate amount that a director is declared to be liable to contribute is the amount by which the company's assets can be discerned to have been depleted by the director's conduct which caused the discretion under s214(1) to arise. But Parliament has indeed chosen very wide words of discretion and it would be undesirable to seek to spell out limits on that discretion, more especially since this is, so far as counsel were aware, the first case to come to judgment under this section. The fact that there was no fraudulent intent is not of itself a reason for fixing the amount at a nominal or low figure, for that would amount to frustrating what I discern as Parliament's intention in adding s214 to s213 in the Insolvency Act 1986, but I am not persuaded that it is right to ignore that fact totally.

I take into account the following factors in addition to those set out above, which give rise to the existence of the court's discretion under s214(1):

1. This was a case of failure to appreciate what should have been clear, rather than a deliberate course of wrongdoing.

2. There were occasions when positive untruths were stated which cannot just be treated as unwarranted optimism. Mr David in particular is given to a flowing turn of phrase. He referred to PMC's continuing to trade as "the ship of state sailing on". That, in itself, is not to be held against him, although it is doubtless a symptom of his inability to see the realities of the current trading position. But when, as happened more than once, a statement of fact was made which was positively untrue, that is to be held against him.

3. The most solemn warning given by the auditor in early February 1987 was effectively ignored. I do not regard Mr Tough's attendance at the bank on 10 February as indicating even tacitly that if the bank agreed to extend facilities it would be proper to carry on trading.

4. Mr David has given a guarantee to the bank with a limit of £50,000. The bank will have a charge over anything which Mr David or Mr Murphy contributes pursuant to my order. Pro tanto that will relieve Mr David from his guarantee liability.

5. The affairs of PMC were conducted during the last seven months of trading in a way which reduced the indebtedness to the bank, to which Mr David had given a guarantee, at the expense of trade creditors and in particular Ramona. The bank is, if not fully, at least substantially secured. If this jurisdiction is to be exercised, as in my judgment it should be in this case, it needs to be exercised in a way which will benefit unsecured creditors.

6. The evidence regarding the disappearance of debtors from the statement of affairs is not entirely clear and there remains in my mind an element of speculation on the extent to which it is right to fix on £22,000 as the amount to be treated as having been overstated in September 1986.

Taking all these circumstances into account I propose to declare that Mr David and Mr Murphy are liable to make a contribution to the assets of PMC of £75,000.

As between the two of them it seems to me right that Mr David should indemnify Mr Murphy as to £50,000 and that above that figure they should be jointly liable. As against the liquidator they should be jointly and severally liable for the whole £75,000. I take this view regarding the indemnity to be given by Mr David partly because Mr David was Mr Murphy's senior in every sense – age, standing in the company and personality – but principally because of the existence of Mr David's guarantee to the bank. Naturally Mr Teverson was not in a position to make submissions to me how matters should be dealt with as between his two clients, and I should be sorry to see the costs, which must already run the risk of eroding the benefits which the section is intended to confer on creditors, further increased.'

Commentary
See also *DKG Contractors Ltd* [1990] BCC 903.

Purpoint Ltd, Re [1991] BCC 121 Chancery Division (Vinelott J)

Section 214 Insolvency Act 1986 – wrongful trading

Facts
The company was an off the shelf company acquired in 1985 by its director Mr Meredith. It carried on a printing business. Mr Meredith and his wife were the only two directors and shareholders. Mr Meredith took responsibility for the customer side of the business and a Mr Froome managed the production side. Mr Meredith admitted that the company was unable to pay its debts as they fell due after December 1986. In May 1987 he was told by the company's accountants of the consequences of trading while insolvent and in June 1987 he took up employment with a firm called Paget Rees Barker ('Pagets') and the company did a substantial amount of printing work for them. The company eventually ceased trading in November 1987 and went into liquidation in May 1988. There were unsecured trade creditors and preferential creditors. The liquidator applied to the court under s212 and the wrongful trading provisions in s214 of the Insolvency Act 1986, that Mr Meredith should make a personal contribution to the assets of the company. The claim under s212 was in respect of cars bought on hire purchase and repossessed and which the liquidator claimed were not needed by the company, sums withdrawn by him in cash and unaccounted for and transactions between the company and Pagets while he was working for the latter.

Held

The director was ordered to pay a total of £12,666.79 under s212, and £53,572.15 under s214.

Vinelott J:

'As I have said, the liquidator seeks orders both under s212 and s214 of the 1986 Act. The claim under s214 gives rise to two difficulties. The first is to determine the date from which Mr Meredith must be taken to have known that there was no reasonable prospect that the company could avoid going into an insolvent liquidation. The second is to determine the amount of the contribution which ought to be made by him, in particular having regard to any amount which he is compelled to pay in the application under s212. It will, I think, be convenient to deal with the s212 claim first.

The s212 claim

This claim is brought under four heads. They relate to:

1. the Nissan Cherry and Nissan Laurel which were brought from the old company or from Mr Froome in October 1986;

2. another car, a Nissan Prairie which was bought new on hire purchase on 6 April 1987;

3. sums withdrawn in cash by Mr Meredith and unaccounted for; and

4. transactions between the company and Pagets in June and July 1987.

As regards (1) the claim first advanced was that the Nissan Cherry appears to have been bought for Mrs Meredith (it was registered in her name), and that there was no justification for providing her with a car. She performed no services for the company. In the course of the hearing it became plain that of the two cars, one, the Nissan Laurel, was bought for the use of Mr Froome, and the other for the use of Mr Meredith who had no other car and needed one for the purpose of the company's business. In the light of this evidence the claim was not pursued. The other car, the Nissan Prairie, was bought new on 6 April 1987 at the cost of £7,833.26. The deposit was £2,500 and the balance was payable with interest by 36 monthly instalments of £221.18. By November, when it was repossessed, the company had paid a total of £4,269.44. Mr Meredith said that when he bought the car he intended to use it for the company's business. The Nissan Cherry had proved too small to carry the loads he sometimes had to transport for the purpose of the company's business. I do not accept that evidence. In my judgment when this car was bought Mr Meredith had already decided to abandon the company and seek employment elsewhere. This car was bought because he thought possession of a new more prestigious car would enhance his prospect of obtaining work elsewhere – in the event with Pagets, who as appears from the letter of 21 April, were not prepared to provide him with a car. The company, in the parlous state it was in, could have struggled on with the Nissan Cherry as before. In my judgment, the purchase of the car was a plain breach of duty by Mr Meredith who is liable to recoup the expenditure. The car was used to some extent for the purposes of the company's business. However, I do not think any allowance should be made in respect of such use; the company still owned the Cherry on which it was paying the hire-purchase instalments and if those payments are allowed no further allowances should be made for the Nissan Prairie.

As to (3), the liquidator has found from the company's records and bank statements that large sums were withdrawn, largely in cash, by Mr Meredith and his wife, which are not accounted for in the company's records. A total of £2,400 was withdrawn before April 1987. However, the liquidator has since satisfied himself that a payment of £2,500 made by Mr Meredith to the company should be treated as repayment of those sums. A further £1,060.93 was withdrawn before 28 May 1987. After 28 May 1987 there were withdrawals totalling £11,482.56. However, the liquidator now accepts Mr Meredith's evidence that sums were withdrawn in cash to meet wages and petty cash expenses to the extent of £6,085.21. That leaves a balance of £5,397.35 unaccounted for and, in my judgment, Mr Meredith is liable to recoup this sum.

(4) The records of the company show that a considerable amount of work was done for Pagets. There are about 30 invoices raised against Pagets. I pause to observe in passing that it is quite clear that there was close contact between Mr Meredith and Pagets during the whole of the company's existence. That must be

borne in mind in evaluating Mr Meredith's claim that an offer of a partnership with Pagets came out of the blue on 20 April 1987. The company went on doing work for Pagets after Mr Meredith had agreed to join them. There are four invoices dated after 20 April. Two are dated 30 April, one 29 May and one 22 June. During the liquidator's enquiries a member of his staff was told by Mr Froome that some of the work covered by the invoices was carried out at a loss to the company – in the case of one invoice at a considerable loss. Mr Froome put the loss on this contract at £11,000. Mr Meredith's evidence was that with one exception the work was costed by Mr Froome and that the contract yielded a profit for the company.

Although I treat Mr Meredith's evidence with considerable reserve, I do not think, on the evidence before the court, it is possible to conclude that (with one exception) the company was paid less than a commercial rate. Mr Froome was not called to give evidence. The exception is the contract on which Mr Froome says the company lost £11,000. Mr Meredith's evidence was that the quotation for this work was a competitive one. Because the company's workforce was unskilled and because the job presented unexpected difficulties there was a great deal of wastage and the quoted price was exceeded. He agreed on behalf of Pagets that the company would charge a price mid-way between the quoted price and the price the company would have charged if the contract had been for a price equal to cost plus its usual profit margin. He claimed that the company covered its cost and made no loss. However he admitted in the course of his oral evidence that the work was done for Pagets in order that Pagets could supply printed material to a client and that Pagets made a profit which he put at £3,000.

In my judgment, on Mr Meredith's own evidence, the transaction was plainly improper. Mr Meredith could not "agree" the price to be paid by Pagets acting both on behalf of Pagets and on behalf of the company. He must accordingly repay to the company an amount equal to the whole profit made by Pagets.

The total of these claims is £12,666.79 (£4,269.44 in respect of the Nissan Prairie, £5,397.35 drawings which are not accounted for, and £3,000 in respect of the work done for Pagets).

Section 214

The first question is as to the date when Mr Meredith ought to have known that there was no reasonable prospect that the company could avoid going into insolvent liquidation. The latest date is 28 May 1987 when Mr Meredith was warned by Adamsons that if the company continued to trade he might be personally liable for its debts. Nothing that happened thereafter would have given any reasonable director ground for hoping that the company could avoid an insolvent liquidation.

I have felt some doubt whether a reasonably prudent director would have allowed the company to commence trading at all. It had no capital base. Its only assets were purchased by bank borrowing or acquired by hire purchase. And its working capital was contributed by a loan from Mr Froome. The business it inherited from Winnersh Printing Services Ltd had proved unprofitable and with the winding-up of that company the creditors, other than the Royal Bank of Scotland, were left with an empty shell. The new company assumed the additional burden of paying a salary to Mr Meredith. However, I do not think it would be right to conclude that Mr Meredith ought to have known that the company was doomed to end in an insolvent winding-up from the moment it started to trade. That would, I think, impose too high a test. Mr Meredith believed that his connections in the advertising and publicity field would enable him to introduce new business and that the failure of the old company had been due not to any want of skill or organising ability on Mr Froome's part, but on his inability to attract custom. I cannot say that was a belief that could not have been entertained by a reasonable and prudent director conscious of his duty to persons to whom the company would incur liabilities in the ordinary course of carrying on its business.

On the other hand, in my judgment, it should have been plain to Mr Meredith by the end of 1986 that the company could not avoid going into insolvent liquidation. The company could not meet its trade debts as they fell due. In addition it owed very large Crown debts and it had no prospect whatever that it could turn its trading into profit sufficiently quickly to pay them off. The difficulty is that it is impossible, because of Mr Meredith's total failure to ensure that proper records were kept and that proper cash flow calculations and net worth calculations were made, to ascertain the precise extent of the company's net liabilities at the end of 1986 or the extent to which the net liabilities were increased by the continuance of the company's trading after the end of 1986.

I think the only solution to this difficulty is to quantify the loss caused by the continuation of trading after the end of 1986 by aggregating the debts owed to creditors incurred after 1 January 1987 and unpaid when the company ceased trading and the amount of the Crown debts incurred after 1 January 1987. Neither of these figures can be precisely ascertained at present. The liquidator has prepared a list of creditors whose debts were incurred after 28 May 1987 and which remained unpaid when the company ceased to trade; this amounts to £13,407.18. But there may be other debts similarly incurred between 1 January 1987 and 28 May 1987 and unpaid when the company ceased to trade. The liquidator has calculated that the PAYE and NIC debts increased after 1 January 1987 by £20,588.51. That is calculating by grossing up the wages paid and money withdrawn by Mr Meredith (treated as remuneration) by 40.5 per cent and treating the amount added as a Crown debt. However, if Mr Meredith has to repay £5,397.35 for his drawings no PAYE or NIC will be payable on that sum. Moreover, the Revenue have not yet quantified their claim and there may be arrears of VAT.

In these circumstances the only course I can take is to stand over this application so that these figures can be calculated and, if possible, agreed with the Revenue. The application will have to be restored briefly so that the figures can be determined by the court and incorporated in the order.

One matter that has troubled me is whether there may not be a degree of overlap or "double counting" if Mr Meredith is called on to pay £12,666.79 in the s212 claim and a further sum in the s214 claim. If £12,666.79 is restored to the company will this not increase the money available to meet liabilities incurred after 1 January 1987 and so decrease the loss to creditors, including the Crown, resulting from Mr Meredith's failure to cease trading not later than 1 January 1987?

I think the answer to this apparent injustice is that if the moneys had not been improperly extracted by Mr Meredith and if the company had not continued to increase its liabilities by trading after 1 January 1987 it would have been in a better position to meet the claims of creditors, including the Crown, whose debts were incurred before 1 January 1987. The liquidator has calculated that the Crown debts alone amounted at 1 January 1987 to almost £20,000. However, it would be unjust to require Mr Meredith to recoup in the s212 application more than is needed to meet the liabilities of the company, other than the debt due to Mr Froome and the bank overdraft which Mr Meredith has been compelled to meet, as at 1 January 1987. When the matter is restored I shall want to be satisfied on this point also.

Mr Craig, who appeared for the liquidator, submitted that Mr Meredith ought to be ordered to pay all the company's creditors and the costs of the liquidation because that is the only way in which creditors whose debts were incurred after Mr Meredith knew or ought to have known that the company was bound to go into insolvent liquidation, can be paid in full. I think that submission is ill-founded. The court, in making an order under s214, is concerned to ensure that any depletion in the assets of the company attributable to the period after the moment when the directors knew or ought to have known that there was no reasonable prospect of avoiding an insolvent winding-up – in effect, while the company's business was being carried on at the risk of creditors – is made good: see *Re Produce Marketing Consortium Ltd* (1989) 5 BCC 569 per Knox J at p597G. The purpose is to recoup the loss to the company so as to benefit the creditors as a whole. The court has no jurisdiction to direct payment to creditors or to direct that moneys paid to the company should be applied in payment of one class of creditors in preference to another. Moreover, creditors whose debts are incurred after the critical date in fact have no stronger claim than those whose debts were incurred before that date. The former class also suffers to the extent that the assets of the company are depleted by wrongful trading.

I do not think it makes any difference in the instant case that some creditors may have afforded credit to the company in reliance on an assurance by Mr Meredith that their debts would be paid and that he would remortgage his house to enable the company to pay them – an assurance which Mr Meredith admitted having given at the meeting of creditors on 25 May 1988. Anybody who gives credit to a company does so in the belief that the company will be in a position to pay its debts when they fall due for payment. Whether these creditors could found a claim against Mr Meredith personally is not a matter on which I am entitled to express an opinion in proceedings by the liquidator under s214.

In addition to the repayment of these sums there must also be a declaration that Mr Meredith's claims against the company in respect of liabilities of the company met by him rank after other creditors.'

Sarflax Ltd, Re [1979] Ch 592 Chancery Division (Oliver J)

Section 213 of the Insolvency Act 1986 – fraudulent trading

Facts

Sarflax was in the business of making machine tools. In 1966 it sold a press to an Italian lock making company. This did not work satisfactorily and the Italian company rescinded the contract. In 1970 the Italian company brought proceedings in the English courts claiming damages but these proceedings were allowed to lapse. In January 1971, pursuant to a resolution, Sarflax ceased to trade as from the close of business on 30 April 1971. Sarflax's assets were sold to its parent company at a price equal to their book value with such price being set off pro tanto against a debt due to the parent company. The remainder of Sarflax's assets were got in over the next two years and applied in discharging Sarflax's other debts but without any acount being taken of the pending claim of the Italian company. In October 1971 the Italian company commenced proceedings in the Italian courts and obtained judgment against Sarflax for £86,000 in November 1973. Meanwhile, in September 1973 Sarflax went into voluntary liquidation. The liquidator admitted proof of the Italian company's judgment debt and applied, inter alia, for a declaration under s332 CA 1948 (now s213 IA 1986) that Sarflax's business had been carried on between January 1971 and September 1973 with intent to defraud creditors. The claim alleged Sarflax could not pay its debts in full but nevertheless caused its assets to be distributed among its creditors with the intent that they should be preferred to the Italian company.

Held

The mere preference of one creditor over another did not amount to an 'intent to defraud' creditors within s332(1) even where a debtor realised he did not have suffcient assets to pay all his creditors in full.

Oliver J:

'... On the face of it counsel's proposition for the liquidator appears both novel and bold. It involves this: that a debtor who reasonably suspects that the value of the assets likely to be available to him is exceeded by the amount of his liabilities must, in effect, suspend payment to all his creditors until the full amount of his liabilities is ascertained or risk a charge of fraud. None of the authorities to which I have been referred give any support to such a proposition and, indeed, the very words of s44 of the Bankruptcy Act 1914 appear to be to militate against it ...'

... Counsel for the liquidator seeks to escape from this by suggesting that there are two types of preference, those which are innocent because the debtor does not necessarily know that the effect will be to defeat other creditors, and those which are fraudulent, where the debtor is aware that the necessary effect of paying one creditor is going to be that another goes short ...'

... I do not think that I can accept that. A preference by definition seems to me to be the payment of one creditor to the exclusion, in whole or in part, of another and it postulates, in its very nature, a deficiency of assets to pay all creditors. A payment "with intent to prefer" or with a view to prefer necessarily, therefore, presupposes a knowledge on the payer that his assets are insufficient to pay all, so that the actual fraudulent intent which counsel for the liquidator ascribes to some of the preferential payments to which the section refers must apply in fact, by definitiion, to all such payments. And if it is in fact fraud intentionally to pay A to the detriment of B, why was it thought necessary to "deem" such payments to be fraudulent ...'

Sherborne Associates Ltd, Re [1995] BCC 40 Bristol District Registry (Mercantile List) (His Honour Judge Jack QC, sitting as an additional High Court judge)

Section 214 Insolvency Act 1986 – wrongful trading – refusal to find non-executive directors liable

Facts

This case was an application by the liquidator of the company for an order that its three non-executive directors, S, I and E, make a contribution to the assets of the company pursuant to s214 IA 1986. The company's business was that of an advertising agency and it was formed in January 1987 with a paid up share capital of £36,000. By early December 1988 the three directors had resigned, and the company was put into liquidation in February 1989 with debts of £178,788.

Board meetings during 1987 illustrated the financial position of the company. At the first board meeting in February, a business plan suggested a required turnover of £450,000 for year ending December 1987. In addition an overdraft of £50,000 was agreed with the bank. At the meeting in March, S stated a turnover of £500,000 was now required to break even and in April the first reference to delaying payments to creditors was made.

At the July meeting, the board was informed that a loss of £27,636 was incurred on first five months trading which S thought 'was a creditable performance'. A turnover of £565,000 was now required to break even. Further losses were considered at the September meeting at which S gave the company until Christmas 'to put things right'. Debtors were now at £25,000 while creditors stood at £45,000.

By the end of September, the company's assets exceeded its liabilities. October, November and December saw further losses and the turnover at the year end was £350,000, a long way short of the forecast.

Two board meetings were held on 22 and 30 January 1988. It was on these dates that the liquidator claimed the directors ought to have concluded that there was no prospect of avoiding liquidation. At the first meeting, S closely examined the three appointed executive directors about their new business prospects and each gave optimistic figures. He also proposed that the company cease trading at the end of February. [The judge found that S did not really mean this and only said it to put pressure on the non-executive directors to drum up new business].The purpose of the second meeting was to decide if the company should cease trading. The net indebtedness was now £78,000. The board went on to approve revised sales forecasts given by the three executive directors, amounting to £1m. Weekly management meetings were agreed to be held with S acting as chief executive. Sherborne continued to trade. The liquidator claimed that these forecasts were wholly unrealistic and that they should not have been accepted.

The company's financial decline continued, despite the recruitment of new people. The figures for the first three months of 1988 showed a loss of £24,859 against a forecast of £7,045. S has a heart attack in may 1988. Despite an encouraging sign in April the results for the first six months of 1988 all showed a loss. The bank then declined to support Sherborne further, although further support was in fact provided by another bank, based on an increase in the company's share capital and the giving of guarantees.

After yet further losses were incurred, at a board meeting in December 1988, I and S resigned and E followed shortly afterwards.

Held

The claim for wrongful trading failed.

1. A wrongful trading claim under s214 IA 1986 survived the death of a director. The claim could therefore be pursued against the personal representatives of S. after his death in 1992.
2. The liquidators claim that I, S and E ought to have realised that there was no reasonable prospect of

avoiding liquidation on the two selected dates of 22 and 30 January 1988 failed. Furthermore, it was not open for the liquidator, or the court, to make such a finding based on alternative selected dates which were not specifically pleaded by the liquidator.

3. S was entitled to conclude, in January 1988, that there was a prospect that the company could achieve a turnaround and make a profit. It was 'a reasonable and not a fanciful prospect'.

His Honour Judge Jack QC:

'The outcome is that I am not satisfied that in January 1988 Mr Squire ought to have concluded that there was no reasonable prospect that Sherborne would avoid going into insolvent liquidation. I am not satisfied that he was not entitled to conclude that there was a prospect for the company achieving the turnaround into profit, which was a reasonable rather than a fanciful prospect. It did not need to make the forecast profit of £55,600 to survive, something better than even would probably have done.

The liquidator's case against Sir Charles Irving and Mr Ellwood must also fail. They were in no better position than Mr Squire to conclude whether the company had reasonable prospects of success and indeed were in a rather worse position. The case having failed against him, the central figure, it must fail also against them. Had I concluded that the case against Mr Squire succeeded, I would have had to consider the difficult question of the extent to which, in such circumstances, they were entitled to say that they looked to and relied on Mr Squire. I do accept that these two non-executive directors were entitled to place reliance on the highly experienced chairman who had far the greater involvement with the company and the figures. In particular it was he who had the discussions with the executive directors between the two January board meetings. In my view, where in circumstances such as here, one director seeks to rely on another, the other director's view or conclusion is a matter to be taken into account with the other matters which the director should be taking into account as required by s214(4). I would here have had to conduct a balancing exercise between the facts which I am presuming for this purpose pointed one way and the conclusion by Mr Squire of the opposite. This is an exercise which can only be done on the basis of actual findings.

I was referred to three decisions on s214 which I have not so far mentioned. They are: *Re Produce Marketing Consortium Ltd* (1989) 5 BCC 569, *Re Purpoint Ltd* [1991] BCC 121 and *Re DKC Contractors Ltd* [1990] BCC 903. In each the liquidator was successful. I will not prolong this judgment by summarising the facts in those cases. It is enough to say that there were in each features which made the conduct of the directors plainly irresponsible as well as other matters which can be used to distinguish them from the present case.'

Commentary

This is a disappointing decision on wrongful trading. All three directors, in contrast to some of the earlier cases on wrongful trading, were experienced businessmen, albeit in different fields. The company had never made a profit and none of the sales forecasts were ever achieved. The judgment itself analyses in detail, whether or not a claim for wrongful trading can survive the death of a director and there is an in-depth analysis of the authorities. The existing case law on wrongful trading, however, is dismissed in a single, final, paragraph of the judgment and is distinguished on the basis that in those cases the directors were 'plainly irresponsible'.

William C Leitch Bros Ltd (No 1), Re [1932] 2 Ch 71 Chancery Division (Maugham J)

Section 213 of the Insolvency Act – fraudulent trading

Facts

In 1927 Leitch sold his business to the company for £5,000 with this sum being satisfied by an allotment of 1,000 £1 fully paid shares and a debenture for £4,000 at 6 per cent pa interest. The business involved the manufacture of perambulators and furniture. Between 1927 and 1930 the business suffered heavy losses and by March 1930 it could not pay its debts as they fell due. At that time the company owed £6,500 for goods and had no means of paying but Leitch ordered some £6,000 of goods and these became subject to the debenture held by him. Creditors of the company issued writs in April and May 1930 and this prompted Leitch to appoint a receiver under his debenture. The receiver appointed Leitch as his manager but he removed goods from the company's shops to other shops and used their proceeds of sale to keep down the interest on his debentures. He was dismissed from this position. In June 1930 an order was made for the compulsory winding-up of the company. The liquidator sought a declaration as to whether Leitch was, in the circumstances, liable for faudulent trading. He was held liable.

Maugham J:

'The conclusion of fact to which I am bound to come is that, at any rate, from 1 March 1930 the company was carrying on business with intent to defraud creditors, to the knowledge, and, indeed, under the direction of the respondent. That leads me to the question of the true construction of s213 Insolvency Act 1986, a question of great difficulty. In my opinion, I must hold with regard to the meaning of the phrase carrying on business "with intent to defraud creditors" that, if a company continues to carry on business and to incur debts at a time when there is, to the knowledge of the directors, no reasonable prospect of the creditors ever receiving payment of those debts, it is in general a proper inference that the company is carrying on business with intent to defraud. As I have intimated, I am satisfied that the respondent knew what the position was from 1 March, 1930; and I hold further, that the respondent deliberately went on trading in the name of the company in order, as he hoped, to safeguard his own position, and without any regard to the interests of the creditors ...'

Preferences and transactions at an undervalue

DKG Contractors Ltd, Re [1990] BCC 903 Chancery Division (John Weeks QC)

Section 214 IA 1986 wrongful trading – s239 IA 1986 preferences – s727 CA 1986 excusing directors when they have acted honestly and reasonably

Facts

The company was formed in March 1986 and went into liquidation in December 1988. Mr and Mrs Gibbons were the only directors and shareholders. The company carried on a business as groundwork subcontractors. No accounts were ever prepared, the company did not have a bank account until 1988 and no annual general meeting was ever held. The creditors were owed £223,871. Between May and November 1988 at least 16 creditors obtained judgments against the company and it was admitted that in the last ten months before liquidation, some £417,763 of the company's money had found its way into Mr Gibbons' hands. Until the company was formed Mr Gibbons was a self employed groundwork contractor and formed the company on his accountants' advice that it would be favourable for tax reasons. However when the company was formed it did not take over his contracts. Instead, he continued to employ men on site and use his own equipment and then invoice the company for these costs. In this way he also became the company's main creditor. The liquidator claimed to recover the £417,763 on the grounds that firstly, it was in breach of his fiduciary duties. Secondly, that it was a wrongful preference within s239 IA and thirdly, that the directors were guilty of wrongful trading under s214 IA. In their defence they claimed that the money was paid to Mr Gibbons to reimburse him for labour, plant and materials supplied to the company. They denied the wrongful preference and wrongful trading allegations and also pleaded to be excused under s727 CA, as they had acted honestly and reasonably.

Held

They were ordered to repay the £417,763 under s212 IA as this was paid in breach of duty. They were also ordered to make a contribution under s214. Mr Gibbons was additionally ordered to pay the same amount under s239. (Payments under s212 and s239 were taken to satisfy the order made under s214).

John Weeks QC:

'I now turn to the law on directors' duties. I start with the proposition that a director is a fiduciary and, as such, unable to contract personally with his company. The articles may authorise such contracts and usually they may make specific provision for remuneration to be paid to directors. It is not suggested that the company's articles authorise any such contract as Mr Gibbons is seeking to uphold in the present case. A fiduciary is entitled to be reimbursed for moneys spent by him on his principal's behalf.

With limited exceptions, this is not what occurred in the present case. Mr Gibbons was not paying men employed by the company. He was paying his own men and using his own machines, and charging the company for his services at rates which he regarded as at least sufficient to cover his own costs. It is argued that the payments can be justified because Mr and Mrs Gibbons were effectively the only shareholders and the beneficial owners of the company.

In *Aveling Barfold Ltd* v *Perion Ltd* (1989) 5 BCC 677 at p682A, Hoffmann J referred to the general rule that any act which falls within the powers of a company, whether or not a breach of duty on the part of the directors, is binding on the company if it is approved by all the shareholders. He went on to explain the limits to the rule. One of them is that creditors are entitled to have the company assets kept intact. Another is that the rule does not extend to cases involving a fraud on creditors.

In my judgment, the system operated in the present case falls within both exceptions to the rule. The company's assets were not preserved for general creditors. The method of operating, particularly at a time when the company was of doubtful solvency, meant that the general creditors were competing on unfair terms with one creditor, who was always likely to be paid ahead of the rest. I therefore conclude that it was a breach of the directors' duties to make the payments to Mr Gibbons in 1988 which totalled £417,763.

I now turn to s212. The section applies if, in the course of winding up, it appears that a person who is or has been a director of the company has misapplied or retained or has become accountable for any money of the company. I am satisfied that Mr and Mrs Gibbons have misapplied £417,763 and accordingly have become accountable for that sum to the company. In subs (3), I have power to compel them to repay, restore or account for the money with interest at such rate as seems just. I propose to exercise that jurisdiction and make an order for repayment of £417,763. I will hear submissions as to interest if the liquidator thinks it worthwhile to make them.

I reach this conclusion with little sympathy for Mr Gibbons. At the outset he was given no information as to his duties as a director but he made no attempt to find out what they might be, and when the going became difficult in April 1988, he sought to pass all responsibility to his wife. I feel more sympathy with Mrs Gibbons, who struggled to keep the books with no outside assistance. However, I feel most sympathy for the many unpaid trade creditors who extended credit to this company in innocence. It would not be fair to them if I did not exercise the discretion to order repayment in full.

In case I should be wrong in any respect under s212, I now turn to consider s239 …

… I have been assisted by the judgment of Millet J in *Re MC Bacon Ltd* [1990] BCC 78. At p87C the judge refers to the previous law which was contained in s44 of the Bankruptcy Act 1914, and continues:

"Section 44(1) has been replaced and its language has been entirely recast. Every single word of significance, whether in the form of statutory definition or in its judicial exposition, has been jettisoned. 'View', 'dominant', 'intention' and even 'to prefer' have all be discarded. These are replaced by 'influenced', 'desire', and 'to produce in relation to that person the effect mentioned in subs (4)(b)'.

I therefore emphatically protest against the citation of cases decided under the old law. They cannot be of any assistance when the language of the statute has been so completely and deliberately changed. It may be that many of the cases which will come before the courts in future will be decided in the same way that they would have been decided under the old law. That may be so, but the grounds of decision will be different. What the court has to do is to interpret the language of the statute and apply it. It will no longer enquire whether there was 'a dominant intention to prefer' the creditor, but whether the company's decision was 'influenced by a desire to produce ... the effect mentioned in subs (4)(b)'.

This is a completely different test. It involves at least two radical departures from the old law. It is no longer necessary to establish a dominant intention to prefer. It is sufficient that the decision was influenced by the requisite desire. That is the first change. The second is that it is no longer sufficient to establish an intention to prefer. There must be a desire to produce the effect mentioned in the subsection.

This second change is made necessary by the first, for without it it would be virtually impossible to uphold the validity of a security taken in exchange for the injection of fresh funds into a company in financial difficulties. A man is taken to intend the necessary consequences of his actions, so that an intention to grant a security to a creditor necessarily involves an intention to prefer that creditor in the event of insolvency. The need to establish that such intention was dominant was essential under the old law to prevent perfectly proper transactions from being struck down. With the abolition of that requirement intention could not remain the relevant test. Desire had been substituted. That is a very different matter. Intention is objective, desire is subjective. A man can choose the lesser of two evils without desiring either.

It is not, however, sufficient to establish a desire to make the payment or grant the security which it is ought to avoid. There must have been a desire to produce the effect mentioned in the subsection, that is to say, to improve the creditor's position in the event of an insolvent liquidation. A man is not to be taken as *desiring* all necessary consequences of his actions. Some consequences may be of advantage to him and be desired by him; others may not affect him and be matters of indifference to him; while still others may be positively disadvantageous to him and not be desired by him, but be regarded by him as the unavoidable price of obtaining the desired advantages. It will still be possible to provide assistance to a company in financial difficulties provided the company is actuated only by proper commercial considerations. Under the new regime a transaction will not be set aside as a voidable preference unless the company positively wished to improve the creditor's position in the event of its own insolvent liquidation.

There is of course no need for there to be direct evidence of the requisite desire. Its existence may be inferred from the circumstances of the case just as the dominant intention could be inferred under the old law. But the mere presence of the requisite desire will not be sufficient by itself. It must have influenced the decision to enter into the transaction. It was submitted on behalf of the bank that it must have been the factor which 'tipped the scales'. I disagree. That is not what subs (5) says; it requires only that the desire should have influenced the decision. That requirement is satisfied if it was one of the factors which operated on the minds of those who made the decision. In my judgment, it is not necessary to prove that, if the requisite desire had not been present, the company would not have entered into the transaction. That would be too high a test."

The question for me, therefore, is whether it has been shown that in making the payments to Mr Gibbons between February and November 1988, the company was not influenced by a desire to put Mr Gibbons in a better position than he would have been in otherwise. The payments until the end of August may well have been influenced by commercial considerations such as the advantages of completing rather than abandoning the contracts. It is, however, impossible to make out any such case for the payments in October and November which in my judgment were inspired solely by a desire to improve Mr Gibbons' position in the event of a liquidation. I infer from those payments that this desire was one of the factors which influenced the earlier payments and, applying Millet J's test, that I find, is sufficient ...

... Mr Gibbons is a connected person and all the relevant payments were made within the two-year period. The time, however, is a relevant time only if the company was at that time unable to pay its debt within the meaning of s123 of the Act. The test here is not balance sheet solvency, but whether the company was able to meet its debts on a day to day basis as they fell due. From the beginning of February, there were unpaid invoices and, in accordance with the Court of Appeal decision in *Re Taylor's Industrial Flooring Ltd* [1990] BCC 44, this is evidence from which I can infer insolvency. Further, Mr Broomfield has given evidence, which I accept, that in February 1988, Mr Gibbons told him that the company had a cash flow crisis and asked him to prepare a schedule of outstanding moneys. They both then went to Keir Moss's surveyor and negotiated a reduction in the retention moneys. They also went to Wilcon and obtained an accelerated payment for the company. I therefore hold that as early as 8 February 1988 the company was unable to pay its debts as they fell due and consequently all the payments to Mr Gibbons were made at a relevant time for the purposes of s239. Under subs (2) the court is directed to make such order as it thinks fit for restoring the position to what it would have been if the company had not given the preference. Accordingly, I propose to make an order that Mr Gibbons pay the sum of £417,763 to the liquidator. Again I will hear any submissions that may be made as to interest.

I now turn to s214 ...

This section was introduced in 1985 as an alternative remedy to fraudulent trading. It carries no criminal sanction and directors are judged not only by their own knowledge and skill and experience, but also by the knowledge, skill and experience that directors in their position could reasonably be expected to have. Patently, Mr and Mrs Gibbons own knowledge, skill and experience were hopelessly inadequate for the task they undertook. That is not sufficient to protect them. It is not argued that subs (3) applies. The only question that arises is whether Mr or Mrs Gibbons knew or ought to have concluded that there was no reasonable prospect that the company would avoid going into insolvent liquidation and, if so, when.

It is argued that the turning point occurred at the end of July when Mr Broomfield and Mr McGarvie left the company and the company was unable to employ any further quantity surveyor to supervise the collection of moneys due to the company. In my judgment, the turning point came earlier. It is admitted that Mrs Gibbons was aware of pressing creditors in April and Mr Knight's first visit to her occurred in May. In April, Mr Gibbons himself became aware of a supplier refusing to make further deliveries to the company and consequently had a row with his wife. It is said that Mrs Gibbons relied on Mr Broomfield's assurances that money would come in, and certainly the money that was eventually received fell well short of the prices which were fixed for the various contracts. Mr Broomfield's job, however, was only to supervise the income. He was never shown the black book or told the state of the company's finances. In my judgment, the warning signs were such that by the end of April the directors should have instituted some form of financial control. If they had done, they would, in my judgment, have concluded then that there was no reasonable prospect of avoiding liquidation. If one applies the standards required by subs (4)(a), therefore, the directors are liable in respect of trading after 31 April. Under subs (1) I have jurisdiction to declare that the directors are to be liable to make such contribution, if any, to the company's assets as I think proper. I therefore propose to make a declaration that the directors are liable, jointly and severally, to make a contribution equal to the amount of the trade debts incurred by the company on or after 1 May 1988. This is not in addition to the orders made under ss212 and 239, and payments under the orders made under those sections are to be taken as satisfying the order under s214 as well.

Finally, I need to consider s727 of the Companies Act 1985. That section provides, so far as material:

"(1) If in any proceedings for negligence, default, breach of duty or breach of trust against an officer of a company ... it appears to the court hearing the case that that officer ... is or may be liable in respect of the negligence, default, breach of duty or breach of trust, but that he has acted honestly and reasonably, and that having regard to all the circumstances of the case (including those connected with his appointment) he ought fairly to be excused for the negligence, default, breach of duty or breach of trust, that could may relieve him, either wholly or partly, from his liability on such terms as it thinks fit."

In my judgment, neither Mr nor Mrs Gibbons acted dishonestly. Neither of them had any knowledge of company law or of the concept of limited liability. Mrs Gibbons did not know to what extent she might be liable for the company's debts. I do not think that they deliberately traded in the manner in which they did in order to avoid personal liability. However, I do not think that they acted reasonably. Before trading in the manner in which they did, they ought to have sought some advice at least, and I think it is significant that the only offer of advice which was made to them was not taken up.

Mr Parker said that he offered to show Mrs Gibbons what books were required for company trading. Mr and Mrs Gibbons, however, chose to trade in a way in which Mr Gibbons has had the lion's share of the company's money, and the outside creditors have been left unpaid. For the same reason, I do not think they ought to be excused and I do not propose to apply s727 of the Companies Act.'

M C Bacon Ltd, Re [1990] BCC 78 Chancery Division (Millet J)

Granting of a debenture – setting aside as a preference – setting aside as a transaction at an undervalue

Facts

This case concerned an application by the liquidator of the company to have a debenture set aside as a preference under s239 Insolvency Act 1986 or as a transaction at an undervalue under s238 Insolvency Act 1986. Until 1986 the company traded profitably but then lost its major customer. In August 1987 it went into creditors' voluntary liquidation at a time when its overdraft with the bank was £235,530. This was secured by a debenture granted in May 1987 at a time when the company could not survive without the overdraft facility. The liquidator claimed that the company was influenced by a desire to improve the bank's position as a creditor in insolvency under s239 Insolvency Act 1986, or alternatively that the granting of the debenture was a transaction at an undervalue within s238(4)(b).

Held

The liquidator's application was unsuccessful. The preference claim failed because the company's directors were not motivated by a desire to improve the position of the bank in the event of insolvency, but by a desire to stay in business which they could not do without the bank's support. The claim that the debenture amounted to a transaction at an undervalue failed because the granting of security over a company's assets does not deplete or diminish their value. What it does do is deprive the company of the ability to apply the proceeds of the assets otherwise than in satisfaction of the secured debt, but this is not capable of monetary valuation.

Millett J:

'11. *Voidable preference*

The Law

Section 239 of the Act provides, so far as material:

"(4) For the purposes of this section and s241, a company gives a preference to a person if –
(a) that person is one of the company's creditors or a surety or guarantor for any of the company's debts or other liabilities, and
(b) the company does anything or suffers anything to be done which (in either case) has the effect of putting that person into a position which, in the event of the company going into insolvent liquidation, will be better than the position he would have been in if that thing had not been done.
(5) The court shall not make an order under this section in respect of a preference given to any person unless the company which gave the preference was influenced in deciding to give it by a desire to produce in relation to that person the effect mentioned in subs (4)(b)."

So far as I am aware, this is the first case under the section and its meaning has been the subject of some debate before me. I shall therefore attempt to provide some guidance.

The section replaces s44(1) of the Bankruptcy Act 1914, which in certain circumstances deemed fraudulent and avoided payments made and other transactions entered into in favour of a creditor "with a view of giving such creditor ... a preference over the other creditors". Section 44(1) and its predecessors had been construed by the courts as requiring the person seeking to avoid the payment or other transaction to establish that it had been made "with the dominant intention to prefer" the creditor.

Section 44(1) has been replaced and its language has been entirely recast. Every single word of significance, whether in the form of statutory definition or in its judicial exposition, has been jettisoned. "View", "dominant", "intention" and even "to prefer" have all been discarded. These are replaced by "influenced", "desire" and "to produce in relation to that person the effect mentioned in subs (4)(b)".

I therefore emphatically protest against the citation of cases decided under the old law. They cannot be of any assistance when the language of the statute has been so completely and deliberately changed. It may be that many of the cases which will come before the courts in future will be decided in the same way that they would have been decided under the old law. That may be so, but the grounds of decision will be different. What the court has to do is to interpret the language of the statute and apply it. It will no longer enquire whether there was "a dominant intention to prefer" the creditor, but whether the company's decision was "influenced by a desire to produce ... the effect mentioned in subs (4)(b)".

This is a completely different test. It involves at least two radical departures from the old law. It is no longer necessary to establish a *dominant* intention to prefer. It is sufficient that the decision was *influenced* by the requisite desire. That is the first change. The second is that it is no longer sufficient to establish an *intention* to prefer. There must be a *desire* to produce the effect mentioned in the subsection.

This second change is made necessary by the first, for without it it would be virtually impossible to uphold the validity of a security taken in exchange for the injection of fresh funds into a company in financial difficulties. A man is taken to intend the necessary consequences of his actions, so that an intention to grant a security to a creditor necessarily involves an intention to prefer that creditor in the event of insolvency. The need to establish that such intention was dominant was essential under the old law to prevent perfectly proper transactions from being struck down. With the abolition of that requirement intention could not remain the relevant test. Desire has been substituted. That is a very different matter. Intention is objective, desire is subjective. A man can choose the lesser of two evils without desiring either.

It is not, however, sufficient to establish a desire to make the payment or grant the security which it is sought to avoid. There must have been a desire to produce the effect mentioned in the subsection, that is to say, to improve the creditor's position in the event of an insolvent liquidation. A man is not to be taken as *desiring* all the necessary consequences of his actions. Some consequences may be of advantage to him and be desired by him; others may not affect him and be matters of indifference to him; while still others may be positively disadvantageous to him and not be desired by him, but be regarded by him as the unavoidable price of obtaining the desired advantages. It will still be possible to provide assistance to a company in financial difficulties provided that the company is actuated only by proper commercial considerations. Under the new regime a transaction will not be set aside as a voidable preference unless the company positively wished to improve the creditor's position in the event of its own insolvent liquidation.

There is, of course, no need for there to be direct evidence of the requisite desire. Its existence may be inferred from the circumstances of the case just as the dominant intention could be inferred under the old law. But the mere presence of the requisite desire will not be sufficient by itself. It must have influenced the decision to enter into the transaction. It was submitted on behalf of the bank that it must have been the factor which "tipped the scales". I disagree. That is not what subs (5) says; it requires only that the desire should have influenced the decision. That requirement is satisfied if it was one of the factors which operated on the minds of those who made the decision. It need not have been the only factor or even the decisive one. In my judgment, it is not necessary to prove that, if the requisite desire had not been present, the company would not have entered into the transaction. That would be too high a test.

It was also submitted that the relevant time was the time when the debenture was created. That cannot be right. The relevant time was the time when the decision to grant it was made. In the present case that is not known with certainty. It was probably some time between 15 April and 20 May, although as early as 3 April Mr Glover and Mr Creal had resigned themselves to its inevitability. But it does not matter. If the requisite desire was operating at all, it was operating throughout.'

[After examining the evidence his Lordship ruled that the granting of the debenture to the bank did not constitute a preference]

'III Transaction at an undervalue
Section 238 of the Act is concerned with the depletion of a company's assets by transactions at an undervalue. Section 238(4) of the Act defines a transaction at an undervalue as follows:

"For the purposes of this section and s241, a company enters into a transaction with a person at an undervalue if –
(a) the company makes a gift to that person or otherwise enters into a transaction with that person on terms that provide for the company to receive no consideration, or
(b) the company enters into a transaction with that person for a consideration the value of which, in money or money's worth, is significantly less than the value, in money or money's worth, of the consideration provided by the company."

The granting of the debenture was not a gift, nor was it without consideration. The consideration consisted of the bank's forbearance from calling in the overdraft and its honouring of cheques and making of fresh advances to the company during the continuance of the facility. The applicant relies therefore on paragraph (b).

To come within that paragraph the transaction must be:

1. entered into by the company;

2. for a consideration;

3. the value of which measured in money or money's worth;

4. is significantly less than the value;

5. also measured in money or money's worth;

6. of the consideration provided by the company.

It requires a comparision to be made between the value obtained by the company for the transaction and the value of consideration provided by the company. Both values must be measurable in money or money's worth and both must be considered from the company's point of view.

In my judgment, the applicant's claim to characterise the granting of the bank's debenture as a transaction at an undervalue is misconceived. The mere creation of a security over a company's assets does not deplete them and does not come within the paragraph. By charging its assets the company appropriates them to meet the liabilities due to the secured creditor and adversely affects the rights of other creditors in the event of insolvency. But it does not deplete its assets or diminish their value. It retains the right to redeem and the right to sell or remortgage the charged assets. All it loses is the ability to apply the proceeds otherwise than in satisfaction of the secured debt. That is not something capable of valuation in monetary terms and is not customarily disposed of for value.

In the present case the company did not suffer that loss by reason of the grant of the debenture. Once the bank had demanded a debenture the company could not have sold or charged its assets without applying the proceeds in reduction of the overdraft; had it attempted to do so, the bank would at once have called in the overdraft. By granting the debenture the company parted with nothing of value, and the value of the consideration which it received in return was incapable of being measured in money or money's worth.

Mr Vos submitted that the consideration which the company received was, with hindsight, of no value. It merely gained time and with it the opportunity to lose more money. But he could not and did not claim that the company ought to have received a fee or other capital sum in return for the debenture. That gives the game away. The applicant's real complaint is not that the company entered into the transaction at an undervalue but that it entered into it at all.

In my judgment, the transaction does not fall within subs (4), and it is unnecessary to consider the application of subs (5) which provides a defence to the claim in certain circumstances.

IV Conclusion:
In my judgment, the granting of the debenture to the bank was neither a void preference nor a transaction at an undervalue and I dismiss the application.

Examinations and assistance under ss235 and 236 of the Insolvency Act 1986

Arrows Ltd (No 4), Re [1994] BCC 641 House of Lords (Lords Keith, Jauncey, Browne-Wilkinson, Lloyd and Nolan)

Insolvency – whether liquidators should supply transcripts of private examination under s236 Insolvency Act 1986 to the Serious Fraud Office

Facts

N was a director and principal shareholder in the company when it went into liquidation. He was examined by the liquidators under s236 Insolvency Act 1986 and the Serious Fraud Office (SFO), under s2(3) of the Criminal Justice Act 1987, asked the liquidators to hand over the transcripts of the examination. The SFO wanted to consider them in order that they might be used in criminal proceedings against N. The trial judge ordered that they should not be handed over, unless the SFO give an undertaking that they would not be used in evidence in criminal proceedings. This decision was reversed by the Court of Appeal and N now appealed to the House of Lords.

Held

N's appeal was dismissed.

1. A judge at first instance, in the companies court, does have a discretion to refuse to permit the liquidators to hand over the transcripts to the SFO, subject to the SFO giving an undertaking not to use them in later criminal proceedings.
2. The judge, however, failed to exercise this discretion properly. It is for the judge in the criminal proceedings to decide whether the admission of the transcripts would prejudice a fair criminal trial. The trial judge will have all the circumstances of the case known to him, which the judge in the companies court will not have.

Lord Nolan:

'I have had the advantage of reading in draft the speech prepared by Lord Browne-Wilkinson. I agree with it in every respect and wish to add only a few words of my own.

It is hard to believe that Parliament, when authorising the director under s2(3) of the Criminal Justice Act 1987 to require the production of "documents" meant that he should have a free hand to obtain the records of admissions made by the defendant to other authorities and to use them as part of the prosecution case. It seems anomalous in the extreme that the director should thus be allowed to obtain and use evidence in the form of admissions made by the defendant to others when by s2(8) Parliament has expressly prohibited, save within narrow limits, the use in evidence of admissions made in response to a requirement under s2(2) from the director himself. Yet that is the result which is produced by the language of s2(3).

For the reasons given by Lord Browne-Wilkinson, I can see no ground in principle to support the distinction thus drawn between admissions obtained by way of s2(2) and evidence of admissions obtained by way of s2(3). There may, in fact, be a stronger case for affording some protection to the defendant in respect of the latter. A defendant responding to inquiries under s236 of the Insolvency Act 1986 may well have been less cautious in his answers than if he were being subjected to a s2(2) inquiry by the director.

The director fully accepts, and to some extent relies upon, the overriding power of the criminal court, under s78 of the Police and Criminal Evidence Act 1984, to exclude the documentary evidence obtained under s2(3) if it would be unfair to admit it. The full terms of s78(1) are that the court may refuse to allow the evidence.

"... if it appears to the court that, having regard to all the circumstances, including the circumstances in which the evidence was obtained, the admission of the evidence would have such an adverse effect on the fairness of the proceedings that the court ought not to admit it."

It seems strange that evidence of admissions by the defendant may be excluded on these grounds, even though it was obtained in strict compliance with an express statutory power. Yet that, as I understand the speech of Lord Mustill in *R v Director of the Serious Fraud Office, ex parte Smith* [1993] AC 1 at p43F–G, is undoubtedly the law in relation to answers obtained from the defendant under s2(2), and is, as I have said, accepted by the director, rightly in my view, as applicable to evidence obtained by way of s2(3). It follows that s78 is the one remaining solid bulwark against the possibility of excessive or unfair use by the director of his powers under s2.

The type of fraud which led to the passing of the Criminal Justice Act 1987 is an exceptionally pernicious form of crime, and those who commit it tend to be as devious as they are wicked. It is not in the least surprising or regrettable that Parliament should have entrusted the SFO with the power to call upon a suspected person to come into the open, and to disclose information which may incriminate him. It would be highly regrettable if the power has, in fact, been created in terms which go significantly wider than was intended. But that is a matter which only Parliament can debate and, if necessary, resolve.'

Bishopsgate Investment Management Ltd v *Maxwell* [1992] 2 WLR 991 Court of Appeal (Dillon, Stuart-Smith and Mann LJJ)

Privilege against self-incrimination

Facts

Bishopsgate Investment Management Ltd (BIM) was the investment trustee of the pension fund of Mirror Group Newspapers Ltd (MGN): Mr Kevin Maxwell (KM) was a director of BIM until he resigned following his father's sudden death. Large sums appeared to be missing from the pension fund and BIM commenced proceedings against, inter alia, KM and obtained the appointment of a provisional liquidator. The provisional liquidator sought information from KM under ss235 and 236(2), (3) of the Insolvency Act 1986 and to require KM to attend a private oral examination. By this time MGN had also commenced proceedings against, inter alia, KM and in those proceedings had obtained an order requiring KM to supply certain information. In both proceedings KM refused to supply the required information, relying on the privilege against self-incrimination.

Held

KM was not entitled to rely on this privilege in the case of the BIM proceedings but, as MGN was not in liquidation, administration or administrative receivership and therefore could not invoke any of the provisions of the 1986 Act, in those proceedings the privilege had not been overridden by statute and KM could take advantage of it and refuse to answer questions.

Stuart-Smith LJ:

'*Bishopsgate Investment Management Ltd* v *Maxwell*. The first issue in this appeal is whether either s235 or s236 of the Insolvency Act 1986 abrogate the privilege against self-incrimination.

The general rule is that "no-one is bound to incriminate himself" in the sense that he is not to be compelled to say anything which "may tend to bring him into the peril and possibility of being convicted as a criminal": per Field J in *Lamb* v *Munster* (1882) 10 QBD 110 at 111 ...

There are exceptions to it; but they are not relevant to this issue. Parliament can abrogate the privilege. It can do so either expressly or by implication. The tendency recently has been for Parliament to do so expressly ...

The presumption is against the abrogation of the privilege. In my judgment the authorities show two somewhat different approaches to the search for the intention of Parliament. The first is what I would call the linguistic approach, the second I shall refer to as the purposive approach ...

The purposive approach is to consider whether the purpose of the section would be frustrated or substantially frustrated if effect was given to the privilege. If the answer is Yes, then by implication the statute abrogates the privilege. This was the approach of Vinelott J in *Re Jeffrey S Levitt Ltd* [1992] 2 WLR 975. In the present case Hoffmann J followed that decision ... and so the present appeal is effectively also against the decision in *Re Jeffrey S Levitt Ltd* ...

I have little doubt that the purpose would be substantially frustrated if the privilege existed in an examination of an officer under s236. Although the office-holder may choose to apply under s236 without having first sought the information under s235, especially perhaps in cases of great urgency, it seems probable that the office-holder will first seek information under s235. If the person who is under the statutory duty to supply such information does so, then there is no need to make an application under s236. It is only if he does not comply with that duty, that the office-holder needs to have recourse to s236. One of the more obvious reasons why there may be failure or refusal to comply or comply fully with that duty is fear of incrimination. Another obvious reason why the office-holder may need to have recourse to s236 is if the accounting records of the company have not been properly kept. There is a statutory obligation on the company to keep proper accounting records; and every officer of a company which fails to do so is guilty of an offence unless he shows that he acted honestly and that in the circumstances in which the company's business was carried on the default was excusable: see s221 (as amended) of the Companies Act 1985. Yet, if the proposition contended for by [counsel for KM] is correct, many if not all questions directed to an officer of the company in such a situation would go unanswered ...

In my judgment an officer or former officer of a company cannot take advantage of the privilege against incrimination in an examination under s236 ...

Mirror Group Newspapers plc v Maxwell. In this appeal [counsel for MGN] submits that [KM] was at the material time in a fiduciary capacity vis-à-vis the plaintiff companies and is liable to account to them. Although [counsel for KM] did not accept that this was so, I have very little doubt on the evidence that it is correct, and in any event I am prepared for the purpose of this appeal to assume that it is.

[Counsel for MGN's] main submission is that there is an exception to the general rule that a person is not compelled to incriminate himself in the case of a person who prior to the material event is in a fiduciary relationship with the plaintiff, that is to say a servant or agent who is liable to account to the plaintiff who is seeking to recover money or property. If this exception exists, it is plain that it is very far-reaching, though in [counsel for MGN's] formulation there are two restricting parameters. First, the relationship of trust must exist before any dishonest act is committed by the servant or agent. Thus an ordinary thief or burglar who is not in a position of trust does not fall within the exception. Secondly, the servant or agent must have undertaken the position of trust in relation to the money or property of his employer or principal such as makes him liable to account ...

Such an exception would, in my judgment, be inconsistent with the underlying principles of the Police and Criminal Evidence Act 1984 ... No distinction in the Act is made between fiduciaries and others. The words of the caution are well-known: "You do not have to say anything unless you wish to do so, but what you say may be given in evidence." Very frequently large organisations have a security or investigation department where members are concerned to question a suspected dishonest employee, not only with a view to investigating whether an offence has been committed, but what has happened to the stolen money or property. It would, I think, be bizarre if in the first capacity they had to tell the employee that he need not answer the question, while in the latter they could apply to the civil court for an order for interrogatories which he was obliged to answer. I therefore agree with [counsel for KM] that these provisions of the Police and Criminal Evidence Act 1984 are inconsistent with the exception contended for by [counsel for MGN], whether as a term to be implied in a contract of service or agency or as being inconsistent with the duties assumed by a person who undertakes responsibilities as a fiduciary.'

After completion of liquidation

Workvale Ltd (in dissolution), Re [1992] 1 WLR 416 Court of Appeal (Sir Stephen Brown P, Stocker and Scott LJJ)

Restoration to register – limitation period

The applicant's late husband allegedly suffered injury at work and, within the primary limitation period under s11 of the Limitation Act 1980, the company, his employers, went into liquidation. Subsequently, but still within the primary limitation period, the husband issued a writ against the company, but this was a nullity as the company no longer existed. The applicant now sought a direction under s651(5) of the Companies Act 1985 that the company be restored to the register and a direction under s651(6) of the 1985 Act that the period of between the dissolution of the company and its restoration to the register be disregarded for the purposes of the 1980 Act.

Held

The application would be successful as, in all the circumstances, there was an arguable case for an order under s33 of the 1980 Act overriding the limitation period.

Scott LJ:

'The words [of s651(5)] "no order shall be made on such an application if it appears to the court that the proceedings would fail by virtue of any enactment as to the time within which the proceedings must be brought" require, in my judgment, that the whole of the relevant provisions be considered. The presence of s33 in the 1980 Act has the consequence that it cannot be predicated that a personal injuries action not commenced within the three-year period "would fail" unless it is clear that s33 does not apply to the case or that an order under s33 would not be made ...

... for the purposes of s651(5) in any case where the primary limitation period has expired the judge should, in my opinion, ask himself whether the applicant has an arguable case for an order under s33. If there is an arguable case for a s33 order, then it cannot, in my judgment, be predicated that "the proceedings would fail". Conversely, if the applicant's case for a s33 order does not appear to be arguable, the statutory language in s651(5) in my opinion bars the making of an order. I would add that where the primary limitation period has expired it is, in my judgment, for the applicant to satisfy the court that a s33 application is arguable.

... in my judgment, the fate of a s33 application in the present case will depend on an exercise of discretion having regard to all the facts of the case and in particular to the matters referred to in s33(3). In my opinion on the facts of the present case a s33 application would be well arguable. I am not impressed by the matters of alleged prejudice or hardship to the defendant caused by the lapse of time since 1983 when the accident happened. The case had been brought to a point ready for trial before the dissolution of the company came to the attention of the solicitors who, on the insurers' instructions, were purporting to act for it. It must be supposed that witness statements had been taken. The difficulties in tracing witnesses are far more likely to prejudice the plaintiff than the defendant. The death of [the husband] will, of course, prevent him being cross-examined on the witness statement that he no doubt gave his solicitors before he died or on the sworn answers to interrogatories that he supplied. But this, too, may prejudice his own case, for the trial judge will be bound to take into account in assessing the weight of his Civil Evidence Act statement the fact that it cannot be tested by cross-examination.

In my judgment therefore the case for a s33 order is well arguable. The learned judge was right to make the order under s651(5) ...

There is, however, an additional matter of procedural practice that I want to mention. As the case now stands, there will have to be an application in the Queen's Bench Division or in the county court, as the case may be, for a s33 order. The material put before the court will be the same material as is now before us. There is, as I understand it, nothing extra that either side will want to adduce for the purpose of the s33 application. So there is no point in putting the parties to the extra expense and continued delay that the further application will inevitably entail. It was, in my opinion, open to Harman J, if satisfied that a s33 application would succeed, to exercise the power conferred on the court by s651(6) and to allow, as asked in para 5 of the notice of motion, that "the period between [the dissolution of the company] and the date of restoration of the company be excluded from the limitation period in respect of the applicant's claim for damages" ... I think that it would have been right for the judge if he had been addressed on the point, which he was not, to make an order under para 5 of the notice of motion.'

12 Accounts and Audit

Liability of auditors

Caparo Industries plc v *Dickman* [1990] 2 WLR 358

Auditor – duty of care

Facts
The plaintiff shareholder in Fidelity plc received the accounts audited by the defendants and at first purchased more shares and then made a successful take-over bid. The plaintiffs alleged that the accounts had been inaccurate and misleading: instead of showing a pre-tax profit for the year of some £1.2m, they should have revealed a loss of over £400,000. Had the defendants owed the plaintiffs a duty of care?

Held
They had not, either as shareholders or potential investors.

Lord Jauncey of Tullichettle

' ... the purpose of annual accounts, so far as members are concerned, is to enable them to question the past management of the company, to exercise their voting rights, if so advised, and to influence future policy and management. Advice to individual shareholders in relation to present or future investment in the company is not part of the statutory purpose of the preparation and distribution of the accounts ...

If the statutory accounts are prepared and distributed for certain limited purposes, can there nevertheless be imposed on auditors an additional common law duty to individual shareholders who choose to use them for another purpose without the prior knowledge of the auditors? The answer must be No. Use for that other purpose would no longer be ... use for the "very transaction" which Denning LJ in *Candler* v *Crane Christmas & Co* [1951] 2 KB 164 at 183 regarded as determinative of the scope of any duty of care. Only where the auditor was aware that the individual shareholder was likely to rely on the accounts for a particular purpose such as his present or future investment in or lending to the company would a duty of care arise. Such a situation does not obtain in the present case.

... it was argued that the relationship of the unwelcome bidder in a potential takeover situation was nearly as proximate to the auditor as was the relationship of a shareholder to whom the report was directed. Since I have concluded that the auditor owed no duty to an individual shareholder, it follows that this argument must also fail. The fact that a company may at a time when the auditor is preparing his report be vulnerable to a takeover bid cannot per se create a relationship of proximity between the auditor and the ultimate successful bidder. Not only is the auditor under no statutory duty to such a bidder but he will have reason at the material time to know neither of his identity nor of the terms of his bid. In this context the recent case of *Al Saudi Banque* v *Clark Pixley* [1990] 2 WLR 344 is in point. There Millett J held that the auditors of a company owed no duty of care to a bank which lent money to the company, regardless of whether the bank was an existing creditor or a potential one, because no sufficient proximity of relationship existed in either case between the auditor and the bank. I have no doubt that this case was correctly decided ...'

Commentary

Al Saudi Banque v *Clark Pixley*: Millett J granted leave to appeal direct to the House of Lords. The appeal was not pursued as the parties reached an out of court settlement.

Galoo Ltd v *Bright Grahame Murray* [1994] 1 WLR 1360 Court of Appeal (Glidewell, Evans and Waite LJJ)

Liability of auditor

Facts

Gamine Ltd owned all the shares in Galoo Ltd. The defendants (BGM) were the companies' auditors. In 1987 Hillsdown Holdings plc purchased 51 per cent of the shares in Gamine. Between March 1987 and January 1993, Hillsdown made loans worth over £30m to Galoo and Gamine. In May 1991 a further 44.3 per cent of Gamine's shares were purchased by Hillsdown. The above transactions were carried out on the basis of the audited accounts of Galoo and Gamine, which were prepared by the defendants, BGM.

The plaintiffs, Galoo, Gamine and Hillsdown, claimed that the audited accounts of Galoo and Gamine were inaccurate and this was caused by the negligence of BGM, who failed to detect a fraud, whereby items were included in the accounts which, in fact, never existed. Actions were commenced for breach of contract and negligence in relation to Galoo and Gamine, and for negligence only in relation to Hillsdown.

These were interlocutory proceedings in which the court had to decide whether there was a reasonable cause of action. In other words, were the plaintiffs' claims bound to fail?

The claims in contract and tort relevant to Galoo and Gamine were:

1. that they incurred loss by accepting loans from Hillsdown of over £30m;
2. that by relying on the audit, they continued to trade and incur losses which they would not otherwise have done. If they had been alerted to fraud they would have put the company into liquidation. Instead they incurred further trading losses of £25m and paid a dividend of £500,000.

The claims in tort relevant to Hillsdown were that they had suffered loss:

3. by their original share purchase in Gamine;
4. by making loans to Gamine;
5. by the purchase of a further 44.3 per cent of Gamine's shares.

The judge at first instance struck out claims (1) and (2). He also struck out claims (4) and (5), but decided that claim (3) did disclose a reasonable cause of action.

The plaintiffs appealed and the defendants cross-appealed.

Held

The appeals and cross-appeal were dismissed.

1. Acceptance of a loan cannot, of itself, be described as a loss causing damage. If anything, it is a benefit to the borrower. Therefore claim (1) was dismissed.
2. Breach of duty by BGM allowed Galoo and Gamine the opportunity to incur trading losses, but it did not *cause* those trading losses in the sense in which the word 'cause' is used in law. Claim (2) was also dismissed.
3. As it was not alleged that the defendants knew or intended that Hillsdown would rely on their accounts for the purpose of making loans and further share purchases in Gamine, claims (4) and (5) disclosed no cause of action.

4. Claim (3) did disclose a reasonable cause of action. In addition to audit purposes, the accounts were prepared for purpose of fixing the share price of the original 51 per cent purchase in Gamine by Hillsdown. The defendants knew that the share purchase agreement contained provisions to calculate the share price by reference to their audited accounts.

The following extract relates to claim (3).

Evans LJ:

'It is tempting to distinguish between the *Caparo* case [1990] 2 AC 605 and the *Morgan Crucible* case [1991] Ch 295 on the basis that in the latter, though not the former case, the identity of a particular purchaser of shares in the company was known to the defendants when they represented that the company's accounts which they had prepared were fair and true. This excludes individual members of the body of existing shareholders to whom the statutory accounts are published (the *Caparo* case), whilst including an identified take-over bidder, as in the *Morgan Crucible* case. But there could be intervening situations, for example, where an existing shareholder is known to be a potential purchaser of more shares, with a view to acquiring the whole or a majority of the shares. The identification test would not provide the answer in such a case. No duty of care would be owed to such a person, in my judgment, on those facts alone, because the third of the four propositions listed by Lord Oliver in the *Caparo* case [1990] 2 AC 605, 638D, already quoted by Glidewell LJ, as it was by Slade LJ in the *Morgan Crucible* case [1991] Ch 295, 318, would not be satisfied: "(3) it is known either actually or inferentially, that the advice so communicated is likely to be acted upon by the advisee for that purpose without independent inquiry", and, vitally, it could not be said that the auditors in such a case "intended that they should act upon it, for that purpose": per Slade LJ in the *Morgan Crucible* case [1991] Ch 295, 320A.

If it is right to confine the duty of care, meaning, to restrict the class of persons who can recover damages if the adviser/representor is negligent, to cases where the defendant is shown not merely to have known that the individual plaintiff would or might rely upon the representation but to have intended that it should be relied upon, by him and for the particular purpose and without intermediate examination, then the resulting analysis comes close to the "voluntary assumption of responsibility" which has been referred to in many of the authorities but which was discounted as a test of liability in *Smith* v *Eric S Bush* [1990] 1 AC 831, 862, per Lord Griffiths:

"... I do not think that voluntary assumption of responsibility is a helpful or realistic test for liability. It is true that reference is made in a number of the speeches in *Hedley Byrne* [1964] AC 465 to the assumption of responsibility as a test of liability but it must be remembered that those speeches were made in the context of a case in which the central issue was whether a duty of care could arise when there had been an express disclaimer of responsibility for the accuracy of the advice ... The phrase 'assumption of responsibility' can only have any real meaning if it is understood as referring to the circumstances in which the law will deem the maker of the statement to have assumed responsibility to the person who acts upon the advice."

Lord Devlin referred in *Hedley Byrne & Co Ltd* v *Heller & Partners Ltd* [1964] AC 465, 530 to "a relationship equivalent to contract" and it is clear from Lord Griffiths's speech in *Smith's* case [1990] 1 AC 831, 862 that the contractual analogy cannot serve as a definition of the cases where the duty of care may arise. But if the statement is made to an identifiable person and the maker not only knows that it will or is likely to be acted upon but also intended that it should be acted upon for a particular purpose, then these may well exemplify "circumstances in which the law will deem the maker of the statement to have assumed responsibility" to the person who acts upon it: per Lord Griffiths, at p862E. The "indeterminate class" of persons referred to by Cardozo CJ in *Ultramares Corporation* v *Touche* (1931) 174 NE 441, 444 is thus reduced to an inter-personal relationship where liability may be imposed, and it would seem unreasonable and even unjust to do so, in my view, if the defendant could not be said to have assumed responsibility towards the plaintiff, not necessarily as an individual, in the circumstances of the case. It is sufficient for present purposes to note that the relationship by definition must be "voluntary" in the sense that no consideration proceeds from the plaintiff for the defendant's advice.'

Commentary

The effect of this case is that, in addition to the issue of proximity between the auditors and those relying on their statements, it is also necessary to consider causation. In particular, the question to be asked is: did the auditors cause the loss or did they merely allow the opportunity for such losses to occur?

James McNaughton Paper Group Ltd v *Hicks Anderson & Co* (1990) The Times 2 October Court of Appeal (Neill, Nourse and Balcombe LJJ)

Draft accounts – duty of care to bidder

Facts

The plaintiffs had been considering the takeover of MK Paper Group Holdings Ltd (MK). MK's chairman had asked the defendant accountants to prepare the accounts for the year as quickly as possible and they duly supplied these accounts in draft form: MK's chairman had given a copy to the plaintiffs' chairman. The plaintiffs had taken over MK and, in an action for negligence, they contended that they had been materially influenced by, inter alia, the defendants' draft accounts, which were found to contain errors.

Held

The plaintiffs' action could not succeed as the defendants had not owed them a duty of care in respect of the preparation of the accounts. Neill LJ said that the natural starting point was *Hedley Byrne & Co Ltd* v *Heller & Partners Ltd* [1963] 3 WLR 101 and he recalled Lord Oliver of Aylmerton's statement as to the guidance which could be obtained from that case in *Caparo Industries plc* v *Dickman* [1990] 2 WLR 358. Neill LJ had also considered the more recent authorities, in particular the speeches in *Smith* v *Eric S Bush* [1989] 2 WLR 790 and in *Caparo* itself. In reaching his decision, Neill LJ had been particularly impressed by matters which included the following:

1. The defendants had been asked to prepare the accounts as quickly as possible and at that stage they were to be produced for MK's chairman.
2. The accounts produced were merely a draft: the plaintiffs had not been entitled to treat them as final accounts and the defendants could not have been expected to foresee that they would so treat them.
3. The transaction had been between experienced businessmen: it was to be anticipated that the plaintiffs would have had access to and would have consulted their own accountancy advisers.

Morgan Crucible Co plc v *Hill Samuel & Co Ltd* (1990) The Times 2 November; [1991] 1 All ER 148 Court of Appeal (Slade, Mustill and Nicholls LJJ)

Takeover – duty of care to bidders

Facts

The plaintiffs made a contested bid for First Castle Electronics plc. Documents were prepared by way of a defence to the bid and the plaintiffs brought a claim in negligence against First Castle's advisers (Hill Samuel), accountants (Judkins) and directors. The gist of the original statement of claim was that the board of First Castle and Judkins were responsible for putting the financial statements into circulation, that they and Hill Samuel were responsible for the profit forecast, and that all of them owed a duty of care to the plaintiffs as persons who could foreseeably rely on them; that the statements and profit forecast were negligently prepared, that the plaintiffs relied on them in making and subsequently increasing their offer and thereby suffered heavy loss (over £50 million). In the light of the decision in *Caparo*

Industries plc v *Dickman* [1990] 2 WLR 358 the plaintiffs applied for leave to amend their statement of claim, the principal purpose being to restrict their claim to representations made by the respective defendants after their bid, that is, during the course of the takeover battle. Hoffmann J refused the application as, in his Lordship's view, the case could not be distinguished from *Caparo* and, despite the proposed amendments, the entire case based on negligence was bound to fail because of the absence of a duty of care owed by any of the defendants to the plaintiffs. The plaintiffs appealed.

Held

The appeal would be allowed as the plaintiffs' action would not be bound to fail. After considering the case against the directors and the relevance of the decision in *Caparo*, their Lordships took the view that with regard to Hill Samuel and Judkins it was arguable for the same reasons, mutatis mutandis, as those relating to the directors, that the existence of a duty of care to the plaintiffs had been established. Their Lordships emphasised that the whole essence of the claim against the several directors was that the representations relied on were made negligently by each of them. Even if a director owed the duty of care alleged, and even if the accounts or the profit forecast were highly misleading, it would not necessarily follow that he was in breach of that duty; that might partly depend on what advice he took and what advice he followed.

Compliance with applications under s236 Insolvency Act 1986

British and Commonwealth Holdings plc v *Spicer & Oppenheim* [1992] 3 WLR 853 House of Lords (Lord Keith of Kinkel, Lord Ackner, Lord Jauncey of Tullichettle, Lord Lowry and Lord Slynn of Hadley)

Administration – production of documents by third party

Facts

British and Commonwealth Holdings plc (B & C) acquired the issued share capital in Atlantic Computers plc (Atlantic). A year or so later administrators of Atlantic were appointed by the court and a month or so after that administrators were appointed for B & C. B & C's administrators sought, pursuant to s236(2) of the Insolvency Act 1986, an order that Atlantic's auditors produce certain recent financial records.

Held

Such an order would be made.

Lord Slynn of Hadley

'The protection for the person called upon to produce documents lies … not in a limitation by category of documents ("reconstituting the company's state of knowledge") but in the fact that the applicant must satisfy the court that, after balancing all the relevant factors, there is a proper case for such an order to be made. The proper case is one where the administrator reasonably requires to see the documents to carry out his functions and the production does not impose an unnecessary and unreasonable burden on the person required to produce them in the light of the administrator's requirements. An application is not necessarily unreasonable because it is inconvenient for the addressee of the application or causes him a lot of work or may make him vulnerable to future claims, or is addressed to a person who is not an officer or employee of or a contractor with the company in administration, but all these will be relevant factors, together no doubt with many others.

It is plain in the present case that Hoffmann J [who heard the appeal from the registrar's order] carried out the balancing exercise on the basis that he was entitled and bound to do so and ... it seems to me that it is impossible to say that in carrying out that exercise he misdirected himself or came to a conclusion to which he could not reasonably have come in the exercise of his discretion ...

This may well be an exceptional order. The size of the financial crash, however, gives rise to an exceptional case. Creditors and investors stood to lose vast sums. It was the administrators' task to investigate "what was the true financial position of Atlantic at the time of its acquisition and, if it was different from the way it was represented, how and why the truth was concealed" (see [1992] BCLC 314 at 317 per Hoffmann J). They need in this very complex situation to check the accuracy of the various financial documents and to know not only what representations were made but how accurate they were. ... I find it difficult to see how the order can be cut down and remain effective. No way has been suggested to achieve this.'